Spreading Buddha's Word in East Asia

To Peggy

with respect and
admiration

Jimmy Wu

3. 1. 2020
Tucson.

THE SHENG YEN SERIES IN CHINESE BUDDHIST STUDIES

THE SHENG YEN SERIES IN CHINESE BUDDHIST STUDIES
Chün-fang Yü, series editor

Following the endowment of the Sheng Yen Professorship in Chinese Buddhist Studies, the Sheng Yen Education Foundation and the Chung Hua Institute of Buddhist Studies in Taiwan jointly endowed a publication series, the Sheng Yen Series in Chinese Buddhist Studies, at Columbia University Press. Its purpose is to publish monographs containing new scholarship and English translations of classical texts in Chinese Buddhism.

Scholars of Chinese Buddhism have traditionally approached the subject through philology, philosophy, and history. In recent decades, however, they have increasingly adopted an interdisciplinary approach, drawing on anthropology, archaeology, art history, religious studies, and gender studies, among other disciplines. This series aims to provide a home for such pioneering studies in the field of Chinese Buddhism.

Michael J. Walsh, *Sacred Economies: Buddhist Business and Religiosity in Medieval China*

Koichi Shinohara, *Spells, Images, and Maṇḍalas: Tracing the Evolution of Esoteric Buddhist Rituals*

Beverley Foulks McGuire, *Living Karma: The Religious Practices of Ouyi Zhixu (1599–1655)*

Paul Copp, *The Body Incantatory: Spells and the Ritual Imagination in Medieval Chinese Buddhism*

N. Harry Rothschild, *Emperor Wu Zhao and Her Pantheon of Devis, Divinities, and Dynastic Mothers*

Erik J. Hammerstrom, *The Science of Chinese Buddhism: Early Twentieth-Century Engagements*

Spreading Buddha's Word in East Asia

THE FORMATION AND TRANSFORMATION OF THE CHINESE BUDDHIST CANON

Edited by Jiang Wu and Lucille Chia

COLUMBIA UNIVERSITY PRESS

NEW YORK

This volume received support from the "New Perspectives in Chinese Culture and Society" program, which is made possible by a grant from the Chiang Ching-kuo Foundation for International Scholarly Exchange to the American Council of Learned Societies.

Columbia University Press
Publishers Since 1893
New York   Chichester, West Sussex
cup.columbia.edu

Library of Congress Cataloging-in-Publication Data
Spreading Buddha's word in East Asia : the formation and transformation of the
Chinese Buddhist canon / Edited by Jiang Wu and Lucille Chia.
pages   cm. — (The Sheng Yen series in Chinese Buddhist studies)
Includes bibliographical references and index.
ISBN 978-0-231-17160-1 (cloth) — ISBN 978-0-231-17161-8 (pbk.) —
ISBN 978-0-231-54019-3 (e-book)
1. Buddhism—Sacred books—History.   2. Buddhism—China—History.   3. Buddhist
literature, Chinese—History and criticism.   I. Wu, Jiang, 1969– editor.   II. Chia, Lucille, editor.
BQ1217.S77   2015
294.3'820951—dc23
2014047857

Cover Design: Jennifer Heuer

This book is dedicated to Lewis Lancaster,
to celebrate his career as a pioneer in many fields.

CONTENTS

PREFACE

Lewis Lancaster

This is a volume in which scholars have approached the topic of the "Chinese Buddhist canon" in a new manner and in some cases with new methods, bringing out a degree of vitality that has not previously been shown in the field. Given the proscription against "canon" that marked the early days of postmodern studies, it was a daring gesture to so openly address an issue that in the past has been held in disrepute. For a few years at the end of the last century, there developed what some have called the "hermeneutics of suspicion." This was particularly applied to canons that were "suspected" of being hopelessly exclusive. In many ways this so-called "postmodern" attitude hardened over time, and the ironic result was loss of flexibility in scholarship. During that time, a response to one of my papers on the Korean version of the canon was the statement: "We don't use the word 'canon' anymore . . . it is not current with our ideas." This signaled a sanction against even talking about what were considered to be "elitist" texts, and it unfortunately expanded into a derisive rejection of the very idea of studying them. However, the purposeful disruption and problematizing of the existing approaches in Buddhist studies was by no means all negative. In those instances where it expanded the vision of what could be done, particularly with often neglected material, the impulse that led to the postmodern appraisal remains valuable.

In the conference presentations and discussion, one could feel the spirit once expressed by Milton as being "in the quiet and still air of delightful studies." There was no attempt to win over the audience with sensationalism that scorned what was fashionable in a previous generation. Instead, the discourse represented the contemporary trend that expands the range of "what can be considered." There was an unstated assumption that a clearly defined boundary of study for the Chinese canon is not the starting point of research. Instead, the leading edge of our advances in knowledge is fluid and is constantly being created by our methodology, expertise, and findings. The papers of this volume outline the frontiers of our current knowledge, and we all recognize that in the future the push into areas not yet considered will require a constant redrawing of boundaries.

In the spirit of exploring the frontiers, the papers included categories, groups, and types without predetermined restrictions. Thus, it would be fair to say that the papers in this conference on the canon of Buddhist texts in Chinese are progressive. They do not represent a retreat to a former state of study but are aids for the field to move forward. The approach can be defined as open to plurality. As a result, the papers present complex views, asking readers to consider politics, social mores, philosophical discourses, material science, and religious values. Can it be determined that all of these are commensurable? What will be the common measure between material science and political strategy? The answers from the authors of this volume show that we can indeed deal with complexity and move among many different spheres of influence. We can handle the complexity of pluralism and view the emerging Chinese Buddhist canon as a product and a still evolving aspect of the commonality that exists among many facets of society.

This effort on the part of the organizers of the conference, where the material in this book was first presented, might be described as shifting from considering the canon as an "object" to recognizing that it may best be approached as an "event." Its story is an account of the way the collection of texts known as the "Chinese Buddhist canon" involves people, whether monks, nuns, officials, craftsmen, or readers; places of translation, sites for archiving, places of birth, routes of dissemination; temporality of years, months, days, dynasties, eras; actions of carving printing blocks, producing paper, shelving volumes in libraries. All such events occur within social, political, and religious frameworks. Once such study is begun, it is soon obvious that the canon "event" involves the whole of society. It is not just an elite activity, nor is it limited to the "rabble." Furthermore, the reports of the conference participants show that the "event" involved thousands of participants who gave support and in some cases direct labor to the creation, maintenance, and ritual reverence of the ever-increasing number of volumes. It might be tempting to reduce the study of the canon to the physical manifestation and thus maintain that while the "object" was revered and supported, few looked beyond it to the content of the texts themselves. But this would ignore the basis for the enormous outlays of resources that were directed toward the texts.

One of the features of the accumulation of so many volumes of texts with Buddhist content is the way the successive additions were accommodated. The point of convergence came to be the place and manner in which the physical manuscripts were housed. Shelving, cataloging, and all the other aspects that we include under library services were in play in the structuring and maintenance of the texts being produced by translation teams over the centuries. As we see in the reports here, the catalogs that were produced, probably first as mere shelf lists, came to be the basis for the early history of Chinese Buddhism. All discussion of the beginning of the tradition in China finds its way to the process by which the literary material was created, including the names of those involved, the date of the activity, and in some cases, the place where it occurred. This information was recorded in the catalogs of the canon collections, and without it we would have little on which to base a history of early Buddhism in East Asia. The accounts of Buddhist origins in China were reached through reflection on the emerging canon as consonant with the rise of an institutional religious structure. For this reason, without studying the Buddhist canon, we cannot understand how the tradition was viewed by those who began to write them.

Although the catalogs played a pivotal role in describing the chronology of Buddhist history, they are not without flaws that impair the completeness and efficiency of our ability to speak intelligibly about the past. There are significant problems of attribution of authorship and dating based on the colophons and catalog entries for certain texts. These anomalies distort the chronicle of causal relationships in both the annals and doctrinal evolution. We are aware that the canon contains translations from India and Central Asia as well as compilations made in East Asia. The compilations have been adjudged as impostures foisted off to others as genuine authentic "translations," so they are called by pejorative titles such as "apocrypha" and even "spurious" or "counterfeit." Any list of texts that have been the most influential in East Asia will contain titles of what I prefer to call "East Asian compilations." The conference delegates fully accepted the presence of such texts in the canon and were far less judgmental than many of the past research reports. These materials are crucial to our understanding of Buddhism, but we must reconsider how they will be dated and attributed in order to have a more accurate view of how doctrinal matters were conceived and included in the canon.

In addition to these issues of the compilations, we have major problems with the attribution of texts that appear to be authentic translations. It is obvious that many translations are not properly assigned or dated in the catalogs and colophons, and this is detrimental to our understanding of the history of word use in the texts. At some time in the future, the Chinese Buddhist canon translations should be fully mined for data that will throw light on how Indian and Central Asian Buddhism was developing from the second century onward. The Sanskrit and Prakrit texts, no less than the "East Asian compilations," show changes over time and multiple sources and authoring hands. The idea that a Sanskrit text is authentic "Buddhism" raises many questions that need to be carefully studied.

In addition to the postmodern complaints about canonicity, there has been the question of who read and studied the texts. Answering it involves trying to ascertain the scope of the "audience" for any given volume. Literacy has often been limited to a small percentage of the population. This was true in East Asia as well as the Indian subcontinent. If few people ever read the texts, then the contemporary academic study of them can hardly be seen as comparable to how they were used in the past. One of the major contributions at the conference was regarding the Jiaxing edition, the string-bound version, made on demand for a growing group of literates who did want to read and study the content. For nearly a century, ordinary people longing for a cheap and easy-to-read edition labored to produce it. This gives us information about the widespread use of the canon and its importance outside the monasteries.

The conference continually returned to issues that touch on questions about the significance of the canon. During the political suppressions of Buddhism in the twentieth century, the canon collections were seen as serving no purpose and therefore had no excuse for being. Consequently, printing blocks and xylograph copies were systematically destroyed. In the anticanon wing of academia, the texts were seen as insignificant to cultural life and destitute of substance for valid study. The canon was thought to be "hollow" and no longer cogent to what was happening in the lives of contemporary people. These criticisms and the subsequent actions often went unanswered; there were no compelling arguments in favor of the pertinence of the canonic collections. With the papers in this volume, one of the most telling examples of the importance of the texts relates to how governments made use of them through the centuries. From the time of the Southern and Northern dynasties, non-Han rulers had had to justify their rule in the face of the historic and long-accepted patterns of inheritance of power through birth. How could these invading peoples find a way to manifest their legitimacy? How the heritage of kingship could be passed on without birthright entitlement was a major problem for new kingdoms being set up on the grounds of the ancient Han culture. Here the Buddhist canon became a constituent of political life. The size of the canon made it worthy of royal attention and the renown associated with copying it in its entirety helped to resolve doubts about the authority of the ruling house. Consequently, the history of the canon is an inescapable part of dynastic histories. This was repeated in Japan in the early twentieth century, when the one-hundred-volume modern printing was named after Emperor Taishō. It was an example of Japan's ability to create a canon with a completely new arrangement, with sophisticated footnotes, and the Taishō edition became one of the major achievements of the empire. When the first digital version of the Pali canon was made in Thailand, it was done for the king's sixtieth birthday in 1987, and he set forward the second phase of the project. The royal acts of support for the canons were not just public. They were also tied to the dictates of the conscience of rulers and often reflected the deep faith of those who held high positions.

No discussion of the canon can be complete without making reference to the major new resource that has effected striking results. The digital age and the consequent production of virtual surrogates of the printed canons in databases has been an actuating power propelling us, willing or not, into different methods of study. Such alterations of centuries-old methods based on codex formats have aroused a certain amount of resistance. The momentum for employing digital data has at times been dilatory, but it is being instilled in scholarship, and lag time between innovation and application has been decreasing. The Chinese Buddhist Electronic Text Association (CBETA) offers a range of applications that are spectacular and ultimately groundbreaking for the study of the canon. The only question is how long it will take the average researcher to incorporate these software options into their studies.

As a longtime student of the Chinese canon, I found listening to these papers a moving experience. We are all deeply grateful to Professors Jiang Wu and Lucille Chia for organizing such an important conference. Through their efforts, the field of Buddhist studies has entered a new phase of appreciation for and understanding of the significance of the Chinese Buddhist canon. Those who read this volume will see the growing edge of current scholarship and the promise for what can be possible in the future.

ACKNOWLEDGMENTS

The editors of this book wish to thank all participants in the First International Conference on the Chinese Buddhist Canon held in Tucson, Arizona, March 26–27, 2011, and acknowledge the support provided by Department of East Asian Studies and the College of Humanities at the University of Arizona. Though their papers are not included in this volume, Robert Gimello, Albert Welter, Miriam Levering, Miroj Shakya, Fang Guangchang, Li Fuhua, He Mei, Chen Huaiyu, and Mario Poceski contributed to the conference, and we deeply appreciate their work. We also want to thank John Kieschnick and Phil Stanley, who coordinated the discussions. Three graduate students in Dr. Wu's seminar on the Chinese Buddhist canon, Shyling Glaze, Xin Zi, and Linjiao Zeng, provided translation and assistance to the conference.

This conference and the publication of this book were supported by the American Council of Learned Societies and the Chiang Ching-kuo Foundation. The Su Wukang Research Fund for East Asian Civilization also provided financial assistance for the publication of this book. Both editors have received general funding from the Chiang Ching-kuo Foundation in recent years, and we deeply appreciate it. Two anonymous reviewers gave us detailed feedback that helped to improve this work. Bryan D. Lowe also read the manuscript and provided detailed comments on several chapters. Finally, we thank all the contributors for their patience and hard work. Many papers have been thoroughly revised. Portions of the introduction and chapter 1 have been adapted from Jiang Wu's chapter on the Chinese Buddhist canon in *Blackwell Companion to East and Inner Asian Buddhism*, edited by Mario Poceski (Blackwell, 2014). An early version of Darui Long's paper has been published in *Hsi Lai Journal of Humanistic Buddhism* 7 (2006). We want to thank both publishers for their permission to use the essays here. Two subsequent conferences on printed editions (University of the West, 2013) and modern canons in East Asia (Brigham Young University, 2015) helped to shape this volume. We want to thank all participants in these two conferences as well.

CONVENTIONS

Transliterations: *pinyin* is used for Chinese names and terms; the standard Revised Hepburn Romanization system for Japanese names and terms; the official Revised Romanization of Korean system for Korean names and terms.

Chinese characters are provided at the first appearance of a term in each chapter and may be repeated later for technical discussion and easy reference. Diacritics are not provided for words that have been incorporated into the English language (such as Tokyo, Kyoto, Mahayana and Hinayana, sutra, sangha, Tripitaka, etc.) except in technical discussions.

Full citations of primary sources from collections such as *Taishō Canon* (*T*), *Korean Canon* (*K*), and other Buddhist collections are given in the following fashion at their first appearance: title, fascicle (*juan* 卷) number (where relevant and abbreviated as "fasc."), serial number, volume number, page number, register (a, b, or c, if necessary), column number; e.g., *Guang hongming ji* 廣弘明集, fasc. 22, *T* 2103, 52: 257a 11–15.

For sources in a canon that uses the traditional "thousand-character" numbering system (*qianziwen* 千字文), the reference to a particular text is given in the following order: case (*han* 函) number, case character (*hanhao* 函號) in Chinese, and volume (*ce* 冊) number. For example, the reference "61 菜 1" means a text that appears in volume 1 of case 61 with the *qianziwen* character *cai*.

For references and quotations obtained and tracked down through the *CBETA Chinese Electronic Tripitaka Collection* (CD-ROM) released by the Chinese Buddhist Electronic Text Association (CBETA), a note of different years is given. For example, *Guang hongming ji, T* (CEBTA 2011) 2103, 52: 257. If all references in a paper come from the CBETA collection, a note is given at the first occurrence of the citation.

The following abbreviations are used for commonly cited titles (full information can be found in the bibliography):

CSZJJ	*Chu sanzang jiji*
JXZ	*Mingban Jiaxing dazang jing*
K	*Goryeo daejanggyeong*
KYL	*Kaiyuan shijiao lu*
SKQS	*Siku quanshu*
T	*Taishō shinshō daizōkyō*
XZJ	*Wan xu zang jing*; reprint of *Dai-Nihon zoku zōkyō*
Z	*Shinsan Dai Nihon zoku zōkyō*

Spreading Buddha's Word in East Asia

Introduction

Jiang Wu and Lucille Chia

The importance of studying the historical development of a religious canon seems obvious. Equally obvious is the daunting challenge of trying to study the many aspects of an immense canon incorporating thousands of works. In the case of the Buddhist canon in Chinese, compiled and recompiled many times and transmitted throughout East Asia,[1] much research remains to be done, especially as the canon continues to evolve in the modern digital age of information. In this volume, we present nine articles of original research on the tradition of the Chinese Buddhist canon that exemplify new directions in studying and understanding the process of canon formation in specific cultural contexts. The chapters are organized into four parts. The first provides an overview of the Chinese canon and highlights some critical issues in canon studies. The second part focuses on the cataloging process during the manuscript age of canon formation. The three chapters in the third part consider the evolution of the Buddhist canon after the advent of printing in imperial China and explore the complex dynamics among the canon, printing technology, the state, and sponsoring communities. The fourth part includes two chapters each on the Korean and Japanese canons, which highlight the East Asian character of the Chinese canon. Finally, the first appendix presents a listing and summaries of the printed editions and the second describes the history of the massive Chinese Buddhist

Electronic Text Association (CBETA) project of digitizing the Chinese Buddhist canon.

As the chapters in this volume show, even topics that have already engaged much scholarly effort merit further exploration, such as the enormously complex issues of textual variants and the changing views on the organization and classification of works in the canon, including the nature of canonicity. Other topics heretofore less examined, such as the technologies used in the physical reproduction of the entire canon and individual works and the socioeconomic history of the publication of different editions of the canon, are now attracting greater attention. In fact, the emergence of the East Asian history of the book and of print culture as areas of study has provided new opportunities for reexamining the Chinese Buddhist canon and its religious, textual, social, and economic contexts.[2] Lastly, although this book focuses on the Buddhist canon in China, the crucial role that the Chinese canon played in the formation of East Asian Buddhism is addressed in two of the chapters. What Kamata Shigeo 鎌田茂雄 termed the "circle of Chinese Buddhism" (Chūgoku bukkyōken 中國佛教圈) developed as other East Asian countries acquired editions of the Chinese canon produced in China and modified its contents in the course of building their own Buddhist textual traditions.[3] Indeed, we cannot fully understand the development of Buddhism in China, Korea, and Japan without understanding the exchanges of canonical texts in Chinese among these regions in Asia.

The remainder of this introduction will discuss briefly three broad topics that will be examined in greater detail in the following essays: the "Cult of the Canon," in which the canon as a physical object is revered and even worshiped; the textual practices used in the compilation of the canon, which reveal how the management of Buddhist knowledge was influenced by and in turn added to the scholarly methods derived from the Chinese textual tradition; and the socioeconomic and political conditions under which official and private editions of the Chinese Buddhist canon were produced and distributed during various historical periods.

THE CULT OF THE CANON

A canon is a work of faith that involves a series of devotional activities in its creation, production, distribution, and maintenance, which can be referred to as the "Cult of the Canon." This religious phenomenon is deeply rooted in the Mahayana tradition of the "Cult of the Book" as defined by Gregory Schopen, who notes that the early Mahayana scriptures placed great emphasis on worshiping written texts.[4] Mahayana scriptures such as the Lotus Sutra and the Diamond Sutra suggest that the place where the written texts were located should become the object of devotion and the merit field. These scriptures also promoted their own production and reproduction as pious activities.

Mahayana scriptures encouraged five devotional actions directly related to the handling of the text: receiving and keeping the sutra, reading it, reciting it, expounding on it, and copying it. All of these actions would result in immeasurable merit in one's next life. Especially meritorious was the act of distributing the physical forms of the sutra, such as by copying it. The promise of a better afterlife no doubt stimulated the propagation of Mahayana scriptures.

In China, the "Cult of the Book" was a long-standing cultural tradition that preceded the advent of Buddhism, and the reverence and even fetishization of works such as the Buddhist and Daoist canons were natural developments. The Buddhist canon represents the ultimate teaching and the essence of the dharma body and is therefore a potent symbol in Buddhist communities, serving as a means to connect with the origin of the tradition and to the ultimate scriptural authority. The state, elite groups, and the common people all aspired to support the production and distribution of the entire set through devotional patronage and sponsorship, ceremonial consecration and worship, ritual writing and reading, etc.[5] Ownership of a canon would greatly enhance the prestige of a monastery, stimulating the growth or revival of religious devotion and attracting more patronage. The sponsors of the canon often invoked the rhetoric of repaying "Four Kindnesses" (si'en 四恩, i.e., the kindness of the Buddha, the rulers, the parents, and all sentient beings) and benefiting the "Three Realms" (sanyou 三有, i.e., the realms of desire, form, and formlessness) as their motive. Thus the production, distribution, and maintenance of the canon and a series of ceremonial routines became an indispensable component of monastic life.

In the process of its creation, the state invested a particular significance in the canon, as it was believed that ownership of such a collection could protect the nation. The Korean kings, for example, had requested *Kaibao Canon* (*Kaibaozang* 開寶藏) from the Song government for the security of the nation and later created their own canon as a way to defend themselves against foreign invasions.

Commoners could also sponsor the project out of their devotion. The creation of *Zhaocheng Canon* (*Zhaochengzang* 趙城藏) in north China during the Jin (Jurchen) Dynasty, for example, was initiated by a little-known Buddhist figure, Yin Shennai 尹矧乃 (?–1176), and continued by his better-known female disciple, Cui Fazhen 崔法珍, who severed her arm at age thirteen and vowed to print a canon. This project was supported by laypeople in Xiezhou 解州 (today's Yuncheng area in Shanxi) and neighboring areas. Legend says that more than fifty followers imitated her devotion and severed their arms as well. They collected funds by "burning arms and fingers," "cutting eyes and livers," and even donating all family property and selling their children. It took them about thirty years to complete the entire canon. Cui Fazhen was allowed to be ordained and awarded a purple robe and an honorific title.⁶

The physical canon could be treated as a sacred object for veneration and sacrifice. Donors could adopt one title, one fascicle, or even one booklet to be given offerings (*gongyang* 供養) for a period of one year, and such an adoption was renewable. During Buddhist holidays, the Hall of Scripture Storage, which was designed for the purpose of devotees' veneration, was opened to these donors for worship.⁷ The canon was also regularly brought out from the cabinets to prevent dampness. This practice developed into the ceremony of "sunning the scripture" (*shaijing* 曬經 or *bakuryō* 曝涼) for public display and respect.

In the Buddhist tradition, texts have served an essential spiritual purpose for believers. The huge number of texts in the canon has been used for ritual reading and writing. Ritual reading of the entire canon developed when it was still in manuscript form. Commonly known as "turning the scripture" (*zhuanjing* 轉經), this activity inspired the invention of the revolving wheel storage cabinet (*zhuanlun zang* 轉輪藏) for symbolic reading of the entire canon. In the Ming Dynasty, it was often referred to as "reading the whole canon in confinement" (*jinbu yuezang* 禁步閱藏), which involved solitude, worship, ablutions, and even fasting. The devotees vowed to read the entire canon in three or four years for the purpose of "benefiting all sentient beings."⁸ Chinese Buddhists also piously devoted themselves to ritual writing, copying the scriptures in the canon. Wealthy donors commissioned manuscript copies written in gold and silver. Poor but zealous devotees paid for the carving of one block or the printing of one fascicle in the canon. Some even went to extremes by using their blood as ink.⁹ The Japanese even invented a speedy method of copying the entire canon in one day by allotting the job to many devotees, who copied their assignments individually at the same time. In 1211, in the presence of Emperor Gotoba 後鳥羽 (1180–1239), 13,315 monks copied the entire canon in one day.¹⁰ Relatively little has been written by modern scholars about the "Cult of the Canon"; the essay by Jiang Wu (chapter 2) redresses this neglect.

TEXTUAL PRACTICES AND TEXTUAL IMPACT OF THE BUDDHIST CANON

The Chinese Buddhist canon has contributed to world Buddhism through its nearly two-thousand-year stewardship of texts translated into or written in Chinese. The compilation of the canon involved meticulous manipulation of thousands of Buddhist texts and developed a textual tradition that forms part of the overall scholarly tradition of East Asian book culture. Textual practices include cataloging, bibliographical study, philological and lexicographical study, and writing annotations to provide information such as pronunciation notes, results of collation with other editions, colophons with donor information, diagrams, illustrations, etc.

Cataloging is one of the most significant textual practices and has attracted scholarly attention. As some bibliographers claim, Buddhist catalogers were even more sophisticated than their Confucian counterparts. The Chinese Buddhist catalogs are not simply an enumerative list of titles; they also contain much historically descriptive information and textual analysis. A typical catalog describes its origins and summarizes or even incorporates works by previous catalogers. These catalogs often pay special attention to different aspects of a text, such as the time and place of translation, the content, and the history of its circulation. Many provide biographies of translators and prefaces to the translated texts as evidence. The records of translations are arranged chronologically or according to the nature of the content, such as Mahayana scriptures and Hinayana scriptures. Notes and discussions about the history and authenticity of the texts are appended. Even those titles that the catalogers have never seen are documented for later research. Texts written in Chinese, though not the emphasis of early catalogers, are recorded as well and put in a separate category. Very often, a list of titles recommended to be included in the canon is also appended and supplies essential information such as titles, number of scrolls, number of sheets of paper, and later the assigned characters from the *Thousand-Character Classic* (*Qianziwen* 千字文). The bibliographical taxonomy is extremely complicated and comprehensive, reflecting the sophistication of the cataloging practice.[11]

A more pressing concern was the authenticity of these "original" texts, because spurious writings produced indigenously often pretended to be of foreign origins, claiming undeserved textual authority and authenticity. The issue of apocrypha has long been recognized, and it became a major task to identify them and prevent their being confused with the Buddha's authentic words. For Buddhist catalogers, the designation "apocrypha" is obviously negative. It means a work to be excluded from the canon, or even barred from further circulation. Generally, the category refers to any indigenously produced Buddhist texts (usually outside India) that claim to be originally transmitted from India. Early catalogers made judgments based on historical records about the translation process or the content of the scripture. For example, in Daoan's 道安 catalog, he attempted to identify indigenous texts based on his knowledge of the translation history. Another cataloger, Sengyou 僧祐, used the category "suspicious and spurious scriptures" to distinguish the apocrypha based on internal evidence, such as style and content, and external evidence, such as authorship and textual provenance. Zhisheng's 智昇 *Record of Buddhist Teachings Compiled During the Kaiyuan Era* (*Kaiyuan shijiao lu* 開元釋教錄, often referred to as *Kaiyuan Catalog*) set the goal of defending the authenticity of the canon, as he barred the apocryphal scriptures from being included in the official edition.[12] In this sense, Buddhist catalogers exercised great bibliographical control over the received Buddhist texts.

In fact, during the first centuries when the Chinese Buddhist canon was formed, a number of highly influential catalogs both described and prescribed the canon's contents and how they were to be organized. Stefano Zacchetti in his essay (chapter 3) argues that in particular, the cataloging efforts of Daoan in the late fourth century C.E. not only imitated earlier Indian organizational models but also provided new ways of classifying and organizing both the existing translations and works that he and other Chinese Buddhists continued to search for, thus formulating "the idea (and ideal) of a canon that was a powerful factor even when it had not yet developed into a fully operational framework for collecting and transmitting scriptures—that is, well before complete collections of Chinese Buddhist scriptures (i.e., actual canons) came into existence during the Southern and Northern dynasties period."

In a different but equally important way, another catalog brought out the canon's Chinese character—Fei Changfang's 費長房 *Record of the Three Treasures Throughout the Successive Dynasties* (*Lidai sanbao ji* 歷代三寶紀), compiled in the late sixth century. As Tanya Storch's reassessment in this volume (chapter 4) points out, Fei's decision to classify Buddhist texts based on the Chinese rulers who sponsored their production and his overgenerous inclusion of far more works in the canon than earlier (and later) catalogers should not be viewed as a totally wrong-headed method, as it has been labeled by many critics up through modern times. Storch examines the historical circumstances in the late sixth century, when Fei and other Buddhists felt the urgent need to defend against what they perceived as Daoist incursions into the political prestige of Buddhism, claims of Daoist historical precedence, and Daoist usurpation of Buddhist literature. Thus Fei's catalog showed clearly his notion of a Chinese Buddhist canon with contents bearing the imprimatur of the political head of the Chinese state and the *chakravartin* ruler, rather than of the sangha—which influenced the important Tang catalogs such as Daoxuan's 道宣 *Great Tang Record of Buddhist Scriptures* (*Da Tang neidian lu* 大唐內典錄) and Zhisheng's *Kaiyuan Catalog*.

PRODUCING A CANON

The complex process of producing an edition of the Chinese Buddhist canon involved mobilizing enormous financial, material, and human resources. How each edition was compiled, the woodblocks cut and stored, and the paper copies printed and disseminated constitutes a unique story that contributes to our overall understanding of the making of the canon both as a revered material object and as the accepted collection of texts recognized by religious communities and the state as the authentic teachings of the Buddha and the essence of the dharma body.

The state's motives for sponsoring an edition of the Buddhist canon were many and varied. Rulers often wished to give imposing and majestic expressions of their religious devotion by directing and funding the compilation and printing of an entire canon. This enterprise also served to remind their subjects of the extension of state power into the religious realm. Other than the state, few political, religious, and social entities could marshal the resources required for such a project. Moreover, the choice of works to be incorporated, including new texts, was subject to state approval, and those texts deemed subversive were excluded. In particular, with the publishing of *Kaibao Canon* (*Kaibaozang* 開寶藏), the first printed edition, in 983, the Song state assumed the authority to determine, with the assistance of accepted Buddhist editors, the canonicity of thousands of Buddhist works and thereby took over the authority of those earlier catalogers discussed above. The importance of *Kaibao Canon* as the exemplar for all subsequent Song-period editions in China and the two Goryeo editions, and its influence on the Khitan Liao, the Tangut, and various Yuan-period editions is undeniable. The prestige of a state edition like the *Kaibao* printing meant that bestowing copies on monasteries, clerics, and foreign states was a signal honor, and in the case of the last, also a powerful diplomatic tool.

Often there were interlocking political and religious motives for the production of a Buddhist canon. For example, the chapter in this volume on *Kaibao Canon* describes how the activities connected with the production of this first printed edition, including a century-long translation project, accorded with the early Song emperors' aim to associate their authority with the dharma and to help pacify and order the country. Moreover, the canon served as the religious work among the large literary compilations intended to bring about a cultural revival after the disruption during the Five Dynasties period. As for the Korean canon, chapter 8 by Wu and Dziwenka illustrates how foreign canons (both *Kaibao* and *Khitan*) had been successfully transformed into a powerful talismanic tradition to serve the royal court in times of national crisis. And the modern *Taishō Canon*, as Wilkinson's chapter 9 informs us, was politically appropriated into Japan's imperialist agenda.

Just as complex but even more varied were the motives for the production of "private" editions of the canon. Both Buddhist clerics and lay devotees took inspiration from *Kaibao Canon* to produce their own printed editions. After all, even more than owning a canon, serving as the headquarters of its compilation and printing would greatly enhance the prestige of a monastery and attract more patronage from both the local elite and commoners. The production, distribution, and maintenance of the canon and a series of ceremonial routines became an indispensable component of Chinese monastic life. Moreover, because reliance on private donors made financial support more tenuous than state sponsorship, the time required for the completion of a private edition varied widely. Lucille Chia's chapter 6 on *Qisha Canon* (*Qishazang* 磧砂藏) describes the complicated history of its compilation and printing (1216–ca. 1332), including the slow progress due to irregular support from devotees in the Suzhou 蘇州 region during the Song and then the significantly faster pace of work during the Yuan, when the project also enjoyed regional government backing and organization.

The production and reproduction of the Chinese Buddhist canon have facilitated religious transformations in Buddhist revival and become a way of defining religious and political identities. The formation of the canon has been a textual and social process that fostered the reification of various kinds of "textual communities," in which members adopted a shared hermeneutic strategy formed through reading and interpreting Buddhist texts. Out of these "textual communities," various ways of interpreting ancient texts emerged, aimed at restoring the "way of antiquity." As a direct result, declining Buddhist traditions, such as Chan Buddhism in the seventeenth century, were revived.[13] The compilation of the canon became a powerful way of asserting sectarian identity as well. The "heretical" White Cloud movement (*Baiyunzong* 白雲宗), for example, was eager to sponsor the publication of the Puning 普寧 edition (1277–90) during the Yuan, and through this effort its new religious identity was recognized (see Chia's chapter 6). In modern times, when new editions were produced in China and Japan, printing using Western technology was largely motivated by the rising nationalism in East Asia.

There were both continuities and changes with the advent of woodblock printing to publish the Buddhist canon. On one level, printing was just another medium for the production of Buddhist texts in order to gain religious merit. Moreover, earlier methods—the carving of sutras on stone or the copying of sutras on paper, sometimes using ink impregnated with gold or silver, or in blood, were common practices that continued into later times. Moreover, printing did not necessarily make the life of an edition less precarious than that of single manuscript copies. While printing allowed more copies to be made more efficiently, woodblocks were often damaged, destroyed, or lost, so that parts or even all of an edition could no longer be printed, and fewer and fewer paper copies survived with the passage of time. By the beginning of the fourteenth century, of the Song-period canons, only the blocks for *Qisha Canon* were extant, and even some of those had to be repaired or recarved. As for the physical format of the printed canon, for reasons of conservatism or practical handling, the scroll and sutra binding remained as popular as it had been for manuscript copies. Not until the late sixteenth century was the string-bound format adopted for *Jiaxing*

Canon (*Jiaxingzang*嘉興藏), which also introduced other notable changes in the ways it was produced, compiled, and presented on the printed page.

One notable change was that the state-sponsored *Kaibao Canon*, the first that was printed, signaled the transfer of authority from the earlier catalogs that had determined the canonicity of scriptures to the canon itself. Thereafter, catalogs continued to be compiled but served as descriptive listings for their respective editions of the canon. Other changes resulted from the nature of block printing. As long as the woodblocks were available, devotees wishing to earn religious merit could choose to have not the entire canon, but just one or a few works reprinted. This way, with the passage of time, the prestige of the woodblocks as the components of an entire canon gave way to a somewhat more ordinary use, to reprint individual texts on demand for donors seeking to gain religious merit with the replication of one sutra (or part thereof)—which happened with the woodblocks for *Qisha Canon*, for instance.

The great size of the Chinese Buddhist canon meant that its production required not only funding and material resources but also well-organized administrative offices to supervise the project. State-sponsored editions were usually handled by a special imperial agency created for the purpose. The Ming government, for example, maintained an office controlled by eunuchs, the scripture factory (*jingchang* 經廠), to manage printing affairs. When such an imperial canon was bestowed upon a monastery, many central and local administrations were necessary to handle the process properly. In the late Ming, the Ministry of Rites in Nanjing was actively involved in creating rules for distributing the canon in Nanjing and treated it as a government duty.

In the private domain, the organization of the printing project could be even more complicated. For example, a sophisticated organization was set up for compiling and printing *Jiaxing Canon* in the late Ming and early Qing. This agency divided responsibilities among various staff members, such as the sponsors, supporters, chief fund raisers, assistant fund raisers, chief monks to manage the canon, chief monks to manage the print blocks, collators and proofreaders, carvers, and printing workers. Darui Long's study (chapter 7) considers three Ming editions and one Qing edition, and provides the most detailed information on how the compilation and printing of these canons were managed. When the canon was distributed, it was often treated as a valuable commodity and thus formed its own "commodity chain" in which private printing shops, merchants, and local literati were involved. In addition, the thriving commercial printers such as scripture shops (*jingpu* 經鋪) and monastic printers played an important role in producing the canon through commissions.[14]

Finally, in historiographic terms, information about the actual production of editions of the canon becomes relatively more abundant beginning with the age of print. Earlier studies of *Kaibao Canon* have discussed its printing, the extant woodcut illustrations, the role of the Song state in sponsoring and supervising its compilation and publication, and the political and diplomatic functions of this first printed edition of the Chinese canon. The essay by Wu, Chia, and Chen (chapter 5) looks in detail at not only the historical circumstances under which *Kaibao Canon* was produced but also its influence on the two editions of *Goryeo Canon* (*Goryeojang* 高麗藏), especially the second one. Indeed, an examination of the collation notes of the Korean monk Sugi 守其 for the second Goryeo edition provides the opportunity for a reevaluation of *Kaibao Canon*.

THE CHINESE BUDDHIST CANON BEYOND CHINA

So far, not only in China but also in Japan and Korea, the study of the Chinese Buddhist canon has largely focused on the bibliographical aspects and empirical descriptions of various editions. No doubt these fundamental studies provide the foundation for further research. However, it is less clear for scholars of Chinese religion and culture how the handling of such a massive body of Buddhist texts affected Buddhist communities in China and beyond.

Although the Chinese Buddhist canon was first produced in Chinese, it became a collection shared and modified by Buddhists throughout East Asia. The Goryeo kingdom, having received *Kaibao Canon* and other Buddhist texts from China, as well as *Khitan Canon*, produced two editions of their own. As the essay by Jiang Wu and Ron Dziwenka (chapter 8) shows, the second Goryeo edition could justifiably claim to be "better than the original"—that is, superior to *Kaibao Canon* in its meticulous collation. Indeed, the Goryeo state used their editions in ways not found in China, including having the canon serve as a gigantic talisman to protect the country against various calamities. As for the modern Taishō edition produced in Japan in the early twentieth century, Greg Wilkinson shows how it was deeply embedded in a nationalist agenda that represented both the country's imperialist aspirations and a new kind of Buddhist scholarship deeply influenced by the Western academic study of religion.

As varied as the topics covered in this volume are, they also serve as an important, if obvious reminder that so much more can be done in examining the history of the Chinese Buddhist canon in East Asia. As Paul Harrison noted, "'the Chinese Buddhist canon' is itself an abstraction of many highly variable collections"[15]—variable in contents, in organization, and in presentation. These changes were often effected as the canon was presented in different media, including oral transmission, hand copies, engravings on stone, block-printed editions, movable-type editions, and now digitized versions. We are reminded that the Chinese Buddhist canon is a complex collection and can but marvel at its continuing transformation even as it preserves the religious teachings of nearly three thousand years.

NOTES

1. For a succinct introduction to the (notions of a) Buddhist canon, see Harrison, "Canon."

2. For recent developments in the history of the book, see Eliot and Rose, eds., *A Companion to the History of the Book,* and Finkelstein and McCleery, *The Book History Reader.* For surveys of studies in the history of the Chinese book, see Brokaw, "Book History in Premodern China" and "On the History of the Book in China," 3–5; Bussotti, "General Survey of the Latest Studies in Western Languages on the History of Publishing in China."

3. Kamata Shigeo formulates this idea in his paper "Chūgoku bukkyōken no keisei."

4. Schopen, "The Phrase 'sa pṛthvīpradeśaṣ caityabhūto bhavet' in the *Vajracchedikā.*"

5. For details, see Fang Guangchang, *Zhongguo xieben dazangjing yanjiu,* 210–22 and 540–44.

6. For details, see Li Fuhua and He Mei, *Hanwen Dazangjing yanjiu,* 98–100; Li Jining, "Jinzang xinziliao kao"; and Zhang, "The Strength of the Forgotten."

7. See Bai Huawen, "Xinxi shidai de zangjing gongyang."

8. Nozawa Yoshimi, *Risshō daigaku toshokan shozō Mindai Nanzō mokuroku,* 73–74. For discussions of different modes of reading scriptures in contemporary Taiwan, see Levering, "Scripture and Its Reception."

9. The allusion is derived from the Avataṃsaka (Huayan) scripture. See Kieschnick, "Blood Writing in Chinese Buddhism," and Yu, *Sanctity and Self-Inflicted Violence in Chinese Religions.*

10. Mizuno, *Buddhist Sutras,* 171.

11. For details, see Liang Qichao, "Fojia jinglu," 21.

12. For details about how each catalog handles the issue of the apocrypha, see Tokuno, "The Evaluation of Indigenous Scriptures in Chinese Buddhist Bibliographical Catalogues."

13. Here we borrow the concept of "textual communities" from European historian Brian Stock, who explains the rise of "heretic" Christian groups in medieval Europe by focusing on how texts were interpreted and literacy functioned in these groups. For discussion of the role of textual communities in the Buddhist revival in the seventeenth century, see Wu, *Enlightenment in Dispute,* 245–56.

14. Nozawa Yoshimi, *Mindai Daizōkyō shi no kenkyū,* 299–320. Chia, "Publishing Activities of Buddhist Monasteries and Sutra Printshops."

15. Harrison, "Canon," 114.

PART I

Overview

1. *The Chinese Buddhist Canon Through the Ages*

ESSENTIAL CATEGORIES AND CRITICAL ISSUES IN THE STUDY OF A TEXTUAL TRADITION

Jiang Wu

The Chinese Buddhist canon is an organized collection of Buddhist texts translated into or written in Chinese. Its main content centers on translated Buddhist works from Indian and Central Asian regions and is supplemented with Buddhist and related texts written in Chinese. In Buddhist communities, a complete set of the canon has also been treated as the object of worship and devotion, acquiring significant textual and spiritual authority. Because of the complexity of its structure and historical evolution, the formation and transformation of the Chinese Buddhist canon can be considered a phenomenon with religious, social, and textual significance in Buddhist history.

In this chapter, I intend to orient readers toward a basic understanding of the Chinese Buddhist canonic tradition and focus on some critical categories and issues in the study of this great textual culture. I first outline the origin of the Chinese Buddhist canon and its historical development. Next I describe the structure of the canon as seen in various catalogs. Because the canon is also a physical object, its material aspects and physical layout will be discussed as well. Finally, I will single out a few critical issues in the study of the Chinese canon.

THE ORIGIN OF THE CHINESE
BUDDHIST CANON

The origin of the Chinese Buddhist canon is an intriguing question because the idea of a canon was clearly brought from India through the translation of various scriptures. But there is little evidence showing that the Chinese modeled their canon on the basis of an existing "Ur-Canon" of non-Chinese origin.

In early history, "Buddha's word" (Buddhavacana) was authenticated during various councils, and the result was the formation of the so-called Tripitaka—the three baskets (sanzang 三藏) comprising Vinaya (pini 毗尼, or lü 律, disciplines), Sutra (xiuduoluo 修多羅, or xiudulu 修妬路, or more commonly jing 經, scripture), and Abhidharma (Apitan 阿毗曇, or lun 論, study of the scripture). The Sutra and Vinaya sections took form during the first council immediately after the Buddha's death at Rājagriha, and the Abhidharma section was gradually developed and added to the canon. Early Buddhist sources also refer to a classification of Buddhist literature into nine or twelve divisions (jiufenjiao 九分教 or shi'erfenjiao 十二分教, shi'erbujing 十二部經) based on literary styles.The formation of the early Buddhist canon, especially the Abhidharma section, was also based on sectarian divisions in Buddhist communities, which reflected sectarian views of early Buddhist orders. One version of the early canon was written down around the first century B.C.E. in Sri Lanka and became today's Pali canon.[1]

Although the Chinese Buddhist canon belongs to a distinctive Chinese textual tradition, the idea of constructing a canon was clearly influenced by Buddhist practice in India. Allusions to the existence of a canon were clear in various accounts of Buddha's parinirvana and the convening of the councils where Buddhist teaching was debated and authenticated.

When the event of Buddha's parinirvana was narrated in various scriptures and Vinaya texts, the formation of a body of Buddha's words and the locations of his teaching were inevitable subjects. It was often hinted in these texts that one of the results of early Buddhist councils was the creation of the canon, yet its nature and contents had been disputed. Some later texts even suggested the existence of a "Mahayana Canon," and this intrigued Chinese Buddhists because the Chinese tradition is overwhelmingly Mahayana. Because Chinese civilization was largely a written culture at the time Buddhism arrived, the Chinese, despite the fact that early Buddhist culture in India was orally based, imagined the canon to be a written collection of scriptures. Various legends emerging during the medieval period promoted the idea of a sacred canon existing in India that was not only written down but also physically stored in mythical and imaginative places such as Dragon King's Palace under the sea. This imaginative mentality gave rise to fervor among Chinese Buddhists to embark on journeys to India in search of such imaginary canons.[2]

It is clear that the idea of a canon was impressed onto the Chinese mind through the numerous references to the existence of an actual "Tripitaka." Chinese Buddhists were aware of the existence of the Buddhist canon during the process of translation and developed an early "Tripitaka Discourse," according to Stefano Zacchetti's paper (chapter 3) in this volume. For example, the fifth-century cataloger Sengyou 僧祐 (445–518) made reference to the compilation of the canon in the first council, recorded in the second fascicle of the *Mahāprajñāpāramitā śāstra* (*Dazhidu lun* 大智度論) and also in the preface to the *Sarvāstivātda Vinaya*. He even mentioned the legend of an eight-section Mahayana canon (*Bodhisattvapiṭaka*) in the translation of *Sutra on the Incarnation of Bodhisattvas* (*Pusa chutai jing* 菩薩出胎經) by Zhu Fonian 竺佛念 in the fourth century.[3]

The formation of the Chinese Buddhist canon is first of all based on massive translations of Buddhist texts imported from India and Central Asia. The translation activities started from the first century, allegedly with the translation of the *Scripture of Forty-two Sections* (*Sishi'er'zhang jing* 四十二章經), and stopped around the eleventh century. Roughly estimated, there are about 194 known translators who translated about 1,484 titles and 5,812 fascicles (Ch. *juan* 卷, literarily "scrolls" or "rolls"), according to a comprehensive catalog compiled in the Yuan Dynasty (*Zhiyuan fabao kantong zonglu* 至元法寶堪同總錄).[4] During this process, the content and structure of the canon evolved into a complicated system. For about a thousand years, translating, cataloging, and digesting these texts became a paramount task for Chinese Buddhists.

However, the imported Indian texts failed to mention a list or catalog upon which Chinese monks could have relied. Recent scholarship has developed a hypothesis that the early Chinese translation projects were tied to the scriptural tradition in the Gandhāran region, where a clear path toward creating a more organized and standardized collection of Buddhist literature, possibly a written Gandhārī canon, emerged during the second century C.E. However, it is also evident that this flourishing textual culture was independent of the Chinese tradition, and no linear link with the creation of a Chinese collection can be established.[5] As Lewis Lancaster shows convincingly, when Chinese encountered missionary monks from India and Central Asia, "the order by which texts were listed was not defined by any of the Indian information available. There was no list to give this order and no rules for making such a list. The Chinese had to invent the rule by which they could determine ordering."[6]

Although the beginning of the Chinese Buddhist canon is still unclear, early records show that the process of canonization in China coincided with the rise of the Mahayana and the transition from oral to written culture in Indian and

Central Asian Buddhism. This transition accelerated when Buddhism was introduced into China and met with the distinctive Chinese textual tradition. The accumulation of translated Buddhist texts resulted in various attempts to examine and classify them. Eventually, Chinese Buddhists organized a unique Chinese canon and continued to produce various editions to update its content and perfect its classification system.

It appears that during the formative age of Chinese Buddhism from the first to the fifth century the only option for the Chinese was to look at their indigenous bibliographical tradition for inspiration about how to organize Buddhist texts. Tanya Storch, in her recent book, shows how deeply the formation of Buddhist canonical catalogs was influenced by Confucian cataloging practice.[7] As she demonstrates, Chinese bibliographers such as Liu Xiang 劉向 (77–6 B.C.E.) profoundly influenced the formation of Buddhist Tripitaka bibliographies. It seems that in this early stage, "Buddhist bibliography in China could take no other course but to emulate Confucian bibliography."[8] Jean-Pierre Drège also suggests that the evolution of Buddhist manuscript culture has to be considered as belonging to the Chinese library and archival tradition, and many Buddhist cataloging activities were first started as part of the archiving efforts in imperial libraries.[9]

The origin of the Chinese canon is still a mystery. To solve it, scholars need to gain better understanding of the Indian textual culture at the time when Buddhism arrived in China. Moreover, the creation of the canon cannot be isolated from the influence of the Chinese bibliographical tradition. It might be futile to search for an "Ur-Canon" or "Ur-Catalog" in the Indian or Central Asian tradition.[10] However, there must be subtle influences from the Indian and Central Asian traditions that we do not fully understand right now. Even though the compilation process appears to have been a Chinese creation, the ways of handling the canon and Buddhist texts might have originated in India and Central Asia because of the continuous influx of Buddhist missionaries and texts to China until the eleventh century. For example, Gregory Schopen speculates that the building of the Revolving Tripitaka Bookcase (Sutra Repository) in China might have been influenced by similar practices in eleventh-century India.[11] Thorough research on the formation of the Chinese canon in the early stage of Chinese Buddhism may offer new insight on the issue of origin.

HISTORICAL DEVELOPMENT OF THE CHINESE BUDDHIST CANON

The Chinese Buddhist canon was often referred to as "Internal Classics" (*neidian* 內典), "Myriad of Scriptures" (*zhongjing* 眾經), "All Scriptures" (*yiqieing*

一切經), or by the more standardized name "the Great Storage of Scriptures" (*dazangjing* 大藏经). Its evolution has been a long process. The appearance of such a complete collection can be traced back to the latter half of the sixth century, when the great number of translated Buddhist texts necessitated a way to classify and catalog them. At first the canon existed as hand-copied manuscripts that were widely distributed to well-established monasteries. The compilation in 730 C.E. of Zhisheng's 智昇 *Catalog of Buddhist Works Compiled During the Kaiyuan Period* (*Kaiyuan shijiao lu* 開元釋教錄) was a landmark event, as this work became the standard catalog according to which later editions organized their contents. In the tenth century, the manuscript editions gave way to the printed editions, which have dominated the Buddhist world until the modern era.

It has been estimated that the total number of works included in all the editions of the canon amounts to 4,878, according to Chinese scholar He Mei's comprehensive catalog.[12] In addition to the Buddha's sacred words, the Chinese Buddhist canon also incorporates a large number of texts written in Chinese by Chinese, Japanese, and Korean Buddhists, both clergy and laypeople, including commentaries, philosophical treatises, philological studies, catalogs, sectarian writings, geographies and travelogues, biographical and genealogical accounts of eminent monks, and encyclopedias and dictionaries. In particular, the canon reflects a tendency to collect all available Buddhist sources—often referred to as an "open canon." (This commonly held "myth" will be discussed later.) In the beginning, it was considered the repository of all genuine translated works brought from India and Central Asia, while writings by Chinese authors were excluded or minimized. In the ninth century, the main content was relatively fixed as the translation process was gradually finished. However, in later times, along with the rise of indigenous traditions such as Tiantai 天臺 and Chan 禪, the canon quickly expanded to include works from these schools, and in modern times it has become an all-inclusive collection of available Buddhist sources translated or written in classical Chinese.

The Chinese Buddhist canon is nonsectarian in that it has incorporated texts from different schools and therefore reflects the overall heritage of Chinese Buddhism, as well as fresh developments through its incorporation of new Buddhist writings. The main section of the canon, which is based on Zhisheng's catalog, contains mostly the translated texts. The new texts that were admitted as supplements, however, reflect the sectarian developments in each stage of the history of Chinese Buddhism. For example, the discovery of *Khitan Canon* (*Qidanzang* 契丹藏) shows the vitality of Liao Buddhism and explains the rise of Buddhist scholasticism represented by Quanxiao 詮曉, Xilin 希麟, Xingjun 行均, and Daochen 道殿, who were active in eleventh-century northern China. Several new editions of the canon produced in the Song, which were sponsored and organized by Linji 臨濟 and Yunmen 雲門 monks in Fuzhou, saw a large-scale inclusion of Chan genealogies and recorded sayings such as *Jianzhong jingguo xudeng lu* 建中靖國續燈錄 (Supplementary record of lamp transmission during the *Jianzhong jingguo* period, 30 fascicles); *Chuanfa zhengzong* 傳法正宗 (The true transmission of the dharma) by Qisong 契嵩; and *Dahui yulu* 大慧語錄 (Recorded sayings of Dahui Zonggao), etc. The inclusion of these Chan texts by imperial decree reflected the rise of Chan Buddhism at that time. In all editions of the Chinese Buddhist canon, there are about 570 Chan works, surpassing all other traditions and showing the momentum of the Chan tradition in Chinese history. However, despite the fact that sectarian preferences influenced its arrangement, the Chinese Buddhist canon is remarkably nonsectarian and remains a valuable resource for all denominations.

The Chinese Buddhist canon exists in three forms: manuscript editions, the stone canon, and the printed editions. Although a few fragments of the manuscript canon and various catalogs have been discovered in Dunhuang, no single complete manuscript edition survived in China, although a great number of transcribed canons based on the imported Chinese texts and catalogs survived in Japan.[13] While the Buddhist canon was written down on paper, some zealous Buddhists also started to carve the entire corpus of Buddhist literature on rocks and stone tablets, hoping that the Buddhist teaching would survive the period of the "Latter-day Dharma" (*mofa* 末法). The tradition of the stone scripture (*shijing* 石經) continued even after the printed editions became popular.[14] After the tenth century, the printed versions predominated.

The manuscript editions were the earliest type, before the spread of printing technology. Because of the lack of physical evidence, it is estimated that the first hand-copied canon might have been created during the first half of the sixth century because there are indications of the existence of individually sponsored canons in the second half of the fifth century. The earliest evidence of the canon is a Dunhuang manuscript, fascicle 6 of the *Saṃyuktābhidharmahṛdaya* (*Za Apitan xin lun* 雜阿毗曇心論, S. 996, *T* 1552), which indicates that the official Feng Xi 馮熙 of the Northern Wei (?–495) created ten sets of the canon in 479. Other pieces of textual evidence show that the emperors in the Northern and Southern dynasties (317–589) sponsored copying the Buddhist canon and distributed it to major monasteries.[15] The great cataloger Sengyou himself was involved in creating three canons in today's Nanjing area: the two canons in Dinglin Monastery 定林寺, created during the Northern Qi (479–502) Dynasty and the Liang Dynasty, and the third in Jianchu Monastery 建初寺.[16] It is clear that Emperor Wu (r. 502–48) in the Liang Dynasty kept an extensive Buddhist library (close to 5,400 fascicles, according to a later source) in his Hualin 華林 Imperial Park, which might have served as a prototype for a canon. This collection has been referred to by the Tang Buddhist scholar Daoxuan 道宣 as

"Sutra Storage at Baoyun Hall" (*Baoyun jingzang* 寶雲經藏).[17] During the Sui (518–618) and Tang (618–907) dynasties, both officially and privately sponsored manuscript editions were widely distributed.

The Chinese scribal culture also profoundly influenced Japan during the Nara period, and the court initiated great efforts to transcribe the canon according to standard Chinese catalogs. The Nara period saw the creation of at least twenty-nine hand-copied canons, and more than forty such transcriptions produced during the Heian period are preserved today.[18] One of the most famous projects was the so-call "May First Canon," which was initiated by Empress Kōmyōshi 光明子 (701–60). The canon was named thus because a prayer dated to the first day of the fifth month of 740 was copied and attached to every transcribed scripture. The canon was organized according to the newly imported *Kaiyuan Catalog* authored by the Tang monk Zhisheng, and about 6,500 scrolls were hand-copied by scribes in the Office of Scripture Transcription, sponsored by the court. Following the Chinese tradition, the copyists were required to ritually purify themselves during the process of transcription. This canon became the model for many transcribed canons in Japan in later periods.[19]

Prior to *Kaibao Canon*, the first printed canon in the tenth century, Chinese Buddhists also started to create a stone version of the canon. The tradition of stone scriptures started in the Northern Qi as a response to persecutions of Buddhism. The greatest project was initiated by Jingwan 靜琬 (?–639), the second Tiantai patriarch Huisi's 天臺慧思 (515–77) disciple, in the Sui Dynasty. The stone tablets of the canon are located in Yunju 雲居寺 Monastery in Fangshan 房山 County of Zhuozhou 涿州, 75 kilometers south of Beijing. After the Sui and Tang dynasties, the stone canon in Fangshan was sponsored by the rulers of the Liao (Khitan, 960–1123), Jin (Jurchen, 1115–1226), and Yuan (Mongol, 1271–1368) dynasties, which had their capitals in the north. The carving project continued in the Ming. This stone version was largely based on 4,000 fascicles of translated texts provided by Zhisheng in the Tang (in manuscript form) with supplemental texts from the Khitan edition (or the Liao edition) of the canon. The earliest tablet is dated to 631, and in the beginning there was no plan to create an entire canon. Under the Liao Dynasty, the stone tablets were rearranged and assigned call numbers according to the "Thousand Character Classic" (*qianziwen*), largely based on the Liao edition of the canon. (See the following discussion for the details of the *qianziwen* system.) The Liao government also followed the format of the printing block by carving 28 columns per tablet and 17 characters per column. (The small-character edition follows 12 columns per half page and 30 characters per column.) Although the Stone Canon in Fangshan lacks the Abhidharma section and is not complete, it is closely related to the manuscript and printed editions. Nowadays, 14,620 stone tablets and 82 inscriptions survive in good condition.[20]

The printed canons dominated the Buddhist textual realm after the tenth century, and Appendix 1 in this volume provides a short introduction to each of these editions, based on Li Fuhua and He Mei's study. All the printed editions were interconnected, since each new edition often relied on the previous editions for content and format. Similar editions formed various "text families" or "lineages" as they borrowed from each other in content, format, and organizing schemes. Some even recycled the blocks of the previous edition or recarved blocks in its exact format. Based on the textual similarities among these editions, Chikusa Masaaki 竺沙雅章 and Fang Guangchang 方廣錩 proposed that all the printed editions can be grouped into "three textual systems": the tradition of central China based on *Kaibao Canon*, the northern tradition based on *Khitan Canon*, and the southern tradition based on *Chongning Canon* (*Chongning zang* 崇寧藏) (see figure 1.1).[21]

In the tenth century, the activities of printing the canon were initiated by the government in the north: *Kaibao Canon* by the Northern Song (960–1127) and *Khitan Canon* by the Liao were completed in 983 and 1068 respectively. Among the canons carved in woodblocks in the north, *Kaibao Canon*, the first of them, stood out as a model for all the later editions and influenced other editions such as *Goryeo Canon* and *Zhaocheng Canon* in the Jin (Jurchen) Dynasty. Under the influence of *Kaibao Canon*, the Goryeo court showed a remarkable inter-

FIGURE 1.1 MAHA-PRAJÑĀPĀRAMITĀ SŪTRA (AROUND 1080) FROM CHONGNING CANON, JUAN 193
Courtesy of Library of Congress. Photo by Jiang Wu, November 2010

est in the canon and created two complete versions, of which the blocks of the second version remain intact. Its superior quality, of which Chinese Buddhists in premodern times were not aware, is widely recognized today through the production of the modern canons in Japan, which have used it as the master copy to collate with other editions.

After the Song government moved to the south in 1127, monasteries in southern China made efforts to carve new editions by their own means. *Chongning Canon*, produced in Fuzhou and completed in 1112, was based on a manuscript edition different from *Kaibao Canon. Pilu Canon* 毗盧藏 and *Sixi Canon* 思溪藏 (including *Yuanjue Canon* 圓覺藏 and *Zifu Canon* 資福藏) in the southern Song, *Qisha Canon* (starting in the Song) and *Puning Canon* 普寧藏 in the Yuan, *Southern Hongwu Canon* (*Hongwu nanzang* 洪武南藏 or *Chuke nanzang* 初刻南藏), and the Japanese *Tenkai Canon* 天海藏 in the early Tokugawa period followed this tradition and formed a "text family." Among these canons carved in the south, *Qisha Canon* was unique because, as Lucille Chia shows, it was largely sponsored by private funds and played a transitional role in continuing this southern tradition from the Song and Yuan to the Ming and Qing.

During the Ming (1368–1644) and Qing (1644–1912) dynasties, several new editions were carved. Among them, under the influence of the *Collated Catalog of Buddhist Works During the Zhiyuan Period* (*Zhiyuan fabao kantong zonglu*), compiled around 1287, *Yongle Southern Canon* (*Yongle nanzang*) modified the classification system created by Zhisheng by making Sutra, Vinaya, and Abhi_dharma the first-order categories, under which texts were further divided as either Mahayana or Hinayana. (See its structure in the next section.) This edition also reorganized the supplemental texts beyond Zhisheng's list. For example, the esoteric texts were put in the category of "Works Written by Western Worthies" (*Xitu shengxian zhuanji* 西土聖賢撰集). These modifications influenced *Yongle Northern Canon* (*Yongle beizang* 永樂北藏), *Jiaxing Canon* (*Jiaxing zang* 嘉興藏 or *Jingshan zang* 徑山藏) in the late Ming and early Qing, *Qing Canon* (*Qing zang*) produced in the Qing, and the Japanese *Ōbaku Canon* (*Ōbakuzō* 黃檗藏) created in the early Edo period. Therefore, Li Fuhua believes that the new structure in *Yongle Southern Canon* represented the fourth system, in addition to the three systems proposed by Chikusa Masaaki and Fang Guangchang.[22]

Despite the frequent production and reproduction of the printed editions in China and Korea, the Japanese canonical tradition prior to 1600 was dominated by a pious scribal culture that privileged the devotional merit of handwriting. Printings of the canon were valued as well, and Japanese monasteries largely relied on imports from China and Korea before the Edo period. Japan's turn to the massive use of printing for canon production occurred during the beginning of the Edo period with the creation of the Tenkai edition in 1648, which utilized the advanced movable-type printing technology, and then the Ōbaku 黄檗 edition in 1681, which was based on the main section of the Chinese *Jiaxing Canon*.

At the turn of the twentieth century, Western printing technology quickly replaced xylography and demanded the creation of new editions of the canon. The Japanese took the initiative to adopt the new technology and created the so-called *"Reduced Print" Canon* (*Shukusatsuzō* 縮刷藏, 1880–85) and *Manji Canon* 卍字藏 (ca. 1912). *Taishō Canon* 大正藏, created in Japan (1922–34), revolutionized the traditional classification system by abolishing the division of Mahayana and Hinayana and the use of the "Thousand-Characters Classic" (*qianziwen*) as its organizing system. The Chinese efforts to create new editions such as *Pinjia Canon* 頻伽藏 and *Puhui Canon* 普慧藏, initiated in Shanghai in the 1910s and 1940s, did not bring any fruitful results until the creation of two editions of *Chinese Tripiṭaka* (*Zhonghua dazangjing* 中華大藏經) across the Taiwan strait, completed in the 1960s and 1980s respectively.

Nowadays the canon embraces the digital revolution. New efforts, such as the Chinese Buddhist Electronic Texts Association (CBETA) project in Taiwan, the *Tripitaka Koreana* project in South Korea, and the SAT Daizōkyō Text Database in Japan, have been made to digitize the entire canon and make it searchable and available online in a technically sophisticated way.[23] Meanwhile, the printed editions continue to play a role, as more beautifully packaged facsimiles and reprints of rare editions have been produced in mainland China in recent years. These new editions, in both digital formats and printed versions, meet the demands of readers for research and devotion.

THE STRUCTURE OF THE CANON AS SEEN FROM THE CATALOGS

Although the Chinese Buddhist canon maintained the tripartite form of Sutra, Vinaya, and Abhidharma, the overall structure is dramatically different from its Indian predecessors and has been adapted to accommodate its unique Chinese concerns. The Sutra section was given greater emphasis as the first part, and the subdivisions and classifications of the canon became more complicated.

The structure of the canon can be seen from various catalogs prepared for organizing Buddhist texts. In preparation for the creation of the canon, catalogs were compiled, an important step toward canonization. The need for a comprehensive catalog was a natural result of the influx of a large number of foreign texts and translations of various origins. Initially, without much sophisticated classification, the Chinese would translate any sources about Buddhism written in Indian and Central Asian languages. While such translations accumulated, issues about classification and authentication arose because obviously a group of texts dealt with similar topics and all had similar structures. Early Chinese Buddhists often had more than one translation of the original text as well.

It is clear that at a very early stage Chinese Buddhists had become conscious of the role of the catalog in creating a canon. Daoan 道安 (312–85) compiled one of the earliest catalogs, *Comprehensive Catalog of All Scriptures* (*Zongli zhongjing mulu* 綜理眾經目錄), also referred to as *Daoan's Catalog*, in 374. It is basically an enumerative catalog arranged chronologically. Although Daoan's work developed useful categories to classify the texts, it lacks principles for classifying the content of these works.[24]

The original catalog is lost. However, its content is preserved in Sengyou's *Collected Records About the Translation of the Tripitaka* (*Chu sanzang jiji* 出三藏記集), compiled in 518 in 15 fascicles, which is often called *Sengyou's Catalog* (*Youlu* 祐錄). In addition to listing all the translations, Sengyou's work describes various editions of the texts based on their translation history and provides prefaces to translations and biographies of the translators. Based on the extensive imperial collection by Emperor Wu of the Liang Dynasty, the monk Baochang 寶唱 authored *The Catalog of All Scriptures* (*Zhongjing mulu* 眾經目錄).

A lost catalog rediscovered in Dunhuang, *Subject Catalog of All Scriptures* (*Zhongjing bielu* 眾經別錄, S. 2872 and P. 3747), is perhaps the first to employ the Huayan theory of the "classification of teaching in five periods" (*wushi panjiao* 五時判教) to divide all texts into Mahayana and Hinayana.[25] Fajing's 法經 *Catalog of All Scriptures* (*Zhongjing mulu* 眾經目錄) in seven fascicles, compiled in 594, continued the division of Mahayana and Hinayana, and under each category titles were further classified as Sutra, Vinaya, or Abhidharma according to their contents. Chinese writings, however, were grouped separately.

The catalogs were directly related to the creation of a canon when a record of the list of titles to be included in the canon was added. In Fei Changfang's 費長房 *Records of the Three Treasures Throughout the Successive Dynasties* (*Lidai sanbao ji* 歷代三寶記) in 15 fascicles, which was compiled in 597 and also referred to as *Records of the Three Treasures During the Kaihuang Period* (*Kaihuang sanbao lu* 開皇三寶錄) or *Fei Changfang's Record* (*Changfang lu* 長房錄 or *Fanglu* 房錄), the "Register of Canonical Texts" (*Ruzang lu* 入藏錄) in two fascicles was included, listing all the titles that should be incorporated into the official canon. Many catalogs in the Tang also list the titles that need to be transcribed, showing that these catalogs had been used as shelf lists of the canon as well.

The monumental catalog that directly contributed to the formation of the content of all later editions was Zhisheng's *Kaiyuan Catalog* in 20 fascicles, compiled in 730. His catalog provides a systematic reevaluation of the authenticity of received Buddhist texts and a comprehensive list of "Register of Canonical Texts" for creating the actual canon. A shorter version based on its list of canonical texts, *Digest of Catalog of Buddhist Works Compiled During the Kaiyuan Period* (*Kaiyuan shijiao lu luechu* 開元釋教錄略出), modified Zhisheng's classification method slightly and for the first time assigned the *qianziwen* characters to the division of cases, showing the popularity of his catalog. Because Zhisheng's catalog became the standard checklist for restoring the canon after the Great Persecution in 845, all the later editions followed its structure with some variations.

Zhisheng's work is divided into two parts. First is the "General Catalog" in 10 fascicles, which classifies titles according to translators and arranges them chronologically according to 19 dynasties. This part also includes biographies of 176 translators. The second part is "Separate Catalog" in 10 fascicles, which studies the bibliographical conditions of each title, both extant and lost. More importantly, Zhisheng discusses each title according to the nature of the content as either Mahayana or Hinayana and further distinguishes them as Sutra, Vinaya, and Abhidharma. In total, Zhisheng's record documents translations from 67 to 730 C.E. and contains 2,278 titles and 7,046 volumes translated by 176 translators. At the end (fascicles 19 and 20) is the "Register of Canonical Texts," which is based on his "Record of Extant Titles with Translation" (*youyi youben lu* 有譯有本錄). It includes 1,076 titles and 5,048 scrolls in 480 cases and became the standard for the main section of the canon in later periods.

Under Zhisheng's organization, Buddhist works are divided into three sections: "Mahayana Works" (*Pusa sanzang lu* 菩薩三藏錄, 638 titles, 2,745 scrolls, and 258 cases), "Hinayana Works" (*Shengwen sanzang lu* 聲聞三藏錄, 330 titles, 1,762 scrolls, 165 cases), and "Works by Worthies" (*Shengxian jizhuan lu* 聖賢集傳錄, 108 titles, 541 scrolls, 57 cases). Under each section, there are subsections and subcategories to classify the texts as illustrated in the following list.[26]

THE STRUCTURE OF ZHISHENG'S CATALOG BASED ON THE OUTLINE OF HIS WORK (*KAIYUAN SHIJIAOLU LÜECHU*)

I. Mahayana Tripitaka
   A. Pitaka of Mahayana Sutra
      1. Mahayana sutras with multiple translations
         a. Sutras of the five major classes
            1) Prajñāpāramiṭa class
            2) Ratnakūṭa class
            3) Mahāsaṃnipāta class
            4) Avataṃsaka class
            5) Nirvāṇa class

　　　　6) Sutras beyond the five major sections with multiple
　　　　　 translations
　　　 b. Mahayana sutras with single translations
　 B. Pitaka of Mahayana Vinaya
　 C. Pitaka of Mahayana Abhidharma
　　　 1. Commentaries on Mahayana sutras
　　　 2. Collections of Mahayana exegesis
II. Hinayana Tripitaka
　 A. Hinayana sutras with multiple translations
　　　 1. The longer Āgama Sutra
　　　 2. The medium Āgama Sutra
　　　 3. The supplementary Āgama Sutra
　　　 4. The miscellaneous Āgama Sutra
　 B. Hinayana sutras with single translations
　 C. Hinayana Vinaya
　 D. Hinayana Abhidharma
III. Tripitaka of Sages and Worthies
　 A. Collections of translated Indian works
　 B. Collections of works in this land (China)

This bibliographical structure was largely followed by later compilers of the Buddhist canon. The main section of the canon thus became fixed. A major development in later times was the inclusion of the majority of the Chinese writings in the supplemental section of the canon. Although there was some confusion about how to classify new translations and added texts, down to the Ming Dynasty (1368–1644), all the later supplements were arranged in chronological order.

The classification system developed by Zhisheng underwent another change in the early Ming Dynasty. Starting from *Yongle Southern Canon* (*Yongle nanzang*), completed in 1420, Zhisheng's structure was modified: the three "baskets," Sutra, Vinaya, and Abhidharma, became the first-order categories, under which Mahayana and Hinayana texts were arranged. An example of this modified structure can be seen from *Yongle Northern Canon* (*Yongle beizhang*) completed in 1440, whose catalog was based on the *Yongle Southern Canon* and translated by Nanjō Bun'yū 南條文雄 into English.

MODIFIED STRUCTURE IN *YONGLE NORTHERN CANON*[27]

　 I. Sutra Pitaka
　　 A. Sutras of the Mahayana
　　 B. Sutras of the Hinayana

    C. Sutras of the Mahayana and Hinayana, admitted into the canon dur-
       ing the Song and Yuan dynasties
II. Vinaya Pitaka
    A. Vinaya of the Mahayana
    B. Vinaya of the Hinayana
III. Abhidharma Pitaka
    A. Abhidharma of the Mahayana
    B. Abhidharma of the Hinayana
    C. Works of the Abhidharma of the Mahayana and Hinayana, succes-
       sively admitted into the canon during the Song and Yuan dynasties
IV. Miscellaneous Works
    A. Works of the sages and wise men of the Western Country (India)
    B. Works of this country (China)
    C. Several Chinese works successively admitted into the canon during
       the great Ming Dynasty
    D. Works wanting in the Northern Collection and now added from the
       Southern Collection with their case numbers (characters)

The Japanese *Taishō Canon*, compiled in modern times, represents a revolutionary change in the structure of the canon. Its cataloging system departs from
Zhisheng's *Kaiyuan Catalog* by abolishing the division of Mahayana and Hinayana and the use of the "Thousand-Character Classic" as its retrieval method.
This newly invented structure contains all the content of the three "baskets"
and makes the sectarian division of Mahayana and Hinayana less apparent. It
also allows more historical works related to Chinese Buddhism, such as non-
Buddhist works, new discoveries in Dunhuang, esoteric liturgical texts, catalogs,
and iconography, to be included, greatly enriching the content of the Chinese
canon. In addition, it highlights the Japanese contribution by creating its own
supplementary sections. This new structure is illustrated below.

THE STRUCTURE OF *TAISHŌ CANON*

I. Main Content (55 volumes)
    (The following sections roughly correspond to the Sutra Pitaka)
    Āgama texts (vol. 1–2)
    Buddha's and his disciples' biographies (vol. 3–4)
    Mahayana sutras in six sections
        Prajñapāramitā section (vols. 5–8)
        Lotus Sutra (Saddharma-puṇḍarīka) section (vol. 9)
        Flower Garland or Avataṃsaka section (vols. 9–10)
        Treasure accumulation (Ratnakūṭa) section (vol. 11)

Mahāparinirvāṇa section (vol. 12)

Great Assembly section (vol. 13)

"Sutra Collection" section (vols. 14–17)

"Esoteric Teaching" section (vols. 18–21)

(The following section roughly corresponds to the Vinaya Pitaka.)

Vinaya section (vols. 22–24)

(The following section roughly corresponds to the Abhidharma Pitaka.)

    Commentaries on Sutras (India) section (vols. 24–26)

    Abhidharma section for Hinayana works (particularly Sarvāstivāda) (vols. 26– 29)

    Madhyamaka section (vol. 30)

    Yogācāra section (vol. 31)

    "Collected Treatises" section (vol. 32)

    Commentaries on Sutras by Chinese authors (vols. 33–39)

    Commentaries on Vinaya by Chinese authors (vol. 40)

    Commentaries on Śāstra by Chinese authors (vols. 40–44)

(The following sections roughly correspond to the supplementary sections of the Chinese canon.)

    "Schools and Lineages" section (vols. 44–48)

    "History and Biography" section (vols. 49–52)

    "Sourcebook" section (vols. 53–54)

    "Non-Buddhist Teachings" section (vol. 54)

    "Catalog" section (vol. 55)

II. Supplementary Content by Japanese authors (30 volumes)

    Supplementary Section of Commentaries on Sutras (vols. 56–61)

    Supplementary Section of Commentaries on Vinayas (vol. 62)

    Supplementary Section of Commentaries on Śāstra (vols. 63–70)

    Supplementary Section of Schools and Lineages (vols. 70–84)

    Siddhaṃ section for liturgical texts (vol. 84)

    "Lost Ancient Texts" section (vol. 85)

    "Suspected Texts" section (vol. 85)

III. Iconographical Content (12 volumes)

IV. General Catalogs (3 volumes)

MATERIAL ASPECTS AND PHYSICAL LAYOUT

The Chinese canon is a unique combination of a series of material and physical elements manifested in aspects such as the media of production and reproduction, the tools of assembly, the layout for transcription and printing, and the use of a numbering system. The early editions of the Chinese Buddhist canon were handwritten and copied by scribes. Jingtai's 靜泰 catalog of the canon stored at Da Jing'ai Monastery 大敬愛寺 in Luoyang (*Da Jing'ai si yiqie jinglun mulu* 大唐東京大敬愛寺一切經論目錄), compiled between 664 and 665, started to record the number of sheets of paper (*zhi* 紙) needed for copying specific titles. Daoxuan's *Catalog of the Inner Classics of the Great Tang Dynasty* (*Da Tang neidian lu* 大唐內典錄) also gave the number of cases (*han* 函). All these pieces of evidence show that the catalogs were intended to be used as shelf lists for curating a hand-copied canon. These activities were usually organized by official agencies and received imperial sponsorship. During the Sui and Tang dynasties, different versions of the canon were available through hand-copying and were stored in royal palaces and Buddhist monasteries. In the tenth century, the major means of production changed to woodblock printing (xylography). In this process, the physical layout and the material characteristics of the canon underwent several changes along with advances in production technologies, such as printing and binding. There are four important aspects of this development: the use of the "Thousand Character Classic" as the call number system, the physical layout, the effects of printing and binding, and the device for storage.

First, as a massive textual production, the creation of a canon requires a sophisticated method to store and retrieve each individual text in a precise way and a system to assign a unique number to each text. Although Zhisheng's *Kaiyuan Catalog* provided a classification system based on subjects, a call number system reflecting the shelf order of each individual text was needed for the Buddhist canon, which resembles a library. Because the Chinese language is not alphabetical, a natural alphabetical order based on titles and author's names cannot be used.Several transitional methods were also employed, according to Fang Guangchang's study. For example, the method of title initials (*jingming biaozhi fa* 經名標誌法 or *jingming zhihao fa* 經名帙號法) employs one character from the title of the text in the canon to mark each individual scroll or case. The method of "fixed shelf storage" (*ding ge chucun fa* 定格儲存法) was used to store different categories of cases in fixed positions in a huge cabinet. The method of verse-based case number (*jisong zhihao fa* 偈頌帙號法) assigned characters in popular liturgical verses to each case. These methods were supposed to distinguish each individual text and provide readers an easy way to retrieve it from the shelf. However, they often resulted in duplicate "call numbers," as the characters were neither unique nor following a sequential order.

Finally, after the Great Persecution of Buddhism in 845, a new method based on the one thousand characters (*qianziwen zhihao fa* 千字文帙號法) was accepted as the most convenient system. The "Thousand Character Classic," authored by Zhou Xingsi 周興嗣 (469?–521) of the Liang Dynasty during the

Southern and Northern dynasties, was a primer for teaching pupils about Chinese language and culture. By definition, it was written using a thousand Chinese characters without duplications, and its contents covered basic knowledge of the natural world, history, ethics, and culture. It became didactic reading material for children, and all educated Chinese were supposed to memorize it.[28] The text was ideal for a call number system because it used one thousand different characters without repetition. The verse is long enough to include all Buddhist works and allows for expansion. (In the case of the seventeenth-century *Jiaxing Canon*, all the thousand characters were used up, and thus some later texts were without assigned characters.) The system based on this essay simply assigns each character to a case. This method first appeared in the anonymous *Digest of Kaiyuan Catalog* (*Kaiyuan shijiao lu luechu*), based on Zhisheng's work, and was widely adopted by the printed editions of the canon in later times. Therefore, one of these characters' appearances in a text became a key marker for identifying whether the text was included in the canon.[29]

Second, in addition to its contents, the Chinese Buddhist canon has some distinctive physical characteristics, such as typographical features and formats. Variations call for special attention and might be clues for dating the edition of the canon. For example, various editions of the canon differ in format (*banshi* 版式). For the manuscript editions and some early printed editions, the layout of a finished page had been standardized as 28 columns per sheet and 17 characters per column. The first printed edition, *Kaibao Canon*, which was still assembled as scrolls, has 23 columns per sheet and 14 characters per column, apparently not following this standard format. *Chongning Canon*, created in Fuzhou, which appeared in an accordion-folding style, has one sheet of paper with 36 columns (some are 30 columns) and 17 characters per column and has been folded into six half-pages, each having six columns. The string-bound *Jiaxing Canon* folds a sheet of paper into two half-pages, each having 10 columns and 20 characters per column. The modern *Taishō Canon*, completely adopting the modern book format, prints three horizontal registers on one page, with 29 columns and 17 characters per column in each register.

At the beginning or the end of a text, a preface (*kanji* 刊記) or colophon (*tiji* 題記) was often appended, including information such as the origin of the text, dates of printing, sponsoring agencies or individuals, and even names of scribes (*xiegong* 寫工), carvers (*kekong* 刻工), printers (*yingong* 印工), and binders (*zhuangbeigong* 裝褙工 or *zhuangdinggong* 裝訂工). Some of this information appears in the center of the printed editions ("heart of the page," *banxin* 版心), where short titles, fascicle numbers, and some of the thousand characters can also be found. Most later editions include illustrations such as a frontispiece image (*feihua* 扉畫) of the Buddha assembly at the beginning of the scroll or fascicle and the image of the protective guardian Weituo 韋陀 at the end. A so-called dragon tablet (*Longpai* 龍牌) in the front or back, which was inscribed with prayers for imperial patronage, greatly enhanced the prestige of such a canon. Some editions also have donation tablets (*Shijing yuanwen pai* 施經願文牌), which were often decorated with a lotus flower (*lianhuapai* 蓮花牌) and recorded the donor's good wishes. (The central area of these tablets was often left blank intentionally, to be filled with donors' names and prayers.) Illustrations were also inserted into the text. One example is the famous landscape woodcuts printed in the Song imperial text *Expounding the Secret Treasure Store* (*Mizangquan* 秘藏詮) in *Kaibao Canon* and the first *Goryeo Canon*, which were preserved at Harvard and in Korea and Japan. (For a discussion of this text and a reprint of one of the pages from the scrolls preserved at the Harvard Art Museum, see chapter 5.)

Third, the production of the canon was also affected by the development of printing technology. Woodblock printing was invented in the seventh century, largely attributed to the need to spread Buddhist scriptures.[30] The mature technology was used for printing the first canon at the printing center Chengdu in Sichuan between 971 and 983, during the Northern Song Dynasty. It was suitable for producing massive projects such as a Buddhist canon because the blocks could be stored and repaired for later use.Binding styles (*zhuangbiao* 裝裱) also changed through history. Early Buddhist texts were often copied on sheets of paper, and several sheets were pasted end to end to form a continuous scroll (*juanzhouzhuang* 卷軸裝). Following the structure of a catalog such as Zhisheng's *Kaiyuan Catalog*, Buddhist texts were divided according to size: a hundred or two hundred sheets of paper, amounting to ten scrolls, were put together into a case (*zhi* 帙 or *han* 函). This collection of scrolls was wrapped with covers (*baoyi* 包衣 or *huyi* 護衣 or *hanyi* 函衣) made of cloth, bamboo, or silk, often in different colors. The earliest printed canon, the Kaibao edition, followed this style. Another early binding style was the so-called Indian style (*fanjia ben* 梵莢本), bundling pages together with strings in imitation of the binding of palm-leaf scriptures. To make it easy to locate a specific section in the text, a long sheet of paper was folded into several pages, called accordion-folding style (*jingzhezhuang* 經折裝), which became the dominant format for binding Buddhist scriptures. In the seventeenth century, *Jiaxing Canon* adopted the popular string-stitched booklet style (*fangcezhuang* 方冊裝 or *xianzhuang* 線裝), similar to the style of popular secular books at that time. One set of *Khitan Canon* created in the twelfth century appeared in the butterfly style (*hudie zhuang* 蝴蝶裝), by which one page is folded and pasted in the center to form a pile.[31] Because of the popularity of the accordion-folding style, many later prints from the early blocks, which were supposed to be assembled as scrolls, adopted this format.The quality of the paper used for copying Buddhist scriptures varies. The common paper used in Dunhuang manuscripts was made of hemp and mulberry. One kind is white sutra paper (*baijing zhi* 白經紙) or stiff white paper (*yingbai zhi* 硬白紙) and the other is stiff yellow paper (*yinghuang zhi* 硬黃紙), which was dyed with Huangbo 黃檗 extracts (*Phellodendrum amurense*). Records suggest that the paper for copying sutras and producing the canon was of better quality. In the Song, the famous Golden-Grain Paper (*Jinsu jian* 金粟牋), a variant of stiff yellow paper, was named after Jinsu Monastery at Haiyan 海鹽 county in Jiangsu and was produced in Suzhou from 1068 to 1094. It was used for copying the canon and became a kind of collectible decorative paper among the literati. This strong and sturdy paper was claimed to be made of silk cocoons but actually had been made with mulberry and hemp. The surface of the paper is smooth and glossy, as both sides are waxed.[32] Korean paper and ink were renowned for their quality as well and had been used for producing *Khitan Canon* in the Liao Dynasty.[33] The woodblocks for printing the canon could be made of pear wood, cherry wood, jujube wood, or catalpa wood; among them, pear wood is the best for carving.

Finally, after its production, the canon was stored in large cabinets and installed in special locations. It is evident that during the seventh century, Buddhist libraries used to store the manuscript canon were prominent buildings in monastic compounds, and some monasteries even had more than one library and canon. According to Daoxuan's account, during the Tang Dynasty, the manuscript editions were kept in a huge cabinet specially designed for storing Buddhist sutras. The cabinet was divided into three vertical sections, each of which was further divided into nine horizontal levels. (The sixth level of the left section and the second and fourth levels on the right were further divided into two small sections.) In total, there were thirty chambers. Following a sequence, the cases and wrappers were stored in fixed places, marked with titles for retrieval.[34]

The earliest surviving Tripitaka cabinet is preserved in the Bhagavad Scripture Storage Hall (*Bojia jiaozang dian* 薄伽教藏殿) at Huayan Monastery in Datong, in today's Shanxi province. The cabinets at this location have been used for storing the Khitan edition. Thirty-eight cabinets were arranged along the wall in the hall. In a large Chinese monastery, a special building called a scripture storage pavilion (*zangjingge* 藏經閣) with two stories, designed for storing the canon, is usually located at the back of the monastic compound. The first floor is the Hall of a Thousand Buddhas, representing the assembly devoted to reading scriptures. On the second floor, cabinets are arranged along the walls in a style called wall storage (*bizang* 壁藏).[35]

Another popular storage method, examined in detail in my chapter on the "Cult of the Canon" in this volume, was wheel storage (*lunzang* 輪藏) or a revolving wheel storage cabinet (*zhuanlunzang* 轉輪藏), invented by Fu Xi 傅翕 or Fu Dashi 傅大士 (497–569). To mark his contribution, his statue was often placed in front of the device, flanked by statues of his two sons. This device makes reading the canon more convenient, done by turning an octagonal revolving cabinet full of Buddhist texts. (There were four-sided and six-sided cabinets in early times.) The cabinet could be as tall as eight feet, and nine feet in diameter. If it was a fixed structure and could not move, devotees would circumambulate around it. Such a device thus served as a shortcut to achieving the benefits of reading the entire canon.[36]

CRITICAL ISSUES IN THE STUDY OF THE CHINESE BUDDHIST CANON

The Chinese Buddhist canon in East Asian context is a familiar but challenging subject. It is familiar because Buddhist scholars deal with the canon on a daily basis in order to make use of its vast textual repertoire. It is challenging because the canon and its various editions constitute a formidable text body with intricate links among themselves and far-reaching impacts on Buddhist communities. Moreover, every text and every edition of the canon has its own life, involving a great number of individuals who devoted themselves to its creation and maintenance. In this chapter, I have summarized some of the basic aspects of this complex tradition based on current scholarship. While research on the canon continues, the accumulation of research on its bibliographic components, discoveries of new editions and texts, and creation of new canons may easily lead to the fragmentation of knowledge and major oversight of some critical issues. At the end of this chapter, I would like to muse upon some of these, which have not yet been addressed sufficiently but need to be studied further. Some of the issues, such as the phenomenon of the Cult of the Canon, have been discussed in the introduction and later chapters and will not be listed below.

1. THE DEFINITION OF THE CHINESE BUDDHIST CANON

So far, there is no commonly accepted definition of the Chinese Buddhist canon. Even the very term "Chinese Buddhist canon" is misleading, because although the canon is based on the classical Chinese language and originated in China, other parts of East Asia, such as Korea and Japan, also engaged in and contributed significantly to this canonical tradition. Here, it should be noted that as a modifier, "Chinese" in the phrase "Chinese Buddhist canon" contains only its linguistic connotation and suggests that the medium of writing down the canon relies on the use of classical Chinese. Geographically, this canonic tradition is best referred to as belonging to the East Asian Buddhist textual culture because the various editions of the canon, originating from China, were brought to neighboring East Asian countries and were further developed. Therefore, some scholars, such as Robert Buswell, prefer to use a term such as "East Asian Buddhist canons," which is much broader in its connotation and extension. Some may object to the use of "canon" as singular with a definite article; as Paul Harrison claims, "there is no such thing as *the* Buddhist canon."[37] The singular form may conceal the fact that there are different editions and textual families within this tradition. The use of the English word "canon" also can be problematic, and the Indic term "Tripitaka" has often been used instead. However, as Lewis Lancaster shows convincingly, "Tripitaka" is not suitable to describe the Chinese Buddhist canon because "the housing and subsequent listing of the texts in the Buddhist libraries of China could not be limited to the three categories of the Sanskrit classification," and "the Chinese Buddhist canon is a complex mixture of Indian and East Asian patterns."[38] More questions can be raised about the nature of the canon: whether the Chinese canon is simply a library, archive, or mere collection of a series of selected texts in comparison with the Western canonical traditions.

To reveal the structural and physical characteristics of this canonical tradition primarily based on texts written in literary Chinese, Professor Fang Guangchang has made an attempt to offer a succinct definition:

> Including essentially the translated Buddhist scriptures of past ages as the core of its content, the Chinese Buddhist canon is the collection of the Chinese Buddhist classics and related literature organized according to certain structures and with some external identification markers.[39]

In this definition, Fang emphasizes "three essential elements" in the composition of a canon: "selection criteria," "systematic structure," and "physical markers." In this light, the Chinese canon is not an arbitrary collection of Buddhist texts but a conscious reassembly of a group of writings according to a well-crafted set of selection criteria articulated in the sophisticated compilation of catalogs, which provide systematic structures that all editions abide by. (In this sense, Jonathan Z. Smith's definition of the canon as an arbitrary list of texts might not apply to the Chinese canon.[40]) Moreover, the canon has a distinctive physical existence with unique external characteristics that can be identified as belonging to a specific variant of a text family. These characteristics include page layout, calligraphic style, binding method, printing format, and the use of a call number system. In his research, Fang has consciously used this definition to study various editions of the canon, especially the manuscript editions. Of course, his definition merits more consideration and needs to be further refined.

For example, although Professor Fang did note the religious aspect of the canon, his definition does not offer a satisfactory explanation regarding the source of its canonicity and authority, not to mention the dynamic interaction between the canon and the religious community.

2. THE MYTH OF AN "OPEN" CANON

The flexibility and the lack of rigid organizing standards in the Buddhist canonical tradition have been observed by many scholars. Paul Harrison believes that all Buddhist canons are basically "open" canons "in which commonly accepted principles of authenticity take the place of a rigidly defined and bounded set of texts in a given linguistic form."[41] The Chinese canon is a notorious example of such an "open" canon. Paul Swanson, for example, summarizes this widely believed idea as follows:

> The Mahayana Buddhist canon is a relatively "open" canon. Compared to the relatively "closed" canon of Christianity or Islam, or even of Theravada Buddhism, it does not have a clear beginning or end. It is not bound by any historical period or geographical area. It is possible to continue to add to the Mahayana Buddhist canon; "scripture" (or more accurately, the "words of the Buddha" [buddhavacana]) is not limited to the actual words of the historical Buddha Śākyamuni.[42]

Swanson's description gives the wrong impression that the Chinese Buddhist canon never faced closure in its long history. One of the historical reasons for such "openness," as Lewis Lancaster points out, is the piecemeal transmission of Buddhist texts into China, which requires Chinese Buddhists to keep their collections "open" in order to search for and include the "missing" texts.[43] It is true that for modern canons given academic merit as collections of essential texts, the structure of the canon tends to be open to change. However, a close look at the canon formation process in East Asia reveals that after the initial "opening" phase of a few centuries, the Chinese canon appears to have reached a point of closure in the mid-eighth century with a series of attempts to create a standardized "Register of Canonical Texts." Eventually, the Chinese canon became based on a core body of texts stipulated by monk Zhisheng's *Kaiyuan Catalog*, which fixed the size of the entire canon at 5,048 fascicles (*juan*) and 480 cases. For centuries, despite the fact that the canon has continued to grow, this core body has remained stable, without much alteration. In the popular consciousness, the canon "closed" with this number of texts listed in Zhisheng's catalog. The number of fascicles was even mythologized in Chinese folklore and became the standard size through the popular Chinese novel *Journey to the West* (*Xiyouji* 西遊記), in which the Chinese canon is described as having exactly 5,048 fascicles.[44]

In reality, texts from Zhisheng's *Kaiyuan Catalog* form the core of the main canon and became a *sine qua non* for all canons in premodern East Asia. The sectarian compilations without this core of translated texts cannot be referred to as the "Great Canon" in Buddhist communities. For example, recent compilations of sectarian writings by Korean and Japanese Buddhists have been duly titled "Complete Collections" (K. *jeonseo* or J. *zensho* 全書) rather than a canon. It is no wonder that Chinese scholar Li Fuhua calls all editions following the *Kaiyuan Catalog* in the premodern era "The Kaiyuan Tripitaka" (*Kaiyuan dazangjing* 開元大藏經).[45] Even within the *Kaiyuan Catalog*, the first four major sections of Mahayana scriptures (Prajñāpāramitā, Ratnakūṭa, Avataṃsaka, and Nirvāṇa), which comprise 840 fascicles in total, were often regarded as the essential core of the entire canon. A canon based on these four sections has been referred to as "Small Canon" (*xiaozang* 小藏) in China. If we borrow Swiss theologian Alexander Schweizer's (1808–88) word, such a small collection of representative texts might be termed "a canon within the canon." So far, little is known about the creation of these "Small Canons" and their relationship to the "Great Canon." They might function as a replacement for the entire canon in small monastic communities, constituting a functional "ritual canon," as Steven Collins calls it.[46] Considering these unique aspects of the Chinese canon, we may say that to some extent, it was indeed a "closed" collection.

The issue of the canon being "open" or "closed" raises an interesting question about the role of catalogs in shaping the structure of the canon. Studies of Western religious canons show that the canon is basically an extension and transformation of a list. Jonathan Z. Smith, for example, tends to reduce the canon to a mere enumerative list or catalog, which has "no necessary beginning or end, and no necessary articulate principles of order."[47] The list or catalog was transformed into a canon only because the "element of closure" was added. Therefore, the notion of a canon implies the idea of closure. For theologian Paul Ricoeur, the canon has to be closed because the closure is "a fundamental structural act that delimits the space for the interplay of forms of discourse and determines the finite configuration within which each form and each pair of forms unfolds its signifying function."[48] These reflections on the nature of the canon as a closed list call for our attention to the role that the catalog played in the formation of the Chinese canon. Moreover, the case of Chinese Tripitaka catalogs is more complicated because a "Register of Canonical Texts" (*Ruzanglu*) was often placed within a much more comprehensive catalog that is both descriptive and enumerative. The nature of the Chinese canon as an open or closed system still awaits further exploration in terms of its historical evolution and structural changes. It is perhaps better to describe the Chinese canonical tradition as a dynamic interplay of openness and closure to avoid simplistic categorizations.

3. THE CANON AND THE
TECHNOLOGY OF PRODUCTION

It has long been ignored that the canon has a distinctive physical dimension involving a process of production and reproduction by utilizing the tools of writing, printing, and digitization in today's world. As Jonathan Z. Smith points out, "[c]anonization, as a secondary process, is inseparable from modes of production; it is as much an affair of technology as theology."[49] Therefore the canon is also a "sacred object" "that is always manufactured and all but infinitely reproducible." Even Wilfred Cantwell Smith, who is not a specialist in the Chinese tradition, recognizes the importance of printing technology in the production of the Chinese collection. He remarks in his famous book *What Is Scripture* that the growth of the Chinese canon "had to do with the decision of financial sponsors, or of particular printers, and not only of imperial authorities or even Buddhist monks, deciding what to include in an edition of the scripture."[50]

At each stage of its development, we can see clearly how the use of new technology transformed the canon as a physical object. During the manuscript era, the canon grew out of a flourishing scribal culture in medieval China in which transcribing Buddhist texts was a social and religious enterprise involving devotional writing and the use of professional scribes and tools for writing, classifying, and binding. Printing was a technological revolution that initiated further changes in the layout and binding style of the canon, the means of social mobilization, and the reading mode of the public. *Jiaxing Canon*, created during the seventeenth and eighteenth centuries, for example, adopted the common format of the string-bound style, which greatly facilitated its circulation and public reading. During the digital age, the canon as a collection of hypertexts has some features that are completely different from the print culture. In the future, as Fang Guangchang predicts, the text will no longer be controlled by a single author, and readers from online communities will participate and interact with the canon collectively as authors. The canon therefore is not fixed, unified, or even coherent. It may become forever open to all possibilities, devoid of any linear and hierarchical structure.[51]

The changes brought by technological revolutions are obvious in the history of the Chinese canon. However, it is still unclear how these technological advances changed the way people interacted with the canon and affected the canon itself. More complex is the interplay between orality, writing, and printing in the past, and digital media in the contemporary world.[52] If the digital trend is continuing, it may suggest that a process of "decanonization" has occurred and tend to lessen the ultimate authority of the canon, leading to the dissipation of the canon as a coherent and consistent whole.

4. THE CANON IN THE COMMUNITY AND ITS PLACE IN EAST ASIAN BUDDHISM

In the English-speaking world, under the influence of scholars of religion such as William Cantwell Smith, the Chinese Buddhist canon has been studied under the rubric of the comparative study of "sacred texts" or "scriptures." However, as Paul Ricoeur aptly pointed out thirty years ago, such an "antihistorical" approach heavily relies on the techniques of textual criticism borrowed from biblical studies. Moreover, such an approach has fundamentally isolated the canon from the community that "constituted" it.[53] Ricoeur's concern alerts us to pay more attention to the role of the canon in Buddhist communities.

The formation of the Chinese Buddhist canon was deeply rooted in Buddhist communities because it was a complicated religious, social, and textual practice involving collective efforts on the national, local, and personal levels. Religiously, the creation of a canon is a work of faith that can be referred to as "the Cult of the Canon," meaning a series of devotional activities involved in its creation, distribution, and maintenance. Such massive production and distribution of texts are facilitated by various social conditions in a particular time period. Each edition is a project that mobilizes local or even national resources and negotiates its relationship with the state and local societies. Textually, the canon is a wonderful display of the skillful management of Buddhist knowledge using scholarly techniques derived from the Chinese textual tradition. This highly sophisticated cataloging practice and classification system resulted from the original bibliographical studies of Buddhist texts by Chinese monk-scholars.

The making of a canon as a social practice involved private and official scriptoria, printing shops, imperial and gentry patronage, monastic and governmental organizations, and nonprofit or commercial distribution. In the premodern era, the creation and distribution of the Chinese Buddhist canon was symbolically tied to state power. On the one hand, the compilation and printing of a canon could only be completed with government support because of the amount of resources involved in the project. On the other hand, official support of the Buddhist canon symbolized the extension of state power into the religious realm.

Through these processes, the Buddhist canon acquired a unique character that reflected various dimensions of social relationships, among which we can see a clear interplay of the symbolic power of state authority, the use of the technology of production, and the social chain of creation and distribution.

To clarify the relationship between the canon and the community requires scholars to be more attentive to these dynamic social relationships rather than being satisfied with superficial descriptions of the canon as a static textual existence. Only through meticulous historical research can we reveal the role of the Chinese canon in the history of East Asian Buddhism. So far, the standard account of East Asian Buddhism remains organized around the formation of different sectarian movements.[54] In this sect-centered narrative, the canon seldom appears relevant. This marginalization contradicts the historical fact that the canon attracted enormous amount of energy toward its production and reproduction, which involved repeated efforts by the imperial court, monasteries, and individuals. The Chinese canon, as symbolic capital for all communities, remained a remarkably nonsectarian textual repertoire of the heritage of Chinese Buddhism. Such a body of texts serves as the spiritual source for religious rejuvenation at the juncture of social and cultural changes. It is no wonder that during Buddhist revivals, efforts to rebuild communities often involved the reproduction of a Buddhist canon, as I have shown in my study of the seventeenth-century Buddhist revival.[55] It is hoped that a reexamination of the history of East Asian Buddhism from the angle of canon formation will help us create an alternative historical narrative independent from the sectarian model.

5. THE CHINESE CANON IN COMPARATIVE PERSPECTIVE

It has to be remembered that the formation of the Chinese Buddhist canon is only one instance of canon formation in East Asian and world religions. To reveal the nature of canon formation and to better understand the Chinese canon itself, there is a great need to conduct comparative studies, as Jonathan Z. Smith recommends: "What we have lacked are comparative studies, the attempt to view canons and processes of canon formation as generic categories in the study of religion."[56]

The Chinese canon has three contexts for comparison. First, within East Asia, there are different processes of canon formation in different cultural areas. Both Korea and Japan, for example, have their distinctive canonic cultures and patterns of canon formation, and their experiences with a foreign textual tradition were different from those of their continental counterpart. Meanwhile, the Chinese canon has to be situated in the process of canon formation in different sectarian backgrounds, as each movement, such as Chan and Tiantai, tended to form its own canon independent of the "great" canon tradition. Second, the Chinese canon belongs to the Buddhist canonical tradition and can be compared with the Tibetan and Pali traditions. Preliminary comparative research shows that although these Buddhist canons share some common characteristics, they differ considerably in their structure and organization. Richard Salomon, for example, points out that these canons stand out for their size, diversity, and flexibility and share similar techniques such as selecting, abridging, and anthologizing texts. However, each tradition is different in its conception and organization of the canon, some more restrictive (Pali) and some more inclusive and encyclopedic (Chinese).[57] Such comparative work has not yet begun and will generate exciting discoveries regarding the characteristics and nature of the Buddhist canon in general. Finally, the study of the Chinese Buddhist canon can be furthered by the comparative study of sacred texts and canon formation in other world religions. Although attempts at such comparative studies have been made in the past, much more can be done based on in-depth studies of each tradition.

The Chinese Buddhist canon is a living tradition. In East Asia, it remains central to Buddhist religious life, especially when the tradition is undergoing significant transformation and Buddhists need to go back to scriptures and canons to seek their spiritual roots and textual authority. We anticipate that the tradition of the Chinese Buddhist canon will continue to evolve with time and serve as the core of the Buddhist tradition in East Asia and beyond. Right now, there is too little Western literature on the history of the Chinese canon, and much more needs to be done to explore the formation and the transformation of the tradition. A thorough study of the Chinese canon can not only enrich our knowledge about Chinese Buddhism but also offer new opportunities for creating an alternative narrative of the history of East Asian Buddhism, different from the traditional sectarian account. This chapter is an initial step to provide an overview of the history and content of the canon and to invite serious discussions about critical issues in the study of this great textual tradition.

NOTES

Part of this chapter has been published as "The Chinese Buddhist Canon" by Jiang Wu in *Blackwell Companion to East and Inner Asian Buddhism*, 363–82. Used with permission.

1. For a brief discussion about the creation of the early Buddhist canon, see Hirakawa Akira, *A History of Indian Buddhism*, 69–75, and Paul Groner's bibliographi-

cal essay on this subject in ibid., 329–30. Lancaster, "Buddhist Literature." Harrison, "Canon." For a study of the "twelve divisions" of Buddhist literature, see Nattier, "The Twelve Divisions of Scriptures." Lamotte, *History of Indian Buddhism*, 148–49. Shimoda, "Some Reflections on the History of Buddhist Canons in Ancient India."

2. For an overall discussion of the characteristics of these Chinese legends about the canon, see Wu, "Imagining Tripitaka."

3. For details about Sengyou's description of the canon, see Link, "The Earliest Chinese Account of the Compilation of the Tripitaka."

4. These statistics only show the extant translations. He Mei, *Lidai hanwen Dazangjing mulu xinkao*, 25. The number of lost translations is very high. In Sengyou's catalog, it is recorded that during the 500 years between the Han and the Liang dynasties, 2,238 titles were translated into Chinese, which amounted to 4,280 fascicles. In Zhisheng's time (around 664), he recorded 2,278 titles and 7,046 fascicles. For details, see Li and He, *Hanwen Fojiao Dazangjing yanjiu*, 52. For discussion about the early translation process of the scriptures, see also Chen, *Chinese Buddhism*, 365–72.

5. For the so-called Gāndhārī hypothesis, see Boucher, "Gandhari and the Early Chinese Buddhist Translations Reconsidered." For an excellent review of recent discoveries and findings about the Gāndhārī documents, see Salomon, "Recent Discoveries of Early Buddhist Manscripts." Salomon suggests that some collections appear to be anthologies derived from a more organized and coherent grouping. Some manuscripts even have folio numbers written on them, indicating some attempts to arrange the texts. He concludes that these new manuscripts "suggests a movement in Gandhāra during or around the reign of Kaniṣka toward a more formalized, comprehensive, and standardized body of written Buddhist scriptures; that is to say, something more like a written canon in the strict sense of the term" (373).

6. Lancaster, "The Movement of Buddhist Texts," 231–32.

7. Storch, *The History of Chinese Buddhist Bibliography*, especially chapter 1.

8. Ibid., 10.

9. Drège, *Les bibliothèque en Chine au temps des manuscrits*, 177.

10. Jens-Uwe Hartmann, in his study of the Bower manuscript collection, concluded that "the texts held in highest esteem by the Buddhists of Northern Turkestan played an amazingly small role in the transmission of Buddhist literature into China, at least as far as can be judged from the surviving Sanskrit fragments." This seems to suggest that the Chinese had quite independent views about what scriptures should be included in their canons. See Hartmann, "Buddhist Sanskrit Texts for Northern Turkestan," 62.

11. Schopen, "A Note on the 'Technology of Prayer.'"

12. He Mei, *Lidai hanwen Dazangjing mulu xinkao*, vol. 1, 5.

13. See Fang Guangchang, "A Personal View." For the Japanese manuscript tradition, see Miyazaki Kenji, *Nihon kodai no shakyō to shakai.*

14. See Harrist, *The Landscape of Words.*

15. See "Prayers for Three Canons in the Northern Qi Dynasty" (*Bei Qi sanbu yiqie jing yuanwen* 北齊三部一切經願文) by Wei Shou 魏收 and "Prayers for the Canon in the Zhou Dynasty" (*Zhou Zangjing yuanwen* 周藏經願文) by Wang Bao 王褒 in *Guang hongming ji* 廣弘明集, fasc. 22. T 2103 52:257.

16. For a brief research note, see Rao Zongyi, "Lun Sengyou," 407. Link, "Shih Seng-yu and His Writing." Sengyou was involved in building the canons in both places, and the Confucian scholar Liu Xie 劉勰 assisted him at Dinglin Monastery. Bai Huawen even speculated that the *Subject Catalog of All Scriptures* (*Zhongjing bielu*) discovered in Duhuang was a product of Sengyou's team in Dinglin Monastery. See Bai, "Dunhuang xieben 'Zhongjing bielu.'"

17. Chen, "Buddhist Establishments," 18–22.

18. For a statistics of Nara-period canon transcription projects, see Miyazaki Kenji, "Nara jidai no Issaikyō ni tsuite," 2–3. Peter Kornicki cited twenty-one such transcriptions during the Nara period. See Kornicki, *The Book in Japan*, 84.

19. *Kaiyuan Catalog* was brought to Japan by the Japanese monk Genbō 玄昉 (?-746) in 735. See Belard, "The May 1st Sutra"; Lowe, "Text and Texture" and "The Discipline of Writing."

20. Lancaster, "The Rock Cut Canon in China." Ledderose, "Carving Sutras Into Stone Before the Catastrophe." Lee, "Transmitting Buddhism to a Future Age."

21. See Chikusa Masaaki, "Sō Gen ban Daizōkyō no keifu." Although Chikusa and Fang worked out these systems independently, Fang Guangchang acknowledged that Chikusa proposed this idea earlier and should be credited for the formulation of the three systems. This view has been accepted by most scholars. See He Mei, *Lidai hanwen dazangjing mulu xinkao*, vol. 1, 7.

22. See his "Yetan Hanwen Fojiao dazangjing de xitong wenti."

23. For a short introduction of various digital projects, see Wittern, "Patterns of Variation," 213.

24. Link, "The Biography of Shi Dao'an."

25. For a transcription of two fragments of this lost catalog, see Fang Guangchang, *Dunhuang Fojiao jinglu*, 12–25 and Tanya Storch's chapter 4 in this volume. Most scholars believe that this recovered work was the same text mentioned in Fei Changfang's *Lidai sanbao ji*, except Tan Shibao. See Tan, *Han Tang Foshi tanzhen*, 197–248.

26. For a description of extant Buddhist catalogs in English, see Nanjio Buyiu (Nanjō Bun'yū), *A Catalogue of the Chinese Translation of the Buddhist Tripitaka*, xi–xxviii. Storch, *History of Chinese Buddhist Bibiography.*

27. This list is modified from the table of contents of Nanjio Buyiu (Nanjō Bunyū), *A Catalogue of the Chinese Translation of the Buddhist Tripitaka*, ix–x. Note that the

edition of this catalog Nanjō worked on was part of *Ōbaku Canon* sent to the Indian Office Library, Britain, by the Japanese government in 1875. Because *Ōbaku Canon* reprinted the main section of *Jiaxing Canon*, which is based on *Yongle Northern Canon*, this catalog has been modified by the compilers of *Jiaxing Canon*, especially the last few titles. For details, see Wu, "Finding the First Chinese Tripitaka in Europe."

28. Drège, "La lecture et l'écriture en Chine et la xylographie," 85.

29. See Fang Guangchang, *Fojiao dazangjing shi*, 304–11, and the revised and updated edition in *Zhongguo xieben dazangjing yanjiu*, 419–513.

30. See Barrett, *The Woman Who Discovered Printing* and "The Rise and Spread of Printing."

31. For details of the binding styles, see Tsien, *Paper and Printing*, 227–34.

32. See Tsien, *Paper and Printing*, 64, 86–88. Pan Jixing, *Zhongguo zaozhi jishu shigao*, 82–83, 96–97. See *Jinsushan dazangjing ji zangjing zhi*. See also Li Jining, *Fojing banben*, 48–52. For the use of Huangbo extract, see Gibbs and Seddon, *Berberine and Huangbo*; Tsien, *Paper and Printing*, 74–76.

33. Zhang Xiumin, *Zhongguo yinshua shi*, 167.

34. T 2149, 55:302–12. For a detailed account, see Drège, *Les bibliothèque en Chine*, 212–14.

35. For a short history of the "Hall of Sutra Storage," see Bai Huawen, "'Jingzang nei.'" Technical details about wall storage and wheel storage are described in fasc. 11 of *Architectural Format and Method* (*Yingzhao fashi* 營造法式), compiled during the Song Dynasty.

36. See Goodrich, "The Revolving Book-Case in China." Nanjio Bunyiu (Nanjō Bun'yū), *A Catalogue of the Chinese Translation of the Buddhist Tripiṭaka*, xxv–xxvi. Prip-Møller, *Chinese Buddhist Monasteries*, 55–60. Daoan, *Zhongguo dazang jing diao-ke shihua*, 150–51.

37. Harrison, "Canon," 111.

38. Lancaster, "The Movement of Buddhist Texts," 237–38.

39. Fang Guangchang, *Zhongguo xieben dazangjing yanjiu*, 10.

40. For his definition, see Smith, "Sacred Persistence."

41. Harrison, "Canon," 112.

42. Swanson, "Apocryphal Texts in Chinese Buddhism," 246.

43. Lancaster, "The Movement of Buddhist Texts," 227.

44. See my discussion of this connection in chapter 2.

45. See Li Fuhua, "An Analysis of the Content and Characteristics of the Chinese Buddhist Canon."

46. Collins, "The Very Idea of a Pali Canon," 104.

47. Smith, "Canon, Catalogues and Classics," 304.

48. Ricoeur, *Figuring the Sacred*, 39.

49. Smith, "Canon, Catalogues and Classics," 307, 298.

50. Smith, *What Is Scripture*, 150.

51. Fang Guangchang, *Zhongguo xieben dazangjing yanjiu*, 36–38.

52. The oral aspect of the canon is also often neglected. As Salomon points out, the Buddhist canon has a primary function of being recited, even though the canon has been written down. See Salomon, "An Unwieldy Canon," 170.

53. Ricoeur, "The Sacred Text and the Community."

54. For an overall critique of such a sectarian view of Chinese Buddhism and its Japanese connection, see Sharf, "On Esoteric Buddhism in China" and Sun Yinggang, "Kuada de lishi tujing."

55. Wu, *Enlightenment in Dispute*.

56. Smith, "Canon, Catalogues and Classics," 296.

57. Salomon, "An Unwieldy Canon."

2. From the "Cult of the Book" to the "Cult of the Canon"

A NEGLECTED TRADITION IN CHINESE BUDDHISM

Jiang Wu

Despite the importance of the canon in Chinese Buddhism, it is still unclear how the making and remaking of a canon initiated new social, cultural, and religious transformations in Buddhist communities. Previous studies have overwhelmingly concentrated on the canon as a collection of sacred texts, without adequate attention to its actual use. It is often neglected that the canon as a whole has become a sacred object, allowing believers to form an intimate relationship through participating in a series of cultic practices.

In the history of Chinese Buddhism, the canon, which primarily contains translated texts and Chinese Buddhist writings, has become the object of devotion and deserves close examination. Here, I use the "Cult of the Canon" to refer to a series of devotional activities involved in the creation, distribution, and maintenance of the canon. During this process, particular legends, myths, rituals, and ceremonies were developed to promote belief in the efficacy of devotion to the canon as a means to secure divine protection and blessing. This phenomenon is closely connected to the concept of the "Cult of the Book," which originated from Mahayana teaching and flourished in China and other parts of East Asia. As Gregory Schopen points out, the "Cult of the Book" was one of the essential characteristics of Mahayana Buddhism, which placed great emphasis on worshiping written texts.[1] In China, the "Cult of the Book" was greatly promoted in medieval times, and popular scriptures such as the *Lotus Sutra* and the *Diamond Sutra* became objects for pious copying. Such precious copies, viewed as the embodiment of "dharma relics" (*fasheli* 法舍利), were reverentially deposited inside stupas.[2]

In this chapter, I consider the "Cult of the Book" as the origin of the "Cult of the Canon" and show that when the "Cult of the Book" met with the Chinese literary tradition, which overwhelmingly valued, even worshiped, written words, the devotion to individual scriptures was extended to the entire canon. To a large extent, the "Cult of the Canon" flourished in China as the Mahayana movement completed its transition from oral to written traditions. The advanced level of social development and the invention of paper and writing techniques in China made well-organized and coordinated reproduction of a large number of Buddhist texts possible. The popularity of printing no doubt further increased the availability of the canon and helped to spread the "Cult of the Canon" in China and other parts of East Asia.

In his seminal paper on the devotional use of sacred texts in early Chinese Buddhism, Robert Campany emphasizes that "the sheer reception, possession, and transmission of the texts was at least as significant as the reading of them or the practice of the teachings they contained."[3] The motifs of the devotional uses he studies, such as scripture recitation; reverent actions toward collection, preservation, and display of texts; the amuletic function of the texts; and miraculous responses caused by the mishandling of the texts can be easily identified in the devotional treatment of the canon as well. As I will explore, the "Cult of the Canon" involves similar types of devotional activities.[4] Among them are five major aspects on which I will focus: patronage and sponsorship, consecration and worship, the cult of the revolving repository, ritual reading and writing, and the promotion of the devotion to the canon in Chan communities.

DEVOTIONAL PATRONAGE AND SPONSORSHIP

IMPERIAL PATRONAGE

In imperial China, Buddhist activities were tied strongly to the protection and blessing of the nation. Most dynasties sponsored their official editions of the canon and used it as "symbolic capital," in Pierre Bourdieu's term. The earliest examples are the emperors in the Northern and Southern dynasties (317–589), who sponsored copying the Buddhist canon and distributed it to major monasteries.[5] All the official editions typically placed the prefaces of royal benediction written by emperors at the beginning of the entire canon. Two exemplar prefaces were written by two Tang emperors: "Preface to the Holy Teaching of

Tripitaka of the Great Tang" (*Da Tang sanzang shengjiao xu* 大唐三藏聖教序) by Taizong 太宗 (599–649), composed in 648 in congratulations on Xuanzang's 玄奘 (602–664) new translations, and "Record of Documenting the 'Preface to the Holy Teaching of Tripitaka of the Great Tang'" (*Shu sanzang shengjiao xu ji* 述三藏聖教序記) by Gaozong 高宗 (628–83), who was the heir apparent at the time he composed it. According to Song historiographer Zhipan 志磐, after these two prefaces were created, they were ordered to be put at the beginning of the canon.[6]

The royal family would sponsor a canon for a variety of reasons. In the prefaces they wrote, imperial rulers often invoked five types of rhetoric to explain their involvement. First, they praised the canon as the embodiment of the most profound teaching that reveals the truth of the universe. Second, they expressed the belief that the creation of the canon could bless their nation and secure peace in the world. Third, they also sponsored a canon out of their personal devotion, for the welfare of their family and deceased family members. Fourth, the rulers believed that Buddha's teaching contains moral instructions that could help their subjects and commoners to rectify their behaviors and thus become less rebellious and harmful to society. Finally, some rulers, claiming to be dharma protectors, were directly involved in the compilation of the canon in order to maintain the purity and accuracy of the content through careful selection and textual collations.[7]

DEVOTION OF THE COMMONERS

Not only the ruling classes fervently supported the creation of the canon; commoners, both clergy and laity, also aspired to create the canon or contribute to its creation. Very often, such a project received royal benediction and was even taken over by the government eventually. The creation of *Fangshan Stone Canon*, located in Yunju Monastery 雲居寺 in Fangshan 房山 County of Beijing, by a devoted monk called Jingwan 靜琬 (?–639) in the Sui Dynasty, shows how an individual, in response to the decline of Buddhist teaching, single-handedly started the project and attracted attention from the court and all walks of society. Jingwan declared his purpose as follows:

> Sakyamuni Buddha's *zhengfa* 正法 (Age of Correct Dharma) and *xiangfa* 像法 (Age of Resemblance Dharma) lasted for more than 1,500 years. Now, in the second year of the Zhenguan era (628), [we have been immersed in] *mofa* 末法 (Age of Latter-Day Dharma) for seventy-five years. The sun of the Buddha has set; the [dark] night is now deep. Blind are sentient beings, and they have consequently lost their way. Jingwan, to preserve the true

dharma, has led his followers, his friends, and those who like [to give alms] to this mountain ridge to carve the *Flower Garland Sutra* and other texts in twelve divisions. [I] hope to rescue the living creatures in the numerous *kalpa* cycles of time and hope all believers and secular people will attain enlightenment.[8]

His devotion even incurred divine assistance. According to the mid-seventh-century collection of Buddhist miracle stories by Tang Lin 唐臨 (600–59), in the middle of the project, a violent rainstorm brought several thousand pine and cypress logs he needed to the construction site before the stone cliff where he wanted to build a wooden Buddha hall.[9]

Such a massive project initiated by the commoners could not be completed without royal support. In 713, Princess Jinxian 金仙 (689–732), a Daoist devotee, gave four thousand fascicles of newly translated scriptures to Fangshan to be carved on stone tablets to commemorate her father, Emperor Xuanzong 玄宗 (r. 712–56). Not only did she ask the government to allocate land to support the project, she also commissioned a monk named Xuanfa 玄法 (fl. 726–55) to recite the entire canon on a yearly basis.[10] After the Sui and Tang dynasties, the *Stone Canon* project in Fangshan was continuously supported by the rulers of the Liao (Khitan, 960–1123), Jin (Jurchen, 1115–1226), and Yuan (Mongol, 1271–1368) dynasties, which based their capitals in the north.[11]

The commoners, without many resources, could also sponsor a project out of their devotion. In the set of *Qisha Canon* preserved in the National Library in Beijing, a colophon dated to the seventh month of 1432 was stamped on the lotus-shaped dedication tablet at the end of the scripture *Vimutti-magga* (*Jietuo dao lun* 解脫道論, case 417) and has the following record:

> Buddhist devotee Dong Fucheng 董福成, a resident at Juxian Alley of Daxing County in Shuntian Prefecture in Beijing of the Great Ming 大明國北京順天府大興縣居賢坊, reverently arouses the sincere mind to donate a set of the venerable Great Canon at the Houchao Gate 後朝門 of Hangzhou Prefecture in Zhejiang. Not doing this for himself, he joyfully gave up his fortune in order to repay the "four kindnesses" (*si'en*) above and the "beings of the three realms" (*sanyou*) below. He wishes all sentient beings in the dharma realm to achieve perfect buddhahood.[12]

Here Dong Fucheng and his family invoked the rhetoric of repaying "Four Kindnesses" (*si'en* 四恩, i.e., the kindness of the Buddha, the rulers, the parents, and all sentient beings) and benefiting the "Three Realms" (*sanyou* 三有, i.e., the desire, form, and formless realms) as the motive for creating the canon, as seen from numerous colophons of various editions. The idea of "Four

Kindnesses" and "Three Realms" was prevalent in medieval China, as seen in Dunhuang manuscripts, and continued as the reason for the sponsorship of various editions of the canon such as *Qisha Canon*. [13]

The creation of *Zhaocheng Canon*, a reprint of the first printed edition of *Kaibao Canon*, in the Jin (Jurchen) Dynasty (1115–26) gave rise to a legend about one of its initiators, a commoner called Cui Fazhen 崔法珍, who severed her arm at thirteen and vowed to print an entire canon. According to a newly discovered stele in Jiangxian 絳縣 in Shanxi, the project was started by Cui Fazhen's teacher, Yin Shennai 尹矧乃, commonly known as Vinaya Master Shigong 實公, who was ordained as a monk when he was twelve. In his youth, he burned his left hand in front of an Avalokiteśvara pagoda and vowed to walk to Mount Wutai with a bow at every step (*buli* 步禮). On his way, he met Emperor Huizong 宋徽宗 (1082–1135), who greatly admired his devotion. At Mount Wutai, his piety moved Bodhisattva Mañjuśrī, who instructed him to carve a new set of blocks of the canon. Back in his hometown, he told his determination to his disciple Layman Liu, who also cut off his left hand out of devotion. When he solicited donations from the Cui family in Changzi County 長子縣 at Luzhou 潞州, their daughter, later known as Cui Fazhen, was so moved that she cut off her left arm to follow him. With the help of his disciples, Vinaya Master Shigong set his base at Tianning Monastery 天寧寺 at Xiezhou and started the project. Before he passed away in 1176, he instructed Cui Fazhen to continue.[14] Cui's project was supported by laypeople in Xiezhou 解州 (today's Yuncheng area in Shanxi) and its neighboring areas. According to a colophon attached to *Qisha Canon* recorded by the monk Bao Shanhui 鮑善恢 in 1411, more than 50 followers imitated her devotion and severed their arms as well. (See chapter 6 for details about Bao's inscription.) The legend says they raised funds through extreme "self-afflicted violence" (Jimmy Yu's term) such as "burning arms and fingers" and "cutting eyes and livers." They even donated all family property and sold their children. It took them about thirty years to complete the entire canon in 1178. Cui Fazhen was then awarded a purple robe and an honorific title.[15] The blocks were soon moved to Beijing and became known as the official *Hongfa Canon* 弘法藏, which was popular in the Jin and Yuan dynasties.

CEREMONIAL CONSECRATION AND WORSHIP

HANDLING THE CANON AS A SACRED OBJECT

In its physical form, the canon has always been treated as a sacred object for veneration and sacrifice. In large monasteries in late imperial China, a special building called Tripitaka Pavilion (*zangjingge* 藏經閣) with two stories was designed for storing the canon; it is usually located at the back of the monastic compound. The first floor was the Hall of a Thousand Buddhas, representing the assembly devoted to reading scriptures. On the second floor, Tripitaka cabinets were arranged along the walls. The canon was also used for consecration of pagodas, sometimes in its entirety. The 1972 discovery of 47 printed scriptures inside the Śākyamuni statue on the fourth floor of a Timber Pagoda in Yingxian 應縣 shows that texts from the three divisions of the canon—Sutra, Vinaya, and Abidharma—were deliberately selected to represent the entire Buddhist canon, perhaps *Liao Canon* because twelve of the scriptures were identified as from *Liao Canon*.[16] In 1976, a whole set of *Qing Canon*, popularly known as *Dragon Canon*, a total of 724 cases, was discovered inside the White Pagoda in Baita Monastery 白塔寺 in Beijing. According to historical records, this was placed inside in 1753.[17]

Devotion to the canon took many forms. A believer could claim one title, or one fascicle, or even one booklet as the object of worship for a period of one year. During Buddhist holidays, the Tripitaka Hall, the place where the canon was kept, was opened to these believers.[18] The scrolls or booklets in the canon had to be taken from the cabinets to the open air to prevent dampness and to kill bookworms. Based on this practice, the ceremony of "Sunning the Scripture" (*shaijing*) was developed for public display and respect. This was most often done on the sixth day of the sixth month, coinciding with the Taoist festival of Heavenly Blessing (*Tianzhujie* 天贶节).[19] In Buddhist communities, the festival was often referred to as "Assembly of Sunning Scriptures" (*shaijinghui* 曬经会) or "Assembly of Turning Scriptures" (*fanjing hui* 翻經會), during which scriptures were moved outside the storage hall and all the pages were turned over to receive enough exposure to sunlight and fresh air to prevent dampness. Usually, a serious ceremony of worship and chanting was organized as well. In the Suzhou area during the late imperial period, such assemblies were especially attractive to women because legend said that if women turned the entire canon ten times, they would be reborn as men in their next life.[20]

Such a ritualized handling of the canon can be dated to early times. On the twenty-ninth day of the twelfth month of 839, the Japanese pilgrim Ennin 圓仁 (794–864), during a trip to China, stayed in a Buddhist monastery built for Korean sojourners at Wendeng 文登 in today's Shandong peninsula and noticed their ceremony of venerating the canon. According to Ennin's travelogue, the Scripture Storage Hall had a special place in this Korean monastery: "In the evening they lighted lamps as offerings at the Buddha Hall and Scripture Storehouse of this Korean Cloister but they did not light lamps elsewhere." Considering that lamp oil was an expensive commodity, the Scripture Hall was treated as a special object for veneration.[21]

ARCHITECTURAL DESIGN OF TRIPITAKA STORAGE

Special buildings to house the scriptures and the canon were also developed during the Tang. As seen from murals in Dunhuang, which reflect the monastic architecture in the Sui and Tang dynasties, the layout of a monastic compound was characterized by "one hall and two pavilions" (*yidian er'lou* 一殿二楼): the Great Hall was flanked by the Bell Tower (*zhonglou* 钟楼, usually on the rear left) and the Tripitaka Tower (*jingge* 经阁 or *jinglou* 經樓, usually on the rear right) behind.[22]

The famous Tang poet Bai Juyi 白居易 wrote the most detailed description of such a structure in Xiangshan Monastery 香山寺 at Longmen 龍門 in Luoyang. According to his "Record of the Rebuilt Tripitaka Hall in Xiangshan Monastery" (Xiangshansi xinxiu jingzangtang ji 香山寺新修经藏堂记), a dilapidated structure with three bays in the northwest corner of the monastery compound was refurbished as the Tripitaka Hall. In the east and west bays, six Tripitaka cabinets with two doors each were placed. In the central bay, an altar with statues of five hundred arhats was displayed. Behind the statues was a mural of the Western Land of Bliss and two pictures of bodhisattvas. Surrounding the altar were twenty-four magnificent canopies. The renovation project was completed on the twenty-fifth day of the ninth month in 840, and a huge ceremony was held to celebrate. To ensure the eternal turning of the dharma wheel, seven people with moral integrity were hired and financially supported for chanting the entire canon, following the order in the catalog.[23] Bai's account shows clearly that the canon was treated as a sacred object with ceremonial solemnity. After its production and transportation to the monastery, the canon was stored in large cabinets and installed in special locations.

Advances in building techniques in China gave rise to more sophisticated Tripitaka storage methods. Based on the idea of the Tripitaka Cabinet, a distinctive storage design appeared in the Song Dynasty and was called "wall storage" (*bizang* 壁藏) because huge cabinets were arranged along the walls. The detailed architectural design was included in a Song state architectural manual, *Official Building Standards* (*Yingzao fashi* 營造法式), by Li Jie 李誡 (1035–1110), published in 1103.[24]

On the twenty-third day of the tenth month of 1072, the Japanese monk Jōjin 成尋 (1011–81) visited Qisheng Chan Cloister 啓聖禪院 to the east of Kaifeng and described how two sets of the canon, probably the newly carved *Kaibao Canon*, was stored there: "On the east, west, south, and north walls, there were two sets of Tripitaka in black ink. Above every bay, a pavilion was built, and each bay was divided into three chambers, under which scriptures were laid on the shelves." The next day, he visited Fusheng Chan Cloister 福聖禪院 and left a record of their way of storing the canon: "Above the cabinets on the four sides [of the room], there was a small four-story pavilion. On the four walls, there were two sets of Tripitaka [printed] in black ink. Above them was a four-storied pavilion, and each bay has three small pavilions."[25]

Here, Jōjin noted a special structure, a four-story wooden pavilion above the cabinet. This kind of arrangement, with miniature pavilions built on top of the Tripitaka Cabinet, was actually an innovative design full of mythological significance. Commonly referred to as "Jeweled Storage in the Heavenly Palace" (*Tiangong baozang* 天宮寶藏), this elaborately decorated wooden structure was believed to be the symbolic place where the Buddhist canon was stored. In the Buddhist encyclopedia *Orthodox Lineage in the Buddhist World* (*Shimen zhengtong* 釋門正統), composed in the eleventh century, such a legend was described as follows:

> Nowadays, this design is called "the Oceanic Storage in Dragon's Palace" (*Longgong haizang* 龍宮海藏). It has been said that this is based on the event when Nāgārjuna dove into the sea [to fetch the sutra]. It was also called "Jeweled Storage in the Heavenly Palace" (*Tiangong baozang*). This saying is based on Śākyamuni's residence there.[26]

The earliest surviving example of wall storage with a miniature wooden model of the Heavenly Palace is preserved in the Bhagavad Scripture Storage Hall (*Bojia jiaozang dian* 薄伽教藏殿) at Huayan Monastery in Datong in today's Shanxi Province. Built in the Liao Dynasty, the cabinets at this location have been used for storing *Liao Canon*. Thirty-eight cabinets were arranged along the wall in the hall.[27]

Here the origin of the canon was further mythologized and popularized, involving the mythological Dragon Kings and Gods. On the basis of this legend, an architectural structure was created to embody a Chinese imagination of the canon.[28] Such an imaginative design was also employed in another, even more popular storage method designed for canon veneration—the revolving repository.

THE CULT OF THE REVOLVING REPOSITORY

INVENTION OF THE TECHNOLOGY OF "TURNING THE CANON"

A remarkable architectural invention was the creation of the revolving repository (*lunzang* 輪藏, J. Rinzō, Kr. Yunjang, or *zhuanlunzang* 轉輪藏, J. Tenrinzō, Kr. Jeonryunjang). This resembles a sutra repository or miniature library but actually was a devotional device. Legend says that it was invented by Fu

Xi 傅翕 (497–569), commonly known as Fu Dashi 傅大士, around 544 to 546. Although Gregory Schopen suspects that the idea of the revolving repository as a "technology of prayer" originated in India in the eleventh century, more Chinese records suggest that Fu Xi was the inventor.[29] At least during the ninth century, the use of the revolving bookcase for storing the canon was documented. For example, Goodrich points out that the device was first mentioned in an inscription dated to 823 and documents the installation of a version of the canon in 5,327 scrolls in a revolving repository in 809.[30] As early as 840, the Japanese pilgrim Ennin saw a hexagon-shaped revolving repository on Mount Wutai.[31] The famous Tang poet Bai Juyi detailed the structure of such a revolving repository in Nanchan Cloister in Suzhou. According to his record, "Stone Inscription of the Revolving Repository at the Thousand-Buddha Hall of Nanchan Monastery in Suzhou" ("Suzhou Nanchanyuan Qianfotang zhuanlun jingzang shiji" 蘇州南禪院千佛堂轉輪經藏石記), this revolving repository was built in 828 and completed in 836, at a total cost of 3,600 strings of coins. Decorated with a thousand small Buddha statues, this nine-story device was painted with colors and surrounded by 62 mirrors. It was octagonal with two doors on each side. The inside cabinet was divided into 64 sections and stored 256 cases and 5,058 scrolls of scriptures.[32]

The revolving repository was most popular during the Song Dynasty, especially after the twelfth century, because it became a significant source of income for Buddhist monasteries.[33] The repository could store either the so-called "small canon," which comprised four major sections of 840 fascicles of Mahayana scriptures, including Prajñāpāramitā Sutras in 600 fascicles, Ratnakūṭa Sutras in 120 fascicles, the Avataṃsaka Sutra in 80 fascicles, and Nirvāṇa Sutras in 40 fascicles, or an entire collection of the canon, which was usually recorded as 5,048 fascicles based on Zhisheng's catalog. For economic reasons, a monastery could acquire a "small canon" first and gradually expanded to the entire collection. Demand for the entire canon to fill the revolving repository may have spurred the printing of private editions after *Kaibao Canon*, such as *Chongning Canon* and *Puning Canon*.

The repository's design was even included in the Song architectural manual *Official Building Standards* (*Yingzao fashi*). According to an illustrated description (figure 2.1), its shape resembles an octagonal pagoda about 20 *chi* (6.4 meters) high and 16 *chi* (5.1 meters) wide, with a central axle connected to an iron pivot and receiver at the base, fixed with lime-clay mortar. Four stories were built to store scriptures, with a structure symbolizing the heavenly palace (*Tiangong louge* 天宮樓閣) on the top.[34] According to Goodrich's study, in early times, the device was four-sided or six-sided. The whole structure could be as high as 8 feet, and 9 feet in diameter. If the cabinet was a fixed structure and could not move, devotees would circumambulate around it.[35]

轉輪經藏

FIGURE 2.1 THE DESIGN OF THE REVOLVING SUTRA REPOSITORY IN
THE SONG DYNASTY
Yingzao fashi, *fasc. 32, 21b*

CIRCUMAMBULATORY READING
AND PATRON GODS

This device indeed made "reading the canon" more convenient. Turning an octagonal revolving cabinet full of Buddhist texts served as a shortcut to achieving the benefits of reading the entire canon. The creation of the revolving repository for storage therefore gave rise to a new mode of religious devotion—a kind of "circumambulatory reading," as Charlotte Eubanks calls it.[36] According to legend, when Fu Xi created the revolving repository, he made three vows. First, if someone entered the gate of the chamber that housed the device three times, that person would remain as a human being for all future reincarnations. Second, if the devotee could push it for one revolution, the merit would equal that from chanting the scriptures. Third, if someone could turn it numerous times, the merit earned would be the same as for reciting the entire canon.[37]

During the Song Dynasty, this device was lavishly decorated, and many sources from the Song described its use as a devotional object. In a preface dated to 1057, the Song literary monk Qisong 契嵩 (1007–72), while commemorating the installation of a revolving repository built in Chongshou Chan Cloister 崇壽禪院 located at Wuwei Commanderate 無為軍, frankly admitted that it was not an invention from Buddha's time. Rather, Fu Xi invented it based on the meaning of "turning the wheel of dharma." He said that such a device was usually installed in a hall and surrounded by several houses. Buddha statues and other instruments were placed inside. The total cost for all the buildings amounted to seven million coins.[38]

The revolving repository gradually evolved into a separate cult, independent from other monastic establishments and protected by its own patron god (zangshen 藏神). On most devices, Fu Xi was worshiped and deified as the reincarnation of Maitreya Buddha. Fu Xi's statue, dressed in Confucian shoes, a Daoist cap, and a Buddhist robe, was often placed in front of the device and flanked by statues of his two sons. Local gods were also incorporated into the pantheon as protectors. For example, eight godly generals and a local god in Yiwu 義烏, where Fu Xi used to be a magistrate—the general of Baojing (Baojing jiangju 保境將軍)—were also erected as guardians for the canon. A Song record by Han Yuanji 韓元吉 (1118–?) describes a popular patron god of the revolving repository erected at Guangjiao Cloister 廣教院 in Xinzhou 信州. This patron god appeared to be a little-known local deity and was described as fierce-looking, with "red hair and dark face" and two horns on his head. Despite the dreadful appearance of the patron god, the revolving repository attracted many local patrons, especially seafaring merchants, because of its efficacy in saving people from disasters.[39]

LEGENDS OF EFFICACY

The revolving repository became increasingly miraculous, and legends developed during the Song. The popularity of the device gave rise to various miracle stories about how it revolved by itself in response to pious devotion. Following the popular theory of resonance and response (ganying 感應), people believed that the revolving repository could move by itself if the devotees were pious enough. Many legends documented this. For example, it was said that in Huili Monastery 惠曆寺 in Linjiang Military Commanderate 臨江軍, a new revolving repository was built and monks charged a thousand coins for the believers to turn it just once. A poor lady wanted to turn the device desperately, for the blessing of her deceased husband before she remarried someone else. However, although she sought donations for several months, she still could not collect enough money to make one turn. The date of her second marriage was approaching quickly, and she could not give up the idea of turning the repository. With no choice, she prostrated in front of the revolving repository and burst into tears, throwing all the coins she had collected on the ground. In response, the revolving repository started to turn by itself. The monks were shocked and thereafter would no longer dare to set a price.[40] Confucian literati were also involved in such devotional activities. Another legend says that in 1088, when the official Yang Jie 楊傑[41] visited the revolving Tripitaka repository believed to have been built by Fu Xi at Shuanglin Monastery 雙林寺, the device suddenly revolved by itself, without anyone pushing it. Yang Jie wrote a eulogy to commemorate the event. The legend says that this was because Yang had faith in the Pure Land and often meditated on the image of Amitabha.[42]

In a magical way, the revolving repository also turned by itself in response to emergencies. According to *Annalist Records of Buddhas and Patriarchs* (*Fozu tongji* 佛祖統紀), when the Jurchen army was about to invade Ningbo, Yuetang Daochang 月堂道昌 (1089–1171), then abbot at Ayuwang Monastery 阿育王寺 and a master in the Yunmen 雲門 line of Chan Buddhism, hid in a pit where the relic of Śākyamuni's ashes (Śarira, Ch. *Sheli* 舍利) was stored. When the Jurchen army started to burn the temple, the Guanyin image on the wall suddenly emitted light and let out water. Moreover, the revolving repository in the monastery also started to revolve by itself. The soldiers then left.[43]

The revolving repository was still popular in late imperial China. One such device in Longfu Monastery 隆福寺 in Beijing was famous in the Ming Dynasty, and Liu Dong 劉侗 (fl. 1634) made a note in his *Survey of Scenic Sights in Beijing* (*Dijing jingwulue* 帝京景物略), published in 1635: "People may read the canon or make donations. If one's virtue or gift is equal to the number of one canon [that is, the number 5,048, the standard size of the canon; see my discussion in the next section], it is sufficient to make one turn of the wheel." Here, "reading" the canon clearly meant to turn the revolving repository physically. This record also indicates that such a devotional activity had become increasingly lucrative, as in the Ming; it was suggested that the fee for turning the device amount to 5,048 coins, matching the total number of scriptures in a standard canon as contained in Zhisheng's *Kaiyuan Catalog*. The miracle story of the canon's self-turning in response to arduous devotion continued to be popular. On the same note, Liu Dong recorded that the canon responded to a poor girl's sincerity: "A poor girl who was not able to read the canon, and was likewise unable to make a donation, was ashamed and contrite, and therefore placed one coin on the revolving mechanism. It then turned without ceasing, which surprised everyone in the temple. They then tried to stop it, but the wheel went *ya ya*, just like the start of a drumroll."[44]

In south China, the most famous revolving repository during the Ming Dynasty was the one erected in Huiyin Monastery 慧因寺 in Hangzhou, commonly known as Korean Temple (Gaolisi 高麗寺) because of its Korean connection. At first, the Korean prince-monk Uicheon 義天 (1055–1101) came to study with the Huayan Master Jingyuan 淨源 (1011–88) from 1085 to 1086. The texts he had collected from China supplemented the first edition of *Goryeo Canon*. Such a Korean connection continued during the Yuan Dynasty: in the winter of 1313, the retired Goryeo king Chungseon 忠宣王, Wang Jang 王璋 (1275–1325), revived the monastery by donating land and a set of the Buddhist canon.[45] A magnificent revolving repository was later erected and became a famous tourist attraction in Hangzhou. Even the renowned late-Ming literatus Zhang Dai 張岱 (1597–1679) visited this place when he was young. As he recorded, the revolving repository was rebuilt in the Wanli reign and was spectacular. He recalled vividly how his mother ordered the service in the following note translated by Jonathan Spence:

> She took out a string of three hundred coins and instructed our sedan chair bearers to set the revolving storage case in motion. At first, the revolving mechanism gave out a groaning sound, like band instruments being played by a beginner. Then, as it began to spin with greater ease, the stored sutras revolved as if in flight, so that those doing the pushing could no longer keep up with it.[46]

RITUAL WRITING AND READING

COPYING THE ENTIRE CANON

In the Buddhist tradition, texts have served an essential spiritual purpose for believers. The huge number of texts in the Buddhist canon has been therefore used for ritual writing and reading. Chinese Buddhists piously devoted themselves to ritual writing of the scriptures in the canon. Many devotees were inspired to copy scriptures by themselves. Wealthy donors commissioned manuscript copies written in gold and silver or even sponsored the carving of blocks for the entire canon. Poor but zealous devotees paid for the carving of one block or the printing of one fascicle in the canon. Legend says that some even went to extremes, using their blood as ink and peeling off their skin as paper.[47]

Early history is replete with such records of ritual writing. For example, when a canon was created in the sixth century, it immediately became an object for pious copying. The prime minister of the Chen Dynasty, Xu Ling 徐陵 (507–83), whose devotion had no parallel, according to the author of *Treatise of Discerning Orthodoxy* (*Bianzheng lun* 辯正論), hand-copied an entire canon. Another prime minister of the Chen, Jiang Zong 江總 (519–94), also copied a canon, which amounted to 3,752 fascicles.[48]

Such devotion to ritual copying was also popular in the Tang Dynasty. The famous Chinese monk who spread the ordination tradition to Japan, Jianzhen 鑒真 (688–763), for example, copied three sets of the whole Tripitaka in 733, which amounted to eleven thousand scrolls.[49] Even Japanese pilgrim Ennin noticed such a popular practice when he traveled in China. On the second day of the seventh month of 840, he ascended Mount Wutai and visited the Tripitaka Hall, in which he saw a set of a complete canon copied and donated by a layperson, who was inspired by the hierophany of the Bodhisattva Mañjuśrī. Ennin recorded it as follows, as Edwin Reischauer translates it:

> There is a Tripitaka in more than six thousand scrolls, all in gold and silver characters on dark blue paper with rollers of white sandalwood, jade, and ivory. I saw the subtitle by the man who had vowed [to have this work done]. It said:
>
> I, Cheng Tao-chüeh 鄭道覺, a man of Ch'ang-an, on the fourteenth day of the fifth moon of the fourteenth year of Ta-li 大曆 (799), while going around the five terraces, personally saw His Holiness [the Bodhisattva Monju (Mañjuśrī)] and the Myriad Bodhisattvas and the "gold-colored world" [of Monju] and accordingly developed faith and copied six thousand scrolls of the Tripitaka in gold and silver characters.[50]

The use of printing as a means to create the canon did not take away the advantage of hand-copying the canon for devotional purposes. Hand-copying with gold and silver ink remained one of the pious acts. The Mongol court of the Yuan Dynasty, in particular, sponsored massive copying projects throughout the country. In the spring of 1294, the Mongol emperor Kublai Khan 忽必烈 (1215–94), for example, asked monks and Confucian literati to hand-copy the canon with gold ink and use "caskets of seven treasures" (*qibaoxia* 七寶匣) to store the scriptures, hoping they would last forever. The Yuan government even sent envoys to Korea to solicit good-quality Korean paper and enlist qualified monk-scribes to copy the canon.[51]

VARIETIES OF READING PRACTICE

Ritual reading of the entire Buddhist canon also developed when the canon was still in manuscript form. One famous example in medieval China was an official during the Chen Dynasty, Yao Cha 姚察 (533–606). He received bodhisattva precepts when he was only fourteen. After he served the Chen Dynasty, he used all his salary to build monasteries and left little when he died. According to his biography in the dynastic history, he had read the entire canon and thoroughly understood the truth.[52] Commonly known as "turning the scripture" (zhuanjing 轉經), the activity of ritual reading inspired the invention of the revolving repository for symbolic reading of the entire canon, as discussed in the previous section. Ritual reading was a routinized activity aiming at eye contact with each page and utterance of the words, without the requirement of understanding the meaning of the text. This was often referred to as "turning the dharma wheel," and its efficacy came from finishing the project as a whole. Sometimes the reader only picked several lines at the top, or in the middle and bottom sections, to recite as a symbolic completion of the reading activity. Therefore, this mode of reading was different from the conventional reading process, which aimed at understanding the content.[53]

There were few reading aids in the texts published in a canon, such as punctuation marks, emphasis, notes, etc. to help readers comprehend the meaning. However, there was one kind of aid: pronunciation notes using the back-cut (fanqie 反切) method of phonetic notation became an indispensable component of the canon and were often appended to the end of each fascicle of the text.[54] This addition, starting with the printing of Chongning Canon in the eleventh century, was clearly an aid for ritual chanting.

It appears that ritual reading of the entire canon had been incorporated into the mortuary ceremony for deceased parents as an expression of filial piety. A newly discovered stele in Chongqing 重庆 (figure 2.2), left by a filial son named Wang Bogui 王伯珪 in the Northern Song Dynasty, detailed such a ceremony for his father, Chief Officer Wang 王長史, which centered on the reading of the entire canon by a group of monks. Dated to 1020, the stele text starts as follows.

> The lonely son [Wang] Bogui and others, for offering to our diseased father Acting Chief Officer (She Changshi 攝長史), starting from the ninth day of the first month, invited thirty-one monks to our house to read the canon once, with vegetarian meals provided every day. On the thirteenth day of the second month, the monks were dismissed after the coffin was interred. This (two characters are missing from the original) was done as a mortuary ritual. Respectfully, I list the number of merits of reading the canon as follows:

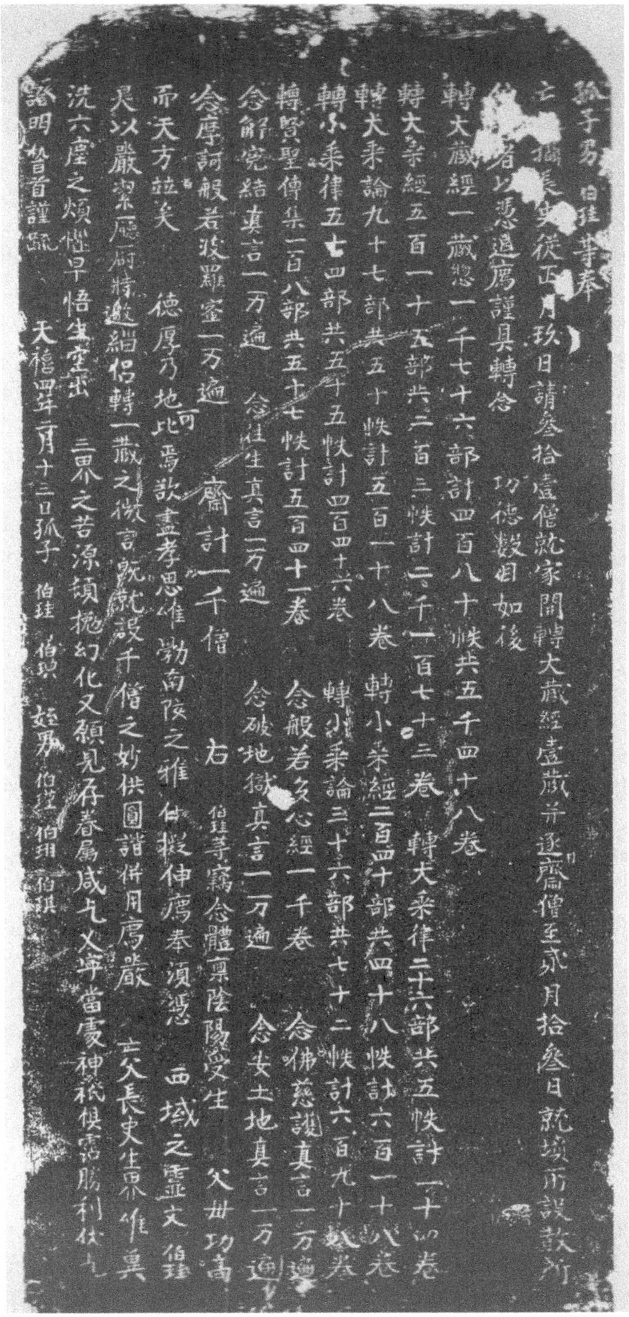

FIGURE 2.2 STELE OF TRIPITAKA RECITATION CEREMONY, DATED TO 1020

Reprint from Xin Zhongguo chutu muzhi. Chongqing, *vol. 9, page 9*

Reading the great canon one time, all together 1,076 titles, 480 cases, and 5,048 fascicles/scrolls in total:

Reading Mahayana Sutras, all together 515 titles, 203 cases, and 2,173 fascicles/scrolls in total; reading Mahayana Vinaya, all together 26 titles, 5 cases, and 14 fascicles/scrolls; reading Mahayana Treatises, all together 97 titles, 50 cases, and 518 fascicles/scrolls;

Reading Hinayana Sutras, all together 240 titles, 48 cases, and 618 fascicles/scrolls; reading Hinayana Vinaya, all together 54 titles, 55 cases, and 446 fascicles/scrolls; reading Hinayana Treatises, all together 36 titles, 72 cases, and 698 fascicles/scrolls.

Reading *Anthology of Sages and Worthies*, all together 108 titles, 57 cases, 541 fascicles/scrolls. . . .

The rest of the text lists a series of magic spells that were chanted ten thousand times, in association with reading the entire canon. On behalf of his relatives, the filial son Wang Bogui wrote down his prayer to repay the kindness of his father and declared that the purpose of reciting the entire canon was to "express his feeling of filial piety."[55]

It is not clear which edition of the canon the reading ceremony was based on. However, the list and numbers provided in this record match those in Zhisheng's *Kaiyuan Catalog*. (The only mistakes is that Mahayana Vinaya should be 54 fascicles and Hinayan Vinaya should be 45 cases.) This suggests that this edition is based on Zhisheng's catalog and might be the newly carved *Kaibao Canon* or a manuscript edition popular in the Sichuan area.

The Mongol emperors in the Yuan Dynasty were among the most pious toward the canon and knew particularly the merits of printing and reciting it. On important occasions, the Mongol emperors would summon monks in the capital to recite the entire canon. For example, in 1272, Kublai Khan requested monks in Beijing to recite the entire canon nine times.[56] In the sixth month of 1307, Emperor Chengzong 成宗, Temür 铁穆耳 (1265–1307), ordered monks in north China, south China, Korea, Sichuan, and Yunnan to recite the canon for the blessing of his harem.[57] Mongol nobles responded to the rulers' passion by donating money for reciting the canon. In 1316, the Uighur official Yighmish (Yihei Mishi 亦黑迷失), a pious Buddhist himself, donated his own money to sponsor a hundred temples to recite the Buddhist canon once a month and pray for the well-being of the Mongol emperors.[58]

In late imperial China, a ceremony of ritual reading of the canon, "reading the whole canon in confinement" (*jinbu yuezang* 禁步閱藏), seems to have been popular. The devotees vowed to read the entire canon in three or four years in solitary living quarters. During the reading process, worship, ritual ablutions, and fasting were often involved. For example, handwritten colophons in *Yongle Southern Canon* indicate that a certain Buddhist devotee named Jueyong 覺詠, who lived in Fujun Temple 府君廟 in Pubo village 蒲箔村—probably located in Changzhi 長治 County in Shanxi—read the entire canon in four years, probably several times. He started on the first day of the third month in 1694 and finished on the first day of the tenth month of 1697. [59]

WHAT IS THE NUMBER OF A CANON?

The "Cult of the Canon" also influenced the "Cult of the Book," as it became popular to recite a particular scripture 5,084 times, the number of scrolls/fascicles in a standard canon based on Zhisheng's *Kaiyuan Catalog*.

In popular Buddhist culture in China, to recite the sutra such a canonical number of times would bring sons to families without them, pacify wandering souls, and ensure a peaceful death and rebirth in the Pure Land. The term *zang* became a standard unit of measurement after most later editions of the canon followed Zhisheng's catalog, which set the number of the entire canon at 5,048 fascicles. Such a unit was often used to count the recitations of a specific scripture. This practice can be dated as early as the eleventh century. For example, according to the biography of the Tiantai monk Congya 從雅, who hailed from Qiantang 錢塘 (Hangzhou) in the Song Dynasty, he recited the *Lotus Sutra* five times the canonical number (*wuzang* 五藏, or 25,280 times), the *Diamond Sutra* four times the canonical number (*sizang* 四藏, or 20,192 times), and the *Amitabha Sutra* ten times the canonical number (*shizang* 十藏 or 50,480 times).[60]

Congya's fellow monk Weiwo 惟渥 (1014–1102), also a native of Qiantang, was devoted to reciting scriptures and the whole canon as well. He started to read the canon in 1041. After reading each fascicle, he would recite the *Heart Sutra* five times. This means that after reading the entire canon of 5,048 scrolls, he had read the *Heart Sutra* five times the canonical number, or 25,280 times. More remarkable was that he read the entire canon like this three times. He also recited many individual scriptures, including the *Heart Sutra* a hundred times the canonical number (504,800 times) and the *Diamond Sutra*, the *Smaller Amitabha Sutra*, and the *Spell of Great Compassion* (*Dabeizhou* 大悲咒) twenty times the canonical number (10,096 times) each.[61]

In the late Qing Dynasty, the famous lay Buddhist reformer Yang Wenhui 楊文會 (1837–1911) noted that many monks and even Daoists claimed that they read a scripture for a canonical number of times, which was 5,048. He wrote in a short note, "Investigating the Number of One Canon" ("Yizang shumu bian" 一藏數目辨):

Nowadays, when clergy and laity recite scriptures and spells, they always claim [that they have recited] the number of "one canon." If you ask about the actual number, they say "five thousand forty-eight." I once checked the catalogs of all the canons. Only *Kaiyuan shijiao lu* (Zhisheng's catalog) has five thousand forty-eight scrolls. The others vary in number, either more or less. Till now, there are still seven thousand two hundred scrolls [in the canon]. The common people stick to the number of five thousand forty-eight because they follow the legend in *Journey to the West* (*Xiyouji*).[62]

Here, Yang Wenhui notes the importance of the total number of scrolls in Zhisheng's *Kaiyuan Catalog* and how the devotees used it as a standard number for recitation. However, he wrongly attributed its origin to the popular novel *Journey to the West*. (See below for the reference to the canon in this novel.)

SHORTCUT READING OF AN APOCRYPHAL SUTRA

A little-known tradition of a shortcut form of ritual reading of the book titles in the canon was based on a type of apocryphal text that provides a fictional list of an imagined canon for recitation and worship. It was first noticed by accident in 1945, when the renowned Buddhist scholar Zhou Shaoliang 周紹良 received a copy of a Buddhist scripture from a monk on a train from Nanjing to Shanghai. Zhou had never heard of this text, entitled *General Catalog of the Great Canon Spoken by the Buddha* (*Foshuo dazangjing zongmu* 佛说大藏經總目). The main content was "Catalog of Scriptures Chinese Monks Took Back from India" (*Tangseng xitian qujing mulu* 唐僧西天取經目錄). Through Zhou Shaoliang's and Fang Guangchang's study, it is now clear that the genesis of this fictional list can be traced back to the Tang Dynasty. The list bears striking resemblance to two Dunhuang manuscripts, S. 3565 and P. 2987, both of which are entitled *The Total Numbers and Catalog of Mahayana and Hinayana Sutra, Vinaya, and Abhidharma in India and China* (*Xitian daxiao cheng jing lü lun bing zaitang dushu mulu* 西天大小乘經律論並在唐都數目錄).[63] This tradition appears to have been extremely popular and was eventually included in Wu Cheng'en's romantic novel *Journey to the West*, which contains two such lists in chapter 98 as the standard catalogs of the canon in India and China.[64]

Not only was the shortcut popular in premodern China, such apocryphal texts are still circulating in China today. A 1998 reprint of a text entitled *Catalog of All Scriptures in the Great Canon* (*Dazang zongjing mulu* 大藏總經目錄) is based on an 1888 woodblock edition (figures 2.3a and 2.3b).[65] The purpose of this apocryphal sutra is to encourage reciting and copying the catalog as a con-

FIGURE 2.3A, FIGURE 2.3B SAMPLE PAGE OF *DAZANG ZONGJING MULU*, 1998 REPRINT
Collection of and photo by Fang Guangchang

densed version of the entire canon. This text is an excellent example illustrating the practice of the "Cult of the Canon." Throughout, in addition to giving fictional details of the canon, the author calls for devotion and dedication to it. The benefit for the cult is described as follows.

> Worshiping the canon can be used to eliminate disasters and destroy obstructions, repent crimes and release mistakes, realize fruition and establish causes, illuminate the mind and see nature. It can repay unrepayable kindness and assist transformation without deliberate effort and action.[66]

The text continues to highlight the efficacy of reciting and copying the catalog itself.

> In case there are good men and women who obtain the titles in this scripture, if they are able to wholeheartedly chant and recite them one time, it is similar to reading the scriptures in an entire canon; if someone is able to copy this text, the accumulated merits will be countless and they will be protected by sages and worthies.[67]

The anonymous author of this text sees that worshiping the catalog is equivalent to devotion to the entire canon. Such devotion includes reciting the titles and copying the text. When a pagoda or a statue is made, this text can be put inside for worship.[68] For those who contract a serious illness, it is recommended that they acquire one copy of this text and put the book in a small bag made of cloth, which they should wear on their chest. After they die and go through the purgatories, King Yama should spare them after he sees that there is a great Buddhist canon on their chest.[69]

CHAN BUDDHISM AND THE "CULT OF THE CANON"

CHAN MONKS' INVOLVEMENT WITH THE CANON

Despite the Chan rhetoric of immediate enlightenment and negative attitude toward scriptural learning, Chan monks played major roles as custodians of the canon and practitioners of the "Cult of the Canon." The Chan connection can be traced to the late Tang. For example, Zongmi 宗密 (780–841) even contemplated compiling a separate "Chan Canon."[70] Ritual reading of the canon was also occasionally referred to in koan literature. In the Chan recorded sayings of Zhaozhou Congshen 趙州從諗 (778–897), it is clear how Chan monasteries operated the ceremony of chanting the entire canon as a business in the ninth century. In one of the most quoted koans about Zhaozhou, an old lady sent money and asked him to "turn" the whole canon. But Zhaozhou, after accepting the money, simply came down from his high chair and walked around it one time, calling this "turning the canon." The old lady, after learning this, replied in a surprised way: "I came to request you to turn the whole canon; why did you only turn half of it?" Zhaozhou was speechless.[71] The meaning of this koan is not the focus of our discussion here. However, this episode shows clearly that the "Cult of the Canon" became a monastic practice that was actually a paid service in monasteries dominated by Chan monks.

During the Song Dynasty, Chan monasteries were among the most enthusiastic in building the revolving repositories. In "Charts of Five Mountains and Ten Monasteries in China" (*Gozan jissatsu zu* 五山十刹圖), brought to Japan in the fourteenth century, a revolving repository structure can be clearly seen in the layout of Jinshan Monastery 金山寺 in Zhenjiang 鎮江 and Lingyin Monastery 靈隱寺 in Hangzhou.[72] It seems that in medieval China, running a revolving repository was a profit-making business for Chan monasteries, and Chan monks, even famous teachers, were caretakers of this device.

Japanese scholar Shiina Kōyū 椎名宏雄 studied fifty-five records of canon acquisition in Song sources and clearly demonstrated that Chan monks were a leading force in promoting the "Cult of the Canon." According to his study, there were more canon-building activities in the Northern Song, especially in the eleventh century, largely due to the carving of *Kaibao Canon*, which spurred enthusiasm. Judging from their sectarian affiliation, Chan monks of the Yunmen 雲門 school were the most active during the Northern Song, followed by monks from the Huanglong 黃龍 lineage in the Linji school. During the Southern Song, monks of the Yangqi 楊岐 lineage showed increased interest in acquiring the canon and managing the library that housed it.[73]

CHAN JUSTIFICATION FOR
CARETAKING THE CANON

However, active involvement in acquiring and maintaining the canon in Chan monasteries entailed a contradiction for Chan monks, as they claimed to have transcended all Buddhist teachings in writing. For example, in a record of building the Tripitaka Hall in Baizhaoshan Monastery 白兆山寺 in Anzhou 安州 in today's Hubei Province, the Yunmen Chan monk Chuisu 垂素 asked himself this hypothetical question: "Bodhidharma's Chan Buddhism did not establish written words and pointed to one's mind [as the way] to become Buddha by seeing his nature. Then why do we have to take all five thousand books [the canon, around 5,048 scrolls] and make it a canon?" Chuisu disagreed and then explained to himself: "All sentient beings have the straightforward mind that is still and illuminating. Therefore, they are equal to the Buddha. However, because their emotions are attached to external things, they thus become ill due to obstructions, and the Buddha is just like a good doctor who knows the root of these illnesses. According to the illness, he prescribed medicines to cure them. . . . Now the Tripitaka Hall is just the place to hold these 'medicines' [the canon]."[74]

For some Chan teachers, having a Tripitaka collection in their monasteries might have been a convenient choice. Around 1095, Chan master Sixin Wuxin 死心悟新 (1043–1114) was invited to Yunyan Chan Cloister 雲巖禪院 in Hongzhou 洪州 in Jiangxi as abbot and had no choice but to support an effort to build a revolving repository, fearing that a pure Chan teaching would not attract many patrons. He consoled himself that to build such a device was to "practice Buddhism during the period of Latter-Day dharma" 末法中作佛事, when there was no correct teaching and practice in Buddhist communities.[75]

The most articulate defense of Chan monks' involvement in caretaking the canon was made by Foguo Weibai 佛國惟白, an orthodox Chan monk who not only authored one of the most influential Chan transmission histories, *Continued Records of Lamp Transmission from the Jianzhong Jingguo Reign* (*Jianzheng jingguo xudenglu* 建中靖國續燈録), but also wrote a comprehensive reading guide to the canon, entitled *Essential Guide and Checklist of the Great Canon* (*Dazangjing gangmu zhiyao lu* 大藏經綱目指要録), in eight fascicles compiled in 1104 after he read *Kaibao Canon* in its entirety. He promoted reading the canon, as it could have "Five Benefits" (*wuli* 五利) and repay "Five Kindnesses" (*wubao* 五報). According to him, compiling such a guide for reading the canon could benefit Chan teachers, dharma lecturers, dharma commentators, canon readers, and those who did not have time to read the entire canon. Moreover, such a project repays the kindness of kings and emperors, dharma protectors, one's parents, teachers, and patrons. Here he listed Chan monks among the first group of beneficiaries because he believed that to spread Chan teaching, a Chan teacher must "rely on broad knowledge [of the canon] to respond to people who have questions."[76] Weibai's example shows that the tension between Chan and the canon was explained away, and being a Chan monk and engaging in studying the canon were no longer contradictory.

THE ROLE OF THE CANON IN
CHAN MONASTIC PRACTICE

Chan monks also became exemplars of ritual reading of the entire canon. The famous Song monk Juefan Huihong 覺范惠洪 (1071–1128) mentioned in his *Record of Chan Grove* (*Linjianlu* 林間錄) a famous Chan monk named Chengti 澄湜 at Qixian Monastery 棲賢寺 in Lushan. When he became old, Chengti read the entire canon three times. Because he regarded reading in a seated position as not reverent enough, he decided to recite it while standing and carried the scripture on his back while walking.[77]

During the Song Dynasty, when Chan Buddhism dominated monastic life, circumambulation around the canon was a ritualized ceremony. In various editions of monastic rules after the Tang, it was incorporated as one of the monastic routines. The ceremony was usually held in the Tripitaka Hall on the first and fifteenth days of the month, after the morning meal. After a novice announced the activity, bells tolled and the assembly was summoned. A special kind of drum was struck to announce the beginning of the ceremony of circumambulating the canon. The rector chanted, "All should keep Mahaprajñāpāramitā (Great Perfection of Wisdom) in mind," and the abbot led the assembly to circumambulate the device three times, symbolizing turning the dharma wheel three times. Then the rector chanted the "Spell of Great Compassion" (Dabeizhou). At the end, the verse of returning the merit to all was chanted together, following a standard format.[78] Very likely, music was played during the ceremony. As the Japanese Zen pilgrim Eisai 榮西 (1141–1215) observed about the Chinese practice in his famous *Treatise for Promoting Zen and Protecting the Nation* (*Kōzen gokoku ron* 興禪護國論), "Monks gathered together to play music and turn the octagonal revolving repository."[79]

It is clear that Chan monks paid special attention to the canon and acted as caretakers of the tradition. Different versions of the Chan Pure Regulations document special rules for handling the canon and the procedure for reading it. In *Pure Regulation of Chan Monasteries* (*Chanyuan qinggui* 禪苑清規), the Director of the Library (*zangzhu* 藏主) was clearly stipulated as the caretaker of the canon. He should set up the reading room and all accessories and arrange seats for readers. The procedure for checking out scriptures was orderly and strict. First, the reader had to check the availability of seats in the sutra hall and then inform the Director of the Library of his intent to read. Then the director led the reader to the sutra hall and they bowed (*chuli* 觸禮) to each other. During the process of reading, they must maintain a high level of reverence.

> After the director of the library has been escorted out, those wishing to read must unfold their sitting mats, place them on the floor before the holy statue, and bow down three times. They must then stand up and do *chuli* one time to the chief seat. They will then circumambulate the hall once and meet the sutra curator to request a time to read the sutras. . . . The monks who are reading the sutras must burn incense in the sutra hall and worship solemnly. While holding the sutras in their hands, the monks must not talk or laugh with others. The desk should not have sutras piled up on it, and there should be no pens, ink, miscellaneous stationery items, or Chan literature alongside the sutras.[80]

The rules went on about how to handle the scriptures respectfully and properly to protect their physical appearance. According to Griffith Foulk, Chan monks during the Song, with the sponsorship of patrons for a particular purpose of merit dedication, held a ceremony called "revolving reading" (*kanzhuan* 看轉) "in which the great assembly of monks chanted scriptures or flipped rapidly through the sutra books."[81]

The reverential reading of the canon was also encouraged when Chan Buddhism was revived in the seventeenth century. For example, in the monastic rules drafted by a famous Chan teacher, Feiyin Tongrong 費隱通容 (1593–1662), the tradition of worshiping the canon was further developed for the revived communities. In his "Rules for the Two Assemblies in Chan Monasteries" (*Conglin liangxu xuzhi* 叢林兩序須知), Feiyin Tongrong made fifteen special rules regarding the duties of the Director of the Library in the regulations he put in place in Jinsu Monastery 金粟寺. These rules include how to arrange the canon in order and details of log keeping, prevention of dampness, repairing damaged books, procedures for checking out and returning scriptures, etc.[82] Yuanhong Yirun 源洪儀潤, the author of a commentary on *Baizhang's Pure Regulations* (*Baizhang qinggui*)—*Baizhang qinggui zhengyi ji* 百丈清規證義記—even suggested that every monastery where a canon was stored should support one monk specializing in reading the canon. This monk must be required to read and recite the canon every day to embody the meaning of "Eternal Turning of the Dharma Wheel."[83]

CONCLUSION

Previous studies of the canon have focused on textual analysis and edition collation and thus neglected its actual use in religious communities. However, as

Wilfred Cantwell Smith points out, "no text is a scripture in itself and as such. People—a given community—make a text into scripture, or keep it scripture: by treating it in a certain way."[84] In a similar vein, the meaning of the canon can only be fully revealed when believers use it in a devotional context. New sources have emerged on the actual use of the canon and show that the "Cult of the Canon" was an essential phenomenon that defined Chinese Buddhism and even spread to other parts of East Asia. The emergence and flourishing of the "Cult of the Canon" in China is a natural outcome of the "Cult of the Book," as the Buddhist devotion to spreading written scriptures interacted with the advanced book culture in China.

In my preliminary research, I found that the "Cult of the Canon" was a prevalent religious phenomenon that developed along with the creation of the Chinese canon in the sixth century and reached its height after the eleventh century, then gradually declined in modern times. This cult centered on the physical existence of the canon and was usually associated with a special kind of mythology or miracle stories about the efficacy of the canon in a given community. Patron gods were deliberately created to expound the efficacy and merits of such a cult. Special rituals and ceremonies, such as worship of the canon and its patron gods, ritual reading and copying, and physically turning the revolving repository or turning the pages of the canon were believed to contribute to merit accumulation. In this context, the textual content of the canon became less important. To summarize, the "Cult of the Canon" had the following salient features.

First, the "Cult of the Canon" was based on the Chinese imagination of the canon derived from translated scriptures, in which the mythological account of the canon, such as its existence in Indra's palace and the Dragon King's palace, stimulated worship and devotion. As I have shown elsewhere, the "Cult of the Canon" has its "root metaphor"—that is, the legends and myths about the origin of the canon based on abundant references in various translated Buddhist texts and further mythologized by Chinese people. These stories continued to ferment in the popular consciousness and were expressed in novels and even apocryphal texts, in which the canon in its entirety was promoted as representing the whole Buddhist teaching and the Buddha's dharma body. Such ideas were popularized in Buddhist encyclopedias and anthologies such as Daoshi's 道世 *Pearl Forest of the Dharma Grove* (*Fayuan Zhulin* 法苑珠林) and were even preserved in Dunhuang manuscripts and popular novels such as *Journey to the West* (*Xiyouji*). More importantly, it was believed that devotion to the entire canon would bring considerable blessing and merit. This kind of popular consciousness thus motivated both the elite and common people to participate in the production and distribution of the entire canon.[85]

Second, the "Cult of the Canon" emerged from advances in architectural and printing technology that made possible the massive production of the canon and innovative storage devices, such as the revolving repository. The creation of the canon was a remarkable invention involving tremendous intellectual, technological, and manual power, such as the organization of textual criticism, cataloging, collations, use of scribes and printing technology, the combination of private and government resources, etc. The distribution and maintenance of the canon also required architectural advances and the efficient use of local resources.

Third, the "Cult of the Canon" was most often invoked by emperors and kings in China and other parts of East Asia as a means to strengthen the symbolic power of the state and royal family during empire building. In Korea, for example, the canon has been incorporated seamlessly into the ideology of "Buddhism for National Protection."[86] Such a massive project with symbolic significance was perfect for rulers to display imperial power and acquire political legitimacy as well as divine empowerment.

Fourth, the "Cult of the Canon" was quickly adopted by monastic communities and formed a distinctive type of devotion that centered on the canon and even became independent of other monastic establishments. Activities such as building revolving repositories and holding ceremonies of worshiping the canon were incorporated into monastic rituals. When Chan Buddhism became dominant during the eleventh century and later, Chan monasteries became active in promoting the "Cult of the Canon."

Finally, the community responded to the canon with religious fervor and completely embraced the cult by worshiping the device of the revolving repository and participating in ritual reading and writing. Meanwhile, legends and miracle stories developed about the efficacy of the "Cult of the Canon" and the commoners helped to spread this folklore, which tended to cater to the spiritual concerns of local people. To a large extent, the "Cult of the Canon" became localized in particular regions to address the spiritual needs of local communities. As we have seen from the service of reciting the entire canon by the Wang family in the Song Dynasty, to participate in monastic rituals and ceremonies centering on the "Cult of the Canon" provided opportunities for devotees, including royal family members, to establish their "personal relationship" with the divine and to ensure their own and their families' welfare.[87]

In recent years, intensive research on the cult of relics and images by Buddhist scholars has yielded fruitful results and considerably enriched our understanding of Buddhism as a religion in practice.[88] The Chinese Buddhist canon, however, as a massive collection of written texts, was naturally associated with the abuse of textual authority and the exercise of textual hegemony in a postmodern perspective. Although its textual function has been acknowledged and even further developed in the digital age, it appears that the Chinese Buddhist canon is no longer an interesting and trendy topic to pursue except for the purposes of textual collation and criticism. As Oliver Freiberger observes, "in contemporary academia, the concept of a canon is rather unpopular. The word 'canon' reminds us of elites who use their power to suppress opposing views by labeling them as non-canonical and heretic. It reminds us of colonialism and 'Orientalism,' of the ways Western scholars 'canonized' the knowledge of 'the East.'"[89] As a result, scholars tend to stay away from the "canon" but focus on "practice," which is by itself an abstract construction.

However, the canon is not only a collection of texts but also an object to which religious practices were directed. Together with the relics that represent Buddha's Rūpakāya, the canon represents his Dharmakāya, equally important in Buddhist communities.[90] By shifting our focus to the devotional aspect of the canon, I view Chinese Buddhism from a new perspective, which reveals an important tradition overlooked by scholars of Chinese religion. The Cult of the Canon not only was prevalent in Chinese Buddhism but also became a pan-East Asian phenomenon along with the transmission of the canon to Korea, Japan, and Vietnam. Many of these East Asian countries formed their own unique canonical tradition and developed various forms of devotion to the canon. More in-depth studies in these areas will further deepen our understanding of the Buddhist canon and its actual impact on religious communities.

NOTES

Citations of *Taishō Canon* (1–55, and 85 volumes), *Jiaxing Canon*, *Shinsan Zokuzōkyō* (abbreviated as Z), and *Zhengshi Fojiao ziliao leibian* in this chapter are based on the CBETA Chinese Electronic Tripiṭaka Collection (April 2009 version) unless noted otherwise.

1. Schopen, "The Phrase 'sa pṛthvīpradeṣaṣ caityabhūto bhavet' in the *Vajracchedikā*." Schopen quotes a variety of Mahayana scriptures that suggest that the spot where the written texts were located shall become the object of devotion and the merit field. These scriptures also promoted their own production and reproduction as pious activities.

2. It is common in the Buddhist tradition to bury objects with written words, such as scriptures and *dharani* scripts, in stupas. For examples of inserting scriptures inside statues and stupas during the Liao Dynasty, see Shen, "Realizing the Buddha's Dharma Body" and "Praying for Eternity." Barrett, "Stupa, Sutra and Sarira in China." Tsiang, "Monumentalization of Buddhist Texts."

3. Campany, "Note on the Devotional Uses," 52. Campany made this remark when comparing Buddhist and Daoist practices, and it applies to both traditions regarding their use of sacred texts.

4. Fang Guangchang has noticed this phenomenon and outlined some aspects in his *Zhongguo xieben dazangjing yanjiu*, 210–22 and 540–44.

5. See these prayers preserved in *Guang hongming ji* 廣弘明集, fasc. 22, T 2103, 52: 257.

6. *Guang hongming ji*, fasc. 22, T 52: 258, 259. See also *Fozu tongji*, fasc. 39, T 2035, 49: 366b.

7. For a convenient collection of imperial prefaces to the canon, see Fukuda Gyōkai, *Gyosei daizōkyō jobatsu*.

8. Harrist, *The Landscape of Words*, 181. Translation is based on Ledderose, "Thunder Sound Cave," 241 and Shen, "Realizing the Buddha's Dharma Body," 268n22.

9. See Gjertson, *Miraculous Retribution*, 165–66. His name was mistaken as Zhiwan 智菀 in the original Chinese record. See also Ledderose, "Changing the Audience."

10. For this event and the possible connection with Fazang 法藏, see Chen Jinhua, "A Daoist Princess and a Buddhist Temple."

11. The rubbings of *Fangshan Stone Canon* have been reproduced in China. For studies in English, see Lancaster, "The Rock Cut Canon in China"; Li Jung-hsi, "The Stone Scriptures of Fang-shan"; Ledderose, "Carving Sutras Into Stone Before the Catastrophe."

12. Li Jining, "*Jinzang* xinziliao kao," 447–48. For the carving of *Qisha Canon*, see Lucille Chia's chapter 6 in this volume. For a photo of this colophon, see figure 6.8a.

13. For other examples, see Li Fuhua and He Mei, *Hanwen Fojiao dazangjing yanjiu*, 291, 296, 297, and 302.

14. See Wang Zeqing, "Xiezhouban *Jinzang* muke de zhongyao wenxian."

15. According to Li Jining, Bao's record contains the content of an original stele written by Jin official Zhao Feng 趙渢, dated to 1193. For details, see Li Jining, "*Jinzang* xinziliao kao." See also Li Fuhua and He Mei, *Hanwen Dazangjing yanjiu*, 98–100, 296–302. Bao Shanhui was a monk of Hui'in Monastery, or the popularly known Korean Temple in Hangzhou. His record about Cui Fazhen was inserted as a colophon for the repaired *Qisha Canon*. For a brief account of Hui'in Monastery and its connection with the canon, see below.

16. Shen, "Realizing the Buddha's Dharma Body," 293.

17. See Li Fuhua and He Mei, *Hanwen dazangjing yanjiu*, 527.

18. See Bai Huawen, "Xinxi shidai de zangjing gongyang."

19. The popular festival of Heavenly Blessing was declared a holiday by Song Zhenzong 宋真宗 in 1011. See Zhao Sheng, *Caoye leiyao: Zhujie*, fasc. 1, 2763–64. This became a festival in late imperial China for people to expose their books and clothes under the sun.

20. For this legend, see Gu Lu, *Qing Jia Lu*, fasc. 6, 134.

21. See Ennin's travelogue, fasc. 2, in Reischauer, trans., *Ennin's Diary*, 157.

22. Xiao Mo, *Dunhuang jianzhu yanjiu*, 61–62. This layout was confirmed in the textual sources in Tang literature.

23. *Quan Tang wen*, 676: 4764. See also T 2122, 53: 875–76. For a partial translation in French, see Drège, *Les bibliothèques en Chine au temps des manuscrits*, 211.

24. For a short history of the "Hall of Sutra Storage," see Bai Huawen, "'Jingzang nei.'" Technical details about wall storage and wheel storage are described in fasc. 11 of *Official Building Standards* (*Yingzao fashi* 營造法式), compiled during the Song Dynasty. See Feng, *Chinese Architecture and Metaphor*.

25. Jōjin, *San Tendai Godaisan ki*, fasc. 4, 412–13, 417–18. For Jōjin's connection with the canon during his stay in China, see Demiéville, "Notes additionnelles sur les editions imprimées du canon bouddhique," 128–31. For an account of Jōjin's travel in China, see Verschuer, "Le voyage de Jōjin au mont Tiantai." See also Borgen, "Jōjin's Discoveries in Song China" and "Jōjin's Travels from Center to Center."

26. *Shimen zhengtong*, Z 75: 297b, no. 1513.

27. See Liang, *A Pictorial History*, 61.

28. See Wu, "Imagining Tripitaka."

29. For a thorough discussion of the revolving repository invented by Fu Xi, see Zhang Yong, *Fu Dashi yanjiu*, 442–71. See also Nagai Masashi, "Fu Dashi to Rinzō." For Gregory Schopen's research on the Indian origin of this device based on an eleventh-century Indian reference, see Schopen, "A Note on the 'Technology of Prayer.'" Chinese sources indeed mentioned an Indian monk named Chafuluojie 刹縛羅劫 or Shili Fuluo 室利[口＋縛]囉, who was consulted about building five mechanically connected revolving repositories in Kaifu Monastery 開福寺 in Changsha during the early tenth century. See Sun Di 孫覿, "Chong'an si wu lunzang" 崇安寺五輪藏, in *Hongqing jushi ji*, fasc. 23, *SKQS*, 1135: 242. See also Huihong 慧洪, "Tanzhou Kaifu zhuanlunzang lingyan ji" 潭州開福轉輪藏靈驗記, *Shimen wenzichan* 石門文字禪, fasc. 21, *JXZ* no. 135, 23: 676b–c. See also Huang Minzhi, "Guanyu Songdai siyuan de zhuanlunzang," 378–79.

30. See Goodrich, "The Revolving Book-Case in China." For a convenient collection of historical sources about the revolving repository in China, see Mujaku Dōchū, *Zenrin shōkisen*, 63–66.

31. See Reischauer, trans., *Ennin's Diary*, 247.

32. Bai Juyi, *Bai Juyi ji*, fasc. 70, 1487–88.

33. See Huang Minzhi, "Zailun Songdai siyuan de Zhuanlunzang." Kani Noriyuki, "Sōdai Tenrinzō to sono shinkō."

34. For the architectural aspect of this device, see Qinghua Guo, "The Architecture of Joinery," and Zhang Shiqing, *Zhongguo jiangnan Chanzong siyuan jianzhu*, 252–56.

35. See Goodrich, "The Revolving Book-Case in China." Nanjio Bunyiu (Nanjō Bun'yū), *A Catalogue of the Chinese Translation of the Buddhist Tripiṭaka*, xxv–xxvi. There are a few such examples extant today; see Prip-Møller, *Chinese Buddhist Monasteries*, 55–60. Daoan, *Zhongguo dazangjing diaoke shihua*, 150–51. In Korea, the only surviving structures are the two revolving repositories preserved in Yongmunsa 龍門寺. See Choi Youngsook, "Yongmunsa Yunjangdae yeongu." In Japan, a recent survey shows that there are still sixty-two kinds of revolving repositories extant. See Nozaki Jun, "Nihon no Rinzō nitsuite no oboegaki."

36. Eubanks, *Miracles of Books and Body*, 173–95.

37. *Fozu tongji, T* 2035, 49: 318c.

38. See Qisong, *Tanjin wenji*, fasc. 12, *T* 52: 711b, no. 2115. For a recent study of Qisong, see Morrison, *The Power of Patriarchs*.

39. See Han Yuanji, *Nanjian jiayi gao*, fasc. 16, 315. Native patron gods for the revolving repository were also developed in Japan, and the story of worshiping Rinzō was even incorporated into a classic Noh play called *Rinzō*. See Eubanks, *Miracles of Books and Body*, 184–86.

40. See Fei Gun, *Liangxi manzhi*, fasc. 10, 118. This story was also collected in *Tushu jicheng: Shijiaobu jishi* 圖書集成: 釋教部紀事, fasc. 2, Z 1661, 88: 502b.

41. For Yang Jie and his connection with Buddhism, see Huang Chi-chiang, "Bei Song Jushi Yang Jie yu Fojiao."

42. *Fozu tongji*, fasc. 46, *T* 2035, 49: 417b.

43. Ibid, 424a.

44. Liu Tong, *Dijing jingwu lue*, fasc. 1, 43–44. Both quotations were translated by Goodrich, "The Revolving Book-Case in China," 145.

45. See Huang Chi-chiang, "Ŭich'ŏn's Pilgrimage." See also Bao Zhicheng, *Gaoli si yu Gaoli wangzi*, 55–56, 123–24; Li Fuhua and He Mei, *Hanwen Fojiao dazangjing yanjiu*, 342–43.

46. Spence, *Return to Dragon Mountain*, 79. The idea of the revolving repository has been assimilated into Buddhist and Daoist mortuary rituals in Southeast Asian Chinese communities, as witnessed by Kamata Shigeo in Singapore in 1979. However, the revolving device used in these rituals has nothing to do with the Buddhist canon. See Kamata Shigeo, *Chūgoku no Bukkyō girei*, 236–49.

47. The allusion to this pious devotion to ritual writing is derived from the Avataṃsaka (Huayan) scripture. See Kieschnick, "Blood Writing in Chinese Buddhism"; Yu, *Sanctity and Self-Inflicted Violence*.

48. This must be an early manuscript edition of the canon. See *Bianzheng lun* 辯正論, fasc. 3, *T* 2110, 52: 506b. In these early examples, it might be true that the devotees copied the whole canon by themselves. It is also possible that they commissioned scribes to copy it for them.

49. See Bingenheimer, "A Translation of the *Tōdaiwajō tōseiden*" (Part 2, 2008 PDF version), 17. Bingenheimer believed that Jianzhen ordered the copying rather than doing it himself.

50. See Reischauer, trans., *Ennin's Diary*, 254.

51. *Shishi jigu lue xuji* 釋氏稽古略續集, fasc. 1, *T* 2038, 49: 908a. The Yuan government recruited monks in 1297, 1302, and 1305 and requested a paper supply for copying the canon in 1309, 1338, and 1340. See Kim Changsuk, ed., *Goryeosa Bulgyo gwangye saryojip*, vol. 1, 139, 140, 143, 150, 151.

52. See Yao Cha's biography in *Chenshu* 陳書, quoted from *Zhengshi Fojiao leibian*, vol. 1, 66a.

53. When Holmes Welch inquired about thirty elderly monks who devoted themselves to reading scriptures in the "scripture perusal chamber" at Liuyun Monastery 留雲寺 in Shanghai, his informant simply told him that these monks did not understand the scriptures necessarily, but simply "turn the thousands of pages of the Tripitaka, glancing at each." See Welch, *The Practice of Chinese Buddhism 1900–1950*, 102–3.

54. For the use of *fanqie* in the canon, see Yong and Peng, *Chinese Lexicography*, 198–99, 207–8, 218–20, 369–75.

55. *Xin Zhongguo chu tu mu zhi. Chongqing*, vol. 9, 202–3. For a study of this stele, see Li Xiaoqiang, "*Song Wang Changshi*."

56. See the biography of Kublai Khan in *Yuanshi* 元史, fasc. 7, *Zhengshi Fojiao ziliao leibian*, 1: 454.

57. See the biography of the Wuzong emperor in *Yuanshi* 元史, fasc. 23, *Zhengshi Fojiao ziliao leibian*, 1: 456.

58. This event was recorded in a stone stele and was discovered in Quanzhou. The content of the stele was preserved in *Minzhong jinshi lue* 閩中金石略, fasc. 11, reprinted in *Shike shiliao xinbian* (Series 1), 17: 13030. Yighimish was a Mongol official and merchant. He had been dispatched to South Asian countries as envoy and amassed great wealth from trade. For details, see Chen Dezhi, "Cong Yiheimishi shenfen kan Make Boluo." He also sponsored the recarving of *Pilu Canon* in 1313. See Li and He, *Hanwen dazangjing yanjiu*, 354–55.

59. Nozawa Yoshimi, *Rissō daigaku toshokan shozō Mindai Nanzō mokuroku*, 79–80.

60. *Buxu gaoseng zhuan*, fasc. 2, Z 1524, 77: 375a. See his short biography in *Zhongguo Fojiao renming dacidian*, 654.

61. *Fahua xianying lu*, fasc. 2, Z 1540, 78: 49c. See his short biography in *Zhongguo Fojiao renming dacidian*, 675.

62. Yang Wenhui, *Yang Renshan Ji*, 53. Yang Wenhui was actively involved in the printing of Buddhist texts and the canon. For studies of Yang Weihui and his connection to the printing of the canon, see Chen Jidong, *Shinmatsu Bukkyō no kenkyū: Yō Bunkai o chūshin to shite*. Goldfuss, *Vers un bouddhisme du XXe siecle*.

63. For trascriptions of these texts, see Fang Guangchang, *Dunhuang Fojiao jinglu*, 275–90. Images of both texts can be downloaded from the International Dunhuang Project website. For Zhou's discovery, see Zhou Shaoliang, "De Foshuo dazangjing mulu yinyuanji." According to Zhou's introduction, the Ming version was a reprint by a Beijing devotee, Wang Fuqing 王福慶, in 1427. For a detailed study of these Dunhuang texts, see Fang Guangchang, *Zhongguo xieben dazangjing yanjiu*, 296–316.

64. Wu Cheng'en 吳承恩, the author of *Journey to the West*, gives two lists of the contents of this fictional canon in chapter 98. See Wu Cheng'en, *Journey to the West*, vol. 4, 389–90, 395–96. For a transcription of this list, see Fang Guangchang, *Dunhuang Fojiao jinglu*, 291–94.

65. It is a modern printed edition with seventeen pages, printed in simplified characters with no punctuation. According to its introduction, the full title of this text is *Catalog of All Scriptures in the Great Canon Spoken by the Buddha and Place Names of Sarila, Holy Tooth, Jeweled Pagoda (Foshuo dazang zongjing mulu sheli lingya baota minghao* 佛說大藏總經目錄舍利靈牙寶塔名號). I want to thank Fang Guangchang for providing photos of this version.

66. *Dazang zongjing mulu*, 1998 reprint, 1.

67. Ibid., 7–8.

68. Ibid., 14.

69. Ibid., 10.

70. We only have the preface to this compilation left. For a short account of the creation of *Chan Canon* and a study of the preface, see Broughton, "Tsung-mi's Zen Prolegomenon," 14–15; *Zongmi on Chan*, 22–26, 101–79. See also Gregory, *Tsung-mi and the Sinification of Chinese Buddhism*, 224–43. According to Fang Guangchang, who reconstructed its content, fragments of Zongmi's *Chan Canon* have been preserved in Dunhuang manuscripts. See Fang Guangchang, *Zhongguo xieben dazangjing yanjiu*, 242–79.

71. See *Wudeng huiyuan*, fasc. 4, Z 1565, 80: 92b.

72. Zhang Shiqing, *Wu shan shi cha tu*, 49, and Foulk, "Myth, Ritual, and Monastic Practice," 188.

73. Shiina Kōyū, *Sō Gen-ban zenseki no kenkyū*, 153–65.

74. See the stele written by Fan Chunren 范纯仁 in *Shike shiliao xinbian*, 17: 19–20. For Chuisu's short biography, see *Zhongguo Fojiao renming dacidian*, 381. For a thoughtful reflection on Chan attitudes toward canon and scripture, see Poceski, *Ordinary Mind as the Way*, 139–49.

75. See Huang Tingjian's 黃庭堅 record in *Quan Songwen*, fasc. 2324, 107: 188. For Sixin Wuxin's biography, see *Zhongguo fojiao renming dacidian*, 599.

76. See *Shōwa hōbō sōmokuroku*, 2: 771b. For a brief introduction of his compilation of the Chan lamp history *Jianzhong jingguo xudenglu*, see Schlütter, *How Zen Became Zen*, 24.

77. Z 1624, 87: 0245c23. For his biography, see *Buxu gaoseng zhuan*, Z 1524, 77: 420, and *Zhongguo Fojiao renming dacidian*, 1024–25.

78. See *Chanlin beiyong qinggui*, Z 1250, 63: 620c.

79. T 2543, 80:15b. This reference is obtained through SAT Daizōkyō Text Database. For a study of Eisai, see Welter, "Zen Buddhism as the Ideology of the Japanese State," and "Buddhist Rituals for Protecting the Country in Medieval Japan."

80. Yifa, *The Origins of Buddhist Monastic Codes*, 159–60.

81. Foulk, "Myth, Ritual, and Monastic Practice," 188.

82. Z 1251, 63: 668b. For Feiyin Tongrong and his life, see Wu, *Enlightenment in Dispute*, 92–93.

83. *Baizhang qinggui zhengyi ji*, fasc. 5, Z 1244, 63: 044c15.

84. See Smith, *What Is Scripture*, 18.

85. See Wu, "Imagining Tripitaka."

86. For details, see Wu and Dziwenka, "Better Than the Original," chapter 8 in this volume.

87. Largely based on Robert Hymes's understanding of a "personal model" in Chinese religion, I use "personal relationship" to refer to a direct connection between the devotee and the divine without the mediation of clergy or bureaucratic hierarchy. The devotion based on this personal relationship is often locally based, and the spread of the canon in local societies enabled devotees to develop such relationships and encouraged immediate appropriation of the canon for their personal use. For a detailed discussion, see Hymes, *Way and Byway*. See also Wu, *Enlightenment in Dispute*, 275–76.

88. There are many studies on the relic cult in Buddhism; for a few representative works, see Sharf, "On the Allure of Buddhist Relics"; Schopen, "Monks and the Relic Cult in the Mahaparinibbanasutta"; Strong, *Relics of the Buddha*.

89. Freiberger, "The Buddhist Canon and the Canon of Buddhist Studies," 261.

90. Such an attempt has been noticed by Buddhist scholars. For example, John Strong finds that dharma relic was an important category, as it often converged with other relics cults by inserting a piece of written scripture into the stupa. He also notes that there was a tendency in the tradition to unite Rūpakāya and Dharmakāya as the 84,000 monasteries Asoka built, corresponding to the 84,000 sections of Buddha's teachings, since after Buddha passed into nirvana, the unity of his body was disrupted. Richard Salomon's study of the ritually buried Gandhāran manuscripts also reveals the deliberate association of textual relics with bodily relics in order to perpetuate *Buddhavacana* (Buddha's words). See Strong, *Relics of the Buddha*, 10 and 138–39; Salomon, "Why Did the Gandharan Buddhists Bury Their Manuscripts?" For some discussion about scripture deposits as the embodiment of Dharmakāya, see Shen, "Realizing the Buddha's Dharma Body."

PART II

The Formative Period

3. Notions and Visions of the Canon in Early Chinese Buddhism

Stefano Zacchetti

INTRODUCTION: THE TWOFOLD NATURE OF THE CHINESE BUDDHIST CANON

All the various bodies of scriptures evoked by the name "Buddhist canon"—such as the Pali canon, the Tibetan canon, the Mongolian canon, and the Chinese canon, just to mention those surviving in a more or less complete form—are in fact very different things from the viewpoint of their internal structure and formative principles. They were shaped by different historical forces, in response to different cultural and political conditions. All these differences are partly masked by the use of unifying terms such as "canon," "Tripiṭaka," etc., to refer to these collections. If taken uncritically, all these designations are potentially misleading. Indeed, even within a single tradition, such as that of Chinese Buddhism, we may find significant discrepancies among canons produced in different periods. Thus, for example, a Ming private canon such as the Jiaxing 嘉興 edition is very different from a Tang official canon, not just from a quantitative point of view or for being a printed edition instead of a manuscript one, but because it reflects a very different religious and cultural project.[1]

Nevertheless, I think that in comparison to other Buddhist scriptural collections, the Chinese canon (*Dazangjing* 大藏經)—here meant in the more traditional and stricter sense of the main canon (*zhengzang* 正藏), chiefly consisting of translations officially recognized as canonical[2] — displays two particularly significant (and indeed well known) peculiarities, which I tentatively call its inclusive nature and its conservative nature.[3]

THE INCLUSIVE NATURE OF THE CHINESE CANON

By defining the Chinese canon as an "inclusive" textual body, I mean that it is an essentially trans-sectarian set of texts, which, crossing doctrinal and even institutional borders, includes scriptures reflecting, from an Indian perspective, very diverse historical backgrounds as well as doctrinal and spiritual orientations (perhaps most notably, Mahayana and non-Mahayana). In this respect, the Chinese canon is considerably different from the model represented by the canons of the various schools, such as, for instance, the Theravadin canon.[4] Thus the Chinese canon has preserved texts belonging to nearly all the traditions and schools of Indian Buddhism, and composed over a long span of time.

The inclusive nature of the Chinese canon should not be seen as merely resulting in an inert, passive accumulation of texts, as if the canon were just a container where all sorts of heterogeneous materials came to be stored. On the contrary, it played an active, powerful role in shaping a number of ideas and forms typical of Chinese Buddhism. The integration of diverse translated scriptures into a single canon must be regarded as a highly creative process with important hermeneutical consequences: establishing it in effect entailed the creation of a new context within which translated scriptures could be interpreted in innovative ways. In other words, scriptures translated into Chinese and integrated into the canon became part of a new, differently structured organism. No matter how diverse their original (Indian) backgrounds and doctrinal orientations, they were generally considered and treated as part of a *single* textual body. This fact had significant consequences for their interpretation in China and ultimately came to influence the overall development of Chinese Buddhist thought. For example, the complex systems of "doctrinal classification" (*panjiao* 判教) used sophisticated hermeneutical techniques to try to account for the doctrinal diversity present in the canon, turning this very diversity into an important philosophical asset.

The four so-called "Chinese Āgamas" (*si Ahan* 四阿含) are a case in point. As is well known, the Chinese canon, apart from a number of related sutras and anthologies, contains four main Āgama collections,[5] translated between the fourth and fifth centuries C.E.: the *Dīrghāgama* (*Chang ahan jing* 長阿含經, *T* 1), the *Madhyamāgama* (*Zhong ahan jing* 中阿含經, *T* 26), the *Saṃyuktāgama* (*Za ahan jing* 雜阿含經, *T* 99), and the *Ekottarikāgama* (*Zengyi ahan jing* 增壹阿含經, *T* 125). They belong to different schools and were probably composed in different Indic languages.[6] In other words, no Indian canon has ever included these four Āgamas in its Sūtrapiṭaka. However, in China these translations have been generally considered as forming a homogeneous textual set. This idea, already expressed by Daoan 道安 (312–85),[7] came to play a considerable role in later Buddhist thought. The four Āgamas are frequently mentioned in exegetical works and treatises composed during the Sui-Tang period. For example, Zhiyi's 智顗 (538–97) *Profound Meaning of the Lotus Sutra* (*Miaofa lianhuajing xuanyi* 妙法蓮華經玄義, *T* 1716) gives the four Āgamas the following comprehensive characterization:

> If we are to expound [the characteristics of] the four Āgamas, then while the *Ekottarika*[*-āgama*] clarifies causes and effects relevant to humans and gods, the *Madhyama*[*-āgama*] clarifies the profound meaning of the True Quiescence, the *Saṃyukta*[*-āgama*] clarifies the various forms of meditative practice, and the *Dīrgha*[*-āgama*] refutes the heresies, they jointly expound [the following subjects]: impermanence, knowing suffering, eliminating the source [of suffering], realizing extinction, cultivating the path.[8]

For the celebrated Tang master Zongmi 宗密 (781–841), these four versions of the Āgamas—*as a single whole*—constituted, together with the *Abhidharma*, a particular stage of the Buddha's teaching, that of the "Lesser Vehicle" (*xiaosheng* 小乘, Hinayana).[9] In fact, this traditional view of *the* four "Chinese Āgamas"—more or less consciously articulated—continues to be influential, to a certain extent, especially in modern Japan. This is true of academic scholarship: for example, Akanuma Chizen's still widely used *Comparative Catalogue of Chinese Āgamas and Pāli Nikāyas* (1929) has a programmatic structure and an underlying agenda, which in my opinion betray the residual influence of the old Chinese conceptions of the four translated Āgamas as a coherent set (and, in modern terms, as a sort of equivalent—or perhaps surrogate—of the *Suttapiṭaka* of the Pali canon).[10] That this is true even at a religious level is demonstrated by the movement founded in 1978 by Kiriyama Seiyū 桐山靖雄 and called Agonshū 阿含宗.[11]

Thus, the "Chinese Āgamas" is a designation perhaps more appropriate than generally conceded, for in a sense they are, as a group, an entirely Chinese invention. This is a particularly telling example of the active transforming power generated by the Chinese canon, though certainly not the only one.

THE CONSERVATIVE NATURE
OF THE CHINESE CANON

The definition of the Chinese canon as a "conservative" (or "historically inclusive") body refers to the fact that, for a variety of reasons,[12] it has generally preserved multiple translations of the same scriptures. Even when new translations did supersede the older ones in scholarly or religious use,[13] the latter were not discarded, but continued to be transmitted in the canon. In this respect, the Chinese canon is different from its Tibetan counterpart.[14] Perhaps the most striking example of this attitude is provided by the *Aṣṭasāhasrikā Prajñāpāramitā* (The Perfection of Insight in Eight Thousand Lines), whose seven Chinese versions, produced from the Han to the Song, document the whole history of Chinese Buddhist translations.

In this way the Chinese canon came to encapsulate a historical dimension in its system of religious values. This is quite extraordinary for a body of sacred texts, and no parallel of comparable significance comes to my mind. It tells us much about the way the Chinese decided to see Buddhism and construed their own image of it. Because it is one thing to keep different translations of, say, the Gospels on the shelf of one's library, and to consult them for satisfying one's philological or even theological curiosity; it is another to include different translations in a collection—the canon—that has, in itself and as a whole, predominantly religious functions (such as producing merit). In other words, Chinese Buddhists did not try to dispel history from their holy scriptures. On the contrary, they saw the historical dimension inherent in the transmission of the canon as being fully part of the holiness of scriptures, not as detracting from it.

These two crucial aspects of the Chinese canon are also reflected in the principles of canonicity generally adopted in China,[15] which constitute another of its peculiarities. The Indian tradition, roughly speaking, adopted standards of canonicity based at least partly on doctrinal considerations, such as agreement with the nature of things (*dharmatā*).[16] In contrast, in the Chinese context, the most immediate and basic criterion to establish the "authenticity" of a scripture (as seen from the attempts to define the specular notion of "apocryphal") was whether it had been translated from a foreign original.[17] All this once again points out the obvious foundational role of translations and translation practices in the Chinese Buddhist context: the "classical" Chinese canon that attained its substantially definitive form in 730 C.E., with Zhisheng's 智昇 *Catalog of the Buddhist Teaching Compiled in the Kaiyuan Period* (*Kaiyuan shijiao lu* 開元釋教錄, T 2154; hereafter *KYL*), is essentially a collection of translations, though open to a limited number of Chinese texts (mainly bibliographical and historical works).[18]

The main focus of my study, whose chronological limits are from the mid-second to the late fourth century C.E., will be the analysis of the ideas, models, practices, and visions that played a role, during the early period, in shaping the ideology underlying the Chinese canon and ultimately contributed to producing its distinctive features, particularly those highlighted above. Thus, although I will also deal with some technical, tangible features of the canon (organization, catalogs' structure, circulation and use of texts), my main concern will be the *ideas* underlying those features.

In discussing this subject, the problem of the sources (which is, in turn, closely related to that of the kind of analysis we want to carry out) is particularly vital. We can roughly identify three main levels of discussion/analysis, and hence three typologies of sources:

a. The first level of analysis (predominant in this paper) deals with early statements on the canon. We can analyze the way the early sources available to us (prefaces, colophons, commentaries, etc. from the Han to the time of Daoan, which we can call "type A sources")—those composed during the period at issue—speak and conceive of the canon. The main problem is that, at this level, our sources are few and mostly fragmentary.

b. The existence of a second level of analysis (and of a second type of sources) depends on the fact that the sources at the previous level have been made available mainly through historical and documentary works that were compiled later (especially during what I would call the first "historiographical outpouring" of Chinese Buddhism, during the Liang period) and, what is even more significant, that reflect very different historical and cultural contexts. The single most important source for the study of the early canon is Sengyou's 僧祐 (445–518) complex, multilayered masterpiece, the *Collection of Records on the Translation of the Tripitaka* (*Chu sanzang ji ji* 出三藏記集, *T* 2145, hereafter *CSZJJ*). But apart from having preserved (and selected) for us most of the surviving "type A sources," the *CSZJJ* also embodies, in different ways, Sengyou's own vision of the canon, which in many respects clearly reflected the ideas and expectations of early sixth-century Jiangnan cultivated clergy. In studying any aspect of early Chinese Buddhism, we should remember that we are nearly always looking through "type B sources," and in most cases, through Liang clerical glasses.

c. We can also aim at a more ambitious and more difficult-to-reach level of analysis by trying to study how canonical scriptures were actually used from the second to the fourth century C.E., and to guess which ideas underlie their use. For this purpose, our main sources are the very texts that later came to constitute the canon itself: translations and early commentaries.

CIRCULATION OF SCRIPTURES DURING THE EARLY PERIOD: PATTERNS OF INFLUENCE IN EARLY TRANSLATIONS

We have very few direct sources concerning the way Buddhist scriptures were transmitted and circulated during the period when the earliest translations were produced, in the second and third centuries C.E. Some documents collected in Sengyou's *CSZJJ* contain precious fragments of information on this subject, such as the ancient colophon to the *Da shi'er men jing* 大十二門經. According to Daoan, who quoted it in his preface to the same scripture, a manuscript of this text was "copied in the seventh year of Jiahe 嘉禾 (238 C.E.), at Jianye 建業, in the residence of the Metropolitan Commandant Zhou."[19]

But, all in all, we know very little concerning the scale of circulation of early translations during the third and fourth centuries, which witnessed the crisis and then the disintegration of the unified empire. Yet some information on this issue, so important to the history of the Chinese canon during its formative phase, can be obtained from the philological analysis of translations themselves. For example, if we want to assess the extent to which a certain body of translations circulated and exerted its influence on other translations, an analysis focused on the attestation of rare lexical items can often provide results that we could never get from external sources. This is a largely new research area, made possible by the availability of new tools (especially the CBETA searchable electronic edition of the canon), which, like the telescope for Galileo, enable us to see things we simply could not see and whose existence we did not even suspect earlier.[20]

For example, from the scant biographical information on Zhi Qian 支謙 (third century) provided by Huijiao's 慧皎 (497–554) *Biographies of Eminent Monks* (*Gaoseng zhuan* 高僧傳),[21] one would easily get the impression that he was a fairly marginal figure in the history of Chinese Buddhist translations. The new approach to this research field outlined above has completely changed this assessment. I will propose only one example from Dharmarakṣa's translation of the Larger *Prajñāpāramitā*, the *Guang zan jing* 光讚經 (*T* 222). In chapter 1 there is one passage, listing a number of gifts presented to the Buddha by various categories of gods, which in the Taishō edition (based on the thirteenth-century Korean edition of the canon, the so-called *Palman Daejanggyeong* 八萬大藏經) reads as follows:

> At that moment, in this world system, all the gods of the Śuddhāvāsa-Pure-Abode, . . . having taken spontaneously created heavenly flowers, heavenly perfumed unguents, heavenly mixed perfumes, heavenly pounded perfumes, heavenly blue lotuses, hibiscuses, gorgeous flowers, and all other [sorts of] wonderful heavenly flowers, complete with stalks and leaves, they set out, one by one, to bring [these gifts] to the Thus-Come One, bowed their head at his feet, and strewed them on the Buddha.[22]

Instead of *xian hua* 鮮華, "gorgeous flowers,"[23] all the other editions collated by both the Taishō edition and the modern *Zhonghua dazangjing* 中華大藏經 collection read *heng hua* 蘅華/蘅華, "*heng* flowers." As I have argued elsewhere,[24] the latter is no doubt the correct reading: this is the name of a fragrant plant,[25] probably used in this context as a translation of *saugandhika* (here the name of a kind of water lily, but whose basic meaning is "fragrant")[26] in the corresponding Sanskrit text.[27]

This particular use of *heng* 蘅 is very rare in the canon.[28] Apart from the *Guang zan jing*, it is only attested in three other translations,[29] the earliest of which is Zhi Qian's *Weimojie jing* 維摩詰經, T 474 (*Vimalakīrtinirdeśa*).[30] Therefore, in view of the available evidence, it is very probable that this particular rendition was first coined by Zhi Qian and subsequently adopted by Dharmarakṣa and Tanwulan.

This is a very small example, but it is a good instance of the kind of information we can extract from a minute philological analysis of early translations. It highlights the fundamental function played by precedents in translation procedures since the early period: earlier translations constituted, in effect, a "canon" to which one could refer for rendering terminology and stock phrases when producing new translations, even of different scriptures. This *modus operandi* may have ultimately contributed to the habit of conserving early translations in the later canon.

CANONICAL SCRIPTURES AND EXEGETICAL PRACTICES DURING THE EARLY PERIOD

Further information on our subject can be obtained from the analysis of the interplay between translations and commentaries. It is well known that the work of several important translators embraced scriptures reflecting different typologies and trends in both vehicles and thus played a seminal role in shaping the inclusive canon typical of Chinese Buddhism. This "open" character can already be perceived in the work of some of the earliest translators. An example is provided by An Shigao's translations: within a generally Sarvāstivādin body of scriptures, we find a text such as the *Yin chi ru jing* 陰持入經 (Canonical text on the *Skandhas*, the *Dhātus*, and the *Āyatanas*, T 603) that is clearly not Sarvāstivādin.[31] And yet this somewhat atypical text was crucial in the tradition linked to the activities of the Han translator.

Certainly I would not overstress this fact; after all, An Shigao's corpus is just a group of translations, shaped by reasons (and perhaps by quirks of fate) we cannot know with any precision.[32] But An Shigao's choice of the texts that he happened to render into Chinese became a necessary reference point to the later commentators. And these scriptures, as a group, soon became equally authoritative, a reflection of the translator's authoritative status during the early medieval period. As a result, they were seen by the authors of the few surviving early commentaries to form a hermeneutical continuum. That is, they were perceived as a single scriptural system within which a given text could be legitimately used to shed light on, and interpret, another one. In other words, for some early Chinese commentaries, An Shigao's translations (or at least some of them) worked as a de facto "micro-canon." To a certain extent, this is typical of religious exegesis at large: what, from a strictly historical point of view, may have been the outcome of casual factors—which scripture happened to be translated and made available to certain commentators in a given place at a given time—had become a hermeneutical necessity, and hence the seed of a canon.

Let us consider the following passage from the anonymous preface to the so-called *Yin chi ru jing zhu* 陰持入經註, *T* 1694 (presumably composed during the first half of the third century C.E.),[33] one of the most important early commentaries that have survived in the canon:

> The obscure ones (*yin* 陰, *skandha*) and the constituents (*chi* 持, *dhātu*) are a [comprehensive] name of the practice; [this teaching/scripture, viz. the *Yin chi ru jing*] has the same origin as the *Ānāpāna-[smṛti]*, but represents a separate stream.[34]

As I have argued elsewhere,[35] here the author of the preface, who belonged to a circle with strong ties with An Shigao's tradition, is specifically discussing two of the most significant scriptures translated by the Parthian master, the *Yin chi ru jing* itself (to which the commentary following this very preface is devoted), and the *Anban shouyi jing* 安般守意經 (Canonical scripture on the *Ānāpānasmṛti*). In the passage quoted above, these two texts are clearly regarded as reflecting the same tradition. Looking at them with a modern Buddhological eye, we may well say that this statement is almost certainly wrong. But it made sense in its own context, and in fact it reflects the actual exegetical procedures carried out by the authors of the *Yin chi ru jing zhu*, which contains several references to the *Ānāpānasmṛti*, as well as quotations from both the *Anban shouyi jing* translated by An Shigao[36] and a related early commentary (the *Anban jie* 安般解).[37]

This state of affairs is not restricted to An Shigao's works. Generally speaking, translations produced during the Eastern Han and Three Kingdoms periods constitute a fairly heterogeneous body of texts, not only from a doctrinal and typological point of view but also due to their differences in language and style,[38] which probably reflect the diversity and relative independence of the Buddhist communities engaged in translation activities at Luoyang 洛陽 between the second and third centuries C.E. Be that as it may, there is little doubt that at least some of these texts were soon seen and utilized as a single corpus—that is, as a canon in a nutshell.

The two earliest surviving Chinese Buddhist interlinear commentaries—the already mentioned *Yin chi ru jing zhu* (*T* 1694) and the anonymous commentary to the first chapter of the *Da mingdu jing* 大明度經 (*T* 225)[39]—often quote passages from a variety of scriptures translated during the Han and Wu periods. For example, the *Da mingdu jing* commentary quotes one Mahayana text ascribed in the canon to Lokakṣema (the *Dunzhen jing* 純真經),[40] another one translated by Zhi Qian, the *Huiyin sanmei jing* 慧印三昧經 (*T* 632),[41] the *Anban shouyi jing* translated by An Shigao,[42] and the *Faju jing* 法句經 (*T* 210), an early third-century translation of a *Dharmapada*.[43]

All these miscellaneous scriptures are equally referred to by the authors of the commentary as sources of doctrinal authority. We may say that these early commentaries were in effect based on a certain "micro-canon" that, though seemingly limited from the perspective of later developments, already displayed some of the characteristics, such as inclusiveness, evinced by the fully developed Chinese canon of the later periods.

Another exegetical practice typical of early Chinese Buddhism (especially during the fourth century) worth discussing is that of the "synoptic editions," as Zürcher calls them.[44] Adopted by the fourth-century exegete Zhi Mindu 支愍度 and by Daoan, among others, this particular technique was used when different Chinese translations of the same scripture were available. Taking one translation as the basic text, the commentator would list the main differences with the other versions, thus allowing a better understanding of all the texts compared, as remarked by Zhi Mindu in his "note" to the synoptic edition of the *Śūraṃgama-samādhisūtra*, which is the most important source on this technique.[45] Perhaps these peculiar exegetical works, highlighting the considerable advantages one could get from the existence of multiple versions of the same text, played a role in their preservation, thus bringing forth the distinctive, historically inclusive character of the Chinese canon.

VISIONS OF THE CANON: DAOAN AND THE QUEST FOR COMPLETENESS

The definition of the *Dazangjing* as an inclusive canon, introduced in the preceding sections, ought to be taken with a grain of salt. From a different perspective, this notion of inclusiveness no doubt requires some qualifications. We can say that there are two opposing forces that, while perhaps inherent, to varying degrees, in any body of religious scriptures, played particularly crucial roles in the formation of the Chinese canon (due to its peculiar historical background), one exclusive and the other inclusive. On the one hand, to enforce its prestige, we want a canon to be "pure," free from false representations of the sacred word. On the other hand, we want it to be "complete," that is, as exhaustive as possible. Perhaps at different points in the history of Chinese Buddhism one of these two tendencies prevailed over the other, but both were always present.

During the early period, the second tendency was probably strengthened by the fact that Buddhist scriptures were introduced in China piecemeal: hence completion remained from the outset a goal to be achieved, an ideal or a value, so to speak. This motif surfaces, for example, in Daoan's *Vinaya* preface (*T* 1464, 24: 851a 6–b 7; not included in the *CSZJJ*),[46] which is perhaps the most important source documenting his view of the canon during the last phase of his life:

> The spread of [Buddhist] scriptures to the land of Qin has already had a long history. Scriptures were translated as they happened to be available having been brought here by Indian *śramaṇas*. . . . [I,] Daoan, have always regretted that the Tripitaka was incomplete.[47]

Daoan was already confronted by the problem of apocryphal translations, as is witnessed by his catalog of "scriptures of doubtful authenticity" (*yi jing* 疑經), incorporated into the *CSZJJ*.[48] Yet the issue of apocrypha was still in its infancy, and although later it became a dominant concern for the compilers of Buddhist catalogs, it seems that during the early period, especially up to Daoan, the need to get a larger, more complete canon was, understandably enough, the prevalent one.

In this connection, the significance of quantity in the context of the discourse on canonical scriptures should not be overlooked. Some Buddhist texts refer to the notion that holy texts are in principle (i.e., in their original form) big,[49] and that the existence of smaller versions (or, in some cases, their subsequent shrinking) is due to the lesser faculties of human beings.[50] In other words, the quantitative dimension of scriptures possesses a value of its own: larger is better. An interesting passage at the end of the massive *Prajñāpāramitā* commentary known as *Da zhidu lun* 大智度論 (*T* 1509) provides a doctrinal foundation to this view:

> Moreover, while the Tripitaka contains only 300,000 lines, 9,600,000 *akṣaras* in all, Mahayana [scriptures] are immeasurable and limitless. So, for instance, this medium version of the *Prajñāpāramitā*[51] consists of 22,000 lines, the large version of the *Prajñā[pāramitā]* consists of 100,000 lines, [but] in the palaces of the Nāga and Asura kings, and of all the *devas* there is [a version] in myriads of *koṭīs* of lines. Why? Because the lifespan of all these *devas*, Nāgas,[52] and [other] gods is long, and the force of their memory strong. For human beings of this world, life is short and memory weak:[53] they cannot even read the Lesser *Prajñāpāramitā*, let alone longer versions! Why is the *Prajñāpāramitā* known to the other great bodhisattvas immeasurable and limitless? The Buddha does not preach it with just one body, but may manifest immeasurable

bodies during immeasurable ages, and for this reason what he preaches is also immeasurable.[54]

It would be entirely wrong to assume that the various ideas concerning the canon and canonical scriptures gradually developed in China were merely the outcome of a passive reaction to the external stimulus constituted by the translation activity. As we shall see, from a fairly early stage some complex models acted as a powerful drive to classify, organize, and conceive the body of Buddhist scriptures gradually being made available in Chinese through the work of translators.

One crucial issue in this connection is that of the role played by traditional Indian classifications of canonical scriptures during the early formative phase of the Chinese canon. Here I will just give a preliminary discussion, mainly based on the data included in Sengyou's *CSZJJ*.

The structure of the "classic canon" that gradually developed since the Sui period and was fixed by Zhisheng's *KYL* in 730 C.E. indeed reflects, with important adjustments, the Tripitaka paradigm.[55] But I cannot find any conclusive evidence that during the early period discussed in this chapter the notion of "three baskets" (or other similar Indian organizational principles) played any particular role in organizing *actual collections* of translated scriptures.[56] In fact, during this early period, even the idea of gathering all canonical scriptures into a single, actually existing comprehensive collection (a canon *stricto sensu*) was probably yet to be implemented. According to Li Fuhua and He Mei, the first manuscript copies of the entire canon produced by imperial order date to the Southern and Northern dynasties period.[57]

Yet from a careful analysis of the available sources, a more complex and interesting picture does emerge. The classification of canonical scriptures in twelve classes, or divisions (*aṅga*),[58] is already mentioned in what is, in effect, the earliest surviving Buddhist text composed by a Chinese, Yan Futiao's 嚴浮調 (or, less likely, Fotiao 佛調) *Preface to the Shami shi hui zhangju* 沙彌十慧章句序 (presumably composed during the second half of the second century C.E.):

> Formerly, at the time of the Buddha, the Teaching[59] had not yet been written down, [but] the disciples recited [its] words as they came out of the Venerable One's mouth. The words were simple and their meaning vast, [their] record was new and profound. [However,] once the Buddha had entered nirvana, the subtle words were forever interrupted;[60] it was as if the Gu River[61] had dried up, or the sun and the moon had fallen down. Then all the saints let Ānanda recite what he had heard, and altogether they produced the Dharma in twelve classes.[62]

The main feature of interest in this passage is not just Yan Futiao's reference to the twelve *aṅgas* (probably their earliest mention in a Chinese source of any kind), but the fact that even here this category is already part of perhaps the earliest *Chinese* discourse on the Buddhist teaching. Yet in this passage Yan Futiao is most likely not documenting the way canonical texts were actually classified in the Later Han Buddhist communities of Luoyang. Rather, his reference to the twelve *aṅgas* is part of a mythical depiction of the Buddha and his teaching. This passage constitutes also the archetype (or, more correctly, the earliest available specimen) of a topos that occurs frequently in early Chinese discourse on canonical scriptures, particularly in the initial portion of prefaces (*xu* 序). This recurring and somewhat conventional narrative frame (which we could call the "narrative of the canon") generally has the function of placing a particular text within the broader context of the Buddha's teaching and its subsequent codification,[63] thus suggesting the *idea* of a whole canon even during the early phase of Chinese Buddhism, when the *reality* of actually available translated scriptures, still few and fragmentary, was certainly very different.

Another remarkable early example of this motif can be found in the *Dharmapada* preface, anonymous but generally ascribed to the third-century translator Zhi Qian:[64]

> The Buddha, the omniscient one, was greatly benevolent by nature. Taking pity on all under heaven, he manifested himself in the world. He revealed a doctrine through which he removed [the doubts of] human beings. It consists of twelve classes in all, which summarize its essential meaning, and it is subdivided into several categories. The four Āgamas were transmitted by Ānanda after the Buddha had departed from the world.[65]

Looking at the materials collected by Sengyou in the *CSZJJ*, it seems that the "narrative of the canon" figures with particular prominence in Daoan's prefaces.[66] This is certainly not accidental. The canon as a general ideal and goal, and the notion that each single scripture translated into Chinese made sense insofar it could be seen as a piece of a larger mosaic, are both ideas crucial to Daoan's discourse.

A quick terminological search in the *CSZJJ*—a sort of micro-history of the word *sanzang* 三藏 (Tripitaka) in the documents collected by Sengyou—yields some interesting results: no author earlier than Daoan uses *sanzang*. Then, if we look at the occurrences of this word in these surviving materials from the *CSZJJ*, we must conclude that the Tripitaka, as a significant frame of reference for discussing and classifying (if not concretely organizing) canonical scriptures, became part of the Chinese discourse on the canon essentially with Daoan. This, again, is not surprising: in his late years at Chang'an, Daoan for the first time had a direct glimpse of the "thing itself": important translations of Āgama, Abhidharma, and Vinaya texts and even of entire collections first became available, in China, at one time and in one place.[67] But it is remarkable that the word *sanzang* occurs even in some of his early prefaces.[68]

From what we know of Daoan's activities, the "Tripitaka paradigm"—the overarching notion of a complete canon to be acquired—was certainly more than a mere figure of speech: it was rather something of a polestar, a powerful force that led Daoan into a relentless search for canonical scriptures. Indeed, he sometimes expressed his regret in almost obsessive terms[69] that the canon was incomplete, and the quest for its completeness was a constant leitmotif in his surviving works.

But this ideal had also an important practical side: it provided a frame for classifying translated scriptures. This largely unexplored aspect of Daoan's conception of the canon can be approached through the analysis of his remarks quoted by Sengyou in the *CSZJJ*. As is well known, the catalog section of the *CSZJJ*[70] contains more than sixty glosses introduced by the words "the venerable [Dao]an says" (Angong *yun* 安公云),[71] presumably quoted from Daoan's lost bibliographical works,[72] which were the basis of Sengyou's own catalog.

In terms of content, "Daoan's glosses" can be subdivided into six typologies: scriptural classification;[73] attribution of translations;[74] identification of retranslations; [75] identification of abridgments (*chao* 抄);[76] recording alternative titles;[77] and other typologies.[78]

By far the most numerous (forty-seven) and interesting group of glosses (especially from the viewpoint of the history of the canon) are those on scriptural classification, in which Daoan sought to match one or more translations to a specific Indian canonical subdivision. The categories he used in his classification are eight (see table 3.1): the four Āgamas, Abhidharma, Lüjing 律經 (possibly corresponding to Vinaya),[79] Vaipulya, and Jātaka. The glosses are invariably in the form "[X] *chu* 出 Y" ("[X] comes from Y"), where X is the title of a Chinese translation and Y one of these eight categories.

The most intriguing category employed by Daoan is probably *fangdeng bu* 方等部 (Vaipulya; in one case *jing* 經 occurs as a variant for *bu* 部). In the *CSZJJ*, apart from the title of a scripture ascribed to Lokakṣema,[80] the term *fangdeng bu* occurs only in Daoan's glosses, used after *chu* 出 as a parallel to the names of the various other scriptural categories (Āgamas, Abhidharma, etc.) used in his classifications. As is well known, *fangdeng* 方等 is a common expression corresponding, albeit indirectly, to Sanskrit *vaipulya*,[81] a category belonging to the list of twelve divisions of canonical scriptures already mentioned above.

TABLE 3.1. LIST OF THE SCRIPTURAL CATEGORIES
USED IN DAOAN'S GLOSSES

	長阿含 (Dīrghāgama)	中阿含 (Madhyamāgama)	雜阿含 (Samyuktāgama)	增一阿含 (Ekottarikāgama)	阿毘曇 (Abhidharma)	律經 (Vinaya?)	方等部/經 (Vaipulya)	生經 (Jātaka)
Number of glosses	6 or 7	14	3	1	7 or 8[82]	2	11	2
Number of scriptures	8 or 10	16	49	1[83]	?	2	11	3

The use of *vaipulya* and related words in Indian Buddhist literature is a complex issue,[84] but it seems clear that Daoan used this category with reference to Mahayana sutras.[85] This assumption can be corroborated by an important passage of his already mentioned *Vinaya* preface:

> [Speaking of texts introduced into China,] among the twelve divisions, [scriptures belonging to] the *vaipulya* class (*piyueluo bu* 毘曰羅部; see n. 89) were the most numerous.[86] Because the teachings of Zhuangzi and Laozi, which are fashionable among people of this land, are similar to the [teaching of] complete oblivion[87] [expounded by] *Vaipulyasūtras* (*fangdeng jing* 方等經), [the latter] easily became fashionable.[88]

The expression *fangdeng bu* is very rare in the canon:[89] essentially, it can be regarded as part of Daoan's terminology. It would seem that, confronted by the *tripiṭaka/āgama* classification paradigm, Daoan adopted the *vaipulya* category from the "twelve divisions"—as is suggested by, among other things, the predominant use of *bu* 部 in Daoan's glosses, instead of the more common *jing* 經[90]—in order to find a place, within this general framework, for classifying Mahayana sutras, which were predominant among Chinese translations.[91]

I will not discuss the accuracy of Daoan's classifications.[92] Rather, from the particular perspective of this discussion, the most interesting aspects are the principles underlying them. Fragmentary as they are, these glosses constitute an important source for studying Daoan's ideas on the canon and the more tangible articulations of the "Tripitaka rhetoric" displayed in his prefaces.

We should remember that before the great translation project launched at Chang'an during Daoan's late years, for the most part only individual texts or anthologies (cf. above n. 56) had been rendered into Chinese. While it is probably impossible to date Daoan's glosses with any precision, I would venture to speculate that they mostly reflect this particular historical context. Most of Daoan's classification glosses concern non-Mahayana texts, and, as already mentioned above, we know that it was exactly at the end of the fourth century that the first complete translations of two *Āgamas* (*Madhyamāgama*[93] and *Ekottarikāgama*), as well as of important Vinaya and Abhidharma texts, were accomplished under Daoan's supervision.[94] Thus at that moment the notion of a complete canon, containing a substantial core of non-Mahayana scriptures, probably started to gain more defined contours in Daoan's eyes. His glosses on scriptural classification can therefore be seen as an attempt to match the reality of Chinese translations produced up to that time with the new models of scriptural classifications made available to him either directly, through the recent translations, or through the firsthand information he could presumably have received from the numerous foreign masters then active in Chang'an. No matter when and where

Daoan composed his bibliographical works, it is conceivable that he kept adding data in the form of these glosses even during his late sojourn in Chang'an.

In Tokuno's words, Daoan's catalog was probably "an attempt to make a comprehensive record of translations made during the nearly two-hundred-year period from the beginning of translation activities in China up to the time of its compilation."[95] In other words, Daoan, in composing his catalogs, adopted an essentially historical perspective (reflected by the chronological structure of his main catalog), with the practical aim of recording existing translations and, when possible, ascribing them to known translators. But his glosses on scriptural classification also disclose other, less apparent aspects of his bibliographical work. On a different level, the essentially historical and Chinese side of Daoan's work was ideally linked—through these glosses—to the overall picture of what he considered the Indian tradition as it was accessible to him: i.e., to his particular idea of the canon. No doubt, this is the most interesting aspect of this operation; Daoan made use of certain Indian traditional categories to produce what was, in effect, a highly imaginative and rather "Chinese" notion of the canon (needless to say, any uncritical use of categories such as "Chinese" and "Indian" would be entirely inadequate to describe such a complex process of cultural interaction).

I think that Daoan's project has been largely successful. In this respect, the adoption of *vaipulya* as a classification device is particularly noteworthy. If my interpretation of Daoan's use of this category as an attempt to integrate Mahayana texts into the *tripiṭaka/āgama* paradigm (almost as a sort of Mahayana equivalent of the Āgamas) is correct,[96] then we can say that it had lasting effects and was to play a crucial historical function. In a sense, the categories adopted by Daoan can be seen as the main limbs of *a certain* kind of canon in a nutshell, which prefigured the definitive configuration of the Chinese Buddhist canon, *tripiṭaka*-structured (see above n. 55) and yet capable of integrating both Mahayana and non-Mahayana scriptures into a single textual body.[97]

CONCLUSION

As the Chinese Buddhist canon began to take tangible shape during the fifth and sixth centuries, it was influenced by the interaction of different sets of practices, ideas, and traditions, combined with the need to address a number of practical and theoretical issues—a process traceable partly back to the earliest phase of Buddhist translations into Chinese. Of special interest are the complex patterns of interaction between Chinese practices (translation, exegesis, bibliographical traditions, etc.) and Indian paradigms, both of which—as is particularly apparent in Daoan's work—contributed to shaping the ideology underlying the Chinese Buddhist canon as we know it today.

That each translated scripture was part of a whole—a notion voiced in so many early prefaces through the "narrative of the canon"—was probably the most important legacy in this area inherited from the Indian tradition. Indian organizational models (*Āgamas*, Tripiṭaka, etc.) provided Chinese Buddhists with the idea (and ideal) of a canon that was a powerful factor even when it had not yet developed into a fully operational framework for collecting and transmitting scriptures—that is, well before complete collections of Chinese Buddhist scriptures (i.e., actual canons) came into existence during the Southern and Northern dynasties period.

In this process, as is generally true of Chinese Buddhism, we actually see complex patterns of interaction and adaptation rather than passive acceptance of external models. Daoan's use of the category of *vaipulya* is a case in point.[98] This embryonic but eventually successful attempt to integrate Mahayana sutras into the Tripiṭaka framework also entailed a radical and creative reinterpretation of the very notion of canon as an inclusive scriptural corpus.

NOTES

I wish to express my gratitude to Ven. Dhammadinnā, Jan Nattier, John R. McRae, and Jonathan A. Silk, who read an early draft of this article and made several helpful suggestions. Any errors remaining are mine alone. I would also like to dedicate this small work to the memory of John R. McRae and my father.

1. Suffice it to mention the massive inclusion in *Jiaxing Canon* of works produced in China (e.g., see Li and He, *Dazangjing yanjiu*, 500–8; Li Jining, *Fojing banben*, 174), whose presence in the Tang canons had remained confined to a few items (cf. n. 18 below). On this edition, see also Dai Lianbin, "The Economics of the Jiaxing Edition."

2. This feature is reflected by the sections listing the "[scriptures] included in the canon" (*ruzang lu* 入藏錄) of various Sui and Tang catalogs. See Fang Guangchang, *Zhonggguo xieben dazangjing yanjiu*, 223–27.

3. See also Richard Salomon's excellent discussion ("An Unwieldy Canon," 163–64).

4. This assertion requires some qualifications: even the Pali canon (at least in its Burmese configuration) includes heterogeneous materials, such as the *Nettippakaraṇa*, the *Peṭakopadesa*, and the *Milindapañha*, which (together with the *Suttasaṃgaha*) "have been added to the Khuddakanikāya in Burma" and "may have belonged to a non-Theravāda tradition originally" (von Hinüber, *Handbook of Pāli Literature*, 76, § 156). It is also worth mentioning that the Tibetan canon includes a number of Theravadin scriptures. See Skilling, "Theravādin Literature in Tibetan Translation."

5. The word *Āgama* refers to various collections of discourses of the Buddha, roughly corresponding to the *Nikāyas* of the Pali Suttapiṭaka.

6. See Enomoto, "On the Formation of the Original Texts of the Chinese Āgamas."

7. For example, see the beginning of his *Ekottarikāgama* preface: "the four *Āgamas* have the same doctrinal purport" (quoted in Sengyou's *Collection of Records on the Translation of the Tripiṭaka* (*Chu sanzang ji ji* 出三藏記集 , T 2145, hereafter *CSZJJ*, T 2145, 55: 64b 1; cf. also T 125, 2: 549a 5). Of course, here Daoan is not referring to the four Chinese translations mentioned above: only two *Āgamas* (*Madhyamāgama* and *Ekottarikāgama*) had been translated during his lifetime. But information on the other *Āgamas* was probably easily available in Chang'an, which by the end of the fourth century, during Daoan's last years, had become a major center of Buddhist translation activities. See Zürcher, *Buddhist Conquest*, 200–1 and 202–4; Palumbo, *An Early Chinese Commentary*, 9 ff. (and especially 39–44 on Daoan's *Ekottarikāgama* preface); see also the section on "Visions of the Canon" below.

8. T 1716, 33: 800b 2–5. On the treatment of the four *Āgamas* in Tiantai *panjiao* systems reflecting Zhiyi's teaching, see Mun, *The History of Doctrinal Classification*, 126–27 and 129.

9. In fact, in another work, titled (after Gregory, *Inquiry Into the Origin of Humanity*, 30) *Preface to the Collected Writings on the Source of Chan* (*Chan yuan zhu quan ji du xu* 禪源諸詮集都序), Zongmi's description of "Hīnayāna" literature is even more comprehensive: "All the 618 fascicles of *sūtras* such as the [four] *Āgamas* etc., and the 698 fascicles of treatises such as the [*Abhidharmamahā*]*vibhāṣā*, the [*Abhidharma*]*kośa* etc., merely expound [the teaching of] this Lesser Vehicle and the previous [teaching of] the Causes and Effects and of Humans and Gods" (T 2015, 48: 403b 23–24; cf. also Gregory, *Inquiry Into the Origin of Humanity*, 129, whose translation of this passage I have partly adopted). The figures provided by Zongmi betray the origin of this classification, viz. Zhisheng's entries for the "Sūtrapiṭaka of the Śrāvakas" and the "Abhidharmapiṭaka of the Śrāvakas," in *Kaiyuan shijiao lu* 開元釋教錄, T 2154, 55: 580a 26 and 580b 12. So in this particular case we can directly trace the origins of a specific doctrinal formulation back to a bibliographical classification typical of the Chinese Buddhist canon.

10. Paul Demiéville's discussion of these translations is also, it seems to me, fully in line with this venerable East Asian tradition: "C'est également à cette époque [viz. around the beginning of the fifth century] que fut traduite le Corbeille hīnayāniste des Sūtra, avec ses quatre «Traditions» (*Āgama*)" (Demiéville, "Le bouddhisme—Les sources chinoises," 418, § 2082; cf. also 431–32, § 2108). As observed by Demiéville (431, § 2016), the decision by editors of the Taishō to place the *Āgamas* at the beginning of the canon is a modern innovation due to the influence of the Pali Canon (and, I would add, of its prestige in modern scholarship). For a critical discussion of the Taishō's structure, see Li and He, *Dazangjing yanjiu*, 624–26.

11. See Reader, "The Rise of a Japanese 'New New Religion,'" especially 249–51.

12. That during most of the formative phase of the canon China was politically divided may have played a role in this respect: different collections, reflecting different areas and traditions, initially transmitted independently (and thus established), only at a later stage merged into a single canon.

13. In a number of cases, even after new and philologically more accurate translations had become available, particularly during the Tang Dynasty, older versions continued to remain in use for stylistic, doctrinal, and religious reasons (on this issue see, for example, Cao Shibang, *Zhongguo Fojiao yijing shi lunji*, 190–93, and cf. Gimello, "Chih-yen," 366).

However, the preservation of multiple versions of the "same" scripture was not the only approach adopted in the formative process of the Chinese canon. Occasionally, especially during the early period, we come across revisions of previous translations (see for example Wang Wenyan, *Fodian hanyi zhi yanjiu*, 70–71; Nattier, *A Guide*, 85–86). For a particularly interesting example of early revision, see Harrison, *The Samādhi of Direct Encounter*, 232–33.

14. Old translations were generally revised by Tibetans. See Skilling, "From bKa' bstan bcos to bKa' 'gyur and bsTan 'gyur," 90 with n. 29; Harrison, "A Brief History of the Tibetan bKa' 'gyur," 73, and "Canon," 114.

15. See Kuo Liying, "Sur les apocryphes," 682–84.

16. Lamotte, "Assessment" (esp. 12–13); Davidson, "An Introduction"; Harrison, "Canon," 111.

17. Cf. for example Sengyou's external criterion for distinguishing authentic scriptures from apocrypha: "in the case of authentic texts, this meant there was evidence that they had been transmitted from outside of China" (Tokuno, "Evaluation," 37). As Sengyou states, in the case of apocrypha one "has neither heard that someone went far into the Outer Regions [viz. India or Serindia, to obtain it] nor witnessed its reception from, and translation by, Western visitors [viz. foreign monks]" (*CSZJJ* 39a 2; tr. Tokuno, "Evaluation," 37). It is noteworthy that Sengyou, in the same text, also refers to the four *mahāpadeśas* (四大教法; see Lamotte, "Assessment," 9–13; Cousins, "Pali Oral Literature," 2–3), and particularly to the principle that teachings that contradict the *dharmatā* are not to be regarded as *buddhavacana* (*CSZJJ* 38c 18–20). In fact the Chinese canon contains even some translations of non-Buddhist Indian sources, such as the *Jin qishi lun* 金七十論 T 2137, a version of the *Sāṃkhya-kārikā* translated in the sixth century by Paramārtha (see Radich, "External Evidence," 76). Texts such as this were explicitly recognized as being non-Buddhist (e.g., see *Kaiyuan shijiao lu*, T 2154, 55: 624a 9–11): they were not included in the canon by error. This is indeed revelatory of the strong intrinsic canonizing power of the translations: the fact that these are authentic *Indian* texts was obviously considered more important than the fact that they were not Buddhist.

18. See the list of Chinese works at the end of the *ruzang lu* of the *KYL, T* 2154, 55: 697b 2–698a 2 (cf. also Kuo Liying, "Sur les apocryphes," 683). The progressive increase in the number of Chinese works included in the canon represents one of the most significant trends in its historical development.

19. *CSZJJ* 46b 8–9; also Zürcher, *Buddhist Conquest*, 48–49; Zacchetti, "Rediscovery," 269. Incidentally, this record also provides a first-rate piece of information on the social history of Buddhism in the third-century state of Wu.

20. Cf. Jan Nattier's inspiring discussion of "rhetorical communities" in early Chinese translations in *A Guide*, 166–68.

21. *T* 2059, 50: 325a 18–b 4; the biography of Zhi Qian contained in the *CSZJJ* (97b 13–c 18) is far more detailed.

22. *T* 222, 8: 148a 11–17; cf. Zacchetti, *In Praise of the Light*, 158–59, § 1.71.

23. Apart from the Korean edition, this reading is also attested in the twelfth century *Jin Canon* (*Jinzang* 金藏), and in the *Fangshan* 房山 text of the *Guang zan jing*, which was carved during the Liao Dynasty, in or around 1048 (see Zacchetti, *In Praise of the Light*, 105). On the possible implications of this fact from the viewpoint of textual history and criticism, see Zacchetti, *In Praise of the Light*, 123–27.

24. Zacchetti, *In Praise of the Light*, 268 n. 211.

25. I.e., the *duheng* 杜蘅/杜衡: *Pollia Japonica* Thunb. or *Asarum forbesii* Maxim. according to Gao Mingqian, *Zhiwu guhan ming tu kao*, 140–41.

26. In Guo Pu's 郭璞 (276–324 C.E.) commentary on the *Shanhai jing* 山海經, *duheng* 杜衡 is glossed as 香草也 ("it is a fragrant plant"; quoted in Yuan Ke, *Shanhai jing jiaozhu*, 29 n. 6). Then it is possible to understand why *heng hua* 衡華/蘅華 could be chosen as a rendition of *saugandhika* (obviously interpreted on the basis of its meaning "fragrant").

27. Cf. *Pañcaviṃśatisāhasrikā Prajñāpāramitā*, ed. Dutt, 11, 4–6: . . . *divyāni utpalakumudasaugandhikapuṇḍarīkapadmāni gṛhītvā divyāni ca keśaratamālapatrāṇi gṛhītvā yena tathāgatasyāsecanaka ātmabhāvas tenopasaṃkrāntāḥ.*

28. It is noteworthy that, in translated texts, *heng* occurs nearly always within the string 青蓮 芙蓉 蘅華 (with variants), which suggests that it is used to render the same original term. The only exception is 著蘅華鬘 in the *Zhong ahan jing* (*T* 26, 1: 530a 3 and *passim*), corresponding to *kumudamāliṃ* ("wearing a garland of white water lilies") in *Dīghanikāya*, vol. II, 343. The specific function performed by lists (a nearly ubiquitous feature of Buddhist sutra literature) in the context of Chinese translations is worth further study: they may have been means for cross-referencing and thus stabilizing, at least to a certain extent, translated terminology even in the absence of bilingual glossaries.

29. Apart from that in Zhi Qian's *T* 474, there are two occurrences of this plant name in Dharmarakṣa's translation of the *Ajātaśatrukaukṛtyavinodanāsūtra* (*T* 627, 15: 419b 21 and 419b 28), and one in the *Ji zhi guo jing* 寂志果經 (*T* 22, 1: 274c 19–21), as-

cribed in the canon to Zhu Tanwulan 竺曇無蘭 (*Dharmaratna?), corresponding, according to Akanuma (*The Comparative Catalogue*, 6), to *sutta* no. 2 of the *Dīghanikāya* (Pali Text Society ed., vol. 1, 47 ff.).

30. 譬如，族姓子，高原陸土不生青蓮 芙蓉 蘅華 [with variants] . . . (T 474, 14: 529c 8–9). This corresponds, with fewer words, to *nojjaṅgaleṣu pṛthivī-praveśeṣūtpalapadmakumudapuṇḍarīka**saugandhikāni** virohanti* in the Sanskrit text of the *Vimalakīrtinirdeśa* (folio 47a 6–7; ed. Taisho University, 78).

31. See Zacchetti, "Early Chinese Translation," 83 n. 50; on the Sarvāstivādin scriptures translated by An Shigao, see Harrison, "The *Ekottarikāgama* Translations," 279–80. It is possible to speculate that An Shigao translated this treatise because, being both a compendium of Buddhist doctrine and a text related to the tradition of hermeneutics represented by the *Peṭakopadesa*, it was useful in his exegetical and teaching activities.

32. This situation—which, on the surface, one might be tempted to label as eclecticism—is not, needless to say, limited to Chinese translations. Some Indian Buddhist libraries known to us in one way or another present a similar picture of variety: for instance, the Gilgit manuscript corpus (see Fussman, "Dans quel type de bâtiment," 124–34), or the rich monastic library (or libraries) obviously presupposed by an encyclopedic commentary such as the *Da zhidu lun* 大智度論, T 1509.

33. On this commentary, see Zacchetti, "Some Remarks on the *Peṭaka* Passages," which discusses the preface (151–54) with translation in the appendix on 184–88.

34. T 1694, 33: 9b 14–15.

35. Zacchetti, "Some Remarks," 186 n. 17.

36. See Zacchetti, "A 'New' Early Chinese Buddhist Commentary," 472 n. 160.

37. Ibid., 471–78.

38. Zürcher, "A New Look," 282–84.

39. On the intricate problems posed by this translation of the *Aṣṭasāhasrikā Prajñāpāramitā*, see Nattier, "Who Produced the *Da mingdu jing*?"

40. This scripture, a translation of the *Drumakinnararājaparipṛcchāsūtra*, is included in the present canon with the title *Dunzhentuoluo suowen rulai sanmei jing* 佗 真陀羅所問如來三昧經, T 624. See Harrison, "The Earliest Chinese Translations," 150–52; its traditional attribution to Lokakṣema is, however, in need of revision (see Nattier, *A Guide*, 84–85).

41. This is a translation of the *Tathāgatajñānamudrāsamādhi*. See Nattier, *A Guide*, 141.

42. That is, the text rediscovered in 1999 in the Kongōji 金剛寺 manuscript canon; see Zacchetti, "On the Authenticity of the Kongōji Manuscript," 158, and "A 'New' Early Chinese Buddhist Commentary," 439.

43. On these quotations, see Nattier, "Who Produced the *Da mingdu jing*?" 304–5 n. 19. The *Da mingdu jing* also contains a quotation from a text named *Liaoben* 了本 (T 225, 8: 480a 26), which is quoted four times in the *Yin chi ru jing zhu* (T 1694); in my

opinion, this is probably a commentary (arguably that composed by Zhi Qian) on the *Liaoben shengsi jing* 了本生死經 (*T* 708), as I hope to demonstrate in a forthcoming article devoted to this issue.

44. Zürcher, *Buddhist Conquest*, 99–100. On this exegetical form, see Chen Yinke's seminal study (in *Jinming guan cong gao chubian*, 181–87) and, for a recent critical discussion of Chen's analysis, Wu Jing, "Chen Yinke 'heben zizhu' shuo xintan."

45. *CSZJJ* 49b 9–14.

46. On this scripture and Daoan's preface, cf. Fang Guangchang, *Daoan ping-zhuan*, 231–32.

47. *Binaiye* 鼻奈耶, *T* 1464, 24: 851a 11–15. I follow the punctuation suggested by Ui Hakuju in his translation. See his *Shaku Dōan kenkyū*, 110.

48. "The Evaluation of Indigenous Scriptures," 34; Tan Shibao, *Han-Tang Fo shi tanzhen*, 73 and 76.

49. A well-known example of this view is provided by *Prajñāpāramitā* texts: contrary to the opinion prevalent among modern scholars, in China, the Larger *Prajñāpāramitā* (*Da pin* 大品) was traditionally considered more original than the version in eight thousand lines, the *Aṣṭasāhasrikā* (*Xiao pin* 小品). According to the famous scholar-monk Zhi Dun 支遁 (314–66), the *Aṣṭasāhasrikā* was an abridgment of the Larger version produced after the Buddha's decease (CSZJJ 55b 16–17). For a discussion of the ideas concerning Prajñāpāramitā literature circulating in China during the fourth century, see Zürcher, *Buddhist Conquest*, 339–40 n. 182. Incidentally, although Zürcher seems to consider it a Chinese development ("I do not know of any Indian counterpart of this theory," ibid.), Zhi Dun's view was not unknown in Indo-Tibetan Buddhism. Already Eugène Burnouf mentioned this issue in his seminal study of Indian Buddhism: "Je dis [of the *Aṣṭasāhasrikā*] rédaction plus courte, pour ne rien décider sur la question de savoir, si, comme le veulent les Tibétains, ce n'est qu'un abrégé des collections plus amples, ou si au contraire cette édition est, comme le prétendent les Nepâlais, l'ouvrage primitif dont les autres ne seraient que des développements" (*Introduction*, 464–65 with n. 1 p. 465, quoting Brian Houghton Hodgson as his source of information on this issue). It is of course possible that what Burnouf mentions as the opinion prevalent in Tibet had been influenced by Chinese traditional ideas on Prajñāpāramitā texts.

50. On traditions concerning the loss of sutras, see Lamotte, "Assessment," 8–9.

51. I.e., the *Mohebanreboluomi* 摩訶般若波羅蜜經 translated by Kumārajīva (*T* 223).

52. This passage echoes the well-known tradition on Nāgārjuna's obtaining Mahāyāna texts from the Nāgas (see for example the *Longshu pusa zhuan* 龍樹菩薩傳 *T* 2047, 50: 184c 8–16; cf. also Skilling, "Vaidalya," 89–90).

53. For a similar discussion, in the *Da zhidu lun*, concerning another textual tradition, see *T* 1509, 25: 192b 3–6. On the *Peṭaka*, cf. also Zacchetti, "Some Remarks," 68–69, with n. 11.

54. *T* 1509, 25: 756a 26–b6. On this passage, see also Durt, "The Difference."

55. See Li and He, *Dazangjing yanjiu*, 62–65. The all-important "catalog of [scriptures] included in the canon" (*ruzang lu*) of Zhisheng's *KYL*, which forms the basis of the Chinese canon in its definitive premodern shape, has a Tripitaka structure first applied to Mahāyāna scriptures—*Dasheng ruzang lu* 大乘入藏錄 (see the outline in *T* 2154, 55: 680b 3–8), being composed of sutras (*Dasheng jing* 大乘經), vinaya (*Dasheng lü* 大乘律), and treatises (*Dasheng lun* 大乘論)—and then to "Hīnayāna scriptures"—*Xiaosheng ruzang lu* 小乘入藏錄 (equally subdivided into sutras, vinaya, and treatises; see *T* 2154, 25: 691a 13–20). Actually, this way of organizing canonical scriptures had already been adopted in an earlier catalog, the *Catalog of All Scriptures* (*Zhongjing mulu* 眾經目錄), *T* 2146, completed in 594 C.E. by Fajing 法經 and others. See Tokuno, "Evaluation," 41; Nattier, *A Guide*, 13–14. See also Tanya Storch's chapter 4 in this volume.

56. Recent studies on early Chinese translations and Indic manuscripts have shown that anthologies played a crucial role in the transmission of Buddhist texts: see for example Salomon, "An Unwieldy Canon," 184–203; Allon, *Three Gāndhārī Ekottarikāgama-Type Sūtras*, 23–24; concerning An Shigao's work, see Harrison, "The *Ekottarikāgama* Translations." It is remarkable that this widespread method of textual organization and transmission was not officially acknowledged—that is, listed among traditional Indian Buddhist scriptural typologies. This throws light on a possible hiatus between notional (such as Tripitaka) and real models of textual transmission that deserves further study.

57. Li and He, *Dazangjing yanjiu*, 61–62; cf. also Fang Guangchang, *Zhonggguo xieben dazangjing yanjiu*, 17–19; Ji Yun, *Huijiao* Gaoseng zhuan *yanjiu*, 67–71. Incidentally, all the data discussed by these authors show the close relationship between the birth of the canon and the process of bringing Buddhism under the control of the state, in full swing during the sixth century, especially in North China. An early document mentioning multiple copies of an entire canon (*yiqiejing* 一切經) in 1464 fascicles is the colophon of Dunhuang manuscript S. 996, containing the final part of fascicle 6 of the *Za apitan xin lun* 雜阿毘曇心論 (*T* 1552, *Saṃyuktābhidharmahṛdaya*). This manuscript was copied in 479 C.E., during the Northern Wei Dynasty (Fujieda, "The Tunhuang Manuscripts," 23–24; for an edition of the colophon see Ikeda, *Chūgoku kodai shahon shikigo shūroku*, 92, entry no. 101).

58. This is a system for classifying the *buddhavacana* (Word of the Buddha) according to partly overlapping and variously defined typological categories called *aṅgas* ("divisions"). The system attested in Pali sources consists of nine divisions, while the list of twelve divisions is prevalent, though not without exceptions, in Sanskrit sources. For a detailed discussion see Lamotte, *Traité*, vol. 5, 2281–2303; on this category in early Chinese translations, see Nattier, "Twelve Divisions." Another early mention of the twelve divisions is that contained in the ancient commentary (Zacchetti, "A 'New' Early Chinese Buddhist Commentary") transmitted in the canon as the *Anban shouyi jing* (*T* 602, 15: 172c 4–5; cf. also Nattier, "Twelve Divisions," 173).

59. On the term *jingfa* 經法, widely used in early translations as a rendition of *dharma*, see Vetter and Zacchetti, "On *Jingfa*."

60. 佛既泥曰，微言永絕. This is a common topos; cf. for example the reference to Confucius' death at the beginning of the *Yiwen zhi* 藝文志, the bibliographic monograph included in the *History of the Han* (*Han shu*, 1701): 昔仲尼沒而微言絕 ("Long ago Zhongni [Confucius] died and the subtle words [*wei yan* 微言] were cut off"; tr. Lewis, *Writing and Authority*, 327).

61. As Antonello Palumbo pointed out to me, Gu shui 穀水 is the name of a river near Luoyang; see Li Daoyuan 酈道元 (469?–527), *Commentary on Book of the Rivers* (*Shui jing zhu* 水經注), fasc. 16, *Shui jing zhu jiaozheng*, 388 ff.

62. *CSZJJ* 69c 19–24. For a complete translation of this preface, see Nagajima Ryūzō, *Shutsu sanzō kishū*, 244–46.

63. This recurring motif is also probably to be explained, at least in part, on the basis of the well-established conventions typical of prefaces as a codified genre in Han and early medieval Chinese literature. As shown by Kogachi's detailed study ("Gokan Gi Shin chūshakusho no jobun," 5–7), prefaces to commentaries composed in this period generally contained an account of the history of the text object of the commentary.

64. See, for example, Zürcher, *Buddhist Conquest*, 47–48.

65. *T* 210, 4: 566b 19–22 and *CSZJJ* 49c 24–27; for complete translations of this preface, see Willemen, "The Prefaces," 210–13, and Nakajima Ryūzō, *Shutsu sanzō kishū*, 64–68.

66. *Zengyi ahan xu* 增一阿含序 (*CSZJJ* 64b 17–22; translated by Palumbo, *An Early Chinese Commentary*, 42–43); *Yin chi ru jing xu* 陰持入經序 (*CSZJJ* 44c 10–12); *Shi'er men jing xu* 十二門經序 (*CSZJJ* 45c 22–26; cf. Zacchetti, "Rediscovery," 283); *Daodi jing xu* 道地經序 (*CSZJJ* 69b 9–15; translated by Link, "Shyh Daw-an's Preface," 6–7); *Apitan xu* 阿毘曇序 (*CSZJJ* 72a 13–17); *Biposha xu* 鞞婆沙序 (*CSZJJ* 73b 15–20); *Biqiu da jie xu* 比丘大戒序 (*CSZJJ* 80a 17–21); *Binaiye xu* 鼻奈耶序 (*T* 1464, 24: 851a 3–9).

67. Zürcher, *Buddhist Conquest*, 203–4; for a recent, masterful discussion of the translation activities carried out in Chang'an under Daoan's direction, see Palumbo, *An Early Chinese Commentary*, 9–66.

68. E.g., see the preface to the *Yin chi ru jing* (*CSZJJ* 44c 12).

69. Cf. Zacchetti, *In Praise of the Light*, 69 n. 101, on the frequent use of *hen* 恨 in Daoan's prefaces to express regret for the fact that some scriptures were not available to him.

70. These notes are only found in fascicles 2–3 of the *CSZJJ*.

71. In some cases the glosses are introduced by the words "[Dao']an's Catalog says" (*An lu yun* 安錄云); see *CSZJJ* 5c 23; 7a 6; 8a 1.

72. As argued by Tan Shibao (*Han-Tang Fo shi tanzhen*, 69–74), Daoan probably composed several different catalogs, and the title *Zongli zhongjing mulu* 綜理眾經目錄, generally ascribed to Daoan's catalog, is not original.

73. *CSZJJ* 6a 7; 6a 9; 6a 12–13; 6a 24; 6b 16; 6b 18; 6b 23–24; 6c 3; 6c 15; 7a 4; 7a 6; 7a 9; 7a 15; 7b 15; 8a 7; 8a 15–16; 8c 20; 15b 22; 15b 24–25; 15c 7; 15c 9; 16b 17; 16b 23; 16c 23; 16c 25–17a 1; 17b 17–20; 17b 22; 17b 24–25; 17c 25; 17c 27; 18a 6–9; 18a 23; 18b 6; 18b 13; 18b 14.

74. Three glosses are examples of Daoan's conjectural criticism: he tentatively proposes (*CSZJJ* 6b 5–6; 6b 26–27) or rejects (*CSZJJ* 8c 6) the attribution of some scriptures to a certain translator, using a cautious formulation (*si* 似, "it seems that").

75. There are three glosses quoted by Sengyou (*CSZJJ* 7b 25; 8a 1; 9a 1), in which Daoan identifies a certain scripture as the retranslation of a text that had already been rendered into Chinese. The expression Daoan used to refer to these retranslations is *gengchu* 更出, not *chongyi* 重譯, which later became the standard term (e.g., in the *KYL*) and is already used by Sengyou (e.g., *CSZJJ* 96a 27–28). As is well known, *chu* 出 is a crucial word in early terminology on Buddhist translations (see, for example, Chen Jinhua, "Some Aspects"). Daoan used *gengchu* also in his prefaces (*CSZJJ* 52b 19–20 and 72, b3; cf. also 62b 4, in the anonymous *Jianbei jing shizhu huming bing shuxu* 漸備經十住胡名并書敘, also ascribable to Daoan; on this important document and its authorship, see Zacchetti, *In Praise of the Light*, 53–62 and 69–73). *Gengchu* occurs also in other documents, not by Daoan, collected by Sengyou (e.g., *CSZJJ* 64a 3–13).

76. *CSZJJ* 5c 28 and 6b 7. Note that in both glosses (relevant to the [*Da*] *daodi jing* [大]道地經 *T* 607 and the *Daoxing jing* 道行經 *T* 224), Daoan used the verb *chao* 抄 to describe what he considered a process of abridgment from the originals, carried out outside China and preceding the translation. However, this word was generally used with reference to "condensations" based on Chinese translations (see, for example, Tokuno, "Evaluation," 39).

77. *CSZJJ* 5c 23 and 6b 17; cf. also 15a 22.

78. Sengyou quotes a few other remarks by Daoan that do not seem to fit any of the preceding typologies. See *CSZJJ* 9a 10; 9c 3–4; 16c 18.

79. It is not entirely clear what Daoan meant with this expression (see *CSZJJ* 16c 27–17a 1), also because one of the two scriptures to which he appended this label, the *Liu jing jing* 六淨經, is lost, while the other, the *Sanshiqi pin jing* 三十七品經, is of difficult identification. The canon contains a short sutra ascribed (probably wrongly, in my view) to An Shigao, named *Chan xing sanshiqi pin jing* 禪行三十七品經 *T* 604, while a scripture with a similar title (*Fo shuo sanshiqi pin jing* 佛說三十七品經), not included in the canon and preserved in a fifth-century Dunhuang manuscript, has been recently published by Fang Guangchang (Fang, "Sanshiqi pin jing"). Both these texts deal with the same subject, viz. the thirty-seven factors conducive to awakening (*bodhipākṣikā dharmāḥ*), a fundamental category of Buddhist practice. This must also have been the topic of the *Sanshiqi pin jing* referred to in Daoan's gloss, but it is impossible to identify with certainty the latter as any of these two surviving scriptures. It is worth noting that Fang Guangchang takes *lüjing* 律經 in the gloss as referring to

the *Yi jue lü* 義決律, a lost translation by An Shigao listed in Sengyou's catalog (see Zacchetti, "A 'New' Early Chinese Buddhist Commentary," 432) which also included a discussion of the thirty-seven factors (Fang, "Sanshiqi pin jing," 177). While this is not impossible, early uses of this word in the canon seem to suggest a different interpretation. The term *lüjing* 律經 occurs in the Han translation of the *Kāśyapaparivarta* (*Yiyue monibao jing* 遺曰摩尼寶經), where 若比丘悉知律經 (*T* 350, 12: 193a 20) corresponds to *ekatyo bhikṣur vinay[a]dharo bhavati* in the Sanskrit text (*Kāśyapaparivarta* § 134, folio 67r 1–2, ed. Vorobyova-Desyatovskaya, 46); i.e., here *lüjing* = *vinaya*. It is also clearly used in the same sense in a passage of the anonymous preface to the *Sifen lü* 四分律, *T* 1428, describing the relative scarcity of vinaya texts among the Buddhist scriptures introduced in China during the early period: 自大教東流, 幾五百載 雖蒙 餘暉, 然律經未備 (*T* 1428, 22: 567a 18–19).

80. *CSZJJ* 6b 14; according to Nattier, *A Guide*, 88, this title, recorded by Sengyou as 方等部古品曰遺曰說般若經, might be an alternative one for the early Chinese version of the *Kāśyapaparivarta* (*T* 350).

81. As pointed out by Seishi Karashima (*The Textual Study*, 278, and *A Glossary of Dharmarakṣa's Translation*, 133–34; cf. Edgerton, *Dictionary*, 510 a–b), this translation reflects the form *vaitulya*, attested as an alternative form for *vaipulya* (see note 84).

82. The number of Daoan's glosses employing the categories *Abhidharma* and *Dīrghāgama* (as well as the number of scriptures allotted to these categories) cannot be determined with certainty, due to some variants mentioned by Sengyou or present in the textual tradition of the *CSZJJ*. See *CSZJJ* 15c 7 and 15c 9. On the problems posed by the category *Abhidharma* in these glosses, see note 92.

83. This is the *Ekottarikāgama* anthology, consisting of 44 sutras, translated by An Shigao (the *Za jing sishisi pian* 雜經四十四篇, on which see Harrison, "The *Ekottarikāgama* Translations").

84. The most recent and detailed discussion of this issue known to me is by Peter Skilling ("Vaidalya," 84–97; cf. also Skilling, *Mahāsūtras*, vol. II, Parts I–II, 31–42). Among other things, Skilling discusses at length the Sanskrit words used interchangeably to refer to this scriptural category (*vaidalya*, *vaitulya*, and *vaipulya*) and their Pali counterparts (*vedalla*, *vetulla*, and *vepulla*). According to him, "both sets derive from a single term, but are no longer etymologically cognate" ("Vaidalya," 85 with n. 77). Skilling further argues that "it is likely that the earliest form was Vedalla/Vaidalya," while "in later manuscript traditions, the most common Sanskrit form by far is Vaipulya." For the sake of convenience, throughout my discussion I will use the form *vaipulya*.

85. This is also the interpretation of *vaipulya* provided by the *Da zhidu lun* (*T* 1509, 25: 308a 4–8; cf. Lamotte, *Traité*, vol. 5, 2301): "[the name] 'extended scriptures' (*guang jing* 廣經, *vaipulya*) refers to Mahāyāna [scriptures] such as the *Prajñāpāramitā*, etc." Cf. also the *Mahāparinirvāṇasūtra* (*Dabanniepan jing* 大般涅槃經, *T* 374, 12:

472b 6–8; *T* 375, 12: 715a 18–20); Skilling, "Vaidalya," 90–92, and *Mahāsūtras*, vol. II, Parts I–II, 38–41.

86. Perhaps here Daoan had in mind particularly *Prajñāpāramitā* texts. See Zürcher, *Buddhist Conquest*, 389 n. 42.

87. This expression, *jian wang* 兼忘, which in this context should refer to the doctrine of emptiness propounded by *Prajñāpāramitā* scriptures, is quoted from chapter 14 of the *Zhuangzi* 莊子 (*Tian yun* 天運); see Guo Qingfan, *Zhuangzi jishi*, vol. 2: 498–99. Cf. also Link, "Evidence for Doctrinal Continuity," 83–84 n. 91.

88. *T* 1464, 24: 851a 12–14.

89. Apart from Daoan's glosses, *fangdengbu* 方等部 only occurs in some later exegetical texts, particularly Tiantai (e.g., *T* 1716, 33: 813c 4; *T* 1717, 33: 832c 3 and *passim*; *T* 1719, 34: 186c 26, etc.); the equivalent transcription *piyueluo* 毘曰羅部 (possibly reflecting a Gāndhārī form, *vivula*: cf. Karashima, "Was the *Aṣṭasāhasrikā Prajñāpāramitā* Compiled in Gandhāra in Gāndhārī?", 176 with n. 14) is only attested in the above quoted passage of Daoan's *Vinaya* preface.

90. The expression *fangdeng jing* 方等經 (cf. also Zacchetti, *In Praise of the Light*, 311 n. 527) is rather common, and already attested in the *Banzhou sanmei jing* 般舟三昧經 (*Pratyutpannasamādhi*) ascribed to Lokakṣema (*T* 418, 13: 911c 13), even if it occurs in the verse portion of this text, which is to be seen as a later addition to the original Han translation (see Harrison, *The Samādhi of Direct Encounter*, 229–35; Nattier, *A Guide*, 81–83).

91. Nevertheless, Daoan's use of this category is not free from problems. We do not know either how systematic was the adoption of this classification in Daoan's bibliographical work or to what extent it would correspond to our current notion of "Mahāyāna texts." For example, one is left wondering why Daoan—if we are to trust Sengyou's quotations—classified as *vaipulya* only two of Lokakṣema's translations (viz., *Wen shu jing* 問署經, *T* 458, and *Neizang baipin jing* 內藏百品經, *T* 807), whereas we would classify the whole group as belonging to the Great Vehicle. See Harrison, "The Earliest Chinese Translations."

92. Apart from Daoan's use of *fangdeng bu*—not entirely clear, as observed in the preceding note—his classification of some scriptures as belonging to the *Abhidharma* is also quite puzzling. This is the case with the *Qi nü jing* 七女經, *T* 556, and the *Lao nüren jing* 老女人經, *T* 559 (see *CSZJJ* 7a 4 and 7a 9), both ascribed to Zhi Qian. As remarked by Jan Nattier (*A Guide*, 143–45), these texts are of the *avadāna* type and do not seem to have anything to do with the *Abhidharma*. In fact, Nattier wonders if Daoan's glosses might not be due to "a possible confusion between the terms *abhidharma* and *avadāna* in the course of transmission of information concerning these texts."

93. Perhaps it is not entirely by chance that *Madhyamāgama* is the category with the highest number of occurrences in the glosses on scriptural classification (14 times).

94. See above, n. 67.

95. Tokuno, "Evaluation," 33.

96. This must remain, however, a working hypothesis, and further research is needed to understand Daoan's adoption of *fangdeng bu/vaipulya* in all its implications, and especially in its relationship with Indian uses of related categories. As is clear from the materials collected and analyzed by Skilling (see above, n. 84), this cluster of categories (*vedalla, vaipulya,* etc.) was employed in a rather fluid, complex way across Buddhist institutional and doctrinal boundaries.

97. I think that Tokuno's assessment ("Evaluation," 35), that "his attempt to distinguish indigenous scriptures from translated texts was probably the most significant influence exerted by his catalog," does not fully appreciate the historical function achieved in Daoan's truly seminal work.

98. In fact, the use of *vaidalya/vaipulya* by followers of the Mahayana in India, as described by Peter Skilling (cf. also above n. 84–85), is in part reminiscent of Daoan's application to the Chinese context of *fangdeng bu/vaipulya*: "For Mahāyānists, Vaidalya was the nexus that linked the Mahāyāna to the 'official,' or at least traditional, categories of the Buddha's teaching" (Skilling, "Vaidalya," 86). In this connection, it is interesting to observe that the term *vaipulyapiṭaka* (cf. Skilling, "Vaidalya," 89–90) is attested in the colophon of a sutra included in a very interesting Sanskrit manuscript— a collection of twenty short Mahayana sutras recently edited by Bhikṣuṇī Vinītā (*A Unique Collection*, 582): *buddhāvataṃsakād vaipulyapiṭakād anantabuddhakṣetraguṇodbhāvanaṃ nāma mahāyānasūtram*, etc. ("the Mahayana Sutra entitled *The Manifestation of the Qualities of Infinite Buddha-fields*, from the *Buddhāvataṃsaka vaipulyapiṭaka*"). On the significance of this colophon see Vinītā, *A Unique Collection*, xix and 585 n. a; Silk, "Review Article," 64. One can also think of the notion of Bodhisattvapiṭaka as a canonical repository of Mahayana sutras, discussed in a text produced in Daoan's circle, the *Fenbie gongde lun* 分別功德論 T 1507 (see Palumbo, *An Early Chinese Commentary*, 221–28; cf. also Pagel, *The Bodhisattvapiṭaka*, 10–16).

[Since it appeared only at the moment when I was correcting the final proofs of this article, I was not able to take account of an important article on *vaipulya* and related terms: Seishi Karashima, "Who Composed the Mahāyāna Scriptures?—The Mahāsāṃghikas and *Vaitulya* scriptures." *Annual Report of the International Research Institute for Advanced Buddhology at Soka University* 18 (2015): 113–162.]

4. *Fei Changfang's* Records of the Three Treasures Throughout the Successive Dynasties (Lidai sanbao ji 歷代三寶紀) *and Its Role in the Formation of the Chinese Buddhist Canon*

Tanya Storch

It can be argued that the proper history of the Chinese Buddhist canon be-gins with its printed editions because the printed format allows for easier access, wider dissemination, standardization of the contents, and preservation of textual stability. But before the earliest printed editions appeared, for a period of more than five hundred years, Chinese scholars zealously labored over the creation of the principles of textual criticism and taxonomic organization, which they applied to the handwritten canon and which eventually affected the contents and structure of the printed version. In the canon catalogs, various manuscripts of translated Buddhist texts, as well as Chinese works, were listed, classified, and evaluated with respect to their doctrinal truth. As Kyoko Tokuno put it, such catalogs were "both prescriptive and proscriptive in their function, in that they classified texts to be either included in or excluded from the canon. In a real sense, they held the key to the fate of texts and, by extension, the formation of the Buddhist canon in China."[1]

Close to a hundred scriptural catalogs were written from the late third century through the Northern Song Dynasty (960–1127), at which point printed editions began to seriously take on their functions and almost entirely replaced them.[2] Each scholar who had made a catalog of the handwritten Tripitaka assumed some religious and scriptural authority, leaving the canon with a somewhat different shape and meaning as far as the whole collection of texts was concerned. These differences were insignificant at certain times, yet dramatic at others. Antonino Forte evaluated the effects of Zhisheng's 智昇 (fl. ca. 730) approach to the Tripitaka by saying, "We must not forget that Chih-sheng's [Zhisheng's] standards of objectivity, no matter how high they may have been, were nonetheless subordinated to the demands of orthodoxy as defined at *that historic moment.*"[3] And Eric Zürcher issued a warning against taking at face value even the earliest of scriptural catalogs: "the excellent quality of this catalogue [viz., *Daoan lu* 道安錄] and its comparatively early date have led all later authorities to accept Tao-an's [Daoan's] statements as unquestionable facts. . . . We must never forget that . . . we have to do with *attributions.*"[4]

This situation should not discourage a scholar of the Chinese Buddhist canon. Rather, it calls for recognition of the simple fact that the processes by which this canon was created are parallel to such processes in other religions. For instance, specialists in Christianity speak of the New Testament as it was envisioned by Marcion, or Eusebius, or Jerome. Every time a new arrangement of Christian writings was provided by a particular compiler, it reflected a new perspective on the roles the Christian community, its leaders, and its texts played in society.

With this in mind, I focus here on one influential catalog of the Sui Dynasty (581–618)—Fei Changfang's 費長房 (fl. late sixth century) *Records of the Three Treasures Throughout the Successive Dynasties* (*Lidai sanbao ji* 歷代三寶紀; henceforth *Records of the Three Treasures*), published around 597. Neglected by most Western scholars due to "historical forgeries" committed by its author, this catalog established a new outlook on the issue of the authenticity of Buddhist texts in China. It classified all Buddhist texts according to the dynastic rulers who had sponsored their production, who were now viewed as the ultimate authority in deciding which texts deserved inclusion in the canon. This trend, along with several other innovations implemented in this catalog, deeply affected the Tang Dynasty's (618–907) approach to the Tripitaka. Even Zhisheng, who was critical of Fei Changfang, followed the dynastic approach that Fei had imposed on the Tripitaka and kept most of the new features the latter had added to the traditional ways of cataloging. To fully recognize the role the *Records of the Three Treasures* played in the history of the formation of the Chinese Buddhist canon, this chapter analyzes it against the background of other Sui Dynasty and pre-Sui Dynasty catalogs, as well as through comparison with the catalogs of the Tang era, with a special emphasis on Daoxuan's 道宣 (596–667) *Catalog of the Inner Canon of the Great Tang Dynasty* (*Da Tang neidian lu* 大唐內典錄, henceforth *Inner Canon Catalog*) and Zhisheng's *Catalog of Buddhist Teachings Compiled During the Kaiyuan Era* (*Kaiyuan shijiao lu* 開元釋教錄, henceforth *Kaiyuan Catalog*).

FEI CHANGFANG'S WORK AND THE PRE-SUI DYNASTY TRIPITAKA CATALOGS

Our study of the role of the *Record of the Three Treasures* in the development of the Chinese Tripitaka would be incomplete without discussing its account of the previous catalogs of the Chinese Buddhist canon. Before Fei Changfang, Chinese Buddhists do not seem to have paid serious attention to the history of Buddhist bibliography. For instance, Sengyou 僧祐 (445–518), who had a chance to provide an earlier account of Buddhist catalogs in his *Collection of Records About the Translation of the Tripitaka* (*Chu Sanzang jiji* 出三藏集記, ca. 515; henceforth *Collection of Records*), spoke in detail only of the one compiled ca. 374 by monk Daoan (312–85). We can therefore say that Fei Changfang was the first scholar to put together a collection of data about all scriptural catalogs compiled throughout the centuries before his own work was published circa 597. After Fei, accounts of Buddhist bibliography were canonized and published as part of the Tripitaka. Both Daoxuan in the *Inner Canon Catalog* and Zhisheng in the *Kaiyuan Catalog* provided complete histories of Buddhist bibliography, relying heavily on Fei Changfang's work for the pre-Tang period.

Although Fei Changfang forged information concerning the two catalogs he considered to be the oldest, most of his data appear to be historically correct and can be verified through comparisons with other sources. But even the information now deemed historically incorrect provides an important insight into Fei's contribution to the Buddhist bibliographic tradition. For example, he suggested that the first bibliographic account of Buddhist scriptures was written by the Han Dynasty Confucian scholar Liu Xiang 劉向 (ca. 77–ca. 6 B.C.E.). Liu Xiang was a seminal figure in the Confucian bibliographic tradition, whose *Subject Catalog* (*Bielu* 別錄) of the Han imperial library is widely accepted by Confucian scholars as the oldest work of its kind.[5] In this *Subject Catalog*, Confucian classics were given a prominent position among other works of national literature. Thus, by saying that Liu Xiang wrote a catalog of Buddhist scriptures, Fei Changfang meant to place them in a position of importance and respect similar to that of the Confucian classics.

The second catalog, which, likewise, was never written, was ascribed by Fei Changfang to Kāśyapa Mātanga (Shemoteng 攝摩騰), a legendary monk who, according to most Buddhist sources, brought the first scripture, *Sutra in Forty-Two Sections* (*Sishi'er zhang jing* 四十二章經), to the court of the Han Emperor Ming 明帝 (r. 58–75).[6] This statement, although historically incorrect, clearly expressed Fei Changfang's belief that the cataloging of scriptures began at the same point in history as their translation.

Looking at more reliable data from Fei Changfang's history of the Chinese Buddhist bibliography, one may or may not accept that the earliest catalog of scriptures actually written belonged to Zhu Shixing 朱士行, a Chinese monk who lived during the Wei 魏 Dynasty of the Three Kingdoms (220–265) period. Direct statements by Fei Changfang about the *Catalog by Zhu Shixing* (*Zhu Shixing lu* 朱士行錄)[7] are too short to make a convincing case for its actual contents. Scattered throughout the *Records of the Three Treasures*, however, are other references to this catalog[8] concerning the translations from the Latter Han Dynasty (25–220) that suggest it could have been a comprehensive catalog of translations made in Luoyang. From Zhu Shixing's biography, we know that he left for Khotan in search of the Mahayana scriptures around 260. Thus it is reasonable to suggest that his list of translations might have been compiled prior to his departure, in order to compare the existing contents of the Chinese Tripitaka with what he hoped to find in other countries.[9]

The next title from Fei Changfang's history of Buddhist bibliography is *Catalog of Zhu Fahu* (*Zhu Fahu lu* 竺法護錄),[10] which, most likely, was written by the translator Zhu Fahu, also known as Dharmarakṣa (ca. 233–310).[11] Huang Biji indicated it could have been compiled between 284 and 313, but Men'shikov gave a more specific date of 305.[12] Men'shikov also suggested that it was the earliest catalog of a privately owned collection of the Tripitaka, not necessarily a list of Zhu Fahu's actual translations. If so, this would mean that translator Zhu Fahu served as a "parameter of the canon," as Stefano Zacchetti has suggested.[13] This would also explain why Sengyou's *Collection of Records* claims more translations in Zhu Fahu's name than in the name of any other translator. Sixteen undocumented texts discovered by Jinhua Chen could have been copied from this catalog.[14]

Fei Changfang also wrote about *Catalog of Nie Daozhen* (*Nie Daozhen lu* 聶道真錄).[15] He indicated it was put together by Nie Daozhen, who lived in Chang'an during the Western Jin 西晉 Dynasty (265–317).[16] He was a son of Nie Chengyuan 聶承遠, one of Zhu Fahu's most famous disciples, who had helped him with the translations.[17] The *Catalog of Nie Daozhen* was most likely compiled between 307 and 312 and is described in more detail in Daoxuan's *Inner Canon Catalog*, where the actual number of translations is given as fifty-four in sixty-six fascicles.[18]

Zhi Mindu 支敏度 (d.u.), according to Fei Changfang, wrote his own catalog circa 326. This work was known to Fei Changfang under two different titles— *Catalog by Zhi Mindu* (*Zhi Mindu lu* 支敏度錄) and *Catalog of All Scriptures and Commentaries* (*Jinglun doulu* 經論都錄). The second title described perhaps Zhi's particular approach to the Chinese Tripitaka. From the information provided by Fei Changfang[19] and several passages of Zhi's writings preserved in Sengyou's *Collection of Records*,[20] we may speculate that Zhi envisioned a canon where the Chinese indigenous writings, such as commentaries to the translated sutras and prefaces written by famous Chinese scholars, would be esteemed (nearly) as much as the translations.

Fei Changfang also included information about a catalog by monk Daoan, which, unlike all the catalogs previously discussed, has been the center of academic attention for quite some time.[21] Because Fei Changfang's account does not add anything of significance to what we already know, I will simply summarize the most important points about this work: Daoan must be credited with the very idea of assessing the authenticity of each Chinese translation using knowledge about the person who had translated it. In essence, this decision parallels developments in Christian history, where the early Roman Church relied on "apostolic transmission" in evaluating the texts considered for the canon. Daoan was not merely the inventor of a similar idea in Chinese Buddhism; he actually implemented it by attributing hundreds of the anonymously translated texts to certain individuals he knew were involved in the translation activities. Daoan then organized his catalog so that scriptures attributed to the known translators appeared in the first part and were regarded as a more authentic part of the canon. He gathered scriptures that could not be attributed to a known translator in the second part, placing them in close proximity to the texts he openly condemned as "suspicious."[22]

Although the *Records of the Three Treasures* does not include the table of contents of Daoan's catalog, it appears in Sengyou's *Collection of Records*.[23] According to Sengyou, in the first division, Daoan had listed all the translations that he was able to attribute to known translators and called this type of text *jing* 經, which can be translated as "scripture."[24] In the second part, he gathered a plethora of anonymous translations that he classified, on the basis of the texts' additional characteristics, as a) "ancient different [translations] of scriptures" (*gu yi chu jing* 古異出經); b) [contemporary] anonymous scriptures (*shi yi jing* 失譯經);[25] c) different [anonymous] scriptures, *Liangtu yi jing* 涼土異經, from Liangzhou (in modern Gansu); and d) different [anonymous] scriptures, *Guanzhong yi jing* 關中異經, from Guanzhong (in southern Shaanxi). After that, he created a division for what he described as the "suspicious scriptures" (*yi jing* 疑經). This was followed by writings of Chinese Buddhists, including commentaries and historical records.

The real value of Fei Changfang's history of Buddhist bibliography becomes apparent in its discussion of other catalogs of the same time period, which had not been mentioned by Sengyou and about whose existence very little information is available. These include such an important work as *Catalog of All Scriptures by Zhu Daozu* (*Zhu Daozu zhongjing lu* 竺道祖眾經錄, ca. 419). It was produced in the community located on Mount Lushan under the guidance of Daoan's most prominent student, monk Huiyuan 慧遠 (ca. 336–416).[26] Apparently, those who left Daoan in the north and moved south with Huiyuan were without scriptures, as described in Huiyuan's biography in Sengyou's *Collection of Records*. An actual story about the creation of this catalog is provided not merely by Fei Changfang but also by Daoxuan, who wrote about it in his *Inner Canon Catalog*.[27] After Huiyuan sent people in search of scriptures and the scriptures were delivered,[28] he ordered monk Daoliu 道流 to write a catalog of the Tripitaka. Daoliu did not complete it before he died, and Zhu Daozu 竺道祖 finished the work, giving it the title *Catalog of All Scriptures* (*Zhongjing lu* 眾經錄). It was the largest catalog of Chinese Buddhist literature ever produced in China, and at four fascicles, far lengthier than earlier catalogs, which were only one fascicle long. It classified the texts of the Tripitaka on the basis of the Chinese dynasties during which their translations were made. It also had a division where scriptures made in the Gansu corridor were listed and identified as false.

Fei Changfang provided information about yet another significant bibliographic work: *Subject Catalog of All Scriptures* (*Zhongjing bielu* 眾經別錄), an anonymous compilation from the Liu Song Dynasty (420–479).[29] This information is crucial because it attests to the earliest known use by the Chinese of the Indian tripartite structure of the Tripitaka in its practical application to all translated texts. Sengyou gave his bibliographic work a title that reflected that he knew the Tripitaka was made of the "three baskets," although he did not organize the scriptures accordingly. By contrast, the author of the *Subject Catalog of All Scriptures* arranged Chinese Buddhist literature by following, as closely as he could, the original tripartite structure of the Tripitaka. He divided the catalog according to the Mahayana scriptures (438 texts in 914 fascicles); Hinayana scriptures (651 texts in 1,682 fascicles); and scriptures he could not attribute to either Mahayana or Hinayana (174 texts in 184 fascicles). He also provided separate divisions for the suspicious texts, of which he counted 17 in 20 fascicles; and texts on divination (6 works in 121 fascicles). Additionally, this author provided separate lists for the vinaya literature (12 texts in 195 fascicles) and Abhidharma literature (6 texts in 152 fascicles).[30]

Sengyou, the author of *Collection of Records*, the oldest extant catalog, made no mention of this *Subject Catalog of All Scriptures* in his discussion of how the cataloging of scriptures had developed in China. The *Subject Catalog* was extant during Sengyou's time and later when Fei Changfang was writing his history of Buddhist bibliography. In light of this, one is hard pressed to find the reason Sengyou neglected such an excellent work of Buddhist bibliography and chose as his model a catalog written by Daoan—a much older and shorter work, far from complete in terms of the number of scriptures it counted, as well as its taxonomic divisions. One explanation may be that the standards of scriptural authenticity used by the author of the *Subject Catalog* seemed too loose to Sengyou.[31] He preferred a more rigid and rigorous evaluation of each text's authority, which was provided by Daoan's method, and he considered this to be a model for the truly authoritative catalog of the Tripitaka. If so, then by providing information about all catalogs written in China, Fei Changfang effectively acted as a counteragent to Daoan's and Sengyou's approaches and actively sought to expand the range of the historiographical bibliographical tools with which to measure the authenticity of the Tripitaka.

As we know today, Sengyou's *Collection of Records* was published sometime between 515 and 519.[32] Its author was a monk who held a high position within the Buddhist community and was personally responsible for the persecution of the Chinese Buddhists who, in his view, committed the crime of forging the words of the Buddha.[33] Rather than reviewing the extensive body of studies on Sengyou's catalog,[34] I focus here on the summary of Sengyou's data by Fei Changfang as part of the discussion on the latter's approach to the history of Buddhist bibliography.[35]

According to Fei, *Collection of Records* counted 2,162 texts in 4,328 fascicles and was organized in the following way ("Venerable An" refers to Daoan below):

1. Newly compiled list of scriptures and treatises.[36]
2. Newly compiled list of different translations of the [same] scriptures.[37]
3. Newly compiled list of the vinaya [texts organized according to] four schools with an introduction.
4. Newly compiled list of the different ancient translations of scriptures from the Venerable An [catalog].[38]
5. Newly compiled list of the anonymous translations from the Venerable An [catalog].
6. Newly compiled list of different translations made in Liangzhou 涼州 from the Venerable An [catalog].
7. Newly compiled list of different translations made in Guanzhong 關中 from the Venerable An [catalog].
8. Newly compiled additions to the list of the anonymous translations of scriptures.
9. Newly compiled list of "digest-translations" of scriptures.
10. Newly compiled list of suspicious scriptures from the Venerable An [catalog].
11. Newly compiled list of suspicious scriptures and false compilations.
12. Newly compiled list of commentaries to the scriptures and various [historical] records from the Venerable An [catalog].[39]

Throughout the *Record of the Three Treasures*, Fei Changfang paid homage to Sengyou by praising his accomplishments, listing divisions of his catalog, and counting the exact number of texts and fascicles in each division. Yet he did not choose Sengyou's approach as an exclusive model for himself, as Sengyou had with Daoan's catalog. In fact, Fei Changfang recorded an important struggle between Sengyou's position and what can be called the imperial approach to the Tripitaka in his discussion of monks Sengshao 僧紹 and Baochang 寶唱, both of whom received orders from Emperor Wu of the Southern Liang Dynasty (502–557) to compile an official catalog of Buddhist works in the dynasty almost immediately after Sengyou's work was completed. According to Fei Changfang, in 516, Sengshao began compiling a new account of the Tripitaka that was expected to be based primarily on the emperor's own collection of scriptures.[40] As a result, *Catalog of Scriptures from the Palace in the Jetavana Park* (*Hualin fodian zhongjing mulu* 華林佛殿眾經目錄) was presented at the court but was not deemed unsatisfactory.[41] At this point, Baochang was ordered to write a new catalog of the Tripitaka, which he presented to the court around 519: *Catalog of Scriptures of the Liang Era* (*Liangshi zhongjing mulu* 梁世眾經目錄), an official catalog of the Tripitaka of the Southern Liang Dynasty.[42]

We can only speculate about the emperor's motives for not fully embracing Sengyou's position and placing the name of his dynasty on the catalog written by Baochang instead. One motive can be found in Sengyou's rejection of the sutras associated with the nun Sengfa 僧法, who was the emperor's favorite.[43] Sengyou's version of the Tripitaka could also have been less acceptable to the emperor because Sengyou, unlike Baochang, did not give the *dharani* literature (for which the emperor had a great fondness) a prominent place in the textual hierarchy. Third, Sengyou had also spoken critically about the abridged redactions of the sutras (*chao jing* 抄經), most of which were made by famous court aristocrats and enjoyed by the emperor.

Fei Changfang's approach to the history of Buddhist bibliography must be considered truly ecumenical because he included *all* known catalogs from both southern and northern territories despite the fact that he was personally persecuted by the Northern Zhou 北周 (557–581) government. According to him, during the Northern Wei Dynasty (386–535) an important catalog was produced under the supervision of Li Kuo 李廓 (fl. mid-sixth century), who (much like Fei Changfang himself) was a lay scholar in charge of the enterprise, which took more than two decades to complete. This *Catalog of All Scriptures of the Wei Era* (*Weishi zhongjing mulu* 魏世眾經目錄) counted only 427 translations in 2,053 fascicles and was arranged according to the Mahayana and Hinayana forms of Buddhism and according to the "three baskets," but translations from the vinaya were listed only for the Hinayana part of the canon, while the Mahayana scriptures were divided according to the sutra, Abhidharma, and Chinese commentaries. This account of the Tripitaka also separated works actually in existence and actively used by Buddhists of the time from those described by the earlier catalogers but no longer extant. Fei Changfang's study of Li Kuo's catalog undoubtedly affected his own approach to the Tripitaka. Fei and Li, however, were diametrically opposed in their views of nonorthodox literature. Among Buddhist catalogers, Li Kuo was one of the least tolerant of texts he considered unorthodox. He provided one division for "totally untrustworthy sutras" and another for "totally untrustworthy Abhidharma literature." These were topped by yet another list that condemned the texts that were "absolutely nonscriptural and only fooled people and made a mockery of their titles."[44]

Fei Changfang also described a major catalog of the Northern Qi Dynasty ordered by Emperor Wenxuan 文宣 (r. 550–559): *Catalog of All Scriptures of the Qi Era* (*Qishi zhongjing mulu,* 齊世眾經目錄, 576), which was ascribed to monk Fashang 法上 (496–581). It listed 787 texts in 2,335 fascicles, organized into the following sections: 1) heterogeneous scriptures; 2) sutras; 3) vinaya; 4) Abhidharma; 5) "separate parts" (literally, *biesheng* 別生); 6) abridged sutras; 7) collections of sutras; and 8) works created by people (i.e., not the words of the Buddha).[45]

In summary, this review of pre-Sui period Tripitaka catalogs reveals the extraordinary significance of Fei Changfang's history of Buddhist bibliography. First, Fei must be credited with establishing the Buddhist bibliographic tradition that kept records from earlier catalogs of the Tripitaka. Many outstanding scholars of the Tang Dynasty, including Daoxuan and Zhisheng, followed his example by creating their own accounts of all previous Buddhist catalogs. This tradition provided a fuller history of the canon. Second, Fei Changfang established a tradition of Buddhist textual criticism that resembled and, in many respects, paralleled the pre-existing Confucian studies, where the paramount importance of the classics was emphasized by detailed attention to these texts' recensions in meticulous records in all significant book catalogs. Creating a corresponding bibliographic tradition for Buddhism was extremely important because Confucian bibliographers refused to include the Tripitaka in most of their catalogs and practically never listed titles of Buddhist texts in dynastic histories.[46] The only way to represent the Tripitaka within the framework of the Chinese national book collection was by developing Buddhists' own body of bibliographic studies.

Finally, Fei Changfang's scrupulous study of the entire history of Buddhist catalogs enriched his knowledge of and widened his approach to the collections of texts identified with the Tripitaka. We know that Sengyou selected one exclusive model—he used Daoan's idea of the known authorship of the translations as a foundation for all textual classifications imposed on all existing texts. By comparison, Fei Changfang's way of dealing with the Tripitaka was multidimensional because he had studied, described, and incorporated into his work accomplishments of those catalogers whose views were different from Daoan's and Sengyou's. For instance, he followed Zhu Daozu's emphasis on the dynasty that sponsored the production of the text and guaranteed its doctrinal status. He used Zhi Mindu's position with respect to Chinese indigenous writings. And from Li Kuo's catalog, he learned how to distinguish between the significance of extant texts in use by believers and that of other works that were listed in the canon but no longer existed.

FEI CHANGFANG'S WORK AND OTHER SUI DYNASTY CATALOGS

The rise of the Sui Dynasty (581–618) brought big changes in the history of Chinese Buddhism. No longer a foreign religion exalted by some rulers and rejected by others, Buddhism became an integral part of Chinese society. It is telling that the Sui rulers looked to Buddhism as an ideology to unite the country after more than three centuries of disunion and turmoil. Fei Changfang proudly quoted in his catalog one of the edicts of the founder of the dynasty, Emperor Wen 文帝 (r. 581–604):

> With the armed might of a chakravartin king, We spread the ideals of the ultimately enlightened one. With a hundred victories in a hundred battles, We promote the practice of the ten Buddhist virtues. Therefore We regard the weapons of war as having become like the offerings of incense and flowers presented to the Buddha, and the fields of this world as becoming forever identical with the Buddha-land.[47]

Such an elevation of Buddhism's political importance explains why, during the short four decades of the Sui Dynasty, four comprehensive catalogs of the Tripitaka were compiled. Three of them resulted from direct imperial orders. In response to Emperor Wen's request, *Catalog of Scriptures of the Great Sui Dynasty* (*Da Sui zhongjing mulu* 大隋眾經目錄) was presented by monk Fajing 法經 in 594, and *Catalog of the Inner Canon of the Renshou Era of the Sui Dynasty* (*Sui Renshou nian neidian lu* 隋仁壽年內典錄) was presented by monk Yancong 彥悰 in 602; at the request of Emperor Yang 煬帝 (r. 605–616), *Catalog of Scriptures* (*Zhongjing mulu* 眾經目錄), which had a longer official title in its original form, was presented by monk Zhiguo 智果 in 617, only a year before the collapse of the dynasty.[48]

In contrast, Fei Changfang's *Record of the Three Treasures*, although the largest and most famous catalog of the Sui era, was not compiled under imperial auspices. It was presented to Emperor Wen and had his approval, but it was not granted the status of an official catalog of the dynasty on par with Fajing's and Yancong's works.[49] The reason may be found in Fei's biography. According to all available sources, he became a monk early in life but lost his clerical status during the Northern Zhou Dynasty's persecution of Buddhism.[50] The loss became permanent. None of the sources explains why it was not restored after Emperor Wen came to power, but in any case, Fei Changfang's precarious position within the contemporary sangha was probably the reason prominent monk-scholars, such as Fajing and Yancong (but not Fei Changfang), were given the honor of writing official accounts of the Sui Dynasty's Tripitaka.

Despite the persecution he had suffered from the imperial government of the previous dynasty, Fei Changfang was a staunch supporter of the Sui Dynasty and its founder. He portrayed the destruction of the Northern Zhou Dynasty as a triumph of the dharma in China and Emperor Wen as a "heavenly emissary appointed to rule the world and restore Buddhism."[51] He also boasted of a title, "scholar of translations" (*fanjing xueshi* 翻經學士),[52] received from Emperor Wen. Still, he did not enjoy the same degree of imperial favor and material support as Fajing and Yancong, both of whom employed large teams of assistants, including collators, translators, and copyists, in compiling their catalogs. Nevertheless, or perhaps because Fei lacked such resources in his work, *Records of the Three Treasures* turned out to provide a unique overall representation of the Tripitaka, although it shared many features in common with other Sui Dynasty catalogs. To better understand their differences and similarities, it is useful to compare how the three catalogs organized the contents of the Chinese Buddhist canon.

Records of the Three Treasures comprises 15 fascicles and accounts for 2,268 texts in 6,417 fascicles. It classifies the Tripitaka as shown in table 4.1.

Fajing's *Catalog of Scriptures of the Great Sui Dynasty* is 7 fascicles long, but accounts for 2,257 texts in 5,310 fascicles. Fajing had much better access to the imperial archives and a great number of assistants who counted every piece of translation and commentary written throughout the history of Buddhism in China—privileges unavailable to Fei Changfang.[53] In Fajing's catalog, the Tripitaka was organized as follows:

Mahayana
1. Sutra-pitaka:
a) available in one translation
b) available in different translations
c) anonymous translations
d) translations of separate parts
2. Vinaya-pitaka: subdivided into the same categories as the Sutra-pitaka
Hinayana: Divisions and subdivisions identical with the Mahayana part of
    the catalog
[Works collected] after the Buddha's Nirvana
Compilations of the Western Sages
Compilations of all the virtuous people of this land (i.e., China)

TABLE 4.1. CONTENT OF *RECORDS OF THE THREE TREASURES*

Fascicle	Content
1	Historical survey and chronological table of the most important events in the history of Buddhism in China during the Zhou 周 (ca. 1100–221 B.C.E.) and Qin 秦 (221–7 B.C.E.) dynasties
2	Historical survey and chronological table of the most important events in the history of Buddhism in China during the Han Dynasty
3	Historical survey and chronological table of the most important events in the history of Buddhism in China from the end of the Han Dynasty up to the year 597 (when the catalog was completed)
4	Catalog of all Buddhist texts produced during the Latter Han Dynasty
5	Catalog of all Buddhist texts produced during the Wei and Wu 吳 kingdoms
6	Catalog of all Buddhist texts produced during the Western Jin Dynasty
7	Catalog of all Buddhist texts produced during the Eastern Jin Dynasty
8	Catalog of all Buddhist texts produced during the Former and Later Qin 前,後秦 dynasties
9	Catalog of all Buddhist texts produced during the Western Qin 西秦, Northern Liang 北涼, Wei, Qi 齊, and Chen 陳 dynasties
10	Catalog of all Buddhist texts produced during the Liu Song 劉宋 Dynasty
11	Catalog of all Buddhist texts produced during the Southern Qi 南齊 and Liang 梁 dynasties
12	Catalog of all Buddhist texts produced during the Sui Dynasty
13	The Mahayana scriptures entered into the canon: 1) Sutra-pitaka: a) by known translators b) anonymous 2) Vinaya-pitaka: a) by known translators b) anonymous 3) Abhidharma-pitaka: a) by known translators b) anonymous
14	The Hinayana scriptures entered into the canon: 1) Sutra-pitaka: a) by known translators b) anonymous 2) Vinaya-pitaka: a) by known translators b) anonymous 3) Abhidharma-pitaka: a) by known translators b) anonymous
15	Afterword to the catalog; table of content of the catalog; list of catalogs compiled prior to the *Records of the Three Treasures*

Yancong's *Inner Canon Catalog* is also 5 fascicles long, with 2,180 texts in 5,058 fascicles, fewer than in Fei Changfang's catalog despite the fact that Yancong added titles of new texts written in the years between the publications of these two volumes. Yancong organized his catalog in a much simpler manner than Fajing and Fei Changfang, arranging the Tripitaka according to the following five categories:

1. Scriptures available only in one translation
2. Scriptures available in many translations
3. Compilations of the sages
4. Translations of the separate parts of the scriptures
5. Suspicious and false compilations

The last Sui Dynasty catalog, published by Zhiguo in 617, was not preserved in its entirety, but a table of its contents found in the Sui dynastic history shows the following count of scriptures and organization of the Tripitaka:

Mahayana sutras: 617 translations in 2,076 fascicles
Hinayana sutras: 87 translations in 852 fascicles
Miscellaneous sutras: 380 translations in 716 fascicles
Suspicious sutras: 172 translations in 36 fascicles
Mahayana vinaya: 52 translations in 91 fascicles
Hinayana vinaya: 80 translations in 478 fascicles
Mahayana *śastras*: 35 translations in 141 fascicles
Miscellaneous *śastras*: 51 translations in 437 fascicles[54]

The differences between Fei Changfang's approach to the Chinese Buddhist canon and that of other Sui Dynasty Buddhist bibliographers are evident from the above lists. The main distinctive feature in Fei's catalog is that he used the sequence of Chinese dynasties (*lidai* 歷代) as a fundamental classification principle with which to organize the entire canon. Thus he presented the Chinese Buddhist canon so that a text's association with the dynasty that authorized its production and circulation qualified it for inclusion. Fei did not pay any serious attention to the Indian tripartite structure of the canon until the very end of his catalog. Only in fascicles 13–14, where he presented the "List of [Scriptures] That Entered the Collection" (*ru zang mu* 入藏目), did he utilize the tripartite approach that served as the main organizational principle in the Sui Dynasty catalogs written by Fajing and Zhiguo. Fei equally disregarded in the first twelve fascicles of his catalog the classifications based on the qualities of different redactions of the translated texts that served as the main principle in

Yancong's organization of the Tripitaka. Yancong paid very serious attention to issues concerning different redactions, but Fei Changfang included all Buddhist texts—whether they appeared in different translations or just one, and whether they were translations of the separated parts of a longer text or complete translations—in the chronological category if they were produced during the same dynasty. In using this dynastic classification rather than the tripartite classification, Fei was declaring that the proof of the text's authenticity was its recognition and approval by a legitimate dynasty that guaranteed its doctrinal truth.[55]

Although other Sui catalogers followed the dynastic sequence within their own bibliographical categories, none of them turned Chinese historical chronology into a fundamental organizational principle that acted inside the Buddhist canon like a spinal cord within a body, holding the entire collection together. The consequences of this dynastic approach to the Tripitaka had great significance. In the decades following the creation of Fei Changfang's catalog, it became much easier for the Chinese to "own" the translated Buddhist canon. While ideas about the Vinaya, Sutra, and Abhidharma remained new and difficult to grasp for the majority of Chinese readers, their own historical chronology was a familiar and easy-to-follow principle that pervaded so much of Chinese scholarship and culture. Fei Changfang's new emphasis on chronology is also related to the further development of indigenous Chinese ways of classifying the Buddha's teachings in the *panjiao* 判教 (classification of teaching) system. The *panjiao* divided Buddhist teachings into chronological periods, each of which was identified with a particular form of wisdom that was revealed. Some elements of the *panjiao* approach were already present in Fei Changfang's description of the canon.[56]

Another of Fei Changfang's innovations is that he elevated the status of non-translated literature, i.e., indigenous works written by Chinese Buddhists. Historically, Chinese indigenous works were considered inferior to the translated Tripitaka. Daoan and Sengyou had ranked works by Chinese authors below even the texts they considered to be suspicious and false translations. In their minds, these could at least be somehow connected to the original words of the Buddha, albeit twisted in transmission; but the words of Chinese authors clearly could not be the original teachings. Usually, Fajing is credited with adding a separate division to the Chinese Tripitaka where the "works of the sages," both Chinese and foreign, were respectfully introduced.[57] But actually the ranking that Fajing gave these texts within a hierarchy observed throughout his catalog is still lower than that of the Hinayana scriptures, considered by Chinese to be of somewhat lesser importance than the Mahayana canon. Fei Changfang's approach to the literature written by Chinese Buddhists must be considered far more respectful than Fajing's, for he listed Chinese works *alongside* the translated scriptures and *inside* the dynasty-based periodical classifications found in fascicles 4–12 of his catalog. Thus, his message concerning Chinese-written Buddhist literature was clear. According to his vision of the Tripitaka, there was no significant difference between the translated scriptures and the Chinese indigenous writings. Effectively, he had moved the writings by Chinese authors to their highest-ranked position yet in the history of Chinese Buddhism.[58] This pioneering decision affected the development of Buddhism in China by speeding up the process of canonization of indigenous texts, especially historiographical and commentarial literature.

Another innovation that made Fei Changfang's description of the Tripitaka unique is his addition of a history of Buddhist bibliography in China. Evidently, neither Fajing's nor Yancong's nor Zhiguo's catalog contains a section dedicated to Buddhist catalogs, so Fei must be credited with the canonization of scriptural catalogs themselves.

Fei Changfang was also the only Sui bibliographer who wrote the canon registry *ru zang mu* 入藏目 (fascicles 13–14), in which he successfully separated the actual canon—used on a regular basis by practitioners—from the contents that mainly represented the process by which the canon was put together and were of little use to a regular practitioner. This proved extremely efficient at a time when catalogs of the Tripitaka were getting longer and longer and their contents more and more sophisticated. Fei Changfang's *ru zang mu* was imitated by the Tang Dynasty's catalogers, and this in turn helped establish the contents of the first printed edition.

Finally, a very important difference between Fei Changfang's approach to the Tripitaka and that of other Sui Dynasty Buddhist bibliographers was that Fei Changfang seriously softened the judgment on the so-called suspicious and false scriptures. A comparative reading of the tables of contents of the four Sui catalogs shows that Fei's was the only one that did not provide a division for the suspicious and false scriptures. Although all catalogers before and during the Sui Dynasty felt obliged to expose and condemn those texts that could not be considered "authentic" by the standards imposed by Daoan and Sengyou, Fei Changfang decided to rid the canon of them by deftly reassigning the texts declared by his predecessors to be suspicious and false to other categories, such as "digest redactions" and "anonymous redactions." This decision, which earned him a bad reputation among certain scholars, was certainly helpful in restoring the good reputation of the Tripitaka among audiences who were not scholastically trained. This was urgently needed, as the number of suspicious and false scriptures had grown nearly eightfold in the period between Daoan and Fajing.[59] Fei Changfang's new approach to the issues of scriptural authenticity set a bibliographic trend even in his own time. His contemporary, Yancong, was the first to subscribe to it, as he left the bulk of the scriptures reassigned by Fei Changfang in their respective categories. The trend was also widely followed during the Tang Dynasty, as Daoxuan and Mingquan 明佺 (?–712) adopted it in their catalogs, and even Zhisheng, the person most critical of Fei Changfang's "reassignments," did not go as far as to eradicate them all.

FEI CHANGFANG'S WORK AND THE DYNASTIC-PERIODICAL APPROACH TO THE TRIPITAKA

What sets the *Records of the Three Treasures* apart from not just other corresponding Sui works but all Chinese Buddhist catalogs is that it was intended to be more than merely a catalog of Buddhist texts. Although many Chinese catalogers were in the habit of adding some historical information to the lists of translated texts, they did not incorporate dynastic tables into their work, as did Fei. Nor did they provide extensive accounts covering all the Chinese dynasties with the aim of illustrating how each dynasty had contributed to the spread of Buddhism by sponsoring the production of scriptures and propagating Buddha's word. What Fei accomplished in his fifteen-fascicle-long compilation was so different from what other catalogers had done that his work was often classified outside of the genre of Buddhist catalogs and published alongside Buddhist genealogies and other historical texts.[60]

The truly gigantic scope of Fei Changfang's dynastic-periodical approach to the canon becomes evident when one reads carefully through the first three fascicles. Although Fajing had already begun weaving together some stories about the creation of the Buddhist canon in China and certain accounts found in Chinese traditional histories,[61] he built just a few parallels between the events of the traditional history and Buddhist events, while Fei Changfang attempted a monumental task of connecting *almost every important event* of Chinese history described in such texts as *Shu jing* 書經, *Shiji* 史記, *Zuo zhuan* 左傳, *Han shu* 漢書, and *Sanguo zhi* 三國志 with the events believed to have happened in the process of translating the Tripitaka into Chinese. His account reads as a viable alternative to the Confucian view of Chinese history because it rewrites traditional history from a distinctly Buddhist perspective. This makes it comparable to the Christian "Histories of the Church" or Sri Lankan histories, such as *Dipavamsa*, because in these texts, the entire national history is reinterpreted through religious ideals.

Fei Changfang began the process of reshaping Chinese historiography starting from the Zhou Dynasty, considered by the Chinese to be the foundation of their civilization. In order to change old, well-known accounts of the Zhou era and re-present events as Buddhist, Fei Changfang inserted numerous new elements such as dreams, prophecies, premonitions, birthmarks, and other allusions to Buddhism. This transformation of the old historical accounts served the purpose of persuading readers to acknowledge that Buddhist dharma was present in the life of the Chinese nation from its very beginning, although it was not as fully revealed at that time as later on. On one hand, Fei Changfang's method is reminiscent of the work Origen of Alexandria (185–232) conducted in the Christian world in order to successfully merge the messages of the Old Testament with those of the New Testament, the so-called "allegorical method."[62] On the other hand, it rested on the ancient and well-respected Chinese philosophical idea that the cosmos functioned as "gnomon and shape," "sound and echo," "stimulus and response."[63]

Fei Changfang interpreted several important events in China's early history as the "shadows," "echoes," and "responses" that corresponded to the "gnomon," "sound," and "stimulus" of the Buddhist events happening in India. For example, while describing the birth of Houji 后稷, the legendary founder of the Zhou Dynasty, Fei explained that Houji's mother became pregnant because she saw a gigantic figure in her dream.[64] The apparent "Buddhicization" of Chinese history happened in this instance because *Shiji* recorded that Houji's mother had stepped into a gigantic footprint and thus became pregnant. Changing the "gigantic footprint" into a "gigantic figure" altered the meaning of this record in two ways. First, it made a connection to the Buddha's own mother, who, according to the Buddhist tradition, saw a gigantic white elephant before she became pregnant with the Buddha. Second, it related Houji to the Han Dynasty's Emperor Ming, who saw a gigantic figure in his dream and sent the first expedition in search of Buddhist scriptures. In addition, Fei Changfang detailed birthmarks on Houji's body, providing information unavailable in other historical accounts. This allusion is unmistakably Buddhist in nature, and it created a vivid connection between Houji and the Buddha, who was famous for his thirty-two birthmarks.

The most important "Buddhist" event of the Zhou period, however, was placed by Fei Changfang in the years of Zhuangwang's 莊王 rule (696–682 B.C.E.). Here, he connected a moment recorded in Chinese history with a specific moment when the Buddha was born in what is now Nepal. He interpreted the description of the "star rain" known to have happened during the reign of Zhuangwang, according to the *Zuo zhuan*, to refer to the same magnificent "star rain" recorded in the *Fangguang da zhuangyan jing* 方廣大莊嚴經 (Skt. *Lalitavistara*) as a cosmic celebration of the birth of the Buddha.[65]

Fei employed similar means to sufficiently Buddhicize the Qin Dynasty part of Chinese history. For instance, he made good use of a famous Confucian story about a persecution of their doctrine by the Qin emperor, Shi Huangdi 始皇帝. He used the story to conclude that the earliest Buddhist stupas (which, according to him, were built during the Zhou Dynasty) were destroyed by Shi Huangdi. He explained that the earliest Buddhist texts in China disappeared for the same reason as the Confucian classics—they were burned by the "evil" emperor. And he masterfully capitalized on one particular aspect of this story describing how Shi Huangdi mistreated scholars who upheld Confucian values. Fei Changfang created a parallel story that became rather famous later on, in which Buddhism was revealed to be a much stronger doctrine than Confucianism because it was capable of giving magical protection to its followers. Specifically, Fei described a group of monks who arrived in China during the reign of Shi Huangdi in order to spread Buddhism but ended up in prison. Unlike the Confucian scholars, whose lives were destroyed, however, the Buddhist monks were miraculously released by a tall diamond figure—clearly an allusion to the image of the Buddha.

Fei Changfang Buddhicized historical events that happened during each subsequent dynasty, arriving finally at his own, declaring its founder, Emperor Wen, to be a heavenly emissary appointed to rule the world and rescue Buddhism from the perils under the Northern Zhou Dynasty. It is extremely important that we recognize these attempts by Fei at rewriting Chinese history through the Buddhist lens. By doing so, he laid a strong ideological foundation for actively reshaping the content and structure of the Tripitaka. Specifically, as we know, he used the dynastic-periodical principle to organize all known Buddhist texts in fascicles 4 through 12 of his catalog, where the texts were classified and authorized on the basis of the ruling dynasty that sponsored their production and legitimized their distribution; thus he guaranteed their status as reliable Buddhist texts. This new arrangement brought about a significant change in the very nature of the chronological data provided in scriptural catalogs. During earlier times when Buddhist bibliography was still modeled after the Daoan-Sengyou approach, catalogers made an effort to record dates pertaining to the beginning and end of the translation work. However, for Fei Changfang, dates when the translated texts received imperial authorization were far more significant.[66]

The dynastic principle also served to justify giving higher scriptural status to Chinese indigenous writings, such as commentaries and historical records. These were actually included in the canon, according to Fei, because they had been officially approved by a ruler of the dynasty when they were written. For instance, in the seventh fascicle of Fei's catalog, along with the translated scriptures of the Eastern Jin Dynasty (317–420), are treatises written by Sengrui 僧睿 and Zhidun 支遁, as well as catalogs by Daoliu 道流 and Daozu 道祖;[67] while in fascicles 8 and 9, along with the translations authorized by the Former and Later Qin dynasties, there are writings by Sengzhao 僧肇 and Sengrui, and a detailed account of the catalog by Li Kuo.[68]

Another intended consequence of this paramount emphasis on the dynastic-periodical dimension of the Tripitaka was the restoration of doctrinal status to several dozen texts pronounced suspicious and false by the previous catalogers. While it is easy to see why this move caused some scholars to criticize Fei Changfang's scholastic scrupulousness,[69] his new approach to the nonorthodox literature was a direct result of his vision of the Tripitaka being the *production of the successive dynasties* rather than just a collection of texts made by individual translators. Fei championed the idea that there was no need to condemn Buddhist texts that were approved by the ruling *chakravartin*, whom he identified with Emperor Wen. His position marked a shift from a belief that the sangha was in charge of the authenticity of the canon to a belief that the emperor was the one charged with the responsibility to guard its authenticity. This was also a sign of Buddhism transforming into a state religion. As Jinhua Chen pointed out, both the founder of the Sui Dynasty and the founder of the Zhou Dynasty, Empress Wu, usurped the throne and built their political legitimacy on the idea of the *chakravartin*, a legitimate protector of the universal Buddhism.[70] However, while Fei Changfang relied on the state's authority to admit works into the Buddhist canon, he did not use this same principle for the opposite purpose: exclusion of texts from the Tripitaka. This, in fact, occurred under Empress Wu 武后 (r. 684–704), who demanded that her official catalog of the Tripitaka be free of the suspicious and false scriptures. As a result, many such texts were reassigned to different categories, while those the empress personally condemned were described in a separate catalog, outside of the officially approved content of the Tripitaka (see below).[71]

FEI CHANGFANG'S WORK AND THE TANG DYNASTY CATALOGS

The Tang Dynasty is usually called the "Golden Age" of Chinese Buddhism, yet by comparison with the Sui, its political support for Buddhism was weaker. Many Tang rulers, including its second powerful ruler, Taizong 太宗 (r. 627–649), sought to disassociate themselves from Buddhist teachings, used by the Sui emperors as the main ideological support for their government's legitimacy, preferring to rely instead on more traditional systems of beliefs and governance.[72] During the Tang, laws were passed that subjected the Buddhist community to the strictest regulations it had seen since the Eastern Jin Dynasty, when the intense debates about "whether monks should bow to the emperor" began.[73] In the mid-ninth century under Emperor Wuzong 武宗 (r. 841–846), land and other properties owned by Buddhist monasteries were confiscated, depriving the sangha, at least temporarily, of its former social, cultural, and economic influences.

The distancing between the Tang Dynasty's imperial ideology and Buddhist religious ideals and institutions is evident in how this dynasty compiled its catalogs of the Tripitaka. Although about half a dozen significant Buddhist bibliographic works were created, the rate at which this dynasty produced such works over some three centuries pales by comparison with the far shorter-lived Sui, during which four catalogs were made in less than four decades. Furthermore, most of the classification schemes and methods of doctrinal and scriptural taxonomy used in the Tang were mostly borrowings from and refinement of what was already in place in the Sui catalogs, particularly those by Fei Changfang and Yancong. Under the Tang, most efforts toward developing the Tripitaka were made in the technical areas of reproducing, indexing, and storing its texts,[74] and few *new ideas* concerning its textual classifications were advanced. Before a more detailed comparison between the Sui and Tang bibliographic traditions is possible, we must briefly review the most significant Tang catalogs.[75]

1. *Catalog of Scriptures of the Tang Era* (*Tang zhongjing mulu* 唐眾經目錄; not extant) by monk Xuanwan 玄琬 (526–636) is the only catalog written during the reign of Taizong, the second Tang emperor; none was produced during the rule of the first emperor, Gaozu 高祖 (r. 619–626). This suggests how little interest the founders of this dynasty had in the Buddhist canon, especially in comparison with the founder of the Sui Dynasty, who ordered the compilation of two major catalogs within eight years. Moreover, by the year that Zhisheng's *Kaiyuan Catalog* appeared, Xuanwan's work was no longer in circulation.[76]

2. *Catalog of the Inner Canon of the Great Tang* (*Da Tang neidian lu* 大唐內典錄; 2,487 works in 8,476 fascicles; *T* 2149) was issued in 664 by Daoxuan during the reign of Gaozong 高宗 (r. 650–684), a known patron of Buddhism. Before it was overshadowed by Zhisheng's monumental work, it was the most important bibliographic compilation of the Tang Dynasty. It will be discussed below.

3. *Catalog of All Sutras and Śastras of the Da Jing'ai Monastery* (*Da Jing'ai si yiqie jinglun mulu* 大敬愛寺一切經論目錄; 2,291 works in 6,994 fascicles; *T* 2148) is another catalog of the Gaozong era. It was compiled by Jingtai 靜泰 in 664 at imperial order. According to the *Kaiyuan Catalog*, its main purpose was to add Xuanzang's[77] translations to the canon. Without those, it is largely a repeat of Yancong's catalog.

4. *Notes on the Illustrations to the Translations of Scriptures of the Old and Modern Times* (*Gujin yijing tuji* 古今譯經圖記; 1,602 works in 5,552 fascicles; *T* 2151) written by Jingmai 靖邁 (d.u.). The story of this catalog is unique. At the Da Ci'en Monastery 大慈恩寺 in Chang'an, in the famous "translation court,"

the walls were covered with portraits of the most famous translators of the Tripi-taka, beginning from Kāśyapa Mātanga and ending with Xuanzang 玄奘 (ca. 600–664).[78] Jingmai, by the order of Gaozong, created this catalog as an expla-nation of this series of fresco portraits.

5. *Corrected and Authorized Catalog of Scriptures of the Great Zhou Dynasty* (*Da Zhou kanding zhongjing mulu* 大周刊定眾經目錄; 3,616 works in 8,641 fascicles; *T* 2153) was presented to the court in 695 by monk Mingquan 明佺, fol-lowing the order of Empress Wu.[79] Its purported primary goal was to supersede all Tang catalogs and catalog the most correct, as well as the largest, Tripitaka of all times. As a result, it contained the most titles of any catalog of the Chinese Buddhist canon. In its original form, it included only scriptures and writings considered orthodox by Empress Wu. Suspicious and false texts were ordered to be collected separately in what was known then as the *Corrected and Authorized Catalog of False Scriptures of the Great Zhou* (*Da Zhou kanding weijing mulu* 大周刊定偽經目錄).

6. *Catalog of Buddhist Teaching Compiled During the Kaiyuan Reign of the Great Tang* (*Da Tang Kaiyuan shijiao lu* 大唐開元釋教錄; 2,278 works in 7,046 fascicles; *T* 2154), issued by Zhisheng 智昇 in 730, contained fewer works than Empress Wu's catalog.[80] This work is considered by modern scholars to be the pinnacle in the development of the cataloging of the Chinese Buddhist canon in manuscript form, and its classification schemes were dutifully emulated by the editors of the printed editions of the Tripitaka. As Jiang Wu put it, it was "the monumental catalog that directly contributed to the formation of the content of all later editions."[81]

7. *Digest of the Catalog of Buddhist Teaching Compiled During the Kaiyuan Reign* (*Kaiyuan shijiaolu luechu* 開元釋教錄略出; 1,076 works in 5,048 fasci-cles; *T* 2155) was most likely compiled by an anonymous scholar but is attributed to Zhisheng. It is an extraction of a particular division from the *Kaiyuan Cata-log*, comprising only works by known translators. All texts are divided according to Mahayana, Hinayana, and works of Indian and Chinese authors, following the "three baskets" structure previously seen in most Sui and Tang catalogs.[82]

8. *Newly Authorized Catalog of Śākyamuni's Teaching of the Zhenyuan Era of the Great Tang* (*Da Tang Zhenyuan xinding shijiao mulu* 大唐貞元新定釋教 目錄; henceforth *Zhenyuan Catalog*; 1,213 works in 5,390 fascicles; *T* 2157) was presented by monk Yuanzhao 圓照 (d.u.) in 794 during the reign of Emperor Dezong 德宗 (r. 780–804). It was intended to serve as a continuation of the *Kai-yuan Catalog*, adding new indigenous texts and translations. It was also meant to correct and improve Zhisheng's catalog and send a message that, under De-zong's rule, the Tripitaka reached its highest point in terms of the clarity of its classifications and doctrinal reliability. Despite its declared ambitions, however, this gigantic 30-fascicle-long catalog contains significantly less than the number

of works in the *Kaiyuan Catalog*, whose classification schemes it clearly followed. According to Yuanzhao's biography in Zanning's 贊寧 (920–1001) *Song [Version of the] Biographies of Eminent Monks* (*Song Gaoseng zhuan* 宋高僧傳), his contemporaries did not hold this work in high esteem.[83]

9. *Catalog of the Inner Canon* (*Neidian mulu* 內典目錄; number of works and fascicles unknown; not extant), which had a longer official title when it was published, was the last bibliographic work of the Tang era. It was ordered by Emperor Wenzong 文宗 (r. 827–840). Apparently it was lost soon after it was published, so it probably exerted little influence on the development of the Buddhist canon.

From this brief overview, it seems that the Tang-era Buddhist bibliography heavily relied on the work of the Sui Dynasty catalogers. The first Tang catalog was merely a reproduction of Yancong's *Inner Catalog* of 602, to which only a few new translations were added. A catalog by Jingtai (no. 3 in our list) reproduced most of Yancong's textual selections and classifications, the only addition being the translations made by Xuanzang. At the same time, the two most influential Tang catalogs, by Daoxuan and by Zhisheng, developed their classifications by embracing Fei Changfang's dynastic-periodical approach to the Tripitaka. This becomes evident when we look at their tables of contents. For instance, Daoxuan's *Inner Canon Catalog* divided the texts as follows:

1. Translations of Buddhist scriptures *throughout the successive dynasties* [author's emphasis].
2. Scriptures *throughout the successive dynasties* classified by number of fascicles and by whether the translator(s) were known or anonymous.
3. Scriptures *throughout the successive dynasties* that have been "entered into the canon."
4. Most important Buddhist scriptures *throughout the successive dynasties*.
5. Buddhist scriptures *throughout the successive dynasties* that are referred to in the catalogs but no longer extant.
6. Compilations and commentaries made by both clergy and laypeople *throughout the successive dynasties*.
7. Scriptures *throughout the successive dynasties* that appeared as a result of rearrangements [made to the original texts of the scriptures] through the process of their independent circulation.[84]
8. Suspicious and false sutras and *śastras* produced among the translations *throughout the successive dynasties*.
9. Catalogs of the scriptures *throughout the successive dynasties*, starting from the present and going back to the very beginning.
10. China's responses to the Buddhist teachings *throughout the successive dynasties*.

The term "throughout the successive dynasties," coined by Fei Changfang in order to express the Tripitaka's dependence on the rulers of Chinese dynasties, appears in the title of each division of Daoxuan's catalog. Apparently, Daoxuan accepted Fei Changfang's approach to the Tripitaka as a collection of texts whose legitimacy was approved by the successive rulers, rather than a collection of texts made by individual translators and approved by the sangha. This change in the criteria of canonization reflected the important ideological switch from deifying the arhat-like translators to deifying the ruler as the *chakravartin* and protector of the authenticity of the canon. From this perspective, it can be said that Daoxuan was more a follower of Fei Changfang than of Sengyou and Fajing.

Daoxuan also emulated Fei Changfang by canonizing scriptural catalogs and including them (in division 9) in the body of the Tripitaka. And in division 3, he imitated Fei by offering his own version of what can be referred to as the "practical canon," which both men called the "list [of scriptures] that can be entered into a collection" (*ru zang mu*).[85]

A significant point of difference between Daoxuan and Fei Changfang is that the former paid more attention to distinguishing and delineating various textual redactions of translations (the "Daoan-Sengyou approach"), while the latter considered this less important for the main part of his catalog. But Daoxuan went further than Fei in his effort to condense the number of core scriptures considered crucial for a regular practitioner, as seen in his division 4, which gives a list of texts "considered to be most important"—an even more compressed version of the Tripitaka than the *ru zang mu*. Another difference between these two catalogs is that while Fei's work heavily Buddhicized lives of Chinese rulers to indicate a complete merge of imperial and Buddhist ideologies, Daoxuan's noticeably toned down this approach—a politically motivated caution, given that some Tang emperors were not ardent Buddhists or were even anti-Buddhist. Nonetheless, one gets a strong sense of Daoxuan's longing for Fei Changfang's ways of looking at Chinese history because, in division 10, he describes various miraculous events that occurred in China in response to the spread of Buddhism. Thus, although he no longer dared to Buddhicize the most famous events of ancient Chinese history, he followed Fei by using the concepts of "gnomon and shadow" and "sound and echo" in describing how the Tripitaka spread in China and produced many miracles among its population.

The *Kaiyuan Catalog* is widely recognized as a hallmark of Buddhist bibliography, but not enough recognition is given to Zhisheng's predecessors, who helped him build this monumental description of the Tripitaka. This lack of understanding of how closely Zhisheng followed the path they had laid down is largely due to the fact that Zhisheng's original twenty-fascicle catalog is usually known to readers in its abridged, four-fascicle *Digest* form (no. 7 above). In the original catalog, he envisioned the structure of the Tripitaka as in table 4.2.

TABLE 4.2. CONTENT OF ZHISHENG'S *KAIYUAN CATALOG*

Fascicle	Content
1	Translations and compilations by both monks and laymen of Sutra, Vinaya, and Abhidharma, indicating old and new, whether anonymous or made by known translators, along with the biographies of the translators [whose scriptures were] produced during the Han Dynasty
2	same as fascicle 1, but for the Wu and [Western] Jin dynasties
3	same as fascicle 1, but for the Eastern Jin and Fu Qin 符秦 (351–94) dynasties
4	same as fascicle 1, but for the (Yao) Qin 姚秦 (384–417), Western Qin, Former Liang 前涼 (314–76), and Northern Liang 北涼 (398–439) dynasties
5	same as fascicle 1, but for the [Liu] Song Dynasty
6	same as fascicle 1, but for the Qi, Liang 梁, (Yuan) Wei (元) 魏 (471–534), and (Gao) Qi (高)齊 (550–77) dynasties
7	same as fascicle 1, but for the [Northern] Zhou, Chen, and Sui dynasties
8-9	same as fascicle 1, but for the Tang Dynasty
10	List of [all scriptural] catalogs written before the *Kaiyuan Catalog*
11-12	Extant translations of the Mahayana Sutra, Vinaya, and Abhidharma texts; dates of the translators' lives indicated
13	Extant translations of the Hinayana Sutra, Vinaya, and Abhidharma texts, as well as collections and biographies of the sages and worthy men; dates of the translators' lives indicated
14	Lost translations of the Mahayana Sutra, Vinaya, and Abhidharma texts
15	Lost translations of the Hinayana Sutra, Vinaya, and Abhidharma texts, as well as collections and biographies of the sages and worthy men
16	Separate parts of the Mahayana and Hinayana scriptures, as well as collections and biographies of the sages and worthy men, which became independent scriptures
17	Different kinds of redactions of the Mahayana and Hinayana scriptures
18	Suspicious and false scriptures
19	Entered into the canon collection (*ru zang*) of the Mahayana
20	Entered into the canon collection (*ru zang*) of the Hinayana

Clearly, Zhisheng utilized Fei Changfang's dynastic-periodical approach to the Tripitaka as the primary organizing principle, with all other types of taxonomic classification being secondary, used to subdivide the works in fascicles 1–7 already organized according to dynasties. The first time the "three baskets" principle is used as the main taxonomic rule is in fascicles 8–9, where translations made during the Tang Dynasty are described. And distinctions between the Mahayana and Hinayana canons are not made apparent until fascicles 11–17 and 19–20.

The contents of Zhisheng's fascicle 10 likewise pay tribute to Fei Changfang, as Zhisheng continued to describe and canonize scriptural catalogs that were written before his own. Fei Changfang's example apparently persuaded Zhisheng to adopt the idea of the canon register (*ru zang mu*), as can be seen from the contents of fascicles 19–20.[86] Comparing Zhisheng's, Fei Changfang's, and Daoxuan's versions of the *ru zang mu* helps us understand the important changes effected in the structure of the canon during the century or so before the advent of printed editions. We can bring together all the relevant data after reconciling the three catalogers' somewhat different ways of counting works.[87]

Table 4.3 compares the three catalogs' figures in the Sutra, Vinaya, and Abhidharma divisions for both the Mahayana and Hinayana parts of the canon.

First, it is easy to see that in Fei's catalog, the Hinayana texts outnumber the Mahayana texts: 603 to 511. This situation was reversed in the Tang; both Daoxuan and Zhisheng recorded more Mahayana than Hinayana texts. Daoxuan's ratio of 492 Mahayana texts versus 272 Hinayana ones is surpassed by Zhisheng's ratio of 638 Mahayana works to only 330 Hinayana ones.

Another trend in table 4.3 shows the growth of the Sutra-pitaka with time. The disproportion between the Sutra-pitaka and other types of canonical literature already existed in Fei Changfang's catalog in both the Mahayana part (11 Abhidharma, 31 Vinaya, and 469 Sutra texts) and the Hinayana part (31 Abhidharma, 70 Vinaya, and 502 Sutra texts). Although the reason is not clear, this

TABLE 4.3. COMPARISON OF FEI CHANGFANG, DAOXUAN, AND ZHISHENG CATALOGS

	Mahayana			Hinayana		
	Sutra	Vinaya	Abhidharma	Sutra	Vinaya	Abhidharma
Fei Changfang	469	31	11	502	70	31
Daoxuan	386	34	72	204	35	33
Zhisheng	515	26	97	240	54	36

pattern was broken by Daoxuan,[88] who actually reduced the number of scriptures in the Mahayana Sutra-pitaka to 386 and in the Hinayana Sutra-pitaka to 204. Daoxuan also increased the number of Mahayana Abhidharma texts to 72 and Vinaya texts to 34. Zhisheng, however, for the Mahayana part, reduced the number of Vinaya texts to 26, increased the number of the Abhidharma texts to 97, and made the largest increase in the Sutra-pitaka. He raised the overall number of the sutra texts to 515, the highest in all three catalogs.[89]

Statistical comparisons of this kind serve to prove the point made at the start of this chapter: catalogers often decided the fate of a particular text in the Tripitaka, and they also shaped the contents of each division of the canon. It is obvious that their collective efforts over time helped guide the evolution of the Chinese Buddhist canon. The figures presented above show that the literature of the Sutra-pitaka was so important to the Chinese catalogers that they lowered the status of the Vinaya-pitaka (which had been designated the first division of the canon during the First Buddhist Council in the sixth century B.C.E.) and made the Sutra-pitaka into a predominant class of literature in the canon. By the early decades of the eighth century, the disproportion between the sutra and vinaya literature was rendered so dramatic that, in the *ru zang mu* by Zhisheng, the Sutra-pitaka was nearly twenty times the size of the Vinaya-pitaka.

At the same time, the supreme importance of scriptures associated with the older forms of Buddhism (which Chinese catalogers referred to as Hinayana) was upheld by the catalogers of the Sui Dynasty: Fei Changfang counted 92 more scriptures in the Hinayana canon than in the Mahayana. But the Tang dynasty's catalogers already undermined the importance of the Hinayana texts rather seriously, for in Zhisheng's *ru zang mu*, there were nearly twice as many Mahayana texts as Hinayana.

CONCLUSION

Studying the *Records of the Three Treasures Throughout the Successive Dynasties* offers a unique perspective on early phases of the Chinese Buddhist canon's development. It becomes apparent that Fei Changfang modified the Daoan-Sengyou approach to the Tripitaka because he considered it too rigid in its treatment of the anonymous and so-called suspicious and false texts. According to Fei Changfang's new vision of the canon, the ruler of the dynasty was ultimately responsible for the truthfulness of the texts the canon included. In his view, it was no longer necessary for the Buddhist community to condemn those texts that were not condemned by the dynastic rulers. This approach resulted in Fei Changfang's restoring many texts that had been rendered nonauthentic by Daoan-Sengyou's measurements, making them a legitimate part of the canon.

The *Record of the Three Treasures Throughout Successive Dynasties* also provided the first historical account of all Buddhist catalogs ever written in China, thus contributing to the incorporation of scriptural catalogs themselves into the canon during the Tang era. The Buddhists' own tradition of bibliography became a crucial factor in elevating the social and cultural prestige of the Tripitaka, particularly because it filled the lacuna left by the Confucian historians unwilling to include information about the Buddhist canon in dynastic chronicles.

Fei Changfang's catalog also created a shift in the overall development of the Tripitaka by offering its practitioners a shortened version of the canon, called the canon registry (*ru zang mu*, lit. list of scriptures entered into a collection), which included only those texts that were in use by Chinese practitioners. This trend was further developed by Daoxuan and Zhisheng in the Tang Dynasty, eventually leading to the establishment of the parameters for the most essential contents of the canon, making it ready for reproduction by printing.

NOTES

The author wishes to express her heartfelt gratitude to Lucille Chia, Jiang Wu, Jinhua Chen, and Ling-ling Kuo for their invaluable assistance in preparing this essay.

1. Tokuno, "Catalogues of Scriptures," 116.

2. Quite a number of Buddhist scriptural catalogs were still written during the Southern Song, Yuan, Ming, and Qing dynasties (late twelfth through the early twentieth centuries); however, unlike earlier catalogs, they diminished in importance and served primarily as an auxiliary tool accompanying the printed editions. In other words, these later catalogs followed the contents of the printed canons rather than prescribed them. See also He Mei, *Lidai hanwen Dazangjing mulu xinkao*.

3. Forte, "The Relativity of the Concept of Orthodoxy in Chinese Buddhism," 240.

4. Zürcher, *The Buddhist Conquest of China*, 30.

5. Liu Xiang died before he finished his catalog, which was revised by his son, Liu Xin 劉歆 (?–23 C.E.), who renamed it *Seven Epitomes* (*Qi lue* 七略). In turn, this work was modified and incorporated into the *Han shu* 漢書 as the Bibliographic Treatise (*Yiwen zhi* 藝文志). On Liu Xiang's and Liu Xin's catalogs, see Hu Chusheng, *Zhongguo muluxue yanjiu*; and Wang Bijiang, *Muluxue yanjiu*.

6. This legend about Kāśyapa Mātanga bringing the *Sutra in Forty-Two Sections* to the court of Emperor Ming is best covered in Ch'en, *Buddhism in China*, 29–31.

7. *T* 2034, 49: 127b, and 76b. Fei Changfang referred to this work as *Catalog by Zhu Shixing* (*Zhu Shixing lu*) or as *Catalog of the Han [Dynasty's Translations] by Zhu Shixing* (*Zhu Shixing Han lu*).

8. See instances in *T* 2034, 49: 50a–b; 52c; and 53b–c.

9. More information is in *Catalog of the Inner Canon of the Great Tang Dynasty*. See *T* 2149, 55: 221a–24b.

10. *T* 2034, 49: 127c, and 63a–64b.

11. About Dharmarakṣa, see Boucher, "Dharmaraksha," and "Gandhari and the Early Chinese Buddhist Translations Reconsidered."

12. Huang Biji, "Fei Changfang *Lidai sanbao ji* yanjiu," 20; Men'shikov, *Rukopisnaia Kniga v Kulture Narodov Vostoka*, 176.

13. See Zacchetti's chapter in this volume.

14. See Chen Jinhua, "Some Aspects of the Buddhist Translation Procedure in Early Medieval China," 645.

15. *T* 2034, 49: 127c.

16. *T* 2034, 49: 64c.

17. Boucher described how the two worked together. See "Gandhari and the Early Chinese Buddhist Translations Reconsidered," 487.

18. *T* 2149, 55: 232b.

19. *T* 2034, 49: 74a.

20. *T* 2045, 55: 49 a–b; 58 b–c.

21. For a bibliography of studies on Daoan's catalog, see Storch, "Daoan"; Tokuno, "Catalogues of Scriptures," 116; and Zacchetti's chapter in this volume.

22. As Sengyou described it, "if the scripture had the name of the translator, [Daoan] put it in the first part of the [catalog]. If it was anonymous, he put it toward the end of the catalog." See *T* 2145, 55: 16c.

23. Ui Hakuju attempted a complete reconstruction of Daoan's catalog, based on Sengyou's quotations. See his *Shaku Dōan kenkyū*.

24. Another appropriate translation would be "Buddhist classic." He definitely did not use it to mean "sutra" as a distinctive class of Buddhist literature, as it became known in the later centuries. Corless was the first to point at this in "The Meaning of Ching (Sutra?) in Buddhist Chinese," 67–72. Fang Guangchang gives a detailed analysis of the meaning of *jing* during various stages of the canon's formation, agreeing that it had a different meaning during the earliest stages. See his *Zhongguo xieben Dazangjing yanjiu*, 2–4.

25. That is, anonymous translations that he considered to be contemporary (and not ancient) based on their language and style of translation.

26. *T* 2034, 49: 127c.

27. *T* 2149, 55: 336c.

28. Evidently, some of the texts collected were original manuscripts, but it could also have been misunderstanding on the part of Fei Changfang and Daoxuan, who reported this.

29. About this catalog, also see chapter 1 by Jiang Wu in this volume.

30. *T* 2034, 49: 125b–c.

31. For instance, the author of the *Subject Catalog* included texts on divination, which Sengyou rejected. Also, Sengyou counted significantly more suspicious and false texts than the author of the *Subject Catalog* did.

32. The actual dates of its compilation are still open to dispute. For the beginning of this dispute, see Naitō Ryūo, "*Shutsu sanzō kishu* senshu nenji nitsuite."

33. In Sengyou's catalog, he listed titles of nearly twenty texts ascribed to the monk Miaoguang, all of which were proclaimed false at a trial where Sengyou himself was a supreme judge. Afterward, all Miaoguang's writings were burned. See T 2145, 55: 40c.

34. For a summary of these studies in English, see Kyoko Tokuno, "Catalogues of Scriptures"; Jinhua Chen, "Some Aspects of the Buddhist Translation Procedure in Early Medieval China," 603–62; and Jan Nattier, *Guide to the Earliest Chinese Buddhist Translations,* 9–12.

35. T 2034, 49: 125c–26a.

36. The word "treatise" (*śastra* or *lun* 論) was added by later scholars, possibly Fei Changfang himself, so as to amend the lack of the Abhidharma division in Sengyou's original catalog. In the earliest editions of Sengyou's catalog, this first division does not have the word "*śastra*" in the title.

37. In the Taishō edition, a mistake is evident here, as the word *yi* (different) is replaced with *zhuan* 撰 (compile, put together).

38. Old translations, possibly considered to be different versions of the texts known by their contemporary translations.

39. When we compare this table of content with the one found in the *Collection of Records About the Translation of the Tripitaka,* we observe several differences. For instance, according to Fei Changfang's information, Sengyou had placed the vinaya texts right after the authored translations of the sutras, yet in the actual Sengyou catalog, the vinaya texts are much farther down in the textual hierarchy. It appears that Fei Changfang tried to "correct" Sengyou by giving the vinaya division a higher position than it originally had in Sengyou's catalog. There are other noteworthy differences, which cannot be discussed in this chapter but are discussed in my book *The History of Chinese Buddhist Bibliography.*

40. For discussion of this library, see Jinhua Chen, "Buddhist Establishments Within Liang Wudi's Imperial Park," 18–22.

41. It is difficult to know with certainty why Sengshao's catalog did not satisfy the emperor. One explanation is that the emperor sought to get away from Sengyou's rigid approach to the Tripitaka, but Sengshao was unable to bring in a new approach. Instead, he reduced Sengyou's catalog from fifteen to four fascicles and added new titles from the library kept in the imperial palace. Detailed analysis of Chinese sources on this Sengshao catalog is in Jinhua Chen, "Buddhist Establishments Within Liang Wudi's Imperial Park," 19.

42. Besides Fei Changfang, information about Baochang's catalog is found in the *Sui shu* 35: 1098, and Daoxuan's *Xu Gaoseng zhuan* 續高僧傳 (*Continuation of the*

Biographies of Eminent Monks, T 2060, 50: 426c). According to the *Sui shu*, the emperor's library contained 5,400 fascicles of Buddhist literature, several hundred fascicles more than the number in Sengyou's catalog.

43. On Sengfa, see Campany, "Notes on the Devotional Uses and Symbolic Functions of Sutra Texts," 44–46.

44. T 2034, 49: 126a.

45. Fashang, Chief Buddhist Controller, was also responsible for selecting sutras to be carved in stone near Capital Ye 鄴 in southern Hebei (and some are still preserved at the nearby Xiangtangshan 響堂山 caves). This underscores the fact that, during the Northern and Southern Dynasties, the Tripitaka was slowly becoming an object of imperial pride and imperial control. For more on this, see Tsiang, "Monumentalization of Buddhist Texts in the Northern Qi Dynasty."

46. For the period from the beginning of the Eastern Jin to the end of the Tang, only one dynastic history included information about the Tripitaka—*History of the Sui Dynasty* (*Sui shu* 隨書). Its author, Zhangsun Wuji 長孫無忌 (594?–659), gave an account of the Tripitaka after all books in the *"sibu"* 四部 classification were listed. Buddhist catalogs, however, are found in the *"Shi"* 史 (History) and *"Zi"* 子 (Philosophers) divisions of this catalog. Some bibliographies not in the dynastic histories, such as *Seven Registers* (*Qi zhi* 七志, 473) by Wang Jian 王儉 (452–89), did include information about the Tripitaka scriptures.

47. T 2034, 49: 107c. Translation from Wright, *Buddhism in Chinese History*, 67.

48. For the first two catalogs, see T 2146 and 2147. Note that, in both cases, the titles have been reduced to just four characters. Zhiguo's catalog appears to be lost, but a portion of it is reproduced by Zhangsun Wuji in the book catalog written for the *Sui shu*, 1094–95.

49. Both Fajing's and Yancong's catalogs originally included the name of the dynasty in their titles, indicating their official imperial status. Beginning in the Northern and Southern Dynasties period (420–589), there were two different trends in catalog writing—one coming from the sangha and the other from the state. In my book *History of Chinese Buddhist Bibliography*, I provide a detailed analysis of these trends. Here, I will just cite Bunyiu Nanjio (Nanjō Bun'yū 南條文雄), the first scholar to mark catalogs "made by a Sovereign of China" (*A Catalogue of the Chinese Translation*, XVII–XXIII) as opposed to other types of catalogs.

50. This is reported in *Kaiyuan Catalog*, *Zhenyuan xinding shijiao mulu* 貞元新定釋教目錄 (see below), and Zhipan's 志磐 *Fozu tongji* 佛祖統紀 (1269; T 2035.49.1291–475c), among other sources. See a comparative chart of these sources in Huang Biji's "Fei Changfang *Lidai sanbao ji* yanjiu," 8–9.

51. Quoted from Jinhua Chen, "Śarīra and Scepter," 123.

52. According to the *Kaiyuan shijiao lu*, *Zhenyuan xinding shijiao mulu*, and *Fozu tongji*, his title was *fanjing xueshi*. In the Taishō edition, one more character (*chen* 臣) was added by mistake.

53. It was suggested by Yamazaki Hiroshi that the *Records of Three Treasures* was compiled mainly on the basis of the collection stored at Da Xingshan Temple 大興善寺. See his line of argumentation in *Zui Tō no Bukkyō shi no kenkyū*, 66–89. However, it seems that Fei Changfang used multiple sources and did not confine his account to one particular collection.

54. *Sui shu*, vol. 4, 1094–95.

55. Fei Changfang discriminated between the anonymous and authored translations, and between scriptures available in one or many translations, only in the *ru zang mu*. See my analysis of this part of his catalog later in this chapter.

56. See Fang Guangchang, "Defining the Chinese Buddhist Canon," for a discussion of connections between the early *panjiao* systems and the classifications of scriptures adopted in the Liu Song Dynasty catalog, *Zhongjing Bielu* 眾經別錄. Connections between the *panjiao* and scriptural classifications used in other Tripitaka catalogs are still awaiting proper investigation. Two recent monographs on the *panjiao*—Chanju Mun's *The History of Doctrinal Classification in Chinese Buddhism* and Petzold's *The Classification of Buddhism: Comprising the Classification of Buddhist Doctrines in India, China, and Japan*—do not discuss this subject.

57. See the "After the Buddha's Nirvana" part of his catalog in table 4.1.

58. This was one of several reasons a new catalog of the Tripitaka was ordered by Emperor Wen. Its author, Yancong, lowered the status of indigenous literature and made it comparable to Fajing's textual classification.

59. Daoan condemned 26 texts and Fajing, 197.

60. We find it in the "Philosophers" (*zi*) section in the "Jingji zhi" 經籍志, in the Taishō edition, vol. 49, where genealogies of Buddhist schools and their patriarchs are also collected.

61. In fascicle 7, Fajing told a story about Emperor Wu 武帝 (r. 140–87 B.C.E.) of the Former Han Dynasty and the court astrologer, Dongfang Shuo 東方朔 (154–93 B.C.E.), meant to assert that Buddhism existed in China from the beginning of its history. Fajing also wrote a story about Liu Xiang examining Buddhist scriptures during Emperor Cheng's 成帝 (r. 32–7 B.C.E.) reign. (Fajing erred, because it was actually Emperor Ai 哀帝 [r. 6–1 B.C.E.] who gave this order.) Several other stories in this fascicle are clearly meant to provide an account in which Buddhist events and Chinese political events were connected.

62. Origen of Alexandria is known widely for his use of allegorical interpretation, which developed sets of correspondences between the Hebrew Bible and the New Testament; he believed that the events described in the Hebrew Bible had occurred in order to prefigure events in the life of Jesus Christ. Apparently, Fei Changfang employed a similar technique in writing about correspondences between the events of Chinese history, recorded in traditional sources, and Buddhist events, recorded in Buddhist texts. On Origen's method of scriptural allegorism, see Heine, *Origen: Scholarship in the Service of the Church*.

63. For more on this concept, see Henderson, *Development and Decline of Chinese Cosmology*, 22–28.

64. *T* 2034, 49: 23a.

65. *T* 2034, 49: 23c.

66. Forte comments on this trend in *A Jewel in Indra's Net*, 57–58; Jinhua Chen also notes this change in the nature of dates provided in the Tang Dynasty's catalogs in "Some Aspects of the Buddhist Translation," 648.

67. These are the two catalogs produced in the Lushan community according to the instructions from the monk Huiyuan, discussed earlier in this chapter.

68. A catalog of the Northern Wei Dynasty, also discussed earlier in this chapter.

69. See, for example, Tan Shibao, *Han-Tang foshi tanzhen*, and Hayashiya Tomojirō, *Kyōroku Kenkyū*.

70. See Jinhua Chen, "Śarīra and Scepter," 117–23.

71. This monumental bibliographic work that counted the largest number of Buddhist texts ever known in China had the title *Corrected and Authorized Catalog of Scriptures of the Great Zhou Dynasty*; it will be discussed in the following part of this chapter.

72. See Weinstein, *Buddhism Under the T'ang*; and Wright, "T'ang T'ai-tsung and Buddhism."

73. See Storch, "Law and Religious Freedom in Medieval China."

74. See Jiang Wu's chapter 1 in this volume.

75. While the review offered here is very brief, more detailed accounts of the Tang Dynasty's catalogs can be found in Liang Qichao, "Fojia jinglu zai zhongguo muluxueshang zhi weizhi;" Yao Mingda, *Zhongguo mulu xueshi*; Hayashiya Tomojirō, *Kyōroku kenkyū*; Kuraishi Takeshiro, *Mokuroku gaku*; Hu Chusheng, *Zhongguo muluxue yanjiu*; Lu Shaoyu, *Zhongguo muluxue shiqiao*; and Fang Guangchang, *Zhongguo xieben Dazangjing yanjiu*.

76. In fascicle 10 of his catalog, Zhisheng described all bibliographic works written before his, including this one, which he states was based on the Sui Dynasty catalog of Yancong.

77. Xuanzang was a renowned Chinese pilgrim to India and one of the most prolific translators of the Tang Dynasty. For a bibliography of studies about him, see Mayer, "Xuanzang," 910.

78. The specific date of its compilation is unknown; it must be during Gaozong's reign (650–683). So far, no one has found these portraits of the translators painted in Da Ci'en Monastery.

79. As for Empress Wu, her rule (684–704) could be considered an interruption of the Tang Dynasty, especially with her announcement of a new dynasty in 690—the Zhou. In the Confucian world, women were not allowed to become rulers, but Empress Wu found ideological justification for her enthronement in Dharmakṣema's translation of the *Great Cloud Sutra*, which predicted that a female divinity who reached

enlightenment would be reborn as ruler of the entire human world. Understandably, because of Empress Wu's support, Buddhism flourished under her rule more than under Tang rulers before and after her. On the political uses of Buddhism by Empress Wu, see Forte, *Political Propaganda and Ideology in China*, especially 153–68 for the bodhisattva prophecy, and Jinhua Chen's "Śarīra and Scepter," 123–25, for the quote from the *Great Cloud Sutra*.

80. A few scholars who commented on Empress Wu's catalog believe this was a result of forgeries admitted, yet no comprehensive study has being conducted to demonstrate what exactly was added to the Tripitaka to make it larger than any other collection of Buddhist manuscripts.

81. See Jiang Wu's chapter 1 in this volume for a detailed table of contents of this catalog and comments on its quality. For a complete study of Zhisheng's contribution to the formation of the Chinese Tripitaka, see Fang Guangchang, *Zhongguo xieben Dazangjing*, 39–71.

82. There is a general misunderstanding about the structure of Zhisheng's original twenty-fascicle-long catalog because of this digest catalog, which is not a condensed version, as widely believed. In the original *Kaiyuan Catalog*, the differences between the Hinayana and Mahayana canons are recognized only in the last ten fascicles of the work, where Zhisheng accounted for the extant scriptures. In the first ten fascicles, he actually followed Fei Changfang's dynastic-periodical principle and did not divide scriptures according to their Mahayana or Hinayana teachings. Similarly, in the original catalog, the contents of the Sutra-, Vinaya-, and Abhidharma-pitaka are not outlined until fascicles 8–9, where Zhisheng listed translations made during the Tang Dynasty. Zhisheng's original catalog is examined below.

83. T 2061, 50: 804b.

84. This particular taxonomic category, *zhiliu chenhua* 支流陳化, is rather loosely defined by Daoxuan and difficult to translate. In a nutshell, in division 7, he collected various pieces that Chinese Buddhists took out of the translations and adapted for various religious uses. These included various chants, gathas, and other relatively small parts, used separately in rituals and for magic protection. Some texts were modified for the specific purposes for which they were used. Daoxuan himself admitted it was difficult to describe the type of texts this group represented, but felt strongly they must be cataloged. In the attention he paid to this literature, he was similar to Baochang, who also compiled separate lists of magical formulas and prayers to the Buddhist deities. In a sense, this collection by Daoxuan is comparable to a book of hymns and verses found in the pews in a Christian church, although it cannot be called a Buddhist hymnal in the full sense of this term.

85. See below for detailed comparison of Fei Changfang's, Daoxuan's, and Zhisheng's *ru zang mu*.

86. For a detailed study of Zhisheng's *ru zang mu*, see Fang Guangchang, *Zhongguo xieben dazangjing yanjiu*, 547–640, where he provides a list of its entire contents.

87. For example, Fei separates his figures of scriptures that were anonymous from those by known authors, but Zhisheng and Daoxuan put both kinds together in their *ru zang mu*. The latter two men indicated these texts' authored or anonymous status by providing individual commentaries written underneath the title of each text. Also, Fei, by reclassifying many anonymous works in the *ru zang mu*, "rehabilitated" them, i.e., rescued them from being condemned as false or suspicious works by earlier catalogers. Specifically, in the Mahayana division, Fei included 234 authored vs. 235 anonymous sutra texts; in the vinaya, 19 authored vs. 12 anonymous; and in the Abhidharma, 5 authored vs. 6 anonymous works.

Fei, Zhisheng, and Daoxuan also counted fascicles and cases differently. Fei noted the number of texts and fascicles in each division of the Tripitaka that he included in his *ru zang mu*, but not the number of cases used for storing these texts. In contrast, Daoxuan and Zhisheng both counted the number of cases used for storing the actual manuscripts. Daoxuan was inconsistent in his count of cases, but Zhisheng seems to have provided these numbers for nearly all scriptures included in the *ru zang mu*.

88. One explanation is that he was the Vinaya Master; the head of the Vinaya School.

89. In his *ru zang mu*, he also gave a separate list of compilations made by foreign and Chinese Buddhist writers; it included 68 foreign and 40 Chinese texts.

PART III

The Advent of Printing

5. *The Birth of the First Printed Canon*

THE KAIBAO EDITION AND ITS IMPACT

Jiang Wu, Lucille Chia, and Chen Zhichao

In the fourth year of the Kaibao 開寶 reign (971), Emperor Taizu (r. 960–975) of the Song Dynasty 宋太祖 ordered the first carving of a set of woodblocks for the Chinese Buddhist canon. Thus this edition is referred to as *Kaibao Canon*, or the Shu (i.e., Sichuan) edition (*Shuban* 蜀版)—since it was collated and the blocks were carved in Sichuan. In 1127, Kaifeng, the Northern Song capital, was sacked by the invading Jurchens, who abducted the two emperors and carted off many treasures. The imperial libraries were looted and many of their books and woodblocks taken north. One of the greatest prizes was the over 130,000 blocks of *Kaibao Canon*, which were subsequently lost.[1] In the century and a half during which the original canon and its supplements were compiled and printed, copies had been bestowed on monasteries throughout China and on envoys from other Asian states, such as Goryeo, the Khitan Liao and Tangut Xi Xia empires, Japan, and Annam (now Vietnam). This inspired both private groups in China and the rulers of Goryeo and the Liao to produce their own editions of the Chinese Buddhist canon, which were by no means replicas of *Kaibao Canon*. Indeed, among the "text lineages" of the Chinese Buddhist canon, *Kaibao Canon* represents the "Central Plain lineage," as distinguished from the "Northern lineage" epitomized by *Khitan Canon* and the "Southern lineage" including various editions derived from *Kaibao Canon*, such as

Chongning Canon 崇寧藏 and *Qisha Canon* 磧砂藏, carved in the Song and Yuan dynasties.[2]

Today, *Kaibao Canon* is represented by extant single copies of only about a dozen fascicles, mostly from different works.[3] Its fame and influence, however, continued long after its woodblocks had disappeared and its printed copies became increasingly rare. And the combined length of studies on *Kaibao Canon* since its creation may now be approaching that of the work itself. Most thorough have been the examinations by East Asian scholars.[4] In the West, scholars of the twentieth century, such as Paul Demiéville, L. C. Goodrich, and Kenneth Ch'en, noted the importance of the canon. In addition, the illustrations of some remaining scrolls were intensively studied by art historians such as Max Loehr.[5]

In this chapter, we focus not only on textual analysis of *Kaibao Canon* but also on the history of its creation against the background of the rise of print culture in China during the ninth and tenth centuries, and on its influence on the subsequent printed editions of the canon, especially those produced from the tenth through thirteenth centuries in East Asia. We reveal that the newly founded Song state was eager to define a new policy toward Buddhism after the persecution in the Later Zhou Dynasty, and the creation of *Kaibao Canon* was instrumental in shaping this new policy. Moreover, the creation of the canon helped to reestablish the link with China's cultural past and had been employed as a diplomatic tool to show the Song's state's cultural superiority over her neighbors.

EARLY SONG RELIGIOUS POLICIES AND THE RISE OF THE SICHUAN AREA AS A PRINTING CENTER

BUDDHIST POLICIES IN THE EARLY SONG DYNASTY

In the history of Chinese Buddhism, the last of the four major persecutions, which occurred under Emperor Shizong (r. 954–958) in the Later Zhou Dynasty 後周世宗, less than two decades preceding the carving of *Kaibao Canon*, exerted an important impact on the production of this work. The histories record that in 955, Shizong ordered the closing of some 30,336 monasteries, leaving open only 2,694,[6] which must have resulted in the loss or scattering of Buddhist works from the monastic libraries. Although historical sources do not mention any particular government action to destroy Buddhist canons in manuscript form, it is possible that these were also damaged or destroyed.

Upon seizing power from the Later Zhou in a coup shortly after Shizong's death and establishing the new Song Dynasty, the first emperor, Taizu, quickly publicized his somewhat ambivalent policy toward Buddhism and Buddhist institutions.[7] In order to strengthen his rule and stabilize the society, Taizu needed Buddhism to "assist governance and promulgate morality" (*zhushi quanshan* 助世勸善). However, while promoting Buddhism, Taizu and the other early Song emperors also took measures to restrain Buddhism (and Daoism) by imposing state control over religious institutions.[8] In the sixth month of 960, the first year of the new dynasty, he declared: "Keep intact all the local temples that were not closed down in the second year of the Xiande 顯德 period [of the Later Zhou, 955]." His decree of 967 repealed Shizong's order to destroy bronze Buddhist statues but also forbade casting new ones.[9] In 966, Taizu also officially sent a group of 157 monks under the leadership of the monk Xingqin 行勤 to India to collect texts for translation.[10] Subsequently, Indian monks, some of whom came from the renowned Nālandā University, were brought to the capital, Kaifeng, in 971, 973, and 980.[11] The translation work under the auspices of the state will be discussed below, in connection with *Kaibao Canon*; of all the measures that Taizu and his successors took in defining the Song state's relationship with Buddhism, this was the most ambitious.

Thus, Song Taizu, although later mythologized as a Confucian ruler, was also deeply involved in Buddhism personally and even identified himself as a "Wheel-turning Monarch" (*chakravartin*, Ch. *zhuanlunwang* 轉輪王).[12] He copied the *Diamond Sutra* by himself and chanted it, and summoned monks to lecture on the sutras. During his reign, state examinations were reinstated as a requirement for the ordination of monks. In 967, Taizu decreed that Buddhist monks had priority in court ranking. He and his brother and successor, Taizong 太宗, also patronized the cult of the Tang sage Sengjia 僧伽, called the Great Sage of Sizhou (Sizhou Dasheng 泗州大聖), and greatly promoted its popularity in the Song.[13]

THE EARLY SONG STATE'S EMPHASIS ON WEN

Rulers establishing a new dynasty in imperial China often felt obliged to demonstrate the legitimacy of their new state; this nearly always involved linking it to older dynasties through championing and continuing the traditions of high culture. The first Song emperors were no exception. As Albert Welter points out, the early Song emperors consistently "championed *wen* (the literary/civil) over *wu* (martial prowess) as the defining feature of their mandate, reviving the model of the *wen* official who implements policy on the basis of knowledge and moral character in preference to that of the military warlord who governs by virtue of sheer force of arms."[14]

The Song state's activities in the promotion of *wen* ranged from restocking the greatly diminished holdings of the imperial libraries to sponsoring numerous literary and scholastic compilation and publishing projects, including the "Four Great Works of the Song"[15] (see below), as well as the Confucian Classics and commentaries and lexicographical works, medical texts, and Daoist works. While most of these projects began or were completed under the second emperor, Taizong, the largest one, *Kaibao Canon*, preceded nearly all the others and was inaugurated by the first emperor. We can argue that the urgency with which *Kaibao Canon* was begun had to do at least as much, or more, with political and diplomatic motives as with religious or cultural ones.[16] Thus, although Taizu had initiated the acquisition of Buddhist texts from India, he did not wait for these works to be translated into Chinese before starting the compilation and woodblock carving of *Kaibao Canon*. Nor did he wait until the surrender of southern states like the Southern Tang (976) and Wu-Yue (978), whose wealth of Buddhist texts, especially of the growing Chinese Tiantai 天台 and Chan 禪 schools, became available. Many of the works not included in the first printing of this canon were incorporated into the later versions, so Taizu's intention in rushing the canon into print was to claim not so much the state's authority to determine the texts included but rather the state's authority to issue the physical canon and use it as a political and diplomatic tool.

Taizu's successor, Taizong, a "bibliomaniac," as John Haeger called him,[17] and an even greater enthusiast of Buddhism, further promoted the translation activities. Shortly before the blocks of *Kaibao Canon* arrived at the capital, he set up a new institution, Institute of Scripture Translation (Yijingyuan 譯經院), in 980 at Taiping Xingguo Monastery 太平興國寺 to house foreign monks such as Tianxizai 天息災 (later renamed by Taizong as Faxian 法賢 or Dharmabhadra, ?–1000), Shihu 施護 (Dānapāla, fl. 970s) and Fahu 法護 (Dharmarakṣa, 963–1058, not to be confused with an early translator with the same name) and allowed them to manage translation projects.[18] An additional building was set up west of the institute to house the blocks of *Kaibao Canon*, which had been transported from Sichuan. The entire facility, together with the printing office (Yinjingyuan 印經院) for *Kaibao Canon*, was then renamed Institute of Dharma Propagation (Chuanfayuan 傳法院).[19] This office was in charge of printing until the blocks were moved to Xiansheng Monastery 顯聖寺 in 1071. The activities of the Institute of Scripture Translation apparently ended in 1082, due to lack of funding, qualified Indian translators, and scriptures in Indian and Central Asian languages, and to the opposition of Confucian officials, who objected to the expenses incurred.[20]

The history of the institute was closely intertwined with that of *Kaibao Canon*, since almost all the Northern Song translations of Buddhist works incorporated into the canon supplements were produced there. Indeed, even toward the end of its existence, the institute was active in revising *Kaibao Canon* in 1069–78.[21] Once editorial work ceased, the driving force for the institute was lost.

According to Huang Chi-chiang's study,[22] Taizong's patronage of *Kaibao Canon* was motivated by both his personal interest in Buddhism and his intention to show himself a capable ruler. In 983, when the canon was finished, Taizong had just been defeated in a war with the Khitans and was eager to recover his image as a supreme sovereign. One of his strategies was to sponsor large-scale literary projects. Only the first of these works was promptly printed after its compilation. Among the imperially sponsored literary compilations were the "Four Great Works of the Song"—*Extensive Records of the Taiping Reign (Taiping guangji* 太平廣記), *Collections Read by the Emperor During the Taiping Reign (Taiping yulan* 太平御覽), both begun in 977, and *Best Essay Collections from the Literary World (Wenyuan yinghua* 文苑英華), begun in 982. The fourth work, *Outstanding Models from the Storehouse of Literature (Cefu yuangui* 冊府元龜), was compiled starting in 1005 under the third Song emperor, Zhenzong 真宗 (r. 998–1022). Taizong declared that his purpose for sponsoring such projects was to "spread civilization throughout the empire," and personally demonstrated his serious commitment by activities such as reading three *juans* of *Taiping yulan* daily for a year until he finished it, thus giving it its final title. Upon being admonished by his officials for spending too much time on the project, he claimed, "My nature is to delight in reading. . . . This work consists of one thousand chapters and I desire to complete it in one year."[23]

In light of Taizong's strategic use of these cultural enterprises, religious texts fitted his agenda perfectly. His motive for supporting the Buddhist translation projects and the continuing compilation of *Kaibao Canon* and its supplements, as he proclaimed, was to promote Buddhist teachings. Upon the completion of the first batch of translations in 983, he wrote:

I have made a modest investigation of this teaching and have come up with this view: he who rules as a monarch is standing in the Buddha's shoes. Should he do one good thing, all under heaven would benefit [from his act]. This is what Buddhists call "benefiting others." . . . A ruler should nurture myriads of things, like innocent children, indiscriminately, putting each in the place it deserves. Shouldn't this be a way of practicing Buddhism? Buddhist words, although they are beyond the pale of this world, have points worth contemplating. Try reading these [translations] just for the sake of preserving [the Buddha's] teaching, rather than being captivated by it.[24]

He also declared contentedly:

Recently, both domestic and foreign affairs have been under steady control; officials near and far, in the capital and in remote districts, have been standing in awe of me. When my thought stops here, I am quite thrilled. Doing good things every day so people can benefit from [our work] is a way of participating in Buddhism.[25]

Taizong, seeing himself as an "emperor of letters," even composed Buddhist poems and commentaries that were included in *Kaibao Canon*. He wrote *Expounding the Secret Treasure Store* (*Mizangquan* 秘藏詮) in 983, and *Conditions and Perceptions* (*Yuanshi* 緣識) and *Verses in Praise of Happy Excursions* (*Xiaoyaoyong* 逍遥詠), all of which, together with commentaries by eminent monks in the capital, were incorporated into *Kaibao Canon* in 996.[26] In 1013, Buddhist essays written by Taizu and Taizong were included in the canon. Taizong also wrote *Collection of Marvelous Enlightenment* (*Miaojue ji* 妙覺集), which was added in 1015. Both Emperor Zhenzong 真宗 and Emperor Renzong 仁宗 (r. 1023–1063) continued to patronize Buddhism by writing prefaces to new translations, despite a short period of suppression of Buddhism during Zhenzong's reign.[27] Zhenzong also commented on *Sutra of Forty-two Chapters* (*Sishi erzhang jing* 四十二章經) and *Sutra of Buddha's Remaining Teaching* (*Yijiaojing* 遺教經), and even compiled a collection of phonetic notes of Buddhist scriptures, *Collection of Pronunciations in Buddhist Scriptures* (*Shidian fayin ji* 釋典法音集), which amounted to thirty fascicles after it was supplemented by monks. These works were included in the canon in 1019 and 1020. In 1037, Emperor Renzong wrote a preface for *Catalog of Dharma Treasure Newly Compiled During the Jingyou Reign* (*Jingyou xinxiu fabao mulu* 景祐新修法寶目錄), a catalog for the new translations completed during the Jingyou reign.

To support these Buddhist projects, the Song emperors asked for participation by their high officials, also known as accomplished literati. They were appointed "Officials of Translation and Embellishment" (*yijing runwen guan* 譯經潤文官)[28] to supervise the translation projects and compile new catalogs for *Kaibao Canon*.

SICHUAN AS A PRINTING CENTER

Kaibao Canon was carved in Sichuan, which had formed a unique regional culture since early imperial times. When the carving was ordered in 971, the Song court apparently deemed prominent printing centers such as Hangzhou and Fuzhou in the Wu-Yue kingdom not to be good choices for political reasons. Although Wu-Yue would not be subjugated until 978, it had since its founding in 907 followed a diplomatic policy of submitting as a vassal to the rulers of the Five Dynasties in north China, and it continued to do so with the Song. Thus its last ruler, Qian Chu 錢俶 (929–988), a devout Buddhist, would probably have welcomed such an important project as the compilation and printing of the canon if Song Taizu had chosen Hangzhou for this work.[29] Moreover, the religious convictions of the Wu-Yue rulers meant that they fully embraced the notion of making theirs a Buddhist state proclaimed through religious and cultural projects that would make it distinctive among the Ten Kingdoms. Along with the rival state of Southern Tang, Wu-Yue had preserved much more of Chinese written culture, including Buddhist works, than the north central part of China in the tumultuous period of the late Tang and Five Dynasties. Wu-Yue was also the home of the Tiantai school and had numerous economic, diplomatic, and religious ties with other regions of East Asia, including Goryeo and Japan.[30] Thus, from a production point of view, Hangzhou had much to offer, but the Song state would have had to relinquish control of the project, thereby defeating one of the chief reasons for the production of the canon. Indeed, it is possible that if the Song had not succeeded in reuniting the country or done so a few decades later than 960, the Wu-Yue court might have been the first to sponsor the compilation and printing of the Chinese Buddhist canon.[31]

Nor did Song Taizu choose to have the woodblocks for *Kaibao Canon* carved in the capital, Kaifeng 開封, or Luoyang 洛陽, although these were also important book centers in tenth-century China. It is likely that the recent persecution of Emperor Shizong of the Later Zhou Dynasty was the culmination of decades of destruction of many Buddhist works in north central China that had begun in the turmoil of the late Tang, so that the task of compiling texts for a new canon would have been more difficult than in other areas of the empire.

One other area that seems to have preserved enough Buddhist texts, on paper or on stone (carved on Fangshan 房山),[32] was around modern Beijing and controlled by the Khitan Liao Empire, whose rulers had been receiving copies of Buddhist scriptures from the Tang court that had been preserved, in contrast to those destroyed in north central China. Again for political reasons, the Song state could not consider this region for the carving of its new canon, although once completed, it would be bestowed on the Khitan court and inspire the latter to compile their own edition, as mentioned above.

For these reasons, Song Taizu may have decided to have the new canon's woodblocks carved in Chengdu 成都, the capital of Sichuan, whose ruler, the second and last ruler of the Later Shu 後蜀, Meng Chang 孟昶, surrendered to Taizu after a long and relatively peaceful reign (934–65). The conquest of Sichuan, a major state among the Ten Kingdoms, was significant for the newly founded Song regime and marked Taizu's transformation from a regional warlord to an emperor. For Taizu to order the collation and the block carving for a new canon done in Chengdu may have been intended as a gesture of reconciliation to the area after putting down a rebellion as well as a mutiny by Song troops that cost some 87,000 lives.[33] Exactly how the carving of *Kaibao Canon* in Sichuan fitted into Taizu's agenda to unify his empire is unclear, but the choice

of Chengdu as the carving center made sense, given the region's history of printing for over two centuries.

The facts about the early Sichuan printing industry have been recounted in
various secondary works, so we will only mention briefly some of the evidence.[34]
One of the earliest prints is a charm, dated to 757, of a six-armed bodhisattva surrounded by Sanskrit words in the Lantsa script, which was discovered
in 1944 in a Tang tomb in Chengdu. From the ninth century, we have more
examples of Sichuan printing, such as the fragment of a calendar for 882, also
from Chengdu, that was discovered in Dunhuang.[35]

The lively Chengdu printing industry in the ninth century is suggested by
various pieces of anecdotal evidence. In 835, Feng Su 馮宿 (767–836), a military
commissioner in Sichuan, memorialized that privately printed calendars were
being sold even before the official one issued by the government's Astronomy
Bureau, and that this was to be prohibited. In the same year, Emperor Wenzong 文宗 of the Tang decreed that the provincial authorities should forbid the
carving of woodblocks for such works. Nearly fifty years later, in 883, again in
Sichuan, another Tang official, Liu Pian 柳玭, reported seeing poorly block-
printed character books, divination works, and other imprints for sale.[36]

Indeed, in the waning years of the Tang Dynasty, when the emperor Xizong
僖宗 (r. 873–88) fled to Chengdu from Chang'an and the Huang Chao 黃巢 rebellion, many of his officials went with him, and the court's presence in Sichuan
further stimulated the printing industry there, an influence that continued when
the region became independent in the early tenth century. One well-known
work was by the court Daoist, Du Guangting 杜光庭 (850–933), who in 913 had
printed his *Guangsheng yi* 廣聖義, a subcommentary on the commentary of
Tang Xuanzong 玄宗 (r. 712–756) on the *Daodejing*, with financial support from
a court official and favorable remarks from the first ruler of the Former Shu—a
significant change in official attitude from the irritation expressed by earlier
Tang officials. Ten years later, a posthumous collection of verses by an eminent
Buddhist monk, Guanxiu 貫休 (823–913), was also printed in Chengdu.[37]

The most important development in the early printing history of Sichuan
was the publication of the "Nine Classics" 九經. During the early imperial period, carefully collated copies of Chinese Confucian Classics were carved in
stone slabs as early as 175 and could be copied for studying. Of course, it was far
more convenient for the reader to have their own paper copy; these, however,
were manuscripts until the first printings of the classics in the tenth century,
which occurred as two different projects, one in Kaifeng and one in Sichuan.
In addition to the printing of the nine Confucian Classics initiated by the Later
Tang ministers, Feng Dao (882–954) 馮道 and Li Yu 李愚 (d. 935), in Kaifeng
from 932 to 953, Wu Zhaoyi 毋昭裔 (d. 967), minister under the Later Shu in
Chengdu, supervised not only the carving of the woodblocks for a set of the

Confucian Classics but also a stone inscription of these works.[38] The Song historian Sima Guang 司馬光 (1019–1086) considered this event, along with Wu Zhaoyi's huge private donation to build schools, as the causes of the "Literature Revival" in the Sichuan area.[39] Wu certainly enlisted a large number of skilled carvers and private print shops for this project, the scale of which showed that the Sichuan printing industry was technologically ready to produce an even larger work like *Kaibao Canon*.

The existing scrolls of *Kaibao Canon* adopted a new printed format with 14 or 15 characters per column and 23 columns per sheet, making it appear more spacious than the standard manuscript format of 17 characters per column and 28 columns per sheet, as was popular for Buddhist manuscripts from the Tang and is seen in many Dunhuang texts. Obviously, the *Kaibao Canon* format had been influenced by the large-character editions (*daziben* 大字本) produced in Sichuan, which usually had 16 characters per column. The calligraphic style also matches those Sichuan works: the layout is clear and loose, and characters are slightly slim with sharp turns and long and strong brushstrokes.[40] In addition, scholars have suggested that the deluxe handwritten copies in gold and silver ink ordered to be produced in Sichuan by Song Taizu just before the start of the Kaibao project may have had the same format.[41]

THE BIRTH OF *KAIBAO CANON*

THE CREATION OF KAIBAO CANON *IN CHENGDU*

Despite the importance of *Kaibao Canon*, Song official records and the Song dynastic history contain no references to its creation in Chengdu. Several Buddhist works compiled in the Song and Yuan, however, provide information on this history. According to these sources, the compilation of and then the carving of the woodblocks for *Kaibao Canon* were ordered shortly after the Song conquered Sichuan.

The earliest known record is a passing reference in *Records of Northern Mountain* (*Beishan lu* 北山錄) by the Tang scholar-monk Shenqing 神清 (?–820), which was annotated and printed in 1068, according to its preface. The reference to *Kaibao Canon* was made in chapter 16 by the work's annotator, a Sichuan monk named Huibao 慧寶 (d.u.):

> Recently the emperor of the Great Song has produced several canons made of gold and silver ink [*jin yin zi* 金銀字], and carved over 130,000 woodblocks of the canon in order to enhance and glorify the monasteries in the empire.[42]

As Chen Yuan has already pointed out, Huibao must have been living in the early Song,[43] and this brief note, the chronologically closest to the *Kaibao Canon* project, reveals significant information about its carving in Sichuan.

All other references to the carving of the canon are found in much later works. Among them, three are often quoted, and each provides one or two more scraps of information not in the Huibao annotation.[44] For example, Tiantai monk Zhipan's 志盤 *Annalist Records of Buddhas and Patriarchs* (*Fozu tongji* 佛祖統記), compiled in 1269, mentions the name of a eunuch official who supervised the carving and that the blocks were delivered to Kaifeng in 983.[45] Another source, found in Nianchang's 念常 *Comprehensive Chronicle of Buddhist Patriarchs* (*Fozu lidai tongzai* 佛祖歷代通載), compiled in 1341, connects the order to carve *Kaibao Canon* with the writing of Buddhist sutras in gold and silver characters.[46] Yet another record comes from monk Jue'an's 覺岸 (1286–?) *Outline of the Investigation of the Buddhist Past* (*Shishi jigulue* 釋氏稽古略), compiled in 1354, and describes the carving largely based on information recorded in previous documents.

> In the first year of the Kaibao era, *mou-ch'en* 戊辰 [968] . . . on the twenty-seventh day of the ninth month, an imperial order [was issued] to the authorities of Chengdu Prefecture to produce two sets of the Buddhist scriptures written [respectively] in gold and silver characters under the supervision of the Executive of the Ministry of War, Liu Xigu 劉熙古.[47] . . . In the fourth year of Kaibao, *xinwei* 辛未 [971], on the eleventh day of the sixth month, an imperial command for another set written in gold characters [was issued]. ([cited from] *Songseng shilue* 宋僧史略 and *Xinianlu* 繫年錄). In the fifth year of Kaibao, *renshen* 壬申 [972], [the emperor] having succeeded in pacifying the various states by his use of military might, had several canons written in gold and silver characters. In the fifth year of Kaibao [972], an imperial order [commanded that] the Buddhist sutra be cut in woodblocks and the entire canon be printed. The blocks numbered 130,000. ([cited from] "Chapter on External Believers" in *Records of Northern Mountain* [*Beishan lu*] 北山錄外信篇)[48]

This last record is perhaps the most complete and comprehensive, and is valuable for providing the sources on which it is based: Zanning's 贊寧 (920–1001) *Brief History of Song Buddhism*; a lost book named *Annalist Records* (*Xinianlu*); and the note in *Beishan lu* discussed above. *Annalist Records* is no longer extant. According to references to it in *Shishi jigulue*, the full title of this book is *Fofa xinianlu* 佛法繫年錄, and it was written by Huijian 慧鑒, a Tiantai monk who lived in Upper Tianzhu Monastery 上天竺寺 in Hangzhou and served as the head lecturer. It appears that this work contained the most detailed account of Buddhist affairs in the early Song, and the author of *Shishi jigu lue* frequently referred to it.[49]

Finally, one stele inscription from 1690 written by the Chan monk Zhangxue Tongzui 丈雪通醉 (1610–1696) has linked the carving of *Kaibao Canon* to a monastery in Chengdu.

> In the past, the founding emperor of the Song ordered that blocks be cut for the Great Canon in Yibu 益部 (Chengdu). In the eighth year of the Taiping xingguo reign, the work was completed. The blocks were stored in Zhengyin 正因 Monastery, which is today's Wanfu 萬福 Monastery.[50]

In this note, the temple name Zhengyin is a misprint of Jingyin 淨因, which is another name of the famous Jingzhong Monastery 淨眾寺 during the late Southern Song and Yuan dynasties. Jingzhong Monastery had been established in the Tang by the Korean Chan monk Wuxiang 無相 (K. Musang, 684–762), commonly known as Master Kim. Wuxiang transmitted Chan patriarch Zhishen's 智詵 teaching to Wuzhu 無住 and established the Jingzhong/Baotang 保唐 tradition, as documented in *Records of Dharma Treasures Through Successive Generations* (*Lidai fabao ji* 歷代法寶記). He was extremely popular in Chengdu and was even noted in Tibetan sources. Wuxiang and his dharma heir, Jingzhong Shenhui 淨眾神會 (720–794), resided in Jingzhong Monastery and attracted great support from the local government and the Tang court. According to Zongmi 宗密 (780–841), who was heavily influenced by Jingzhong Shenhui, the temple acquired a certain official status in the Tang by offering large ordination ceremonies.[51] In the Song, its name was changed to Jingyin Monastery 淨因寺. Tradition says that it was also popularly known as Wanfo Monastery 萬佛寺 because many Buddha statues were located in the temple; this was confirmed when numerous Buddha statues were excavated in the 1950s. During the Ming, "Wanfo" was erroneously pronounced "Wanfu," and the rebuilt temple therefore was given this name.[52]

In Zhangxue Tongzui's inscription, written to commemorate the reinstallation of *Hongwu Southern Canon*, he mistakenly assumed this edition had been printed from the blocks of *Kaibao Canon* and thus made a reference to where its blocks were stored. However, his attribution of Jingyin 淨因/Jingzhong 淨眾/Wanfo 萬佛 monastery as the storage place of the *Kaibao Canon* blocks may have been based on local folklore with no hard evidence, but recent studies on Jingzhong Monastery in the Song, especially the claim that the first paper currency in the world (*jiaozi* 交子) was produced there, point strongly to its role as a printing center.[53] Thus Jingzhong Monastery not only may have been the birthplace of *jiaozi*, but the close relationship between government printing activities and the monastery suggests that it may also have been used for earlier printing projects, such as the engraving of the *Kaibao Canon* blocks. It is highly plausible that the Song court authorized one of the leading monasteries in Chengdu to organize the entire production. In the history of canon production, Buddhist monasteries have always played a leading role in collating, carving, and printing the canon because they often possessed a copy or copies of the canon to serve as exemplar(s) and had available established networks of block carvers to facilitate the project. Therefore, it can be hypothesized that Jingzhong Monastery may have been the headquarters for the *Kaibao Canon* project, where the engraving was done and the blocks were kept before they were transported to Kaifeng.

Despite the enticing but scanty information from these Buddhist records, the creation of *Kaibao Canon* in Chengdu is still shrouded in mystery, especially because the city was devastated by the Wang Xiaobo 王小波 and Li Shun 李順 rebellion[54] soon after the blocks were transferred to Kaifeng. Questions remain about the creation of these blocks: given the advanced printing industry in Chengdu, how was the printing project managed under government supervision? What was the relationship between *Kaibao Canon* and the existing manuscript canon tradition in the Chengdu area? At this point, without further evidence, we can only say that the Song state availed itself of the resources in Chengdu: the relative abundance of manuscript (and possibly some printed) Buddhist works in the region's monasteries; the editorial skills of the Buddhist clerics there; and the raw materials, labor, and organizational skills necessary for carving some 130,000 woodblocks in just twelve years—a pace unmatched by any subsequent Song or Yuan edition of the canon.

KAIBAO CANON *IN KAIFENG*

The more detailed information we have on *Kaibao Canon* after its woodblocks were transported from Chengdu to Kaifeng, the Northern Song capital, allows us to trace the history of the Song state's management of this collection, the largest of the literary compilations it sponsored. State control began with setting up special quasi-official agencies in charge of printing and translation under firm court supervision. By the late Northern Song, however, government supervision was eased and the control of the canon was transferred to big monasteries and private printshops in Kaifeng. Finally, by the early twelfth century, all translation activities ceased, marking the end of nearly a century and half of the Song state's involvement in producing the first printed Buddhist canon. Even as the first "edition" of *Kaibao Canon* was being printed starting in 983, the collection continued to be supplemented several times up through the beginning of the twelfth century. Various catalogs were compiled to list the works that were incorporated into the canon (table 5.1).

The post-983 additions included some older works not found in Zhisheng's 智昇 *Kaiyuan Catalog* (*Kaiyuan shijiao lu* 開元釋教錄), compiled in 730;[55] new translations made during the Song; writings from some of the major

TABLE 5.1. TRIPITAKA CATALOGS COMPILED DURING
THE NORTHERN SONG

Year	Catalog Title	Compilation Information
1013	*Dazhong xiangfu fabao lu* 大中祥符法寶錄 (*Catalog of Dharma Treasure During the Dazhong xiangfu Reign*)	This catalog was compiled by Yang Yi 楊憶 and the monk Weijing 惟淨. It includes the list of translations made between 983 and 1013, compiled under Translation Officer Zhao Anren 趙安仁.
1022	*Dazangjing suihan suoyin* 大藏經隨函索引 (*Case-by-Case Index to the Great Canon*)	The monk Wensheng 文勝 was in charge of this project, an attempt by Emperor Zhenzong to collate the entire canon that stopped later.
1036	*Jingyou xinxiu fabao mulu* 景佑新修法寶目錄 (*Catalog of Newly Compiled Dharma Treasures During the Jingyou Reign*)	This catalog was compiled by Translation Officer Lü Yijian 呂夷簡 (979–1044) following an imperial decree. It includes new translations (total of 161 fascicles) from 1011 to 1036.
1062	*Tiansheng shijiao lu* 天聖釋教錄 (*Catalog of Buddhist Teaching During the Tiansheng Reign*; two of three fascicles extant)	This catalog was compiled based on *Kaiyuan Catalog, Zhenyuan Catalog* 貞元錄, and *Supplementary Zhenyuan Catalog* 續貞元錄, indicating the total size of *Kaibao Canon* around that year to be 6,197 fascicles.
1078	*Yuanfeng fabao lu* 元豐法寶錄 (*Catalog of Dharma Treasure During the Yuanfeng Reign*)	This lost catalog was compiled to reflect the translation of seventeen titles from 1038 to 1080. The essays composed by previous emperors such as Emperor Taizong were also included in the canon.
1104	*Dazangjing gangmu zhiyaolu* 大藏經綱目指要錄 (*Essential Guide and Checklist of the Great Canon*)	This is a private catalog written by the Chan monk Foguo Weibai 佛國惟白 (d.u.) based on his reading of *Kaibao Canon*.

Note: Dazhong xiangfu fabao lu *is cited in* Fozu tongji, *fasc. 44,* T 49: 404c. *This catalog was reprinted in* Zhonghua dazangjing, *vol. 73, fasc. 3–16. Weijing was a Chinese monk who was educated at the institute and became a major translator after the three Indian translators passed away. See Nakamura Kikunoshin, "Sō Denpoin yakukyō sanzō Yuijō no denki oyobi nenpu." For translations omitted from this catalog, see Orzech, "The Trouble with Tantra in China," esp. 316–19. For more information on* Dazangjing suihan suoyin 大藏經隨函索引 (Case-by-Case Index to the Great Canon), *see Lü Cheng, "Songzang shuban yinben kao."*

Chinese Buddhist schools, including those of the Tiantai, Huayan 華嚴, and Faxiang 法相 patriarchs, as well as compositions by several of the Song emperors.[56] Some new works in Chinese, such as *Expounding the Secret Treasure Store* (*Mizangquan*), written by Emperor Taizong, and Qisong's 契嵩 (1007–1071) literary collection *Tanjin wenji* 鐔津文集, were included by imperial decree or upon personal petition. Very often, these new texts would be carved and printed for circulation individually, sometimes even before permission to include them in the canon was granted. Again, there seems to have been no rush to canonize these additional works. For example, earlier dissemination of *Mizangquan* as a single work did not mean it was immediately incorporated into the canon because the *qianziwen* characters had not yet been assigned to these individual texts and translations.[57]

Moreover, the meticulously compiled catalogs for the canon and supplements are highly useful for tracing not only the history of the canon but also the Song state's attitude toward controlling the dissemination of Buddhist texts. As scholars have observed, some translations were omitted from, say, the *Catalog of Dharma Treasure During the Dazhong Xiangfu Reign* (*Dazhong xiangfu fabao lu* 大中祥符法寶錄), compiled around 1013, and other translations were listed in the catalog but did not make it into *Kaibao Canon*.[58] These translations, however, were produced by the Yijingyuan/Chuanfayuan and apparently printed and put into limited circulation, and even presented at times to foreign visitors, like Chōnen 奝然 (938–1016). We may argue therefore that the Song state's main concern was less about assuming the authority of determining the canonicity of each and every Buddhist text but much more over its dissemination both within and outside China.

Printing of the canon and other Buddhist works was originally entrusted to the Printing Office, where the entire canon was produced by imperial order or by request. At the end of the eleventh century, this duty was transferred to a local temple in Kaifeng. During this process, the printing business was also separated from the Institute of Dharma Propagation. In 1071, due to financial constraints, the court decided to abolish the Institute of Sutra Printing. In the following year, the responsibility for printing the canon and other Buddhist works was transferred to Shengshou Chan Cloister in Xiansheng Monastery 顯聖寺聖壽禪院 in Kaifeng, and the court appointed eminent monks Huimin 慧敏 and Huaijin 懷謹 as "Printing Administrators" (Yinzao tixia 印造提轄) in charge of printing the canon in Xiansheng's own Institute of Sutra Printing 管勾印經院事.[59] (This can be seen from the ink stamp of fasc. 1 of *Aweiyuezhizhe jing* 阿維越致遮經 in figure 5.1). Upon arriving at the Song court in 1073, the Japanese Tendai monk Jōjin 成尋 (1011–1081) requested *Kaibao Canon* by petitioning the Institute of Dharma Propagation, which then sent a missive to Xiansheng Monastery to start the printing.[60]

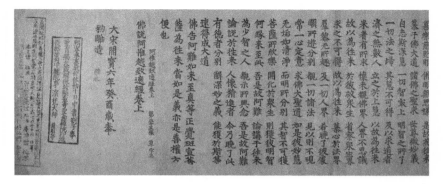

FIGURE 5.1 FASCICLE 1 OF *AWEIYUEZHIZHE JING* 阿惟越致遮经 IN
KAIBAO CANON, NATIONAL LIBRARY AT BEIJING
Reprint from Fojiao wenxian liuzhen.

It seems that Xiansheng Monastery, the new home of the *Kaibao* blocks, continued to carve new blocks. A *Kaibao* colophon reprinted at the end of *Dacheng zhiyin jing* 大乘智印經 in *Zhaocheng Canon* (Case 625 雁), a replica of *Kaibao* carved during the Jin Dynasty, clearly indicated that the block was carved in 1095 at Xiansheng Monastery. However, in the last years of *Kaibao Canon*, most blocks were not carved in Kaifeng by official temples but were collected from Hangzhou, where they had been carved by private sponsors. Therefore, the page format of the canon also changed. For example, in *Zhaocheng Canon*, Li Tongxuan's 李通玄 *Jointed Commentary of Avataṃsaka Sutra* (*Huayan helun* 華嚴合論*) has the format of 30 columns and 17 characters per column, while works by Tiantai patriarchs have only 26 columns and 20 characters per column. This irregularity indicates that the blocks of these texts were not carved in the official printing office in Xiansheng Monastery. Instead, they were probably carved by private print shops and acquired by Song officials who were in charge of the canon in this last stage.[61] All these changes suggest that by the third quarter of the eleventh century, the state's impetus for translating, compiling, and adding works to *Kaibao Canon*, and printing them, had significantly slackened after nearly a century of intense work on the canon.

Finally, one extant part of *Kaibao Canon* is worth discussing briefly for additional insight into the Song state's attitude toward the creation of this collection. This is *Mizangquan*, an imperial commentary on the canon written by Emperor Taizong in 983, then annotated by a group of eminent monks in Kaifeng by 988. In 995, it was ordered to be printed in the institute and included in the canon. Two completed copies were found in the first and second editions of *Goryeo Canon*. In addition, the Harvard Art Museum has only fascicle 13 (fig. 5.2), which was the subject of Max Loehr's intensive study.[62]

FIGURE 5.2 LEAF 15 FROM CHAPTER 13 OF THE IMPERIAL COM-
MENTARY ON THE BUDDHIST CANON (TRIPITAKA) COMMISSIONED
BY EMPEROR TAIZONG (R. 976–97)
*Date: 1108, overall dimensions (approximate): 31.3 x 333.7 cm (12 5/16 x 131 3/8 in.), Harvard
Art Museums/Arthur M. Sackler Museum, Louise H. Daly, Anonymous and Alpheus
Hyatt Funds, 1962.11.3. Photo by Imaging Department © President and Fellows of Harvard
College*

The Harvard copy of fascicle 13 presents a mystery for researchers: first, it has
no *qianziwen* characters in all leaves, which shows that it was very likely printed
before its incorporation into the canon; second, there is no 1071 stamp to indicate the transfer of blocks to Xiansheng Monastery, as in some other printings.
Rather, a much later stamp of acquisition by monk Jianluan 鑒孿 in Qinglian
Monastery青蓮寺, dated to 1108, can be clearly seen. Third, the illustrations
for this fascicle were reproduced in the first *Goryeo Canon* but not the second
Goryeo Canon.[63] Most scholars agree that the illustrations were created later, to
be pasted into the text pages. The fascicle was only decreed to be included in the
canon in 995 and very likely excluded the illustrations, as we have seen from the
second Goryeo edition. It is possible that when it was first printed, it had no *qianziwen* characters, because these were only given when the *Dazhong xiangfu* and
Tiansheng catalogs were compiled. Both catalogs assign the characters *jia* 假,
tu 途, and *mie*滅 to the text. It is also clear that *Mizangquan* had been circulated
as an individual text independent of the canon, as a gift to the emperor's close
officials and to the Korean envoy Han Eongong韓彥恭 in 991.[64] According to
Chen Yuquan, it is likely that monks from Qinglian Monastery acquired this
early print without *qianziwen* and stamped it with their own colophon bearing
the Daguan 大觀 reign name (1107–10).[65]

In his analysis of the woodcut illustrations, Loehr observed that the designs,
dating from 984–991, "were conservative or even somewhat archaizing works"
that may thus have received the approbation of the imperial court, the Buddhist

establishment, and at least some of the scholar-official elite. What is striking, however, is the dearth of images referring to Buddhism and how different these illustrations are from the frontispieces of sutras and the well-known *dharanis* from Hangzhou during the Five Dynasties and Song periods[66] and single-leaf prayer sheets of the late Tang onward. From these illustrations we can clearly trace the subsequent development of illustrations in Buddhist texts, but certainly not from the *Mizangquan* images. Given that *Mizangquan* was a part of *Kaibao Canon* but also apart from the main body of the canon proper, it may be unfair to argue that the woodcuts are atypical of Buddhist illustrations from that period. Nevertheless, it is possible that, like the format of the text in *Kaibao Canon*, the *Mizangquan* illustrations differed from earlier Buddhist manuscripts and prints because the entire canon project was the first of its kind, directed by and for the Song state.[67]

THE CIRCULATION OF KAIBAO CANON IN THE SONG

Although the details about the circulation of *Kaibao Canon* within China are sketchy, it was probably widely distributed to temples throughout the country. Among the twelve extant fascicles reprinted in *Kaibao yizhen* 開寶遺珍, six had colophons indicating that the majority of the extant copies came from Qinglian Monastery at Jincheng 晉城in Shanxi, whose monks had sponsored a reprinting from blocks at the capital. According to the colophon of fascicle 1 of the *Avataṃsaka Sutra*, *Kaibao Canon* had been circulating as early as 983, the year the blocks were brought to Kaifeng. Other colophons show that the canon continued to be circulated until 1108, the second year of the Daguan reign.[68] Judging from available evidence, the canon was in popular demand, in particular due to the widespread construction of revolving sutra repositories in China.[69] For example, the Southern Song monk Zhongwen Xiaoying 仲温晓莹, a disciple of Dahui Zonggao 大慧宗杲, in his miscellaneous notes *Recorded Remarks at Yunwo Chapel* (*Yunwo jitan* 雲臥紀譚), claimed that "scriptures and texts in the Great Canon that are circulated in the empire were originally printed and circulated by Taizu and Taizong."[70] This indicates clearly that the canon in circulation was *Kaibao Canon*. It was also available to readers to consult; the Chan monk Foguo Weibai 佛國惟白 (d.u.) spent the whole summer of 1104 reading *Kaibao Canon* in a monastery and compiled a comprehensive catalog, *Outline and Essential Record of the Great Canon* (*Dazangjing gangmu zhiyaolu* 大藏經綱目指要錄).

Initially the Song government placed the printing of the canon under the strict control of the Institute of Dharma Propagation. Special permission was still needed for printing requests even after the institute's printing office closed in 1071 and the Shengshou Cloister in Xiansheng Monastery in Kaifeng was put in charge. This rule was not relaxed until 1108, when government permission was no longer required, as suggested by the absence of any mention of the institute in the colophons.[71]

The production of *Kaibao Canon* was not only for domestic consumption. The canon's most important function was as a gift to other countries, a way of demonstrating Song China's cultural superiority. In the third month of the first year of the Yongxi 雍熙 period (984), a set of the canon was bestowed to Japanese monk Chōnen at his request.[72] Nearly ninety years later, in 1073, Jōjin obtained the new supplements in thirty cases, together with other Chinese writings. The Goryeo court managed, between 989 and 1099, to receive *Kaibao Canon* some eight times, including at least three copies during the production of the first Goryeo edition (1011–1028).[73] The Song court also gave the canon to Xi Xia (Tangut) at least six times.[74] Annam received an entire set of the canon at least eight times; it must have been the newly carved *Kaibao Canon*.[75] In 1019, even the rising Jurchen state came to request the canon.[76] These international outflows not only enhanced the cultural prestige of the Song among its neighbors in Asia but also stimulated other Asian regimes to create their own editions, in Chinese by the Koreans and Khitans, and in their own language by the Tanguts.

THE STRUCTURE AND CONTENT
OF *KAIBAO CANON*

THE MAIN CANON AND ITS SUPPLEMENTS

No complete set of *Kaibao Canon* exists, so although scholars agree that the main canon follows the order of *Kaiyuan Catalog*, disputes arise about its exact contents and size, especially the supplementary sections. Based on different estimates, scholars have reconstructed its catalog differently and speculated on the exact size of the canon, as exemplified by the figures listed in table 5.2, which also shows that the greatest uncertainties arise concerning the three supplements.

In the discussion below, we give a summary of *Kaibao Canon*'s structure rather than attempting a full reconstruction of its contents, including those of the three supplements.

1. MAIN CANON BASED ON ZHISHENG'S *KAIYUAN CATALOG*

As *Kaibao Canon* was the first printed Buddhist canon and was issued by the Song state, the organization of its contents exerted great influence on later editions. In turn, its main contents followed *Kaiyuan Catalog*, which was highly

TABLE 5.2. ESTIMATES OF THE SIZE OF KAIBAO CANON

	Kaiyuan Catalog	Loehr	Tong Wei	Nakamura Kikunoshin	Li Fuhua and He Mei	He Mei 2014
Main canon (completed ca. 983)	1,076 titles	1,124 titles/ 5,048 fascicles/ 480 cases	1,081 titles/ 5,057 fascicles/ 480 cases	5,048 fascicles/ 481 cases (later changed to 480 cases)	1,076 titles/ 5,048 fascicles/ 480 cases	1,087 titles/ 5,041 fascicles/ 480 cases
First supplement (completed ca. 999)		—	142 titles/ 503 fascicles/ 51 cases		316 titles/ 554 fascicles/ 57 cases	315 titles/ 573 fascicles/ 57 cases
Second supplement (completed 1073)		—	274 titles/ 696 fascicles/ 71 cases		104 titles/ 880 fascicles/ 87 cases	105 titles/ 882 fascicles/ 87 cases
Third supplement (completed by 1108)		—	33 titles/ 348 fascicles/ 37 cases		60 titles/ 480 fascicles/ 58 cases	67 titles/ 477 fascicles/ 58 cases
TOTAL		—	1,529 titles/ 6,604 fascicles/ 639 cases		1,565 titles/ 6,962 fascicles/ 682 cases	1,574 titles/ 6,973 fascicles/ 682 cases

Sources: Data for Kaiyuan Catalog (comp. 730 by Zhisheng) from T 2154:55: 477–724. Data for Loehr from Loehr, Chinese Landscape Woodcuts, 15. Loehr based his estimate primarily on Tokiwa Daijō's work. Data for Tong Wei 童瑋 from Tong Wei, Bei Song Kaibao dazangjing diaoyin kaoshi ji mulu huanyuan, 15. Data for Nakamura Kikunoshin 中村菊之進 from Nakamura Kikunoshin, "Sō Kaihōpan Daizōkyō kōsei kō." Nakamura divided the supplements of Kaibao Canon into twenty-three sections to discuss their composition. For a summary of data from Li Fuhua 李富華 and He Mei何梅, see Li and He, Hanwen Fojiao dazangjing yanjiu, 83. Data for He Mei 2014 is from He Mei, Lidai hanwen dazangjing mulu xinkao, vol. 1, 42. Fang Guangchang is also writing a monograph about Kaibao Canon with a new constructed catalog (Jiang Wu, personal communication with Fang, Dec. 25, 2011).

influential after the Huichang persecution of 845 as Buddhist institutions attempted to recover texts.[77] Nevertheless, examining Foguo Weibai's catalog (*Dazangjing gangmu zhiyaolu*) and those of *Zhaocheng Canon* and *Goryeo Canon* and comparing them with *Kaiyuan Catalog* shows that *Kaibao Canon* did diverge somewhat from *Kaiyuan Catalog*, for several possible reasons.

First, *Kaibao Canon* simply deleted a few titles from *Kaiyuan Catalog*. For example, Tong Wei believed that *Kaibao Canon* included five titles not in *Kaiyuan Catalog* while omitting two other titles.[78] Second, *Kaibao Canon* used different versions of the same titles that contained more or fewer fascicles than listed in *Kaiyuan Catalog*. This often resulted in different organization when the works were arranged into cases. Traditionally, 10 fascicles would constitute one case, but because of the length of a given text, sometimes a case contains fewer than 10 fascicles. This caused some confusion about the exact numbers of cases and fascicles contained in the main canon. For example, although the total numbers of titles and cases of *Kaibao Canon* and *Kaiyuan Catalog* were very close, in the catalog reconstructed by Tong Wei, Case 281 容 and Case 282 止 have no content because Tong believed that different ways of dividing fascicles and cases left the compilers of *Kaibao Canon* no choice but to leave them empty.[79] Nakamura Kikunoshin noticed that when Chōnen first received the canon, its main section contained 481 cases rather than the standard 480 cases. He thus suggested that a rearrangement of its content occurred shortly after its creation to make it into 480 cases.[80]

2. SUPPLEMENTS

The supplements incorporated the translations of new titles from India sponsored by the Northern Song court, older translations from the Tang and earlier not included in *Kaiyuan Catalog*, and Chinese texts that reflected the new changes in religious communities, especially the rise of Chan Buddhism and the revival of Tiantai Buddhism. This last group included imperially commissioned works from the early Song, such as Zanning's *Eminent Monks of the Song* (*Song Gaosengzhuan* 宋高僧傳), begun in 988. The Song court's support of Chan Buddhism is revealed in the compilation of the Chan genealogies such as *Record of Lamp Transmission During the Jingde Reign* (*Jingde chuandeng lu*), originally compiled by Daoyuan in 1004 and edited under Yang Yi and incorporated into the canon in 1009; *Tiansheng Guangdeng lu* 天聖廣燈錄 in 1029; and *Chuandeng yuying ji* 傳燈玉英集 in 1034, all included in the supplemented sections of *Kaibao Canon*. In 1034, an abbreviated version of *Jingde chuandeng lu* compiled by Wang Sui 王隨 was included as well.[81] In 1024, several classics of the Tiantai school were included.

A few surviving sources allow us to study the canon supplements. First, there are the records left by the Japanese monks Chōnen and Jōjin. Second, a series of catalogs of translations compiled by the Institute of Sutra Translation list the titles of new texts to be included in the supplements: *Catalog of Dharma Treasure During the Dazhong Xiangfu Reign* (*Dazhong Xiangfu fabao lu*, 1013), and *Catalog of Dharma Treasure Newly Compiled During the Jingyou Reign* (*Jingyou xinxiu fabao lu*, 1036). Third are the catalogs produced by the Song monk Weibai 惟白 and the Korean monk Sugi 守其 (d.u.). The latter produced a catalog with detailed collation notes (*Goryeoguk sinjo Daejang Gyojeong byeollok* 高麗國新雕大藏校正別錄, referred hereafter as *Collation Notes*) after carefully studying *Kaibao Canon* and comparing it with other editions. In addition, the catalog of the rediscovered *Zhaocheng Canon*, first reconstructed by Jiang Weixin 蔣唯心 and recently by Li Fuhua, has also been extremely helpful. Finally, the first Goryeo and the Zhaocheng Jin editions, being close copies of the *Kaibao* edition, serve as important references.[82] Based on these catalogs, we give a brief summary of their major supplements in the following.

A. FIRST SUPPLEMENT The first supplement, completed circa 999, consisted of two parts: the first included translations from Indic languages made between 982 and 999, and the second contained older translations made in the Tang or earlier, which had not been listed in *Kaiyuan Catalog* but appeared in *Zhenyuan Catalog* (*Da Tang Zhenyuan xu Kaiyuan shijao lu* 大唐貞元續開元釋教錄, 798), which supplements Zhisheng's *Kaiyuan Catalog*. More specifically, Li Fuhua and He Mei, using their examination of *Zhaocheng Canon* and *Goryeo Canon*, determined that the 187 titles and 279 fascicles of Song translations are found in cases 481 杜 through 510 轂, and the ensuing cases 511 振 through 537 奄 contain 129 titles and 275 fascicles of the earlier translations.[83] These findings are consistent with Weibai's catalog, which describes the two parts as comprising supplemental "scriptures and biographies" and other texts previously not included the canon (nor *Kaiyuan Catalog*).[84]

We may speculate about why the older translations from the Tang and earlier were *not* incorporated into the main canon completed in 983. Was it because the original compilers made the editorial decision to include only what was in *Kaiyuan Catalog*? After all, it should have been easy enough to collect the works listed in the Zhenyuan supplement to *Kaiyuan Catalog*. Or perhaps it again also had to do with the rush to finish what could be considered the "main" part of the canon.

B. SECOND SUPPLEMENT The second major supplement, completed in 1073, included new translations from 1000 to 1073, as well as Chinese writings by monks that were approved by the court to be included in the canon. In total, in this supplement has 104 titles, 880 fascicles, and 87 cases, from case 538 宅 to 624 亭.[85]

C. THIRD SUPPLEMENT The third supplement, produced circa 1105–1113, included a few new translations from 1074–1106 (625 雁–628 塞) and Chinese writings by Tiantai, Huayan, and Yogacara (Faxiang) teachers (629 雞–682 幾). In particular, 15 cases from 646 岫 through 660 畝 contain 150 fascicles of works by the Tiantai patriarch Zhiyi 智顗 (538–597) and his disciple Zhanran 湛然 (711–782), retrieved from Korea by the last King of Wu-Yue, Qian Chu.

KAIBAO CANON AS SEEN FROM SUGI'S COLLATION NOTES

Several valuable Korean sources are useful for reconstructing *Kaibao Canon*, especially the two editions of *Goryeo Canon* and Sugi's notes made when he collated *Kaibao Canon* with *Khitan Canon* and the first *Goryeo Canon*. A careful examination of these catalogs reveals that *Kaibao Canon* was created in a hasty fashion and was not given a thorough textual collation. Therefore, textual discrepancies and various typographical errors remain throughout.

Sugi's notes are especially useful, as they reveal the variations between the Kaibao and Khitan editions. Sugi found that of the seventy-six mistakes in sixty-five texts from all three editions, forty-six come from *Kaibao Canon*.[86] As Robert Buswell's study shows, Sugi's collation notes provide crucial information for helping us reconstruct *Kaibao Canon* and in particular, clues about the nature of its manuscript exemplar. We discuss below textual problems found in *Kaibao Canon* according to Sugi, including:

1. complete or partial omission of a text
2. disordered transposition
3. dittography
4. erroneous attribution of authors, titles, and fascicle numbers

(The references for the texts mentioned in the following discussion are summarized in table 5.3.)

One text in *Kaibao Canon* that exhibited all these problems is the *Apidamo dabiposha lun* 阿毘達磨大毗婆沙論 (Abhidharma Mahāvibhāṣā Śāstra). Sugi noted three sections with missing passages, three transposed passages, one dittography, and two sections with incorrect characters.[87] The missing texts in the last fascicle consisted of four different segments, the first three with seventeen missing characters each and the fourth with sixteen missing characters, strongly

TABLE 5.3. EXAMPLES OF TEXTUAL PROBLEMS IN *KAIBAO CANON*

Work	Textual Problems	References
Apidamo dabiposha lun 阿毘達磨大毘婆沙論	missing passages; transposed passages; dittography; sections with incorrect characters	*Kaibao* 947 (千字文:造-疲); K 952; T 1545; Buswell 169–70
Shi Moheyan lun 釋摩訶衍論	missing from *Kaibao Canon*	*Khitan Canon*; *Fangshan shijing* 1073; K 1397; T 1668; Buswell 141; *Digital Dictionary of Buddhism*
Apitan ba jiandulun 阿毘曇八犍度論	dittography	*Kaibao* 938; K 943; T 1543
Jueding pinijing 決定毘尼經	transposed passages	*Kaibao* 36; K 35; T 325; Buswell 139, 153
Shousui jing 受歲經	confusion of two works with similar titles	*Kaibao* 677 (若); *Khitan Canon*; K 688; T 50; Buswell 163–64
Shou xinsui jing 受新歲經		K 871; T 61; Buswell 165
Dabaoji jing 大寶積經	verse in leaf 28 of fasc. 110 missing last line	*Kaibao* 23; K 22, T 310
Suxidi jieluo gongyang fa 蘇悉地羯羅供養法 *Suxidi jieluo jing* 蘇悉地羯羅經	not in *Kaiyuan Catalog* or *Kaibao Canon*, but in *Khitan Canon*; Sugi keeps both in the second Goryeo edition	*Fangshan shijing* 1054; K 431; T 894 *Kaibao* 427; *Fangshan shijing* 574; K 432; T 893

suggesting that the copyist(s) simply missed entire columns of characters from an exemplar with the common format of seventeen characters per column, and that clerical errors probably were harder to check given the fourteen-to-fifteen characters per column format of *Kaibao Canon*.[88]

Occasionally entire works were missing from *Kaibao Canon*. For instance, *Shi Moheyan lun* 釋摩訶衍論, a commentary on the *Awakening of Faith* (*Dacheng qixin lun* 大乘起信论), was incorporated into the second Goryeo edition from *Khitan Canon*. That no premodern edition of the canon compiled in China has this work strengthens the view that the traditional attribution of the translation to Vṛddhimata 筏提摩多 during the Yao Qin 姚秦 Dynasty (384–417) is incorrect and that it was actually written by the Silla monk Weolchung 月忠 in the ninth century.[89] Thus the work was available in northeast China, in the Khitan empire, where it was carved in stone on Fangshan.

Dittography was another serious problem. For example, according to Sugi, fascicle 8 of *Apitan ba jiandulun* 阿毘曇八犍度論 (*Abhidharmajñāna-prasthānaśāstra*) has thirty-five lines of text copied verbatim from Zhu Fonian's 竺佛念 initial translation, which had already been corrected, according to Daoan's preface.[90] Thus the error in *Kaibao Canon* meant that probably its exemplar had preserved the uncorrected translation.

Sometimes errors in *Kaibao Canon* exhibited a longevity of centuries, suggesting how problematic were the compilations of subsequent printed editions of the canon in Song and Yuan China. For example, in *Jueding pinijing* 決定毗尼經 (*Upāliparipṛcchāsūtra*), Sugi identified three passages in which "the text is corrupt, the meaning cannot be reconstructed and it is difficult to find a way of interpreting them." After checking with two other versions, he found that *Kaibao Canon* simply transposed two large paragraphs of the text, the first involving 487 characters and the later 517 characters. Thanks to Sugi, these had been corrected in *Goryeo Canon* and then preserved in *Taishō Canon*. Later Chinese editions published in south China, however, persisted with this mistake.[91]

Finally, the pressure to complete their work quickly caused the compilers of *Kaibao Canon* to make careless mistakes, by wrong attribution of authors, titles, or fascicle numbers. Thus *Kaibao Canon* confused two works with similar titles but very different contents, *Shousuijing* 受歲經 and *Shou xinsuijing* 受新歲經 (*Pravāraṇasūtra*), and placed the latter where the former should have been. Having caught this mistake, Sugi corrected it and rearranged in the second Goryeo edition.[92]

These and other textual problems, discussed in the detailed appendix at the end of Buswell's article, provide useful information about how *Kaibao Canon* was compiled. First, based on Sugi's notes and his editorial choices for the second Goryeo edition, the Khitan edition, though imperfect, was textually superior to the Kaibao. Clearly, there were more texts and better collated versions available in the region of northeast China controlled by the Liao Empire than in Sichuan.

Sugi's collation notes show that the compilers of *Kaibao Canon* did try to organize the canon and do their best to find manuscripts to match the bibliographical records in Zhisheng's *Kaiyuan Catalog*. But apparently their efforts were not always successful. For example, in leaf 28 of fasc. 110 of *Dabao-jijing* 大寶積經 (*Mahāratnakūṭa*), there was a verse preserved in the standard version in *Taishō Canon*.

Although the delusions of sentient beings are abundant,
Buddhas will not detest and abandon them.

They make vows with great compassion
To ferry all across the sea of life and death.

眾生雖垢重　　諸佛不厭捨
願以大慈悲　　度脫生死海 (T 310, 11:630b)

The Kaibao version of this verse, which has survived and is reprinted in *Kaibao yizhen*, is missing the last line, so the Kaibao collator merely noted that "All canons are missing one sentence" 諸藏皆少一句.[93] It seems therefore that the compilers of *Kaibao Canon* noticed this lacuna and failed to find the missing line in various existing manuscript copies.

Sometimes *Khitan Canon* actually retained works missing from *Kaibao Canon*, as revealed with two texts translated by Shanwuwei 善無畏 (Śubhakarasiṃha). *Suxidi jieluo jing* 蘇悉地羯羅經 (*Susiddhikaramahātantra sādhanopāyikapaṭalasūtra*) in three fascicles is found in both the Kaibao and Khitan editions. The Khitan edition, however, includes another text by Shanwuwei, *Suxidi jieluo gongyang fa* 蘇悉地羯羅供養法 (*Susiddhikarapūjāvidhi*), whose content is completely different from the Kaibao version. Sugi checked *Kaiyuan Catalog* and noticed that the latter work in the Khitan edition was not listed. After examining the text, however, Sugi believed that this title was not a wrongly attributed text or an apocryphon, so he kept both works in the second Goryeo edition. This discrepancy only shows that *Kaibao Canon* was based on a manuscript edition different from the one on which *Khitan Canon* was based, and not that either canon was "incorrect."[94]

In general, however, that the Song state was in a hurry to begin and complete work on the Kaibao project so early in the dynasty resulted in sacrificing the slow and arduous process of careful collation and a thorough search for works catalogued in *Kaiyuan Catalog*. As Buswell points out, it is to Sugi's credit that he used an objective, astute, and flexible approach to editing that made the second Goryeo edition better than the Kaibao, Khitan, and the first Goryeo edition.[95] What is intriguing—and more an issue for further exploration than for mere criticism—is why the textual problems in *Kaibao Canon* persisted far more in the canons printed later in imperial China.

CONCLUDING REMARKS: THE LEGACY OF *KAIBAO CANON*

The first printing of the Chinese Buddhist canon expanded into new dimensions existing issues about the production and transmission of this vast collection, the nature of a religious canon, and the uses of a religious canon by a political state. Indeed, *Kaibao Canon* was first and foremost a state enterprise, meant to serve different purposes of the newly established Song Dynasty. First, it represented a new state attitude toward Buddhism, one that looked favorably on Buddhism and intended to revive it after the recent persecution under Shizong in the Later Zhou. Second, *Kaibao Canon* served as a powerful diplomatic tool, especially in light of the Song failure to subjugate militarily the various states, such as the Khitan Liao and the Tangut Xi Xia, that challenged its supremacy in East and Inner Asia. Third, the early Song emperors, starting with Taizong, envisioned Buddhist texts as integral to their aim of connecting their dynasty to the cultural and literary accomplishments of past regimes, and of reuniting the scholarship of the north and south, which had been separated in the late Tang and Five Dynasties.

In view of these goals, especially the first two, it was more important to finish the canon project by compiling and carving woodblocks for (almost) all the Buddhist works catalogued in *Kaiyuan Catalog* than to make the new edition textually perfect and complete. Indeed, completeness had to wait as the Song emperors dispatched Chinese monks to Inner Asia and India and welcomed Indian monks to China, with both groups bringing new Buddhist works to be translated and incorporated as supplements to the original *Kaibao Canon*. The idea that the Chinese Buddhist canon was a work in progress, whose compilation was an open-ended process, was not new in the Song, but it certainly suited the state's purposes in producing this first printed edition together with its three supplements—a process that took some 130 years.

The first Song emperor felt a sense of urgency in publishing—that is, printing and distributing—the main body of texts early in the dynasty. This made Sichuan a reasonable if not ideal choice for the compilation and block carving of the canon. The region had the necessary material resources and the skilled labor needed for such an enormous printing project. And if Sichuan certainly lacked some of the manuscript texts needed for thorough collation work, its Buddhist collections were probably in better shape than those in north central China, where even more texts went missing as a result of the turmoil during the late Tang and Five Dynasties, especially the Later Zhou persecution. Other areas that had more complete collections of Buddhist works than Sichuan were not chosen for political reasons: the northeast continued to be under the control of the Khitans, directly or indirectly; and states in the south, like the Southern Tang or Wu-Yue, were yet to be fully integrated into the new Song empire. That the finished blocks were promptly transported from Chengdu to the imperial capital of Kaifeng shows that the Song state intended to keep full control over the production and dissemination of the canon, at least until around 1082, when the translation project ended.

The main part of *Kaibao Canon* was completed in 983—pre-dating the production of the "Four Great Works of the Song" and the recompilation of the Song *Daoist Canon* 道藏. Moreover, the printing of *Kaibao Canon* began immediately after its woodblocks were transferred to Kaifeng, while the Dao-ist canon was not printed until circa 1121.[96] In fact, even the new Institute of Scripture Translation was not established in Kaifeng until 980–981, when the project in Sichuan was mostly completed. The chronological sequence of these events again supports the argument that the Buddhist canon served political and diplomatic purposes that the other projects did not, at least to the same extent. After all, most of the states surrounding Song China had a pronounced Bud-dhist inclination. And one could argue that the first two Song emperors were emulating the very pronounced Buddhist bent of the Wu-Yue rulers, which was clearly expressed and put to good use in their diplomatic and commercial ties to Goryeo and Japan.

The Song state's inevitable loss of control over the reproduction and dis-semination of the canon occurred both inside and outside of China. Within China, the bestowal of copies of *Kaibao Canon* to favored temples and monas-teries broadcasted texts that could be copied, reproduced through cutting new woodblocks, and inspired efforts to recover lost texts and produce new ones. The first printing of the Chinese Buddhist canon also became an enterprise to emulate, though not to copy slavishly. For example, of the subsequent Song and Yuan canons printed in China, only the twelfth-century *Zhaocheng Canon* (*Jin Canon*), produced in Shanxi in north China,[97] followed the *Kaibao* format of fourteen to fifteen characters per column and is considered a copy of *Kaibao Canon* in terms of content and the order of works. All the other editions, which were produced in central and southern China, reverted to the popular older ar-rangement of seventeen characters per column, and, more importantly, differed from *Kaibao Canon* in the choice and ordering of the works. In China, the first printed edition after *Kaibao Canon* was *Chongning Canon*, privately financed and produced under the auspices of the Eastern Chan Monastery 東禪寺 in Fuzhou 福州. The carved woodblocks were kept at this monastery, even though upon completion in 1103, it was granted the imperial title of *Great Canon of the Imperial Birthday in the Chongning Era* [1102–1106] (*Chongning wanshou da-zang* 崇寧萬壽大藏), perhaps an indication of official approval of a canon that incorporated more works than *Kaibao Canon* and would be the model for later Song and Yuan editions.

It is telling that during the Southern Song, the state did not sponsor the compilation and printing of another edition of the canon to replace the *Kaibao Canon* blocks lost to the Jurchens. *Yuanjue Canon* 圓覺藏,[98] begun in Huzhou 湖州 (in Zhejiang) in 1132, that might have been intended as a replacement to *Kaibao Canon* was a private initiative. It seems that after *Kaibao Canon*, the Song state did not have any strong motive for producing another edition—in contrast to the Goryeo state, which began work on the second edition of the canon within two years of the Mongols' destruction of the first one in 1234.

Indeed, the Song state's sponsorship of translations and original Chinese works of Buddhism also declined precipitously after the 1080s.

The Song state never published another official edition of the canon for a variety of reasons. First, *Kaibao Canon* fulfilled the early Song state's political and diplomatic aims. Second, an enormous project such as the recompilation and recarving of the canon almost certainly would have faced the opposition of the growing power of the Confucian scholar-officials—an attitude already expressed toward the *Kaibao* project and the Institute of Scripture Translation. And even for those officials and literati who were Buddhist in inclination or sympathy, supporting the recompilation of the entire canon became less important than their attention to individual Buddhist texts written in their own time, for which they could advocate by presenting them to the emperor and supporting their printing and distribution.[99] Inclusion of such works in the canon was desirable, but not so urgent as to require a new edition of the canon. Thus, just as the canon catalogs lost their significance and vitality in defining canonicity after the Tang, the canon itself lost much relevance as a repository of Buddhist texts in the Song. Even the Tiantai works championed by the Hangzhou master Ciyun Zunshi 慈雲遵式 (964–1032), with support from the well-known scholar-official Wang Qinruo 王欽若 (962–1025), and the Chan "lamp histories" truly attained their significance independent of their incorporation into the *Kaibao Canon* supplements. Indeed, Albert Welter argues that after the reign of Taizong, literati interested in promoting *wen* sought literary styles and expressions to distinguish their times from the Tang.[100] This also meant moving away from the huge compilations that enjoyed imperial sponsorship under the first two Song emperors, such as *Kaibao Canon* and the "Four Great Works of the Song."

The canon continued to enjoy prestige as a generous gift to temples and monasteries or as a way for these institutions to gain distinction by producing private editions.[101] Generally speaking, however, these later Song and Yuan editions did not undergo rigorous recompilation; none could match the editorial work that so distinguished the second Goryeo edition.

Bestowal of copies of *Kaibao Canon* to other Asian states also spurred them to compile and print their own editions. The Khitan Liao court actually carved at least two different editions, one that has been found in a scroll format in larger characters and one in a string-bound format with smaller characters. Because we have only remnants of both editions, it is difficult to date their carving and printing, but the main edition may have been started soon after the Khitans received a copy of *Kaibao Canon* in 1019 and completed as early as 1030.[102] As Li Fuhua and He Mei argue, because of the loss of Buddhist texts in north central China, from the time of the persecution under Tang Wuzong 武宗 in 845 through the turmoil and destruction during the Five Dynasties, in particular under Shizong of the Later Zhou, the region in northeastern China under Khitan control actually managed to preserve more Buddhist materials, either in manuscript or in stone at Fangshan. These texts included many that were produced or collated under official auspices. Thus one may argue that the Khitan edition rather than the Kaibao was more faithful to the *Kaiyuan Catalog* and carried on a more complete canonical tradition—what Chikusa Masaaki referred to as the Northern Tradition.[103]

The first Goryeo edition was carved between circa 1011–1087 and, based on the extant remnants, was a faithful copy of the *Kaibao* edition, first sent to Goryeo in 989. Although Goryeo received a copy of *Liao Canon* in 1064, apparently it was not used for collation purposes until the compilation of the second edition, as described in Sugi's notes. In the *Supplementary Canon* compiled by Uicheon 義天 (1055–1101), which contains works in the seventeen-character-per-column format, we probably see earlier influences of *Liao Canon*.[104] Thus both the Khitan and Goryeo Buddhists involved in compiling their own canons were well aware of when to take from and when to diverge from *Kaibao Canon*. Indeed, the rapidity with which the second Goryeo canon was begun contrasts tellingly with the absence of any Chinese state-sponsored replacement for *Kaibao Canon* in the Southern Song.

NOTES

1. The woodblocks of both the first printed Buddhist and Daoist *Zhenghe Wanshou Daozang* 政和萬壽道藏 canons were brought by the Jurchens to Beijing. See Su Bai, *Tang-Song shiqi de diaoban yinshua*, 60–63; and also Patricia Ebrey's vivid description of the fall of Kaifeng and the loss of books to Jurchen soldiers in *Accumulating Culture*, 318–19.

2. Chikusa Masaaki, "Sō-Gen ban Daizōkyō no keifu." On the influence of *Kaibao Canon* on the Khitan edition, see also Xu Shiyi, "Kaibaozang and Liaozang de chuancheng yuanyuan kao." See also Ledderose, "Competing with the Northern Sung."

3. These extant fascicles have been reproduced in Fang Guangchang and Li Jining, eds., *Kaibao yizhen*. For a few more remnants not reproduced in this publication, see Li Fuhua and He Mei, *Hanwen fojiao dazangjing yanjiu*, 70–71. In addition to surviving copies from the original *Kaibao Canon*, there are hand-copied or reprinted copies preserved in the Dunhuang and Turfan manuscript archives and in Japan, such as Ishiyamadera 石山寺, Nanatsudera 七寺, and Seikadō bunko 靜嘉堂文庫.

4. For a thorough summary of the bibliographic details of *Kaibao Canon*, see Li Fuhua and He Mei, *Hanwen fojiao dazangjing*, 69–91.

5. Demiéville, "Notes additionnelles," 128–31; Ch'en, "Notes on the Sung and Yuan Tripitaka"; Goodrich, "Earliest Printed Editions of the Tripitaka"; Loehr, *Chinese Landscape Woodcuts*.

6. *Jiu wudai shi*, 1529–31; Sima Guang, *Zizhi tongjian*, 9527; *Xin wudai shi*, 125. This reprinted version of *Xin wudai shi* mistakenly records the number of closed monasteries as 3,336.

7. Buddhist legends concerning Song Taizu's establishment of the new dynasty abounded. For example, stories had prophesied Taizu's rise to power, including the idea that he was the incarnation of Dīpaṃkara Buddha (Dingguangfo 定光佛 or Randengfo 燃燈佛), the twenty-fourth of the past buddhas before Śākyamuni Buddha, and thus was destined to reunite China. Other legends referred to Taizu's visit to a magic monk called "Hemp Cloth" (Mayi 麻衣), who was skillful in divination and was the alleged founder of a divination tradition named "Mayi physiognomy" (*mayi xiangfa* 麻衣相法). These legends linked Taizu's success to a reversal of Shizong's anti-Buddhist policy. For a thorough discussion, see Liu Changdong, *Songdai fojiao zhengce yanjiu*, 1–55. One prophecy claimed that even the sixth-century monk Baozhi 寶誌 (418–514) during Liang Wudi's 梁武帝 (r. 502–549) time had predicted that 21 rulers from the Zhao 趙 family, from which Taizu hailed, would rule China for 799 years. It seems the Song rulers took these predictions seriously, and the second emperor Taizong even founded a new temple to store Baozhi's mummy and staff and claimed to have had a vision of him in the palace. See Vermeersch, "Buddhism and State-Building in Song China and Goryeo Korea," 5.

8. See Wang Shengduo, *Songdai zhengjiao guanxi yanjiu*, 4–7.

9. For the 960 decree, see Li Tao, *Xu Zizhi tongjian changbian*, 1.17; 967 decree: ibid., 8.195.

10. *Fozu tongji*, T 49: 395b.

11. For relations between Song China and India, see Jan, "Buddhist Relations Between India and Sung China." For the translation of Buddhist works from Indic languages to Chinese, see Bowring, "Brief Note: Buddhist Translations in the Northern Sung"; Sen, "The Revival and Failure of Buddhist Translations During the Song Dynasty"; Huang, "Imperial Rulership and Buddhism in the Early Northern Sung."

12. In Buddhism, the notion of a *chakravartin* king who upholds the dharma and possesses the wheel that rolls across the lands that he conquers has been used by rulers in different regions since at least the fourth century B.C.E., with the Indian king Aśoka (r. 268–232 B.C.E.) as the best-known early example. Chinese rulers such as Liang Wendi 梁文帝 (r. 502–549 C.E.) and Sui Wendi 隋文帝 (r. 581–604) have also claimed this title.

13. Huang, *Sizhou dasheng yu Songxue daoren*, 13–80.

14. Welter, "A Buddhist Response to the Confucian Revival," 21. See also Bickford, "Making the Chinese Cultural Heritage at the Courts of Northern Sung China."

15. See Kurz, "The Politics of Collecting Knowledge" and "The Compilation and Publication of the *Taiping yulan* and the *Cefu yuangui*."

16. Sen, "The Revival and Failure of Buddhist Translations," 32.

17. Haeger, "The Significance of Confusion," 407.

18. Actually, translations from Indic languages began earlier in the Song. In 973, Wang Guicong 王龜從, the prefect of Fuzhou 鄜州 (in Shaanxi), presented two translations by an Indian and a Chinese monk to Taizu. See Sen, "The Revival and Failure of Buddhist Translations," 34.

19. Demiéville, "Notes additionnelles," 121–22; Sen, "The Revival and Failure of Buddhist Translations," esp. 34–39.

20. See, e.g., Nakamura Kikunoshin, "Sō Denpoin yakukyō sanzō Yuijō," which has a detailed chronology up through 1051.

21. For the end date of 1082, see Bowring, "Brief Note," 81 and 93.

22. Huang, "Imperial Rulership and Buddhism," esp. 151–55.

23. Ibid., 407.

24. *Fozu tongzai*, *T* 49:339a, translated by Huang, "Imperial Rulership and Buddhism," 153. See also his "Song Taizong yu Fojiao."

25. Ibid., 339a.

26. Ibid., fasc. 43. All these works were preserved in *Goryeo Canon* and reprinted in *Goryeo daejanggyeong*, vol. 35.

27. For Zhenzong's interest in Daoism, see Shi, "Huizong and the Divine Empyrean Palace Temple Network."

28. This position was referred to as "Translation Envoy" (*yijing runwenshi* 譯經潤文使) as well. These high-ranking officials, who were often also involved in other state-sponsored literary projects, included Lü Yijian 呂夷簡 (979–1044), Song Shou 宋綬 (991–1040), Wang Shu 王曙 (963–1043), Zhang Ji 張洎 (934–97), Yang Li 楊礪 (930–99), Li Wei 李維 (d.u., *jinshi* 985), Zhu Ang 朱昂 (925–1007), Liang Zhouhan 梁周翰 (929–1009), Xia Song 夏竦, Zhao Anren (958–1018), Chao Jiong 晁迥 (948–1031), Yang Yi 楊億 (974–1020), Fu Bi 富弼 (1004–83), and Wang Anshi 王安石 (1021–86). See Liang Tianxi, *Bei Song Chuan fa yuan ji qi yi jing zhi du*, 54–58; Huang, "Songdai runwen yijingguan yu Fojiao."

29. On the Wu-Yue kingdom, see Worthy, "Diplomacy for Survival."

30. See the works cited in Shih-shan Susan Huang, "Early Buddhist Illustrated Prints in Hangzhou." For the exchanges in Buddhist texts, including the recovery from Japan and Korea of Tiantai texts lost in China in the late Tang and Five Dynasties, see esp. ch. 7 of Brose, "Buddhist Empires."

31. The other possible choice among the southern states was the Southern Tang, which, however, had offered (some) military resistance to Song troops before surrendering in 976. See Kurz, *China's Southern Tang Dynasty, 937–976*, esp. ch. 4. It is significant that carting off the holdings of the imperial libraries of the Southern Tang and Wu-Yue to Kaifeng more than doubled the Song state libraries' works. We do not, however, have comparable information about Buddhist works from these southern states.

32. For a brief introduction to the Fangshan sutras, see Lancaster, "The Rock Cut Canon in China."

33. Lorge, "From Warlord to Emperor."

34. Su Yongqiang, *Beisong shuji kanke yu guwen yundong*, 84–88.

35. For Bodhisattva charm, see *Zhongguo banke tulu*, fig. 1; For calendar, see Giles, *Descriptive Catalogue*, serial no. 8100.

36. For Feng Su and Liu Pian, see Pelliot, *Débuts*, 33–41; Tsien, *Paper and Printing*, 151–52. Liu Pian's note is preserved in *Airizhai cong chao* 愛日齋叢抄 (attributed to Ye Zhi 葉寘). For Wenzong's decree, see Seo Tatsuhiko, "Printing Industry," 14. For Sichuan printing in the Song, see also Gu Yongxin, "Song Shuke jingshu banben yanjiu"; Gu Tinglong, "Tang Song Shuke banben jianshu."

37. See Barrett, "Daoism and the Origins of State Printing."

38. The most thorough discussion of the sources remains Pelliot, *Débuts*, 61–81; see also Tsien, *Paper and Printing*, 156–57, and Zhang Xiumin, *Zhongguo yinshua shi*, 40 and 43–44.

39. Sima Guang, *Zizhi tongjian*, fasc. 291, 9495.

40. Gu Yongxin, "Song Shuke jingshu banben yanjiu," esp. 28–39. Gu, who focuses on imprints of the Confucian Classics produced in Sichuan in the Song, argues that the Shu-style large-character works were considered among the superior publications of the period.

41. See Li Fuhua and He Mei, *Hanwen Fojiao dazangjing yanjiu*, 86.

42. *T* 2113, 52:632a; also Shenqing, *Beishan lu* (Song reprint edition), 296. The gold and silver ink manuscript canons were a far more ambitious project than a *Diamond Sutra* in the same style that had been submitted earlier in 963 by Shen Lun 沈倫 (909–87), a Fiscal Intendant of Shaanxi (Huang Chi-chiang, "Imperial Rulership and Buddhism," 151).

43. Chen Yuan, *Zhongguo fojiao shiji gailun*, 94. Chen Yuan noticed the early event Huibao mentioned is dated to 973, and he quoted Zanning's *Dasong sengshilue* 大宋僧史略 and Daoyuan's *Jingde chuandelu* (1004). Therefore, Huibao was most likely active between 973 and 1004. See also Li Fuhua and He Mei, *Hanwen fojiao dazangjing yanjiu*, 86–87.

44. Max Loehr, in *Chinese Landscape Woodcuts*, 13–14, translated them into English based on Tokiwa Daijō's work "Daizōkyō chōin-kō" without noticing that some of the important references were only contained in notes rather than in the main text.

45. *T* 2035 49: 396a.

46. *Fozu lidai tongzai*, fasc. 18, *T* 2036 49: 656c. Loehr did not translate the sentence I italicized in the translated passage, which has been checked against the Taishō edition. The original notes are marked inside parentheses.

47. Liu was prefect of Chengdu Prefecture around 967. See *Song shi*, fasc. 263, biography 22, 9100–02.

48. Loehr, *Chinese Landscape Woodcuts*, 14; *T* 2037, 49:859c.

49. *T* 49: 859a.

50. "Guangyan si zangjinglou ji" 光嚴寺藏經樓記, in *Bashu Fojiao beiwen jicheng*, 537.

51. See Adamek, *The Mystique of Transmission*, 276–90. See also Gregory, *Tsung-mi and the Sinification of Buddhism*, 37–54. See also Faure, "Ch'an Master Musang."

52. For Buddhist excavation of the Buddha statues, see Liu Zhiyuan and Liu Tingbi, *Chengdu Wanfosi shike yishu*, 1–7. For an English introduction to the Wanfosi stele and art, see Wong, "Four Sichuan Buddhist Steles."

53. See the Yuan work *Chubipu* 楮幣譜 by Fei Zhu 費著, which has a passing reference to the monastery: "In the first year of Longxing reign (1163), [the government] began sending an official to supervise [the production of paper], and he moved his office to Jingzhong Monastery located in the east of the city. In the fifth year of the Shaoxi 紹熙 period (1194), [the government] began to build a paper factory at the side of the monastery and sent an official to supervise the business inside the monastery." In *Quanshu yiwen zhi* 全蜀藝文志, fasc. 57, quoted from Luo Tianyun and Deng Zhongshu, "Chengdu Jingzhongsi." For more cautious research, see Hu Zhaoyi, "Songdai jiaozi."

54. Schifferli, "La politique économique des Song du Nord au Sichuan (965–1000)," esp. 132–36.

55. *T* 2154, 27: 572a. Among the many studies of *Kaiyuan Catalog*, see Kyoko Tokuno, "The Evaluation of Indigenous Scriptures in Chinese Buddhist Bibliographical Catalogues," esp. 52–58.

56. Li and He, *Hanwen Fojiao dazangjing yanjiu*, 83–91. The additions were then assigned their own *qianziwen* case numbers. Scrolls were grouped into ten per case and assigned a case number from *qianziwen*. On the translations (and sometimes retranslations) of the Yijingyuan/Chuanfayuan, see also Jan, "Buddhist Relations Between India and Sung China"; Sen, "Revival and Failure"; and Orzech, "Looking for Bhairava."

57. This can be seen in the 985 record of the Japanese monk Chōnen, in which he listed works in the canon and the new translations separately, indicating that the latter were not yet formally incorporated into the canon.

58. See, for example, Orzech's "Looking for Bhairava," in which he discusses the circulation of esoteric texts translated by the Yijingyuan/Chuanfayuan.

59. See *Songhui yao: zhiguan* 宋会要 职官, fasc. 25. This has been confirmed in the ink stamp in fasc. 1 of *Aweiyuezhizhe jing* 阿維越致遮經 (*Qianziwen* 草), also in the stamp of fasc. 19 of *Fobenxingjing* 佛本行經. For a convenient collection of all colophons, see Fang's introduction for *Kaibao yizhen*. Reprinted in Fang Guangchuang, *Suiyuan zuoqu*, 91–96.

60. The Japanese pilgrim Jōjin recorded the requesting procedure in fascicles 7 and 8 of his travelogue.

61. This scenario has been corroborated by an account in fasc. 17 of *Jingyou Catalog* that gives a detailed explanation of this process. *Zhonghua dazangjing*, vol. 73, 579.

62. Loehr, *Chinese Landscape Woodcuts*. For the *Mizangquan* in the first *Goryeo Canon* preserved in Nanzenji, see Egami Yasushi and Kobayashi Hiromitsu, eds., *Nanzenji shozō "Hizōsen" no mokuhanga*; and Loehr, *Chinese Landscape Woodcuts*, 55–69

and plates 18–27. Susan Huang also discussed this piece of woodcut in the transition from Tang to Song, "Tang Song shiqi Fojiao banhua," 396–400.

63. For the *Mizangquan* in the first *Goryeo Canon* preserved in Nanzenji, see Egami Yasushi and Kobayashi Hiromitsu, eds., *Nanzenji shozō "Hizōsen" no mokuhanga*; and Loehr, *Chinese Landscape Woodcuts*, 55–69 and plates 18–27.

64. For a short review of the inclusion of Taizong's work into the canon, see Su Bai, *Tang-Song shiqi de diaoban yinshua*, 80–81.

65. Chen Yuquan, "Bei Song 'Yuzhi Mizang quan' banhua yanjiu," 168.

66. See Shih-shan Susan Huang, "Early Buddhist Illustrated Prints in Hangzhou."

67. For a detailed study of *Mizangquan* illustrations, see Chen Yuquan, "Bei Song 'Yuzhi Mizangquan' banhua yanjiu."

68. For Qinglian Monastery, see Li Huizhi and Gao Tian, "Shanxi Jincheng Qingliansi Fojiao fazhan zhi mailuo" and "Shanxi Jincheng Qingliansi kao."

69. For the spread of the canon in the Song, see Cao Ganghua, "Dazangjing zai liangsong minjian shehui de liuchuan" and *Songdai fojiao shiji yanjiu*, 26–28, 41–49. Most of the references to the revolving sutra repositories did not specify the version of the canon stored inside the device. For revolving repositories, see Jiang Wu's chapter 2 in this volume and Huihui, "Cong *Kaibaozang* kan guanke dazangjing de diaoyin."

70. X 1610, 86:664a, compiled between 1131 and 1162.

71. Su Bai, *Tang-Song shiqi diaoban yinshua*, 55–56.

72. See Demiéville, "Sur les éditions imprimées du canon chinois," 127.

73. The Goryeo court was also successful in obtaining six copies of *Khitan Canon*; Zhang Hongwei, "Shi zhi shisi shiji Zhongguo," esp. 36–39.

74. See Dunnell, *The Great State of White and High*, esp. 36–37 and 62–63. The Tanguts were inspired to develop a writing system and to translate Buddhist works into Tangut, many of which were printed in the later eleventh century. It is quite possible that a Buddhist canon in Tangut was compiled during this time, but the extant printed edition was completed much later, in 1302 in Hangzhou. See Lucille Chia's chapter 6 on *Qisha Canon* in this volume.

75. For an overview of the Ly Dynasty's effort to seek the canon from the Song court and building of repositories, see Minh Chi et al., *Buddhism in Vietnam*, 69–70. Tài Thư Nguyễn, Thi Thơ Hoàng, et al., *The History of Buddhism in Vietnam*, 95–96. See also Kawakami Seishi, "So chokuhan zōkyō Annan denrai kō."

76. *Fozu tongji*, fasc. 44, T 2035, 49:406b. It was recorded as "Dong Nüzhenguo" 東女真國, which should not be confused with the short-lived Eastern Jurchen state (1215–1233) founded by Puxian Wannu.

77. Fang Guangchang, *Zhongguo xieben dazangjing yanjiu*, 90–104.

78. See Tong Wei, *Bei Song Kaibao dazangjing diaoyin kaoshi*, 7.

79. Ibid., 84, 131–32. Tong Wei's reconstruction and explanation are problematic and need further investigation. It seems that he was unable to consult Sugi's *Collation Notes*. In Sugi's notes, case 281 容 has at least *Xinshousui jing* 新受歲經, which was

placed in case 677 若 in Tong Wei's catalog (86), and *Si weicengyoufa jing* 四未曾有法經 is in case 285 言 in Tong Wei's catalog (90). Similarly, case 282 止 has at least *Foshuo pinbosuo luowang yi fo gongyang jing* 佛说頻婆娑羅王詣佛供養經 but was put in case 284 思 by Tong Wei (89). See also Sugi's *Collation Notes*, fasc. 18.

80. Nakamura Kikunoshin, "Sō Kaihōpan Daizōkyō kōsei kō."

81. See Welter, *Monks, Rulers, and Literati*, 115–208. As Welter's detailed discussions show, incorporating a text into the Chinese Buddhist canon did not guarantee textual stability. The contents of the *Jingde chuandeng lu* differed in the various versions. Not only was Daoyuan's original text revised by Yang Yi, but Yang's version underwent further revisions, and Wang Sui's abbreviated version may be closer to the Daoyuan original.

82. See Jiang Weixin and Cai Yunchen, *Songzang yizhen xumu*; Li Fuhua, *Jin zang*.

83. Li Fuhua and He Mei, *Hanwen Fojiao dazangjing yanjiu*, 80–81.

84. *Shōwa hōhō sōmokuroku*, vol. 2, 768.

85. Li Fuhua and He Mei, *Hanwen Fojiao dazangjing yanjiu*, esp. 81–83.

86. Buswell, "Sugi's Collation Notes." The textual problems of *Kaibao Canon* have also been discussed in Lü Cheng, "Songzang Shuban yinben kao." See also Zhu Zifang, "Liaochao yu Gaoli de foxue jiaoliu."

87. Buswell, "Sugi's Collation Notes," 169–70.

88. For a different editorial approach, see Lancaster, "Comparison of the Two Carvings of the Korean Buddhist Canon," for a description of the practice of preserving the format (number of characters per column and number of columns per page) of the first Goryeo edition in the second one.

89. See the entry for this work in the *Digital Dictionary of Buddhism*, edited by Charles Muller.

90. Buswell, "Sugi's Collation Notes," 140 and 168.

91. Ibid., 139.

92. Ibid., 165.

93. Fang Guangchang, "Guanyu Kaibaozang kanke de jige wenti," 16.

94. Buswell, "Sugi's Collation Notes," 159, actually reverses the two titles and says that it is the *gongyang* text that is in *Kaibao Canon*.

95. Ibid., esp. 151–52.

96. It is true, however, that the compilation of a new catalog for *Daozang* was completed quite early in the Song, around 1016, and the entire canon was hand copied in the ensuing decades. Although Daoist clergy were involved in the compilation of the Song *Daozang*, no corresponding special institute like the Buddhist Institute of Dharma Propagation was established for this project. It is interesting that the compilation of the catalog was managed in the Chongwen yuan 崇文院, which included the various imperial libraries, and under the direction of Wang Qinruo, who, along with Yang Yi, was among the chief compilers of the *Cefu yuangui* 冊府元龜. Both men were also involved in state compilations of Buddhist works. For the Daoist canon, see

van der Loon, *Taoist Books in the Libraries of the Sung Period*, esp. 29–50; and Schipper, "General Introduction," in *The Taoist Canon*, esp. 26–32.

97. The emergence of new sources suggests the process of compilation is more complicated. See Dewei Zhang, "The Strength of the Forgotten."

98. For the complicated history of this edition, variously referred to as the Huzhou edition 湖州本, *Sixi Yuanjue Canon* 思溪圓覺藏, or the *Zifu Canon* 資福藏, see Li Fuhua and He Mei, *Hanwen dazangjing yanjiu*, 223–51.

99. See Huang Chi-chiang, "Experiment in Syncretism," for a discussion of officials and literati sympathetic to Buddhism (71–101) and those opposing (some aspects of) Buddhism (101–15).

100. Welter, *Monks, Rulers, and Literati*, esp. ch. 6.

101. See, for example, Lucille Chia's chapter 6 on *Qisha Canon* in this volume.

102. See the chapter on the Liao canons in Li Fuhua and He Mei, *Hanwen dazangjing yanjiu*, 127–60. Li and He (138) argue that the earlier "large character" 大字 canon up through the works listed in the *Kaiyuan Catalog* was completed by 1030, with the remaining portions finished by the reign of Daozong 道宗 (1055–1100).

103. See Chikusa, "Sō-Gen ban Daizōkyōno keifu."

104. See chapter 8 in this volume on *Goryeo Canon* by Jiang Wu and Ron Dziwenka. According to Buswell, "Sugi's Collation Notes," 178n10, *Kaibao Canon* was bestowed on Goryeo several times (989, 991, 1019, and 1098–1100). The later copies included the supplements to *Kaibao Canon*. On *Liao Canon* in Goryeo, and Uicheon, see Buswell, "Sugi's Collation Notes," 130 and 138.

6. The Life and Afterlife of Qisha Canon (Qishazang 磧砂藏)

Lucille Chia

Given the great size of the Chinese Buddhist canon—the printed editions of which usually comprise five to six thousand volumes (*ce* 冊) in the traditional sutra binding—it is somewhat astounding to consider the low survival rate for both the woodblocks and the printed copies of these works. Between the tenth and fourteenth centuries, the Chinese Buddhist canon was printed in China in at least seven different woodblock editions, yet not one of them is extant in its entirety.[1] We are therefore fortunate to have, among the editions of the Chinese Buddhist canon printed in the Song and Yuan, three nearly complete sets of *Qisha Canon* (*Qishazang*, 1216–ca. 1322), as well as six other sets in China and Japan, containing several thousand to several hundred fascicles.[2] Consequently, scholars have been able to study this edition in some detail and learn how Buddhist clergy and lay believers went about compiling, collating, printing, and funding such a great enterprise. Paratextual information has also helped to unravel the complexities that link *Qisha Canon* in many ways to other editions of the canon or smaller sutra collections produced during the Song and Yuan and reprinted in later periods.

This chapter grew out of my examination of the fairly complete copy of *Qisha Canon* in the Gest Collection at Princeton University. Since this set has been previously examined by other scholars,[3] I shall not be presenting new information about undiscovered or unexamined volumes. Instead, I hope to contribute to the discussion about how the monasteries and the individuals and groups involved in its production affected the compilation and publication of an edition of the Buddhist canon in imperial China—that is, to add to what we know of the local and regional history of *Qisha Canon*.

Let us begin with the first group of sutras in the Chinese Buddhist canon, *Da bore boluomiduo jing* 大般若波羅蜜多經 (henceforth *Da bore jing*). As Li Jining points out,[4] in many extant copies of *Qisha Canon*, these volumes are impressions made not from the original woodblocks but from the blocks carved over a century later, in the 1330s, at Miaoyan Monastery 妙嚴寺 in Wuxing District 吳興縣 in Huzhou Circuit 湖州路. The colophon inscription (*kanji* 刊記) at the end of the first fascicle is dated 1332 and was written at the sutra printing office of Miaoyan Monastery. The inscription refers to carving woodblocks not for an entire canon, but for four of the most important and popular sutras (abbreviated titles: *Bore jing* 般若經, *Niepan jing* 涅槃經, *Huayan jing* 華嚴經, and *Dabao ji jing* 大寶積經), after the texts had been recollated using five editions of the canon printed in the Song and Yuan: the one at Hongfa Monastery in the imperial capital Dadu 大都弘法寺, the one from Puning Monastery at Nanshan in Hangzhou 南山普寧寺, the one from Yuanjue Monastery 圓覺寺 in Sixi 思溪 in Huzhou, the one from Dong Chan Monastery in Fuzhou 福州 in Fujian 古閩東禪寺, and finally, the one from Yansheng Monastery in Qisha in Suzhou 磧砂延聖寺. This printing project at Miaoyan Monastery lasted about twenty-six years (1324–49), somewhat longer than needed for the entire *Puning Canon* (*Puningzang* 普寧藏, 1277–90), or *Kaibao Canon* (*Kaibaozang* 開寶藏, 972–83), the first printed Chinese Tripitaka.

In fact, the inscription at the end of fascicle 1 of *Da Bore jing* in *Qisha Canon* raises a number of important issues about the convoluted publishing history of so many editions of the Buddhist canon. First, the blocks for *Da Bore jing* in the original edition of *Qisha Canon* were carved over a century earlier, starting in 1216, a fact we know from the copy held in Saidai Monastery 西大寺 in Nara, Japan.[5] Second, in less than 120 years after the *Qisha Canon* project had begun, and very shortly after most of this edition had been finished (ca. 1322),[6] at least some of the original woodblocks for the sutras most in demand for reprinting had been either lost or too damaged to be used. Nevertheless, the vicissitudes of the woodblocks for *Qisha Canon* appear to have been no greater, or perhaps even less than for the other Song and Yuan editions of the canon. By the 1330s, woodblocks for three of the editions (*Puningzang*, *Yuanjuezang*, and *Dongchanzang*) mentioned in the colophon inscription in the Miaoyan Monastery edition of *Bore jing* were all gone. Third, the usual response to destroyed woodblocks was to carve new ones, produced after collating different available editions. Fourth, at least two projects were launched, at Miaoyan Monastery and

Baoen Wanshou Hall in Houshan in Jianyang County 建陽縣后山報恩萬壽堂 in northern Fujian, to recarve the four great sutras (rather than the entire canon), as discussed below. Most likely, neither endeavor was intended to make up for the lost or damaged woodblocks of *Qisha Canon* but to make available for reprinting those sutras most in demand by donors. The question arises, then, who felt it necessary to produce the entire canon rather than just the sutras most in demand? We shall explore these issues below, after first considering the history of the *Qisha Canon* project.

QISHA CANON DURING THE SONG

Yansheng Cloister 延聖院, as the monastery was designated during the period in the Song when *Qisha Canon* was produced (1216–ca. 1272),[7] was first established as a chapel (*an* 庵) in 1172 by a Chan Preceptor, Jitang 寂堂, a native of Huating County 華亭縣 in Pingjiang Prefecture 平江府 (modern Suzhou). From a family named Fei 費, he acquired a sandy islet called Qisha 磧砂 off the northern shore of Chen Lake 陳湖 in Wu County 吳縣, about twenty kilometers southeast of the prefectural seat.[8] Until the late twelfth century, this area lagged behind that around Lake Tai 太湖, west of the city, and only began to grow into the fabled land of rice and fish as water-control measures by the Song state resulted in Chen Lake approximating its modern contours and concurrent linkage to the numerous surrounding waterways, including the Wusong River 吳松江 slightly to the north and the larger Dianshan Lake 澱山湖 to the south. For the monastery to be situated on the shore of Chen Lake seemed a little precarious, given the dangers of flooding and that the lake itself was created as a result of the sinking of the land, probably in a period of heavy rainfall and flooding, around 747 in the Tang.[9] In fact, only one other monastery, Yongshou si 永壽寺, established in the Tang, was located on the shore of the lake.[10]

Yansheng Monastery did not even earn a mention in the regional gazetteers of the times, such as *Wu jun zhi* 吳郡志 (1192).[11] Indeed, one incentive for the monks and lay devotees to begin an ambitious printing project might have been to earn renown for a rather obscure monastery that was located outside the prefectural seat, in a region that, into the Southern Song, was economically lagging behind nearby Huzhou Prefecture and even more, the Hangzhou area, a trend that correlated well with the number of Buddhist monasteries in these localities. In contrast to more than 770 monasteries in Hangzhou and 110 in Huzhou, Pingjiang had only 60 in the Song, about half within the prefectural seat.[12]

It is unclear whether the initial objective of Qisha Yansheng Monastery was to publish an edition of the entire canon, or just of the four important and popular sutras to earn some income and recognition for the monastery in the local area. During the first several decades of printing and publishing, there seem to have been very few major donors. The most prominent was Zhao Anguo 趙安國, who held the government title *Baoyi lang* 保義郎 (Gentleman protecting righteousness) and later *Chengzhong lang* 成忠郎 (Gentleman of complete loyalty),[13] and who was referred to in the colophons as *da tanyue* 大檀越, or great benefactor. The colophon inscriptions from the original *Qisha* edition of *Da Bore jing* state that he contributed to the block carving of the work's 600 fascicles. In other works in *Qisha Canon* up through the 1260s, Zhao Anguo continued to be listed as either a donor or a fund raiser. It seems likely that by 1232, when the blocks for the four important sutras had been carved, the monastery's abbot and important contributors like Zhao Anguo conceived of the more ambitious project of printing a complete canon and compiled a table of content (1234–36), essentially duplicating that of the earlier *Yuanjue Canon*.[14] Indeed, a comparison of the catalogs of the *Yuanjue* and *Qisha* editions is revealing. At times, both erred in dividing a single work or conflating two or more works; at other times, the *Qisha Canon* catalog made mistakes not in the *Yuanjue Canon* catalog. These details suggest that perhaps the *Qisha Canon* catalog was produced somewhat hurriedly as a prospectus for donors interested in contributing to the production of the remaining works to complete an entire canon.[15] In any case, as Li and He estimate, only about one-fifth of *Qisha Canon* was completed before work was halted in 1273, and the works produced in the Yuan would follow the catalog for *Puning Canon*.

During the late Southern Song, many more donors contributed on a far smaller scale than Zhao Anguo did. For example, one Jin Zhu 金鑄, a native of Fengchi Village in Changzhou County 長洲縣鳳池鄉 (figure 6.1), gave 257 strings and 730 cash to have 8,591 characters carved for the fifth fascicle of *Fangguang bore boluo mi jing* 放光般若波羅蜜經.[16] In this and several other colophons, Zhao Anguo is also mentioned, but as a fund raiser (*du quanyuan* 都勸緣). Interestingly, we find more small-scale donors like Jin Zhu in the works in *Qisha Canon* carved in the Song than in the Yuan, and these donors came primarily from nearby areas, in Pingjiang and Huzhou prefectures. Among the lay Buddhists who donated relatively small amounts to the production of *Qisha Canon* were those whom Barend ter Haar terms "People of the Way," identifiable by the character *dao* 道 in their self-designations or autonyms, who were primarily active in Huating and Wujiang 吳江 counties of Pingjiang Prefecture. Unlike in two other large Buddhist publishing projects in the Yuan, however, these donors did not constitute the main driving force or even an important supporting group for *Qisha Canon*. Indeed, one reason work stopped on *Qisha Canon* and did not resume until 1297 may have been that lay Buddhist donors were attracted to the *Puning Canon* project, discussed below.[17]

In general, large-scale donors, both private and official, seem few in the Southern Song compared to the Yuan. In fact, the dates of the inscriptions in

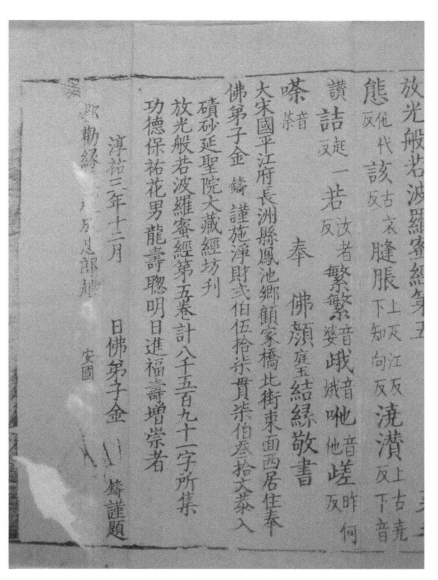

FIGURE 6.1 *QISHAZANG* 61菜3: COLOPHON INSCRIPTION AT THE
END OF THE FIFTH *JUAN* OF *FANGGUANG MOHE BORUO BOLUOMI
JING* 放光摩訶般若波羅蜜經, DATED 1243
Courtesy of the East Asian Library and the Gest Collection, Princeton University

works completed in the Song by no means followed the ordering of the case numbers, suggesting how dependent the *Qisha Canon* project was on less-than-steady donations during this period. Actually, even the individual volumes of a single work were not necessarily engraved in order. For example, the *Fayuan zhulin* 法苑珠林 has inscriptions ranging from 1233 to 1256, with consecutive volumes sometimes engraved over a decade apart.[18]

Moreover, the fire in 1258 that destroyed much of Yansheng Monastery probably damaged some of the woodblocks. The colophons in most fascicles of *Fang-guang bore boluo mi jing* (which immediately follows *Da bore jing*, the first sutra in *Qisha Canon*) are all dated 1243–45, but the eighth fascicle has a colophon dated 1265, suggesting that the blocks for this fascicle were recarved after the fire.[19] The fairly long time to effect this repair suggests that by the 1260s it was increasingly difficult to obtain contributions in the Jiangnan area as the government weakened and worries about the Mongol invasion mounted.

QISHA CANON DURING THE YUAN

The hiatus of twenty-four years (1273–96) lengthened the total time elapsed between the inception and completion of *Qisha Canon* to over a hundred years. Thus this edition took longer to finish than any other printed edition of the Chinese Buddhist canon from the Song and Yuan, even if we choose the earlier end date of 1322, rather than 1363 when the last of the esoteric sutras were incorporated. By comparison, the first printed edition, *Kaibao Canon*, took far less time, about eleven years (972–83), to carve the woodblocks for the main canon. Similarly, the first Korean edition took about three-quarters of a century (1010–87), even counting the time the Goryeo state was waiting for the Song supplements to arrive.[20]

Perhaps the best comparison, however, would be with *Puning Canon*, which took only fourteen years (1277–90)[21] to finish. Both the Qisha and Puning editions of the canon were initiated by private groups, and both had support from active Buddhist movements with prominent lay members. In the case of *Puning Canon*, the moving spirit was the monk Daoan 道安 (?–d. 1281), a leader of the White Cloud Movement that was especially active in areas of Jiangnan, such as Huzhou and Jiaxing 嘉興 prefectures, but had as its center Puning Monastery in Nanshan in Yuhang 餘杭 in Hangzhou.[22] Before becoming the abbot at Puning Monastery in 1257, Daoan had been at Miaoyan Monastery, which had its own tradition of sutra publishing and apparently possessed at least portions of the earlier printed canons, as implied in the 1332 colophon inscriptions of its own edition of *Da Bore jing*, discussed earlier. Moreover, Miaoyan Monastery was located in Huzhou, as was Yuanjue Monastery, where the fourth Song edition of the canon was produced in the 1130s, and where a printing office continued to be active at least into the early thirteenth century.[23] In his vigorous efforts to promote the White Cloud Movement, Daoan not surprisingly included the ambitious plan to reprint the Buddhist canon, although it was at a time when southern China was about to be conquered by the Mongols. As evidence of his political astuteness, even before the final demise of the Southern Song, Daoan had traveled north to the Mongol capital of Dadu (modern Beijing) and gained support for the White Cloud Movement and for the reprinting of the canon.[24] In fact, when Daoan died in Dadu, about four years after the start of the project, it was continued with equal fervor by four of his disciples who succeeded him one after another as the abbot at Puning Monastery. Thus *Puning Canon* was begun and finished well within the time when work had been suspended on *Qisha Canon*. Furthermore, even though the White Cloud Movement was proscribed and its leader executed in 1320, *Puning Canon* continued to be printed, and other works were added to this edition up through 1335 (see below).[25] At the end of the Yuan, however, the *Puning Canon* blocks were burned along with the entire monastery, so that in another twist of fate, *Qisha Canon* became the one edition whose woodblocks survived into the Ming and became the basis of *Hongwu Southern Canon* (*Hongwu nanzang* 洪武南藏), the first printed edition of the new dynasty.[26] Nevertheless, the legacy of *Puning Canon* lived on in *Qisha Canon*, because when work resumed on the latter in 1297, the sequence of texts followed that in the *Puning Canon* catalogue.[27] Moreover, the collation of texts and the phonological glosses in the Yuan portions of *Qisha Canon* were largely the same as in *Puning Canon*.

The completion of *Qisha Canon* in the Yuan presents a more complex story than the preceding Song chapter, with more interesting details available in the extant sources. This information also reveals *Qisha Canon*'s many complex connections to various collections of Buddhist works, including several other editions of the Buddhist canon, in Chinese, Tibetan, and Tangut. Furthermore, the story involves both institutional Buddhist activities supported by the Mongol court as well as Buddhist movements led by clerics or lay devotees that had more problematic relationships with the Yuan state.

The compilation and the block carving took on some of the energetic efficiency that informed the production of *Puning Canon*, for a variety of reasons. First, the Suzhou region continued its economic growth as its lands and its dense network of waterways increasingly benefited from the land reclamation and water-control projects, state and private, that had begun in the Song. It seems that Suzhou Prefecture suffered less from the turmoil of the Song-Yuan transition than the Hangzhou area. For example, during the Yuan, one of the water-control projects most important for the area just around Yansheng Monastery was the continued and regular dredging of the Wusong River, into which boats could enter. The Wusong River was, of course, connected to the Grand Canal and Lake Tai, as well as to the seacoast at Baoshan 寶山 in Jiading County 嘉定縣. Consequently, in comparison to Song times, Changzhou County became more economically competitive with the area between the Pingjiang prefectural seat and farther west into Lake Tai.[28]

The active role of the local and regional government officials in effecting these land and water improvement programs also indicated interest among some of them in supporting other local projects, including the continuation of *Qisha Canon*. When work resumed around 1297,[29] it seems that several donors, both monks and laymen, provided much of the needed funding. For example, one Zhu Wenqing 朱文清, an Assistant Director of the Left of the Branch Secretariat, and members of his family donated funds to have 1,000 fascicles of sutras carved for *Qisha Canon*. In the following year, another official from the Branch Secretariat, Zhang Wenhu 張文虎, made a large contribution to the carving of blocks for *Qisha Canon*.[30] Similarly, from about 1310 to 1311, a group of monks from Yansheng Monastery itself used the funds left by their deceased preceptor for carving another 1,000 fascicles.[31] It seems that clerics in Qisha Monastery continued to supervise practical aspects of the engraving and printing work. Moreover, we have no donor inscriptions from 1303 until early 1306, suggesting that work on *Qisha Canon* might have proceeded in fits and starts, similar to what occurred during the Song. But around 1306, the pace quickened due to the infusion of funds by and administrative energy of Guan Zhuba 管主八,[32] who held the position of Registrar of Monks in Songjiang Prefecture 松江府僧錄.[33]

Before discussing Guan Zhuba's involvement with *Qisha Canon*, however, it is useful to mention briefly the roles played by two other non-Han clerics in Buddhist activities in the Jiangnan area, who were instrumental in promoting the development of esoteric Buddhism in Yuan China. Although Tantric Buddhist texts had been translated into Chinese since at least the latter part of the sixth century,[34] the incorporation of such works into editions of the Chinese Buddhist canon only began in earnest in the Yuan, due to the efforts of Lamaist Buddhist clerics. These men included not only Tibetan monks, such as those of the Sa-skya sect, particularly the extremely influential and powerful 'Phags-pa (Ch. Basiba 八思巴, 1225–80), who held the title of Imperial Preceptor (*Dishi* 帝師), but also Tangut monks such as Shaluoba 沙囉巴 (1259–1314),[35] possibly Yang Lianzhenjia 楊璉真加 (late thirteenth century), as well as Guan Zhuba. All three held official positions supervising Buddhist institutions in the Jiangnan area. Yang has been excoriated in Chinese historiography as the despoiler of the Southern Song imperial tombs near Hangzhou and the overzealous restorer of Buddhist monasteries in the same region, the lands of which he mismanaged, grossly enriching himself in the process.[36] In contrast, Shaluoba and the lesser-

known Guan Zhuba managed to gain neutral or even somewhat benign reputa-
tions for their contributions to the Chinese Buddhist canon.

Shaluoba, who had studied Tibetan Lamaist Buddhism under 'Phags-pa
and was appointed the Inspector-General of Buddhism in the Jiang-Zhe region
(Jiang-Zhe deng chu Shijiao zongtong 江浙等處釋教總統)[37] in 1295—a few
years after Yang Lianzhenjia's disgrace—apparently assumed a much more con-
ciliatory approach toward the Chinese Buddhists in the area. He was most noted
as a translator of Buddhist works into Chinese, including six texts incorporated
by imperial command into *Puning Canon*, in 1310 and 1313.[38] Only one of these,
'Phags-pa's *Zhang suo zhi lun* 彰所知論, written to instruct Kubilai's crown
prince Jinggim (Zhenjin 真金, 1243–85) in the basics of Sa-skya Buddhism, was
also incorporated into *Qisha Canon*. The inclusion of Shaluoba's translations
in *Puning Canon* suggests that Buddhist officials in central and southern China
during the late thirteenth and early fourteenth centuries favored this edition
of the canon, if only for the practical reason that it was the most recently completed version, with the woodblocks still available.[39] The blocks for Shaluoba's
translations may have been engraved and stored at Puning Monastery, which
was entirely destroyed at the end of the Yuan. This would explain why these
works did not reappear in any subsequent edition of the canon until the late
nineteenth century.[40]

In contrast, works added to *Qisha Canon* during the Yuan, including *Zhang
suo zhi lun* and more than 90 esoteric sutras, appear in almost all the premodern
editions of the canon produced during the Ming and Qing, as well as modern
editions. These supplements to *Qisha Canon* were the work of Guan Zhuba.[41]
By 1306, when his name began appearing in *Qisha Canon* lists of the personnel
involved in the collating, editing, block carving, and fund raising (figure 6.2)
and as a major donor himself (figure 6.3),[42] Guan Zhuba already had extensive experience in compiling and collating numerous other Buddhist collections in Tangut, Tibetan, Chinese, and possibly Uighur, as enumerated in his
inscriptions at the end of several of the works in *Qisha Canon*.[43] For example,
by 1302, he had finished engraving woodblocks for the Tangut Buddhist canon
in Hangzhou and had ordered that 100 copies be printed, as well as up to a
thousand copies of individual works from the canon for distribution in Ningxia,
in today's northwest China, where the Tangut Xi Xia empire (1033–1227) had
been located.[44] In the same year, he was officially authorized to set up a printing
office at Wanshou Monastery 萬壽寺[45] in Hangzhou Circuit to continue printing Buddhist works in various languages. Guan Zhuba's inscription states that
since *Qisha Canon* was not yet completed, he contributed his own funds and
raised funds from other donors to carve another 1,000 fascicles.[46] Other prominent fund raisers included government officials such as Zhang Lü 張閭, whose
title, given in figure 6.2 (leftmost column), was Assistant Director of the Left of

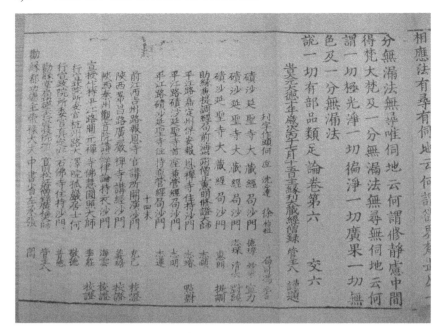

FIGURE 6.2 *QISHAZANG* 361交6: *APIDAMO PINLEI ZULUN*
阿毗達磨品類足論. END OF *JUAN* 6, LISTING BLOCK CARVERS,
EDITORIAL STAFF, AND FUND RAISERS. DATE OF CARVING: 1306.
GUAN ZHUBA'S 管主八 NAME APPEARS ON THE LAST COLUMN OF
THE PENULTIMATE SHEET AND ON THE PENULTIMATE COLUMN OF
THE LAST SHEET.
Courtesy of the East Asian Library and the Gest Collection, Princeton University

the Central Secretariat (Zhongshusheng zuocheng 中書省左承) and who apparently was in the Jiangnan area around 1306, since *Qisha Canon* colophons
mentioning him are only dated to that year.[47]

Furthermore, there is good evidence to support Li Jining's contention that
while monks at Qisha Yansheng Monastery were deeply involved in the collation and compiling of sutras and commentaries to incorporate into *Qisha
Canon*, they no longer supervised the work of cutting the woodblocks and printing the copies, which was done in the printing office that Guan Zhuba had
established in Hangzhou.[48] The colophon inscriptions in some works of *Qisha
Canon* carved in the Yuan, however, suggest that some of the blocks were still
being carved at Yansheng Monastery's printing office (*kanjing ju* 刊經局). For
example, a monk at the monastery donated not money, but seventy-six *dan* 石 of
white rice to feed the carvers in 1306 (figure 6.4).

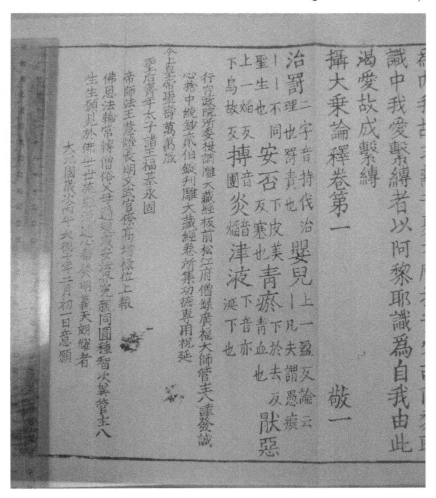

FIGURE 6.3 *QISHAZANG* 248 敬1: *SHE DASHENG LUNSHI* 攝大乘論釋.
INSCRIPTION AT THE END OF *JUAN* 1 SHOWING GUAN ZHUBA'S
DONATION.
Courtesy of the East Asian Library and the Gest Collection, Princeton University

Nevertheless, the supposition that far more of the works were carved in Hangzhou is supported by considering the names of block carvers recorded in volumes
of *Qisha Canon* dated around the early fourteenth century. Three examples are
shown in this chapter's appendix, which lists carvers who worked not only on *Qisha Canon* but also on repairing the blocks for three other works in the Hangzhou
area. For instance, the first work, *Liji zhengyi* 禮記正義 (Correct meaning of the

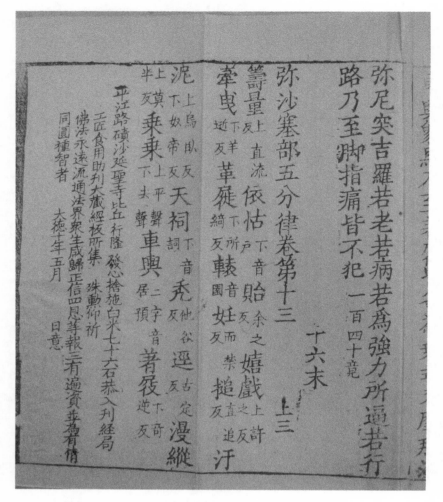

FIGURE 6.4 *QISHAZANG* 329 上3: COLOPHON INSCRIPTION AT THE END
OF *JUAN* 13 OF *MISHA SAI BU HEXI WUFEN LÜ* 彌沙塞部和醯五分律,
INDICATING THE DONATION BY A MONK XINGLU 行路 OF 76 *DAN* OF
WHITE RICE TO FEED THE CARVERS AT THE PRINTING OFFICE OF
YANSHENG MONASTERY, DATED 1306.
Courtesy of the East Asian Library and the Gest Collection, Princeton University

Book of Rites), was originally printed in 1191 by Huang Tang 黃唐, an official in the
Southern Song Tea and Salt Supervisorate for the Liangzhe East Circuit (Liang
Zhe donglu chayansi 兩浙東路茶鹽司).[49] Since the repair of the woodblocks for
Liji zhengyi was done in Hangzhou, it seems almost certain that the block carvers
in the appendix would have been working there, rather than in the Suzhou area.[50]

It was natural, if not inevitable, that Guan Zhuba set up his printing office in Hangzhou. This area had been one of China's largest and most important printing centers since the tenth century, when Hangzhou served as the capital of the Wu-Yue 吳越 kingdom, whose rulers expressed their Buddhist devotion in part through the mass production of religious sculptures, images, and texts. By the late thirteenth century, the abundance of skilled labor for the printing industry—copyists, illustrators, engravers—and the numerous print shops connected to government offices, religious institutions, and private individuals and selling both religious and secular imprints all carried on firmly established traditions of block printing.[51] Access to the abundant local resources for printing very likely explains how *Puning Canon* was completed in an astonishingly short time.

Not surprisingly, Hangzhou printers also led in developing the iconography and stylistic language in religious printed images.[52] Indeed, if there was any other area that could rival Hangzhou in the inventiveness and productiveness of its religious imprints, it was not in Song China but in the Tangut Xi Xia empire, where Buddhism was the state religion and where one conspicuous manifestation of imperial patronage was the massive production of printed religious texts and images.[53] Thus, Guan Zhuba's printing projects in Hangzhou represented the fusion of two rich and distinctive traditions of Buddhist publishing.

In particular, nine of the ten known frontispieces (*feihua* 扉畫) drawn and engraved for *Qisha Canon* during the Yuan display religious iconography and stylistic elements seen in Tibetan Buddhist art that had not previously appeared in Chinese artworks. Two obvious examples in figure 6.5 are the style of the lotus throne with the *vajra* symbol on which Śākyamuni is seated, and the presence of Tibetan (or Indian) monks among the audience listening to the Buddha's preaching. Actually, printed illustrations in Tangut Buddhist imprints produced earlier already showed the multicultural influences at work in the Xi Xia region, and very likely the illustrators and engravers there mastered a variety of artistic styles, whatever their own ethnic backgrounds.

Similarly, craftsmen and commercial print shops in Hangzhou worked together with the printing office established by Guan Zhuba to produce Buddhist texts and illustrations in various styles and different languages.[54] For instance, on the lower left corner of the frontispiece in figure 6.5, the print shop is identified quite precisely: "Printed by the Yang family at the north end of Zhong'an Bridge in Hangzhou" (Hangzhou Zhong'an qiao bei Yang jia yinxing 杭州眾安橋北 楊家印行), and the name of the illustrator, Yang Dechun 楊德春, is given on the lower right. The Yang family print shop, which remained active into at least the early Ming, was located in a commercial area of the city together with other printers, markets, temples, the government examination office, and a public hospital.[55] The exact dates for Yang Dechun are unknown, but the style of the drawing and the figures depicted show great similarity to frontispieces in the Tangut canon, also completed in Hangzhou around 1302 under Guan Zhuba's

FIGURE 6.5 *QISHAZANG* 160 傷2: FRONTISPIECE IN A NUMBER OF WORKS, INCLUDING THIS ONE: *ZUI WU BIJING* 最無比經. BLOCKS FOR TEXT CARVED 1239.
Courtesy of the East Asian Library and the Gest Collection, Princeton University

supervision. Furthermore, a recut of figure 6.5, with the narrow cartouches originally giving the names of the shop and of the illustrator blacked out, appears in some extant copies of *Qisha Canon*. In the volumes of *Qisha Canon* in the National Library of China, there are works with a similar frontispiece, but the artist is Yang Xinzhen 楊信真, who probably recarved the illustration sometime later, perhaps later in the Yuan or in the Ming.[56]

Recarving of frontispieces was probably routine and frequent, since these woodblocks were used to make impressions attached to any number of Buddhist works, including popular sutras in great demand by donors willing to pay for up to thousands of copies. Consequently, these woodblocks would have been worn out quite quickly, and this may explain why no Song-period frontispieces for *Qisha Canon* seem to be extant. Although there are no dates given in the pictures, stylistic similarities and the names of block carvers in several of the illustrations suggest that the "original" woodblocks probably all date to around the first decade of the fourteenth century.[57] Once cut, impressions from these blocks could be attached to sutras that had been printed at an earlier or later date. Thus the date of an inscription in the text cannot be assumed to be that of the frontispiece.[58]

Three other *Qisha Canon* frontispieces list the name of the illustrator, Chen Sheng 陳昇, and one also gives the name of the carver, Chen Ning 陳寧.

The latter's name is also given (in Chinese characters) on an illustration in the sutra *Bayang jing* 八陽經 in Uighur script.[59] Although the remnants of the only known copy of this work were retrieved in the Turfan area in northwest China, it is most likely that at least the blocks for the frontispiece, if not the sutra itself, were carved in Hangzhou[60]—further attesting to Guan Zhuba's vigorous efforts to disseminate Buddhist works in different languages throughout the empire.

By around 1322, most of *Qisha Canon* was completed—a far quicker effort than what had been done in the late Southern Song. Furthermore, Guan Zhuba's intention was not limited to completing that *Qisha Canon* as it originally had been intended by the monks of that monastery, but extended to incorporating esoteric sutras, vinaya, and *sāstras* missing in the *Qisha, Puning,* and other editions of the canon compiled in central and southern China, as well as distributing these works to monasteries throughout the country, not necessarily as parts of the canon. He accomplished this by copying the available works from the edition of the canon in Hongfa Monastery in Dadu, as well as compiling several in the Hangzhou printing office.[61] The broad dissemination of these esoteric works is suggested in the inscription at the end of *Biqiu xixue luefa* 苾蒭習學略法 with commentary by 'Phags-pa (figure 6.6). The blocks engraved for these works were probably kept in Hangzhou and were not moved to Yansheng Monastery until 1363 by Guan Zhuba's son, Guan Nianzhenchila 管輦真吃剌.[62]

Another instance of a large Buddhist printing project in the early fourteenth century with possible connections to *Qisha Canon* was the recutting of parts of *Pilu Canon* (*Piluzang* 毗盧藏), which was originally produced in the Song (1120–51).[63] The sponsors of the reproduction in 1315 were members of the White Lotus Movement, led by one Chen Juelin 陳覺琳 at Bao'en Wanshou Hall in Houshan in Jianyang County in Jianning Prefecture in northern Fujian (figure 6.7a), which had been established in 1239.[64] The evidence for connections between *Qisha Canon* and the White Lotus Movement is plausible, if circumstantial. According to Barend ter Haar, the inspiration for the White Lotus Movement can be traced to the monk Mao Ziyuan 茅子元 (ca. 1088–1166) in the Southern Song, whose White Lotus Penance Hall (Bailian chanting 白蓮懺堂) was located near Lake Dianshan, about eight kilometers southwest of Chen Lake. In addition, the Chan master Jitang, who founded Yansheng Chapel 延聖庵 at Qisha, had advocated the Lotus Tradition (*Lianzong* 蓮宗). Then in the Southern Song during the early decades of the carving of *Qisha Canon,* some of the donors from Wujiang and Huating districts had names with the affiliation characters *pu* 普 and *jue* 覺, as noted in the colophons of the works in *Qisha Canon.* It was not until around 1315 in the Yuan, however, that Houshan Hall began its printing project.

In fact, rather than creating an entire canon, the plan was to recut the same four great sutras as Miaoyan Monastery in Huzhou would do less than two

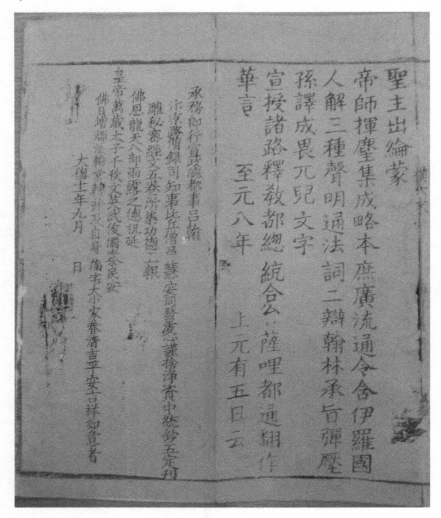

FIGURE 6.6 *QISHAZANG* 576横6: *DA YUAN DISHI SHUO GENBEN YIQIE YOUBU BIQIU XIXUE LUEFA*大元帝師說根本一切有部苾蒭習學略法
Courtesy of the East Asian Library and the Gest Collection, Princeton University

decades later. The sponsors at Bao'en wanshou Hall (or Houshan Hall) probably conceived of their task as a reprinting of *Pilu Canon* because they had access to copies of this edition, which had been printed in Fuzhou 福州.[65] Houshan Hall was a highly suitable choice as headquarters, since it was located in the same district (Chongtai li 崇泰里) as the Jianyang printing industry, which had become, next to Hangzhou, the largest book center in the country starting in

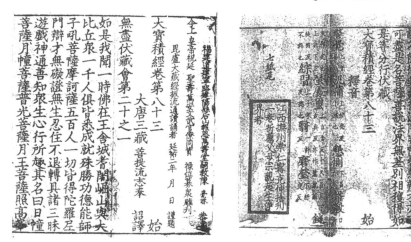

FIGURE 6.7A AND FIGURE 6.7B COLOPHON INSCRIPTIONS FROM *DA BAO JIJING* 大寶積經: A) END OF *JUAN* 83, INSCRIPTION IDENTIFY-ING CHEN JUELIN AT THE WANSHOU BAO'EN TANG IN HOUSHAN IN JIANYANG DISTRICT, DATED 1315; B) END OF *JUAN* 50, INSCRIPTION IDENTIFYING A DONOR FROM FUZHOU 撫州 IN JIANGXI.
Taibei: National Central Library, Rare Book #08666

the late twelfth century.[66] The colophons at the end of many *juan* of the sutras show, however, that the donors who contributed to the carving or printing of the Houshan Hall project came from a wide geographical region. Although many were natives of northern Fujian — from other districts in Jianning Prefecture and from Shaowu Prefecture 邵武路 — others identified themselves as from various circuits, including Fuzhou lu 撫州路 across the border in modern Jiangxi (figure 6.7b), Guangzhou, Hubei, and Henan. One of the donors from Henan, named Chen Jueyuan 陳覺圓, may have been a relative of Chen Juelin, or just another member of the White Cloud Movement who also used the affiliation characters *jue* and *yuan* popular with White Lotus adherents.[67]

The White Lotus adherents of Houshan Hall can also be linked indirectly with other Buddhist printing activities, such as through their connections with an eminent patron, King Chungseon 忠宣王 (r. 1308–11) of Goryeo, a close relative of the Mongol imperial family who spent far more of his life in China than in his own country.[68] In 1308, when the White Lotus Movement was temporarily banned and members of Houshan Hall were accused of insidious and surreptitious religious activities, King Chungseon came to their defense at the imperial court and helped win them a reprieve.[69] It is not clear why he did so, but as a devout Buddhist who continually demonstrated his piety by donating scriptures and even entire sets of the Buddhist canon to many monasteries, especially in the Hangzhou region, he may have become interested in the printing venture of Houshan Hall. In fact, although Huiyin Monastery 慧因寺 in Hangzhou, which had become known as Goryeo Monastery (Gaoli si 高麗寺) by the Northern Song, was the focus of patronage by Goryeo kings and officials, other temples, including major ones in the Hangzhou area as well as Daqingshou Monastery 大慶壽寺 in Dadu, also received gifts of Buddhist works. Except for one instance, in 1312 when King Chungseon apparently commissioned the carving of woodblocks for a large collection of sutras in Dadu, it is unclear whether he had blocks carved or merely had impressions made from existing blocks. For the Hangzhou monasteries, both King Chungseon and a retired Goryeo prime minister, Weon Kwan 元瓘, donated copies of the canon as well as land.[70]

Thus by the first half of the fourteenth century, even as Guan Zhuba was making strenuous efforts to complete *Qisha Canon*, other groups, including the lay adherents of the White Lotus Movement at Houshan Hall in northern Fujian and the White Cloud followers at Miaoyan Monastery, were also active in producing not entire editions of the canon, but only works that were deemed the most important, such as the four great sutras. Because these were the most often reprinted, the woodblocks for older editions wore out more quickly or had been damaged or destroyed. The questions then arise: Why print an entire canon, and in particular, why complete *Qisha Canon?* One reason had to do with the far greater religious merit and prestige accrued by a monastery that compiled and published an entire canon, rather than a collection of Buddhist works or short booklets of parts of sutras or *dharani* sutras, or single prayer sheets and images. It seems that Yansheng Monastery was noted primarily for the canon compiled there and not for much else. And for Guan Zhuba and his staff, the opportunity to see to completion an edition that incorporated three hundred fascicles of esoteric sutras into *Qisha Canon* must have been a powerful incentive. Once it was finished, copies could have been printed to serve as donations from eminent donors to various monasteries both in China and abroad, in Japan and possibly in Korea.[71]

Perhaps the more urgent reason was the need for complete canonical collections of Buddhist writings for which the woodblocks would be available for reprinting. As mentioned earlier, woodblocks for so many editions of the Buddhist canon, both in China and elsewhere in East Asia, suffered perilously short lifetimes. Within China, by the early fourteenth century, apparently the only editions of the Buddhist canon with a complete set of woodblocks were *Puning Canon* and *Qisha Canon* in the south and two or three in the north, produced under imperial auspices. Judging from extant portions of those editions produced in Dadu, they were probably not disseminated as widely as the southern editions. For example, the edition produced in the last quarter of the thirteenth century and kept at the capital's Hongfa Monastery 弘法寺 (also dubbed by modern scholars as *Hongfa Canon* 弘法藏),[72] was obviously not very accessible for ordinary Buddhists, even if some monasteries in China, Korea, and Japan were fortunate recipients. Neither was the edition produced around the Yanyou 延祐 period (1314–20), remnants of which were discovered at Beijing's Zhihua Monastery 智化寺 in 1984.[73] Thus there was good reason to finish *Qisha Canon* and to repair the older blocks that had been damaged or destroyed. Where and by whom the works that lacked printing blocks were repaired during the Ming constitutes another complex chapter in the story of *Qisha Canon*.

QISHA CANON DURING THE MING

During the Ming, one of the earliest and perhaps most notable use of *Qisha Canon* was as the exemplar for *Hongwu Southern Canon*, the dynasty's first official edition of the Buddhist canon, which was compiled and carved in Nanjing between circa 1372 and circa 1403. In fact, the contents of the first 591 cases of the Hongwu edition were essentially facsimile recuts of *Qisha Canon*, with some editorial revisions.[74] Despite some revisions and rearrangements of the contents from *Qisha Canon*, most of the official edition was a facsimile recut of the earlier canon, so that in some volumes details such as block carvers' names and donor information from the latter were reproduced. The *Hongwu nanzang* compilers in the early Ming may have chosen to reproduce *Qisha Canon* over other Song, Yuan, Jin, or Liao editions for the practical reason that both the paper copies and many of the woodblocks for the *Qisha* edition were available in the Jiangnan area. Moreover, *Qisha Canon* was itself the heir to the compilation efforts from *Kaibao Canon* through the other southern Chinese editions of the Song and Yuan.

Of course, by the early Ming, not all the original woodblocks for *Qisha Canon* were extant. As noted earlier, *Da Bore jing* was one of the first group of sutras carved at Yansheng Monastery, during the Southern Song, circa 1216–29. By the second decade of the fourteenth century, the original blocks apparently were no longer available. Thus monasteries and other institutions holding or wishing to acquire copies of *Qisha Canon* had to fill in the missing volumes using other printed editions, such as that from Houshan Hall or Miaoyan Monastery. But within a century or less, even the blocks for these two sets apparently were no longer available, because around 1411–12, a group of Buddhist devotees in Hangzhou, led by a novice monk, Bao Shanhui 鮑善恢, had the blocks for several works recarved.[75] According to an inscription dated 1411, Shanhui was at the time associated with Xianlin Monastery for doctrinal study (Xianlin jiangsi 仙林講寺),[76] located east of Yanqiao 鹽橋 (Salt [market] bridge) inside the

Hangzhou city walls. But from another inscription,[77] by the following year, he was associated with Gaoli Huiyin Monastery for doctrinal study (Gaoli Huiyin jiangsi 高麗慧因講寺, see above), which had been destroyed at the end of the Yuan and only slowly rebuilt during the Ming—a process that was completed around the end of the sixteenth century. Thus it is no surprise that the set(s) of the canon donated by King Chungseon and by the retired minister Weon Kwan a century earlier were no longer complete.[78]

In the colophon inscriptions for the recut portions of *Qisha Canon* that his group sponsored, Shanhui noted that he tried to replace missing works in Xianlin Monastery's collection of sutras by looking for copies from both Qisha Yansheng and Miaoyan monasteries, but found that many of the blocks were worn and could no longer be used.[79] From the way that Shanhui worded his colophons ("sui wang Qisha, Miaoyan er sha buyin zangdian" 遂往磧砂 妙嚴二刹 補印藏典), it seems that the surviving blocks of *Qisha Canon* and the Miaoyan works remained at their respective temples.[80]

In another of Bao Shanhui's inscriptions appearing in *Qisha Canon*, he included a historically valuable text that contributed to the entangled history of the different editions of the canon.[81] This particular inscription, also dated 1411, incorporated part of a text that had been composed far earlier, in 1183, by Zhao Feng 趙渢, an official in the Jurchen Jin government. The 1183 text comes from a stele erected to commemorate the efforts of the nun Cui Fazhen 崔法珍, who was instrumental in raising funds for the engraving of *Zhaocheng (Jin) Canon* 趙城 (金)藏 (ca. 1148–73) in south-central Shanxi. Nearly two and half centuries later, Bao Shanhui copied part of the stele text, to praise her efforts and perhaps suggest that he was, on a smaller scale, emulating her accomplishment. The text may have been available in *Hongfa Canon*, held in Dadu during the Yuan, from which Guan Zhuba copied works to help complete *Qisha Canon*. In turn, of course, *Hongfa Canon* was an elaboration of *Zhaocheng Canon*, the woodblocks of which had been eventually transported to Dadu.[82]

During the Ming, print shops in Hangzhou continued to play an important role in reprinting portions of *Qisha Canon*. Figure 6.8a shows an end sheet pasted on a re-engraved portion of *Qisha Canon* during the Ming or later by the Yang family print shop, still at the same address as given in the frontispiece of figure 6.5, near the Houchao Gate 候朝門. We do not know when the impression in figure 6.8 was made, but if it was paid for by the devotee who had the dedication written inside the large lotus colophon block, then the date would be 1432 (Xuande 宣德 7, given in the last column). The figure of Weituo 韋馱, however, had been carved ten years earlier (Yongle 永樂 20, i.e., 1422), as indicated by the small inscription at the lower left corner. From the information in figures 6.5 and 6.8, we know therefore that the Yang family's print shop was in business for at least a century. The donor, one Dong Fucheng 董福成, identified himself

FIGURE 6.8A AND FIGURE 6.8B *QISHAZANG* 417背 1: *JIETUO DAO LUN* 解脫道論: A) DONOR DEDICATION (1432), PRINTER COLO-PHON, AND WEITUO (CARVED 1422); B) BEGINNING OF *JUAN* 1. *Courtesy of the East Asian Library and the Gest Collection, Princeton University*

as from Daxing County 大興縣 in the Beijing area, so he was rather far from home, possibly on a pilgrimage to the famous temples in Hangzhou and the surrounding areas. He vowed, together with a bevy of family members—wife, younger brother, sons and their wives, etc.—to have printed one *zang* (5,048 copies) of the sutra.[83] Actually, Dong Fucheng had several different works from *Qisha Canon* reprinted, and the calligraphy in those recarved versions clearly distinguishes them from the earlier Song and Yuan parts of the edition.[84]

Puzzles yet to be fully resolved abound when we examine Ming impressions of volumes found in extant holdings of *Qisha Canon*. For instance, attached to the end of a number of volumes of other parts of *Qisha Canon* is the colophon block and Weituo of the Jiang family, a print shop in Nanjing, close to the Jubao Gate in southern Nanjing (聚寶門來寶樓姜家印行) and near the famous Bao'en Monastery 報恩寺 (figure 6.9a). In fact, the text of the sutra itself (figure 6.9b) looks like an early Ming reprint, judging from the calligraphic style. The exact same colophon box, identification of the Jiang family, and Weituo appear at the end of fascicle 41 of *Da Bore jing* in the Gest copy of *Qisha Canon*, but there the colophon box is blank and the calligraphic style is different.

Another example is the inscription at the end of *Dazang shengjiao fabao biaomu* 大藏聖教法寶標目, shown in figure 6.10a, which is not from the original printing of *Qisha Canon* done in 1306 but quite likely a reprint from the early or mid-Ming made in Beijing, with a date of 1436 for this particular impression.[85]

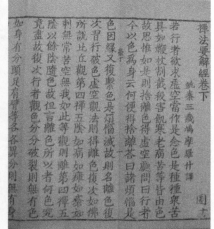

禪法要解經卷下

姚秦三藏鳩摩羅什譯

若行者欲求虛空當作是念色是種種衆苦
其如癰相刺截殺害飢渴衆老病苦等皆由色
故思惟如是則捨離色得虛空處問曰行者
今以色爲身云何便捨離苍曰諸煩惱是
色因緣又復緊色是煩惱減故則名離色復
次冒行破色虛空觀法則得離色復次如佛
所說比立觀第四禪五陰如病如癰如瘡如箭如
刺無常苦空無我如此等觀則離第四禪五
陰以除陰隨色故但言離色所以者何色究
竟盡故復次此行者觀色分分破裂則無有色
如身有分頭足有形等各各異分則無有身

圖七

三寶弟子太監吳誠謹施

正統十年二月十七日

FIGURE 6.9A AND FIGURE 6.9B *QISHAZANG* 433圖4: *CHANFA YAOJIE JING* 禪法要解經, *JUAN* 2. THE JIANG FAMILY PRINT SHOP WAS LOCATED IN THE SOUTH OF NANJING NEAR THE BAO'EN SI 寶恩寺.
Courtesy of the East Asian Library and the Gest Collection, Princeton University

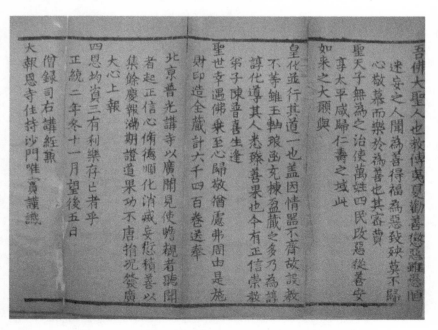

FIGURE 6.10A *QISHAZANG* 586遵 1: *DAZANG SHENGJIAO FABAO BIAOMU* 大藏聖教法寶標目. PRINTING DATED 1437.
Courtesy of the East Asian Library and the Gest Collection, Princeton University

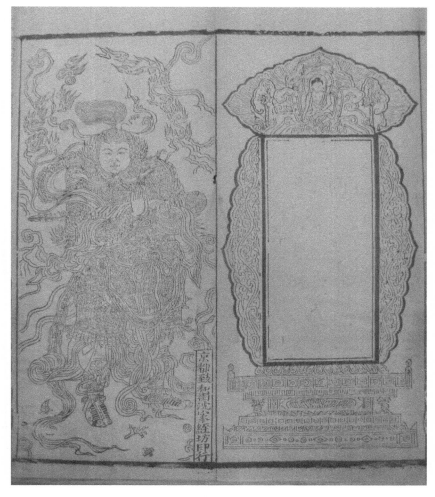

FIGURE 6.10B *QISHAZANG* 586遵 10: BLANK CARTOUCHE AND
WEITUO
Courtesy of the East Asian Library and the Gest Collection, Princeton University

Judging from the figure of 6,400 fascicles for the entire canon mentioned by the
donor, the blocks for this copy of the work may not have been cut expressly to
make up for lost parts of *Qisha Canon* but possibly for the short-lived Hongwu
edition compiled under imperial auspices (1372–98).[86] The blank cartouche
(figure 6.10b) at the end lacks a donor inscription, but at the lower right corner
of the Weituo panel, the print shop is identified as that of the Shen family on
Zhihe Street in Beijing.

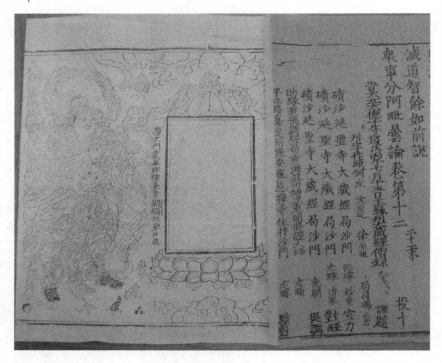

FIGURE 6.11 *QISHAZANG* 363投 10: *ZHONGSHIFEN APITAN LUN*
眾事分阿毘曇論, *JUAN* 12 (CARVED 1306). WHITE SHEET (LAST
TWO FOLDS) ATTACHED BY HU FAMILY SUTRA PRINT SHOP IN
BEIJING DURING THE MING.
Courtesy of the East Asian Library and the Gest Collection, Princeton University

Also located in Beijing was the Hu 胡 family print shop inside the Chongwen
Gate 崇文門 (figure 6.11). But apparently either this copy was not paid for by a
donor or that information was not recorded. That the preceding sheet with the
original list of block carvers, editorial staff, and fund raisers (same as that in figure
6.2) was cut off shows the recycling through reprinting of Buddhist works by print
shops for later donors seeking to earn merit. The Hu print shop also issued the
Qisha Canon copy of *Sifen lüzang* 四分律藏 (336 隨 1–10) shown in figure 6.12,
of which the first nine volumes are impressions from the original 1306 blocks.
The tenth volume, however, came from *Yongle Southern Canon* 永樂南藏 or a
copy thereof, because the original *qianziwen* designation (in the center fold in
figure 6.12: "姑六") corresponds to that edition. Since the volume was used for a
set of *Qisha Canon*, however, the case number had to be changed to "隨十," as
indicated by the small square of paper at the bottom of the first column.

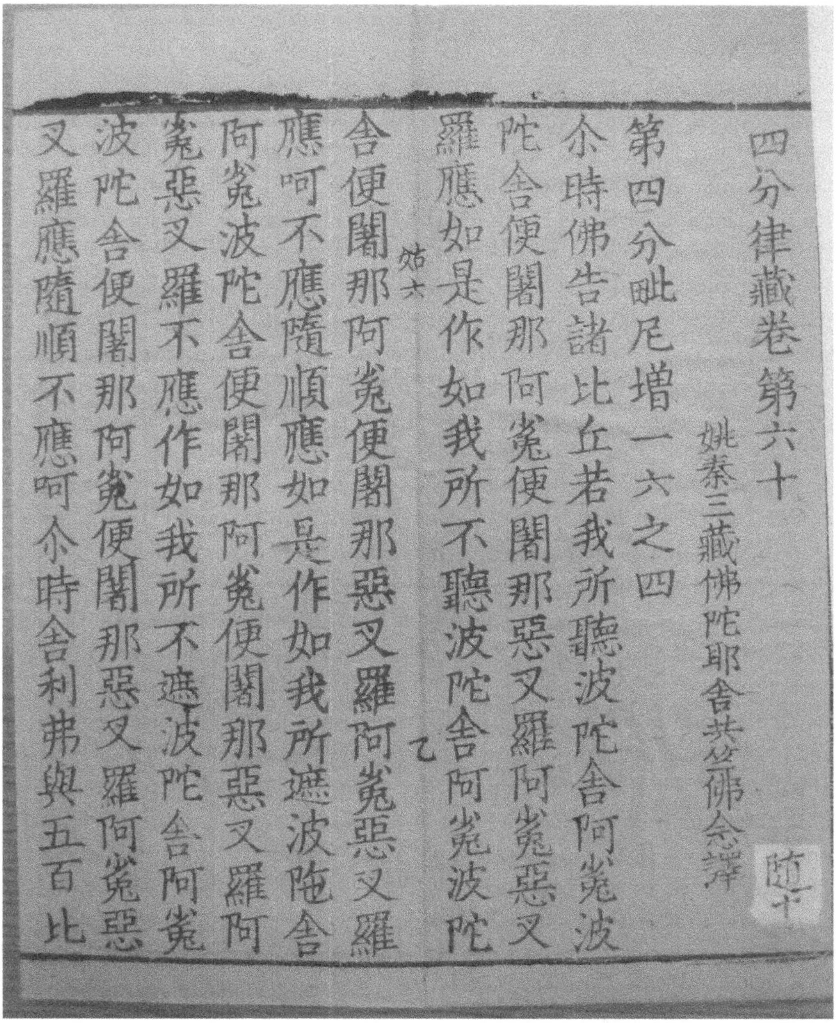

四分律藏卷第六十

姚秦三藏佛陀耶舍共竺佛念譯

第四分毗尼增一六之四

尔時佛告諸比丘若我所聽波陀舍阿㲰波
陀舍便闥那阿㲰便闥那惡叉羅阿㲰惡叉
羅應如是作如我所不聽波陀舍阿㲰波陀

舍便闥那阿㲰便闥那惡叉羅阿㲰惡叉羅
應呵不應隨順應如是作如我所遮波陀舍
阿㲰波陀舍便闥那阿㲰便闥那惡叉羅阿
㲰惡叉羅不應作如我所不遮波陀舍阿㲰
波陀舍便闥那阿㲰便闥那惡叉羅阿㲰惡
又羅應隨順不應呵尔時舍利弗與五百比

姑六

乙

How did print shops obtain copies of works from *Qisha Canon* (or any other edition of the canon)? Most likely, the blocks were kept in one location (or possibly several locations — usually monasteries — close to each other). Print shops throughout the country could then pay for making a number of impressions of works, to which they could add their own end sheet with a colophon block and picture of Weituo. Thus they would have a ready-made supply of various works from the canon, particularly popular texts such as the *Lotus Sutra* or even the most popular part of that work (*Pumen pin* 普門品 or "Gate of universal salvation")[87] to anticipate customer demand. It is also possible that the print shops recarved woodblocks to make facsimile copies of the works from a canon, or sometimes made hand copies. The blocks for *Yongle Southern Canon* were kept in Nanjing at Bao'en Monastery, so the Hu print shop may have bought copies of works from this edition and transported them back to Beijing for prospective donors' use.[88] It is difficult to guess when this tenth fascicle of *Sifen lüzang* was printed, but the calligraphy suggests the first half of the fifteenth century, perhaps before the third official edition of the canon, *Yongle Northern Canon*, was completed around 1440 in Beijing. Although this northern edition corrected many of the textual errors in the preceding southern edition and was generally considered to be better collated, its blocks were kept within the Forbidden City and very difficult for ordinary people and print shops to access to make copies.

This explains why copies of works from *Qisha Canon* continued to be issued until the end of the sixteenth century, like that shown in figure 6.13. The colophon does not identify the print shop but does have information about the donor, a monk from Zhifo Cloister 芝佛院 in Macheng County 麻城縣 in Huguang 湖廣, and is dated 1599, nearly three centuries after the original carving of this sutra, the first in the canon. We do not know, however, whether the *Qisha Canon* woodblocks were still in existence in 1599. Yansheng Monastery had been repaired in 1417 but probably fell into neglect thereafter. Several poems from later in the fifteenth century paint a melancholy scene of a dilapidated monastery by the shore of Lake Chen. Wu Kuan's 吳寬 (1435–1504) verses mention that there was a sutra print shop on the premises which the birds did not dare to fly into, because there were still woodblocks or copies of sutras. In any case, it would seem that either the roof or part of the walls had already fallen in. By the mid-Chongzhen period (1628–44), the monastery was in ruins.[89]

Thus *Qisha Canon* during the Ming progressed from its early prestigious role as the exemplar for the first official Ming edition to a humbler one as the storehouse of sutras that were mostly printed individually for donors. In its place in the late sixteenth century came *Jiaxing Canon*, different in its page layout and string-bound format from the earlier editions in scroll and sutra binding formats, as well as in its methods of acquiring donations for the initial block carving.

FIGURE 6.13 QISHAZANG 1 天 1: MING WANLI 27 (1599) COLOPHON
INSCRIPTION AND WEITUO ATTACHED TO END OF *DA BORE*
BOLUOMIDUO JING 大般若波羅蜜多經, *JUAN* 1.
Courtesy of the East Asian Library and the Gest Collection, Princeton University

CONCLUSION

Qisha Canon enjoyed a life and an afterlife of nearly four centuries in all, unmatched by any other set of woodblocks for a premodern edition of the Chinese
Buddhist canon, other than the second Goryeo edition. This longevity afforded
opportunities for *Qisha Canon* to influence and be influenced by other editions

of the canon. For example, the more direct exemplars used to collate *Qisha Canon* included *Sixi Canon*, *Puning Canon*, and *Hongfa Canon*. In turn, *Qisha Canon* became the exemplar from which *Hongwu Southern Canon* was copied. Furthermore, in any extant set of *Qisha Canon*, we find a physical commingling of volumes printed from its original woodblocks as well as from several other canon editions and other large collections that were engraved before or after *Qisha Canon*.

Because of Guan Zhuba's work, this edition also became one of the first that included a significant number of esoteric sutras and the Tibetan-Nepalese artistic influence in the design of its frontispieces. In fact, in the Yuan Dynasty, the reunion of north and south China afforded Buddhists opportunities to assemble a larger Chinese Buddhist canon than ever, by incorporating new works translated or written during that period, such as esoteric sutras from Tibet, and by recovering works previously missing from editions in a particular region. Works that had only been available in north China or the Liao or Xi Xia empires or Goryeo, but not in south China, were now added to *Qisha Canon*, making it an East Asian canon in Chinese.

Finally, since we have more extant volumes of *Qisha Canon* than of any other edition until the advent of *Jiaxing Canon*, we can, as has already been done to some extent, mine the donor inscriptions to learn more about how and precisely why Buddhist clergy and laity supported the enormous enterprise of printing an entire canon. But like so many Chinese block-printed works, religious and secular, the extant *Qisha Canon* volumes are later reprints, probably from the Ming, so that we also learn about the more commercial aspects of this kind of publishing on demand. In effect, the history of *Qisha Canon* allows us to understand not just the Buddhist cult of the book but more broadly, the Chinese obsession with the written word.

APPENDIX

BLOCK CARVERS RECORDED IN WORKS IN
QISHA CANON CUT DURING THE YUAN AND
IN THE FOLLOWING WORKS:

1. *Liji zhengyi* 禮記正義, 70 fascicles. Originally carved in 1191 (宋紹熙 2); repaired in the Yuan.

   Chen Bangqing 陳邦卿   Wang Gui 王桂
   Chen Wen 陳文   Xu Jin 徐進
   Chen Xiu 陳琇   Xu Ren 徐仁

Chen Yunsheng 陳允升   Xu Yong 徐泳

Fan Hua 范華   Xu Yuan 徐囦

He Hou 何屋   Yang Ming 楊明 (S)

Hu Chang 胡昶   Yu Rong 俞榮

Jiang Folao 蔣佛老   Zhang Wen 章文

Mao Wenlong 茅文龍   Zhang Zhen 張珍

Shen Zhen 沈珍   Zhu Wen 朱文 (S)

Shi Bogong 史伯恭

2. *Shiji* 史記, 130 fascicles. Originally carved in the Song; repaired in the Yuan.

Chen Bangqing 陳邦卿   Wang Hui 汪惠

Chen Riyu 陳日裕   Wang Xing 王興

He Jiuwan 何九萬   Xiong Daoqiong 熊道瓊

He Tong 何通   Xu Yong 徐泳

Hu Chang 胡昶   Xu Yuezu 徐悅祖

Hu Qing 胡慶   Yang Cai 楊采

Mao Wenlong 茅文龍   Ying Zihua 應子華

Pan Yong 潘用   Yu Rong 俞榮

Shen Zhen 沈珍   Zhang Zhuo 章著

Wang Gui 王桂

3. *Hou Han shu* 後漢書, 90 fascicles. Originally carved in the Southern Song Shaoxing period (1131–62); repaired in the Yuan.

Chen Bangqing 陳邦卿   Ren Wei 壬韋

Chen Riyu 陳日裕   Wang Xing 王興

Chen Xiu 陳琇   Xiong Daoqiong 熊道瓊

Chen Yunsheng 陳允升   Xu Ren 徐仁

Fan Hua 范華   Xu Yong 徐泳

He Hao 何浩   Xu Youshan 徐友山

He Tong 何通   Ying De 應德

He Zong 何宗   Yu Rong 俞榮

Hu Chang 胡昶   Zhang Wen 章文

Jiang Folao 蔣佛老   Zhang Zhen 張珍

Pan Yong 潘用   Zhang Zhuo 章著

Qi Ming 齊明   Zhu Zi 朱梓

NOTES

I thank Jiang Wu, Jennifer Eichman, the two readers of the submitted manuscript, and especially Hua Kaiqi for their comments and corrections.

1. On the Chinese Buddhist canon, see Li and He, *Dazangjing yanjiu*, for a thorough introduction covering much recent scholarship. A shorter but amply illustrated work is Li Jining, *Fojing banben*. See the introduction in this volume for a list of block-printed editions of the Tripitaka produced in China in the Song and Yuan. There were also *Liaozang* 遼藏 (ca. 1031–60) printed by the Khitan state, and the two Goryeo editions (1011–87 and 1236–51). Only the woodblocks of the second Goryeo edition survive. But even today, scholars continue to discover volumes that seem to belong to previously unidentified editions, as Li Jining discusses in his book.

2. The three nearly complete sets are held by Chongshan Monastery 崇善寺 in Taiyuan, Shanxi Province, in China (5,418 volumes); by the Gest Collection in the Princeton University East Asian Library (5,323 volumes in the set plus about another dozen miscellaneous volumes); and the Shaanxi Provincial Library (combined from the holdings of Kaiyuan 開元寺 and Wolong monasteries 臥龍寺 in Chang'an 長安). This last set (about 5,000 fascicles), with the missing parts supplied from other editions of the canon, as well as other sutra collections printed in the Song, Yuan, and Ming, formed the basis of the photofacsimile edition first published in 1933–35, then reprinted in 1962–65 and in 1987. The last reprint includes materials from the Princeton Gest holdings. (See under *Qishazang* in the bibliography for these reprints.) The next largest collection is that of the Kyō-u Library 杏雨書屋 in Osaka, Japan (4,548 fascicles). See Li and He, *Dazangjing yanjiu*, 254–56, for a listing of the libraries with sizeable portions of *Qisha Canon*.

3. In addition to Li and He, *Dazangjing yanjiu*, esp. 253–315, and Li Jining, *Fojing banben*, esp. 119–34, see also the essays included in the photofacsimile reprint *Yingyin Song Qisha zangjing*. Other works discussing *Qisha Canon* will be mentioned in the course of this chapter.

4. Li Jining, *Fojing banben*, 127. The colophon inscription (*kanji* 刊記) is reproduced in *Yingyin Song Qisha zangjing*, as well as Tekiya Katsu, *Sekisha zōkyō*, 50–51, and Li and He, *Dazangjing yanjiu*, 286. Tekiya's work is a useful and convenient collection of the inscriptions from the *Yingyin Song Qisha zangjing*.

5. Li and He, *Dazangjing yanjiu*, 263.

6. Most of *Qisha Canon* was completed by 1322, but additions, including a number of sutras of the esoteric schools (*mimi jing* 秘密經), were not fully incorporated until 1363. These esoteric sutras took up most of the last 28 cases (*han* 函) of a total of 591 cases. See below for further discussion. In this chapter, the works in *Qisha Canon* will be designated by case number (*hanhao* 函號), the *qianziwen* 千字文 character, and the volume (*ce* 冊) number. For example, *Pusa dichi jing* 菩薩地持經 in *Qisha Canon* is 203 維 1–203 維 8. That is, this sutra is found in case 203, corresponding to the *qianziwen* 維, volumes 1–8 in *Qisha Canon* (and to no. 1581 in *Taishō Canon*).

7. By the early sixteenth century, the monastery was referred to as the Qisha (chan) si 磧砂 (禪) 寺 in gazetteers such as *Changzhou xianzhi*, 10.14a, and *Gusu zhi*, 29.82b–83a.

8. The history of Yansheng Monastery has been discussed in the various modern essays written for the photofacsimile edition (1931–35) of *Qisha Canon* and more recently in Li and He, *Dazangjing yanjiu*, 256–61. The two texts closest in time to the period when the canon was produced at the monastery are the records by the monk Yuanzhi 圓至 toward the end of the Zhiyuan 至元 period (1264–94) of the Yuan. These two texts from Yuanzhi's *Muqian ji* 牧潛集 have been reproduced in full in *Yingyin Song Qisha zangjing* and in Li and He, *Dazangjing yanjiu*, 257–59. Among the gazetteers, the longest description of the monastery is in the *(Tongzhi) Suzhou fuzhi*, 42.32b–33a.

9. *Zhouzhuang zhenzhi* 1882, 1.15b–16b. The lake has been variously named Chen hu 陳湖, supposedly in memory of the submerged land (Chen xian 陳縣 or Chen zhou 陳州); or Chen hu 沉湖 (Sunken Lake); or Cheng hu 澄湖. The last name is preferred today and suggests how clearly one can see to the bottom of the lake, which is usually only about 2 meters deep. According to tradition, when the lake is calm, it is possible to see below the water streets and houses of villages submerged long ago.

10. *Gusu zhi*, 29.78a.

11. It is not clear when the chapel was elevated to the status of a cloister (*yuan* 院), but by the time the carving of sutras started in 1216, the inscriptions recorded a Yansheng yuan.

12. Liu Xinru, "Buddhist Institutions," table 8, 46. Of course, taken as a whole, the entire lower Yangzi region was the Buddhist heartland of China in the Song, and by no means was Pingjiang Prefecture economically undeveloped in Southern Song China. But within the Jiangnan region, it is useful to differentiate more precisely among localities (prefectures and the counties within). Liu argues that there is a significant correlation between the number of Buddhist monasteries and the economic and demographic growth in each locality, based on his data for the Song.

13. Hucker, *Dictionary*, 126a, says that *Chengzhong lang* (no. 469) was a prestige title to fix the holder's rank status, in this case, a lowly rank 9a. Zhao Anguo may have been a Song imperial clansman, but I have not found information about him in Song sources.

14. The story of the Yuanjue edition (Li and He, *Dazangjing yanjiu*, 233–51) of the canon makes that of the Qisha edition look simple. Work on the woodblocks for the Yuanjue edition began in 1132 in the Southern Song and may have taken several decades to complete. The blocks were originally engraved in what was first known as Yuanjue Chan Cloister (Yuanjue Chan yuan 圓覺禪院) in Sixi 思溪 in Huzhou 湖州. The cloister was later elevated to a monastery and renamed Fabao Chan Monastery (Fabao Chan si 法寶禪寺). This partly explains the various names by which this edition of the canon is known: *Yuanjuezang, Sixizang, Fabaozang*, etc. Confusion also abounds as to whether the woodblocks for the complete canon were cut more than once or the original set of blocks was repaired as needed over time.

15. Li and He, *Dazangjing yanjiu*, 278–79, gives a table detailing the differences between the two catalogues.

16. 61 菜 1–63 芥 10; *T* 221.

17. See ter Haar, *White Lotus*, 33 and 35, which distinguishes the "People of the Way" from other lay Buddhists who were active in the White Lotus Movement. The latter were involved in possibly reprinting *Qisha Canon* during the Yuan, as discussed later in this chapter.

18. *Fayuan zhulin*: *Qishazang* 481 杜 1–490 羅 10; *T* 2122. The very useful appendices 7 (for the Song) and 8 (for the Yuan) in Li and He, *Dazangjing yanjiu*, 702–42, provide available dates of the inscriptions for works in *Qisha Canon*.

19. Tekiya, *Sekisha zōkyō*, 61, entry for 61 菜. Li and He, *Dazangjing yanjiu*, 260, suggest that since we have surviving copies of works dating from before the 1258 fire, the earlier blocks were not (all) destroyed, but it may be that some were damaged. In the Princeton Gest holdings, all the fascicles of 61 菜, which are hand copies that faithfully reproduced the original inscriptions, were probably produced after the blocks were destroyed.

20. Lancaster, "Buddhist Canon," 176–77.

21. Li and He, *Dazangjing yanjiu*, 319.

22. There is a substantial secondary literature on the White Cloud Movement, e.g., Ogawa Kan'ichi, "Gendai Hakuunshū"; Overmyer, "White Cloud Sect"; and ter Haar, *White Lotus*, esp. 32–37.

23. Liu Xinru, "Buddhist Institutions," 45, citing *Wuxing zhi* 吳興志 (1201), 13.34a.

24. Ogawa Kan'ichi, "Gendai Hakuunshū," 9–16; Li and He, *Dazangjing yanjiu*, 316–54; Overmyer, "White Cloud Sect," 634–36.

25. Li and He, *Dazangjing yanjiu*, esp. 347–49.

26. *Hongwu nanzang* is almost entirely a copy of *Qishazang*, with the same ordering of works. In their discussion of this first Ming edition, Li and He, *Dazangjing yanjiu*, 375–406, argue that it would be more accurate to deem it *Jianwen nanzang* 建文南藏, based on the engraving dates from the second Ming emperor's reign (1399–1402).

27. Overmyer, "White Cloud Sect," 635. At least two works—those by Qingjue 清覺 (1043–1121), the founder of the White Cloud Movement—that had been added to the end of *Puning Canon* do not seem to have been incorporated in *Qisha Canon*, quite possibly for political reasons, since the movement was proscribed by 1319 (see below).

28. Liang Gengyao, "Suzhou de nongye fazhan," 265–66; Marmé, *Suzhou*, 45–59.

29. 1297 is the earliest date for fascicles of *Qisha Canon* produced in the Yuan. See appendix 8 of Li and He, *Dazangjing yanjiu*, 726.

30. Zhu Wenqing's exact official title was the Assistant Director of the Left in the Branch Secretariat for Henan, Jiangbei, and other regions 河南江北等處行中書省左承. Wenqing's son, Xianzu 顯祖, is the only other family member whose name is given. So far, I have not found Wenqing in any Yuan source other than *Qisha Canon*. I am uncertain why Chikusa Masaaki (*Sō-Gen bukkyō bunkashi*, 354) identifies this man with a Zhu Qing 朱清, who was a pirate on Chongming Island 崇明島 in the mouth of the Yangzi River (and now part of Shanghai municipality). Zhang Wenhu's official title

was Assistant Administrator of the Branch Secretariat for Jiangbei and other regions 江北等處行中書省參知政事. He was a native of Jiading 嘉定 (*Yuanren zuanji*, 1117). If Chikusa is correct, then both men were natives of the area close to Yansheng Monastery. Zhu Wenqing's name appears in inscriptions in fascicles of *Qisha Canon* dated in 1301, and that of Zhang Wenhu for those dated 1302. See Li and He, *Dazangjing yanjiu*, appendix 8, which lists the principal donors for many of the works in *Qisha Canon* during the Yuan.

31. For example, one of the works funded by these donors, *Apidamo da piposha lun* 阿毗達摩大毗婆沙論 (372 惻 1–391 神 10; *T* 1545), has colophon inscriptions almost all dated 1310 or 1311. See, e.g., Tekiya, "Sekisha zōkyō," 130 (373 造 1).

32. Although "Guanzhuba" may be more consistent with "Shaluoba" than "Guan Zhuba," I have adopted the second version, not to imply that that Guan was a surname but for legibility's sake, especially given that his son's name is more easily read as Guan Nianzhenchila than Guannianzhenchila 管輦真吃剌.

33. It is unclear how long Guan Zhuba remained at this post. At least two works in *Qisha Canon* have prefaces, both by the monk collator (Wu) Keji (吳) 克己 and both dated 1306, that refer to Guan Zhuba as the "former" (*qian* 前) Monk Registrar. Portions of these prefaces are quoted in Li and He, *Dazangjing yanjiu*, 294. But in a 1307 donor's colophon by Guan Zhuba himself (*Qishazang* 585 何 10), he does not use *qian* in front of his title. It may be that he left the position of Monk Registrar of Songjiang around 1306–7, but continued his work of supervising various religious printing projects in Hangzhou. This slight discrepancy has already been noted by Pelliot, "Les Débuts," 90–91.

34. See, e.g., Gimello, "'Canonization' of Zhǔntí."

35. See Franke, "Sha-lo-pa," in which Shaluoba's biography from Nian Chang's 念常 *Comprehensive Chronicle of Buddhist Patriarchs* (*Fozu lidai tongzai* 佛祖歷代通載; *T* [CBETA 2011] no. 2036, 49: 729–30) is translated.

36. For Yang Lianzhenjia, who was the Supervisor of Buddhism in Jiangnan (*Jiangnan zongshe zhang shijiao* 江南總攝掌釋教) from 1277–91. See Franke, "Tibetans in Yüan China," esp. 321–25. It is unclear whether Yang was Tibetan or Tangut. There is one connection between Yang and *Qisha Canon*. A frontispiece shown in Zheng Zhenduo, *Zhongguo gudai mukehua xuanji*, vol. 9, 14, was supposedly carved for this edition of the canon in 1290 under Yang's direction. There is no date on the illustration, but since Yang was removed from office by 1291, the date is possible. If so, then it is more than a decade earlier than the *Qisha Canon* frontispieces produced under Guan Zhuba's supervision (see below).

37. Before 1298, Shaluoba was appointed to a similar position in Fujian (Franke, "Sha-luo-pa," 204).

38. Ogawa Kan'ichi, "Gendai Hakuunshū kyōdan," 8.

39. The six works translated by Shaluoba (*T* 925, 926, 976, 1189, 1417, and 1645) are briefly discussed by Franke ("Sha-lo-pa," 209–12), who points out that other than the

Zhang suo zhi lun, it is unclear from what language(s) Shaluoba translated these works, but all the translations were made under imperial command. In 1310, the crown prince ordered that the printing be done by Shen Mingren 沈明仁 the leader of the White Cloud Movement at that time. Ten years later, however, Shen had completely fallen out of favor and was executed, and the White Cloud Movement died out (Franke, "Sha-lo-pa," 210; Overmyer, "White Cloud Sect," 636–39).

40. After *Puning Canon*, the works translated by Shaluoba first appeared in the reduced print (*shukusatsu* 縮刷) edition of the canon printed in 1880–85 in Tokyo.

41. See Li and He, *Dazangjing yanjiu*, 275, 290–95; Li Jining, *Fojing banben*, 122–23. Other than Guan Zhuba's own inscription at the end of Buddhist works that he helped to compile or publish, we have no information on him. See Xu Rucong, "Fojiao zhushi xiang," concerning the evidence of the introduction of esoteric Buddhism into the Jiangnan area during the Yuan and the role of Guan Zhuba and his son.

42. This list and a similar one from 1299 are reproduced in Li and He, *Dazangjing yanjiu*, 264–65.

43. This inscription appears, for instance, at the end of fascicle 3 of *Dazongdixuan wen benlun* 大宗地玄文本論 (581 踐 3) and is reproduced in Li and He, *Dazangjing yanjiu*, 291–92. A more complete version appears at the end of a Buddhist work (which is in Tangut) found in the Mogao Cave in Dunhuang and has been translated in full in Karmay, *Early Sino-Tibetan Art*, 43–44 (with the Chinese text on 119). This inscription, like the shorter one in *Qisha Canon*, is dated 1307, when Guan Zhuba was in Hangzhou.

44. Wang Han, "Kanke *Dazangjing*," gives a starting date of 1293 for the Tangut canon, which is quite possible, but I have not seen any Yuan record noting that Guan Zhuba was in the Hangzhou area at that date.

45. Wanshou Monastery, on Gushan Island 孤山 off the north shore of the West Lake in Hangzhou, was one of the Buddhist monasteries restored by Yang Lianzhenjia in the Dade 大德 period (1297–1307), after it had been converted to a Daoist temple in the Southern Song (Tian Rucheng, *Xihu youlan zhi*, 19: 12a; Liang Shizheng et al., *Xihu zhi zuan*, 3: 21b).

46. Two such colophons are reproduced in Li and He, *Dazangjing yanjiu*, 291–93.

47. Zhang Lü's official titles varied in different colophons in *Qisha Canon*. In addition to the title given in figure 6.2, at the end of fascicle 64 of *Yujia shi di lun* 瑜伽師地論 (229 福 4), he is described as an official of the Commission for Buddhist and Tibetan Affairs (Xuanzheng yuan 宣政院).

48. Li Jining, *Fojing banben*, 123.

49. See the lists of block carvers for the original blocks and the blocks in the Yuan in Wang Zhaowen, *Song-Yuan kangong*, 305b–306b. See also the early work on *Qisha Canon* engravers by Yang Shengxin, "*Qishazang* keyin" and "Lun *Qishazang*," as well as the critique of Yang by Zhang Xinying, "Lun *Qishazhang* du hou."

50. Many block carvers were itinerant, and traveling from Hangzhou to Suzhou by water took only about eight days. But the appendix is only one of about six such lists I have so far compiled. It is unlikely that these block carvers who worked on other imprints in Hangzhou were all traveling to Suzhou during the early fourteenth century.

51. The engraving and printing of the second edition of a Quanzhen Daoist work, *Xuanfeng qinghui tu* 玄風慶會圖, in 1305 attests to the reputation of Hangzhou as the premier publishing center of the time. Rather than have the work produced in north China, where the Quanzhen Daoists had compiled a printed edition of the Daoist canon (1234–77), the Daoist cleric who organized the fund raising and work for the *Xuanfeng qinghui tu* did so in the Hangzhou area. See Katz, "Writing History," and Chia, "The Uses of Print," 193–201.

52. Hangzhou printing in early imperial China has been well studied; see Huang, "Early Buddhist Illustrated Prints in Hangzhou," and the references therein.

53. As the scholars in the growing field of Tangutology and Xi Xia printing point out, the multicultural and multilingual nature of the Xi Xia empire (Tangut, Tibetan, Uighur, Chinese, etc.) also provides a fascinating and enlightening perspective for considering Han Chinese Buddhism and printing. On imperially sponsored Buddhist printing during the Xi Xia period, see, among others, Dunnell, *Great State*, esp. 50–83, and Saliceti-Collins, "Xi Xia Buddhist Woodblock Prints," and references therein. I thank Anne Saliceti-Collins for giving me a copy of her M.A. thesis.

54. The most detailed discussion of these frontispieces and of their similarities to those in the 1302 Tangut canon is Karmay, *Early Sino-Tibetan Art*, 41–54. In addition to Karmay's list of the eight illustrations shown throughout the photofacsimile reprint *Yingyin Song Qisha zangjing*, there are at least two others—shown in Lee and Ho, *Chinese Art Under the Mongols*, figs. 279 and 281. Given the stylistic similarities of all ten known frontispieces, the "original" blocks were probably all cut around the first decade of the fourteenth century.

55. For a brief discussion of the Yang family print shop and a number of other commercial printers in this area of northern Hangzhou during the Southern Song, see Edgren, "Southern Song Printing at Hangzhou," 36–37.

56. Recut with blacked-out cartouches in Monnet, *L'empire du trait*, 128 (fig. 85b). Li Jining, "*Qishazang* yanjiu," 73, argues for a Ming date for the Yang Xinzhen engraving.

57. Re-engravings, such as Karmay, *Early Sino-Tibetan Art*, 47 (fig. 28), and Monnet, *L'empire du trait*, 128 (figs. 85a–b), were made in the later Yuan and the Ming.

58. Thus the dates for figs. 276–81 in Lee and Ho, *Chinese Art Under the Mongols*, which come from the inscriptions at the end of the sutra texts, are not the dates for the frontispieces. For example, although the frontispiece in fig. 278 was probably engraved ca. 1306, the blocks for the text of the sutra *Daban niepan jing* 大般涅槃經 (122 遍 1–125 率 10) were probably all cut in the Song, in the 1260s–early 1270s, just before work halted on *Qisha Canon*. As for figs. 276–77, *Foshuo mimi sanmei dajiao wang jing*

佛說秘密三昧大教王經 (541 微 1–4) has an inscription dated 1301 for the text, which was probably engraved in Qisha Yansheng Cloister, but the frontispieces were most likely carved some years later in Hangzhou. Karmay, *Early Sino-Tibetan Art*, 48; and Edgren, *Chinese Rare Books*, 80, and "Southern Song Printing at Hangzhou," 36, have made much the same observation.

59. Karmay, *Early Sino-Tibetan Art*, 48, and Feng Jiasheng, "Bayang shen zou jing," in which the illustration is not sufficiently clear to show the engraver's name.

60. Chen Ning's name appears among block carvers for at least one other imprint produced in Hangzhou during the Yuan Zhida 至大 period (1308–11); see Wang Zhao-wen, *Song-Yuan kangong xingming*, 258b.

61. See Guan Nianzhenchila's inscription at the end of fascicle 7 of *Dasheng liqu liu boluo miduojing* 大乘理趣六波羅蜜多經 (565 多 7), reprinted in Li and He, *Da-zangjing yanjiu*, 295.

62. The 1363 inscription is given in Li and He, *Dazangjing yanjiu*, 295, and Tekiya, "Sekisha zōkyō," 157.

63. Li and He, *Dazangjing yanjiu*, 207.

64. Ter Haar, *White Lotus*, 65, 69. But there is no evidence that clerical or lay adherents of the movement were prominent active supporters of the *Qisha Canon* printing project during the Southern Song. Date of founding and location of Houshan Hall given in *Jianyang xianzhi* 1553: 7.25a.

65. See ter Haar, *White Lotus*, esp. 72–89, and "Buddhist-Inspired Options," 140–47.

66. Despite the large printing enterprise of Houshan Hall, none of the known commercial printers of Jianyang is associated with religious publishing. It may be that these printers did produce Buddhist works but did not identify their own names in these imprints. Furthermore, several important printing families were related to more prominent men connected to Zhu Xi (who lived in the area) and the Neo-Confucian movement, and may have not wanted association with a movement like the White Lotus. On Jianyang commercial publishing in the Song and Yuan, see Chia, *Printing for Profit*, chs. 3–4.

67. Many of the genealogies from northern Fujian claim that the ancestors of the lineage came from Gushi District 固始縣 in Henan, so the speculation (Li and He, *Dazangjing yanjiu*, 356) that Chen Juelin and Chen Jueyuan were kinsmen may be correct.

68. On King Chungseon, see Huang Chi-chiang, "Ŭich'ŏn's Pilgrimage," 259–62.

69. Ter Haar, *White Lotus*, 76.

70. *Huiyin si zhi*, 6.6a–9a, on Weon Kwan's donation of copy of the canon to Huiyin Monastery; 7.5a–6a on donation by Weon Kwan and King Chungseon of land to the same monastery; 7.8b–9b on King Chungseon's donation of fifty copies of the canon to monasteries in the Hangzhou area. These commemorative essays (all dated 1314) use the phrase *yinzao* 印造 but not *ke* 刻 or *kan* 刊, so the copies of the canon were probably made from existing blocks, with those of *Puning Canon* being the most likely

choice, since they were stored in Puning Monastery in Hangzhou Prefecture. This is borne out by the discovery of a volume of *Fu fa zang yinyuan jing* 付法藏因緣經 from *Puning Canon* inside a statue of the Buddha in Zhihua Monastery 智化寺 in Beijing (Xu Huili, "Zhihua si faxian Yuandai zangjing," 1–2). Another possibility was *Qisha Canon*, which would have been almost finished by the time of the Goryeo donations. In any case, it seems far more likely that the copies were made from woodblocks available in China, rather than from those for the second Goryeo edition, if only for practical reasons.

71. One might argue that the need in Goryeo was less since by the mid-thirteenth century, the blocks for the second Goryeo edition of the canon had been carved. Nevertheless, works newly translated into Chinese from Tibetan and other languages, and works missing for other reasons, were sent to Goryeo to supplement that country's canon. Moreover, the flow of Buddhist works went in both directions to supply texts lost or missing in both countries, although by the Yuan, this traffic had abated compared to earlier periods. See Brose, "Crossing Thousands of *Li*"; Jorgensen, "Regeneration of Chinese Buddhism"; Faure, "Ch'an Master Musang"; Huang, "Ŭich'ŏn's Pilgrimage"; and Wu and Dziwenka, "'Better Than the Original'" (chapter 8 in this volume).

72. Li and He, *Dazangjing yanjiu*, 356–74; Li Jining, *Fojing banben*, 138–39. The *Hongfa Canon* 弘法藏 was an expansion of the earlier *Zhaocheng Canon* 趙城藏 produced in the twelfth century in central Shanxi. The latter in turn was based on *Kaibao Canon*, the woodblocks for which were taken from Kaifeng by the Jurchens when they invaded the Northern Song capital.

73. Xu Huili, "Yuan dai zangjing"; Li Jining, *Fojing banben*, 139. In fact, extant portions of both *Hongfa Canon* and the edition at Zhihua Monastery were discovered only in the late twentieth century, although Japanese holdings for both have been noted earlier.

74. See Li and He, *Dazangjing yanjiu*, 375–406, and Long Darui, "A Note on the Hongwu Nanzang." The blocks for *Hongwu nanzang* were cut most probably in Nanjing at Jiangshan Monastery 蔣山寺 (later renamed Linggusi 靈谷寺) and then stored in Tianxi Monastery 天喜寺 until the latter was completely destroyed by fire in 1408. Thus ironically *Hongwu nanzang* had a far shorter lifetime than *Qishazang*. In addition to the first 591 cases, *Hongwu nanzang* also had texts contained in a further 87 cases.

75. As for Bao Shanhui, who referred to himself as a novice (*shami* 沙彌), the inscriptions at the end of the sutras that he helped recarve contain the only information we have about him.

76. For the classification of Buddhist monasteries into *chan* 禪, *jiao* 教 (practical instruction), and *jiang* 講 (doctrine), see Yü Chün-fang, *Renewal of Buddhism in China*, 148–50.

77. See Li Jining, *Fojing banben*, 131–32, concerning both inscriptions found in the recarved fascicle 528 of *Da bore boluomiduo jing*.

78. *Huiyin sizhi*, 1.2a claims that eight- to nine-tenths of the monastery was destroyed in the Yuan Zhizheng 至正 period (1341–67) and rebuilt in the early Ming; Wu Jingzhi, *Wulin fanzhi*, 3.7a. Note that the first work gives the characters for the monastery's name Huiyin as 慧因, while the second work has 惠因.

79. Two such inscriptions are reproduced in Li and He, *Dazangjing yanjiu*, 296–99, and in part in Li Jining, *Fojing banben*, 131–33 (with fig. 55 showing the inscription at the end of fascicle 528 of the *Da Bore jing*).

80. The quotation is from the 1411 colophon found in a number of works for which Bao Shanhui and his associates paid to have new blocks carved, including sections of *Da Bore jing* (e.g., fascicle 528).

81. The inscription is reprinted in full in Li and He, *Dazangjing yanjiu*, 297–99, and in Li Jining, *Fojing banben*, 109–10, with fig. 48 showing Bao Shanhui's inscription. The inscription is the longest extant remnant of the original 1193 text; shorter notices are given in other works, such as *Yongle Dadian* 永樂大典.

82. For the relationship between *Zhaocheng Canon* and *Hongfa Canon*, see Li and He, *Dazangjing yanjiu*, 103–10.

83. Dong talks of "dazang zun jing yi zang" 大藏尊經一藏, and one *zang* corresponds to 5,048—the number of fascicles in *Kaibao Canon*, the first printed edition. Although the term used by Dong, "(Dazang) zun jing" (大藏) 尊經" (preeminent sutra) often refers specifically to *Zhengfa hua jing* 正法華經, he clearly was using this term to mean the sutra he had printed.

84. See fig. 56 in Li Jining, *Fojing banben*, 133, for another example of a recarved work sponsored by Dong Fucheng: *Fo jixiang de zan* 佛吉祥德讚 (522 功1).

85. Figure 6.10 shows the end of fascicle 1 of the copy held in the Gest Collection. The *Yingyin Song Qisha zang jing* gives a colophon by Guan Zhuba at the end of fascicle 9 dated 1306 (Tekiya, *Sekisha zōkyō*, 160 [586 遵 9]), which was the first time that this Northern Song work was incorporated into the Buddhist canon.

86. The Hongwu edition was largely copied from *Qisha Canon*, retaining the latter's case numbering (*hanhao* 函號) and *qianziwen* designations, but its total number of fascicles amounted to over seven thousand.

87. The *Pumen pin* chapter circulated separately for quite some centuries and was often published as a stand-alone work, known by titles such as *Guanshiyin Sutra*. See Yü Chün-fang, *Kuan-yin*, 75.

88. The blocks for the second official Ming edition, *Yongle Southern Canon* 永樂南藏, were apparently fairly accessible for printing, but they deteriorated quickly due to poor storage conditions. Moreover, the edition was criticized for numerous mistakes in the texts. See, for example, Feng Mengzhen's 馮夢禎 (1548–1605) prefatory essay to the late Ming *Jiaxing Canon* 嘉興藏. Also see Long Darui, "Managing the Dharma Treasure" (chapter 7 in this volume).

89. The poems and the monastery falling into ruins are given in *Suzhou fuzhi*, 42: 31b–32a.

7. *Managing the Dharma Treasure*

COLLATION, CARVING, PRINTING, AND DISTRIBUTION OF THE CANON IN LATE IMPERIAL CHINA

Darui Long

The Chinese produced the first woodblock edition of the Buddhist canon during the early Song Dynasty (972–83), and over the next thousand years, more than thirteen other editions were carved. These are considered invaluable treasures in both the Chinese cultural heritage and Buddhist literature. Although many scholars today use *Taishō Canon* printed in modern movable type,[1] further research on the earlier woodblock editions will help us understand how the Chinese imperial court, Buddhist monks, and laypeople managed such a huge printing project.

The production of any edition of the Chinese Buddhist canon was a massive undertaking, requiring decades to raise the needed funds, to collect and collate the works included, and to organize and carry out the actual work of carving the woodblocks and printing the canon. For a court edition, fund raising was not a problem because the emperors were rich enough to donate sufficient funds for the project. For the editions initiated by common people, this was no easy job. Even when the carving of woodblocks was completed, the managers of the printing house had to preserve the blocks, keeping them safe from fire, worms, and humidity.

The printing of the Buddhist canon is usually considered a pious religious activity. Many Buddhists, monks, nuns, and laypeople would be involved in the project. They showed respect to the scriptures and the Buddhist canon and took this as merit-making in the worship of the so-called "Three Treasures," Buddha, Dharma, and Sangha. Common people and emperors also would copy scriptures to earn merit. The temple would organize activities involved in making and preserving individual scriptures or an edition of the Buddhist canon: fund raising, copying, carving, and printing, as well as maintaining the woodblocks and the imprints (including sunning the latter).

In this essay, I discuss practical issues of handling the canon, including textual collation, project management, and the managerial work after an edition of the canon was carved by focusing on the canons created during the later periods: *Yongle Southern Canon* (*Yongle nanzang* 永樂南藏), produced in 1420; *Yongle Northern Canon* (*Yongle beizang* 永樂北藏), produced circa 1440; *Jiaxing Canon* (*Jiaxingzang* 嘉興藏), begun in the late sixteenth century;[2] and *Qing Canon* (*Qingzang* 清藏, or *Qianlong dazangjing* 乾隆大藏經, or *Longzang* 龍藏) of the eighteenth century. *Yongle Southern Canon*, *Yongle Northern Canon*, and *Qing Canon* were imperially sponsored editions, while *Jiaxing Canon* was privately sponsored by clergy, elite, and common believers.

I will rely mainly on two sources. For the imperial editions, I will frequently refer to *Qingjing tiaoli* 請經條例 (Rules for requesting a Buddhist canon), an appendix to the catalog of *Yongle Southern Canon*.[3] The rules in *Qingjing tiaoli* were set down by the Ministry of Rites in Nanjing and contain useful information on how a regular customer could obtain a copy of the Buddhist canon from Bao'en Monastery 報恩寺 and the associated printing houses. The other source is *Kezang yuanqi* 刻藏緣起 (The [account of the] origin of production of the Buddhist canon), which collects all the relevant prefaces and essays written for the purpose of fund raising and organizing the printing process of the private *Jiaxing Canon*.[4] In addition, I will also use some new sources that I have discovered in Zhiguo Temple 智果寺 in Yangxian 洋縣, Shaanxi Province; in the Chongqing 重慶 Library; and in the Regenstein Library at the University of Chicago.

COLLATING THE CANON

THE COLLATION WORK FOR THE COURT EDITIONS

Emperor Chengzu成祖 (r. 1403–24) ascended the throne after he wiped out the forces loyal to the previous Emperor Huidi惠帝 (Jianwen 建文, r. 1399–1402), who was his nephew. He tried by all means to claim his legitimacy. Emperor Chengzu's father, Zhu Yuanzhang (r. 1368–98), initiated the creation of *Hongwu Southern Canon* in 1372.[5] The final engraving of this edition was completed in the third year of Emperor Huidi (1401). The woodblocks were kept at Tianxi Monastery for printing and distribution. However, a mad monk set fire to the temple in 1408 and all the blocks were destroyed. Emperor Chengzu immediately felt the need to construct another edition of the Buddhist canon, following his father's example. He probably also took up this project to show that he was a filial son. He wanted to cover up the fact that he had usurped the throne of his nephew by violating his father's will. During his reign, Emperor Chengzu sponsored two editions of the Buddhist canon. The one constructed earlier in Nanjing in the south was called *Yongle Southern Canon*, and the one engraved in Beijing in northern China was called *Yongle Northern Canon*.

The collation for the court editions was closely supervised by offices in the imperial government. The production of *Yongle Southern Canon* was under the guidance of the Buddhist Registry Office (Seng lu si 僧錄司), affiliated with the Ministry of Rites, usually run by eminent monks. Thus Daoyan 道衍 (1335–1418, also named Yao Guangxiao 姚廣孝), a famous monk and advisor to Emperor Chengzu, was responsible for the engraving of *Yongle Southern Canon*. Monk Daocheng 道成 participated in the construction of three editions of the Buddhist canon, including *Hongwu Southern Canon*, *Yongle Southern Canon*, and *Yongle Northern Canon*.[6] Monk Jingjie 淨戒 (ca. 1418) was responsible for the collation work of *Hongwu Southern Canon* and *Yongle Southern Canon*. Monk Yiru 一如 and Monk Sikuo 思擴 were responsible for both *Yongle Southern Canon* and *Yongle Northern Canon*.[7]

The initial work for *Yongle Southern Canon* began in 1409. The carving work was probably finished in 1419. The emperor moved the capital from Nanjing to Beijing in 1420; even before this, he felt the need to carve a new Buddhist canon in Beijing. Thus, it was in the third month of the seventeenth year of Yongle (1419) that Emperor Chengzu asked monk Daocheng and monk Yiru to prepare the format of a new canon. This was *Yongle Northern Canon*, which was completed in 1440, long after Emperor Chengzu's death in 1424. Both canons contain a total of 636 *han* 函 (cases) with 6,361 volumes.[8] The woodblocks were kept in the Imperial Storehouse (*neifu* 內府). In fascicle 2, *Jinling fancha zhi* 金陵梵剎志 (Gazetteer of monasteries in Nanjing), there are many records of the dialogues between Emperor Chengzu and the monks, which provide important information on how this edition of the Buddhist canon was compiled, under not only the auspices but also the active attention of Emperor Chengzu. He was particularly well versed in Buddhist scriptures and wrote more than thirty prefaces and essays concerning Buddhist literature. Never in Chinese history was there another emperor who made so many detailed suggestions for the production of a Buddhist canon.

For example, on the eighteenth of the seventh month in the eighteenth year of the Yongle reign period (1420), the emperor asked how much time would be needed to complete the carving of the woodblocks. The monks responded by saying that it depended upon how many carvers could come to work together. The emperor then asked whether or not 2,500 workers could finish the carving in one year, to which no one could answer in the affirmative. The emperor suggested that one set of woodblocks should be placed in Beijing and another in Nanjing, and a set of stone carvings should be kept.

Emperor Chengzu also determined the format of *Yongle Northern Canon* — five lines with seventeen characters in each column, and a larger page size than for the previous *Hongwu Southern Canon* and *Yongle Southern Canon*, both of which had six columns with seventeen characters per column. The emperor also decided the style of the cases, which were made of silk. He sent monks and officials to get old editions of the Buddhist canon from Suzhou and elsewhere for collation, as two months before, monks had told him that the old set of the Buddhist canon kept at Qingshou Temple 慶壽寺 was incomplete. Eighty-nine monks were summoned from various temples for the collation work. Monks Yiru An一如庵 and Jingfazhu 進法主 were responsible. A record in *Jinling fancha zhi* indicates that more than one hundred and twenty monks and scholars had collated the scriptures one time before the fifteenth day of the sixth month in the seventeenth year of the Yongle reign (1419). When the emperor heard that the monks planned to start cross-proofreading at the beginning of the seventh month, he dismissed the idea by saying that they could start it at the end of the month. The cross-proofreading was completed on the seventh day of the first month of the eighteenth year of the Yongle reign (1420). Venerable Yiru and others made a memorial to the emperor by proofreading seven times.[9] The emperor also was concerned about the calligraphers. He ordered them to show the quality of their work by samples. More than sixty-four monks were involved in copying the scriptures.

An issue arose about including the prefaces from earlier editions of the canon written by the emperors of previous dynasties. The monks in charge of constructing *Yongle Northern Canon* asked the emperor whether they should include all these prefaces. Emperor Chengzu agreed to include those written by Emperor Tang Taizong 唐太宗 (r. 627–49), Emperor Song Taizong 宋太宗 (r. 976–97), and Emperor Ming Taizu 明太祖 (r. 1368–98). It is telling that he ordered the monks to delete some of the scriptures or prefaces relating to the time of his predecessor, Emperor Huidi, his nephew.[10]

During the following Qing Dynasty (1644–1911), the Manchu rulers also understood the political significance of the canon and wanted to proclaim the state's authority over the cultures of the peoples within the empire through massive publishing projects, including religious works. The Qing emperors sponsored not only an official Chinese edition of the Buddhist canon but also editions in the Manchu, Mongolian, and Tibetan languages.

Let us now focus on *Qing Canon*, sponsored by Emperor Yongzheng 雍正 (r. 1723–35). In 1734, the collating work began at Xianliang Monastery 賢良寺 outside Dong'an Gate 東安門 in Beijing. Emperor Yongzheng wrote five prefaces in three years for the canon. He ordered the setting up of an institution for the production of the Buddhist canon in the court named Office of Tripitaka Repository (Zangjing guan 藏經館) with officials, monks, and lamas, totaling 133 people.

In the second month of the thirteenth year of the Yongzheng period (1735), Prince Yunlu 允祿 (1695–1767) and Prince Hongzhou 弘晝 (1712–70) were appointed officials in charge of the production of the Buddhist canon.[11] Both men were close relatives of the emperor, and their appointments indicated the great importance that the imperial court attached to the project. Under the two princes, a special team was set up for the work. Gongbu Cha 工布查 and three others were officers responsible for proofreading. He De 赫德 and nine others were supervisors. Sixty-four monks were proofreaders; many of them were abbots of famous monasteries in China. Abbot Chaosheng 超聖 of Xianliang Monastery, on whom the emperor conferred the title of Chan Master Wuhe Yongjue 無閡永覺, and four other eminent monks supervised the work as follows:

Chaoding 超鼎 and three others were responsible for classification of recorded sayings;
Yuanman 源滿 and four others were responsible for proofreading the canon;
Zu'an 祖安 and six others were in charge of division of the proofreading;
Zhenqian 真乾 and thirty-eight people participated in proofreading.[12]

Both Emperor Yongzheng and Emperor Qianlong made decisions to delete some important Buddhist works. For instance, *Chu sanzang jiji* 出三藏記集 (Collection of notes on the translation of the Tripitaka), *Gujin yijing tu ji* 古今譯經圖記 (Illustrated accounts of the translation of Buddhist scriptures from the past to the present), *Wuzhou kanding zhongjing mulu* 武周刊定眾經目錄 (Catalogue of Buddhist scriptures compiled in Empress Wu Zetian's reign), *Yiqie jing yinyi* 一切經音義 (Dictionary of pronunciation and meaning of all scriptures), and *Guoqing bailu* 國清百錄 (Hundred records of Guoqing Monastery) were all deleted by the decision of Emperor Yongzheng. Arrogant in his own knowledge of Buddhism, he believed that the monks who compiled previous editions of the Buddhist canon had been wrong to select works by certain eminent monks whom they respected. In all, more than thirty-two works were deleted by Emperor Yongzheng, causing a heavy loss to the textual value of the Buddhist canon. Modern scholars feel that Emperor Yongzheng was wrong in doing so.[13]

Emperor Qianlong also asserted his authority in censoring the contents of the Buddhist canon. In 1769, he decided to delete a number of works by the famous late Ming and early Qing literatus Qian Qianyi 錢謙益 (1582–1664), who had surrendered himself to the Manchu regime but remained loyal to the previous dynasty in his heart; his mixed feelings came out in his works. When Emperor Qianlong found Qian's commentary to the *Śūraṃgama Sutra* (*Da fo ding shou lengyan jing shujie meng chao* 大佛頂首楞嚴經疏解蒙鈔) in *Qing Canon*, he issued an order in 1765 that all woodblocks carved with Qian's works be destroyed and the works not be circulated. Thus 660 woodblocks were destroyed.[14] When I checked *Yongle Northern Canon* in the Chongqing Library in 2009, I found a colophon in the "mixed catalog of *Yongle Northern Canon* and *Qing Canon*" indicating that Qian's work, totaling 6 *han*,was deleted at the order of Emperor Qianlong in 1765.[15] Thus, the Qing emperors' interference in the re-compilation of the Buddhist canon had greatly decreased the academic value of this *Qing Canon*.[16]

THE COLLATION OF A PRIVATE EDITION: JIAXING CANON

Certain private editions of the canon, such as *Jiaxing Canon*, also underwent careful collation. By the mid-Ming Dynasty, the woodblocks for the extant *Yongle Southern Canon* were seriously worn from excessive use. It was reported that twenty copies were printed each year. These were poor in quality, with many blurred and illegible characters. Moreover, access to *Yongle Northern Canon*, which was a court edition, was difficult. Thus, in the first year of the Wanli period (1573), Yuan Liaofan 袁了凡 (1533–1606), a high-level official, discussed with monk Huanyu 幻餘 the possibility of carving woodblocks for a string-bound edition of the Buddhist canon. Yuan suggested the change from the traditional sutra binding to string binding in order to reduce the cost. Feng Mengzhen 馮夢禎 (1548–1605), another eminent official, described the situation as follows:

> Ever since the engraving of the woodblocks for the Buddhist canon, the scriptures have been gradually disseminated far and wide. Aside from one set of woodblocks kept at the capital, seven or eight sets of woodblocks were made during the Song (960–1279) and Yuan (1279–1368). For example, Qisha 磧砂 Monastery in Pingjiang County 平江縣, a temple in Wujiang County 吳江縣, and a temple in Shaoxing 紹興, Zhejiang Province, and so forth have kept woodblocks of the Buddhist canon. We can see the flourishing of Buddhism in those periods.
>
> In the present dynasty of Ming, two woodblock editions were made in the capitals[17] when all the woodblocks kept at local temples, as discussed above, were destroyed. *Yongle Northern Canon* in Beijing was much better than

Yongle Southern Canon kept in Nanjing in the south. However, it has been extremely difficult to request a set to be printed because this *Yongle Northern Canon* was kept in the court.[18] We notice that many monasteries in southern China have kept this *Yongle Northern Canon*, which was donated by imperial edict during the Jingtai reign (1450–57) of Emperor Daizong 代宗. It has been comparatively easier to get permission to print *Yongle Southern Canon*. However, there are many mistakes in it. Even if one tries to correct them, one probably will make more errors and the words become unreadable due to the difficulty in punctuation. Furthermore, there is the price: it costs over one hundred *liang* 兩[19] of silver for the printing and binding. It is no wonder that people in remote and poor rural areas cannot read the Buddhist canon all year round. I regret to note this.[20]

The plan to produce a string-bound edition of the canon, however, was not put into action until 1584. Eminent monks Zibo Zhenke 紫柏真可 (1543–1603), Mizang Daokai 密藏道開 (fl. 1593),[21] and Huanyu 幻餘 first drew up a plan to raise funds. Then in 1576, Mizang Daokai and the official Fu Guangzhai 傅光宅 (1547–1604)[22] suggested a scheme: they would ask ten influential Buddhist believers each to persuade three more to join the group and to donate money for the project. They then modified this idea to find 40 great donors, each contributing 100 *liang* of silver every year. They hoped that each year they could raise more than 4,000 *liang* of silver. Twenty people in Hebei, Shanxi, and Shandong provinces joined. They asked 10 people to join in this enterprise in Jintan 金壇 (Zhejiang Province), Danyang 丹陽, Wujiang 吳江, and Songjiang 松江 (all in Jiangsu Province). Ten other individuals from Huizhou 徽州 and Puzhou 蒲州 also joined in. This plan, however, was not easy to implement because some of the donors delayed their contributions and some of the silver obtained was of low quality. Master Mizang and lay Buddhists then decided to expand the plan and find another 20 donors from northern China and another 20 from southern China. Each year 40 people in the north and another 40 people in the south tried to meet the quota. When some donors dropped out, the organizers would add others to make up the loss.[23] The leading donors, usually local officials who were devout Buddhists, gave money regularly and mobilized gentry members, officials, and other Buddhists in their areas to help raise more funds. Each year, they sent lists of donors' names with the amount of money they had given to monk Tansheng 曇生, abbot of Huacheng Monastery 化城寺 at Jingshan near Hangzhou. As Tansheng gathered all the money and other contributions, he sent these funds and materials to Mount Wutai 五台山 in Shanxi, or purchased goods in the south for the production of the canon. This way of fund raising was important for the first stage of carving the woodblocks of the Buddhist canon.[24]

Zibo Zhenke and Mizang Daokai went to Beijing. They paid a visit to Emperor Shenzong's 神宗 mother for support.[25] The empress wanted to donate money for their canon project, but Zibo declined politely. Zibo believed that the merit of making a Buddhist canon could be shared not only by the imperial family but also by ordinary people.

The organizers decided in the beginning that they would use the money they earned from the printed scriptures to pay for the carving of subsequent blocks. In 1609, Wu Yongxian 吳用先 suggested that the printing houses make a joint list of the scriptures with the prices. Those who came to purchase the scriptures should follow the rules about payment so that the printing houses could manage their income and use the profit to carve more scriptures. During the Qing, in the fourth year of Emperor Shunzhi 順治 (1647), Zhu Maoshi 朱茂時 and Zhu Maojing 朱茂曍 compiled a catalog of the canon with the prices for the scriptures printed in various temples.[26] They noted that the cost of the Buddhist canon rose because the price for paper went up rapidly, as did other expenses such as labor costs, the transport of materials, etc., and felt it necessary to set new prices. Checking the inscriptions on the prices, we can see that the price of the Buddhist canon was indeed adjusted accordingly, which facilitated the carving of more scriptures.

As early as 1587, the ten most influential scholar-officials gathered in Yanjing 燕京 (modern Beijing) to discuss issues concerning the construction of the Buddhist canon in the string-bound style. Ten participants made a vow to follow eight regulations on which they fully agreed:

1. They would meet regularly on the seventeenth of each odd-numbered month to discuss the issues concerning the project. Those who were absent without asking for leave would be fined.

2. They would cross-review (*Huxiang choudui* 互相抽對) the collated scriptures on the following day.

3. The participants must finish proofreading the scripture they chose on time.

4. The proofreader must note every discrepancy in characters by referring to the original sources.

5. A second cross-review must be carried out.

6. When encountering difficult and complicated cases, they would gather together to discuss.

7. The proofreaders should take care of the scriptures they borrowed for proofreading, and no lending to others was allowed.

8. Monks or laypeople supporting the project could donate two *liang* of silver and two *dan* 擔 (100 kg) of rice for the meeting.[27]

For the collation work, these ten scholar-officials and monks decided to use *Yongle Northern Canon* as the exemplar. The regulations say:

We shall first collate the Northern and Southern [*Yongle*] editions and use
Song and Yuan editions for further collation with the Northern and Southern
editions. If we cannot find copies of the Song and Yuan editions, then we
will use the Northern and Southern editions. If we find any discrepancy in
one character, one sentence, or even the title of the scripture, between what
they called "the Southern Song edition," the "Yuan edition," and the "Ming
Northern edition," most likely referring to *Sixi Canon*, *Qisha Canon*, and
Yongle Northern Canon, we shall put a movable label on the top of the page
of the Northern edition, irrespective of which edition is correct or wrong. We
will just note the difference between the Song or Yuan edition and Northern
edition in this way: certain words were written in such a way in the Song
or Yuan editions, whereas the Northern edition is written in another way, or
the Song or Yuan editions have extra words or some missing words, or sometimes, there is a space specially designed for emperors' names of the Song and
Yuan dynasties.[28] There we should note the differences in format, spacing,
and other problems; for example, there are likely to be some wrong words or
substitutes. If we are not sure of the correct usage of the words, we may write
down what we have in mind; for instance, we may say that there might be
some extra words or missing words. If we are sure of the mistakes in certain
words, we may say so straightforwardly. We should write them down on a
movable label. We should copy it in regular script so that other editors may
re-collate the page. We should paste the movable label in order to prevent it
from falling off. We should never scribble on the copies of the sutra binding
of the Buddhist canon.[29]

The editorial committee also formulated strict rules for proofreading. After
the second proofreading, they would have the texts cross-reviewed. Anyone
who made mistakes in proofreading would be fined. Then the calligrapher
would make a copy of the texts, after which there would be another round of
proofreading. The carving would not start until the written copy was considered
error-free.

More than 150 people participated in the collation work. Among them were
eminent monks, lay Buddhists, scholars, and officials, including:

1. Qu Ruji 瞿汝稷 (1548–1610), secretary of the Ministry of Justice and Salt
   Distribution Commissioner, who was well versed in both Confucian and
   Buddhist studies. He was the author of *Record of Pointing at the Moon*
   (*Zhiyue lu* 指月錄), an important Chan text.
2. Wang Kentang 王肯堂 (1549–1613), a famous doctor of medicine. He
   wrote a commentary on a Yogācāra text (*Cheng weishilun zhengyi*
   成唯識論證義).

3. Qian Qianyi 錢謙益, a great scholar, whose works include *Complete Works of Muzhai (Qian Qianyi)(Muzhai quanji* 牧齋全集) and *Commentary on Śūraṃgama Sutra (Shou lengyan meng chao* 首楞嚴蒙鈔). Qian was responsible for proofreading *Commentary on the Nirvana Sutra (Niepan jing shu* 涅槃經疏). He compiled and wrote a preface for *Complete Works of Great Master Hanshan Deqing (Hanshan dashi mengyou quanji* 憨山大師夢遊全集).

4. Mao Jin 毛晉 (1599–1659), a famous publisher of the time, who also collated many scriptures.

The participation of these scholars in the collation work contributed to the high quality of the contents, classification, carving, and readability of *Jiaxing Canon*.[30]

THE CARVING OF THE CANON

THE CARVING OF QING CANON

After the collation, the next stage was carving the blocks, during which concrete issues such as the choice of wood, coordinating the carvers' work, etc., had to be considered to ensure the quality of the printed canon. The carving of *Qing Canon* exemplified careful management under imperial control.

After discussion with their staff, Prince Yunlu and Prince Hongzhou, the heads of the project, estimated that they would need 73,100 blocks of pear wood. The size for each woodblock was 2.4 *chi* 尺 (0.8 m) long, 0.9 *chi* (0.3 m) wide, and 0.11 *chi* (3.6 cm) thick. Because it was difficult to gather sufficient wood for 73,100 blocks at one time, the two princes sent three officials of the Imperial Household Department to places where pear trees were available in Zhili 直隸 (now Hebei Province) and Shandong with 7,000 *liang* of silver, where they spent a year purchasing about 10,000 woodblocks, far smaller than the needed quota.

The court then asked the governors of Zhili and Shandong to purchase more woodblocks and promised to pay for them when all were gathered. The governors apportioned the number of woodblocks acquired to prefectures and counties. Soon the local officials and people felt bothered by this. An official of the Censorate in Sichuan suggested that it would be much easier to collect so many woodblocks if the court accepted the assembled blocks. Emperor Qianlong, who had just ascended the throne, immediately ordered the two princes to take action. The princes, however, disagreed. Prince Yunlu explained to the emperor in his memorial that to guarantee the quality of the woodblocks for the canon, he had visited many carvers and asked about their experience. The carvers told him, "The woodblocks will expand. For the purpose of maintaining high quality, blocks that are wet or have knots are not usable. Joined blocks are certainly not acceptable. For now, you may only be concerned about finishing the job, but later, the woodblocks are likely to warp or crack, so that you will spend much money, but they will not last for a long time."[31] On hearing these words, the prince examined old woodblocks stored in the warehouse that had been engraved in the Ming Yongle period (1403–24). Each block was made of one whole piece of wood, but still, because they had been used for a long time, some of them had decayed. In the forty-second year of Kangxi (1703), people started to repair them, using smaller blocks joined together. Finding that the characters carved on these blocks were damaged, the prince then told the emperor that if they used joined blocks for convenience in producing the new canon, the blocks would break in two or three years. Thus he opposed the use of joined blocks, wet blocks, and blocks with knots. He told the local governors to collect pear wood blocks only in the fall instead of other seasons, to maintain the quality of the wood.[32]

Upon hearing the explanation of Prince Yunlu, the emperor changed his previous decision. He told officials to accept only the blocks that were qualified for the construction of the Buddhist canon. As for blocks that did not meet the requirements, the officials would simply accept them for other printing purposes. The Imperial Storehouse thus received 37,400 good blocks sent from 117 counties in Zhili Province and from 107 counties in Shandong Province. Another 16,000 blocks did not meet the requirements for use in carving the canon.[33]

For the construction of *Qing Canon*, the Imperial Storehouse gathered over a thousand people, organized into groups for different tasks. First, seven official supervisors were responsible for copying the scriptures, and for the tasks of carving, printing, folding, and binding. More than 869 workers, including carvers, printers, carpenters, folders, painters, etc., were employed in the project. Among them were 691 carvers, 71 printers, 9 carpenters, 50 printing assistants, 36 painters, and 12 folders. Most of the carvers were recruited from east China, where printing was a well-developed industry.[34]

The entire project cost 24,290 *liang* of silver for the woodblocks and 56,900 *liang* for the labor, totaling 81,190 *liang* of silver. A carver received 7.2 *qian* 錢[35] of silver for each block carved. The cost for printing one set of the canon was 625 *liang*, and the price for one printed set was 668 *liang*, giving the Inner Court a profit of 42.4 *liang* for "selling" each set.

Prince Yunlu was right to decline the use of joined, wet, and knotty blocks. The woodblocks of this *Qing Canon* have been in general well preserved for over 250 years since their carving.[36]

THE CARVING OF THE PRIVATE JIAXING CANON

Jiaxing Canon is a good example of the well-managed carving process conducted by producers of some of the private editions. Although this edition was named after Jiaxing County, where the bulk of the canon was produced, the project actually started at Miaode Chapel 妙德庵 on Mount Wutai in Shanxi Province in 1589.

There were quite a number of big monasteries that could be used for engraving the Buddhist canon in eastern China then. Mizang Daokai and Zibo Zhenke had no intention of staying at Mount Wutai; it was far away, and transportation was not easy. Daokai prayed before the Buddha image to seek answers. Three times he prayed and three times the answers he received were for Mount Wutai—a sacred shrine for Mañjuśrī Bodhisattva.[37] Apparently, the organizers wished to attract more donors by using the name of this famous mountain. In addition, Venerable Deqing (1546–1623), an eminent monk of the Ming Dynasty, had stayed at Mount Wutai in the earlier years of Emperor Wanli's reign (r. 1573–1620). Venerable Deqing was highly respected by Emperor Wanli's mother, who was a faithful devotee of Buddhism. For these reasons, Mount Wutai was chosen as the site for constructing the Buddhist canon at the beginning.

The first book to be carved, *Huayan jing helun* 華嚴經合論, totaling 120 fascicles, was completed in 1591. More than 70 workers were involved in the carving of this scripture alone, not counting calligraphers, proofreaders, carpenters for the woodblocks, porters, and others.[38] The following year, *Huayan jing* 華嚴經 and other lengthy scriptures were carved. The donors for these huge scriptures were 10 major Buddhist officials and a large number of Buddhist devotees whom they had helped to connect.

The living and working conditions at Mount Wutai, however, were poor. The extreme cold in winter meant that the carvers could only work for about half the year. In any case, many of them came from the south. Moreover, the paper for printing was transported from southern China. There were fewer donors in the north than in the south. Finally, the outbreak of peasant uprisings in north China made the area unstable. Thus, in 1592 the project's sponsors decided to move the workshop to Jizhao Chapel 寂照庵 in Jingshan Monastery 徑山寺, Jiaxing County, Zhejiang Province. By this time, blocks for about 1,200 fascicles were already carved.

Regulations were drawn up for the construction of *Jiaxing Canon*, including rules translated from *Kezang yuanqi*:

1. The woodblocks must be wood of pear trees one *cun* 寸 (3.3 cm) thick. Wet wood or blocks thinner than this measurement are not acceptable

because the wood will shrink when they dry. Blocks that have knots and blocks that are secured by two boards to make them bigger will not be accepted even if they are carved.

2. Qualified calligraphers will be paid for the ink, paper, and brushes they use and for their food.

3. Carvers will be paid for their work by each hundred characters.

4. One honest carver from a respected family will be chosen as a leader.

5. New carvers must submit as samples two verses in praise of the Buddha.

6. The newly carved sample woodblocks must be examined character by character and page by page. If they are of superior quality, the carver will be rewarded with two *fen* of silver per page. If the quality is good, one *fen* will be awarded. If so-so, the woodblock might be accepted, but the carver will be urged to improve his work. If the carver fails to produce woodblocks of the same quality as the sample work he submitted at the beginning, he will not be paid but fined for the pieces of wood and the written copy of the text used.

7. The carver should submit his samples after carving thirty pages and show them to persons responsible for the team. He will then be paid for work and food. There should be no borrowing of money. He will be paid after carving a scripture. If a scripture has fewer than thirty pages, he will be paid by the number of pages carved.

8. The carver should engrave his name at the left side of the centerfold and the number of characters cut on that leaf at the right side of the center-fold, to facilitate checking.

9. When carvers have quarrels or fights or are engaged in illegal activities, the leader must report it to the organizers of the Buddhist canon project. The [appropriate] government office will be informed of what happened if the matter was serious. The persons involved must be dismissed. If the head carvers try to conceal misconduct and cause more serious incidents, all persons involved will be sent to the government office for punishment.

10. Two *fen* of silver will be paid when ten woodblocks are carved.[39]

These detailed regulations show how concerned the project organizers were about the quality of the block carving and the smooth management and supervision of the carvers, the rules for whose work and conduct were clearly laid out, including calling upon the local government if necessary. Apparently such care was effective: eminent Buddhist scholar Lü Cheng 呂澂 (1896–1989) praised the quality of the work done at the first stage by saying that before the death of monk Zibo in 1603 the rules were strictly followed in each carving workshop.[40]

MANAGING THE PRINTING AND DISTRIBUTION

THE PRINTING OF YONGLE SOUTHERN CANON

After the carving of a Buddhist canon was accomplished, those involved in the project might celebrate its great success, but much work remained. For example, the woodblocks had to be stored in a dry, well-ventilated place, where the staff also had to guard against fire and termites.

After the woodblocks of *Hongwu Southern Canon* were destroyed in a fire at Tianxi Monastery 天禧寺 in 1408, *Yongle Southern Canon* was begun by the imperial court[41] and completed around 1419. The woodblocks were kept in the Meditation Hall (Chandian 禪殿 or Chantang 禪堂) of the same monastery (renamed Bao'en Monastery in 1413) until the early years of the Qing Dynasty. These blocks were so poorly maintained, however, that many of them were damaged. Records show that the blocks of *Yongle Southern Canon* were repaired twice. Ge Yinliang 葛寅亮 (1570–1646) of the Ministry of Rites in Nanjing[42] initiated the first repair in 1606. The second repair was reported by Chen Kaiyu 陳開虞, the magistrate of Jiangning 江寧 Prefecture around 1663. A long stele inscription describes the status of the woodblocks of this *Yongle Southern Canon* in the Kangxi period (1662–1722). The monk Songying 松影 and others spent years repairing the damaged blocks. Since it was an arduous and costly task, they decided to set up an institution to repair the Buddhist canon.[43]

Existing records reveal that it was much easier to obtain a set of *Yongle Southern Canon* in Nanjing than the imperial northern edition in Beijing, which was far less accessible. In Nanjing, many commercial print shops were involved in the printing and binding of the southern edition.[44] Customers coming to Nanjing for a set of the Buddhist canon would pay the printing house for the materials and labor and also give a block-rental fee (*bantou qian* 板頭錢)[45] for the support of the monks in Bao'en Monastery. This suggests that the monastery derived a substantial annual income from the requests for printing the canon.

As time passed, however, the pursuit of profit by monks at Bao'en Monastery and the private printing houses led to corruption, as reported by customers in their complaints to the authorities. The monastery probably raised the rental fee for the woodblocks, and the printing houses the fees for printing and binding. To coordinate and facilitate the process of printing and distribution, the Ministry of Rites drew up "The Rules for Requesting a Buddhist Canon" (*Qingjing tiaoli*) in 1605. These rules established the proper procedure for requesting a set of the printed canon and clarified the roles of Bao'en Monastery, which held the blocks, and the commercial print shops, which borrowed the blocks and printed copies using paper and ink of different qualities, as requested by customers. The Ministry of Rites was also hoping to correct corrupt practices, such as those described in the complaints contained in "The Rules for Requesting a Buddhist Canon." One case recorded that three monks from Hubei, Guangdong, and Sichuan complained about malpractice of printers. One shop used low-quality paper and silk, but charged an extra forty *liang* of silver. Another print shop delayed its work by two months. A third shop used paper instead of silk for the volume covering. On hearing the complaints, the Ministry of Rites ordered the shops to pay back the overcharged amounts, and the monks in charge of the woodblocks were censured.

For purchasing *Yongle Southern Canon*, the Ministry of Rites set up detailed rules and regulations. Thus the different prices for three kinds of paper (subdivided into three grades each) used for printing the canon were fixed, as was the schedule for the printing and binding: three months for an entire set of the canon. The monks who came to buy the canon would first get a registration number, which they would return before leaving Nanjing. They could then examine available printing materials—paper, silk, etc.—and choose a print shop, with whom any private transaction was forbidden. Then the official in the Ministry of Rites would issue a registration ticket to the customers, to the Meditation Hall, and to the print shop, which then was given permission to do the printing and binding.[46]

The format of the printed volumes, as stipulated by the regulations, was 33 cm high and 10.1 cm wide, and all the materials were measured according to official standards. The total cost was given a more liberal estimate of the budget in accordance with the market price of the time period (*congkuan gusuan* 從寬估算).[47] Although the costs of some materials might have fluctuated with time, the high and low prices might be complementary. There should be no way, for example, to increase the price due to the rise in price of one or two materials. There were cases where, because the prices were fixed, the print shops might use good papers and silks but do poor-quality binding work. Moreover, dishonest practices, such as using low-quality materials in what should be a high-quality copy, might occur. Indeed, the complete assortment of tricks by the monastery and the print shops could not be enumerated, so the purchasers must examine their copy of the canon carefully and report any problems to the officials.

When the work was done, the customer and the printer both had to double-check all items and hand in the registration ticket. If the buyer wished to express dissatisfaction and complaints about the quality of the work, he might write a note stating that it failed to meet the standards and send it to the office with a sample case of scriptures, sample prints of scriptures, and silk. The printer had to return the money he overcharged the customer and would be punished by having a cangue fastened around his neck. If the printing time exceeded the three-month limit, the print shop managers and workers would be reprimanded. If the incorrect kinds of paper and silk were used, the monk in charge would be responsible for the misconduct if he did not report it.

Rather than the entire canon, some customers wanted only the Four Major Sections (*Si da bu* 四大部, or *Si jing* 四經), which consisted of the Prajñāpāramitā 般若部, Ratnakūta 寶積部, Avataṃsaka 華嚴部, and Nirvāṇa 涅槃部. These sutras totaled 84 cases 函 containing 843 *juan*. The cost was greatly reduced. For the entire canon, the cost of each case was determined in accordance with the nine grades of printing quality, in addition to one *liang* and eight *qian* of the woodblock-rental fee (*bantou qian*). Finally, if a customer wanted to print miscellaneous supplementary sections of the canon, the fees were calculated accordingly.[48]

In addition to the original canon, there was the *Xuzang* section 續藏 (the supplement of the Buddhist Canon), consisting of forty-one cases. The blocks that had to be carved for these works were fixed at a cost of three *qian* 錢 and six *fen* 分 each, and the *bantou qian* was eight *liang* for the set.[49] If the work was to carve twenty-five woodblocks, the following words would be carved on each block: "monk so-and-so offered *bantou qian* for engraving the blocks,"[50] indicating it was ready for further examination. The monk in charge of the canon would come to the supervising office with the carvers to obtain the registration number when it was issued, and the carving was to be done in ten days. The finished woodblocks and printing materials would then be examined, and an overall report, including the income and expenditures, would be filed on the first day of the month. When a carver had engraved twenty-two blocks, eight *fen* of silver was given (presumably to the print shop) for the purchase of papers, ink, and glue; printing samples; and labor costs. The organizers also settled the accounts of the profit made from the printing and gave what was left to the monks for their daily necessities.[51]

Qingjing tiaoli set down very specific instructions on the copying and engraving work, and the fees charged. Copyists wrote in Song-style characters and were paid for their work and for the paper they used. The dimensions of the well-polished pear woodblocks, which were carved on both sides, and how deep the carvers should carve into the blocks were specified, as was the pay of the carver, calculated on the basis of the number of characters and number of columns. The work of the copyists and carvers was proofread by monks, and characters written or cut hastily and carelessly had to be redone. A finished woodblock earned three *qian* of silver.

Each set of the canon earned 12 *liang* of the woodblock-rental fee (*bantou qian*), and *Qingjing tiaoli* estimated that each year, about 20 sets of the entire Buddhist canon were produced, yielding a sum of 240 *liang*. In addition, approximately 20 sets of the *Four Sections* of the canon were printed each year, yielding about 36 *liang* of the woodblock-rental fee (*bantou qian*).[52] This money went to pay for the food of the 76 monks working in the Meditation Hall.[53]

A brief note describes the renovation of the rooms in the monastery where the woodblocks were stored, where the business of ordering and purchasing the canon was conducted, and where monks who came to buy the printings were housed. In fact, *Qingjing tiaoli* was probably compiled after these renovations, at the end of 1605. Registration books and a wooden cupboard were placed in the hall.[54]

The Ministry of Rites also allocated funds for the living expenses of the monks who came to Nanjing to buy the canon. They were to live in the seven rooms built to house them in the Meditation Hall of Bao'en Monastery. Also fixed was the cost of their food, provided by the Meditation Hall. As for miscellaneous fees, the regulations stated that the expenses of the monk purchasing the Buddhist canon, including food and accommodations, should be computed on a daily basis. Thus there should be no extra expenses not recorded in the registration book; asking for even a single penny more was considered a crime of dishonesty.[55] The monks purchasing the Buddhist canon were allowed to report the abuse to the office for further examination.

Qingjing tiaoli also observed that previously the customers had been reluctant to complete the questionnaire evaluating the quality of the canon they bought because it would entail a long waiting period before they could leave Nanjing. Thus the rule now allowed them to submit their report on the day when they handed in the registration number, and ask the office to issue a permit without delay. And if any doormen guards at the entrance of the monastery demanded a bribe and made trouble for the monks, the latter could immediately report it and the doormen guards would receive severe punishment.

THE DISTRIBUTION OF YONGLE NORTHERN CANON

Yongle Northern Canon, completed in 1440, has 637 cases, totaling 1,615 works in 6,361 fascicles. This edition was presented to big temples throughout the country in the name of the emperor. An imperial decree would be given to present the canon. A temple that received it would build a monument in memory of the event and a library to house the canon. Three imperial decrees were issued for the protection of the Buddhist canon. The first was written by Emperor Yingzong 英宗 (r. 1436–49 and 1457–64) in 1440, for the famous Linggu Monastery 靈谷寺 in Nanjing:

> I, the emperor, understand the wish that Heaven and Earth protect the people. I respectfully followed the will of Emperor Chengzu, my grandfather, to print the Buddhist canon and distribute it in the world. Now I have decided to present a set to Linggu Monastery, Nanjing, to always be consecrated

there. Buddhist officials and monks should read and praise the canon, and pray that the nation may enjoy prosperity and the common people may enjoy happiness. You must protect the Buddhist canon with respect. You must not contrive to allow indiscriminately any person to borrow the Buddhist canon because they may make light of and cause blasphemy against it, thus harming the canon. Anyone who violates the rules must be seriously interrogated and punished. Thus decreed.[56]

Stele inscriptions of this decree can be also found in many other monasteries in China, such as Fayuan Monastery in Beijing 北京法源寺[57] and Nanhua Temple in Shaoguan in Guangdong Province 韶關南華寺.[58] Japanese scholar Nozawa Yoshimi recorded that 139 temples received *Yongle Northern Canon*.[59] Local gazetteers also show that many temples received this *Yongle Northern Canon* twice: the first time around 1445, during the reign of Emperor Yingzong, and the second time at the end of the sixteenth century, when Dowager Empress Li 李氏 (mother of Emperor Shenzong 神宗) had the last 41 cases carved and distributed their prints throughout the empire.

Emperor Shenzong (r. 1573–1620) issued an imperial decree to the abbot, monks, and lay congregation of Zhiguo Temple in Yangxian, Shaanxi Province (figure 7.1):

The Emperor's Decree

To abbots, monks, and others at Zhiguo Monastery:

I, the emperor, believe that the teachings of the Buddha lie in the Buddhist scriptures. They serve to guide the good people and enlighten the broad masses who may have lost their way. The Buddha's teachings aim at protecting the nation and people. Otherwise, the teachings are useless. Hence, our beloved great saint mother, the elegant and well-cultured Empress Dowager, ordered printers to construct supplementary scriptures, totaling 41 *han* 函, together with the previously engraved Buddhist scriptures totaling 637 *han*. Now these scriptures are presented to your temple. You should take great care of them and always read them in a solemn way. You must not indiscriminately allow any persons to disrespect the canon to the point of causing damage. Protect and preserve the canon so that it will endure through the ages. This is the royal decree. Issued in the fourteenth year of the Wanli reign (1586), the ninth month, and day _____.[60]

It was generally believed that *Yongle Northern Canon* was presented only by the imperial court to the major monasteries in the country. However, He Mei mentions an incomplete *Yongle Northern Canon* kept at Yunju Temple, Fangshan 房山雲居寺, near Beijing. A colophon indicates that eunuchs in the court donated money to print this copy of *Yongle Northern Canon* for merit:

FIGURE 7.1 ZHIGUO MONASTERY STELE IN YANG COUNTY
Photo by Darui Long

Lu Shou, imperial commissioner, commander of Eastern Depot and head eunuch of the Department of Rites, donated money to print the Buddhist canon with a sincere heart in the hope of realizing the ultimate wisdom so that he may alight on the other shore of Bodhi. On the day when the Buddha obtained enlightenment, 1613.[61]

Another colophon shows that *Yongle Northern Canon* was printed at the order of the emperor in 1598.[62] He Mei believed that the fact that this eunuch was involved in the printing of the Buddhist canon implied that the imperial court had become economically weak, because Lu Shou's donation was given in the late years of Emperor Shenzong. However, I found colophons at the Regenstein Library at the University of Chicago stating that a court maid donated money to print this *Yongle Northern Canon* in 1584, when the economy was not so bad (figure 7.2).

Court Maid Li, a disciple of Buddhism and attendant in charge of registration for the memorials of the Interior Court, makes a vow: she heartily donates the money to print the Buddhist canon and spread it in the world. With this merit and good condition, she wishes to be reborn in the best place in the Western Paradise, where the lotus will transform her in a new birth—she will see Amitabha and receive instructions from him. Let all living beings in the dharma world share the same conditions of Buddha knowledge.

The fourth month, the twelfth year of Wanli (1584)[63]

FIGURE 7.2 COURT MAID LI'S COLOPHON IN *YONGLE NORTHERN CANON* AT REGENSTEIN LIBRARY, UNIVERSITY OF CHICAGO
Photo by Darui Long

The woodblocks of this set of *Yongle Northern Canon* were probably still printable in the early years of the Qing Dynasty. In 2009, I found in a copy at Chongqing Library a colophon stating: "Revised on the eighteenth day, the third month, the forty-fifth year of Emperor Kangxi (1706)."[64] This colophon is significant because it indicates that the woodblocks of *Yongle Northern Canon* were still in use. Unlike the recent facsimile reprint,[65] it has no prefaces written by the Ming Emperor Chengzu and Emperor Yingzong and was probably one of the last copies of *Yongle Northern Canon*. A memorial to the Qing Emperor Yongzheng indicates that most of the woodblocks originally carved in the Ming Yongle period had decayed, so that in 1703, the Qing court arranged for carpenters to repair the damaged blocks. After a few years, however, they were damaged again and were no longer printable.[66] When I visited Yongquan Temple 湧泉寺 in Fuzhou, Fujian Province, July 2, 2013, the monk did not show me any scriptures, but allowed me to visit the hall where they were stored in big cabinets. The words carved on the cabinet indicate that its collection of *Yongle Northern Canon* was shipped to the temple in the fifty-third year of Emperor Kangxi (1714). I could figure out that the date for printing this copy of *Yongle Northern Canon* should be in the early eighteenth century.

The woodblocks of *Yongle Northern Canon* apparently were still in use in the early period of the Qing Dynasty (1644–1911). Later, they all disappeared. How could this happen? When did they disappear? Since there were over 70,000 woodblocks for one set of the Buddhist canon, the imperial court must have provided a big hall to house them. When I visited Mr. Weng Lianxi 翁連溪, curator of the Imperial Palace Library, in June 2012, I raised the issue. He told me that a high-ranking official submitted a memorial to ask the emperor to allow them to use the woodblocks of *Yongle Northern Canon* as charcoal for making glaze tiles for the imperial court. This took place after the woodblocks of *Qing Canon* were engraved in 1735. The memorial said that the woodblocks of *Yongle Northern Canon* were used for three hundred years and now they were no longer usable. They were replaced by *Qing Canon*. The ministers suggested that the woodblocks of *Yongle Northern Canon* be used as charcoal to make glazed tiles for the Forbidden City. They told the emperor that this could save thousands of silver money. The emperor agreed. Thus all the woodblocks of *Yongle Northern Canon* were shipped to Liulichang Street 琉璃廠街 as their final resting place.[67]

The production of an edition of the Buddhist canon was an arduous task that needed many resources, manpower, and devoted sponsors. The cases described in this chapter demonstrate how Chinese monks managed these huge projects of collating, carving, printing, and distributing the Buddhist canon. Their efforts to preserve Buddhist literature marked their contribution to a great tradition that has exerted a huge influence on East Asian civilizations.

The production of the Buddhist canon in China was sponsored or often supported by the imperial court. Even the private editions of the canon, initiated by the gentry and the common people, often enlisted support from local authorities and the central government. The entire project involved years of preparation, fund raising, collation, proofreading, printing, binding, and distribution. When the woodblocks were carved, much managerial work was required, including preservation and repair of the blocks, as well as carving blocks for new scriptures to supplement the original edition. This essay is a preliminary investigation of the practical aspects of managing such a project; more in-depth studies should reveal further how a canon was actually created and circulated.

NOTES

I would like to express my hearty thanks to Professor Lucille Chia for her kind advice and suggestions for my chapter, which was written in 2006. She sent a long list of references to widen my horizon for this topic. I would also thank Professor Jiang Wu, who kindly sent Professor Nozawa Yoshimi's paper to me. Dr. Ananda Guruge (1928–2014) kindly proofread my paper twice and made suggestions for further improvements, for which I am always grateful. He passed away on August 6, 2014. I am sorry that I can no longer show this publication to him. An early version of this paper was published in *Hsi Lai Journal of Humanistic Buddhism* 7 (2006): 329–51 and is reprinted here with permission. After this chapter was almost finalized, I found more research on the construction of the Chinese Buddhist canon, including Zhang Hongwei's 章宏偉 and Chen Yunü's 陳玉女 works. Due to limited time, I realized that I could not expand on the topic of fund raising in this chapter. I believe that more research should be done on this in the future.

1. On *Taishō Canon*, see Wilkinson's chapter 9 in this volume.

2. The name of *Jiaxing Canon* (*Jiaxingzang* 嘉興藏) refers to Jiaxing 嘉興 County, where much of the work of carving and printing of the canon was done. The edition is also referred to as *Jingshan Canon* (*Jingshan dazingjing* 徑山大藏經) for the name of a monastery near Hangzhou, where the woodblocks were housed; or as *String-bound Canon* (*Fangce dazangjing* 方冊大藏經) for its style of binding, which differs from other woodblock editions of the Chinese Buddhist canon that were in either scroll or sutra-binding format.

3. This document can be found in Ge Yinliang's 葛寅亮 *Jinling fancha zhi* 金陵梵刹志 (1607), *juan* 49, and has also been reprinted in *Shōwa hōhō sōmōkuroku* 昭和法寶總目錄. When I translated it into English in 2001, I compared the two versions and found at least three mistakes in the latter, which make it incomprehensible.

4. *Kezang yuanqi* was first engraved during the Ming Wanli period (1573–1619), possibly more than once. Most of the articles in this book are included in *Jingshan zhi* 徑山志 (1624), compiled by Song Kuiguang 宋奎光. This *Jingshan zhi* contains fourteen articles written by two eminent monks and twelve scholar-officials. However, it does not contain the last sections concerning the rules of how to collate, proofread, carve, and print the Buddhist canon. Among modern reprinted editions are the 1919 version by Yangzhou Tripitaka Institute (Yangzhou zangjing yuan 揚州藏經院) in Yangzhou and the 1932 version from Jinling Sutra Printing Agency (Jinling kejing chu

金陵刻經處) in Nanjing, which was recarved with a donation from General Liu Xiang 劉湘 (1890?–1938) from Sichuan. It includes an appendix with the chronology of the construction of this canon, not available in other editions. I am grateful to my late father, Professor Long Hui 龍晦, for having photocopied it for me from the Sichuan Provincial Library in 1998. The various versions of *Kezang yuanqi* have been collated in Nakajima Ryūzō, *Minbanreki kakōzō no shuppan to sono eikyō*.

5. Emperor Taizu (r. 1368–98), also called Emperor Hongwu, was a Buddhist monk before joining the rebel army. Apparently he was greatly influenced by Buddhism.

6. Li and He, *Dazangjing yanjiu*, 387, 409, 439.

7. Li and He, *Dazangjing yanjiu*, 409. Detailed dialogues between these monks and Emperor Chengzu can be found in Ge Yinliang, *Jinling fancha zhi*, collated by He Xiaorong, 76–80. Monk Jinjie's 淨戒 and monk Yiru's 一如 biographies are found in *Gaoseng zhuan heji*, 632 and 840. Both Jingjie and Yiru were *you shanshi* 右善世 (the Buddhist Patriarch to the right) in the Buddhist Registry Department. Yiru was responsible for editing *Da Ming sanzang fa shu* 大明三藏法數 and Sikuo 思擴 was one of the editors.

8. This was the so-called *Zhengzang* 正藏 (the main part of the Buddhist canon). In the reign of Emperor Wanli, 41 cases were added. This part was called *Xuzang* 續藏 (Supplement to the *Yongle Northern Canon*).

9. Ge Yinliang, *Jinling fancha zhi*, 75.

10. Li and He, *Dazangjing yanjiu*, 441. Emperor Huidi was overthrown by his uncle Zhu Di 朱棣, who then ascended the throne as Emperor Chengzu (r. 1403–24). The *Hongwu Southern Canon* (*Hongwu nanzang* 洪武南藏) had been completed in the third year of Emperor Huidi (Jianwen). During his brief time on the throne, the young emperor was intent on reducing the power of his uncles, especially Zhu Di, who controlled the Beijing area. Thus Emperor Huidi may not have invested much of his resources into the completion of *Hongwu Southern Canon*, which had been initiated in the reign of his grandfather and predecessor, Emperor Taizu. We do not have records of when this *Hongwu Southern Canon* was completed—no dated colophon exists in the extant copy in the Sichuan Provincial Library. However, at an antiques auction in Beijing in 1997, a colophon at the end of *Da fangguang huayan jing* 大方廣華嚴經 in fascicle 67 clearly indicates the date of the eighteenth year of the Hongwu 洪武 reign period (1385). For information about this colophon, see Huang Yansheng, *Guji shanben*, 87.

11. Prince Yunlu was the sixteenth son of the Kangxi Emperor and was on good terms with his brother Yinzhen 胤禛, who later became the Yongzheng Emperor. Prince Hongzhou was the fifth son of Emperor Yongzheng and a brother of Emperor Qianlong.

12. Yang Jian, *Qing wangchao fojiao shiwu guanli*, 256.

13. Li and He, *Dazangjing yanjiu*, 523–25.

14. See Goodrich, *The Literary Inquisition of Ch'ien-Lung*, 102–4.

15. Of course, the original *Yongle Northern Canon* does not have Qian Qianyi's work. But the copy of *Yongle Northern Canon* kept at Chongqing Library actually includes parts of *Qing Canon*, so that its colophon records the deletion of Qian Qianyi's work. Qian's work was first included in *Jiaxing Canon* and early printings of *Qing Canon*. Emperor Qianlong issued a decree to destroy the woodblocks in 1765. Qian's work was allowed to be reprinted again in the fifteenth year of Emperor Guangxu (1889). In 1988 the Chinese Buddhists decided to reprint this *Qing Canon*. They found an intact copy of Qian's work in Kaiyuan Temple, Chaozhou, Guangdong Province 廣東潮州開元寺. Thus, we can gain access to Qian's work in this 1988 modern reprint.

16. Lü Cheng, *Lü Cheng foxue lunzhu xuanji*, 1492. Emperor Yongzheng was most aggressive in editing Chan texts in the canon; see Jiang Wu, *Enlightenment in Dispute*, ch. 6.

17. There were two capitals in the Ming Dynasty. The first capital was established in Nanjing by Emperor Taizu. Later, in 1420, Emperor Chengzu announced his decision to move the capital to Beijing, but Nanjing remained a secondary capital for the duration of the Ming Dynasty. See Farmer, *Early Ming Government*.

18. Those who requested the court edition of the Buddhist canon had to get permission from the emperor. When they obtained it, they had to build a library to house the Buddhist canon and a monument to commemorate the event. When I visited Zhiguo Temple in Yangxian, Shaanxi Province 陝西洋縣智果寺, in 2010, I found that Emperor Shenzong's decree was engraved on a stele. When I visited Zhiti Temple, Ningde City, Fujian Province 福建寧德支提寺, July 2012, I found that three decrees issued by Emperor Yingzong and Emperor Shenzong were engraved on a big wooden board.

19. *Liang* 兩 is translated as *tael*, a unit of weight (ounce) for silver and gold in imperial China and other East Asian countries.

20. *Kezang yuanqi* (Sichuan Provincial Library), 5a. This part can be found in *Jingshan zhi* 徑山志 (Gazetteers of Jingshan), *juan* 5, 434–39. On the production of *Jiaxing Canon*, see also Dai Lianbin, "The Economics of the Jiaxing Edition of the Buddhist Tripitaka" and the references therein.

21. Mizang Daokai's birth and death dates are unknown. He decided to leave the *Jiaxing Canon* project and become a hermit, probably around 1597. See Li and He, *Dazangjing yanjiu*, 488–90.

22. Fu Guangzhai, one of the first donors to the *Jiaxingzang* project, was a native of Liaocheng 聊城, Shandong Province, and Itinerary Censorate of Shanxi Province.

23. Venerable Mizang made efforts to contact quite a number of powerful lay devotees. He asked them to find more donors. See *Mizang Kai chanshi yigao* 密藏開禪師遺稿 (Collection of letters by Venerable Mizang), JXZ (CBETA) no. 118, 23: 16c, 17a, and 18c.

24. Yang Yuliang, "Gugong bowuyuan cang *Jiaxingzang* chutan."

25. Empress Dowager Li 李氏 (1546–1614) was an ardent supporter of Buddhism. Her biography is found in *Mingshi*, 3534–36. Also see Goodrich and Fang, *Dictionary*

of Ming Biography, 856–59. See Nie Furong's 聶福榮 comprehensive study on Empress Dowager Li and her belief in Buddhism in her M.A. thesis. On her involvement with supplementing *Yongle Northern Canon*, see below.

26. *Shōwa hōhō sōmōkuroku*, vol. 2, 300.

27. *Kezang yuanqi* (Sichuan Provincial Library), 79b–81b.

28. Whenever the name of an emperor of the current dynasty was mentioned, the writers had to give it special prominence in the book format, which was not necessary for emperors of previous dynasties. That serves as a way to identify the different editions published in different dynasties. For *Jiaxing Canon*, the compilation of which began in the Ming Dynasty, the editors were not obliged to put the names of the Song and Yuan dynasties in prominent positions. The edition of *Kezang yuanqi* I used was a photocopy of the original copy from the Sichuan Provincial Library. Whenever it mentions Emperor Taizu, Emperor Chengzu, and Śākyamuni or Tathāgata, it leaves a certain space for them. I collected two photocopies of the same book in modern reprints from 1912 and 1932. They do not follow this pattern at all.

29. *Kezang yuanqi* (Sichuan Provincial Library), 80a–81b.

30. Yang Yuliang, "Gugong bowuyuan cang *Jiaxingzang* chutan." For the connection with Mao Jin, see Mao Wen'ao, "Mao Jin yu senglü zhi jiaoyou ji kejing kao."

31. Rough translation from Li and He, *Hanwen dazangjing yanjiu*, 516. It is a record from the Qing Imperial Archive.

32. Li and He, *Hanwen dazangjing yanjiu*, 516.

33. Yang Yuliang, "Qing *Longzang jing* de kanshua qingkuang shiyi," 74. Yang's source comes from *Neiwufu Wuyingdian xiushuchu dang* 內務府武英殿修書處檔.

34. Ibid. Also see Weng Lianxi, *Qingdai neifu keshu tulu*, appendix: "Qingdai neifu keshu gaishu," 55.

35. In units of mass, there are ten *qian* in one *liang*.

36. The woodblocks were kept in Bolin Temple 柏林寺 for some years. In 1988, it was reprinted in China. The blocks were then moved to Yunju Temple in Fangshan 房山雲居寺. Now they are kept in the Beijing *Bangpu zhiban yinshua youxian gongsi* 北京邦普制版印刷有限公司 (Bangpu Printing Company) in Daxing County 大興縣 on the outskirts of Beijing. This publishing house has been reprinting copies of this edition since 1988.

37. *Kezang yuanqi*, 69b. Also see Zhang Hongwei, *Shiliu—shijiu shiji Zhongguo chuban yanjiu*, 164.

38. Li and He, *Hanwen dazangjing yanjiu*, 481.

39. *Kezang yuanqi* (Sichuan Provincial Library), 84a–85b.

40. Lü Cheng, *Lü Cheng foxue lunzhu xuanji*, 1484–89. These rules were relaxed in later periods. See Dai, "The Economics of the Jiaxing Edition."

41. Nozawa Yoshimi (*Mindai Daizōkyō shi no kenkyū*, 148–52) disputes this, arguing that not all the blocks were destroyed, and some of them were actually recycled for use in *Yongle Southern Canon*.

42. Ge Yinliang was also the compiler of *Jinling fancha zhi*.

43. Li and He, *Dazangjing yanjiu*, 414–19.

44. Li Jining, *Fojing banben*, 157, lists fifteen print shops in Nanjing, all near Bao'en Monastery.

45. *Bantou qian* 板頭錢 refers to the money paid for the woodblocks to be lent out to the printing shops for printing. The buyer had to pay this block-rental fee to the temple where the blocks were kept and a printing fee to the printing shop.

46. Ge Yinliang, *Jinling fancha zhi*, 736–37.

47. Again, *Shōwa hōhō sōmōkuroku* (vol. 2, 358) misprints the word 佸 as 佑, causing grave misunderstanding. It is untranslatable because 佸 means to estimate while 佑 means to support. Also see *Jinling fancha zhi*, 737.

48. Ibid., 737.

49. Apparently the blocks for the *Xuzang* section were missing at the time, and the carvers were ordered to carve them.

50. *Shōwa hōhō sōmōkuroku* (vol. 2, 359) misprints the word *ban* 板 as *zhi* 枝. *Ban* 板 means blocks while *zhi* 枝 means branch.

51. Ibid., 737–38.

52. Each set would yield 12 *liang* of silver. Ibid., 729. And each *Four Sections* of the canon would yield 1.8 *liang* of silver. Ibid., 737.

53. Ibid., 738.

54. Here *Shōwa hōhō sōmōkuroku* uses the Japanese word 丗 for the original Chinese word *wù* 丗. The Japanese Kanji looks slightly different from the Chinese. The Chinese readers might feel strange with this word. They might misread it as *mu* 母, which means "mother" in Chinese. Cf. Ge Yinliang, *Jinling fancha zhi*, 738.

55. *Shōwa hōhō sōmōkuroku* (vol. 2, 358) has one printing mistake and two missing words here. It misprints 分 as 八, causing confusion. The missing words are 毫者.

56. Ge Yinliang, *Jinling fancha zhi*, 100.

57. Lü Tiegang and Huang Chunhe, *Fayuan si*, 344–45.

58. Foyuan and Chuanzheng, *Xinxiu Caoxi tongzhi*, 725.

59. Nozawa Yoshimi, "Mindai Kitazō kō," 85–91. Nozawa has made a very comprehensive examination of the temples that received the canon. Two sets may be added to his list. Shengjing Monastery 聖境寺 in Xixian 隰縣, Shanxi Province, obtained a set in the twenty-sixth year of the Wanli reign (1598). The local gentry and Buddhists raised funds to request a set of the Buddhist canon from the imperial court. See Dang Baohai, "Shanxi Xixian Qianfo an Ming-Qing fodian yu baojuan." There is a similar imperial decree kept at Yuanguang Monastery 圓光寺, Xumi Mountain 須彌山, Guyuan County 固原縣, Ningxia Hui Autonomous Region. See Xie Jisheng, "Ningxia Guyuan Xumishan Yuanguang si ji xiangguan fan seng kao."

60. The blank at the end of the stele was left intentionally, to be filled on the day of the stele's erection. Comparing the photos I took at Zhiguo Monastery during my visit in the summer of 2010 with those from the Princeton University copy of *Yongle*

Northern Canon, I find that the text of this decree is the same, except that the inscription on the stele in front of the building where the canon is stored at Zhiguo Monastery has a date.

61. Li and He, *Dazangjing yanjiu,* 462.

62. Li and He, *Dazangjing yanjiu,* 462. The text ends with the line "大明萬曆戊戌年七月吉日奉旨印造施行。"

63. I found this colophon at Regenstein Library, where I spent almost three weeks in May–June 2011.

64. The original Chinese in the colophon reads as follows: "康熙四十五年三月十八日重修。"

65. Reprint edition published by Xianzhuang shuju 綫裝書局 in 2005. See the description of this reprint in Li and He, *Dazangjing yanjiu,* 462–64.

66. See Liang Yuquan et al., "Fabao chongguang."

67. *Qinggong neiwufu zaobanchu dang'an zonghui,* vol. 8, 259–60. Thanks are due to Mr. Weng Lianxi for his generous help.

PART IV

The Canon Beyond China

8. *Better Than the Original*

THE CREATION OF *GORYEO CANON* AND THE FORMATION OF *GIYANG BULGYO* 祈禳佛教

Jiang Wu and Ron Dziwenka

In 1884, U.S. Navy officer George Clayton Foulk (1856–93), one of the first Westerners who toured the Korean peninsula, visited Haeinsa 海印寺 after hearing about its great reputation. Although the monastery seems to have been a disappointment for him, he was impressed by its collection of a huge number of woodblocks.

> Behind the main building was a high hall, on top of which were two long buildings, each 250 feet, parallel, and apart say 100 feet. The eaves are lined with brass bells which ring quite loudly in the wind. In these buildings, well arranged in suitable racks by divisions, are an enormous number of board-engravings, the printing blocks for printing the whole Buddhist classics. The boards are about 28 inches long and 10 wide, corners bound with iron, and very black, with characters to fill two pages, generally, being cut on each side of the board. The priests do not know how many boards there are. By an estimate of the number of racks and boards in each, I calculated 77,080, which falls short I am quite sure. There must be 80,000 of them in all. This "library" is the most wonderful feature of the temple. The boards are beautifully cut and the work required to make them all must have been amazing.[1]

Foulk's description, though not perfectly accurate, was perhaps the first report about the Korean canon by a Westerner. However, his diary had been "buried" in the Bancroft Library at the University of California, Berkeley, until its publication in 2008, and had virtually no impact on Western knowledge about the Korean canon, formally known as *Goryeo Canon* (Tripitaka Koreana, 高麗大藏經). Most Westerners learned about the Korean canon through the intensive study by Japanese scholars such as Ono Genmyō, Ōya Tokujō, and Ikeuchi Hiroshi, when Korea was under Japanese colonial rule from 1910 to 1945.[2] Their works informed the world that there had actually been three attempts in Korea to create the canon, and the extant blocks are from the final attempt. *Goryeo Canon* then attracted the attention of Western scholars and became a subject of study in the works of the French scholars Maurice Courant and Paul Demiéville, and later, the American scholar Lewis Lancaster. Courant left a detailed note about the Korean canon in his Korean bibliography, published in 1896, and Demiéville wrote a short introduction of its history in his comprehensive survey of various printed editions of the Chinese canon. In 1979, Lewis Lancaster and Sung-bae Park published their monumental catalog of *Goryeo Canon*, greatly facilitated research on it, and enhanced its visibility in the burgeoning field of Buddhist studies at that time.[3] After the liberation of Korea from Japanese rule, the canon became a national treasure for preservation and research.[4] After the Depositories for the Tripitaka Koreana Woodblocks at Haein Temple were added to the UNESCO World Heritage List in 1995 and the digitization project was completed in 2000, *Goryeo Canon* became even more prominent, and 2011 marked the millennium anniversary of the beginning of its creation.

Despite its importance and the publicity surrounding it, there are still many issues to be resolved concerning its content and history. One of the crucial issues is how the study of the canon will contribute to our understanding of Korean Buddhism in general. Many scholars consider the role of *Goryeo Canon* in terms of the paradigm of "Buddhism for nation protection" (*hoguk bulgyo* 護國佛教) and believe that the canon functioned as a tool of state protection in Goryeo history. As Henrik Sørenson correctly points out, "*Hoguk pulgyo* understood as Buddhism functioning on behalf of the ruler and the kingdom was clearly a reality under the Koryŏ."[5] However, there has been a growing trend in studies of Korean Buddhism to critique this concept as a fundamental aspect of Korean Buddhism, specifically concerning its recent origin during Japanese colonial rule and the postliberation era.[6] In light of these new scholarly works, the discourse on "nation protection" needs to be substantiated by analyzing how *Goryeo Canon* functions in historical contexts.

In this chapter, we intend to reconceptualize the role of the canon in the Buddhism-state relationship in Goryeo society by situating the canon in its historical context and examining how it was utilized in different situations and for various purposes during the Goryeo and beyond. Our study shows that its creation and active use were successfully assimilated into a general Buddhist culture characterized by ritual performance in the court for the purposes of "praying for divine blessing and exorcising calamities" (*gibok yangjae* 祈福禳災). Loosely termed *Giyang Bulgyo* 祈禳佛教, this form of Buddhist culture penetrated Goryeo society and functioned as part of the elaborate ceremonial system that helped sustain the political hierarchy.[7] In this system, *Goryeo Canon* played an active role through the creation of the Tripitaka Assembly (Janggyeong Doryang 藏經道場 or Janggyeong Hoe 藏經會), a unique Korean invention shaped by the belief that the blocks of the canon could serve as a talisman with magical powers to dispel foreign invasions and astral calamities. During times of peace, the canon, through ritual chanting and worship in Tripitaka Assemblies as well as active editing and reproduction, functioned as a means of religious expression to pray for divine blessing and to assert Korea's cultural supremacy. During times of foreign invasion, there was a perceived necessity to amass divine power to combat military threats and their manifestations in heaven and on earth. As Lancaster suggests, the "existence of such a revered object in the nation must have been a source of pride and have encouraged the people to hope for better days with the power of their talisman."[8] In light of this new understanding, the concept of "Buddhism for nation protection," though not necessarily inaccurate, is misleading in the study of *Goryeo Canon*, and a more refined and contextualized interpretation needs to be reached. Among the various reasons for commissioning the collection and copying of various Buddhist texts, it is clear that "nation protection" was but one. After a short overview of the history of its creation, we will focus on the various historical and religious backgrounds of the creation of the first and the second *Goryeo Canon* editions.

HISTORICAL OVERVIEW

The presence of a Buddhist canon on the peninsula can be traced back as early as the seventh century. According to the *Memorabilia of the Three Kingdoms* (*Samguk yusa* 三國遺事), the earliest reference to the arrival of the canon in Korea, most likely the manuscript edition, was in 643, when Jajang 慈藏 (590–658) brought a set of four hundred cases from Tang China and stored them at Tongdo Monastery 通度寺 at the southern tip of the peninsula.[9] In 928, in the eleventh year of the reign of King Taejo太祖, a Silla monk brought a Tripitaka from the Later Tang Dynasty in Fujian, and it was stored in the Hall of Śakra Devendra (Jeseonwon 帝释院).[10] Although it is not known how these imported canons influenced Silla and early Goryeo Buddhism, these frequent references to the canon show the early Korean interest in and attention to it.

THE FIRST GORYEO CANON

The true stimulus for the creation of a Korean edition was the printing of *Kaibao Canon* 開寶藏 by the Northern Song (960–1127), completed in 983. The 989 entry in *Song History* (*Songshi* 宋史, 387th book) tells of the Goryeo King Wang Chi 王治 (temple name Seongjong 成宗, r. 981–997) sending the Buddhist monk Yeoga 如可 to the Song, ahead of an official Song envoy visit to the peninsula, with a memorial of respectful salutations and a request to receive a set of the newly printed Tripitaka. Again, in 991, King Seongjong sent his own envoy, Han Eongong 韓彥恭, to the Song court, and Han brought back another set of the printed *Kaibao Canon* consisting of 2,500 fascicles in 481 cases. Copies of *Kaibao Canon* consisting of varying numbers of volumes were brought to Korea six times during the Goryeo era.[11]

According to the standard narrative based on a prayer by Yi Gyubo 李奎報 (1168–1241), the publication of the first edition of *Goryeo Canon* began within the next decade, in the spring of 1011 during the Khitan invasion of Korea, and was completed in 1029. King Hyeonjong 顯宗 (1009–1031) initially garnered the support of the elites to commission the first *Goryeo Canon*. The immediate historical background was the invasion of the emboldened Khitans, who established their dynasty as Liao 遼. This gave rise to a view that the purpose of carving the canon was to repel the Khitan army. According to a later recounting of the event in Yi Gyubo's prayer, which we will examine later, King Hyeonjong issued the order to make a Goryeo canon to quell the Khitan Liao aggression.

The project continued during the reign of King Munjong 文宗, who directed the monk Dowon 道元 to establish rooms for storage of the woodblocks in Heungwang Temple 興王寺. Then, in 1067, after twelve years of national effort, the construction of the *Goryeo Canon* woodblock sutra hall, or future repository for the completed *Goryeo Canon*, at Heungwang Temple was finished.[12]

Pilgrimages and commemorative events for the first edition were carried out in 1087, during the reign of King Seonjong 宣宗 (r. 1083–94). That year, three commemorative ceremonies were held: in the second month at Gaeguk Monastery 開國寺, a Buddhist ceremony to celebrate the carving of blocks for *Goryeo Canon*; in the third month, a ceremony at Heungwang Monastery to celebrate the completion of this edition; and in the fourth month at Guibeop Monastery 歸法寺, a ceremony to enshrine the printed *Goryeo Canon*.[13]

This first *Goryeo Canon*, however, was burned during a Mongol invasion in 1232 at Buin Monastery 符仁寺 on Palgong Mountain 八公山 near today's city of Daegu 大邱 in the Republic of Korea. It was the most comprehensive canon at the time and comprised 5,924 fascicles in 570 cases. At present, about 300 fascicles have been discovered in South Korea. In Japan, about

1,800 fascicles of this edition are preserved in Nanzen Monastery in Kyoto, and 551 scrolls are at the Tsushima Provincial Museum. In total, about 2,700 fascicles are extant.[14]

THE SUPPLEMENTARY GORYEO CANON

After the completion of the first canon, new editions and supplements continued to arrive from the mainland. Khitan Liao emperor Daozong 道宗 (1055–1100) sent a complete edition of the Khitan Buddhist canon to Goryeo in 1063. In 1067, the Khitan court again sent a set of the Tripitaka to Goryeo, and in 1083 another set arrived and was stored in Gakguk Monastery 覺國寺. In 1083, King Munjong imported the Song Kaibao edition of the canon and other Buddhist texts.[15]

The arrival of new texts spurred an effort to supplement the newly completed canon. During the reign of King Munjong, *Supplementary Goryeo Canon* (*Goryeo Sokjanggyeong* 高麗續藏經), also known as *Storehouse of Teaching of the Buddhist Canon* (*Gyojang Daejangyeong* 教藏大藏經) and *Supplementary Pitaka* (*Sokjanggyeong* 續藏經), was compiled. This project was carried out by National Preceptor Uicheon 義天 (1055–1101), the son of Munjong, who went to the Song in 1085 to collect commentaries and treatises and returned with over three thousand of them.[16] Uicheon's effort resulted in the compilation of an exhaustive catalog of doctrinal teachings and commentaries entitled *Newly Compiled Comprehensive Record of the Canonical Works of the Various Schools* (*Sinpyeon Jejonggyojang Chongnok* 新編諸宗教藏總錄).[17] If the entire supplementary canon from 1086 exists, it should contain 1,010 titles in 4,740 fascicles, according to Uicheon's catalog.

After the completion of his catalog, which served as the blueprint of his project, and with Munjong's support, Uicheon then organized the Tripitaka Supervising Office (Gyojangdogam 教藏都監). In 1091, the Tripitaka Bureau (Gyojangsa 教藏司) was set up at Heungwangsa 興王寺 as the center for cutting and carving the woodblocks for publishing *Supplementary Goryeo Canon* at Heungwangsa.[18] Uicheon put Damjin 曇眞, a student of Nanwon 爛圓, in charge of collating the text and making corrections in the supplementary edition. During this process, his disciple Nakjin 樂眞 (1045–1114) assisted him with the editing. Because Uicheon had collected texts from Song China, Liao, and Japan, the supplementary canon contained many lost texts. For example, of the Khitan Buddhist books known to exist in Goryeo, he selected 39 types and 139 specific texts to be included in his supplementary edition,[19] which preserved at least the titles of commentaries that had been written by Korean and Khitan monks but have since been lost. However, the blocks of the supplementary edition were also destroyed by fires in the late twelfth century, and only some of its copy prints are extant in Korea and Japan.

THE SECOND GORYEO CANON

The creation of the second canon was directly related to the Mongol invasions of the Korean peninsula, which occurred six times between 1231 and 1258 during the reign of King Gojong 高宗 (r. 1213–59), who lived in the shadow of the military rule of the Choe family. When the first Mongol invasion began in 1231, the powerful military autocrat Choe U 崔瑀 (1179?–1249) forced the royal family and government officials to flee the capital of Gaeseong 開城 (also known as Songdo 松都) to Ganghwa Island 江華島, knowing that the Mongols could not launch an effective naval assault there. (The court did not move back until 1270, when a coup ended the Choe family rule and the new government decided to surrender to the Mongols.) However, as already mentioned, the blocks of the first *Goryeo Canon* were not moved to the new capital and were destroyed in a fire during the invasion.

After the destruction of this first *Goryeo Canon*, King Gojong, with the support of the nobility, decided in 1236 to commission the carving of another Korean canon in woodblocks based on the first Goryeo edition, and this later came to be known as *Eighty-Thousand Tripiṭaka* (*Palman Daejanggyeong* 八萬大藏經), or *Second Goryeo Canon*. To oversee the carving project, Gojong ordered the establishment of the Tripitaka Publication Bureau (Changgyeong dogam 藏經都監) at Seonwon Monastery 禪源寺 on Ganghwa Island. A branch office at Nami Island 南怡島 was set up in 1236 by Jeong Yeon 鄭宴, who spent a great deal of his fortune in doing so.[20] In addition, there were a number of suborganizations or branch offices of the supervisory organization to carve the woodblocks in the Jinju 晉州 region on the mainland of the peninsula. The carving process began in 1247 and was completed in 1251. Throughout, the completed blocks were brought to and stored in a hall near the city of Ganghwa.[21]

To oversee the editing of the entire project, King Gojong commissioned the monk Sugi 守其 at Gaetae Temple 開泰寺 in today's Daejeon. Sugi composed a work commonly referred to in short as *Collation Notes*, which was based on a careful collation of *Kaibao Canon*, the first *Goryeo Canon*, and *Khitan Canon*.[22] Due to Sugi's meticulous work, this second version achieved a high scholarly standard. According to Lancaster's study, some key improvements in readability of the text of the Korean edition include more evenly spaced characters (with more space between them), far fewer errors, and the inclusion of a comprehensive catalog. The complete canon comprises 81,250 woodblocks, each weighing just over 3 kilograms, and includes

6,791 printed volumes containing 52,382,960 Hanja characters. In total, this edition includes 1,512 titles.

The entire process of the editing of the texts and the carving of this new set of xylographs took place from 1236 to 1251. After completion of the second *Goryeo Canon* project, the blocks were kept at the Tripitaka Hall outside the West Gate of the city of Gangwha. After a time, they were moved to Seonwon Monastery 禪源寺,[23] where they remained until the founding king of the Joseon Dynasty, King Taejo (r. 1392–98, birth name Yi Seonggye 李成桂), ordered in 1398 that the entire set be moved to Jicheon Monastery 支天寺.[24] In the following year, during the reign of the second Joseon king, Jeongjong 定宗 (r. 1398–1400), the blocks were moved again to Haein Monastery, where they have remained until today.[25] Prints from this set of blocks were widely available, and an example can be seen in figures 8.1a and 8.1b.

FIGURE 8.1A, FIGURE 8.1B COLOPHON OF THE PRINTS FROM THE SECOND GORYEO EDITION IN THE HARVARD-YENCHING LIBRARY: A) THE COLOPHON OF FASCICLE 231 FROM THE *MAHA-PRAJÑĀPĀRAMITĀ SŪTRA* 大般若經, PRINTED BY COURT LADY CHEONG 鄭 AND OFFICIAL GIM HEUN 金瓘 (1238–1310), DATED TO 1300; B) THE COLOPHON OF FASCICLE 565 FROM THE *MAHA-PRAJÑĀPĀRAMITĀ SŪTRA*, BROUGHT TO JAPAN BY TSUJIMA LORD SŌ SADAMORI 宗貞盛 (1385–1452) AND FORMERLY BELONGING TO CHEONHWASA 天和寺.
Photos by Jiang Wu, November 2012

DEBATES OVER THE INTERPRETATION
OF THE FIRST *GORYEO CANON*

The account above would appear to provide a standard history of *Goryeo Canon* without dispute. Actually, there are still many unsolved issues because the entire process lasted more than two hundred and fifty years, and credible sources about it are scarce. Moreover, Goryeo society also underwent significant social, political, and religious changes during this time.

The blocks of the first carving no longer exist, so we are left with many mysteries, particularly the exact purpose for which the canon was created. The conventional view principally relies on Yi Gyubo's prayer for the carving of the second canon, in which he asserted that the canon had been created for the purpose of repelling the invading Khitan army and that it worked magically. However, Japanese scholar Ikeuchi Hiroshi 池內宏, through a careful reading, doubted this widely accepted theory and thus initiated a debate that has continued until today. Not finding any compelling evidence of the purpose for creating the first canon in 1011, he noticed that King Hyeonjong had started to print certain major Buddhist sutras, such as the *Maha-Prajñāpāramitā Sūtra* 大般若經, for Hyeonhwa Monastery 玄化寺 expansion project, which was started in 1018 and completed in 1022. He speculated that the canon printing project must have started and expanded from the printing project in Hyeonhwa Monastery, thus disputing the traditional view that the first canon had been created for defense against the Khitans. Therefore, Ikeuchi concluded that the carving of the first *Goryeo Canon* had begun in 1020 or 1021 and continued for about thirty-seven or thirty-eight years until its completion, and that the motivation had been to pray for divine blessing for Hyeonjong's deceased parents rather than to repel the Khitan army.[26] Moreover, the carving project of the complete canon spanned two generations, from King Hyeonjong to King Munjong, and thus outlasted the Khitan invasion by decades.[27]

Ikeuchi's view is provocative and debatable, considering the colonial agenda of Japanese scholars during his time. Hyebong Cheon, for example, sees this argument as problematic, and instead defends the traditional statement that Hyeonjong's motivation was to repel the Khitan invasions through the power of Buddhism.[28] Gyeong-hyun Mun suggests that the initial motivation for the printing project at Hyeonhwa Temple was to commemorate Hyeonjong's parents as well as to consolidate political power with the aid of Buddhism. Moreover, the project demonstrates the cultural achievements of Goryeo as an independent state.[29]

A resolution of the debate Ikeuchi initiated hinges upon how one reads Yi's prayer and the purpose of the printing project at Hyeonhwa Monastery for the king and the nation. Our interpretation shows that it is highly probable that the first canon project was not initiated in 1011 but at a later time, after the founding of Hyeonhwa Monastery in 1018. The canon was conceived first of all as a way for the king to offer his personal blessing for his parents, then as a gesture to assume a cultural status equal to that of the neighboring Song and Liao.

YI GYUBO'S PRAYER REVISITED

Goryeo Canon was widely believed to be a direct product of "Buddhism for nation protection," and Yi Gyubo's prayer written for the ceremony to commemorate the creation of the second printing has been frequently cited as compelling supporting evidence. To some extent, Yi helped to perpetuate the myth of the canon for nation protection.[30] It is clear from his writing that the recarving of the canon blocks expressed the wish of the Goryeo kings and the court to resist the Mongol invasions. However, it remains unclear how this event fits into the historical context and the Goryeo belief system that allowed the canon to function as such a tool.

Yi's works often highlight the centrality of the ruler in festivals and especially rituals, thus emphasizing that the "Koryo ruler's ontological role in sustaining the country was also made explicit, for he 'extended and protected the life of the country.'"[31] The activities he wrote about were first and foremost connected to the ruler and royal ancestor worship, and only peripherally to the state, Buddhism, or other themes. In 1237, Yi Gyubo wrote the official prayer offered by King Gojong and his ministers as well as the prayer for the commencement of the work on the woodblocks of the second *Goryeo Canon* edition, this time to protect the nation from the Mongols. Here are relevant portions of Yi Gyubo's text, *Prayer to Buddha from the King and Subjects of Goryeo on the Occasion of Engraving the Tripitaka Koreana*, translated by Ki-yong Rhi:

> Let us look back upon the history of the making of the scriptures. It was first begun in the 2nd year of King Hyeonjong. The massive invasion of Khitan troops forced King Hyeonjong to take flight southward, and they held Songak 松岳 (the capital) captive for a long time. When the king and court officials invoked the help of heaven by promising to engrave Tripitaka blocks, the Khitan forces withdrew of their own accord.[32]

According to Yi's prayer, the sole motive behind the carving of the first *Goryeo Canon* was pure reverence of Buddhism and a burning desire to protect the nation and people. In the above passage, Yi Gyubo connects the decision to commission the publication of the second edition to the "success" the first edition had in expelling the Khitans. He seems to clearly state that the carving of both canons was for protecting the nation. The period of the Khitan invasions was from 993 to 1019, while the period of making the first *Goryeo Canon* edition was from 1011 (a year after Khitan's second and largest invasion) to 1029; eighteen years of compilation until completion. However, the Khitans had voluntarily ceased their aggression by 1019! As the next section will reveal, the carving of the second canon had a much more specific purpose that tied it more closely to the state.

Ikeuchi's main concern about the date and purpose of Yi Gyubo's prayer was that it was written 226 years after the alleged event happened in 1011. A host of historical facts prior to the decision to initiate the *Goryeo Canon* project suggest that the Goryeo-Khitan (Liao) war had less to do directly with that decision. The Khitan had first invaded Goryeo in 993, but a treaty established relations between the states, forcing Goryeo to accept the Liao's suzerainty. The Liao then invaded China in 1004, successfully forcing tribute from the Song. A second invasion of the peninsula occurred in 1009, triggered by a military coup by General Gang Jo 康兆 (974–1010), which gave the Khitan a pretext to invade again. The Khitan army led by Emperor Shengzong 聖宗 of the Liao invaded in the eleventh month, just after Hyeonjong was enthroned. They captured Pyeongyang in the twelfth month and marched to Gaeseong on the first day of the first month of 1011. The Goryeo court had decided to leave Gaeseong on the twenty-eighth day of the twelfth month of 1010. Three days later, the Khitan army marched into the capital, but then was forced to retreat after ten days. King Hyeonjong escaped to the south and sent his envoys to persuade Emperor Shengzong to withdraw. Shengzong relented, and left on the eleventh day and crossed the Yalu River 鴨綠江 on the twenty-ninth day.[33]

Though devastating, it was a short invasion, lasting only two and a half months. If Yi's assertion is to be seen as correct, the vow to carve the canon must have occurred during the eleven days that the Khitan army occupied the capital. From the sixth year to the tenth year of King Hyeonjong's reign, the Khitans invaded four times. However, there is little evidence that the canon was carved to repel any of the invasions. In particular, royal collections of books were destroyed when the capital was occupied by the Khitans in 1011, and this left few resources for the court to undertake such a massive project.[34] It appears likely that the Liao had more of an issue with Gang Jo than a desire to conquer the Goryeo, and in their 1010 incursion during an internal Goryeo power struggle, Gang Jo was killed. The Liao did not take over the Goryeo, and Hyeonjong remained king. The Liao's main purpose was to stabilize Goryeo politics and the border, fortify trade, and draw Goryeo more into its sphere of influence and infrastructure. The 1029 completion of this first *Goryeo Canon* edition and the 1031 ceremony to commemorate it took place long after the normalization of relations between the Goryeo and the Liao, which had begun in 1022.

Historical records during this period reveal that King Hyeonjong did resort to "using" or appealing to divine power to resist the invasion, but he did not appeal to the Buddhist canon. For example, he built shrines and conducted a series of rituals to deter the Khitan army. According to *Goryeosa* 高麗史 (*Goryeo History*), in the second month of the second year of his reign, just after he returned to the capital, King Hyeonjong ordered his officials to repair and offer sacrifice at a local shrine dedicated to the spirit of Gamak Mountain (Gamak Sinsa 紺岳神祠, close to today's Seoul) because "when the Khitan army arrived in Jangdan 长湍, suddenly a storm struck as if there were flags, cavalry, and horses in the spirit shrine of Gamak Mountain, and so the Khitan army therefore did not dare march forward."[35]

In addition, for dispelling foreign invasions, a special ceremony called "Ceremony of Suppressing Armies" (*Yabyeongje* 压兵祭) was developed in the tenth month of 1008 by King Munjong. It was held again in 1048 by King Munjong 文宗, in 1117 by King Yejong 睿宗, in 1203 by King Sinjong 神宗, and in 1227 by King Gojong.[36] Although it is not clear if King Hyeonjong resorted to this ritual to repel the Khitan, this means of summoning divine power was available for him to use.

All these pieces of evidence indicate that the belief in the canon as a divine means of repelling enemies had not yet developed during the period of the Khitan invasions, which were not as perilous to the continued existence of the Goryeo as the Mongol invasions would be three centuries later. After the first two Khitan invasions, the Goryeo court was able to fortify its military, give it a more prominent position in society, and prepare for war. Moreover, the Liao was soundly defeated in their third and final main incursion in 1018, half a year before the completion of the construction of Hyeonhwa Monastery.

THE PRINTING PROJECT IN HYEONHWA MONASTERY

The defeat of the Khitan resulted in a period of peace and stability as well as an atmosphere of cultural celebration in Goryeo Korea. From 1030 to 1070, as Michael Rogers points out, "the idea that the peninsular kingdom was no longer a satellite but had developed an independent orbit and was a planet (a 'Little China') in its own right seems to have emerged."[37] The fall of northern China to the Jurchen and the abduction of Song emperors gave Goryeo another reason to assume a nativist identity of cultural independence and "an autonomous national legitimacy," as Rogers puts it. Such cultural confidence was fully displayed after Goryeo and Song resumed unofficial contact in 1069, after about a forty-year hiatus. The creation of the first *Goryeo Canon* therefore should be understood within this context. As early as 1022, when the aforementioned

Hyeonhwa Monastery stele was erected, such a sense of cultural superiority had already become manifested in the celebration of the founding of the temple. As the Minister of Personnel, Chae Chungsun 蔡忠順, indicated, the king and his courtiers wrote eulogies and poems together and posted them on the walls of the halls for public display. It appears that the king also wrote a record for the great canon and asked Gang Gamchan 姜邯贊 (948–1031), the general who had defeated the Khitan invaders in previous campaigns, to compile a full record of it.

The Great Hyeonhwa Monastery was founded in the sixth month of the ninth year, 1018, and had been established to commemorate King Hyeonjong's parents. For this purpose, annual events were decreed by the king, such as the three-day and three-night Maitreya Bodhisattva Assembly each spring, on April eighth, to hold a ceremony to pray for the prosperity and peace of the country and the royal family. The implication was also to raise the authority of Hyeonjong's reign. In addition, on July fifteenth of every year, a three-night Amitābha Assembly was convened to hold a ceremony to pray for the repose of his parents.

An important source, the "Hyeonhwa Monastery Stele" (Hyeonhwasa bieum gi 玄化寺碑陰記), shows that the beginning of a printing project coincided with the Hyeonhwa Monastery expansion project, and that it was initiated in 1018 and included the printing of various sutras. Both projects were commissioned by King Hyeonjong early in his reign, and at a time when the war with the Khitan Liao was winding down. This stele makes explicit reference to a printing project associated with the Goryeo receiving the Song *Kaibao Canon* from China.

According to the Hyeonhwasa stele statements composed by Hallim 翰林 academician Zhou Zhu 周佇 (K. Ju Jeo, d. 1024), compiled in the seventh month of 1021, and in the inscription on its back by Minister of Personnel Chae Chungsun in 1022,[38] the temple had clearly been built to commemorate King Hyeonjong's father, King Anjong 安宗, and his mother, Empress Heonjeong 獻貞, whose love affair led to his birth and the tragic death of both of them. (King Anjong was never enthroned. King Hyeonjong was his illegitimate child with Gyeongjong's 景宗 consort Heonjeong.) However, after the completion of construction and the appointment of eminent monks to serve in the temple, the king decreed that the "true principle of the dragon canon" (Ryongjang ji jinjeon 龍藏之眞詮) must be found:

> The king decreed again: "Since we have gathered a great number of monks in this wonderful place, we must seek the 'true principle of the dragon canon' to help to glorify the great event in this monastery." Therefore, [the king] sent a special envoy [to China] and documented the reason [for requesting the canon]. By riding the wind and steering the waves, the envoy crossed the deep sea and sailed afar to pay a visit to the Central Kingdom to request the Buddhist canon with a memorial. The [Chinese] emperor read the memorial

and praised his filial piety. [His majesty] bestowed a royal decree in ten lines of Chinese characters to praise the king and gave him a set of the Buddhist canon for assistance.[39]

According to the stele, the Goryeo king sent ink and paper to China and expected to receive a printed *Kaibao Canon*. This shows that the king was aware of the recent carving of *Kaibao Canon* and must have been impressed by the project. However, the Song emperor was so generous that he did not even take the paper and ink sent for printing the canon.[40] Importing the Song canon was intended to express the king's filial devotion to his parents, and so was the subsequent printed project he initiated. On the back of the stele, Chae Chungsun elaborated further:

> The king again made a vow to commemorate his parents. . . . In particular, he ordered workers to carve the printing blocks for *Maha-Prajñāpāramitā Sūtra* in six hundred fascicles and three versions of *Avataṃsaka Sutra*, *Gold Light Sutra*, and *Lotus Sutra* at this monastery. He gave it a special title called "Sutra Treasure of Perfect Wisdom" (Banyo gyeonbo 般若經寶) to allow it to be printed and spread for the entire world.[41]

It is clear that the construction of Hyeonwang Monastery and the initiation of the printing project were significant at this time, when the relationship with the Khitan had already become stabilized and cultural communication had been reestablished with Song China. The importation of a new canon must have inspired the king to emulate the Song example of carving *Kaibao Canon*. As Mun Gyeonghyun points out, because Goryeo had very advanced woodblock printing technology, "it naturally developed the religious devotion, cultural desire, and consciousness to want to make [its own] Buddhist canon." [42] The decision to commission the carving of the voluminous *Prajñāpāramitā Sūtra* was not accidental, because it took up the first 600 fascicles, almost 20 percent of the entire canon, and that project could naturally be expanded to the carving of a full canon.

THE INVENTION OF THE TRIPITAKA ASSEMBLY AND THE USE OF THE CANON FOR GIBOK 祈福

One of the little-explored issues concerning the carving of the canon is how the printed canon was actually used in the ritual context. Historical sources suggest that the first canon was created primarily as another instrument for praying for blessings and good fortune, for both the king and the nation. Such a religious culture, loosely referred to as *gibok* Buddhism, was a significant part of the Go-ryeo ritual system. As Hyeonjong gradually expanded on the initial Hyeonhwa Monastery project, the Buddhist scripture printing project was also developed and expanded over time into the carving of a complete canon edition. More-over, the canon came to be used in the unique Goryeo ritual, the Tripitaka Assembly, to pray for the peace and stability of the country.

In Goryeo history, one of the events frequently referred to is the Tripitaka Assembly, which was held in conjunction with a series of Buddhist ceremonies. The Tripitaka Assembly was a unique Korean creation and cannot be found in the dynastic histories of the Song, Liao, and Jin, or even in the later Mongol courts. According to Jongmyung Kim's study, Tripitaka Assemblies were often held in the Goryeo court. From 1029 to 1348, they were held twenty-four times, seven times during King Chungryeol's reign (1274–1308) alone.[43] The perfor-mance of this ritual demonstrates that the Korean rulers were devoted to the canon and were actually incorporating it into the state ceremonial system. A 1029 entry in *Goryeo History*[44] offers further clarification concerning the main rationale behind the decision to create and carve the first Goryeo Buddhist canon. In 1029, the first stage of the project was almost completed. Then, two years later, in 1031, a Tripitaka Assembly for the donation of sutras was held at a celebratory hall (Hoegyeong Jeon 會慶殿), and this was overseen by King Hyeonjong. Another entry in the *Goryeo History* states that in the seventh year of King Jeongjong 靖宗 (r. 1034–46), or 1041, Jeongjong held a celebratory as-sembly meeting for the donation of the Buddhist canon.[45]

Because the ceremony was a regular event, it created a great need for numer-ous copies of the canon. Historical sources show that the Goryeo court imported more than ten complete sets from the Song and Liao. These were placed in the palaces and important temples, very likely for holding Tripitaka Assembly ceremonies.[46] Because the entire canon was chanted while the ceremony was going on, it was expected that the copies made on paper would easily wear out and would need to be repaired or replaced. Possession of a set of blocks would no doubt provide a steady supply of copies of scriptures independent of foreign suppliers.

The Tripitaka Assembly was usually held twice a year, in the spring and the autumn. The ceremony originally lasted for six or seven days and was extended to ten days in 1311, during Wang Jang's reign.[47] The details of its proceedings are not recorded in *Goryeosa* and are not known to us, except for some occasional references. Other sources, especially literary collections, contain much richer information. Uicheon, for example, described that "every spring and fall, in Hoegyeong Hall of the Inner Palace, a hundred eminent monks are invited to organize the assembly for reading the great canon and other Buddhist ceremonies."⁴⁸ From these fragmented sources, the following can be said about the assembly.

First, these types of ceremonies were held in places in Gaeseong and Ganghwa such as Hoegyeong Hall, Daeseong Hall 大成殿, Seongyeong Hall 宣慶殿, Myeongin Hall 明仁殿, Main Palace (Bongwol 本闕), Outer Palace (Oeyeon 外緣), Suryeong Palace 壽寧宮, and Gangan Hall 康安殿 (in Ganghwa). During the ceremony, incense was presented. Moreover, monks were offered vegetarian meals, usually in the polo court (Gujeong 毬庭).⁴⁹ Second, according to Kim Busik's 金富軾 (1075–1151) record, the ritual area was beautifully decorated, and a statue of Śākyamuni was the focus of worship as the leading deity, along with statues of other worthies. Eminent monks were invited to recite the canon.⁵⁰ Third, the king often participated in person by offering incense and even reciting the scriptures himself. Yi Gyubo indicates in his poem that the king bowed in person, offered incense, and circumambulated around the Buddha statues while holding the scriptures.⁵¹ Finally, prayers were written by famous literary Hallim academicians, and the king even composed poems himself to demonstrate his reverence. These prayers are an important source for us to understand how the canon was used in ritual settings.

Existing prayers written for Tripitaka Assembly ceremonies illustrate that the reasons for having the carved canon present and its ritual use were not so narrowly defined as exclusively to repel the Khitan army. The application of the canon was clearly celebrated in the mid-twelfth century, when civilian bureaucrats dominated the court and the state was relatively peaceful and stable. For example, Kim Busik,⁵² who lived in the period between the two carvings of *Goryeo Canon* editions, was commissioned to write a prayer for a Tripitaka Assembly to be held in Hoegyeong Hall, probably during the reign of King Injong 仁宗. Although the year of its actual occurrence cannot be identified, at the beginning of his prayer Kim declared that the ceremony was held for "the longevity of the state and the prosperity of all countrymen." He then wrote, "I humbly wish that Heaven bestows happiness on us and the whole nation celebrates together. . . . Yin and yang reach their harmony and the foundation of the capital is reinforced. [May] Foreign barbarians be at peace and weapons be melted. [Let] Joy and peace reach and benefit all people."⁵³

The poet Jeong Jisang 鄭知常 (?–1135), in his prayer written for a Tripitaka Assembly held on the tenth day of the month of an unknown year, most likely during Injong's reign, also appealed for the good fortune of the nation. He wrote at the end:

> I humbly wish that disasters disappear immediately and blessings be abundant. Heaven regards Your Majesty as a son, and that you graciously enjoy the

retirement of an old person and protect your people forever without limitation. Your decree will cover the north where barbarians live, and your territory will reach the corner where the sun rises. [I wish] the rain, sun, warm, and cold winds all move according to their natural order; that the five agents of metal, wood, water, fire, and earth find their right places. Auspicious Vital Force arrives to bring the harvest of all grains; virtuous teachings propagate in all four directions to ensure [there is] no invasion. The foundation of the country [will] last for ten thousand generations, and royal governance encompasses the entire nation.[54]

Based on these prayers, it is clear that the canons, including both the imported canons and the locally made *Goryeo Canon* editions, were frequently used in the newly invented ceremony held during the Tripitaka Assembly, during which the canon was chanted in unison by a group of monks. In particular, at least during times of peace without the threat of foreign invasion, the assembly was held to express good will and ensure good fortune. It is therefore problematic to simply assert that "nation protection" was the only rationale for the generation and carving of the first Goryeo Buddhist canon.

In addition to these prayers, such an intention can be also seen among the populace when the printed first edition was dedicated. In the extant copy of *Prajñāpāramitā Sūtra* 大般若波羅密多經 from the first edition, a prayer was handwritten at the end of fascicle 110 (Case Ying 盈). A village head and temple-visiting envoy from Kimhae Prefecture 金海府 named Heo Jinsu 許諗壽 made the following vow, dated to 1046:

> [I pray that] our Lord be sagely and our country peaceful; that battles disappear and crops be in good harvest; that parents be loving and live long; that all my deceased ancestors ascend to heaven; that my own blessings be abundant; and that all relatives enjoy longevity. I humbly offer the *Maha-Prajñāpāramitā Sūtra* in six hundred fascicles. The fourth month of the fifteen year [1046] of the reign of Chongxi 重熙. [55]

Although sources concerning the first canon are scarce, it can be hypothesized that it was carved in an atmosphere of celebration rather than of desperation. During times of peace, as in this instance, the canon was primarily used as an instrument for expressing good will and for the blessing of the nation. Our conclusion suggests that Ikeuchi's position cannot be ignored lightly. As Sem Vermeersch stated recently after reexamining the issues surrounding the first edition, even if Ikeuchi may have read the Hyeonhwasa stele erroneously, his thesis remains useful for us to study various conditions that led to the creation of the first canon.[56]

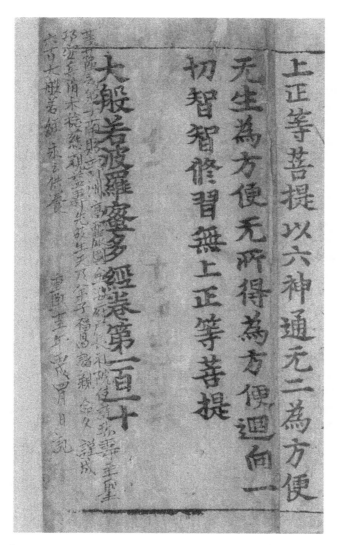

FIGURE 8.2 HANDWRITTEN COLOPHON BY HEO JINSU IN THE FIRST *GORYEO CANON*, DATED 1046. REPRINT FROM *GORYEO CHOJO DAEJANGGYEONG JIPSEONG*, VOL. 1, 82

THE TALISMANIC USE OF THE
SECOND GORYEO CANON

The period during which the second canon was created was a critical moment in Goryeo history, and Korea was facing a tremendous crisis. First, domestically, the country was under the military rule of the Choe house, which had manipulated the state apparatus and usurped the power traditionally held by the Korean kings and aristocrats. Second, internationally, conflicts with the rising Mongols had become unavoidable, and the devastating 1231 invasion engendered a time of nationwide terror and despair. Third, the nation had exhausted its resources to engage in large-scale military resistance and had to consider all possible strategies for defense, including invoking divine power. Under this desperate circumstance, various court rituals, including both Buddhist and Daoist rituals, were arranged to "dispel disasters" (*haeyang* 解禳). The carving of the second canon was therefore not an isolated event but an integral part of the military government's strategy to rescue the country from disasters. Moreover, such disasters were not simply viewed as human affairs on earth. Rather, a cosmological vision of the correspondence between the human world and heavenly power led to an interpretation of Goryeo's plight as a manifestation of "astral calamities" (*seongjae* 星災) or "the disharmony of the five agents." The Goryeo court performed various rituals and ceremonies, including carving the canon as a gigantic talismanic object, to rectify human wrongdoings on earth. The nation-protection function of the canon was thus carried out by incorporating it into a cosmological vision that was deeply rooted in the East Asian practices of geomancy and astrology.

THE CHOE MILITARY HOUSE AND THE
CARVING OF THE SECOND GORYEO CANON

The carving of the second canon was directly related to the policies of the Choe 崔 military house concerning its patronage and application of Buddhism. In 1170, a military coup overturned the rule of the civilian government of King Uijong 毅宗 (r. 1146–70) and established military rule that lasted a century. From the last years of the twelfth century to the first half of the thirteenth century, actual power was controlled and exercised by the Choe family, led by Choe Chungheon 崔忠獻 (1149–1219),[57] who rose to power in 1196, and his son, Choe U (initially known as Choe I 崔怡), who controlled King Gojong as a puppet ruler.

During this time, the collapse of the Jurchen Jin Dynasty led to a series of incursions along Goryeo's northern border. In 1215, the Eastern Xia 東夏, founded by Puxian Wannu 蒲鮮萬奴 (?–1233), attacked. In 1216, the Khitan people under Jurchen rule rebelled and invaded Goryeo. Soon after, the Mongols marched into Goryeo on the pretext of chasing the Khitans. Under the leadership of the Choe house, Goryeo was able to repel these incursions. However, the Mongols launched more devastating attacks, which forced the Goryeo court to consider all possible means to defend the country. In 1231, the Mongols launched a full-scale attack led by Sartaq 撒禮塔. Despite fierce resistance, the Mongol army defeated the Goryeo forces and captured the capital, Gaeseong. The Goryeo court surrendered for peace, but the Mongols demanded a heavy tribute that the Koreans felt difficult to fulfill. In 1232, soon after Sartaq withdrew from Gaeseong, Choe U decided to move the capital to Ganghwa Island and ordered that all the Mongol governors (Darughachi, C. Daluhuachi 達魯花赤) be killed. Sartaq invaded again but was killed in battle by a Goryeo monk. Although several peace treaties for Mongol withdrawal were negotiated, the Koreans repeatedly delayed meeting the demands to move the capital out of Ganghwa Island, pay tribute, and supply royal hostages. The Mongols invaded again in 1235, 1247, 1253, and 1254 on the excuse of Korea's half-hearted submission.

The recarving project was initiated during the Mongols' 1235 invasion, led by Tanqut-Bātur 唐古 and Prince Yekü 也窟. The assault started in the seventh month of 1235, and by the winter of 1236 the Mongol army had conquered most of the northern part of Goryeo. The fighting did not stop until peace talks began in the winter of 1238. It appears that the Goryeo court and the military regime had lost the ability to organize large-scale frontier resistance and could only launch guerrilla-type raids and ambushes to merely harass the invaders. Finally pro-Mongol generals killed the warlord Choe Ui 崔竩 (?–1258), and Goryeo fully submitted to Mongol rule in 1259. It was in the context of this urgent need to resist the Mongols that Goryeo utilized its patronization of Buddhism and promoted the enactment of Buddhist rituals.[58]

As William Henthorn noticed, during this time the Goryeo court began to carry out with greater frequency activities of a religious nature, such as Buddhist rituals, the carving of the second canon, and the organizing of various "vegetarian assemblies" (jaehoe 齋會), astrological observations, and divinations. As he notes, "one astrologer submitted the suggestion that the sun be worshipped during the morning hours from 7 a.m. to 11 a.m. in order to exorcise the Mongol troops from the peninsula."[59] Here, Henthorn erroneously suggests that "it was largely the Court and not the military government which devoted themselves to these activities. In fact, the frequent Buddhist ceremonies in which the King participated are evidence that his power was symbolic rather than actual at this time."[60] Instead, a careful reading of Goryeo History reveals that the military rulers considered patronizing religion, in particular sponsoring the carving of the second canon, as an integral part of their strategy of governing the country and resisting foreign invasions.

An important but overlooked decree issued by King Gojong in the forty-second year (1255) to Choe U's son, Choe Hang 崔沆 (?–1257), reveals that the Choe military house sponsored the project and the king listed this as one of the great achievements, along with a series of military measures, it had undertaken. The following is the translation of a portion of this decree:

> Just like Duke Dan 旦 and Duke Shi 奭 assisted the Zhou Dynasty and Xiao He 蕭何 and Cao Can 曹參 helped the Han Dynasty, sovereigns and their officials helping each other is the same from the past to the present. Since the date that my holy father ascended the throne and the time I became the king, Choe I (Choe U), the Duke of Jinyang 晉陽, has guarded the nation with utmost sincerity and assisted the court with virtue. In the year 1231, frontier generals failed to defend [the border] and the Mongol army thus entered. With godlike planning, Choe I, disputing all oppositions, unilaterally decided to escort me in person to the new capital chosen according to geomancy. Within a few years, large palaces and missing official buildings were established, laws and policies were restored, and the Goryeo nation was thus reestablished.

After praising the Choe family father and son for governing the country and helping the king, the decree immediately describes the process of remaking the canon and clearly indicates that this was a distinctive achievement completely due to the Choe family's private effort.

> Furthermore, the "army-quelling" (jinbyeong 鎮兵) blocks of the Great Canon transmitted through successive generations were all burned by the barbarian soldiers. Because our country has been experiencing many changes, there has been no time to renew it. Choe I, setting up a separate Supervising Office and donating all his personal property, carved almost half of the blocks. [His effort] benefited and blessed the country and his family, and his accomplishment is not to be forgotten. His son, Prime Minster Choe Hang, continued this family project to rescue me from disasters by carving the blocks of the Great Canon. He donated money and supervised the project. Upon its completion, he celebrated and praised it, [in order] to make the world benefit from it. [61]

In the rest of the decree, the king highlighted the importance of carving the canon by associating it with other military strategies adopted by Choe Hang, such as deploying warships along the island and building up fortifications on the outskirts of Ganghwa.

This decree indicates that the Choe family military rulers were closely involved in the recarving of the canon. Father and sons continued to sponsor the project by financing and supervising it. A significant number of blocks were carved on the island of Namhae 南海 in Jinju 晉州, which was the fiefdom of the Choe family and the place where a branch office of the Tripitaka Supervising Office was established. In particular, this decree emphasizes that the purpose of the project had been to quell an invading army and exorcise the enemy, and that the project was initiated by the Choe family itself rather than the king or the Goryeo court. More intriguing is that in the narrative relating the Choe family's accomplishments, the carving of the canon was singled out as a project as important as their military defense of the nation.

Then, an interesting question arises: Why were the military rulers so enthusiastic about recarving the canon? Our reading suggests that the Choe family's use of the canon was consistent with their patronage of Buddhism, especially Seon Buddhism, as a strategy to resist the Mongol invasion. A prayer Yi Gyubo wrote for a Seon Assembly held in Changboksa 昌福寺 and sponsored by Choe U reveals the secret intention that the military rulers wanted to not only patronize but also make use of Buddhism at this critical point. Yi points out that the purpose of holding these types of Buddhist ceremonies was to "quell armies" or "repel the northern army" (*gakbokbyeong* 卻北兵), as King Gojong's decree had mentioned. Moreover, Yi insinuates that a consensus had been reached in the court that Confucian governance alone would not be able to guarantee the eternal peace of Goryeo, and so Buddhism must be utilized as an essential method to do so.

> Those who are prime ministers and court officials cannot solely rely on [Confucian measures of] benevolence, righteousness, ritual, and music to transform people and establish conventions. They must also use the Buddha dharma to quell human hearts, and thus prosperity follows. To use Buddhism to guard the country and to strengthen it [to be] as firm as a metal-made city is also the governor's unorthodox strategy (*gichaek* 奇策).[62]

Here, Yi uses a military term, "unorthodox strategy" or "clever scheme," to describe Choe U's use of Buddhism. The fundamental premise was to create and carry out an "unorthodox strategy" of surprise, like those used in military operations, to put one's opponent off balance. This way of thinking, as Ralph Sawyer points out, was deeply influenced by Chinese military thought and strategic culture, which emphasized such methods to overcome formidable enemies.[63] Although Yi mentions this connection in passing in this passage, it is reasonable to assume that the desperate military situation in the battlefields had necessitated invoking the spiritual power of Buddhism.

In the face of continuous Mongol invasions and disastrous military defeats, the court officials led by Choe U seem to have been serious about applying this strategy, and even to have indulged in the delusion that supporting Buddhism would be even more effective for defense than supplying and fortifying the military. Yi Gyubo expresses this type of wishful thinking clearly and directly:

"transporting supplies and food to feed an army of ten thousand soldiers is not even comparable to supporting one Seon monk, which first [and foremost] saves money."[64] Another court academician, Gim Gu 金坵 (1211–78), wrote similar poems to praise the power of chanting the canon, with lines like, "One canon excels by far an army of a million soldiers."[65] Yi and Gim might have exaggerated the situation. Nonetheless, these passages demonstrate that the court seriously considered utilizing Buddhism, especially carving the canon, together with military plans as means to combat invasions. Under these circumstances, the carving of the second canon has to be considered a military strategy, along with other similar religious rituals and ceremonies, aimed at resisting foreign military incursions.

THE CANON AS A TALISMAN TO SUBDUE ENEMIES

It is clear that *Goryeo Canon* was included in a series of religious measures adopted by the Choe military government. However, the reasoning behind how the canon could have played a role in resisting invasions is still not clear. Based on our reading of historical sources, we offer that the canon was conceived as a powerful talisman, as Lancaster has suggested. Such a creative use was firmly grounded in the geomancy culture on the Korean peninsula.

Here, we again have to focus on Yi Gyubo's writings, because as the most celebrated literatus he drafted numerous ritual texts for the execution of ceremonies, and these reflect the context within which the canon was recarved. Yi had also written many official documents for the court, especially for the power holder Choe U. Yi may have been the best person to write a prayer for the second canon, because of his literary talent and his deep connection with the canon. Not only did he write the prayer when he was 70 years old, in 1237 (he formally retired in the twelfth month of that year),[66] he also kept a close relationship with the chief editor, Sugi, and left many poems referring to him.[67] Moreover, Yi and his son were directly involved in the operation of the Tripitaka Publication Bureau, which also printed Yi Gyubo's literary collection.[68] His many writings concerning religious affairs in the court reveal important background information for the carving of the second canon. In particular, fascicles 39, 40, and 41 of Yi Gyubo's literary collection include all the prayers he wrote for various religious ceremonies. In total, Yi wrote one hundred and twenty-five prayers for various ritual settings on behalf of the sponsors. Among these, about fifty-six can be clearly identified as Buddhist rituals and forty-four as Daoist rituals. Eighteen of them written for both Buddhist and Daoist rituals were related to the exorcism of disasters brought on by irregular star movements, two were prayers written for Tripitaka Assemblies, and eight were written for Choe

Chungheon and Choe U to pray for dispelling the Khitan and Mongol armies.[69]
It is certain that Tripitaka Assemblies were held with greater frequency than is
recorded in *Goryeosa*, especially during times of foreign invasion. For example,
in Yi Gyubo's collection, there are fourteen such regulated verses, each consisting of seven characters in eight lines. If we assume he wrote one poem for each
ceremony, then in the eighteen years from 1215 to 1233, at least fourteen Tripitaka Assemblies were held in the court.[70] Yi's writings thus help us to situate the
canon in this historical context.

The relationship between the second canon and nation protection can be
clearly seen in Yi's prayer below:

> On the strength of our combined devotion, we entreat all buddhas, Bud-
> dhist saints, and the thirty-three gods to invoke divine powers to drive out the
> wicked and ugly enemy from this land so that peace may prevail over it, the
> queen and prince may enjoy good health, and the foundation of Three Hans
> [referring to the Korean nation] may remain secure forever. We, the disciples,
> are duty bound to strive more to follow the ways of Buddha, thus repaying
> even an iota of the grace of Buddha. We pray with all our heart, appealing for
> your generous attention.[71]

However, he neither specifies nor explains which belief system was the basis
on which the canon was used to protect the nation and the divine power invoked. More strikingly, Yi's linking the canon with invoking supernatural power
appears to be unique in the entire history of the Chinese Buddhist canon. In
Song China, for example, *Kaibao Canon* had never been used in this kind of
context even when the Song court was facing tremendous political and military
difficulties. Therefore, we need to continue to read and study Yi's work more
carefully.

The crucial hint for us to understand the role of the canon in the Goryeo
belief system is the use of the term "suppressing" or "quelling" the enemy to
describe its function. Here, the use of the canon as an instrument of "exorcism"
(*jin* 鎮) is closely associated with the use of a talisman to dispel calamities in geomancy. According to the geomantic principle, when an evil force is threatening,
an "exorcism technique" (*jinbeop* 鎮法 or *yeomseung sul* 厭勝术) must be used,
involving the careful placement of various "talismanic objects" (*jinmul* 鎮物 or
yeomseung mul 厭勝物). This type of knowledge had most probably been transmitted from China, and by the eleventh century some Koreans had become
deeply influenced by such superstitions. *Goryeosa* records that a certain Chinese from Fuzhou of Song China named Hu Zongdan 胡宗旦 came to serve
King Yejong 睿宗 and was appointed as a Hallim scholar. He was particularly
skillful in exorcism techniques and demonstrated them to the king.[72] The Song

envoy Xu Jing 徐兢 (1091–1153), during his visit to Goryeo in 1123, commented that the Koreans were believers in the supernatural, and in particular relied on "curses and exorcism" (*jujeo yeomseung* 咒詛厭勝).[73]

It seems that the court and the military government took these geomantic techniques seriously and even applied them during the wars against the Mongols. Choe Chungheon, for example, was deeply influenced by geomantic numerology and yin-yang theory. To repel foreign invasions, he trusted diviners and adopted their advice, which included destroying existing monasteries, moving the king's tablets to new temples, and building new palaces in different locations to achieve better geomantic fortunes. A general called Kim Deokmyeong 金德明 was promoted to Director of the Grand Diviner Bureau because he was able to flatter Choe with his expertise in the use of geomancy. When the Khitan army arrived at the capital in 1217, Kim proposed to Choe Chungheon that the coming of the Khitans had been due to the bad location of the royal tombs, and he attributed this invasion to King Hyeonjong's moving King Anjong's tomb, which had also incurred the earlier Khitan invasion in 1010. At that time, the tomb of King Gangjong 康宗 was buried beside it, causing bad *feng-shui* (*pungsu* 風水). He thus suggested moving the tomb to another place. The third military ruler, Choe U, also patronized a certain Ju Yeonji 周演之, who was a former monk and famous for his divination ability.[74] In addition, the military rulers sought to apply witchcraft to the battlefield. In 1253, in the wake of the Mongol invasion led by Jalairtai (Cheluoda 車羅大, also known as Zhalaer 札剌兒 in Chinese sources), the court "sent an 'astrological officer' (Il Kwan 日官) to bury three stones at strategically important locations, to dispel the barbarian armies."[75] In this passage, we see evidence that sending the king's astrological officers to bury stones can be only explained by the witchcraft technique of "placing a talisman" (*bangjin* 放鎮) to deter the enemy.[76]

Against this background, the blocks of the canon must have been considered collectively as a gigantic talisman. Their talismanic magical function can be attributed to three characteristics. First, the blocks had Chinese characters with Buddha's message carved onto them, in a way similar to Daoist talismanic writings. Second, the sheer number of woodblocks of the canon, which amounted to more than eighty thousand, was large enough to counter the number of soldiers in the threatening invading army. Third, the power of the canon could be released through the chanting of the entire canon in unison during Tripitaka Assemblies. It was believed that the sound of chanting had special powers to invoke divine assistance.

Such power has been attested in various prayers and eulogies for Tripitaka Assemblies. For example, literati such as Yi Gyubo had been asked to write many "Sound Eulogies" (*Eumchansi* 音讚詩) in praise of the power of chanting. In one such poem written for Tripitaka Assemblies, Yi wrote, "The chanting of Buddha's words seems to be [summoning] gods to join and soldiers [who] have been hidden, and our country has revived." He continued: "Don't bother to have the defense of thousands of soldiers with iron armor; just rely on the descent of Buddha's golden body with ten powers." Moreover, the effect of the invocation manifested immediately: "Six heavenly gods surround us in a formidable defensive formation"; and "Eight sections of spirit soldiers guard the sacred altar."[77] It is not surprising that in Goryeo Korea, a unique "Cult of the Canon" emerged based on its talismanic function. (See Jiang Wu's chapter 2 for discussion of this phenomenon.)

THE CANON FOR DISPELLING ASTRAL DISASTERS

Scholars have long documented the fact that Goryeo rulers had to take into consideration geomancy in all aspects of their rule. Research shows that Goryeo rulers were deeply committed to geomancy and applied it in choosing the locations and orientations of Buddhist monasteries throughout the state, as expressed in King Taejo's second injunction.[78] Less known is the fact that the development of astrology also deeply influenced Buddhism. There is ample research to demonstrate that Korean esoteric Buddhism had a close connection to astrology.[79] In the following, we try to explain how the Buddhist canon was invoked in many ceremonies held in response to unfavorable interpretations of astral observations.[80]

Goryeo Buddhism, especially esoteric Buddhism, was significantly influenced by astrology, as demonstrated in the worship of the seven stars of the Northern Dipper, which had originated in Daoism and had been adopted by Buddhists in the eighth century. According to Sørensen, in the mid-twelfth century, especially under King Uijong's reign (1146–1217), this cult became popular in the court. During King Gojong's reign, when the second canon was carved, rituals dedicated to the Northern Dipper were held more than one hundred and twenty five times.[81] A few decades before the carving of the first canon, the Khitan envoy Yelü Chun 耶律纯 visited the Goryeo court in 984 to negotiate border issues. He noted the advanced culture of astrology in Goryeo, and even studied under a Goryeo national preceptor. Yelü compiled his notes into an astrological text entitled *Compendia of Astrology and Divination* (*Xingming zongkuo* 星命總括), which came to be included in the Chinese imperial collections *Yongle Encyclopedia* (*Yongle Dadian* 永樂大典) and *The Complete Collection of Four Treasures* (*Siku quanshu* 四庫全書).[82] The inclusion of a Korean work in Chinese imperial collections testifies to the Korean achievements in astrology and divination.

During Yi Gyubo's time, the frequent foreign invasions and peasant rebellions were compounded by an increase in the number of observed astrological anomalies. Many of Yi's prayers for ritual ceremonies fall into the category of "praying for exorcism," *giyang*. One of the special categories was the rituals aimed at exorcising astral disasters, whose purpose was to reverse the negative impact of abnormal star movements, and as a result, to avoid human-generated disasters in the world. In Yi Gyubo's two prayers written for the Tripitaka Assembly around the time the second canon was created, he makes explicit allusion to the astrological movements in the sky as the reason for holding such ceremonies.

In a prayer he wrote for an undated Tripitaka Assembly, Yi states the reason for holding such a ceremony as follows:

> Because disasters arise from their embryos, we have to admonish ourselves about the gradual emergence of dangers such as this due to minute changes. However, [as described] in astrological records, the lack of many [successful] policies and governance has frequently resulted in the appearance of ominous stars. The "Metal Star" (Geumseong 金星, Venus) suddenly invaded the Grand Forbidden Palace (Daemi 大微) and the Wood Star (Mokseong 木星, Jupiter) again interfered with the "Shimmering Perplexer" (Heonghok 熒惑, Mars). We therefore became very worried and terrified. It is absolutely appropriate to devote ourselves to the most subtle teaching [of Buddhism] and to rely humbly on the help of [Buddha's] compassion to dispel the calamities.[83]

In another prayer for the performance of a Tripitaka Assembly, Yi again refers to the recent astrological changes and unusual events on earth.

> Successive reports indicate that the movement of the moon is out of order. It will either interfere with the constellation occupied by lords or enter into the path of the Grand Forbidden Palace. Again we read the sudden report from the secondary capital (Pyongyong) that a great boulder moved by itself and objects without feet walked. All these are odder than usual. . . . We believe that in order to exorcise [them] we must rely on the best of all our karmic connections.[84]

Yi's comments link the Buddhist canon and the holding of the related Tripitaka Assemblies to the cosmic order, especially the movements of the stars. According to traditional East Asian astrology and astronomy, the sky is imagined as reflecting the imperial hierarchy in the human world, and is further divided into three star clusters or "enclosures" (*won* 垣): the Purple Forbidden Palace (Jami gung 紫薇宮)—the heavenly sovereign's main palace; the Grand Forbidden Palace (Taemi gung 太微宮)—the heavenly sovereign's governing office; and the Celestial Market (Cheonsi 天市). Each "enclosure" contains many stars that were named after official titles in the Chinese bureaucratic system. In addition, there are twenty-eight constellations (*suk* 宿) in four directions. Five planets move across the sky and form different relationships with these palaces and constellations. When a planet enters a particular celestial region marked by three "enclosures" and twenty-eight constellations, they form the relationship of conjunction, which was referred to as "violation" (*rungbeom* 凌犯). In addition, comets and meteorites, usually referred to as "bushy stars" (*paeseong* 孛星), "broom stars" (*hyeseong* 彗星), "guest stars" (*gaekseong* 客星), or "flowing stars" (*yuseong* 流星), have paths of movement that indicate upcoming dangers in the human world. Other celestial phenomena such as solar and lunar eclipses, sunspots, and Venus being visible in the daytime were also observed and interpreted. Based on complicated interpretations of these astrological events by the state observatory, which was monopolized by the court, the Grand Historian (Taesa 太史) presented a report on the celestial phenomena (*cheonmun* 天文) and divination interpretations (*jeomsa* 占词) to the king.[85] Theoretically, all changes in the human world, such as the change of a dynasty, the death of a ruler or minister, natural disasters such as floods and droughts, and military operations and invasions can be predicted in advance based on sophisticated observations of star patterns.

Under the influence of an astrological culture, Goryeo government offices widely employed astrologers. They were even hired onto the command staff of the military to follow and report on erratic star movements as well as signs and phenomena perceivable in the wind and clouds, in order to make prognostications for military operations and to avoid disasters.[86] There are many entries pertaining to astronomical events in *Goryeosa*, which clearly indicates the corresponding relationship among heaven, earth, and the human world. Systematic Korean astronomical records were mostly preserved in the *Astrological Gazetteer* (*Cheonmun Ji* 天文志), in fascicle 48 of *Goryeosa*. In most cases, the astronomers offered unembellished recordings of their observations. Occasionally, an interpretation offered by the Grand Historian, along with the king's reaction, was inserted, thus leaving important information about how the Goryeo court reacted to astrological changes. If a divination indicated an oncoming astral disaster, a ruler had to take immediate action to avert such ill fortune. Although there were also long-term remedies available, such as reforming policies and governance, often the immediate response was to perform special "rituals of exorcism" (*suyeong* 修禳), especially when the resources for more comprehensive responses were exhausted. The Goryeo court and military rulers were fully convinced by the interpretation of star patterns and hoped to change their fate by influencing the stars' movements. Even the mighty military ruler Choe Chungheon had to face the inevitability of his fate. In the fourth day of the ninth month of 1219, the violation of Mars by the moon was observed and the astrological officer reported to the court: "A prominent person will die." Believing this to be the prediction of his death, Choe Chungheon was so scared that he summoned musicians to play all day to reverse his fate. However, he died eventually, late in the night.[87]

Yi's deliberate linking of the use of the Buddhist canon to recent astrological observations shows the prevalent influence of an astrological culture in Korea. Yi's prayers for holding the Tripitaka Assembly clearly demonstrate that the series of ritual events conducted in and by the Goryeo court epitomized systematic responses to recent urgent domestic events and situations that the court interpreted as evidence of disorder. The chanting of the entire canon was considered an integral part of these ritual events, and they were entered into astrological records. Considering this deeply rooted cosmological vision, the carving of the canon cannot be separated from these exorcism rituals. Rather, it must be seen as an essential part of the response to the astrological changes. The entries of these ritual events in records indicate that Buddhist rituals, including those concerning the carving and use of *Goryeo Canon*, had become incorporated into a series of rituals aimed at dispelling calamities.

On the occasion of the millennium celebration of the creation of *Goryeo Canon*, Oh Yunhui, former director of the Tripitaka Koreana Research Institute, made a controversial observation about the *Goryeo Canon* edition in an interview published in the February 10, 2011, issue of the *Joongang Ilbo* newspaper: "The Goryeo Buddhist Canon is a 'fake' copied from China. . . . It is excellent because it is better than the original." [88] What Mr. Oh meant is that the Goryeo edition was not produced by any one nation. Instead, it was produced based on input from earlier preexisting editions that had been translated and compiled by other countries, and thus "was born of the mutual interaction among East Asian nations" to advance the "global religion" of Buddhism.

As Mr. Oh points out, the Goryeo edition was indeed a "better" version than the "original" *Kaibao Canon* in many ways. Because of Sugi's meticulous work, the quality of its textual collation has been widely recognized in the scholarly world, and it became the master copy for a series of modern editions printed in Japan, especially the Taishō edition. In addition, as this chapter reveals, Goryeo people used the canon in innovative ways in response to their own situation. In contrast to China, where the canon had never been conceived or applied as an effective means of warding off disasters, in Korea people incorporated the canon into their own belief system and used it for venerating ancestors, praying for blessings, and repelling foreign invasions. Using the carving of the canon as a means of repelling disasters was clearly a Korean invention; the canon, used primarily to appeal for blessings and to spread Buddha's word in China, was never considered by the Chinese court to function in this way. Even during the Song, when *Kaibao Canon* was created, while the government suffered from many military defeats by the Khitans, Tanguts, Jurchens, and later the Mongols, the court never considered using the canon as a symbolic ritual means to ease the crisis.[89] In this sense, the canon was a tool to assist in the rule of the state through its moral and spiritual message in China. However, in Korea, the canon was incorporated into an indigenous belief system, and thus functioned as part of "Buddhism of praying for blessing and exorcising calamities" (*Giyang Bulgyo*).

NOTES

The authors wish to thank Lucille Chia and Sem Vermeersch for their comments on early drafts. Mr. Xiaohe Ma provided assistance for Jiang Wu's research at the Harvard-Yenching Library in April 2012, and we thank him for his help.

1. Hawley, *Inside the Hermit Kingdom*, 100.

2. Ono Genmyō, "Kōrai daizō chōin kō," 1–4; Ōya Tokujō, *Kōrai zokuzō chōzō kō*; and Ikeuchi Hiroshi, "Kōraichō daizōkyō," 483–614. Japanese scholars claimed that the canon and its blocks had been first discovered by the Japanese historian Sekino Tadashi 関野貞 in 1902. See Ikeuchi, "Kōraichō daizōkyō," 572.

3. Demiéville, "Sur les éditions imprimées du canon chinois," 190–207; Courant, *Bibliographie coréenne*, 215–19; Lancaster and Park, *The Korean Buddhist Canon*.

4. It is currently designated as National Treasure No. 32. Most studies of the canon in Korean have been collected in three volumes, in *Goryeo Daejanggyeong Jaryojip*. Most primary sources are collected in Yi Chi-kwan, ed., *Gayasan Haeinsa ji*, 1992.

5. Sørensen, "Esoteric Buddhism Under the Koryŏ," 85.

6. For a summary of recent debates, see Mohan, "Beyond the 'Nation-Protecting' Paradigm," 49–67.

7. This concept was used in the work of Lü Jianfu, "Gaoli wangchao de qirang fojiao yu dongchuan zhi mijiao," 406–33. This was first published in *Bulgyu yonggu*, 139–60. The Korean scholar Shim Jaeryong also used the concept of "Buddhism for good fortune" (*gibok Bulgyo* 祈福佛教) to characterize Korean Buddhism. See Shim Jaeryong, *Korean Buddhism Tradition and Transformation*, 148–56. For a study of a similar culture in China, see Tao Siyan, *Qirang*.

8. The talismanic use of *Goryeo Canon* was first suggested by Lewis Lancaster. See Lancaster and Park, *The Korean Buddhist Canon*, xii–xiii.

9. This source also mentions a canon set brought to the peninsula in 928. See Paik Nak-choon, "Tripiṭaka Koreana," 63. For other Tripitaka texts brought to the peninsula, see Rhi Ki-yong, "An Introduction to the Tripiṭaka Koreana," 18–19.

10. Paik Nak-choon, "Tripiṭaka Koreana," 63. In the third year of the Later Tang (Hou Tang Tiencheng 后唐天成), "Silent Monk" (Muk Hwasang 默和僧) brought the text to the peninsula. See Ha Tae-Hung and Grafton K. Mintz, *Samguk Yusa*, 233.

11. For a list of eight Chinese canons, including *Kaibao Canon* and *Khitan Canon*, introduced in Korea from 989 to 1107, a period that includes the reigns of King Sonjong to Yejong, see Rhi Ki-yong, "An Introduction to the Tripiṭaka Koreana," 18–19. The standard content of *Kaibao Canon* was about 480 cases and 5,084 fascicles. It is not known why Han brought back only 2,500 fascicles.

12. Kim Yeongmi, "11segi huban–12segi cho Goryeo," 47–77.

13. Demiéville believed that in the later part of the eleventh century the Goryeo court carved another edition, and Sugi distinguished the two as "former national edition" (*gugjeonbon* 國前本) and "latter national edition" (*gukhubon* 國後本). See Demiéville, "Sur les éditions imprimées du canon chinois," 195. He was largely influenced by the Japanese scholar Tsumaki Naoyoshi 妻木直良, who had published an influential article on *Khitan Canon* in 1912. Tsumaki had based his hypothesis on his reading of a dubious phrase in Uicheon's essay. His view was refuted by Ikeuchi. See Tsumaki Naoyoshi, "Kittan ni okeru daizōkyō chōzon no jijitsu o ronzu," 317–40; Ikeuchi, "Kōraichō daizōkyō," 519–22.

14. According to Jong-myung Kim, additional extant copies have recently been found in Korea. See Kim Jong-myung, "The Tripiṭaka Koreana," 156; Cheon Hyebong, *Horim Bangmulgwan sojang*. The Nanzenji editions have been digitized and are available on the Tripitaka Koreana Research Institute website, http://kb.sutra.re.kr.

15. Mun Gyeonghyun, "Goryeo Daejanggyeong reojo ui sajeok gochal," 38.

16. Lancaster, "The Buddhist Canon in the Koryo Period," 44.

17. For this work, see *T* 55, no. 2184. For a partial listing of the main texts, see An Kai-hyon, "Publication of Buddhist Scriptures in the Koryo Period," 84–86.

18. Japanese scholar Ōya Tokujō questioned the assertion that this supplement had been completed, pointing out that the remaining copies from Heungwang Temple did not have case characters from *Thousand-Character Classic*. Moreover, some texts carved were not in Uicheon's catalog, and some were not carved at Heungwang Temple. Ōya also pointed out that Uicheon indicated that when he drafted his catalog he did not start the project as a supplement to the main canon. See Ōya Tokujō, "Kaiinji kyōban kō," 355–60. Reprinted in his *Bukkyō kobankyō no kenkyū*, 57–196, especially 155–71. See also his thorough study of the supplementary canon in *Kōrai zokuzō chōzō kō*.

19. An Kai-hyon, "Publication of Buddhist Scriptures in the Koryo Period," 86–87.

20. Ibid., 87.

21. Bulgyo Bangsong, ed., *Namhae bunsa dogam gwannyeon gicho josa bogosoeo*; Paik Nak-choon, "Tripiṭaka Koreana," 69.

22. Lancaster suspects that Sugi had only two editions to work from: the Northern Song Kaibao edition and the Liao/Khitan edition. See Lancaster, "The Koryo Edition of the Buddhist Canon," 322–33. Lancaster also observed through comparing two versions of *Daoxing bore jing* 道行般若經, from the first edition and the second edition, that the first edition follows the format of *Kaibao Canon* and the editors of the second

edition intended to maintain the same format, including the number of characters in columns and pages. Therefore, in compiling the second edition, the editors altered the format of the original texts of the first edition probably based on "the principle of providing the best reading possible within a format rather than a reading based solely on textual witness." Lancaster, "Comparison of the Two Carvings of the Korean Buddhist Canon," 34–38. Lancaster also notes that the first *Goryeo Canon* edition is like a photocopy of the Kaibao edition. Where no changes were made, the carvers of the blocks of the second Goryeo edition used the old technique of tracing to produce the images. See Lancaster, "The Koryo Edition of the Buddhist Canon," 326.

23. Seonwon Temple is located just south of today's capital city of Seoul, near Suwon. It is not far from the west coast of the peninsula, and near Ganghwa Island. See Hwang Suyoung and Mun Myoungdae, *Goryeo seonwonsaji ui balgyeol gwa goryeo daejanggyeongpan ui yurae*, 37; Chae Sangsik, "Ganghwa seonwonsa ui wichi ye jaekeomto," 138–40; Paik Nak-choon, "Tripitaka Koreana," 70.

24. Jicheon Monastery was located at that time in Namgyeong 南京, today's Seoul. It has been suspected that two sets of blocks were created at the same time, one by the Tripiṭaka Supervising Office and stored in Seonwon Temple and the other by Choe U in 1254 and stored in Jicheon Temple. See Yi Chi-kwan, ed., *Kayasan Haeinsa ji*, 277. See also Sugano Ginhachi, "Kōrai-ban Daizōkyo ni tsuite," 236–37; Paik Nak-choon, "Tripiṭaka Koreana," 70–72.

25. The transfer of the blocks to Haeinsa is not clear either, and the conventional view presented here has been challenged by Ven. Sung Ahn (Deug Guen Yim). He argues that the blocks must have been moved to Haeinsa between 1318 and 1360 because the majority of them were not stored in Seonwonsa, which was sacked by the Japanese in 1360. It is possible that the 1399 move only involved other sets of blocks such as those of esoteric scriptures and the annotated *Avataṃsaka Sutra*. See Yim Deug Guen, "The Enshrinement of the Tripitaka Koreana."

26. See also Lancaster, "The Buddhist Canon in the Koryo Period," 175, 189.

27. Also, Ikeuchi Hiroshi refused to acknowledge the "trustworthiness" of the writings of Yi Gyubo. See Ikeuchi Hiroshi, "Kōraichō daizōkyō," 512, and the discussion below. For a summary of Ikeuchi's argument in English, see Lancaster and Park, *The Korean Buddhist Canon*, xi–xii. Although we consulted the works of Japanese colonial authors such as Ikeuchi, we are aware of their colonial influence and political agenda. For an evaluation of Ikeuchi's "objective" research and colonial agenda, see Breuker, "Contested Objectivities," especially 85–95.

28. Cheon Hyebong, *Raryo inswaesul ui yeongu*, 62; and "Chojo Daejanggyeong ui Hyeonjonbon gwa geu Teukseong," 5.

29. Mun Gyeonghyun, "Goryeo Daejanggyeong reojo ui sajeok gochal," 21–74. For an explanation of the complicated court infighting surrounding the carving of the first canon, see Okamoto Keiji, "Kōrai daizōkyōban no kokusei," 14–23.

30. Ikeuchi Hiroshi, "Kōraichō no daizōkyō," 483–614.

31. Breuker, *Establishing a Pluralist Society in Medieval Korea*, 181. For Yi's literary achievement, see Evon, "Dialogues with God and Stone," 1–48; Bak Changhi, "Ri Gyubo no shūkan to sono shakai ishiki," 785–90; Bak Changhi, "Saishi seiken to kanryōsō," 124–27.

32. Rhi Ki-yong, "An Introduction to the Tripiṭaka Koreana," 14. Yi's prayer for recarving the canon was also translated by Paik Nak-choon, "Tripiṭaka Koreana," 66; and by Lee and De Bary, *Sources of Korean Tradition*, 239. We chose Rhi's translation because it is the most complete and accurate.

33. The 1010 invasion was the largest campaign the Khitans had launched, and it was after King Hyeonjong had just ascended the throne and was engaged in an internal power struggle. However, the Khitans had a limited objective. The coup and assassination by Gang Jo of Liao's Goryeo vassal-king, Mokjong 穆宗 (r. 997–1009), Hyeonjong's father, offered the Khitan justification for the second military incursion in 1009. For details, see Twitchett and Tietze, "The Liao," 43–153. Also see Wright, *From War to Diplomatic Parity in Eleventh-Century China*, and Kim Dangtaek, "Goryeo Mokchong 12 nyeon ui jeongbyeon e daehan ilgochal," 82–97. For details about Shengzong's invasion, see Ikeuchi Hiroshi, "Kittanseisou no Kōrai seibatsu," 199–264. See also Vermeersch, "Royal Ancestor Worship and Buddhist Politics." We thank Sem Vermeersch for sharing his paper with us before its publication.

34. Ikeuchi Hiroshi, "Kōraichō daizōkyō," 506–13.

35. *Goryeosa*, fasc. 63, vol. 2, 352b.

36. *Goryeosa*, fasc. 63, vol. 2, 352b, 353a; fasc. 22, vol. 1, 339a; and fasc. 14, vol. 1, 208b. The details involved in the performance of this ritual are not known.

37. Rogers, "National Consciousness in Medieval Korea," 158; Breuker, "The Emperor's Clothes?" 48–84.

38. Zhou Zhu hailed from Wenzhou 溫州 in China. He came to Goryeo from the Song in 1005, and was appointed to draft official documents. For his short biography, see *Goryeosa*, fasc. 94, vol. 3, 88b.

39. Heo Hungsik, *Hanguk Geumseok Jeonmun*, 445.

40. Ikeuchi thought that the edition the Goryeo king received was a gold-ink canon because the term *kimmun* 金文 was mentioned on the stele. However, this usually referred to Buddha's word in general, and cannot be used as evidence to prove it was a gold-ink edition. Also, he believed that this imported canon was the one Choe Wonsin 崔元信 requested in the tenth year of Hyeonjong. See Ikeuchi, "Kōraichō daizōkyō," 495.

41. Heo Hungsik, *Hanguk Geumseok Jeonmun*, 450. Vermeersch translated the same passage in his "Royal Ancestor Worship and Buddhist Politics" with a slightly different reading.

42. Mun Gyeonghyun, "Goryeo Daejanggyeong reojo," 35–36.

43. See Kim Jongmyung, "Buddhist Rituals in Medieval Korea (918–1392)," 59–63; Hong Yunsik, *Kankoku Bukkyō girei no kenkyū*, 127.

44. See also ibid., 36–37.

45. *Goryeosa*, vol. 1, 88b. See also Mun Gyeonghyeon, "Goryeo Daejanggyeong reojo," 36.

46. Some records of the ceremonies indicate that various copies of the canon other than *Goryeo Canon*, such as a hand-copied, gold-ink version and the Khitan edition, were used in the ceremonies. See Baba Hisayuki, "Kōraiban daizōkyō to zōkyō dōjō," 24–28. Baba points out that the Tripitaka Assembly was not held exclusively for celebrating the carving, copying, printing, and praying for the second canon. From 1029 to 1347, there were twenty-five ceremonies held in the court. For example, the canon was printed in 1316, 1380, and 1381, but there are no entries about the Tripitaka Assembly in official records.

47. *Goryeosa*, vol. 1, 525a. Such ceremonies must have been important events at court in which all officials and palace guards were involved. A coup to overthrow the warlord Jeong Jungbu 鄭仲夫 (1106–79) was thus planned on the night of a Tripitaka Assembly held in 1179. See *Goryeosa*, vol. 100, fasc. 13, 2.

48. See Uicheon's preface to "Wonjong munryu" in Huang Chunyan, ed., *Gaoli dajue guoshi wenji*, 2.

49. Kim Changsuk, ed., *Goryeosa Bulgyo gwangye saryojip*, 138, 140, 141, 144.

50. Yi Chikwan, *Gayasan Haeinsa ji*, 270.

51. For Yi's reference to the king's presence, see Yi Gyubo, *Dongguk I sangguk jip*, fasc. 18, vol. 1, 272. Vermeersch notes in *Goryeosa* 26.37a that in 1270, when a Tripitaka Assembly was held, the king could not afford a music troupe. This shows that music was usually being played while the assembly was in session. See Vermeersch, *The Power of the Buddha*, 333 note 57.

52. For a summary of Kim Busik's clan's ties to the Unified Silla and its capital of Gyeongju, and his practice of Buddhism while supporting Confucianism as a governing principle, see Shultz, "An Introduction to the Samguk-Sagi."

53. Yi Chikwan, *Gayasan Haeinsa ji*, 270.

54. Yi Chikwan, *Gayasan Haeinsa ji*, 270–71.

55. http://kb.sutra.re.kr/ritk/sutra/sutraMain.do (accessed March 23, 2012). Chongxi is the reign name of Emperor Xingzong 興宗 of the Liao Dynasty, and Goryeo started to use the Liao reign name in 993. See Gwon Huigyeong, "Dongjang-sa sojang ui Gamjigeumja," 27; *Goryeo Chojo Daejanggyeong Jipseong*, vol. 1, 82. This piece is preserved at Cheongju Museum of Ancient Prints (Cheongju Goinswae Pangmulgwan 清州古印刷博物館).

56. See Vermeersch, "Royal Ancestor Worship and Buddhist Politics."

57. Choe Chungheon (1149–1214) initiated a successful military coup d'état in 1196, after which the Choe military family effectively ruled Goryeo for the next sixty years. Under the Choe, Goryeo was able to resist the Mongol invasions. For a study of the Choe military house, see Shultz, *Generals and Scholars*.

58. Rockstein, "The Mongol Invasions of Korea: 1231," 42–49. Rockstein translated the relevant descriptions of the 1231 invasion from *Goryeosa*, fasc. 23.

59. Henthorn, *Korea: The Mongol Invasions*, 103.

60. Ibid., 103.

61. *Goryeosa*, fasc. 129, vol. 3, 641a–b.

62. Yi Gyubo, *Dongguk I sangguk jip*, fasc. 25, vol. 2, 9.

63. On the Chinese mainland, the tenth and eleventh centuries saw a surge of interest in military manuals and strategy studies, culminating in the publication and standardization of the *Seven Military Classics* (*Wujing qishu* 武經七書) compiled by the Song court. These studies must have influenced Goryeo Korea as well, as the Goryeo court distributed its own military manual, *Gimhae Byeongseo* 金海兵書, to its generals in 1024. For an explanation of the use of unorthodox strategies, see Sawyer, *Unorthodox Strategies for the Everyday Warrior*. Also, Jiang Wu, personal communications with Sawyer, Feb. 17 and 21, 2012. For the reference to *Gimhae Byeongseo*, see *Goryeosa*, fasc. 81, vol. 2, 638a; and Courant, *Bibliographie coréenne*, 64.

64. Yi Gyubo, *Dongguk I sangguk jip*, fasc. 25, vol. 2, 10. In addition to this record, Yi wrote six prayers for Choe U to commemorate various ceremonies organized for suppressing the Khitan army. For these prayers, see *Dongguk I sangguk jip*, fasc. 39 and 41, vol. 2, especially 227, 256, and 258.

65. Gim Gu, *Jibojip*, fasc. 1, *Hanguo wenji zhong de Meng Yuan shiliao*, vol. 1, 63a.

66. Yi Gyubo, *Dongguk I sangguk jip*, fasc. 25, vol. 2, 14–5. For his chronological biography, see *Dongguk I sangguk jip*, vol. 1, 16.

67. See Yi Gyubo, *Dongguk I sangguk jip*, vol. 1, 260; vol. 2, 353, 374, 387, 403, 205. One of the poems has been translated by O'Rourke in *Singing Like a Cricket*, 69.

68. See the colophon of his collection, Yi Gyubo, *Dongguk I sangguk jip*, vol. 2, 271.

69. For these ritual texts, see Yi Gyubo, *Dongguk I sangguk jip*, vol. 2, 223–41.

70. It was noted that these poems were written from the time he was appointed as "Exhorter of the Right" (Ujeongeon 右正言) in 1215 until 1233, when he was promoted to the third rank. Only the last poem was dated to the year the court moved the capital to Ganghwa, in 1232.

71. Rhi Ki-yong, "An Introduction to the Tripiṭaka Koreana," 13–14; Yi Gyubo, *Dongguk I sangguk jip*, 14–15.

72. *Goryeosa*, fasc. 97, vol. 3, 129a.

73. Xu Jing, *Xuanhe fengshi Gaoli tujing*, 1.

74. *Goryeosa*, fasc. 129, vol. 3, 631b; fasc. 129, vol. 3, 634b. See also *Goryeosa jeolyo*, 350a–352a, 355a. Murayama Chijun, *Chosen no fūsui*, vol. 2, 60–61, 743.

75. *Goryeosa*, fasc. 24, vol. 1, 362a.

76. In this context, talismans should not be narrowly understood as the Daoist talismanic writing, *fu* 符. Rather, the concept includes a variety of objects and substances such as stones, blood, pieces of peach wood, etc. This popular practice can be traced to the Han Dynasty, when such a talisman was made of metal, shaped like the Northern Dipper, and used to suppress enemies. More popular talismans were shaped like coins (*yashengqian* 厭勝錢). See Tao Siyan, *Qirang*, 12. For an introduction to talismanic writings, see Robson, "Talismans in Chinese Esoteric Buddhism." We thank Livia Kohn and Stephan Peter Bumbacher for answering our questions on this.

77. Yi Gyubo, *Dongguk I sangguk jip*, fasc. 18, vol. 1, 271.

78. See Vermeersch, *The Power of the Buddha*, 101–12 and 295–305.

79. For details, see Sørensen, "Esoteric Buddhism Under the Koryŏ," 55–94, especially 71–74. This was also published by Sørensen in *Korean Buddhism in East Asian Perspective*, 85–117. See Sørensen, "On the Sinin and Ch'ongji Schools," 54–60. See also Sørensen, "Worshiping the Cosmos"; "Astrology and the Worship of the Planets," 230–44.

80. At the beginning of the Goryeo Dynasty, the Supervising Office of Divination (Taebokgam 太卜監 — after 1023, it was called Platform of Astral Observation, Sacheon dae 司天臺) and Bureau of Grand Diviners (Taesaguk 太史局) were established to be in charge of observing the sky and interpreting the results. Under King Munjong, both agencies were expanded and promoted, and under King Chungseon 忠宣, the two agencies merged into one institution of astronomy, which was called Seoungwan 書雲館. See Yu Kyung-Loh, "A Brief History of the Bureau of Astronomy," 77.

81. Sørensen, "The Worship of the Great Dipper," 71–105, especially 82–83.

82. For the full text, see *Siku quanshu*, 809: 191–236. The author, Yelü Chun, claims that he was a Hanlin scholar during Emperor Shengzong's reign and his Korean teacher was Wonjae 元齋. The compilers of *Siku quanshu* questioned the authenticity of the Korean origin of this text. However, the name Yelü Chun and his mission never appear in any Chinese dynastic history. That and the fact that the text itself includes a detailed preface and essays appended at the end are evidence that strongly suggest its connection to Korea. Sørensen discusses the text, *Xingming zongkuo*, briefly in note 28 in his "Esoteric Buddhism Under the Koryŏ."

83. Yi Gyubo, *Dongguk I sangguk jip*, vol. 2, 251.

84. Ibid., vol. 2, 252.

85. For a brief summary of such astrological reports, see Needham, et al., *The Hall of Heavenly Records*, 1–15.

86. For a brief discussion of its military use, see Sawyer, "Martial Prognostication," 45–64.

87. *Goryeosa Jeolyo*, fasc. 15, 359a.

88. See his interview by the reporter Baek Sung-ho from the *Joongang Ilbo* newspaper in South Korea about his new book on the *Goryeo Canon* edition. See also Oh Yunhui, *Daejanggyeong*.

89. The Song court often organized various Buddhist and Daoist ceremonies to pray for the longevity of the royal house and to dispel disasters. However, there is no reference to using the Buddhist canon for such a purpose. For a detailed study of Song court rituals, see Wang Shengduo, *Songdai zhengjiao guanxi yanjiu*, 276–96, 343–76.

9. Taishō Canon

DEVOTION, SCHOLARSHIP, AND NATIONALISM
IN THE CREATION OF THE MODERN
BUDDHIST CANON IN JAPAN

Greg Wilkinson

Taishō Canon (*Taishō Shinshū Daizōkyō* 大正新修大蔵經), published between 1924 and 1932, was one of several projects in modern Japan aimed at creating a revised edition of the Chinese Tripitaka. This new edition has become a standard for academic research and devotional study, simply known as "*T*" in academic notation. Less known is how the production of the modern Japanese edition was influenced by a combination of religious devotion, Western-style academic scholarship, and Japan's rising nationalism. In religious terms, Buddhist priests and intellectuals in Japan believed that these new printings of the Chinese Tripitaka would not only elevate Buddhism and Japan but also aid Buddhist evangelism throughout Asia and into the West. They also believed that the canon could unify Buddhism at both sectarian and philosophical levels. In academic terms, these scholars believed that they were setting a new standard in Buddhist studies by creating the most complete and verifiably accurate collection of Buddhist scriptures available, improving its ease of use, and expanding the canon's compilation or catalog. In political terms, they asserted that the canon would elevate the position of Japan in Asia and aid Japan's prominence in the world. It was common for editors of these projects to argue that the canon would defend the nation and help establish peace and prosperity.[1] These new printings of the Chinese Buddhist canon challenged the sectarianism of traditional Japanese Buddhism with a view that was more ecumenical, academic, Western, and global. Although these new editions are based almost entirely on canons imported from China and Korea, the religious, academic, and political motivations of this new Buddhist studies movement created a Buddhist canon that was uniquely Japanese.

To understand the significance and relevance of *Taishō Canon* to the study of printed editions of the Chinese canon, one must first look at the unique historical context of the Meiji period (1868–1912). With the restoration of the Japanese emperor came persecution of Buddhism, as the new imperial regime promoted Shinto or indigenous religious beliefs and traditions over Buddhism as a way to distinguish themselves from the previous feudal regime. In response to this challenge, Buddhist institutions and clergy took several steps. First, they revitalized Buddhist religious devotion to include not simply liturgy or ritual efficacy but also the intellectual study of Buddhist texts and philosophy. Second, they made attempts to connect Buddhism to Western academic methods and theories. Third, within a rhetoric of Japanese nationalism, they propounded the combination of these new devotional and academic agendas as a means to create a uniquely Japanese kind of "Buddhist studies," which promoted canonical projects culminating in *Taishō Canon*. To fully understand its religious and historical significance, we will look at the steps in its creation and the motivations of its creators, as well as the *Taishō Canon*'s influence on contemporary Buddhist canon devotion and study and on contemporary publications of the canon, including digital editions. In doing so, this chapter uses several unique and previously unanalyzed sources, including a newsletter produced for members of the *Taishō Canon* research and scholastic community as well as personal letters between editors of *Taishō Canon* and scholars in Europe. These new sources help illustrate the international cooperation that was essential in the completion of the project.

"BUDDHIST STUDIES" IN MODERN JAPAN

FROM MEIJI TO TAISHŌ

The replacement of the Tokugawa Shogunate (1603–1868) with the Meiji Imperial State (1868– 1912) brought many changes for Japanese Buddhism. Under the Tokugawa regime, Buddhism played many important roles. Institutionally, Buddhist temples served as the central registrar or census office; all families, including the shogun's, had to report to their local temples under the temple parishioner system (*danka seidō* 檀家制度). Through this system, Buddhist temples gained not only political position and state support but also considerable resources and influence from mandatory universal patronage and a monopoly on funeral rites.[2] In particular, Zōjōji 増上寺 in Edo served as the family temple for the Tokugawa shoguns and played an important role in establishing Buddhist doctrines and archiving Buddhist texts. Over two centuries, state support and mandatory public patronage empowered Buddhism both politically and financially but also largely bankrupted it intellectually and morally. The rigorous study of Buddhist texts had been marginalized by esoteric and meditation rituals that sought to understand Buddhist truth with the body rather than the mind. Furthermore, Buddhist monks often disregarded ethical rules and the intellectual discipline expected from Buddhist monastics.

The political roles of Buddhism drastically changed under the new Meiji state. The new regime wanted to modernize Japan and saw secularization and Westernization as essential steps in that process. They also wanted to politically legitimize the new imperial regime while disparaging the Shogunate it supplanted. Replacing Buddhism with Shinto as the state-sponsored religion was believed to be essential for transforming political authority. Buddhism was labeled as old, foreign (Chinese), superstitious, and feudal by a new political order moving toward modernity, nationalism, secularism, and equality. For the early part of the Meiji era, Buddhist organizations were subject to political and social marginalization and even persecution. Termed *haibutsu kishaku* 廃仏毀釈 (abolish Buddhism and destroy Śākyamuni), Meiji persecution of Buddhism included violence against priests and destruction of temples.[3] Some scholars estimate that tens of thousands of sutras, paintings, and other Buddhists artifacts were destroyed, damaged, or lost through persecution and neglect during the early Meiji period.[4]

This persecution awakened many Buddhist monks to the challenges that modernity would present to their institutions and traditions. Buddhism would first need to revitalize religious devotion. Several temples began to stress and improve the intellectual rigor of their monastic training. All of the Buddhist scholars who would later study in Europe, write or edit Buddhist books and periodicals, and hold academic positions at private academies and imperial universities would first learn Buddhism within the traditional temple system. Pure Land was more active than other sects in promoting the intellectual discipline of monastic training. Many Pure Land Buddhist monasteries understood that the task of responding to the challenge of modernity presented by the new Japanese state and the West would be monumental. Modern academic and research standards would require their monks to have confidence in the truth and efficacy of Buddhist texts and philosophies as well as the skills to analyze texts with modern research methods and academic theories. Most notably, the Nishi Honganji 西本願寺 and Higashi Honganji 東本願寺 educated the monks who would become the new academic elite of modern Buddhism. Both monasteries taught hundreds of monks within their school systems not only about Buddhist texts but also about Western disciplines, including social sciences, history, and literary analysis. The Buddhist scholars who would hold academic positions in Japan's imperial universities, like Murakami Senshō 村上専精 (1851–1929), and edit several editions of the Buddhist canon during the Meiji period, like Maeda Eun 前田慧雲 (1857–1930), all received their first training in devotional and scholastic discipline within Buddhist monasteries.[5]

BUDDHIST PRIESTS STUDYING ABROAD

Pure Land monasteries sent dozens of their students to study in Europe. Buddhist monks from Japan studied in France, Germany, and England, most notably with Max Müller at Oxford University, who emphasized the standards of Western scholarship. He taught young Japanese monks the importance of academic objectivity in historical study and textual analysis, training them in the new discipline of comparative religion and in religious theories and philosophies.[6]

Müller believed that the root of Buddhism was to be found in India. This was a novel theory, because Buddhism as a practiced religion had died out in India and Indic Buddhist texts were not as complete or extensive as archives found in Tibet, China, Korea, or Japan. Müller nevertheless believed that Indic Buddhism was the original and purest form of the religion and searched Pali and Sanskrit texts in order to discover the original teachings of Śākyamuni. Japanese Buddhists were attracted to this view because it allowed them to expand their study beyond a complete reliance on the Buddhist texts imported from China and Korea.

Müller also maintained that Buddhism was a universal evangelical religion on par with Christianity and Islam. He argued that characteristics intrinsic in Buddhism and consistent with those in Christianity and Islam had allowed it to spread quickly from northern India to South and East Asia. His Japanese students remained dedicated to evangelical expansion and development of Buddhism in their home countries and internationally.[7]

One of Müller's earliest students was Nanjō Bun'yū 南條文雄 (1849–1927).[8] A student of the Ōtani 大谷 sect of Pure Land Buddhism, Nanjō traveled to England in 1876 and studied at Oxford, where he met a Buddhist scholar from China, Yang Wenhui 楊文會 (1835–1911), who was instrumental in modernizing Buddhist studies in China in much the same way that Nanjō would in Japan.[9] The two men collaborated in the exchange of texts between Japan and China, and many of Nanjō's letters describe their professional cooperation and personal friendship.[10] For instance, Nanjō provided several texts to Yang that had been lost in China, and Yang helped Nanjō and Maeda Eun to locate canonical texts only available in China or Tibet during later canonical projects in Japan.[11] Without a doubt, Müller and other European scholars created a context for ecumenical cooperation between Japanese and Chinese scholars that would not normally have arisen.[12] Nanjō's subsequent scholarship and research showed a direct influence from Müller in scholarly standards, focus on Indic texts and language, and the importance of Buddhist evangelical expansion, all of which shaped the processes and motivations of Japanese scholars who led Buddhist canon-publishing projects.

Nanjō was followed by other Japanese Buddhist scholars at Oxford and other universities in Europe. The editors of *Taishō Canon*, Takakusu Junjirō 高楠 順次郎 (1866–1945) and Watanabe Kaikyoku 渡辺海旭 (1872–1933), studied in Europe, and the writings and works of both clearly reflect Müller's emphasis on academic standards, Indic studies, and evangelical imperative.

Despite these Western influences, however, the ultimate goal of editors like Takakusu and Watanabe was not to Westernize or to modernize Buddhist thought but to show Buddhism to be the truth, regardless of theory or methodology. Buddhism, if understood and presented correctly, could surpass the teachings and principles found in Western philosophies and religions.[13] Takakusu argued that "the totalism of Buddhism is a thoroughgoing, perfect principle . . . there is no need to import into Japan the anomalous autocratic systems of the West . . . if such a principle is needed, there is a perfect one in Buddhism."[14] Thus Japanese Buddhism was complex and complete enough to compete with Western ideas and beliefs and could provide an ideology that formed the foundation for modern advances equal to those in the West.

THE BIRTH OF "BUDDHIST STUDIES" IN JAPAN

Modern "Buddhist studies" in Japan was tasked with balancing devotional and academic interests in order to appease the government and the monasteries. This field, and especially canonical research and publishing activities, combined both Buddhist and national evangelism. Murakami Senshō, the first professor of Buddhist studies (Indic philosophy) at Tokyo University and a student of the Ōtani branch of the Higashi Honganji Pure Land Temple, described the devotional and academic elements of Japan's new Buddhist studies. He tried to appease both the academics of the national universities and the clergy of the major monasteries by asserting that Buddhist scholars cannot evaluate Buddhist truths exclusively through historical positivism and that the religious or "Buddhistic" perspective must be respected. The goals, according to Murakami, were first, to withstand criticism according to modern academic standards; second, to provide deference to religious narratives that include tales of visions, miracles, and wonders; and third, to promote the unity of Buddhist doctrines and teachings while analyzing the unique features of each branch or school.[15] From Murakami we see that the development of Buddhist studies in Japan was not a sudden or immediate change from devotional to academic standards but a gradual process that led to an emphasis on and the primacy of academic processes and theories learned in the universities of Europe, which, however, never completely replaced devotional concerns.

Other Tokyo University scholars, like Inoue Enryō 井上円了 (1858–1919), argued that far from being obsolete, Buddhism represented the sole advantage Japan had in comparison to the West and its Asian neighbors. In 1887, Inoue stated:

> Buddhism is now our so-called strong point. . . . Material commodities are an advantage of the West; scholarship is also one of their strong points. The only advantage we have is religion. This fine product of ours excels those of other countries; the fact that its good strain died out in India and China may be considered an unexpected blessing for our country. If we continue to nurture it in Japan and disseminate it some day in foreign countries, we will not only add to the honor of our nation but will also infuse the spirit of our land into the hearts of and minds of foreigners. I am convinced that the consequences will be considerable.[16]

This new form of Buddhist studies would often adroitly use modern academic theories and methods but not the strict rules of empirical study or historical positivism. For example, most Buddhist scholars, even those who studied extensively abroad, would relate the mythological elements of the life of Shōtoku Taishi 聖徳太子 (574–622) as historical narratives without the least support for their verity, so that Shōtoku Taishi became a central figure in defining the unique essence of Japanese Buddhism. Takakusu Junjirō also edited a new collection of Shōtoku's writings and biographies.[17] He argued that Japan, during the Nara period (810–894), had become a land of naturalized foreigners and that Shōtoku overcame this foreign-dominated culture by asserting a new Japanese Buddhism that became the core of a new national culture.[18] Takakusu looked to Shōtoku's expositions on Buddhist texts to identify and defend a unique Japanese Buddhist ideology.[19]

Ui Hakuju 宇井伯壽 (1882–1963), who took over Murakami's chair at Tokyo University, would argue that Japanese Buddhist studies and *Taishō Canon* were exceptional, unlike the Buddhism of India or China: "Buddhist studies are no longer an import, but something Japan has thoroughly integrated and absorbed."[20] Essentially, Ui and others were stating that Japan had a unique way of looking at Buddhism because their intellectuals had both in-depth devotional and academic experiences. Sometimes, however, that rhetoric became strident, causing many to conclude that Buddhist scholars were providing more fuel to the fire of prewar Japanese essentialism (*Nihonjinron* 日本人論). On the other hand, such ardent championship of Buddhism could also be seen as a reaction to Meiji persecution and Western evangelism.

As this new form of Buddhist studies developed in the monasteries of Japan and the academies of Europe, the Meiji state returned to Buddhism to serve several objectives not satisfactorily completed by Shinto priests. For example, Shinto shrines were ill equipped to assist in developing new state ideologies; the independence of the shrines made them very difficult to organize into an effective bureaucratic arm of the government. Buddhism, however, was already structured into denominational hierarchies; the temple-parishioner system had effectively organized the entire Japanese population into manageable localities, and Buddhist monks were well versed in preaching and ideological instruction. Thus although the state maintained the symbol of Shinto to support their political legitimacy, they resorted to the services provided by the Buddhist institutions to implement several key objectives. The Buddhist temples and clergy gained state support through the Ministry of Education and in turn offered loyalty and propagated national ideologies and the administration of education, taxes, and conscription.[21]

The zealous attempts of the Meiji state to modernize and Westernize opened Japan to the influence of Christian evangelicals. Some argued that Christianity had supported remarkable advancements of the West in science, technology, and learning while Buddhism had helped foster feudalism and isolation, making Japan unprepared to meet the demands of the modern world.[22] Many Japanese intellectuals shunned Buddhism and advocated the spread of Western religions and philosophies along with the adoption of Western science and technology. Christian evangelicals entered Japan after the ban on foreign missionaries was lifted in 1873 and attracted many Japanese converts, probably more by their modern schools and hospitals than by their religious proselytizing. In response to this increased influence, the Japanese state increased its reliance on Buddhism in promoting a national ideology that could also compete with the attractions of modern scholarship. As a result, Buddhism began to be touted as evidence of Japan's superiority over its Asian neighbors and the West.

For example, Shimaji Mokurai 島地黙雷 (1838–1911), a leader of the Jōdo Shinshū's 淨土真宗 Nishi Honganji and one of the first Pure Land Buddhists to travel and study in Europe, advocated a unique form of Buddhist-Japanese nationalism. In his two petitions calling for a special link between Buddhism and the emperor in 1872 and 1873, Shimaji stated that Buddhism was the best source of Japanese exceptionalism and that the emperor could use Japan's preservation of Buddhist texts and practices to show its superiority internationally, promote nationalism and patriotism domestically, and defend the country against foreign influences like Christianity.[23] Similarly, Takakusu argued that only in Japan was all of Buddhism preserved and practiced. Archives and artifacts preserved in treasure houses of Kyoto and Nara had not been subject to domestic destruction due to prolonged persecution or pilfered by foreign archeologists or treasure hunters. Therefore Takakusu believed that Japan held an important place in the preservation and expansion of Buddhism.[24]

The short persecution of Japanese Buddhism actually helped shape its new essential relationship with the state and had an important influence on how the Buddhist canon was understood and used in prewar Japan. Canonical research and national evangelism became intertwined: Buddhist scholars justified canonical projects by arguing that they uniquely served nationalist objectives, and the state supported and sponsored canon projects and Buddhist studies as a way to illustrate Japan's leading role in Asia as well as its ability to excel in specific spheres of modern scholarship.

PRE-*TAISHŌ* CANON PROJECTS

Before the creation of the Taishō edition, several earlier projects to compile and publish a complete Buddhist canon were undertaken in the late nineteenth and early twentieth centuries in Japan, including the Reduced Print edition started in 1877 and the Manji edition in 1902.[25] These projects were influenced by the Western scholarship described above, and each had specific academic, religious, and political motivations or justifications for its production. The compilation process included authenticating the texts by collating previous manuscript and printed editions of the canon and then determining the most verifiably authentic or accurate version. Hence, the term *kōtei* 校訂 was often used in the full name of these Japanese editions to assert that the texts had been authenticated using the most rigorous and objective standards. Sometimes for passages whose meaning varied among the earlier texts, footnotes would explain the disagreements among editions and possible issues with interpretation or meaning. Collators of the new editions would use one previous edition as its principal source and then check that exemplar against other editions. Whether the source was from Korea or China could sometimes create disputes or controversies because of opinions about the validity of certain editions or simply due to national or sectarian preconceptions.

THE REDUCED PRINT EDITION

The Reduced Print edition (*Dai Nihon kōtei shukusatsu daizōkyō* 大日本校訂縮刷大藏經), published from 1880 to 1885 under the direction of Shimada

Mitsune/Bankon 島田みつね / 蕃根 (1827–1907) in Tokyo, was collated (*kōtei*) using the premodern second Goryeo edition as the exemplar; then the most authentic words and meanings were selected from among earlier editions and educated decisions to resolve textual discrepancies were made. This process included the laborious task of having one researcher read a text in a particular edition of the canon while two other researchers checked the same text in two other editions. The result was a new edition that very closely resembles the second Goryeo edition, with minor revisions that were explained in footnotes, especially when discrepancies between editions could greatly alter the meanings or interpretations.[26] It remains the most accurate modern edition, although it did not seek to question the authenticity of a certain edition or to validate particular texts or sutras. Research by Marcus Bingenheimer provides new evidence for the accuracy and significance of the Reduced Print edition (*shukusatsu ban*) as a source text for the Taishō edition. Within a discussion of collation apparatus, Bingenheimer concludes, "it is highly unlikely that the Taishō editors some fifty years later felt the need to completely re-do or even double-check the collation done under Shimada Mitsune."[27]

Perhaps equally significant were the reduced font size and the inclusion of punctuation in the Reduced Print edition. A new small typeface was created for the project. Access, portability, and price were important to the modern canonical scholars because they wanted to make the canon available to both researchers and the general public. Previous editions were unpunctuated, which often led to confusion and sometimes different interpretations of a given text. The lack of punctuation also made the Buddhist canon very difficult to understand for a Japanese reader without special knowledge and training in reading Buddhist texts in Chinese. The producers of the Reduced Print edition openly admitted that the emphasis on portability and price was a reaction to the spread of Christian missionaries in late nineteenth-century Japan. They realized the advantage these missionaries had with a reliable, authoritative text that was easy to transport, carry, and share with potential converts. For Buddhism to spread and respond to the potential growth of Christianity, a portable collection of Buddhist scriptures similar to the Bible would be beneficial.[28]

Interestingly, it was Nanjō Bun'yū who took the Buddhist canon response to the Christian Bible one step further and tried to distill all Buddhist scriptures into a single volume. He and Maeda Eun completed a compilation of essential Buddhist scriptures in a single 500-page volume called the "Buddhist Bible" (*Bukkyō Seiten* 仏教聖典), which would allow Buddhism to respond to the challenge of international evangelism represented by Christianity.[29] The vision of Nanjō's "Buddhist Bible" and the Reduced Print edition was for the modern canon to be not just produced and archived but also widely published and accessible to the clergy, scholars, and the masses. Allowing all readers direct, unfiltered access would have important consequences for the evolution of the comprehension of Buddhism and for religious organizations in Japan.

The Reduced Print edition also illustrates the shift of Buddhist studies away from the monasteries and traditional Buddhist scholars and clergy. The project was led by Shimada Mitsune, who came from a scholar family of Chinese learning and Shugendō 修験道 practitioners.[30] He held several positions in the Meiji government's Ministry of Doctrine (Kyōbushō 教部省) and believed the canon should not only set a new standard of scholarship by correcting mistakes and removing confusion found in previous editions but also elevate the writings of Japan's monks to the level of those included in the Chinese Buddhist canon.[31] Shimada did not necessarily regard creating a new edition of the Buddhist canon as a religious or devotional process and posted ads in local papers, looking for people who could read premodern Chinese texts fluently.[32]

New standards for accuracy, nationalist motives, and editors from government ministries did not mean a complete break from the devotional and religious concerns of Buddhist temples and monks. The canon still represented the *kyōhan* 教判 (doctrinal classification) system of scriptural authority, and the source materials for the compilation were all from Korea and China, archived at the Tokugawa Family Temple Zōjōji. The Zōjōji was also located close to government ministries and was the center of traditional Buddhist scholarship for the Pure Land sect. Its monks maintained close relationships with members of the editorial staffs of nineteenth-century canon projects and were influential in selecting and granting access to source materials, as well as in resolving disputes about unclear or disputed passages. However, they are rarely named as editors or contributors in printed editions.

The Reduced Print edition apparently had a significant influence on the prestige and status of the Japanese state because it could produce a canon comparable to editions from China and Korea. Copies were sent to temples with ties to the imperial family, as a symbol of respect for the emperor. Copies were also sent to the Korean government as an example of the excellence of Japanese Buddhist scholarship.[33]

After the success of the Reduced Print edition, several other canon projects were undertaken in both Kyoto and Tokyo during the early years of the twentieth century. The most notable edition from Tokyo was the *Dai Nihon kōtei Daizōkyō* 大日本校訂大藏經, and in Kyoto the most successful was the Manji edition from Zōkyō shoin 藏經書院 publishing house. The Zōkyō shoin publications[34] were generally seen as more closely tied to the major Buddhist monasteries in Kyoto in order to ensure their commercial success. However, projects in both locations were led not by Buddhist clergy or even men with family or devotional ties to any Buddhist sect but rather by publishers and academic institutions. These projects also widened their collection by including newly discovered texts from China and Japan and sometimes texts that traditionally had been deemed apocryphal.[35]

THE MANJI EDITION

In 1902 the Manji edition, *Dai Nihon kōtei kunten Daizōkyō* 大日本校訂訓点大藏經, of the canon was initiated. This was viewed as an academic or scholastic advance because of its expanded collection of works from later Chinese writers and texts found in earlier versions of the Chinese canon. While some argued that the Manji edition did not improve on the Reduced Print edition in terms of accuracy or verification, the expanded catalog was seen as an improvement for Buddhist studies.[36] The project, completed toward the end of the Meiji period and the Russo-Japanese War (1904–5), exhibited an increasing nationalism. For example, the preface states that the work was published to commemorate the peace brought to Japan through victory in war, and volumes of the canon included the names of those who had lost their lives in battle.[37] Linking the canon to the war shows how it had been appropriated to promote Japan's rising nationalism and war efforts.

The main editors of the Manji edition were Nakano Tatsue 中野達慧 (1871–1934) and Maeda Eun. Both held teaching positions at imperial universities and both remained devout Pure Land Buddhists. Nakano especially was an exceptional combination of academic excellence and religious devotion, who was fervently dedicated to compiling and editing a complete collection of the Buddhist scriptures (*issaikyō* 一切経), believing that Japan was the only country that could accomplish such a project. Although he did not travel to the West to study, he studied Indic languages and German under Nanjō Bun'yū and supported the inclusion of Pali and Sanskrit texts in the canon. Nakano was peculiar among his academic peers because of his strict adherence to Buddhist practice as well as academic study. He never drank or smoked, and ate little as he spent countless hours analyzing Buddhist texts in various languages.[38] Nakano was a renowned example of the academic discipline, religious devotion, and nationalistic fervor that motivated the unbelievably large task of compiling and editing the entire collection of Buddhist scriptures and even increasing it through the addition of texts in other languages. Maeda shared a similar background: he never studied abroad, was also a student of Nanjō, and was extremely devoted to both Pure Land Buddhism and Japan.

Another significant innovation in the Manji edition was a new system of ordering the texts, replacing the traditional method that used the *Thousand-Character Classic* (*Qianzi wen* 千字文) in the earlier Chinese and Korean editions of the canon. The *Thousand-Character Classic* is a Chinese poem containing one thousand different characters, used to teach children and also for ordering lists, much like the letters of the Western alphabet, once the poem is memorized. For a thousand years, one had to memorize it to be able to get access to the canon and to locate the text one wanted. The new method adopted by the *Manji Canon* editors was to simply assign sequential numbers to the cases containing groups of texts. This new way of ordering the texts was a significant advance in recompiling the Buddhist canon and provided evidence for Japanese superiority in Buddhist studies, in comparison with other countries in Asia and the West.

Cooperation with China in expanding the Manji edition's catalog proceeded despite the Japanese scholars' move away from more traditional Chinese approaches, sectarian differences with Chinese Buddhists, and nationalist rhetoric. There are several examples of cooperation with institutions and individuals from China to gain access to earlier Chinese or Tibetan texts, most notably with Yang Wenhui. It seems that at the time of the Manji edition, personal relationships formed in European universities and academic ideals trumped the sectarian and nationalist rhetoric expressed in the prefaces and titles of the finished works. Like the Reduced Print edition, the Manji edition was reprinted and distributed in China shortly after its publication in Japan.

THE *TAISHŌ* CANON PROJECT

Taishō Canon built upon these earlier projects and broke new ground in terms of academic standards, expansion of canonical materials, and research sources as well as connections to the state. The project originated within the Department for Sanskrit and Indian Studies at Tokyo Imperial University, which had initiated the study of Buddhist texts, under the guise of Indian philosophy, with full government support as early as 1879. The project was coedited by Takakusu Junjirō[39] and Watanabe Kaikyoku.[40] Takakusu conceived the idea of *Taishō Canon* and gained support for it from both academic and religious institutions. He also invited Watanabe to work as his coeditor, so that Takakusu is often seen as the leader of the project and receives the majority of attention and credit for its contribution. Takakusu and Watanabe had studied Indic texts as well as scholastic theories and methods in Europe. Both were versed in Sanskrit and Pali, and Watanabe had also studied Tibetan extensively. Moreover, they shared interests in political and social reform as well as Buddhist studies and believed *Taishō Canon* could exert significant political and social influence. Takakusu and Watanabe publicized their objectives as: a wide-reaching and careful collation, a detailed compilation, inclusion of both Indian and Chinese sources, and development of indices and concordances within a published canon that was both portable and affordable.[41]

Taishō Canon represented a monumental project, with over 120 contributors and editing work that involved collating each text through exhaustive use of all available sources. *Taishō Canon* included significant academic and religious advancements. It was based on the Korean canon but was collated using at least four other Chinese editions and many other works and manuscripts in Pali, Sanskrit, and Tibetan. The entire canon was footnoted and punctuated, giving reference to any discrepancies or possible differences in meaning due to translation from Indic languages to Chinese. Following the Manji edition, the *qian-ziwen* call number system was completely abandoned and sequential numbers were assigned to all texts. The new classification method also departed from the Chinese tradition by creating more categories and allowing more content, such as esoteric works and iconography, to be included. Moreover, the preference for Mahayana teaching in the Chinese canonic tradition was downplayed and the Āgama section was placed at the beginning, following chronological order. It is likely that this new emphasis on the importance of translations of early Buddhist teaching was influenced by the predominant European interests in early Buddhist history. The original edition was published as a 55-volume set between 1924 and 1928 with an extensive catalog. Moreover, for the first time a canon was printed and bound into volumes using the modern Western method instead of more traditional formats, such as scrolls or sutra binding. While these publication decisions did not always lend themselves well to ritual use of the sutras, the advances and innovations made *Taishō Canon* the academic standard for Buddhist research both in Japan and around the world, and also made the canon more accessible for religious practice and devotional use.

TAISHŌ CANON AS SEEN FROM THE STEIN COLLECTION

Correspondence with Takakusu Junjirō and an early prospectus of *Taishō Canon* have been found in Aurel Stein's personal papers, archived at Oxford University. These documents provide significant insights into specific processes involved in compiling and publishing *Taishō Canon*. Sir Marc Aurel Stein (1862–1943) was a Hungarian-English archeologist who held positions at several universities and is primarily known for his archeological discoveries in Central Asia, including his 1907 expedition to the Mogao caves near Dunhuang. There he discovered one of the oldest printed Buddhist texts, the Diamond Sutra (868), and tens of thousands of other texts, scrolls, paintings, and relics, which he exported to the British Museum. Stein's finding and successful removal of artifacts from the Dunhuang caves inspired other archeologists and treasure hunters from around the world and greatly depleted the Buddhist texts and relics remaining in China.[42] In a letter to Stein dated March 1, 1924, Takakusu wrote:

You will see from this prospectus that we have taken the liberty to include your name among the patrons and advisors in advance of your permission, for which we crave [*sic*] your kind indulgence. Considering your valuable contributions to the world's knowledge in this field of research, no undertaking of the kind can be launched without the advantage of your moral support, with which we fondly hope you will willingly honor us.[43]

In the following prospectus (figure 9.1), a simple four-page outline of the Taishō project, Takakusu and Watanabe are listed as editors and the canon is listed as being published by the Taishō Tripitaka Association (Taishō Issaikyō Kankōkai 大正一切経刊行会). The scope of the prospectus is described as follows:

The Books comprised in this Edition number 2,633, amounting in the original altogether to nearly 13,000 volumes. They are Chinese translations from Sanskrit, Pāli and other Indian dialects besides the original treaties written in China, Korea and Japan. Of these Books, 487, in 1,489 volumes, represent new additions, being included in none of the previous editions.[44]

Eight sources for the canon's content are then listed. The first three are previous Japanese editions of the Buddhist canon. The fourth is "The texts found in Tun-huang, hitherto unknown, by Sir Aurel Stein and Prof. P. Pelliot."[45] The next source listed is the Imperial Household's copy of the Tripitaka from the Tempyō 天平 period (750). The final three sources are historical inscriptions from Chinese, Korean, and Japanese literati; notes from Buddhist monasteries; and works from the founders of Japanese Buddhist sects or schools. Takakusu states that the Korean (Goryeo) edition of the canon will be compared to Dunhuang and Tempyō copies, "rejecting all the traditional division and order, and clearly distinguishing, as far as possible, the Tripitaka proper from all extraneous works such as commentaries, reference books and helps to study."[46] Sanskrit and Pali terms would be given in footnotes, and a comprehensive subject index would be included in each volume. A list of patrons and advisors is also given, including university scholars both Buddhist and secular, 25 heads of Japanese Buddhist sects or denominations (unnamed), the British and German ambassadors to Japan (Charles Eliot and W. Solf), and other European professors and scholars, including Stein and Pelliot. The prospectus concludes with the terms of the project. The edition would be in 55 volumes of 1,000 pages each for ¥12 and the complete set for ¥594.

The brief and simple prospectus provides a helpful overview of the process and design of the *Taishō Canon* project. It allows us to examine the plan for the project and what changes were made to it. One interesting note is that while the volume numbering in the prospectus agrees with the published work, the actual volumes do not cover all of the sources listed in the contents section of

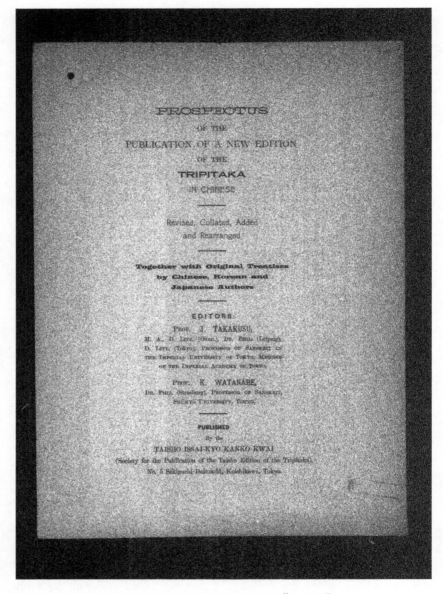

FIGURE 9.1 PHOTO OF THE FIRST PAGE OF "TAISHŌ CANON PROSPECTUS," STEIN MSS NO. 108

The Bodleian Libraries, The University of Oxford; used with permission

the prospectus. It seems that Takakusu's original plan for the canon was much broader and more ambitious than what was eventually published.

Takakusu's letter to Stein reveals another interesting piece of information. At one point he mentions that he is missing notes because of a fire caused by the 1923 Tokyo earthquake. While we know the fires that followed the earthquake were devastating to Tokyo University's Library, we have no other information about the degree of loss or destruction of Takakusu's records. Perhaps this contracted the scope of the original fifty-five-volume edition.

Aurel Stein's records also include a response to Takakusu dated June 23, 1924, which reads in part:

> In the first place let me assure you that I feel honored for finding my name mentioned in the list of distinguished scholars upon whose sympathy and support you count with regard to your big task. Though alas, I am no Sinologue. You may rest convinced that I very thoroughly appreciate the magnitude as well as the exceptional importance of many branches of Eastern research of the work you have charged yourself with. The creation of this great treasury of Buddhist lore in the shape of critical editions of a multitude of texts, many of them hitherto inaccessible will be a monument of your scholarly zeal and a source of true pride for your nation. . . . I am particularly glad to know that it is through Dr. Yabuki's efforts that the hitherto unknown texts among them are to be available for interpretation in your editions. This serves the field for their first publication. Please tell Dr. Yabuki that all Chinese MSS from Dunhuang brought back are now the property of the trustees of the British Museum. And it is their consent which ought to be asked by you. There can be little doubt that it will be readily awarded. At the same time I may be allowed to mention to you personally that if it were possible for you to do your work here at the British Museum you could have access to all MSS texts and facsimiles and perhaps we could facilitate this research through Dr. Yabuki allowing for all of the texts from the far east to be included in your editions.[47]

Two points stand out from this portion of Stein's response. First, he was fully supportive of the Taishō project and completely agreeable to being included as a contributor. Second, Stein mentioned that this edition would be a "true pride for your nation." The national importance of the Taishō edition generally and the inclusion of the texts Stein and Pelliot removed from the Mogao caves specifically were not lost on him. We could speculate about the possible reaction of some Buddhist scholars and adherents in China to assertions of a superior Chinese Buddhist canon published in Japan using the texts taken out of China by Stein and Pelliot. There are instances of criticism of *Taishō Canon* based on the materials acquired by these two men, who were seen in some circles in China as tomb raiders. Such issues continue to be considered, as in recent studies by Fang Guangchang that evaluate *Taishō Canon* and its processes, including cooperation with European archeologists like Stein.[48]

International participation in the *Taishō Canon* project was not limited to Stein. The *Taishō shinshū daizōkyō sōmokuroku sakuin mokuroku Kaiin meibo* 大正新修大藏經總目錄索引目錄会員名簿 (General catalog, indexed catalog, and member directory of Taishō Tripitaka)[49] contains a list of members of the Tokyo Taishō Tripitaka Association. The degree of participation that membership signifies certainly varies, but the list contains names of scholars, Buddhist temples, and academic institutions around the world, divided geographically, starting with Tokyo (over 600 members) and ending with Canada (1 member). While a great majority of members were in Japan or Japanese living in other countries, Korea (Chōsen) has 49 members, Taiwan has 13 members, and China has more than 100 members.[50] Thus the name list (*kaiin meibo*) provides significant evidence that *Taishō Canon* was an international project.

DEVOTION TO TAISHŌ CANON

The academic, religious, and political significance of *Taishō Canon* is illustrated by an event described in the preface to the first volume.[51] Finished in 1924 (Taishō 13), the first volume was presented and dedicated to Shōtoku Taishi at a lecture hall of Tokyo University of the Arts (Tōkyō Geijutsu Daigaku 東京芸術大学), and a member of the imperial family, Kuni no Miya Kuniyoshi 久邇宮邦彦 (1873–1929), attended the ceremony. The academic location for this event seems a little odd. The work of the Taishō edition had been divided among three locations: Zōjōji, the Ueno Imperial Museum, and the library of the Imperial Household. It would seem, therefore, that the library of the Imperial Household or Zōjōji would hold more religious or political significance. However, the lecture hall of Tokyo University of the Arts is adjacent to the Ueno Imperial Museum, and perhaps the size of the hall was necessary. Even if just the contributors to the *Taishō Canon* project attended, there would have been more than 120 people present. The date is also significant because it was believed to be the 1,300th-year commemoration of Shōtoku Taishi's death. The presence of Kuni no Miya Kuniyoshi is also politically notable because although he was not in the direct line of succession to the throne, he was married to an imperial princess, and early in that same year his daughter had married the Crown Prince Hirohito. More importantly, his family was believed to be the direct descendants of Shōtoku Taishi. Kuniyoshi was also an extremely important official of Imperial Shinto. In 1915, he was appointed the curator of ancient texts and the interim Supreme Priest at the Grand Shrine of Ise (Ise Jingū 伊勢神宮).[52] He also held, at that time, the position of President of the Institute for the Japanese Classics at Kokugakuin University 国学院大学.[53] His attendance at this ceremony therefore could be seen as a significant statement of support not only by the imperial government but also by the highest levels of the Shinto establishment.

The dedicatory prayer for this service is recorded in a catalog of *Taishō Canon* and states:

IMPERIAL PRAYER

Which is presented before the statue of Royal Prince-Regent and Dharma King Shōtoku with the first volume of the *Newly Compiled Taishō Canon*

It is the time of April 11 of the thirteenth year of the Taishō reign, the year of Kashi, when Prince Kuniyoshi of the Supreme Order paid homage to Dharma King Shōtoku Toyotomimi 豊聡耳.

It is my (Prince Kuniyoshi's) personal view that in both Great and Small Vehicles, Esoteric and Exoteric Teachings, their languages are either flowery or plain and their meanings are either shallow or profound. As for scriptures, treatises, vinaya, biographies, and various commentaries, there are more than several thousand scrolls. Old and new translations differ in rendition if compared; and the Song edition and Korean edition are obviously different printings that do not match each other, while in our imperial state, the Ōbaku edition was more widespread than any of the previous generations. During the Meiji reign, the canon was compiled and printed twice. However, misprints and mistakes were as many as falling leaves covering the ground; misunderstandings and misreadings were like flying flowers in the sky blown by the wind. This is indeed due to the lack of a canon in the Buddhist world and a great regret in the academic world. Therefore, we searched widely for lost texts and sought out missing documents by either consulting the old manuscripts in Nara's Shōsō-in 正倉院 or collating with the ancient copies from the Dunhuang caves. The accomplishment resulting from all these efforts is precisely this *Newly Compiled Taishō Canon*. In total, it includes 12,864 fascicles in 51 cases. Without exception, all sacred classics from the different schools in Japanese and Chinese are included. Is this not the ferry to cross the dharma ocean and the ladder to ascend the other shore? For this reason, we make a vow with the utmost sincerity: by piously assembling a group of learned people and solemnly endowing this volume, we would like to present the canon in front of the spirit tablet of the Dharma King Shōtoku to be held as the Dharma Treasure in Hōryūji 法隆寺 forever. We offer humbly all the merits produced from this small deed to our current emperor, empress, and prince-regent in order to guarantee their glory as high as the Five Sacred Peaks and their longevity as long as thousands of years. We wish humbly that all sentient beings in the universe will transcend the mundane world and together return to the way leading toward enlightenment.[54]

This dedication of *Taishō Canon* provides a great example of the blend of scholastic discipline, religious devotion, and national patriotism inherent in the project. The sixth-century regent of Empress Suiko, Shōtoku Taishi, was seen by twentieth-century Buddhist scholars as the father of Japanese Buddhism. Takakusu in his *Essentials of Japanese Buddhism* explains that in 594 Shōtoku Taishi established Buddhism as the state religion and set up a classification of Buddhist texts for the proper veneration of specific Mahayana sutras.[55] The ceremony itself shows that Buddhist scholars of the period believed that the canon had real efficacy that could be utilized by including it in religious ritual, and that Japanese Buddhism was unique in East Asia and its historical foundations were worthy of devotion and commemoration. The prayer asks for a religious endowment from Prince Shōtoku and for the canon to be archived at Hōryūji, the sixth-century Buddhist temple complex commissioned by Shōtoku. The arguments within the prayer for *Taishō Canon* are purely intellectual (fixing misprints, referring to all available texts, and resolving contradictions in previous editions). However, great religious devotion and merit will derive from these scholastic standards, and this will result in Japan's supreme place among Buddhist nations. It is also interesting that Dunhuang manuscripts gained through Aurel Stein get a specific mention, thus providing greater evidence for the significance of Stein's role in completing the *Taishō* project.

TAISHŌ CANON AND JAPANESE NATIONALISM

The dedication ceremony of the first volume of the canon confirmed its strong link to Japanese nationalism. Both Watanabe and Takakusu declared not only that *Taishō Canon* was uniquely Japanese but also that Japan was the only place in the Buddhist world capable of producing and understanding all of the Buddhist canon. In *Essentials of Japanese Buddhism*, Takakusu explained the special place of Japan in Buddhist studies:

> In Japan the whole of Buddhism has been preserved—every doctrine of both the Hinayana and Mahayana schools. Although Hinayana Buddhism does not now exist in Japan as an active faith, its doctrines are still studied there by Buddhist scholars. Mikkyō, which we may designate as the Esoteric Doctrine or Mysticism, is fully represented in Japan by Tendai mysticism and Toji mysticism. The point which Japanese mysticism may be proud of is that it does not contain any vulgar elements as does its counterpart in other countries, but stands on a firm philosophical basis. The schools which were best developed in China are Hua-yen (Kegon, the "Wreath" School) and T'ien-t'ai (Tendai, the "Lotus" School). When the Ch'an (Zen) school is added to these two,

the trio represents the highest peak of Buddhism's development. These three flourished in China for a while and then passed away, but in Japan all three are still alive in the people's faiths as well as in academic studies. A rather novel form of Buddhism is the Amita-pietism. It is found to some extent in China, Tibet, Nepal, Mongolia, Manchuria and Annam; but it flourishes most in Japan where it is followed by more than half the population. I believe, therefore, that the only way to exhibit the entire Buddhist philosophy in all its different schools is to give a resume of Buddhism in Japan. It is in Japan that the entire Buddhist literature, the Tripitaka, is preserved and studied.[56]

Takakusu and Watanabe believed that the Taishō edition was necessary in order to advance Japan in the discipline of Buddhology, and that it could effectively advance the status and reputation of Japan within Asia and in the West. Both made statements that the canon could also promote peace in Asia. In the preface to *Taishō Canon*, they jointly declared:

> The completion of the way of benevolence and love, the ultimate principle of perfectly endowed truth, permeates the ten directions and pervades the three existences, encompassing all things and unfolding in all phenomena. How vast and great is the true teaching of the sage Sākyamuni! Moreover, this complete and wondrous teaching which he left behind is transmitted and set forth in our Tripitaka. In this immense work with its more than eight thousand fascicles, its hundred millions of words, the true reality of the universe is thoroughly expounded and the conclusion of life made clear. . . . Yet apart from us, the Buddhist scholars of Japan, who can clarify and spread its teachings? The responsibility of propagation rests on our shoulders. All the more so, after the great world war, when the need to seek the truth presses most urgently upon us, when the study of Buddhism is now on the rise in Europe and America, and when we see so few scholars versed in the Chinese scriptures. The Buddhist scholars of our nation must realize how vast and grave our task has become.[57]

This preface is another significant expression of the coming together of academic, religious, and political motives and influences in the creation of a new Japanese edition of the canon. It is apparent that Takakusu and Watanabe were quite aware of the scholarly achievement of *Taishō Canon* even before its complete publication and that it was not merely an academic exercise or research project. The rhetoric above shows a Buddhist devotional sentiment and a belief that the canon has religious merit and power beyond simply the truths, lessons, or philosophies found in the texts. Also clear is their belief that Japan was uniquely equipped and capable to complete this project. Moreover, they were convinced that although the new discipline of Buddhist studies was advancing in Asia and around the world, *Taishō Canon* proved that Japan was in the van-guard. Takakusu and Watanabe believed that the texts and teachings within the canon should be promoted and proselytized. The state of the world required the printing and dissemination of the canon, which would result in positive political outcomes, including the advancement of Japan and the promotion of world peace.

Reviews of *Taishō Canon* came from both religious and secular circles in Japan, and most praised the work as an example of Japanese leadership and excellence in East Asia and a demonstration of Japan's ability to equal the West in certain areas of academic research. Nationalist statements about the value of *Taishō Canon* included that of Tokutomi Sohō 德富蘇峰 (1863–1957), a famous journalist and historian, who declared that "the Buddhist canon is of more use than military divisions or battleships to enhance the prestige of the Japanese empire."[58] The philosopher Inoue Tetsujirō 井上哲次郎 (1855–1944) declared that Japan's characteristics and history make it uniquely qualified to lead the world in Buddhist studies and thought.[59] The question arises how much of these statements should be attributed to sentiments of Japanese ethnocentrism and imperialism, already growing politically and militarily by the early twentieth century. One could easily assume that these assertions of ethnocentric superior-ity and strident nationalism would weaken the popularity of *Taishō Canon* on the Asian continent. However, *Taishō Canon*, like previous Japanese editions of the Chinese Buddhist canon, was widely and enthusiastically accepted in China back in the 1920s. It sold very well in Korea and China. Records show that several additional printings were requested in China, and in some ways it seems that the texts were being utilized more on the Asian continent than in Japan.[60]

Why doesn't the Japanese national rhetoric and inclusion of texts taken from Chinese monasteries delegitimize *Taishō Canon* for Chinese and Korean Bud-dhists? One explanation might be that *Taishō Canon* really is an effective aca-demic tool. Modern bindings, user-friendly text order, punctuation, footnotes, and volume indices might be enough benefit for Chinese and Korean Bud-dhists to overlook the rhetoric of Japanese nationalism that comes with them. However, another explanation involving the way canons are established and viewed is probably more persuasive. Prior to the Japanese editions, the Chinese Buddhist canon was established by imperial decree. This gave Chinese editions political orthodoxy, which could be seen by some as making them infallible. If the emperor declares the canon complete, discoveries of mistakes or omissions are probably not politically wise. However, a canon that is established by an emperor to whom readers hold no allegiance or reverence can be more openly and aggressively critiqued and analyzed. This might explain the critiques and analysis of *Taishō Canon* by Chinese Buddhists. Japanese Buddhists are more vocal in their praise and devotion to the edition, and the Koreans and Chinese are more vigorous in their academic study of the texts.

This difference in Japanese and Chinese uses of *Taishō Canon* can be seen in the digital databases that contain the edition. The CBETA (Chinese Buddhist Electronic Text Association) digital version, run by a small research group in Taiwan, is seen as a serious digital tool for studying *Taishō Canon*.[61] The group is constantly checking the digital record and fixing issues with transcription, character order, and other errors. The SAT Daizōkyō Text Database operated by Tokyo University is also active in textual verification or improvement of online research tools. The difference in focus between the SAT and CBETA could be motivated by national allegiance and devotionalism. CBETA's Tu Aming described the process for amending the digital record, which is extremely academically rigorous but not devotionally influenced. He explained that every attempt is made to compare all available texts and to consult with leading scholars in the field when changes, addenda, or corrections are made. Whenever these changes are necessary, extensive annotations are made in the footnotes explaining how, when, and why they were made. Whenever discrepancies are found, the differences in editions are provided fully in the footnotes. However, the final say about changes is given independently by Tu Aming and his impressively small staff. This ensures that the highest levels of academic accuracy are upheld without influence from national or devotional interests. It seems that having a Chinese arbitrator of corrections to a Japanese edition of the Buddhist canon has created a balance in which researchers can study the Buddhist texts by the most verifiable and open process possible. A drawback of these digital versions (both SAT and CBETA) is that they often include just the texts. For canonists, often the most important elements are found in the prefaces, inscriptions, and bindings of earlier editions, features that are not preserved in the digital versions. Truly, for understanding the motivations and processes of creating specific editions, like *Taishō Canon*, the information contained in the front and back matter of volumes is essential.

THE LEGACY OF TAISHŌ CANON

We can see the *Taishō Canon*'s impressive legacy in several examples. The first involves the extensive supplements produced after the original edition was completely published in 1928. The response to and sales of the first volumes were so good that the editors and contributors decided to publish additional materials. The subsequent forty-five volumes, published as the "sequel edition of the Shōwa period,"[62] included texts originating in Japan (vols. 56–84) as well as diagrams and pictures of mandalas and Buddhist icons (vols. 86–97). These images are central to understanding specific doctrines of esoteric and Tantric Buddhism, and their inclusion in the canon was seen as essential to a complete representation of Buddhist doctrines. But because of the Japanese texts, the additional volumes are often seen as extracanonical, especially outside of Japan, where Buddhist scholars often only reference the first fifty-five volumes of *Taishō Canon*. For instance, the CBETA digital version of *Taishō Canon* includes only those volumes, as well as volume 85, which contains additional Dunhuang texts.

The completion of the hundredth volume in 1934 was not the end of the *Taishō Canon*–affiliated publications. A continuous stream of indices, concordances, dictionaries, and periodicals focused on *Taishō Canon* continued to be published after that date. Takakusu wrote or edited several books on Southern Buddhism (Indian and South Asian Buddhism) and translated several Pali and Sanskrit works into Japanese.

Since the original publication of *Taishō Canon*, several older editions of the Chinese canon have been found and enthusiastically studied and compared. Several years ago, a treasury of older and yet-to-be-examined texts were discovered at Nanatsu Temple 七寺 in Nagoya, Japan. While the location was unusual in that the temple was not historically a center of serious Buddhist study or a great repository of canonical texts, Buddhist scholars from around Japan intensively studied these texts, compared them to the *Taishō Canon* versions where available, and discussed issues of originality and accuracy.[63]

One of the notable post-project works was a serial newsletter published almost quarterly from 1960 to 1978. The eighty-five issues of the *Taishō Canon Member Newsletter* (*Taishō Shinshū Daizōkyō Kaiin Gappon* 大正新修大藏經会員通信合本)[64] provide a very interesting look at the editors and collaborators of the *Taishō*. Part technical notes, part philosophical essay, part polemical rant, part self-recognition and celebration, the short newsletters were intended for a small group of researchers involved in the continual research and publishing project of *Taishō Canon*. Some of the articles address an important part of Buddhist research, including the importance of Tibetan, Indic, Chinese, or Korean texts. Other articles discuss internal issues about the publication of *Taishō Canon* catalogs or indices. One of the most consistent advertisements in these newsletters is for new printings of Takakusu's translations of the Pali Tripitaka, Upanishads, and Buddhaghosa's commentaries.[65]

A second important example of the national importance of *Taishō Canon* is the awards and recognition that came to its creators. Most often the recognition went to Takakusu, even though the project was completed by more than 100 researchers and coedited by Watanabe Kaikyoku, and many would argue that editorial contribution of Ono Genmyō 小野玄妙 (1883–1939) has been greatly overlooked. Takakusu's efforts in producing *Taishō Canon* and his editorial leadership for the translation of the Pali Tripitaka into Japanese are presented as primary reasons for awarding him first the Asahi Prize in 1932 and later the Imperial Order of Culture in 1944.[66] The Order of Culture is the highest honor that the imperial government can bestow on a civilian. This shows the status and prestige that *Taishō Canon* provided for the Japanese government and the prominence that it brought to Takakusu and Japanese Buddhist studies in the twentieth century.

A posthumous recognition for Takakusu, Watanabe, and Ono was recorded in one of the issues of the *Kaiin Gappon*. On July 26, 1965, members of the *Taishō Canon* Association came together to remember and honor the contribution of these men they referred to as the "three masters." The memorial dinner included statements and messages about each of the editors' contribution, and more generally, how each of these scholars contributed to Buddhist studies and the modern Japanese state.[67]

In modern Japan, Buddhist studies and canonical projects, like *Taishō Canon*, constitute an important and fascinating chapter in the history of Buddhism. Although influence from Buddhist studies in Europe and instances of cooperation with scholars in China provided significant support for Japan's canon projects, the resulting modern editions of the canon became a way for many in that country to assert Japan's academic, religious, and national superiority. In turn, these claims of dominance in Buddhist studies have influenced how *Taishō Canon* has been viewed and utilized by Buddhists around the world. Thus canonical studies contribute to understanding not only the development of academic standards in religious studies but also the rising nationalism and imperialism in Japan; the expanding Buddhist evangelism in Japan, Asia, and the West; and the increased tension between Japan and its neighbors on the Asian continent in the first part of the twentieth century. Newly discovered sources, such as correspondence between Takakusu and Aurel Stein, should spur additional research into *Taishō Canon* as an international project. Greater insight into the influence and possible cooperation of Western and Chinese scholars is needed and would certainly be beneficial to our understanding of the *Taishō* as well as of Buddhist studies in the first part of the twentieth century. Surely this is a great incentive for the continuation of enthusiastic and careful research.

NOTES

I would like to thank Jiang Wu for his guidance, patience, and assistance in researching and writing this chapter. His expertise and efforts have been essential in completing each step of this project. I would also like thank Lucille Chia for her helpful insights and edits to several drafts of this work, Hitoshi Kamada for his help in locating several key Japanese sources, and the participants of the 2011 Tucson conference on the Chinese Buddhist canon for their kind and instructive feedback to my original conference paper.

1. See Ron Dziwenka and Jiang Wu's chapter 8 on the Korean edition for another example of various interpretations about the canon holding national security benefits.

2. Tamamuro, "Local Society," 267–88.

3. Ketelaar, *Of Heretics and Martyrs*, 45–65.

4. Collcutt, "Buddhism," 160.

5. For information on the Buddhist background and training of scholars during the late nineteenth and early twentieth centuries in Japan, see Kōnen Tusnemitsu, *Meiji no Bukkyōsha*.

6. Müller was a forerunner in the fields of Indic studies and comparative religion. He edited *Sacred Books of the East*, a fifty-volume set of English translations of Asian religious classics, and taught and mentored many Buddhist scholars from both China and Japan. See Bosch, *Friedrich Max Müller*, for an in-depth biography.

7. Stone, "A Vast and Grave Task," 219–20.

8. Kōnen, *Meiji no Bukkyōsha*, 245–54.

9. Yang Wenhui was the founder of the Jinling Buddhist Scripture Publishing House (Jinling kejing chu 金陵刻經處) in China.

10. Chen Jidong, *Shinmatsu Bukkyō to Kenkyū*, 469–81.

11. See Goldfuss, *Vers un Bouddhisme du XXe Siècle*, 71–78, for additional specifics of Yang's and Nanjō's relationship and collaboration at Oxford.

12. Despite Nanjō and Yang's personal relationship, deep doctrinal schisms sometimes divided Chinese and Japanese Pure Land scholars. See Nakamura, *Nitchū Jōdokyō ronsō*, 173–75.

13. Kim, *Empire of the Dharma*, 81– 84.

14. Takakusu, *The New Japanism and the Buddhist View on Nationality*, 19.

15. Sueki, "Building a Platform," 13–14.

16. Staggs, "Defend the Nation," 271.

17. Takakusu and Mochizuki, *Shōtoku Taishi Godensōsho*.

18. Takakusu, *The New Japanism*, 31.

19. Takakusu, *The New Japanism*, 38.

20. Ui, *Nihon Bukkyō gaishi*, 217.

21. Hardacre, *Shinto and the State*, 40–48.

22. This rhetoric was common among national learning (*Kokugaku*) and Dutch learning (*Rangaku*) scholars during the late Tokugawa and early Meiji. The ideas of Hirata Atsutane 平田篤胤 (1776–1843) are a good example of using Christian sources to argue against the influence of Buddhism and Confucianism in Japan. See Devine, "Hirata Atsutane and Christian Sources."

23. See Yasumaru and Miyachi, *Shūkyō to kokka*, 234–50.

24. Takakusu, *Essentials of Buddhist Philosophy*, 3.

25. More information about the printing process and source materials for these two editions and the *Taishō* can be found in appendix 1 of this volume ("A Brief Survey of the Printed Editions of the Chinese Buddhist Canon").

26. Kajiura, "Kindai ni okeru Daizōkyō Hensan," 11.

27. Bingenheimer, "Collation Strategies for the Buddhist Canon," 7.

28. Ketelaar, *Of Heretics and Martyrs*, 211.

29. Kōnen Tsunemitsu, *Meiji no Bukkyōsha*, 250–55.

30. Shugendō or the way of acquiring power is a tradition of mountain austerities. The practices are influenced by both Japanese folk beliefs and teachings of esoteric Buddhism.

31. Vita, "Printings of the Buddhist 'Canon' in Modern Japan," 221.

32. Kajiura, "Kindai ni okeru Daizōkyō Hensan," 11.

33. Kajiura, "Kindai ni okeru Daizōkyō Hensan," 10.

34. The Manji edition (1902–5) of the canon was followed by a supplement (*Dai Nihon zoku zōkyō* 大日本續藏經) published 1905–12.

35. Vita, "Printings of the Buddhist 'Canon' in Modern Japan," 225–27.

36. Kajiura, "Kindai ni okeru Daizōkyō Hensan," 12.

37. Vita, "Printings of the Buddhist 'Canon' in Modern Japan," 230.

38. Kōnen, *Meiji no Bukkyōsha*, 138–45.

39. Junjirō was born in Hiroshima and adopted into the Takakusu family. He studied in England, France, and Germany and earned a doctorate in Sanskrit from Oxford. In 1894 he returned to Japan and was appointed Professor of Sanskrit and Indic Philosophy at Tokyo Imperial University. He started the Tokyo Taishō Tripitaka Association (Taishō Issaikyō Kankōkai 大正一切経刊行会), which published *Taishō Canon* and various other works on Buddhism. He also started the Musashino Girls School in 1924, the predecessor of today's Musashino University 武蔵野大学. He was honored by the Japanese government with the Order of Culture prize and by Tokyo, Leipzig, Heidelberg, and Oxford universities with honorary doctorates. See Kōnen, *Meiji no Bukkyosha*, 348–57, for more biographical information on Takakusu.

40. Watanabe studied Indic philosophy, Sanskrit, and Pali at the University of Salzburg. Along with Takakusu, he held appointments at Tokyo Imperial University and was a founding member of the Tokyo Taishō Tripitaka Association and coeditor of *Taishō Canon*. See Kōnen, *Meiji no Bukkyōsha*, 414–24, for more biographical information on Watanabe.

41. Vita, "Printings of the Buddhist 'Canon' in Modern Japan," 233.

42. Mirsky, *Sir Aurel Stein*, 254–78. Chapter 14 of Mirsky's biography describes Stein's expedition to Dunhuang in 1907.

43. Takakusu, in Stein MS. no. 108, 106. I must thank Holly Wilkinson for her assistance in the difficult task of deciphering Takakusu's unique handwriting and reading the poor scans of the Stein letters. The Stein letters have been first examined and translated into Chinese by Chinese scholar Wang Jiqing. See his *Sitanyin yu Riben Dunhuang xue*, 278–93.

44. "Prospectus of the Publication of a New Edition of the Tripitaka in Chinese," in Stein MS. no. 108, 2 (109).

45. Paul Pelliot followed Aurel Stein to Mogao Caves and bought back a large number of texts and artifacts from the area.

46. "Prospectus of the Publication of a New Edition of the Tripitaka in Chinese," Stein MS. no. 108, 3 (110).

47. Stein's letter to Takakutsu, Stein MS. no. 108. The Dr. Yabuki mentioned in the passage is Yabuki Keiki 矢吹慶輝 (1879–1939), a Buddhist scholar from Fukuoka who

studied for several years in England and is listed as one of the members of the Tokyo Taishō Tripitaka Association.

48. Fang Guangchang, "*Dazheng xinxiu dazangjing* pingshu."

49. "Kaiin meibo," in Takakusu and Watanabe, eds., *Taishō shinshū daizōkyō sōmokuroku*, 1–48.

50. The membership from today's mainland China is divided into three groups: Republic of China 中華国民, 111 members; the Kwantung territory 關東洲, 6 members; and Manchukuo 満州, 15 members. The members from China include several leading scholars and intellectuals, notably Hu Shih 胡適 (1891–1962), writer and leader of the May Fourth Movement and China's New Cultural Movement. It is not clear how these names were included. For a brief review of this list, see Xiao Ping, *Jindai Zhongguo fojiao de fuxing*, 151–54. Thanks to Prof. Xiao Ping for passing this reference to Jiang Wu.

51. "Kaiin meibo," in Takakusu and Watanabe, eds., *Taishō shinshū daizōkyō sōmokuroku*, 4–5.

52. Ise is the shrine of Amaterasu, the sun goddess and progenitrix of the Japanese imperial line. The shrine is also the guardian of the imperial regalia and was at the time the most important shrine for the imperial cult and for state Shinto.

53. See *Encyclopedia of Shinto*, http://eos.kokugakuin.ac.jp (accessed July 12, 2012). The Kokugakuin is a Shinto university focused on Shinto and Japanese studies research as well as the education and training of Shinto priests.

54. Takakusu and Watanabe, eds., *Taishō Shinshū daizōkyō sōmokuroku*, 4; translated from classical Chinese by Jiang Wu.

55. Takakusu, *Essentials of Buddhist Philosophy*, 17.

56. Takakusu, *Essentials of Buddhist Philosophy*, 9–10.

57. Stone, "A Vast and Grave Task," 234.

58. Ibid., 231.

59. Kajiura, "Kindai ni okeru Daizōkyō Hensan," 12.

60. Ibid., 13.

61. See Tu, "The Creation of the CBETA Chinese Electronic Tripitaka Collection in Taiwan," appendix 2 in this volume.

62. Vita, "Printings of the Buddhist 'Canon' in Modern Japan," 236. While the rationale or plan for inclusion of texts in this Japanese section is unknown, this was the first time that a large number of Japanese texts were included in the Buddhist canon in a systematic way.

63. Hubbard, "A Report on Newly Discovered Buddhist Texts at Nanatsu-dera," 401–5.

64. *Taishō Shinshū Daizōkyō Kaiin Gappon*, no. 1–85.

65. Ibid., no. 54, 2. Takakusu's translations of Indic texts are often called the *Nanden Daizōkyō* 南伝大蔵經.

66. *Asahi Shinbun*, January 25, 1933, 1, and April 30, 1944, 1.

67. *Taishō Shinshū Daizōkyō Kaiin Gappon*, no. 43, 1.

Appendix 1

A BRIEF SURVEY OF THE PRINTED EDITIONS
OF THE CHINESE BUDDHIST CANON

Li Fuhua and He Mei
Compiled by Jiang Wu

The following descriptions, including major editions printed in Korea and Japan, are based on Li Fuhua and He Mei, *Hanwen Fojiao Dazangjing yanjiu* (2003). He Mei's *Lidai hanwen dazangjing mulu xinkai* (2014) has also been consulted for updated information. Because Li and He checked all catalogs against the actual canon, their calculations of the size of the canon may not agree with the numbers in traditional catalogs. This list follows a chronological order.

Kaibao Canon 開寶藏 (*Song Canon* 宋藏, or the Shu edition 蜀本). This was the first printed edition of the Chinese canon in history, sponsored by the Northern Song government during the Kaibao period. The printing blocks of *Kaibao Canon* were first carved in Sichuan starting in 971 and then moved to the capital, Kaifeng 開封, in 983. This edition was formatted in 23 columns per sheet and 14 characters per column. Multiple pages were pasted together to form a scroll. Its initial content amounts to 5,048 fascicles and 1,076 titles in 480 cases, based on Zhisheng's *Kaiyuan Catalog* (*Kaiyuan shijiao lu*). The final version, which was supplemented with newly translated esoteric texts and sectarian works by Chinese authors, amounts to 1,565 titles and 6,962 fascicles in 682 cases (1,574 titles and 6,973 fascicles, per He Mei 2014). Today, only 14 fascicles survive and are preserved in various libraries and museums in China, Japan, and the United States. This edition was soon sent to the Liao (Khitan) and Xi Xia (Tangut) regimes in north China, and to Japan, Korea, and Vietnam as well.

Goryeo Canon or *Tripitaka Koreana* 高麗大藏經. Based on *Kaibao Canon*, *Tripitaka Koreana* was carved two times in Korean history. The first edition was carved between 1011 and 1029 by King Hyeonjong 顯宗, and its content was identical to the early version of *Kaibao Canon*. This edition was supplemented with new texts that Uicheon 義天 collected. However, the first edition and its supplements were destroyed during the Mongol invasion in 1232. During King Gojong's 高宗 reign (1214–59), the canon was recarved between 1236 and 1251. This new edition includes 1,524 titles and 6,558 fascicles in 628 cases. The entire 86,525 blocks are now preserved in Haeinsa Monastery in South Korea.

Liao Canon 遼藏 or *Khitan Canon* 契丹藏. This edition was printed during the Liao Dynasty (916–1125) shortly after *Kaibao Canon* but following a different manuscript tradition, according to which every half-leaf contains 12 columns and 30 characters per column. Newly discovered copies from this edition in Yingxian 應縣, China, indicate that there were actually two versions of *Khitan Canon*: the large-type version in the scroll form and the small-type version in the string-binding style. The large-type version has 27 columns per page and 17 characters per column, following the standard manuscript format. It was first printed around 987, during Emperor Shengzong's 聖宗 reign (983–1031), under the leadership of Quanxiao 詮曉 and was continued during Emperor Xingzong's 興宗 reign (1031–54) under the leadership of Jueyuan 覺苑. The complete 579 cases with 1,414 titles and 6,054 fascicles were finished in 1068 (1,420 titles, 6,056 fascicles, 579 cases, per He Mei 2014). The small-type version in the butterfly-binding style was basically a reprint of the large-type version. It has a much smaller font and layout and can be packed in fewer than 200 cases. Both versions were brought to Korea in 1062 and 1072 respectively. It was also used as exemplar for *Fangshan Stone Canon*.

Chongning Canon 崇寧藏 (the Dongchan edition 東禪本). The first privately sponsored canon, this edition was produced between 1080 and 1112 in Dongchan Dengjue Monastery (Dongchan dengjue yuan 東禪等覺院) in Fuzhou 福州. In 1103, it was given the title of *Chongning Wanshou Dazang* 崇寧萬壽大藏 by the imperial court. It follows the so-called accordion-binding style, commonly known as sutra-binding style (*jingzhezhuang* 経折裝). One sheet in 36 columns was folded into six pages with six columns per page and 17 characters per column. The complete canon includes 1,451 titles, 6,358 fascicles in 595 cases (1,454 titles, 6,357 fascicles, 595 cases, per He Mei 2014). It is the first canon to include a volume of phonetic explanation at the end of the whole canon.

Pilu Canon 毘盧藏 (the Kaiyuan edition 開元本). Together with *Chongning Canon*, it was often referred to as *Fuzhou Canon* 福州藏 or the Min edition 閩本. Privately sponsored by Chan monks from the Yunmen lineage 雲門宗 due to sectarian rivalry with Dongchan Monastery, which produced *Chongning Canon*, this edition was published between 1112 and 1151 in Kaiyuan Monastery

開元寺 in Fuzhou. Its catalog and format follow *Chongning Canon*. This edition contains 1,452 titles and 6,359 fascicles in 595 cases. The second carving of *Pilu Canon* was done between 1164 and 1176 to supplement it with Chan texts and Tiantai classics. It adopted the popular sutra-binding style with 36 columns a sheet, six columns a half-page, and 17 characters per column.

Yuanjue Canon 圓覺藏 (*Zifu Canon* 資福藏 or *Sixi Canon* 思溪藏, or *Huzhou Canon* 湖州藏, or the Zhe edition 浙本). This edition was often considered as two related versions: first called *Yuanjue Canon* and then renamed *Zifu Canon* or *Later Sixi Canon* (*Hou Sixi zang* 後思溪藏) because of the change of names of the monastery. This project was carried out in Yuanjue Monastery in Sixi in Huzou Prefecture (today's Zhejiang); it was started in 1126 and completed around 1138, with the sponsorship of an individual called Wang Yongcong 王永從 and his clan. The content of this edition follows *Chongning Canon*. Its format, followed by later editions of the canon, was standardized as 30 columns a sheet folded in five or six half-pages, five columns per page, and 17 characters per column. (Some of the early prints have 36 columns a page.) Phonetic explanations were appended at the end of each fascicle. The complete canon contains 1,419 titles, and 5,913 fascicles in 548 cases (1,423 titles, 5,915 fascicles, 548 cases, per He Mei 2014).

Zhaocheng Canon 趙城藏 (*Jin Canon* 金藏). Also based on *Kaibao Canon*, *Zhaocheng Canon* was initiated by the legendary nun Cui Fazhen 崔法珍, who severed her arm. Most of the texts were carved between 1149 and 1178. The total printing blocks number 168,113 and the complete version contains 6,980 fascicles (1,576 titles, 6,972 or 6,975 fascicles, 682 cases, per He Mei 2014). Because it was a reprint of *Kaibao Canon*, its format, binding style, and catalog followed those of *Kaibao Canon*. It was presented to the Jin ruler in 1178, and the complete set of blocks were moved to Beijing and stored in Hongfa Monastery 弘法寺 in 1181. This edition was supplemented several times during the Yuan Dynasty. Therefore, it was commonly referred to as *Hongfa Canon* or *Yanyou Canon* 延佑藏 in Yuan Dynasty sources. A copy of *Zhaocheng Canon* (about 4,800 fascicles extant) was discovered in Zhaocheng County in Shanxi in 1933. Forty-six rare and lost texts from this edition were reprinted in 1935. In the 1980s, this edition also became the basis for the compilation of the Beijing edition of *Chinese Tripitaka* (*Zhonghua dazang jing*) in mainland China.

Qisha Canon 磧砂藏. This edition was completed between 1216 and 1322 and was organized by Qisha Yansheng Monastery 磧砂延聖院 in Pingjiang Prefecture 平江府. It was initiated in 1216 by an official named Zhao Anguo 趙安國 and the abbot Fayin 法音 and finished in 1322. Its early blocks carved in the Song followed *Yuanjue Canon*, and those carved in the Yuan Dynasty followed *Puning Canon*. The complete version contains 1,518 titles and 6,363 fascicles in 592 cases (1,517 titles, 6,363 or 6,372 fascicles, 591 cases, per He Mei 2014). This edition was supplemented several times during the Yuan and Ming dynasties. Its format follows the sutra-binding style with 30 columns a sheet, folded in five half-pages with six columns per half-page and 17 characters per column. The previously discovered copies of the obscure *Wulin Canon* 武林藏 were actually prints from *Qisha Canon*. A near-complete copy was discovered in 1931 in Shanxi and reprinted in 1935.

Puning Canon 普寧藏 (*Hangzhou Canon* 杭州藏, *Yuan Canon* 元藏, the Puningsi edition 普寧寺本). This edition was completed from 1277 to 1290 and contains 1,520 titles and 6,326 fascicles in 590 cases (1,518 titles, 6,352 fascicles, 590 cases, per He Mei 2014). The project was undertaken by a controversial new Buddhist movement named White Clouds Sect (Baiyunzong 白雲宗) in Puning Monastery in Hangzhou. All texts were carefully collated and phonetic explanations were provided. Its format is similar to that of *Qisha Canon*.

Yuan Official Canon 元官藏. The discovery of fragments in the Yunnan Provincial Library in 1979 proves that the Yuan government also produced an official edition that was printed around 1332 to 1336 and sponsored by Great Empress Dowager Pu Da Shi Li 卜答失里. Its content largely follows the newly compiled Yuan catalog *Collated General Catalog of Dharma Treasure During the Zhiyuan Reign* (*Zhiyuan fabao kantong zonglu*). Because it was an imperial edition, its size and font are bigger. A sheet of 42 columns was folded into seven pages with six columns per half-page and 17 characters per column.

Hongwu Southern Canon (*Hongwu nanzang* 洪武南藏 or *First Southern Canon* 初刻南藏). This edition, discovered in a monastery in Chengdu, Sichuan, in 1934, was believed to have been completed in the first emperor Zhu Yuanzhang's Hongwu period (1368–98) in the Ming Dynasty. New studies suggest that this edition was finished in the second emperor's Jianwen 建文 period (1399–1402) rather than in the Hongwu period; therefore it should be called *Jianwen Southern Canon* 建文南藏. This edition, based on the previous Qisha edition with new additions of 87 cases of sectarian texts, was started in 1399, the first year of Jianwen, and finished in 1402. The complete canon includes 1,618 titles and 7,245 fascicles in 678 cases (1,617 titles, 7,239 or 7,161 fascicles, 678 cases, per He Mei 2014). In 1407, the entire set of printing blocks was destroyed in a fire soon after the project was finished.

Yongle Southern Canon (*Yongle nanzang* 永樂南藏). This edition was created from 1413 to 1420 with three supplemental carvings in 1550, 1602, and 1661. It is perhaps the most widely distributed edition because it was available for commercial printing in Nanjing. This edition contains 1,618 titles and 6,325 fascicles in 678 cases (1,656 titles, 7,440 or 7,540 fascicles, 678 cases, per He Mei 2014). Its content was based on *Hongwu Southern Canon*. But the catalog was reorganized to set the division of Sutra, Vinaya, and Sastra as the first order, and all

Hinayana and Mahayana texts and supplemental titles added after Zhisheng's *Kaiyuan Catalog* were put under these categories. This structural change was inherited by the compilers of later canons. It continued the folding style, with five folded pages and 30 columns in one sheet. Thus, there are six columns per half-page with 17 characters per column. The formally misidentified *Wanli Canon* 萬曆藏 was actually part of the supplemental prints from this edition.

Yongle Northern Canon (*Yongle beizang* 永樂北藏 or *Northern Canon* 北藏). This edition was carved between 1419 and 1440, after Zhu Di usurped the throne and moved the capital to Beijing in 1403. It was supplemented between 1577 and 1584 with 41 new cases. In total, this edition includes 6,771 fascicles and 1,615 titles in 677 cases (1,655 titles, 7,504 fascicles, 677 cases, per He Mei 2014). Although the content is almost the same as in the southern edition, the sequence of the texts is different. A few new works produced in the early Ming Dynasty, especially by Zhu Di, were incorporated. Following the standard format, a sheet of paper in 25 columns is folded into five pages and there are five columns per page and 17 characters per column. Because this is the imperial edition, all texts have been collated carefully and its printing quality is very high.

Jiaxing Canon 嘉興藏 or *Jingshan Canon* 徑山藏. This edition was completed between 1589 and 1712 and named after Lengyan Monastery in Jiaxing County 嘉興楞嚴寺, which was the center for printing and distributing its copies. It was also referred to as *Jingshan Canon* because most of its blocks were carved in a monastery in Jingshan, and as the "booklet edition" (*Fangcezang* 方冊藏) because it adopted the popular string-bound style. As a private endeavor, the project was initiated by Yuan Huang 袁潢 (Yuan Liaofan 袁了凡) and a group of literati believers at the beginning of the Wanli period and organized by Zibo Zhenke 紫柏真可 and his disciple Mizang Daokai 密藏道開 at Mount Wutai in the north, and later moved to the south. The complete canon includes the main canon, the supplementary canon, and the additional supplementary canon. The total number of texts reaches an unprecedented number in Chinese history: 2,195 titles and 10,332 fascicles (2,241 titles, 11,612 or 11,952 fascicles, per He Mei 2014). Its main canon follows the content of *Yongle Northern Canon* with a few additions from *Yongle Southern Canon*. Every page was folded into two half-pages with 10 columns and 20 characters per column in each half-page. A new Beijing edition in 377 cases was printed in 2009.

Tenkai Canon (*Tenkaizō* 天海藏), or *Japanese Canon* (*wazō* 倭藏), or the Kan'eiji edition 寬永寺版, or the Tōeizan edition 東睿山版. This edition was sponsored by Tokugawa Iemitsu 德川家光 (1623–51) and undertaken by the powerful monk-advisor Tenkai 天海 (1534–1643). It was based on *Zifu Canon* (*Sixi Canon*) or *Yuanjue Canon* of the Southern Song Dynasty and supplemented with *Puning Canon* of the Yuan Dynasty. The project was started in 1637 and completed in 1648. Printed with movable wood type, this edition adopted the accordion-folding format with 24 columns per sheet of paper, which was folded into four half-pages. Each half-page thus has six columns and 17 characters per column. The complete canon contains 1,453 titles and 6,323 fascicles in 665 cases (1,437 titles, 6,328 fascicles, 599 cases, per *Shōwa hōhō sōmokuroku*).

Ōbaku Canon 黃檗藏 (*Tetsugen Canon* 鐵眼藏). This edition was started in 1669 by Yinyuan Longqi's Japanese disciple Tetsugen Dōkō 鉄眼道光 (1630– 82), who based the new canon on *Jiaxing Canon*, which Yinyuan gave to him in 1668. The printing project was started in 1669 and finished in 1681. It was basically a reprint of the main canon of *Jiaxing Canon*, which was based on *Yongle Northern Canon*. The complete edition contains 2,094 titles and 6,950 fascicles in 274 cases (1,659 titles, 7,674 or 7,826 fascicles. per He Mei 2014). Its format and binding style followed those of *Jiaxing Canon*.

Qing Canon 清藏 (*Dragon Canon* 龍藏, or *Qianlong Canon* 乾隆大藏經). This edition was initiated by Emperor Yongzheng in 1733. Its blocks were carved between 1735 and 1738, based on *Yongle Northern Canon* and *Jiaxing Canon*, and most of them remain intact. The entire canon was carved on 79,036 blocks and contains 7,240 fascicles in 724 cases (1,675 titles, 7,772 or 8,174 fascicles, 724 cases, per He Mei 2014). Yongzheng interfered with the compilation and ordered 54 of his favorite titles to be included, and 32 "problematic" titles excluded. Twelve titles, including his own works, were included in the canon for the first time.

Reduced Print Canon (*Shukusatsuzō* 縮刷藏, full title: *Dai Nihon kōtei shukusatsu dai zōkyō* 大日本校訂縮刷大藏經, or *Gukyō Canon* 弘教藏). This edition was the first modern effort and was edited by Fukuda Gyōkai 福田行誠 (1809–88) in Kōkyō Shoin in Tokyo from 1880 to 1885. For the first time, the Chinese Buddhist canon was printed with modern metal movable type and conformed to modern book standards. The editing work started in 1877 at the suggestion of Shimada Bankon 島田蕃根 (1827–1907) of the Temple and Shrine Bureau of the Meiji government and was based on *Tripitaka Koreana* but collated with *Sixi Canon* (*Zifu Canon*) or *Yuanjue Canon* of the Southern Song Dynasty, *Puning Canon* of the Yuan Dynasty, and *Ōbaku Canon*. Its catalog was based on Zhixu's 智旭 *Guide for Reading the Canon* (*Yuezang zhijin* 閱藏知津) with modifications. Printed with metal type font size 5, it adopted string-bound format with 20 columns per half-page and 45 characters per column. Punctuation was added for the first time. The entire edition contains 1,916 titles and 8,534 fascicles, bound in 418 volumes in 40 cases.

Manji Main Canon 卍字正藏 (full title: *Dai Nihon kōtei kunten Daizōkyō* 大日本校訂訓點大藏經). This edition was initiated in 1902 by Maeda Eun 前田慧雲 (1857–1930) and Nakano Tatsue 中野達慧 (1871–1934) and was based on Ninchō's 忍徵 (?–1711) collation of the Korean edition with *Ōbaku Canon* compiled in 1706–10. Its catalog follows that of *Reduced Print Canon* and *Yongle*

Northern Canon, with modifications. It was the first canon not to adopt the traditional "Thousand-Character Classic" cataloguing method. The complete edition has 347 volumes in 36 cases, printed with metal type, font size 4, in string-bound format. One page is divided into two registers with 20 columns and 22 characters per column. There are 1,617 titles and 7,072 fascicles (He Mei 2014). The main canon was finished in 1905 but soon was destroyed in a fire. However, most of its contents have been incorporated into *Taishō Canon*.

Manji Continued Canon 卍字續藏 or *Japanese Zōkuzōkyō Canon* (*Dai-Nihon zokuzōkyō* 大日本續藏經). This edition was the supplementary canon to *Manji Main Canon*, published between 1905 and 1912. It includes a large number of Chinese texts (about 900 titles) written in later periods, especially sources from the Ming and Qing dynasties, which were provided by Yang Wenhui 楊文會 and monk Shiding 式定 at Lushan Monastery in Zhening 浙寧蘆山寺. It was printed with modern type but was string-bound into 750 volumes in 150 cases, which contain 1,750 titles and 7,140 fascicles. A half-page is divided into two registers with 18 columns and 20 characters per column. After its completion in 1912, it was reprinted in Shanghai in 1925 and in Taiwan in 1976 in 150 volumes. This edition was also reprinted as a new Japanese edition (*Shinsan Dai-Nihon Zōkuzōkyō* 新纂大日本續藏經) from 1980 to 1989 in 88 volumes and was supplemented with a new catalog and index.

Taishō Canon (full title: *Taishō shinshū daizōkyō* 大正新修大藏經). This edition represents a revolutionary change in the history of the Chinese canon. It was edited by Takakusu Junjirō 高楠順次郎 and Watanabe Kaigyoku 渡邊海旭 from 1922 to 1934 and includes sources from India, China, Japan, and Korea; most were written in Chinese before the thirteenth century. More writings by Japanese authors were incorporated to supplement the main content. This edition contains 3,493 titles and 13,520 fascicles in 100 volumes (3,360 titles and 13,101 or 13,534 fascicles, per He Mei 2014). Among these volumes, 55 contain translated texts from Indian and central Asia (vols. 1–32) and Chinese writings (vols. 33–55); 29 (vols. 56–84) include Japanese texts written in Chinese; and one volume (vol. 85) contains newly discovered texts, especially Dunhuang manuscripts. The unique content is the iconography section in 12 volumes, which contains 367 titles and 1,345 fascicles. *Taishō Canon* also includes all surviving catalogs (72 titles in total) in three separate volumes. One printed page has three registers with 29 columns and 17 characters per column, and the results of collation with four other editions were printed at the bottom of the page. All texts were punctuated, which greatly facilitated reading. In this canon, there are about 400 titles of rare sources that never appeared in any previous editions. Among them, 215 are translated Indian sources, 220 are Chinese texts, especially texts in the Sanlun, Pure Land, and Vinaya schools, and the texts discovered in Dunhuang. It is the most authoritative edition and is the standard edition for scholarly citation. The texts incorporated in this canon are based on *Tripitaka Koreana*, which was considered carefully collated and proofread. Texts were also collated with three other editions: *Zifu Canon*, *Puning Canon*, and *Jiaxing Canon*. *Taishō Canon* focuses on translations and early Chinese Buddhist writings, and Japanese writings. More than 150 titles that have appeared in major Chinese editions were excluded from this edition, as were more than 400 titles from the supplementary sections of the previous editions.

Pinjia Canon 頻伽藏. This edition was named after its printer, the Shanghai Pinjia Vihara 頻伽精舍, in the 1910s. Sponsored by a Chinese French lady, Luo Jialing 羅迦陵 (1864–1961), and her husband, Silas Aaron Hardoon (known in Chinese as Hatong 哈同, 1851–1931), a famous French-born Jewish tycoon in Shanghai, this edition was compiled under the direction of monk Zongyang 宗仰. Based on the Japanese *Reduced Print Canon*, it was started in 1909 and finished in 1913. The entire canon contains 414 volumes, 1,916 titles, 8,416 fascicles in 40 cases. This edition, using Chinese type font size 4, adopted the modern printing method but was string-bound with 20 columns per page and 45 characters per column, and was supplemented with some modern translations of Tibetan texts and original Japanese texts.

Puhui Canon 普慧藏. This edition was initiated in Shanghai in 1943 and was named after its sponsor, Sheng You'an 盛幼盒 (1875–1953), whose dharma name was Puhui. His goal was to supplement all existing editions with rare Buddhist texts collected from around the world, including Chinese translations of *Pali Canon* and Tibetan texts. After 1945, the project was continued by Society of Supplementing the Canon of the Republic of China (Minguo zengxiu dazangjing hui 民國增修大藏經會) and lasted until 1955. In total, 104 titles and 100 volumes were published. Printed in font size 4, every page has 16 columns and 41 characters per column. This edition includes some rare Ming and Qing sources together with translations of Theravada and Tibetan texts and writings by contemporary authors.

Chinese Tripitaka (*Zhonghua dazang jing* 中華大藏經): the Taibei edition. The publication of this modern Taiwan edition started in the 1960s and was completed in the 1970s. The project was proposed by Qu Yingguang 屈映光 and Cai Yunchen 蔡運辰, and in 1955 an organization was established to facilitate it. This edition simply facsimiled the existing contents of several editions of the canon without much editing effort. The entire canon, including 4,003 titles (3,976, per He Mei 2014), is divided into four series. The first series (1,581 titles) reprints the newly discovered *Qisha Canon* and some rare sources in *Zhaocheng Canon*. The second series (685 titles) reprints the two supplementary sections of *Jiaxing Canon* for the first time, though excluding titles that already appeared in the first series. The third series (1,337 titles) is a reprint of the Japanese *Manji*

Continued Canon. The fourth series includes supplements of about 400 texts not included in the previous series.

Chinese Tripitaka (Zhonghua dazang jing): the Beijing edition. As a state-sponsored project, this edition was supervised by the prominent Chinese scholar Ren Jiyu 任繼愈 (1916–2009). The original plan was to include the Chinese, Tibetan, Thai, Mongolian, and Manchu editions in one canon to reflect the diversity of the Buddhist tradition in China, though only the Chinese section was finished. For the Chinese section, in addition to the main canon, which facsimiled the remaining titles of the newly discovered *Zhaocheng Canon* of the Jin Dynasty with supplements, the compilers also planned a supplementary canon that would include texts not being cataloged in the "Thousand-character" system and texts preserved in *Fangshan Stone Canon* and the supplementary sections of *Jiaxing Canon, Pinjia Canon, Puhui Canon, Taishō Canon,* and *Manji Zōkuzōkyō Canon.* If accomplished, the complete Chinese section of the canon would include 4,200 titles and 23,000 fascicles. This project was started in 1982, and by 1994 only the main canon (106 volumes) had been completed; a catalog was published in 2004. Because the mother copies from *Zhaocheng Canon* are not complete, the missing texts, including some missing or damaged pages, were photocopied from the Korean edition, which follows the format of *Kaibao Canon.* The compilers of the canon made the decision to maintain the original format of a canon by following the traditional "Thousand-Character Classic" (*qianziwen*) call number system. The current main canon also inserted 340 titles and 3,170 fascicles of texts from eight other editions not included in the original *Zhaocheng Canon.* The completed main section of the Chinese series of this edition includes 1,937 titles and 10,230 fascicles (1,873 titles, per He Mei 2014). All texts are carefully collated with those collected in eight other editions, including *Fangshan Stone Canon, Sixi (Zifu) Canon, Qisha Canon, Puning Canon, Yongle Southern Canon, Jiaxing Canon, Qing Canon,* and *Tripitaka Koreana.* The results of these collations were appended to the end of each text.

Great Buddhist Canon (Fojiao dazangjing 佛教大藏經). Initiated by Taiwan Buddhist teacher Zhihuijian 智慧劍, commonly known as Guangding 廣定, this project was finished between 1977 and 1983. Following the example of *Pinjia Canon,* it aims to include not only Chinese texts but also Chinese translations of Pali and Tibetan sources. Printed in 162 volumes, this edition has 2,643 titles (2,623, per He Mei 2014) and 11,062 fascicles.

Dunhuang Canon 敦煌大藏經. From 1988 to 1990, a new edition based on Dunhuang manuscripts was produced by a collaborative effort of publishers in Beijing and Taiwan. Based on the collection of Dunhuang manuscripts in the National Library in Beijing and supplemented with collections in other libraries around the world, this edition arranges all available Dunhuang manuscripts according to Zhisheng's *Kaiyuan Catalog*. In total, there are 63 volumes, which includes Mahayana scriptures of the Prajñāpāramitā class (vols. 1–20); Mahayana scriptures of Ratnakūta, Mahāsannipāta, Avataṃsaka, and Nirvāṇa classes and other texts outside the five major Mahayana classes (vols. 21–60); and Buddhist texts written in ancient languages such as Sanskrit, ancient Tibetan, Khotan script, and Uighur script (vols. 61–63). Because no complete manuscript canon has been discovered in Dunhuang, there are missing titles in this edition. All texts have been collated with the Beijing editions of *Chinese Tripitaka* and *Taisho Canon* and the results are appended to the end of each fascicle.

Appendix 2

THE CREATION OF THE *CBETA CHINESE ELECTRONIC TRIPITAKA COLLECTION* IN TAIWAN

Aming Tu
Translated by Xin Zi

It has been more than ten years since the Chinese Buddhist Electronic Text Association (CBETA) was founded. CBETA makes every effort to search for and collect Chinese Buddhist texts of the past ages and to develop digital resources for Buddhist studies. CBETA's achievement has won global recognition and can be considered a model of modern digital Buddhist resources. Because of the complexities of the digitization process, the rich content of the final products, and a large number of extended functions and programs, it is difficult for outsiders to understand the digitization of the Tripitaka in depth and to take advantage of these digital resources.

Hereby I review the history of the Tripitaka digitization projects undertaken by CBETA in recent years. I explain the process of digitization, including content development and technical advances, in different stages and categories to help readers keep track of the content of the electronic Tripitaka. Furthermore, by integrating related digital projects and examining the auxiliary application of our catalog project, I provide an overview of the contents of digital resources of the Tripitaka to date. Finally, I discuss the standardization and further development of digitization procedures, hoping that these electronic resources can promote more academic exchanges and research on the Chinese Buddhist canon. This appendix aims to provide a systematic introduction to the digital resources for Buddhist studies created in Taiwan by focusing on the *Chinese Electronic*

Tripitaka Collection and related projects, and to highlight the significance of Tripitaka digitization in our time.

THE EVOLUTION OF THE *CHINESE ELECTRONIC TRIPITAKA COLLECTION*

First, I would like to review the achievement and evolution of the *Chinese Electronic Tripitaka Collection* since the founding of CBETA.[1]

CONCEPTION AND OBJECTIVE OF CBETA

CBETA was founded in 1998. Its goal can be stated as follows: "collect all the Chinese Buddhist classics and establish an electronic collection of the Tripitaka; develop digitization techniques and promote exchange and use of Buddhist texts; facilitate the storage and circulation of Chinese Buddhist texts by taking advantage of electronic media; provide everyone with the opportunity to read Buddhist texts."

A nonprofit organization, CBETA has been working on the full-text digital input of the Chinese Buddhist texts on a large scale for years. Based on the idea of free access and sharing, our essential objective is to establish digital resources in Taiwan and provide free access to the public, allowing all Buddhist scholars to obtain bibliographical information about Buddhist texts and modern readers to have a more convenient, humanized, and interactive interface to read the canon.

PERIODIZATION OF THE DIGITIZATION PROCESS

As a record of the development of Chinese Buddhism, the Chinese Buddhist canon also contains the history of the complex Chinese civilization. According to Fang Guangchang's research, the content, structure, and case numbers of the canon keep changing under the influence of both internal and external factors. Fang suggests that depending on different carriers and means of production, we should divide the history of the development of the Chinese canon into four periods: Handwriting Period, Block-Printing Period, Modern Printing Period, and Digital Period. Based on this, he proposes his own periodization criteria for and definition of the Chinese Buddhist canon.[2]

In contrast, the digitization process of the electronic collection of the Tripitaka at CBETA reversed the order of Fang's periodization. During this process, the CBETA team adhered to the mission of the electronic Tripitaka collection, technical standards, and the characteristics of its digital content to meet the technical challenge of digitizing different text editions. We divided this process into three periods: digitization of modern metal-type printed editions, digitization of block-printed editions, and digitization of handwritten manuscript editions. This division, based on the types of texts, also reveals the history of canon digitization undertaken by CBETA. In the following, I explain these three periods in detail.

THE FIRST PERIOD: DIGITIZATION OF MODERN METAL-TYPE PRINTED EDITIONS

From 1998 to 2007, CBETA accomplished the digitization of *Taishō Canon* (*Taishō shinshū daizōkyō* 大正新修大藏經) and *Manji Continued Canon* (*Manji zokuzōkyō* 卍續藏經), including the full texts of the content and the results of textual collation in the two editions.

During this initial period, CBETA used these two modern metal-type editions as master copies.[3] The total number of Chinese characters in this digital Tripitaka database is over 150,000,000. With high accuracy and markup in XML (Extensible Markup Language), which conforms to the TEI (Text Encoding and Interchange) Standard,[4] this database has become an important tool in the academic world and Buddhist communities in the past decades.

Around the same time we were processing *Manji Continued Canon*, CBETA started the Tripitaka Catalogs Digitization Project from 2005 to 2007[5] to allow future works to go smoothly. Integrating 22 catalogs of different editions of the Chinese Buddhist canon and 21 ancient catalogs, this project is not only the basis of our later works but also a great advance toward the completion of the *Chinese Electronic Tripitaka Collection.*

In addition to posting the digital products on its website for free download on a yearly basis, CBETA also produced more than 10,000 copies of compact disks containing digital resources and a reading software (CBReader) for free distribution. Since users are familiar with the digital resources we distributed in the early years, here I only briefly introduced CEBTA's development in its first 10 years.[6]

THE SECOND PERIOD: DIGITIZATION OF BLOCK-PRINTED EDITIONS AND RELATED TEXTS NOT COLLECTED IN THE CANON

Based on the earlier work of Tripitaka Catalogs Digitization, CBETA planned to start a new project to supplement the current collection with different editions from the past. Therefore, in 2008, we secured funding from the Taiwan E-Learning and Digital Archives Program to work on the *Chinese Buddhist Tripitaka Electronic Text Collection: Taipei Edition* (http://taipei.ddbc .edu.tw/index.php). CBETA has now digitized most essential texts, and the collection is near complete. To follow the plan of *Chinese Electronic Tripitaka Collection*, CBETA set up "Four Steps and Goals": first, finish the digitization of *Taishō Canon* and *Manji Continued Canon*; second, supplement these with all the extant editions of the Tripitaka of the past to present a complete picture of the canon in history; third, compile modern works and texts that are not collected in the Tripitaka in order to go beyond the scope of past editions; and fourth, if allowed, digitize handwritten manuscripts and those produced in other ways.

The product released in 2008 is based on the progress CBETA made in 2007. We had achieved the first goal mentioned above and begun to input and collate other editions of the Tripitaka in that year. The focus of the second step was the digitization of *Jiaxing Canon* because most texts not collected in *Taishō Canon* and *Manji Continued Canon* are contained there. In particular, the digitization of the abundant historical materials on Chan Buddhism in the Ming and Qing dynasties had been greatly anticipated by the academic world. From March 2008 to September 2009, CBETA finished inputting a selected collection of *Jiaxing Canon* in 18 months, including 1,659 fascicles in 285 cases.

The product published in 2009 is based on the digitization of different editions of the Tripitaka in 2008. During this year, we tried to achieve the second and third goals mentioned above, focusing on completing the extant texts in the canon and the texts that were compiled in modern times but were not collected in any editions of the canon. For the latter, we secured authorization to digitize two precious documents: Du Doucheng's 杜斗成 *Collection of Buddhist Sources in Dynastic Histories* (*Zhengshi fojiao ziliao huibian* 正史佛教資料彙編) and Fang Guangchang's 方廣錩 *Buddhist Literature Outside the Canon* (*Zangwai fojiao wenxian* 藏外佛教文獻).[7]

In 2009, we cooperated with the Institute of History and Philology at Academia Sinica to digitize *A Hundred Rubbings of Buddhist Stone Inscriptions of the Northern Dynasty* (*Beichao fojiao shike tapian baipin* 北朝佛教石刻拓片百品), compiled by Yan Juanying 顏娟英.[8] Along with the digitization of Yan's work, CBETA made new progress in adding a full-text search function for special text formats and in presenting the search results.

Based on previous progress and intensive effort in 2010, the latest product presented in 2011 is *Supplementary Tripitaka Collection* (*Lidai zangjing buji* 歷代藏經補輯).[9] Newly added content of supplementary texts, 972 fascicles in 100 cases in total, includes *Fangshan Stone Canon* (*Fangshan shijing* 房山石經),

Zhaocheng Canon (*Zhaochengjinzang* 趙城金藏), *Tripitaka Koreana* (*Gaoli-zang* 高麗藏), *Remaining Treasure of Song Canon* (*Songzang yizhen* 宋藏遺珍), and *Hongwu Southern Canon* (*Hongwu nanzang* 洪武南藏).[10]

THE THIRD PERIOD: DIGITIZATION OF HANDWRITTEN MANUSCRIPTS AND RARE TEXTS

After the digitization of Yan's work, CBETA started a project in collaboration with the National Library in Taiwan in 2010, entitled "Research on the Digitization of Rare Editions of Ancient Books in Taiwan: With a Focus on Rare Buddhist Texts in the Taiwan National Library." This new collaborative project, lasting two years, aimed at upgrading the current collection of rare Buddhist texts in the National Library, both handwritten and block-printed, to digital format by transforming microfilms into digital image files, digitizing full texts, and allowing network access.[11] We hope this project provides the public with access to rare materials in the National Library and enriches the content of the *Chinese Electronic Tripitaka Collection*.

With Dunhuang manuscripts in our digitized collection of handwritten texts, we adopted methods different from those used by European scholars, which only scanned texts into images. In addition to scanning the master copies, our collection allows copying and pasting the textual content and quoting directly from the texts, so that researchers can edit and compose their own works.

THE ACHIEVEMENT OF *CHINESE ELECTRONIC TRIPITAKA COLLECTION*

In this section, discussing the achievements of CBETA in recent years, I will provide substantial details about three aspects of our projects: the guiding principles of collecting, features of the digital content, and the qualitative achievement of our input.

GUIDING PRINCIPLES OF CONTENT COLLECTION

Although Buddhist communities across the Taiwan Strait have made every effort to compile *Chinese Tripitaka* (*Zhonghua Dazangjing* 中華大藏經), which is supposed to be the most complete edition of the Buddhist canon, there are still missing titles and drawbacks. In contrast, a digital Buddhist archive in the information age can present numerous Buddhist texts in new ways unlike their original format and provide unique functions. Therefore, CBETA's guiding principles of content collection are to rectify the deficiencies of cataloging and collation in both the Taiwan edition and the Beijing edition of *Chinese Tripitaka*, and in other paper-based canons, by integrating all catalogs of Buddhist texts, and to construct the most complete digital collection of Buddhist texts including all editions and their contents.

The general principle of content collection is to supplement all the missing titles that the previous collection did not include and to delete those duplicated titles that had been digitized in our previous collection. The process starts with the titles that are easier to digitize. As long as they are included, they will be digitized first. For example, we first digitized *Taishō Canon* and *Manji Continued Canon*. Then when we start to work on *Jiaxing Canon*, we only digitized those titles that were not collected in the first two canons. Following this principle, we will digitize other editions, such as *Zhaocheng Canon* and *Tripitaka Koreana*, to gradually supplement the previous collection. All these supplemental titles collected later are referred to as *Supplementary Tripitaka Collection* (*Lidai zangjing buji*).

FEATURES OF DIGITAL CONTENT

TEI INTERNATIONAL STANDARD

CBETA has adopted the TEI (Text Encoding and Interchange) International Standard as its norm of digitization. TEI is an open-source tag set collectively developed for electronic texts of all languages in any historical period. Users can set up tags by encoding text in XML (Extensible Markup Language), which is useful as a standard to exchange and share information and can preserve the generated digital text for a long time.[12] Using this international tag standard makes it convenient to share the digital Buddhist canon made by CBETA all over the world. After the text is tagged and grammar is checked, digital texts can be exported and saved as HTML files. When supplied with proper style sheets, their content and form can be presented on the web.

XML — EXTENSIBLE MARKUP LANGUAGE

XML is very helpful in managing digital documents because it can process all kinds of programming languages and incorporate all information with abundant tags and markup. For the Tripitaka, if we only digitize the main body of the texts, precious data such as title, time of creation, author and translator's names, and textual collation will be lost. Therefore, CBETA's digitization projects adopt XML to preserve those data for future academic studies.

One of the landmarks of CBETA's digitization projects is the publication of an XML edition. All the data are examined carefully and updated according to the latest TEI version in order to make every single character conform with international open-source standards, so that the documents can be exchanged easily and can be managed by all the tools that meet the XML standard. I hope XML publication can contribute to the future markup standard of Buddhist texts and to the creation of an international Chinese Buddhist canon database for public access and academic research.

QUALITATIVE ACHIEVEMENT OF DIGITIZED TEXTS

Since its founding in 1998, in addition to increasing the quantity of texts in the *Chinese Electronic Tripitaka Collection*, CBETA has made every effort to improve the quality of its content, including Chinese character modification and the adoption of new punctuation marks.

With Chinese characters used in various editions, CBETA modified 204,525 characters through comparing the digital texts of *Taishō Canon* and *Tripitaka Koreana* and adopting readers' feedback.[13] In order to improve the punctuation and paragraph division of ancient texts, CBETA began to process texts using new punctuation marks in 2006. By the end of 2010, 522 texts in 2,203 fascicles had been added with new punctuation marks.[14] CEBTA continues to pay attention to both quantity and quality.

QUANTITATIVE INCREASE

These are the digital products made from 1998 to 2010:[15]

1998–2003: *Taishō Canon*, 2,373 titles in 8,982 fascicles
2004–2007: *Manji Continued Canon*, 1,229 titles in 5,060 fascicles
2008–2010: itemized data of newly digitized content:
 Jiaxing Canon 285 titles, 1,659 fascicles
 Collection of Buddhist Sources in Dynastic Histories 1 title, 10 fascicles
 Buddhist Literature Outside the Canon 77 titles, 136 fascicles
 Hundred Rubbings of Buddhist Stone Inscriptions of the Northern Dynasty 1 title, 100 fascicles
 Supplementary Tripitaka Collection 100 titles, 972 fascicles
 Total 464 titles, 2,877 fascicles

TEXTUAL MODIFICATION

When readers read the same text in different editions of the canon, they can usually identify that in each edition different characters have been used for the same paragraph or sentence. Do we consider these characters wrong? Because the master copies on which different editions of the canon are based were different, discrepancies and mistakes during transcription and printing of the master copies would be kept in different editions and even further spread down to the present time. In addition, although some master copies might be superior in quality and their collation and proofreading were excellent, mistakes and omissions are inevitable in the complicated process of compilation. Since the Chinese language and vocabulary have been evolving dynamically in different historical periods and regions, we need to scrutinize every case when we come across a Chinese character that appears unfamiliar in order to make the right judgment.[16]

In modifying the use of Chinese characters, CBETA respects the integrity of the master copies we chose and the variation of Chinese characters used in different editions. On this premise, we follow the principle of "Three Don'ts" and "Three Dos" as explained in the following.

THE PRINCIPLE OF THREE DON'TS:

- Don't change interchangeable characters that are generally accepted in usage, including variant forms of a Chinese character, old and new characters, and similar characters.
- Don't change characters that do not affect the meaning of the text, even if different characters were used in different editions.
- Don't change the characters when there is not enough evidence. For example, the digital texts and *dharani* spells input by CBETA are based on *Taishō Canon*. The texts and spells had been collated before, with collation results published in book format, indicating that Dunhuang manuscripts, for example, were used as the master copy. We will only revise the text if we see the original texts based on which *Taishō Canon* was compiled or identify the missing texts and spells, or if we have enough evidence.

THE PRINCIPLE OF THREE DOS:

- Do change the mistakes that are not in accord with the master copies and were made during data input.

- Do change the characters that are clearly erroneously used in context. For example, we modify the characters wrongly printed in books such as *Manji Continued Canon*. However, CBETA still preserves the original characters. When using the CBETA CD version, readers can choose to read a given text as it appeared before or after the modification, or show the two versions of the text at the same time.
- Do change if a better version is found. For example, depending on the context, we will modify the text by consulting different versions such as the Ming edition and manuscript edition preserved in the Japanese Shōgozō 聖語藏 collection (handwritten Buddhist manuscripts collection in Shōsō-in 正倉院) listed in *Taishō Canon*'s collation results.

We have tried our best to follow these principles, which are based on rigorous evidential scholarship. Since CBETA's online forum is open to the public, feedback from readers is also helpful for textual revision. Compared with the traditional paperback editions, the electronic canon is much easier to revise. Therefore, CBETA's *Chinese Electronic Tripitaka Collection* not only expands in quantity but also pursues perfection in quality, which is the goal of textual revision.[17]

In addition to the continuous work of input, collation, and tagging, by comparing the electronic versions of *Taishō Canon* and *Tripitaka Koreana*, textual revision has also been carried out without interruption. Besides the revision of *Taishō Canon*, *Manji Continued Canon*, and *Jiaxing Canon*, revision of other texts in the collection is in progress. These results have been published in the CD version of the collection released in April 2011.

THE USE OF NEW PUNCTUATION MARKS

To facilitate reading for modern users, since 2006, CBETA has made further efforts to improve the quality of the collection by applying new punctuation marks to ancient texts and making new divisions of paragraphs. Our goals include[18] adding new punctuation marks in accordance with modern reading habits in order to make texts more readable; and allowing readers to change texts with new punctuation marks back into tradition-style texts and providing references for revising inappropriate punctuation in *Taishō Canon* and *Manji Continued Canon*.

In order to streamline the digitization process and standardize the format of our products, CBETA set up standards for the use of new punctuation marks in two documents: "Explanation of the Application of New Punctuation Marks to CBETA's Buddhist Texts" (CBETA jingwen xinshi biaodian shiwu zuoye shuoming CBETA 經文新式標點實務作業說明) and "Abbreviated Chart of

CBETA's New Punctuation" (CBETA jingwen xinshi biaodian fuhao luebiao CBETA 經文新式標點符號略表).[19]

THE EXTENDED APPLICATION OF THE TRIPITAKA CATALOGS PROJECT

The electronic collection of the Tripitaka is superior to the paper-based editions not only in quantity and quality but also in its advantage of providing retrieval functions for the convenience of readers and users. In addition, the content of the collection is not limited to one canon but incorporates various editions of the canon from all ages. To achieve the goal of building the most complete collection of Buddhist texts, we need to build a comprehensive catalog to manage all the texts. Therefore, we carried out the "cataloging project," which developed a complete catalog database of all editions and revised the catalogs of both editions of the *Chinese Tripitaka* published in mainland China and Taiwan.

BACKGROUND OF THE TRIPITAKA CATALOGS PROJECT

Because Buddhist texts were written in different languages and accepted scriptures are different in different cultures, these texts have been categorized in various cataloging systems without cross-references, even if some of the texts are identical in content. Therefore, it is very difficult to compare them and identify a text. For Buddhist scholars, a digital database that contains catalogs written in Chinese, Sanskrit, Pali, and Tibetan will be a convenient tool for studying Buddhist scriptures.

Therefore, with the help of the National Science Council in Taiwan, CBETA took three years (2005 to 2008) to complete a multilingual digital database of Tripitaka catalogs of multiple editions to provide readers with multiple functions and services, such as online retrieval, full-text links, and related information in time and space.[20]

CONTENT OF THE CATALOG DATABASE

This project integrates the catalogs of all editions of the canon, and other ancient catalogs of Buddhist texts in history. With the aid of modern information technology such as hypertext technique and Metadata and the XML and TEI markup standards, we constructed a knowledge management system of Buddhist canons as the basis of modernization and digitization of Buddhist texts.

We have finished the catalogs of the following 22 canons: *Fangshan Stone Canon (Fangshan shijing* 房山石經*)*, *Tripitaka Koreana (Gaolizang* 高麗藏*)*, *Yongle Northern Canon (Yongle beizang* 永樂北藏*)*, *Qing Canon (Qianlongzang* 乾隆藏*)*, *Manji Canon (Manji shūzō* 卍正藏*)*, *Taishō Canon (Taishōzō* 大正藏*)*, *Buddhist Tripitaka (Fojiaodazangjing* 佛教大藏經*)*, *Chinese Tripitaka (Zhonghuazang* 中華藏*)*, *New Complied Manji Canon (Shinsan Manji zokuzō* 新纂卍續藏*)*, *Kaibao Canon (Kaibaozang* 開寶藏*)*, *Chongning Canon (Chongningzang* 崇寧藏*)*, *Pilu Canon (Piluzang* 毘廬藏*)*, *Yuanjue Canon (Yuanjuezang* 圓覺藏*)*, *Zhaocheng Canon (Zhaochengjinzang* 趙城金藏*)*, *Zifu Canon (Zifuzang* 資福藏*)*, *Qisha Canon (Qishazang* 磧砂藏*)*, *Remaining Treasures from Song Canon (Songzangyizhen* 宋藏遺珍*)*, *Puning Canon (Puningzang* 普寧藏*)*, *Hongwu Southern Canon (Hongwu nanzang* 洪武南藏*)*, *Yongle Southern Canon (Yongle nanzang* 永樂南藏*)*, *Reduced Print Canon (Shukusatsuzō* 縮刻藏*)*, and *Jiaxing Canon (Jiaxingzang* 嘉興藏*)*.[21]

THREE STAGES OF CATALOG DIGITIZATION

Based on CBETA's digital collection, the digital database of Tripitaka catalogs also includes the catalogs of other canons and Buddhist texts that have not yet been planned for digitization by CBETA. There are three stages in this process:[22]

THE FIRST STAGE: CONSTRUCTION OF CHINESE TRIPITAKA CATALOGS

The goal of the first stage was to construct the database and complete the retrieval functions for catalogs written in Chinese. The main work was to collect all catalogs of the Chinese Buddhist canon, related reference books, and Buddhist materials contained in secular books, and convert paper-based texts into electronic form by manual inputting, scanning, digital conversion, and markup. Based on different cataloging systems, databases of each individual canon were established separately. Furthermore, the entries in these separate databases were linked with the corresponding full-text files and images with hyperlinks and functions such as content search and retrieval.

THE SECOND STAGE: CONSTRUCTION OF MULTILINGUAL TRIPITAKA CATALOGS

In the second stage, in addition to supplementing the database of Chinese Tripitaka catalogs, we constructed a database of catalogs written in other languages by following the order of Pali, Tibetan, and Sanskrit. Furthermore, we integrated these databases to make a cross-language database of Buddhist catalogs. Our multilingual retrieval system in Chinese, Sanskrit, Pali, Tibetan, and English is posted online with access to full-text online reading.

THE THIRD STAGE: PERFECTION OF THE DATABASE AND TECHNICAL INTEGRATION

The digital work in the third stage continued on the multilingual catalog system by adding the Manchu Tripitaka catalog database. To strengthen the integration between technology and content, based on the cross-language retrieval of keywords from the catalog database and the technical application of temporal and spatial information processing, we completely break through the functions of the traditional paper-based editions by creating a Buddhist electronic cultural atlas to link keywords, time and location of text production, and the canon.

CONCLUSION: THE SIGNIFICANCE OF CHINESE ELECTRONIC TRIPITAKA COLLECTION

This section introduces the goals and products of the *Chinese Electronic Tripitaka Collection* based on CBETA's digitization experiences and recent progress of Buddhist digital resources in Taiwan. I also explain the challenges and breakthroughs of integrating modern information-processing techniques when managing various versions of texts, and emphasize the service functions of contemporary digital Buddhist resources by focusing on the applications of our cataloging project. As a basic platform for integrating digital Buddhist resources in the world, the *Chinese Electronic Tripitaka Collection* is significant in several ways:

INTEGRATION OF BUDDHIST INFORMATION

At least two kinds of competence—Buddhist knowledge and information-management techniques—are needed for digitizing the Buddhist canon. In the process of digitizing Buddhist texts, we also developed the new academic discipline of contemporary Buddhist information technology to meet the technical demands of our time. Dharma Drum Buddhist College even offers courses on this subject and conducts related academic research.

PERSONNEL TRAINING

Because of the many new functions brought about by digitization, modern Buddhist studies requires certain information skills and knowledge in addition to traditional academic training. We have been trying to create new functions that will assist in reading and research and to provide an open environment for scholars to participate. Meanwhile, we have attempted to utilize our cross-disciplinary experiences to teach students. After many years, we have trained several new scholars and specialists in Buddhist information technology.

INNOVATION OF RESEARCH METHODS

In recent years, we have invented many digital tools for academic research based on new arrangements of Buddhist texts and integration of Buddhist resources. In the process, we realized that the methods of digital research are different from those of paper-based textual study. Therefore, our database not only gives new life to Buddhist texts but also provides new methods of digital research.

COLLABORATIVE CREATION OF INTELLECTUAL PROPERTY

The *Chinese Electronic Tripitaka Collection* is not a simple digitized collection of selected Buddhist texts. We have conducted intensive research on individual texts and compared different editions of the canon written in different languages. In our research, we also explored the "hidden information" behind each canon as a result of repeated compilation and collation throughout its history. Therefore, we aim to construct Buddhist lexicons and parallel corpora for efficient data mining, social networking, and visualization of GIS information through projects such as "Lexical Extraction from Buddhist Texts," "Statistical Lexical Extraction," "Multilingual Lexical Extraction," and "Cross-Language Text Matching."

With the advent of Web 2.0, further development of the *Chinese Electronic Tripitaka Collection* has to consider allowing users to participate in revising digital texts. However, to realize this goal, we need a mature mechanism with sufficient data. In the beginning, we may provide some specialists with the rights to revise our digital texts online. After we perfect this system, we will open our revisable resources to all the users and make it a fully open database that allows simultaneous user interaction, similar to the model of Wikipedia, in order to meet the demands of the new era. In sum, CBETA's work in these years has not only provided new opportunities for reading and studying Buddhist texts in the digital era but also deepened our exploration of these texts by developing new content.

NOTES

1. CBETA's digital resources can be divided into two parts: content and technology. Here I will not describe technical issues at length. For relevant information about technical development, visit CBETA's website at http://www.cbeta.org/tech/index .htm, or see Tu Aming, "Foxue yanjiu ziyuan shuweihua zuoye biaozhun yu guifan" and "Hanwen dianzi dazangjing de zhizuo yuanqi yu zuoye liucheng."

2. Fang Guangchang, *Zhongguo xieben dazangjing yanjiu*, 11–13. This part has been translated in English as "Defining the Chinese Buddhist Canon."

3. Although there are now several types of plate making, such as photocomposition, photographic print, and so on, the original printing method is metal typeset letterpress printing. Therefore, all these editions are referred to as metal-type printed editions.

4. For the TEI Standard and XML language, and relevant technical questions, please refer to http://www.cbeta.org/tech/develop.htm. Or Tu Aming, "Hanwen fodian dianzihua."

5. For details, see the project website: http://jinglu.cbeta.org/.

6. For documents about the history of CBETA in the first 10 years after its founding, see a special collection of papers for the celebration of CBETA's Tenth Anniversary at http://www.cbeta.org/data/cbeta10y/.

7. Up to that point, CBETA had finished the main content of the *Electronic Tripitaka Collection*, including *Supplementary Tripitaka Collection* (*Lidai zangjing buji* 歷代藏經補輯) and *New Series of Modern Texts* (*Jindai wenxian xinbian* 近代文獻新編).

8. Yan Juanying, *Beichao fojiao shike tapian baipin*.

9. For the content of digitized works and specific products of this collection in recent years, please see http://taipei.ddbc.edu.tw/finished.php.

10. For the master copies of the editions used for *Chinese Electronic Tripitaka Collection*, see http://www.cbeta.org/cd/index.php.

11. For a general list of the digitalized items, see http://goo.gl/SzchW.

12. Lou Burnard et al., eds., *TEI shiyong zhinan*, 9–13.

13. For the principle of modifying characters, see http://www.cbeta.org/forum/index/php?topic=31.0.

14. For the use of new punctuation marks, see http://www.cbeta.org/xb/index/htm.

15. These data are collected in CBETA's CD, published in April 2011. For a detailed list, see http://taipei.ddbc.edu.tw/finished.php. For products published before 2008, see http://www.cbeta.org/data/cbeta10y/cdhistory.htm.

16. See http://forum.cbeta.org/index.php?topic31.0.

17. I want to thank the Director-General of CBETA, Wu Baoyuan 吳寶源, for providing this piece of information.

18. For details, see http://www.cbeta.org/xb/content.htm.

19. For these two documents, see http://www.cbeta.org/xb/work.htm; http://www.cbeta.org/xb/table.htm.

20. For details of this project, see http://jinglu.cbeta.org/.

21. For the documents to which the database refers, see http://jinglu.cbeta.org/knowledge/interrelated.htm.

22. For an explanation of the three stages in Chinese, see Tu Aming, "Foxue shuwei ziyuan de fuwu gongneng."

BIBLIOGRAPHY

Adamek, Wendi. *The Mystique of Transmission: On an Early Chan History and Its Contexts*. New York: Columbia University Press, 2007.

Akanuma, Chizen 赤沼智善. *The Comparative Catalogue of Chinese Āgamas & Pāli Nikāyas*. Nagoya: Hajinkaku-shobō, 1929.

Allon, Mark (with a contribution by Andrew Glass). *Three Gāndhārī Ekottarikāgama-Type Sūtras: British Library Kharoṣṭhī Fragments 12 and 14*. Gandhāran Buddhist Texts, Volume 2. Seattle and London: University of Washington Press, 2001.

An, Kai-hyon. "Publication of Buddhist Scriptures in the Koryo Period." *Buddhist Culture in Korea*, ed. International Cultural Foundation, 80–95. Seoul: The Si-sa-yong-o-sa Publishers, Inc., 1982.

Asahi Shinbun 朝日新聞. "Bunka Kunshō" 文化勲章. April 30, 1944, 1.

——. "Takakusu Junjirō no Asahi Shō" 高楠順次郎の朝日章. Jan. 25, 1933, 1.

Baba, Hisayuki 馬場久幸. "Kōraibandaizōkyōtozōkyōdōjō" 高麗版大蔵経と蔵経道場. *Indogaku Bukkyōgaku kenkyū* 57, no. 2 (2009): 24–28 (1119–1115).

Bai, Huawen 白化文. "Dunhuang xieben *Zhongjing bielu* canjuan jiaoshi" 敦煌寫本眾經別錄殘卷校釋. *Dunhuangxue jikan* 敦煌學輯刊 1 (1987): 14–25.

——. "'Jingzang nei,' 'Cangjing ge,' yu 'Tiangong baozang.'" "經藏內," "藏經閣," 與"天宮寶藏." In Bai Huawen, *Fojiao tushu fenlei fa* 佛教圖書分類法, 45–54. Beijing: Beijing tushu guang chubanshe, 2001.

——. "Xinxi shidai de zangjing gongyang yu neiwaidian xuexi" 信息時代的藏經供養與內外典學習. In Bai Huawen, *Fojiao tushu fenlei fa* 佛教圖書分類法, 55–64. Beijing: Beijing tushu guang chubanshe, 2001.

Bai, Juyi 白居易. *Bai Juyi ji* 白居易集. Beijing: Zhonghua shuju, 1979.

Baizhang qinggui zhengyi ji 百丈清規證義集. Z 1244, vol. 63.

Bak, Changhi 朴菖熙. "Ri Gyubo no shūkan to sono shakai ishiki" 李奎報の就官とその社会意識. *Hitotsubashi ronsō* 一橋論叢 57, no. 6 (1967): 785–90.

——. "Saishi seiken to kanryōsō: Saishi seikenka no Ri Gyubo no arikata ni yosete" 崔氏政權と官僚層: 崔氏政權下の李奎報の在り方によせて. *Hitotsubashi ronsō* 一橋論叢 53, no. 1 (1965): 124–27.

Bao, Zhicheng 鮑志成. *Gaolisi yu Gaoli wangzi* 高麗寺與高麗王子. Hangzhou: Hangzhou daxue chubanshe, 1998.

Barrett, Timothy H. "Daoism and the Origins of State Printing: Du Guangting 杜光庭 and the Guang shengyi 廣聖義." In Barrett, *From Religious Ideology to Political Expediency in Early Printing*, 88–115.

——. *From Religious Ideology to Political Expediency in Early Printing: An Aspect of Buddho-Daoist Rivalry*. Watford, UK: Minnow Press, 2012.

——. "The Rise and Spread of Printing: A New Account of Religious Factors." SOAS Working Papers in the Study of Religions. London, 2001.

——. "Stūpa, Sūtra and Sarīra in China, c. 656–706 C.E." *Buddhist Studies Review* 18, no. 1 (2001): 1–64.

——. *The Woman Who Discovered Printing*. New Haven: Yale University Press, 2008.

Beijing tushuguan, ed. *Zhongguo banke tulu* 中國版刻圖錄. 8 vols. 2nd ed. Beijing: Wenwu chubanshe, 1961.

Belard, Regina. "The May 1st Sutra: Conservation of a Nara-period Handscroll." *Journal of the Institute of Conservation* 33, no. 1 (March 2010): 93–109.

Benn, James A. *Burning for the Buddha: Self-immolation in Chinese Buddhism*. Honolulu: University of Hawai'i Press, 2007.

Bickford, Maggie. "Making the Chinese Cultural Heritage at the Courts of Northern Sung China." In *Kaichuang dianfan: Bei Song de yishu yu wenhua yantaohui lunwen ji* 開創典範: 北宋的藝術與文化研討會論文集, ed. Wang Yaoting 王耀庭, 499–535. Taibei: Guoli Gugong bowuyuan, 2008.

Bingenheimer, Marcus. "Collation Strategies for the Buddhist Canon as Seen in the Frequency and Impact of Character Variance in Canonical Editions of the *Song Gaoseng Zhuan* 宋高僧傳 (T. 2061)." *Journal of East Asian Publishing and Society* 4, no. 2 (2014): 1–16.

——. "A Translation of the *Tōdaiwajō tōseiden* 唐大和上東征傳" (Part 1) [Rev. PDF edition (ver. 1)]. *The Indian International Journal of Buddhist Studies* 4 (2003): 168–89.

Blackwell Companion to East and Inner Asian Buddhism. Ed. Mario Poceski. Oxford: Blackwell, 2014.

Borgen, Robert. "Jōjin's Discoveries in Song China." In *Tools of Culture: Japan's Cultural, Intellectual, Medical and Technological Contact in East Asia, 1000–1500s*, ed. Andrew Edmund Goble, Kenneth R. Robinson, and Haruko Wakabayashi, 25–48. Ann Arbor: Association for Asian Studies, 2009.

——. "Jōjin's Travels from Center to Center." In *Heian Japan, Centers and Peripheries*, ed. Mikael Adolphson, Edward Kamens, and Stacie Matsumoto, 384–413. Honolulu: University of Hawai'i Press, 2007.

Bosch, Van Den Lourens. *Friedrich Max Müller: A Devoted Life to the Humanities*. Leiden; Boston: Brill, 2002.

Boucher, Daniel. "Dharmarakṣa." In *Encyclopedia of Buddhism*, ed. Robert E, Buswell, Jr., 225–26. Indianapolis: Macmillan Reference USA, 2003.

——. "Gandhari and the Early Chinese Buddhist Translations Reconsidered: The Case of the Saddharmapuṇḍarīca-sūtra." *Journal of the American Oriental Society* 118, no. 4 (1998): 471–506.

Bowring, Richard. "Brief Note: Buddhist Translations in the Northern Sung." *Asia Major*, 3rd series, 5, no. 2 (1992): 79–93.

Breuker, Remco E. "Contested Objectivities: Ikeuchi Hiroshi, Kim Sanggi and the Tradition of Oriental Historiography (Tōyōshigaku) in Japan and Korea." *East Asian History* 29 (2005): 69–106.

——. "The Emperor's Clothes? Koryŏ as an Independent Realm." *Korean Studies* 27 (2004): 48–84.

——. *Establishing a Pluralist Society in Medieval Korea, 918–1170: History, Ideology, and Identity in the Koryo Dynasty*. Leiden: Brill, 2010.

Brokaw, Cynthia Joanne. "Book History in Premodern China: The State of the Discipline I." *Book History* 10 (2007): 253–90.

——. "On the History of the Book in China." In *Printing and Book Culture in Late Imperial China*, ed. Cynthia J. Brokaw and Kai-wing Chow, 3–54. Berkeley and Los Angeles: University of California Press, 2005.

Brose, Benjamin. "Buddhist Empires: Saṃgha-State Relations in Tenth-Century China." Ph.D. diss., Stanford University, 2009.

——. "Crossing Thousands of *Li* of Waves: The Return of China's Lost Tiantai Texts." *Journal of the International Association of Buddhist Studies* 29, no. 1 (2006): 21–62.

Broughton, Jeff. "Tsung-mi's Zen Prolegomenon: Introduction to an Exemplary Zen Canon." In *The Zen Canon: Understanding the Classic Texts*, ed. Steven Heine and Dale S. Wright, 11–52. New York: Oxford University Press, 2004.

——. *Zongmi on Chan*. New York: Columbia University Press, 2009.

Bulgyeong: Goryeo Daejanggyeong 佛經: 高麗大藏經. Vols. I and II. Ed. Hanguk Bulgyohak yeongu chongseo. Gyeonggido Goyangsi: Bulham Munhwasa, 2004.

Bulgyo Bangsong, ed. *Namhae bunsa dogam gwallyeon gicho josa bogoseo* 南海分司都監關聯基礎調查報告書. Namhae: Bulgyo Bangsong Haksul Josadan Namhae-gun, 1994.

Bumbacher, Stephan Peter. *Empowered Writing: Exorcistic and Apotropaic Rituals in Medieval China*. St. Petersburg, FL: Three Pines Press, 2012.

Burnouf, Eugène. *Introduction a l'histoire du buddhisme indien*. Vol. 1. Paris: Imprimerie Royale, 1844. Translated into English by Katia Buffertrille and Donald S. Lopez Jr. Chicago: University of Chicago Press, 2010.

Bussotti, Michela. "General Survey of the Latest Studies in Western Languages on the History of Publishing in China." *Revue Bibliographique de Sinologie* XVI (1998): 53–68.

Buswell, Robert E. "Sugi's Collation Notes to the Koryŏ Buddhist Canon and Their Significance for Buddhist Textual Criticism." *Journal of Korean Studies* 9, no. 1 (Fall 2004): 129–84.

Buxu gaoseng zhuan 補續高僧傳, Z 77, no. 1524.

Campany, Robert. "Notes on the Devotional Uses and Symbolic Functions of Sutra Texts as Depicted in Early Chinese Buddhist Miracle Tales and Hagiographies." *Journal of the International Association of Buddhist Studies* 14, no. 1 (1991): 44–46.

Canonization and Decanonization. Ed. Arie van der Kooij et al. Leiden; Boston: Brill, 1998.

Cao, Ganghua 曹剛華. "Dazangjing zai liangsong minjian shehui de liuchuan" 大藏經在兩宋民間社會的流傳. *Shehui kexue* 社會科學 10 (2006): 169–77.

——. *Songdai fojiao shiji yanjiu* 宋代佛教史籍研究. Shanghai: Huadong shifan daxue chubanshe, 2006.

Cao, Shibang (Tso Sze-bong) 曹仕邦. *Zhongguo Fojiao yijing shi lunji* 中國佛教譯經史論集. Taibei: Dongchu chubanshe, 1990.

Carter, T. F. *The Invention of Printing in China and Its Spread Westward*. 2nd ed., rev. L. C. Goodrich. New York: Ronald Press, 1955.

Cefu yuangui: jiaoding ben 冊府元龟:校訂本. 11th c. Comp. Wang Ruoqin 王欽若 et al. 12 vols. Hong Kong: Fenghuang chubanshe, 2006.

Chae, Sangsik 蔡尙植. "Ganghwa Seonwonsa ui wichi ye daehan jaegeomto" 江華禪源寺의 위치에 대한 재검토. *Hanguk Minjok Munhwa* 34 (July 2009): 135–70.

Changzhou xianzhi, Longqing 長洲縣志, 隆慶. Huangfu Fang 皇甫汸 et al., comps. *Tianyige Mingdai fangzhi xuankan xubian*, 23. 1571; reprint, Shanghai: Shanghai guji shudian, 1990.

Chanlin beiyong qinggui 禪林備用清規. Z 1250, vol. 63.

Chen, Dezhi 陳得芝. "Cong Yiheimishi shenfen kan Make Boluo: *Yibai dasi kanjing ji bei jiedu*" 從亦黑迷失身份看馬可波羅: 一百大寺看經記碑解讀. *Yanjing xuebao* 燕京學報 26 (2009): 39–54.

Chen, Jidong (Chin Keitō) 陳継東. *Shinmatsu Bukkyō to Kenkyū: Yō Bunkai o chūshin to shite* 清末仏教の研究: 楊文会を中心として. Tokyo: Sankibō Busshorin, 2003.

Chen, Jinhua. "Buddhist Establishments Within Liang Wudi's Imperial Park." In *Development and Practice of Humanitarian Buddhism: Interdiciplinary Perspective*, ed. Jinhua Chen and Lori Meeks, 13–29. Tainan: Tzu Chi University Press, 2007.

——. "A Daoist Princess and a Buddhist Temple: A New Theory on the Causes of the Canon-delivering Mission Originally Proposed by Princess Jinxian (689–732) in 730." *Bulletin of the School of Oriental and African Studies* 69, no. 2 (2006): 267–92.

——. "Śarīra and Scepter: Empress Wu's Political Use of Buddhist Relics." *Journal of the International Association of Buddhist Studies* 25, no. 1–2 (2002): 33–150.

——. "Some Aspects of the Buddhist Translation Procedure in Early Medieval China: With Special Reference to a Longstanding Misreading of a Keyword in the Earliest Extant Buddhist Catalogue in East Asia." *Journal Asiatique* 283, no. 2 (2005): 603–62.

Ch'en, Kenneth. *Buddhism in China*. Princeton: Princeton University Press, 1964.

——. *Chinese Buddhism: A Historical Survey*. Princeton: Princeton University Press, 1965.

——. "Notes on the Sung and Yuan Tripitaka." *Harvard Journal of Asiatic Studies* 14, no. 1/2 (June 1951): 208–14.

Chen, Xinrong 陳心蓉. *Jiaxing cangshu shi* 嘉興藏書史. Beijing: Guojia tushuguan chubanshe, 2010.

Chen, Yinke 陳寅恪. *Jinming guan conggao chubian: Chen Yinke wenji* 金明館叢稿初編: 陳寅恪文集 (vol. 2). Beijing: Sanlian shudian, 2001.

Chen, Yuan 陳垣. *Zhongguo Fojiao shiji gailun* 中國佛教史籍概論. Shanghai: Shanghai shudian, 2001.

Chen, Yunü 陳玉女. *Mingdai fomen neiwai sengsu jiaoshe de changyu* 明代佛門內外僧俗交涉的場域. Taipei: Daoxiang chubanshe, 2010.

Chen, Yuquan 陈昱全. "Bei Song 'Yuzhi Mizangquan' banhua yanjiu" 北宋御製秘藏詮版畫研究. M.A. thesis, Taiwan Shifan daxue, 2009.

Cheon, Hyebong 千惠鳳. "Chojo Daejanggyeong ui Hyeonjonbon gwa geu Teukseong 初雕大藏경의現存本과그特性." *Daedong Munhwa Yeongu* 大東文化研究 11 (1976): 167–221.

——. *Horim Bangmulgwan sojang chojo Daejanggyeong josa yeongu* 湖林博物館所藏初雕大藏經調查研究. Seoul: Seoongbo Munhwa Jaedan, 1988.

——. *Raryeo inswaesul ui yeongu* 羅麗印刷術의研究. Seoul: Gyeongin Munhwasa, 1982.

Chia, Lucille. *Printing for Profit: The Commercial Publishers of Jianyang, Fujian (11th–17th Centuries)*. Cambridge, MA: Harvard University Asia Center, 2002.

——. "Publishing Activities of Buddhist Monasteries and Sutra Printshops (*Jingfang* 經房/經坊)." Paper presented at WACAS annual meeting, Tucson, AZ, October 2009.

——. "The Uses of Print in Early Quanzhen Daoist Texts." In *Knowledge and Text Production in an Age of Print: China, 900–1400*, ed. Lucille Chia and Hilde De Weerdt, 167–213. Leiden: Brill, 2011.

Chia, Lucille and Hilde De Weerdt, eds. *Knowledge and Text Production in an Age of Print: China, 900–1400*. Leiden: Brill, 2011.

Chikusa Masaaki 竺沙雅章. "Sō Gen ban Daizōkyō no keifu" 宋元版大藏經の系譜. In *Sō Gen Bukkyō bunkashi kenkyū* 宋元佛教文化史研究, 271–362. Tokyo: Kyūko Shoin, 2000.

——. *Sō Gen Bukkyō bunkashi kenkyū* 宋元佛教文化史研究. Tokyo: Kyūko Shoin, 2000.

Choi, Youngsook 崔榮淑. "Yongmunsa Yunjangdae yeongu" 龍門寺輪藏臺研究. *Misulsa yeongu* 미술사연구 (美術史研究) 21 (2007): 267–94.

Chu Sanzang jiji 出三藏記集, compiled by Sengyou 僧祐. T 2145, vol. 55.

Ciyi 慈怡, ed. *Foguang dacidian* 佛光大辭典. Beijing: Zhongguo shumu wenxian chubanshe, 1993.

Clart, Philip and Gregory Adam Scott, eds. *Religious Publishing and Print Culture in Modern China: 1800–2012*. Boston: De Gruyter, 2015.

Collcutt, Martin. "Buddhism: The Threat of Eradication." In *Japan in Transition*, ed. Marius Jansen and Gilbert Rozman, 143–67. Princeton: Princeton University Press, 1986.

Collins, Steven. "On the Very Idea of the Pali Canon." *Journal of the Pali Text Society* XV (1990): 89–126.

Corless, Roger. "The Meaning of Ching (Sutra?) in Buddhist Chinese." *Journal of Chinese Philosophy* 3, no. 1 (1975): 67–72.

Courant, Maurice. *Bibliographie coréenne*. 1896; reprint, New York: B. Franklin, 1966.

Cousins, Lance. "Pali Oral Literature." In *Buddhist Studies, Ancient and Modern* (Collected Papers on South Asia, 4), ed. P. Denwood, 1–11. London: Curzon, 1983.

Dai, Lianbin. "The Economics of the Jiaxing Edition of the Buddhist Tripiṭaka." *T'oung Pao* 94, no. 4–5 (2008): 306–59.

Daizōkyō: seiritsu to hensen 大蔵経: 成立と変遷. Ed. Daizōkai. 1964; reprint, Kyōto: Hyakkaen, 1990.

Dang, Baohai 黨寶海. "Shanxi Xixian Qianfo an Ming-Qing fodian yu baojuan" 山西隰縣千佛庵明清佛典與寶卷. *Wenxian* 文獻 2 (2001): 114–32.

Daoan 道安. *Zhongguo dazangjing diaoke shihua* 中國大藏經彫刻史話. Taibei: Lushan chubanshe, 1978.

Daoxuan 道宣. *Da Tang neidian lu* 大唐內典錄. T 2149, vol. 55.

Davidson, Ronald M. "An Introduction to the Standards of Scriptural Authenticity in Indian Buddhism." In *Chinese Buddhist Apocrypha*, ed. Robert E. Buswell, 291–325. Honolulu: University of Hawai'i Press, 1990.

Dazangjing de chengli yu bianqian 大藏經的成立與變遷. Ed. Lan Jifu. Taibei: Huayu chubanshe, 1984.

Dazang zongjing mulu 大藏總經目錄. 1888 woodblock edition. 1998 reprint. Fang Guangchang personal collection.

de Pee, Christian. "Purchase on Power: Imperial Space and Commercial Space in Song-Dynasty Kaifeng, 960–1127." *Journal of the Economic and Social History of the Orient* 53, no. 1/2 (2010): 149–84.

Demiéville, Paul. 1953. "Le bouddhisme—Les sources chinoises." In *L'Inde classique—Manuel des études indiennes*, ed. Louis Renou and Jean Filliozat, 398–463. 1953; reprint, Paris: École française d'Extreme-Oriênt, 2000.

——. "Notes additionnelles sur les editions imprimées du canon bouddhique." Appendix to Paul Pelliot, *Les Débuts de l'Imprimerie en Chine*, 121–38. Paris: Imprimerie Nationale Librairie d'Amérique et d'Orient, 1953.

——. "Sur les éditions imprimées du canon chinois." Appendix to Paul Pelliot, "Les versions chinoises du Milindapañha," *Bulletin de l'Ecole française d'Extrême-Orient* 24 (1924): 190–207.

Devine, Richard. "Hirata Atsutane and Christian Sources." *Monumenta Nipponica* 36, no. 1 (1981): 37–54.

Drège, Jean-Pierre. *Les bibliothèque en Chine au temps des manuscrits (jusqu'au Xe siècle)*. Paris: EFEO, 1991.

——. "La lecture et l'écriture en Chine et la xylographie." In *Études chinoises* 10, no. 1–2 (1991): 77–111.

Dunnell, Ruth W. *The Great State of White and High: Buddhism and State Formation in Eleventh-Century Xia*. Honolulu: University of Hawai'i Press, 1996.

Durt, Hubert. "The Difference Between Hīnayāna and Mahāyāna in the Last Chapter, 'Parīndanā,' of the Ta-chih-tu lun (Mahāprajñāpāramitopadeśa)." *Buddhist Studies Review* 5, no. 2 (1988): 123–38.

Ebrey, Patricia B. *Accumulating Culture: The Collections of Emperor Huizong*. Seattle: University of Washington Press, 2008.

Edgerton, Franklin. *Buddhist Hybrid Sanskrit Grammar and Dictionary*. New Haven: Yale University Press, 1953.

Edgren, Sören. "Southern Song Printing at Hangzhou." *Bulletin of the Museum of Far Eastern Antiquities* 62 (1989): 1–212.

Edgren, Sören, Tsien Tsuen-hsuin, Wang Fang-Yu, and Wan-go H. C. Weng. *Chinese Rare Books in American Collections*. New York: China Institute in America, 1984.

Egami, Yasushi 江上綏 and Kobayashi Hiromitsu 小林宏光. *Nanzenji shozō "Hizōsen" no mokuhanga* 南禅寺所蔵秘蔵詮の木版画. Tokyo: Yamakawa shuppansha, 1994.

Eliot, Simon and Jonathan Rose, eds. *A Companion to the History of the Book*. Oxford: Blackwell, 2007.

Encyclopedia of Buddhism. Ed. Robert E. Buswell, Jr. Indianapolis: Macmillan Reference USA, 2003.

Encyclopedia of Shinto, Ver. 1.3. Kokugakuin University, http://eos.kokugakuin.ac.jp.

Enomoto, Fumio. "On the Formation of the Original Texts of the Chinese Āgamas." *Buddhist Studies Review* 3, no. 1 (1986): 19–30.

Eubanks, Charlotte. *Miracles of Books and Body: Buddhist Textual Culture and Medieval Japan*. Berkeley: University of California Press, 2011.

Evon, Gregory Nicholas. "Dialogues with God and Stone: Self-representation and Eccentricity in the Writings of Yi Kyubo (1168–1241)." KAREC discussion papers 6, no. 1 (2005): 1–48.

Fahua xianying lu 法華經顯應錄. Z 1540, vol. 78.

Fang, Guangchang 方廣錩. *Daoan pingzhuan* 道安評傳. Beijing: Kunlun chuban-she, 2004.

——. "Dazheng xinxiu dazangjing pingshu" 大正新修大藏經評述. In his *Suiyuan quzuo Zhidao xingzhi: Fang Guangchang xuba zawen ji*, 65–78. Beijing: Guojia Tushuguan, 2011.

——. "Defining the Chinese Buddhist Canon: Its Origin, Periodization, and Future." Trans. Xin Zi and Jiang Wu. *Journal of Chinese Buddhist Studies* 28 (2015): 1–34.

——. *Dunhuang Fojiao jinglu jijiao* 敦煌佛教經錄輯挍. Nanjing: Jiangsu gu ji chu ban she, 1997.

——. *Fang Guangchang Dunhuang yishu sanlun* 方廣錩敦煌遺書散论. Shanghai: Shanghai guji chubanshe, 2010.

——. *Fojiao dazangjing shi: Ba zhi Shi shiji* 佛教大藏经史: 八—十世纪. Beijing: Zhongguo shehui kexue chubanshe, 1991.

——. *Fojiao zhi* 佛教志. Shanghai: Shanghai renmin chubanshe, 1998.

——. "Guanyu Dunhuang yishu 'Foshuo Foming jing'" 關於敦煌遺書佛說佛名經. In *Dunhuang Tulufan yanjiu lunwen ji* 敦煌吐魯番學研究論文集, 470–89. Beijing: Hanyu dacidian chubanshe, 1990. Reprint in Fang Guangchang, *Dunhuangxue Fo-jiaoxue luncong* 敦煌學佛教學論叢, vol. 2, 125–153. Hongkong: Zhongguo Fojiao wenhua chubanyouxiangongsi, 1998.

——. "A Personal View of the Reasons for the Closure of the Buddhist Scriptures Cave at Dunhuang." *Social Sciences in China (English Edition)* 中國社會科學英文版 (Autumn 1994): 85–93.

——. "Sanshiqi pin jing" 三十七品經. *Zangwai fojiao wenxian* 藏外佛教文獻, vol. 14, ed. Fang Guangchang, 163–82. Beijing: Zhongguo Renmin daxue chubanshe, 2010.

——. *Suiyuan quzuo, zhidao xingzhi: Fang Guangchang xuba zawen ji* 隨緣去做 直道 行之: 方廣錩序跋雜文集. Beijing: Guangjia tushuguan chubanshe, 2011.

——. *Zhongguo xieben dazangjing* 中國寫本大藏經研究. Shanghai: Shanghai guji chubanshe, 2006.

Farmer, Edward L. *Early Ming Government: The Evolution of Dual Capitals*. Cambridge, MA: Harvard University Press, 1976.

Faure, Bernard. "Ch'an Master Musang: A Korean Monk in East Asian Context." In *Currents and Countercurrents: Korean Influences on the East Asian Buddhist Traditions*, ed. Robert Buswell, 153–72. Honolulu: University of Hawai'i Press, 2005.

Fei, Changfang 費長房. *Lidai sanbao ji* 歷代三寶紀. T 2034, vol. 49.

Fei, Gun 費袞. *Liangxi manzhi* 梁谿漫志. 1192. Shanghai: Shanghai guji chubanshe, 1985.

Feng, Jiasheng 馮家昇. "Keben Huihu wen *Foshuo tiandi bayang shenzoujing yan-jiu*—jian lun Huihu ren duiyu Dazangjing de gongxian" 刻本回鶻文佛說天地 八陽神咒經研究—兼論回鶻人對于大藏經的貢獻. *Kaogu xuebao* 考古學報 1 (1955): 183–92.

Feng, Jiren. *Chinese Architecture and Metaphor: Song Culture in the Yingzao fashi Building Manual*. Honolulu: University of Hawai'i Press, 2012.

Finkelstein, David and Alistair McCleery. *The Book History Reader*. 2nd ed. London and New York: Routledge, 2006.

Fojiao wenxian liuzhen 佛教文獻留真. Ed. Li Jining and Chen Hongyan 陳紅彥. Beijing: Zhongguo guji baohu zhongxi, 2010.

Forte, Antonino. *A Jewel in Indra's Net: The Letter Sent by Fazang in China to Uisang in Korea*. Kyoto: Scuola Italiana di Studi sull'Asia Orientale, 2000.

——. *Political Propaganda and Ideology in China at the End of the Seventh Century*. Napoli: Istituto universitario orientale, Seminario di studi asiatici, 1976.

——. "The Relativity of the Concept of Orthodoxy in Chinese Buddhism: Chih-sheng's Indictment of Shih-li and the Proscription of the *Dharma Mirror Sutra*." In *Chinese Buddhist Apocrypha*, ed. Robert E. Buswell, Jr., 239–50. Honolulu: University of Hawai'i Press, 1990.

Foulk, T. Griffith. "Myth, Ritual, and Monastic Practice in Sung Ch'an Buddhism." In *Religion and Society in T'ang and Sung China*, ed. Patricia Ebrey and Peter Gregory, 147–208. Honolulu: University of Hawai'i Press, 1993.

Foyuan 佛源 and Chuanzheng 傳正. *Xinxiu Caoxi tongzhi* 新修曹溪通志. Beijing: Zongjiao wenhua chubanshe, 2000.

Fozu tongji 佛祖統紀. *T* 2035, vol. 49.

Franke, Herbert. "Sha-lo-pa (1259–1314): A Tangut Buddhist Monk in Yuan China." In *Religion und Philosophie in Ostasien: Festschrift für Hans Steininger zum 65. Geburtstag*, ed. Gert Naundorf, Karl-Heinz Pohl, and Hans-Hermann Schmidt, 201–22. Würzburg: Köningshausen & Neumann, 1985.

——. "Tibetans in Yüan China." In *China Under Mongol Rule*, ed. John D. Langlois, Jr., 296–328. Princeton: Princeton University Press, 1981.

Freiberger, Oliver. "The Buddhist Canon and the Canon of Buddhist Studies." *Journal of the International Association of Buddhist Studies* 27, no. 2 (2004): 261–83.

Fujieda, Akira. "The Tunhuang Manuscripts: A General Description (Part II)." *Zinbun: Memoirs of the Research Institute for Humanistic Studies, Kyoto University* 10 (1969): 17–39.

Fujiyoshi, Masumi 藤善真澄. "Sōchō yakukyō shimatsu kō" 宋朝譯經始末攷. *Kansai Daigaku Bungaku Ronshū* 關西大学文学論集 36, no. 1 (1986): 399–428.

Fukuda Gyōkai 福田行誡. *Gyosei daizōkyō jobatsu* 御制大藏經序跋. In *Shōwa hōbō sōmokuroku* 昭和法寶總目錄, ed. Takakusu Junjirō 高楠順次郎 and Watanabe Kaigyoku 渡邊海旭, 3: 1418–50. 1929–1934; reprint, Taibei: Xinwenfeng chuban gongsi, 1983.

Fussman, Gérard. 2004. "Dans quel type de bâtiment furent trouvés les manuscrits de Gilgit?" *Journal Asiatique* 292, no. 1–2 (2004): 101–50.

Gao, Mingqian 高明乾, ed. *Zhiwu guhan ming tu kao* 植物古漢名圖考. Zhengzhou: Daxiang chubanshe, 2006.

Gaoseng zhuan heji 高僧傳合集. Shanghai: Shanghai guji chubanshe, 1991.

Ge Yinliang 葛寅亮, comp. *Jinling fancha zhi* 金陵梵刹志. Collated by He Xiaorong 何孝榮. 1607; reprint, Tianjin: Tianjin Renmin chubanshe, 2007.

Gibbs, Peter J. and Kenneth R. Seddon. *Berberine and Huangbo: Ancient Colorants and Dyes*. British Library Studies in Conservation Science, Vol. 2. London: British Library, 1998.

Giles, Lionel and Eric D. Grinstead. *Descriptive Catalogue of the Chinese Manuscripts from Tunhuang in the British Museum*. London: Trustees of the British Museum, 1957.

Gim, Gu 金坵. *Jibojip* 止浦集. In *Hanguo wenji zhong de Meng Yuan shiliao* 韩國文集中的蒙元史料, ed. Du Honggang 杜宏剛, Qiu Ruizhong 邱瑞中, and Choe Changweon 崔昌源. Guilin: Guangxi shifan daxue chubanshe, 2004.

Gimello, Robert M. "The 'Canonization' of Zhǔntí: The History of an Esoteric Cult Told in the Development of Its Canonical Corpus, from the Seventh Through the Seventeenth Century." Paper presented at the first international conference on the Chinese Buddhist canon, University of Arizona, Tucson, AZ, March 25–27, 2011.

——. "Chih-yen (602–668) and the Foundations of Hua-yen Buddhism." Ph.D. diss., Columbia University, 1976.

Gjertson, Donald E. *Miraculous Retribution: A Study and Translation of T'ang Lin's Ming-pao chi*. Berkeley: Centers for South and Southeast Asia Studies, 1989.

Goldfuss, Gabriele. *Vers un Bouddhisme du XXe Siècle. Yang Wenhui (1837–1911), Réformateur Laïque et Imprimeur*. Mémoire de l'Institut des Hautes Études Chinoises. Paris: Collège de France, Institut des Hautes Études Chinoises, 2001.

Goodrich, Luther Carrington. "Earliest Printed Editions of the Tripitaka." *Visva-Bharati Quarterly* 19 (1953–4): 215–20.

——. *The Literary Inquisition of Ch'ien-Lung*. Baltimore: Waverly Press, 1935.

——. "The Revolving Book-Case in China." *Harvard Journal of Asiatic Studies* 7, no. 2 (July 1942): 130–61.

Goodrich, L. Carrington and Chaoying Fang. *Dictionary of Ming Biography, 1368–1644*. New York: Columbia University Press, 1976.

Goryeo Chojo Daejanggyeong jipseong 高麗初雕大藏經集成. Ed. Goryeo Chojo Daejanggyeong Jipseong Pyeonchan Wiwonhoe. Seoul: Goryeo Daejanggyeong Yeonguso, 2005.

Goryeo Daejanggyeong 高麗大藏經.Seoul: Dongguk Daehakkyo, 1976.

Goryeo Daejanggyeong Jaryojip 高麗大藏經資料集. Vols. I and II. Goryeo Gyeongnam Hapcheon-gun: Goryeo Daejanggyeong Yeonguhoe, 1987.

Goryeosa 高麗史. Ed. Jeong Inji 鄭麟趾. 1955; reprint, Taibei: Wenshizhe chubanshe, 1972.

Goryeosa Jeolyo 高麗史節要. Ed. Kim Jongseo 金宗瑞. Seoul-teukbyeolsi: Myeongmundang, 1959.

Gregory, Peter N. *Inquiry Into the Origin of Humanity: An Annotated Translation of Tsung-mi's* Yüan jen lun *with a Modern Commentary*. Honolulu: University of Hawai'i Press, 1995.

——. *Tsung-mi and the Sinification of Buddhism*. 1991; reprint, Honolulu: University of Hawai'i Press, 2002.

Gu, Lu 顧祿. *Qing Jia Lu* 清嘉錄. In *Qing Jia Lu Tongqiao yizhuo lu* 清嘉錄 桐橋倚棹錄. Beijing: Zhonghua shuju, 2008.

Gu, Tinglong 顧聽龍. "Tang-Song Shukeben jianshu" 唐宋蜀刻本簡述. *Sichun tushuguan xuebao* 四川圖書館學報 3 (1979). Reprinted in *Zhuangding yuanliu he buyi* 裝订源流和补遗, ed. Shanghai Xinsijun lishi yanjiuhui. Yinshua yinchao fenhui 上海新四軍歷史研究會印刷印钞分會, 216–22. Beijing: Zhongguo shuji chubanshe, 1993.

Gu, Yongxin 顧永新. "Song Shuke jingshu banben yanjiu" 宋蜀刻經書版本研究. In *Beijing Daxue Zhongguo gu wenxian yanjiu zhongxin jikan* 北京大學中國古文獻研究中心集刊, 8: 24–50. Beijing: Beijing daxue chubanshe, 2009.

Guang hongming ji 廣弘明集. T 2103, vol. 52.

Guo, Qingfan 郭慶藩, ed. *Zhuangzi jishi* 莊子集釋. 4 vols. Beijing: Zhonghua shuju, 1997.

Guo, Qinghua. "The Architecture of Joinery: The Form and Construction of Rotating Sutra-Case Cabinets." *Architectural History* 42 (1999): 96–109.

Gusu zhi, Zhengde 正德姑蘇志. 1506. Comp. Wang Ao 王鏊 et al. *SKQS*, vol. 493.

Guy, Kent R. *The Emperor's Four Treasuries: Scholars and the State in the Late Ch'ien-lung Era*. Cambridge, MA: Council on East Asian Studies, Harvard University, 1987.

Gwon, Huigyeong 權熹耕. "Dongjang-sa sojang ui Gamjigeumja 'Bulseolmireuk-seongbulgyeong' e gwanhan ilgochal" 東長寺所藏의 紺紙金字 '佛說彌勒成佛經'에 關한 一考察. *Misul sahak yeongu* 美術史學研究 (*Gogo misul* 考古美術) 165 (1985): 22–60.

Ha, Tae-Hung. *Samguk Yusa: Legends and History of the Three Kingdoms of Ancient Korea*. Trans. Grafton K. Mintz. Seoul: Yonsei University Press, 1972.

Haeger, John Winthrop. "The Significance of Confusion: The Origins of the *T'ai-p'ing yü-lan*." *Journal of the American Oriental Society* 88, no. 3 (July–Sept. 1968): 401–10.

Han shu 漢書. 1st century C.E. Comp. Ban Gu 班固 et al. Beijing: Zhonghua shuju, 1962.

Han, Yuanji 韓元吉. *Nanjian jiayi gao* 南澗甲乙稿. Beijing: Zhonghua shuju, 1985.

Hardacre, Helen. *Shinto and the State 1868-1988*. Princeton: Princeton University Press, 1989.

Harrison, Paul. "A Brief History of the Tibetan bKa' 'gyur." In *Tibetan Literature: Studies in Genre. Essays in Honor of Geshe Lhundup Sopa*, ed. José Ignacio Cabezón and Roger R. Jackson, 70–94. Ithaca, NY: Snow Lion, 1996.

——. "Canon." In *Encyclopedia of Buddhism*, ed. Robert E. Buswell, Jr., 111–15. Indianapolis: Macmillan Reference USA, 2003.

——. "The Earliest Chinese Translations of Mahāyāna Buddhist Sūtras: Some Notes on the Works of Lokakṣema." *Buddhist Studies Review* 10, no. 2 (1993): 135–77.

——. "The *Ekottarikāgama* Translations of An Shigao." In *Bauddhavidyāsudhākaraḥ: Studies in Honour of Heinz Bechert on the Occasion of His 65th Birthday*, ed. Petra Kieffer-Pülz and Jens-Uwe Hartmann, 261–84. Swisttal-Odendorf: Indica and Tibetica Verlag, 1997.

——. *The Samādhi of Direct Encounter with the Buddhas of the Present: An Annotated English Translation of the Tibetan Version of the Pratyutpanna-Buddha-Saṃmukhāvasthita-Samādhi-Sūtra with Several Appendices Relating to the History of the Text*. Studia Philologica Buddhica—Monograph Series V. Tokyo: The International Institute for Buddhist Studies, 1990.

Harrison, Paul M. and Jens-Uwe Hartmann, eds. *From Birch Bark to Digital Data: Recent Advances in Buddhist Manuscript Research*. Wien: Verlag der Österreichischen Akademie der Wissenschaften, 2014.

Harrist, Robert E. *The Landscape of Words: Stone Inscriptions from Early and Medieval China*. Seattle: University of Washington Press, 2008.

Hartmann, Jens-Uwe. "Buddhist Sanskrit Texts from Northern Turkestan and Their Relation to the Chinese Tripiṭaka." In *Buddhism Across Boundaries: The Interplay of Indian, Chinese, and Central Asian Source Materials*, ed. John R. McRae and Jan Nattier. *Sino-Platonic Papers* 222 (March 2012): 50–63.

Hawley, Samuel. *Inside the Hermit Kingdom: The 1884 Korea Travel Diary of George Clayton Foulk*. Lanham, MD: Lexington Books, 2008.

Hayashiya, Tomojirō 林屋友次郎. *Kyōroku kenkyū* 經錄研究. Tokyo: Iwanami shoten, 1941.

He, Mei何梅. *Lidai Hanwen dazangjing mulu xinkao* 歷代漢文大藏經目錄新考. Beijing: Shehui kexue wenxian chubanshe, 2014.

Heine, Ronald. *Origen: Scholarship in the Service of the Church*. Oxford: Oxford University Press, 2010.

Henderson, John B. *The Development and Decline of Chinese Cosmology*. New York: Columbia University Press, 1984.

Henthorn, William E. *Korea: The Mongol Invasions*. Leiden: E. J. Brill Archive, 1963.

Heo, Hungsik 許興植. *Hanguk Geumseok Jeonmun* 韓國金石全文. Seoul: Asea Munhwasa, 1984.

von Hinüber, Oskar. *A Handbook of Pāli Literature*. Berlin; New York: Walter de Gruyter, 1996.

Hirakawa, Akira. *A History of Indian Buddhism from Śākyamuni to Early Mahāyāna*. Trans. Paul Groner. Honolulu: University of Hawaiʻi Press, 1990.

Hong, Yunsik 洪潤植. *Kankoku Bukkyō girei no kenkyū* 韓国仏教儀礼の研究. Tōkyō: Ryūbunkan, 1976.

Hu, Chusheng 胡楚生. *Zhongguo muluxue yanjiu* 中國目錄學研究. Taibei: Huazheng shuju, 1987.

Hu, Zhaoxi 胡昭曦. "Songdai jiaozi juti danshengdi tankao zashi" 宋代交子具體誕生地探考雜識. In Hu Zhaoxi, *Bashu lishi kaocha yanjiu* 巴蜀歷史考察研究, 351–66. Chengdu: Ba-Shu shushe, 2007.

Huang, Biji 黃碧姬. *Fei Changfang* Lidai sanbao ji *yanjiu* 費長房《歷代三寶紀》研究. Taibei: Huamulan wenhua chubanshe, 2009.

Huang, Chi-chiang [Huang Qijiang] 黃啟江. *Bei Song Fojiao shi lungao*北宋佛教史論稿. Taibei: Taiwan shang wu yin shu guan, 1997.

——. "Bei Song Jushi Yang Jie yu Fojiao: Jianbu *Song Shi* Yang Jie benzhuan zhique" 北宋居士楊傑與佛教—兼補宋史楊傑本傳之缺. *Hanxue yanjiu* 漢學研究 21, no. 1 (2003): 253–77.

——. "Experiment in Syncretism: Ch'i-sung (1007–1072) and Eleventh-Century Chinese Buddhism." Ph.D. diss., University of Arizona, 1986.

——. "Imperial Rulership and Buddhism in the Early Northern Sung." In *Imperial Rulership and Cultural Change in Traditional China*, ed. Frederick P. Brandauer and Chun-chieh Huang, 144–87. Seattle and London: University of Washington Press, 1994.

——. *Sizhou dasheng yu Songxue daoren: Song-Yuan shehui jingying de Fojiao xinyang yu Fojiao wenhua* 泗洲大聖與松雪道人:宋元社會菁英的佛教信仰與佛教文化. Taibei: Taiwan Xuesheng shuju, 2009.

——. "Song Taizong yu Fojiao" 宋太宗與佛教. *Gugong xueshu jikan*故宮學術季刊 12, no. 2 (1992): 107–33. Reprinted in Huang Chi-chiang, *Bei Song fojiao shi lun gao* 北宋佛教史論稿, 31–67. Taibei: Taiwan Shangwu yinshu guan, 1997.

——. "Songdai runwen yijingguan yu Fojiao" 宋代潤文譯經官與佛教. *Gugong xueshu jikan* 故宮學術季刊 7, no. 4 (Summer 1990): 13–31. Reprinted in Huang Chi-chiang, *Bei Song fojiao shi lungao*, 68–93. Taibei: Taiwan shang wu yin shu guan, 1997.

——. "Ŭich'ŏn's Pilgrimage and the Rising Prominence of the Korean Monastery in Hang-chow During the Sung and Yüan Periods." In *Currents and Countercurrents: Korean Influences on the East Asian Buddhist Traditions*, ed. Robert Buswell, 242–76. Honolulu: University of Hawai'i Press, 2005.

Huang, Chunyan 黃純燕, ed. *Gaoli dajue guoshi wenji* 高麗大覺國師文集. Lanzhou: Ganshu renmin chubanshe, 2008.

Huang, Minzhi 黃敏枝. "Guanyu Songdai Fojiao siyuan de Zhuanlun zang" 關於宋代佛教寺院的轉輪藏. In *1995 nian Foxue yanjiu lunwen ji: Fojiao xiandaihua* 一九九五年佛學研究論文集: 佛教現代化, 360–96. Taibei: Foguanshan wenjiao jijin hui, 1995.

——. "Zailun Songdai siyuan de Zhuanlunzang" 再論宋代寺院的轉輪藏 (A & B). *Qinghua xuebao* 清華學報 26, no. 2 & 3 (1996): 149–88 and 265–96.

Huang, Shih-shan Susan. "Early Buddhist Illustrated Prints in Hangzhou." In *Knowledge and Text Production in an Age of Print: China, 900–1400*, ed. Lucille Chia and Hilde De Weerdt, 135–65. Leiden: Brill, 2011.

——. "Tang Song shiqi Fojiao banhua zhong suojian de meijie zhuanhua yu zimuo sheji" 唐宋時期佛教版畫中所見的媒介轉化與子模設計. In *Yishushi zhong de Han Jin yu Tang Song zhi bian* 藝術史中的漢晉與唐宋之變, ed. Shi Shouqian 石守謙 and Yan Juanying顏娟英, 385–434. Taibei: Shitou chubanshe, 2014.

Huang, Yansheng 黃燕生. *Guji shanben* 古籍善本. Beijing: Zhongguo shuili shuidian chubanshe, 2005.

Hubbard, Jamie. "A Report on Newly Discovered Buddhist Texts at Nanatsu-dera." *Japanese Journal of Religious Studies* 18, no. 4 (1991): 401–6.

Hucker, Charles O. *A Dictionary of Official Titles in Imperial China*. Stanford: Stanford University Press, 1985.

Huihong 惠洪. "Tanzhou Kaifu zhuanlunzang lingyan ji" 潭州開福轉輪藏靈驗記. *Shimen wenzichan* 石門文字禪, fasc. 21. *Mingban Jiaxing dazangjing*, no. 135, 23: 676b–c.

Huihui 惠慧. "Cong *Kaibaozang* kan guanke dazangjing de diaoyin, yinshua, liutong zhidu" 從開寶藏看官刻大藏經的雕刻、印刷、流通制度. *Shaanxi shifan daxue xuebao* 陝西師範大學學報 36 (July 2007): 309–11.

Huiyin Gaoli Huayan jiaosi zhi 慧因高麗華嚴教寺志. 1627. Comp. Li Zhu 李翥. *Zhongguo fosi shizhi huikan*, vol. 20. 1881; reprint, Taibei: Mingwen shuju, 1980.

Hwang, Suyoung 黃壽永 and Mun Myoungdae 文明大. *Goryeo seonwonsaji ui balgyeon gwa goryeo daejanggyeongpan ui yurae, Ganghwado haksul josa bogoseo* 高麗 禪源寺址의 發見과 高麗大藏經板의 由來, 江華島學術調查報告書. Seoul: Dongguk Daehakkyo, Ganghwado Haksul Josadan, 1977.

Hymes, Robert. *Way and Byway: Taoism, Local Religion, and Models of Divinity in Sung and Modern China*. Berkeley: University of California Press, 2002.

Ikeda, On 池田温, *Chūgoku kodai shahon shikigo shūroku* 中國古代寫本識語集錄. Tōkyō: Ōkura Shuppan, 1990.

Ikeuchi, Hiroshi 池内宏. "Kittan Seishū no Kōrai seibatsu" 契丹聖宗の高麗征伐. In *Man-Sen shi kenkyū: Chusei*滿鮮史研究: 中世, vol. 2, 199–264. Tōkyō: Yoshikawa Kōbunkan, 1933.

——. "Kōraichō no daizōkyō" 高麗朝の大藏經. *Man-Sen shi kenkyū: Chusei* 滿鮮史研究: 中世, vol. 2, 483–614. Tōkyō: Yoshikawa Kōbunkan, 1933.

Jaffe, Richard M. "Seeking Sākyamuni: Travel and the Reconstruction of Japanese Buddhism." *Journal of Japanese Studies* 30, no. 1 (2004): 65–96.

Jan, Yün-hua. "Buddhist Relations Between India and Sung China." Pts. I & II. *History of Religions* 6, no. 1 (Aug. 1966): 24–42; 6, no. 2 (Nov. 1966): 135–68.

Ji, Yun 紀贇. *Huijiao Gaoseng zhuan yanjiu* 慧皎《高僧傳》研究. Shanghai: Shanghai guji chubanshe, 2009.

Jiang, Weixin 蔣唯心 and Cai Yunchen 蔡運辰. *Songzang yizhen xumu Jinzang mulu jiaoshi hekan* 宋藏遺珍叙目金藏目錄校釋合刊. Taibei: Xin Wenfeng chuban gufen youxian gongsi 新文豐出版股份有限公司, 1976.

Jianyang xianzhi 建陽縣志. Comp. Feng Jike 馮繼科 et al. 1553; reprinted as vol. 31 of *Tianyige Mingdai fangzhi xuankanben* 天一閣明代方志選刊本. Shanghai: Guji chubanshe, 1964.

Jingshan zhi 徑山志. Comp. Song Kuiguang 宋奎光. *Zhongguo fosi shizhi congkan* 中國佛寺史志叢刊, 1st series, vols. 31–32. 1624; reprint, Taibei: Mingwen shuju, 1980.

Jinsushan dazangjing ji zangjing zhi 金粟山大藏經及藏經紙. In *Jinsusi shiliao* 金粟寺史料 no. 2. Shanghai: Shanghai guji chubanshe, 2008.

Jiu Wudai shi 舊五代史. 10th c. Comp. Xue Juzheng 薛居正. Beijing: Zhonghua shuju, 1976.

Jōjin 成尋. *San Tendai Godaisan ki* 参天台五臺山記. In *Jōjin Ajari no Haha no shū, San Tendai Godaisan ki no kenkyū* 成尋阿闍梨母集 参天台五臺山記の研究, ed. Shimazu Kusako 島津草子, 223–651. Tōkyō: Hatsubaijo Daizō Shuppan, 1959.

Jorgensen, John. "Korea as a Source for the Regeneration of Chinese Buddhism: The Evidence of Ch'an and Sŏn Literature." In *Currents and Countercurrents: Korean Influences on the East Asian Buddhist Traditions*, ed. Robert Buswell, 73–152. Honolulu: University of Hawai'i Press, 2005.

Kaibao yizhen 開寶遺珍. Ed. Fang Guangchang and Li Jining. Beijing: Wenwu chubanshe, 2010.

Kajiura, Susumu 梶浦晋. "Kindai ni okeru Daizōkyō Hensan" 近代における大藏經編纂. *Jyosho* 常照 51 (Spring 2002): 11–14.

Kamata, Shigeo 鎌田茂雄. *Chūgoku no Bukkyō girei* 中国の仏教儀礼. Tōkyō: Daizō Shuppan, 1986.

——. "Chūgoku Bukkyōken no keisei: so no rekeshi to genjō" 中國佛教圈の形成: その歷史と現狀. *Tōyō gakujutsu kenkyū* 14, no. 3 (1976). Reprinted in Kamata Shigeo, *Chūgoku no Bukkyō girei* 中國の佛教儀禮. Tōkyō: Tōyō bunka kenkyū shō, 1986, 3–10.

Kani, Noriyuki 金井德幸. "Sōdai Tenrinzō to sono shinkō" 宋代転輪蔵とその信仰. *Rissho shigaku* 立正史学 104 (2008): 1–18.

Karashima, Seishi. *A Glossary of Dharmarakṣa's Translation of the Lotus Sutra*. Bibliotheca Philologica et Philosophica Buddhica I. Tokyo: The International Research Institute for Advanced Buddhology-Soka University, 1998.

——. *The Textual Study of the Chinese Versions of the Saddharmapuṇḍarīkasūtra — in the Light of the Sanskrit and Tibetan Versions*. Tokyo: The Sankibo Press, 1992.

——. "Was the Aṣṭasāhasrikā Prajñāpāramitā Compiled in Gandhāra in Gāndhārī?" *Annual Report of The International Research Institute for Advanced Buddhology at Soka University* 16 (2013): 171–88.

Karmay, Heather. *Early Sino-Tibetan Art*. Warminster, UK: Aris and Phillips, 1975.

Katz, Paul R. "Writing History, Creating Identity: A Case Study of *Xuanfeng qinghui tu*." *Journal of Chinese Religions* 29 (2001): 161–78.

Kawakami, Seishi 川上正史. "Sō chokuhan zōkyō Annan denrai kō" 宋勅版蔵経安南伝来考. *Shina Bukkyō shigaku* 支那佛教史學 7, no. 1 (1944): 59–62.

Ketelaar, James Edward. *Of Heretics and Martyrs in Meiji Japan: Buddhism and Its Persecution*. Princeton: Princeton University Press, 1990.

Kezang yuanqi 刻藏緣起. Ca. 1595. Sichuan Provincial Library.

Kieschnick, John. "Blood Writing in Chinese Buddhism." *Journal of the International Association of Buddhist Studies* 23, no. 2 (2000): 177–94.

Kim, Changsuk 金昌淑, ed. *Goryeosa Bulgyo gwangye saryojip* 高麗史佛教關係史料集. Seoul: Minjoksa, 2001.

Kim, Dangtaek 金唐澤. "Goryeo Mokjong 12 nyeon ui jeongbyeon e daehan ilgochal" 高麗穆宗 12 年의 政變에 대한 一考察. *Hanguk hakbo* 18 (1980): 82–97.

Kim, Hwansoo Ilmee. *Empire of the Dharma: Korean and Japanese Buddhism, 1877–1912*. Cambridge, MA: Harvard University Asia Center, 2013.

Kim, Jongmyung. "Buddhist Rituals in Medieval Korea (918–1392)." Ph.D. diss., University of California, Los Angeles, 1994.

——. "The Tripitaka Koreana: Its Computerization and Significance for the Cultural Sciences in a Modern Globalized World." In *Korea and Globalization: Politics, Economics and Culture*, ed. James Lewis and Amadu Sesay, 154–81. London: Routledge Curzon, 2002.

Kim, Yeongmi 김영미. "11segi huban-12segi cho Goryeo-Yo oegyo gwangye wa bulgyeong gyoryu" 11세기 후반-12세기 초 고려·요 외교관계와 불경교류. *Yoksa wa Hyeunsil* 43 (2002): 47–77.

Kogachi, Ryūichi 古勝隆一. "Gokan Gi Shin chūshakusho no jobun" 後漢魏晋注釈書の序文. *Tōhō gakuhō* 東方學報 73 (2001): 1–48.

Kōnen, Tsunemitsu 常光浩然. *Meiji no Bukkyōsha* 明治の仏教者. Tokyo: Shunjūsha, 1968.

Kornicki, Peter. *The Book in Japan: A Cultural History from the Beginnings to the Nineteenth Century*. Leiden: Brill, 1998.

Kuo, Liying. "Sur les apocryphes bouddhiques chinois." *Bulletin de l'École française d'Extrême-Orient* 87, no. 2 (2000): 677–705.

Kuraishi, Takeshiro 倉石武四郎. *Mokuroku gaku* 目録学. Tokyo: Tokyō Daigaku tōyō bunka kenkyūjo, 1973.

Kurz, Johannes L. *China's Southern Tang Dynasty, 937–976*. Abingdon, Oxon; New York: Routledge, 2011.

——. "The Compilation and Publication of the *Taiping yulan* and the *Cefu yuangui*." *Extrême-Orient, Extrême-Occident* 1 (2007): 39–76.

——. "The Politics of Collecting Knowledge: Song Taizong's Compilations Project." *T'oung Pao* 87, no. 4/5 (2001): 289–316.

Lamotte, Étienne. "The Assessment of Textual Authenticity in Buddhism." *Buddhist Studies Review* 1, no. 1 (1983–84): 4–15.

——. *History of Indian Buddhism*. Trans. Sara Webb-Boin. Louvain-la-Neuve: Institut Orientaliste, 1988.

——. *Le Traité de la Grande Vertu de Sagesse de Nāgārjuna (Mahāprajñāpāramitāśāstra)*, vol. 5. Louvain: Institut Orientaliste, 1980.

Lan Jifu 藍吉富, ed. *Zhonghua Fojiao baikequanshu* 中華佛教百科全書. Tainan: Zhonghua Fojiao baike wenxian jijinhui, 1994.

Lancaster, Lewis R. "The Buddhist Canon in the Koryŏ Period." In *Buddhism in Koryo: A Royal Religion*, ed. Lewis R. Lancaster, Suh Kikun, and Yu Chai-Shin, 173–93. Korea Research Monograph, 22. Berkeley: Institute of East Asian Studies, University of California, 1996.

——. "Buddhist Literature: Canonization." In *The Encyclopedia of Religion*, ed. Mircea Eliade, 2: 504–9. New York: Macmillan, 1987.

——. "Comparison of the Two Carvings of the Korean Buddhist Canon." *Korean Journal* 23, no. 8 (Aug. 1983): 34–38.

——. "The Koryo Edition of the Buddhist Canon: New Sources for Research." In *Perspectives on Korea*, eds. Sang-Oak Lee and Duk-Soo Park, 320–32. Sydney: Wild Peony, 1998.

——. "The Movement of Buddhist Texts from India to China and the Construction of the Chinese Buddhist Canon." In *Buddhism Across Boundaries: The Interplay of Indian, Chinese, and Central Asian Source Materials*, ed. John R. McRae and Jan Nattier. *Sino-Platonic Papers* 222 (March 2012): 226–38.

——. "The Rock Cut Canon in China: Findings at Fang-shan." In *Buddhist Heritage: Papers Delivered at the School of Oriental and African Studies in November 1985*, ed. Tadeusz Skorupski, 143–56. London: Institute of Buddhist Studies, 1989.

Lancaster, Lewis and Park Sung-bae. *The Korean Buddhist Canon: A Descriptive Catalogue*. Berkeley: University of California Press, 1979.

Ledderose, Lothar. "Carving Sutras Into Stone Before the Catastrophe." *Proceedings of the British Academy* 125 (2004): 381–454.

——. "Changing the Audience: A Pivotal Period in the Great Sutra Carving Project at the Cloud Dwelling Monastery Near Beijing." In *Religion and Chinese Society*, ed. John Lagerway, 1: 385–409. Hong Kong: Chinese University Press, 2004.

——. "Competing with the Northern Sung: The Liao Buddhist Canon." In *Kaichuang dianfan: Bei Song de yishu yu wenhua yantaohui lunwen ji* 開創典範: 北宋的藝術與文化研討會論文集, ed. Wang Yaoting 王耀庭, 77–109. Taibei: Guoli Gugong bowuyuan, 2008.

Lee, Peter H. and Wm. Theodore De Bary, eds. *Sources of Korean Tradition, Vol. 1: From Early Times Through the Sixteenth Century*. New York: Columbia University Press, 1997.

Lee, Sherman and Wai-kam Ho. *Chinese Art Under the Mongols: The Yüan Dynasty, 1279–1368*. Cleveland: Cleveland Museum of Art, 1968.

Lee, Sonya. "Transmitting Buddhism to a Future Age: The Leiyin Cave at Fangshan and Cave-Temples with Stone Scriptures in Sixth-Century China." *Archives of Asian Art* 60 (2010): 43–78.

Levering, Miriam. "Scripture and Its Reception: A Buddhist Case." In *Rethinking Scripture: Essays from a Comparative Perspective*, ed. Miriam Levering, 29–57. Albany: State University of New York Press, 1989.

Lewis, Mark Edward. *Writing and Authority in Early China*. Albany: State University of New York Press, 1999.

Li, Daoyuan 酈道元. *Shui jing zhu* 水經注. Ca. 520. In *Shui jing zhu jiaozheng* 水經注校證, ed. Chen Qiaoyi 陳橋驛. Beijing: Zhonghua shuju, 2007.

Li, Fuhua. "An Analysis of the Content and Characteristics of the Chinese Buddhist Canon." Paper presented at the First International Conference on the Chinese Buddhist Canon, March 26, 2011, Tucson, AZ.

——. *Jinzang: mulu huanyuan ji yanjiu* 金藏:目錄還原及研究. Shanghai: Zhongxi shuju, 2012.

——. "Yetan Hanwen Fojiao dazangjing de xitong wenti" 也談漢文佛教大藏經的系統問題. Paper presented at the International Conference on the Study of the Chinese Buddhist Canon, Shanghai, Sept. 16–20, 2007.

Li Fuhua 李富華 and He Mei 何梅. *Hanwen Fojiao dazangjing yanjiu* 漢文佛教大藏經研究. Beijing: Zongjiao wenhua chubanshe, 2003.

Li, Huizhi 李會智. "Shanxi Jincheng Qingliansi kao" 山西晉城青蓮寺史考. *Wenwu shijie* 文物世界 1 (2003): 24–32.

Li, Huizhi 李會智 and Gao Tian 高天. "Shanxi Jincheng Qingliansi Fojiao fazhan zhi mailuo" 山西晉城青蓮寺佛教發展之脈絡. *Wenwu shijie* 文物世界 3 (2003): 18–23.

Li Jie 李誡. *Yingzao fashi* 營造法式. 36 fascs. Beijing: Zhongguo shu dian, 1989.

Li, Jining 李際寧. "Beijing tushuguan cang *Qishazang* yanjiu" 北京圖書館藏磧砂藏研究. *Beijing tushuguan guankan* 北京圖書館館刊 3 (1998): 70–73.

——. *Fojing banben* 佛經版本. Nanjing: Jiangsu guji chubanshe, 2002.

——. "*Jinzang* xinziliao kao" 金藏新資料考. *Zangwai Fojiao wenxian* 藏外佛教文獻, ed. Fang Guangchang, vol. 3, 446–63. Beijing: Zongjiao wenhua chubanshe, 1997.

Li, Jung-hsi. "The Stone Scriptures of Fang-shan." *Eastern Buddhist* 12 (1979): 104–13.

Li, Tao 李燾. *Xu Zizhi tongjian changbian* 續資治通鑑長編. Beijing: Zhonghua shuju, 1979.

Li, Xiaoqiang 李小強. "*Song Wang Changshi zhuannian gongde bie* dazangjing shiliao zaji" 宋王長史轉念功德碑 "大藏經" 史料札記. *Zhongguo dianji yu wenhua* 中國典籍與文化 1 (2011): 148–51.

Liang, Gengyao 梁庚堯. "Song-Yuan shidai de Suzhou" 宋元時代的蘇州. *Wenshi zhexue bao* 文史哲學報 31 (1982): 223–325.

——. "Song-Yuan shidai Suzhou de nongye fazhan" 宋元時代蘇州的農業發展. In *Dierjie Zhongguo shehui jingji shi yantaohui lunwenji* 第二屆中國社會經濟史研

討會論文集, ed. Xu Zhuoyun 許倬雲, Mao Hanguang 毛漢光, and Liu Cuirong 劉翠溶, 257–81. Taibei: Hanxue yanjiu ziliao ji fuwu zhongxin, 1983.

Liang, Qichao 梁啟超. "Fojia jinglu zai Zhongguo muluxue zhi weizhi" 佛家經錄 在中國目錄學之位置. In *Fojiao muluxue shuyao* 佛教目錄學述要, *Xiandai Fojiao xueshu chongkan*, no. 40, ed. Zhang Mantao 張曼濤, 21–52. Taibei: Dacheng wenhua, 1978.

Liang, Sicheng. *A Pictorial History of Chinese Architecture: A Study of the Development of Its Structural System and the Evolution of Its Types*. Trans. Wilma Fairbank. Cambridge, MA: MIT Press, 1984.

Liang, Shizheng 梁詩正 et al., comps. *Xihu zhi zuan* 西湖志纂. SKQS, vol. 586.

Liang, Tianxi 梁天錫. *Bei Song Chuanfayuan jiqi yijing zhidu* 北宋傳法院及其譯經 制度. Hong Kong: Zhi lianjing yuan, 2003.

Liang, Yuquan 梁玉泉, et al. "Fabao chongguang: zai chongyin *Longzang* de shihou tan *Longzang*" 法寶重光–在重印龍藏的時候談龍藏. *Fayin* 法音 10 (1988): 24–27.

Link, Arthur E. "The Biography of Shi Dao'an." *T'oung Pao* 46, no. 1/2 (1958): 1–48.

——. "The Earliest Chinese Account of the Compilation of the *Tripiṭaka* (I)." *Journal of the American Oriental Society* 81 no. 2 (April–June 1961): 87–103.

——. "The Earliest Chinese Account of the Compilation of the *Tripiṭaka* (II)." *Journal of the American Oriental Society* 81, no. 3 (Aug.–Sept. 1961): 281–99.

——. "Evidence for Doctrinal Continuity of Han Buddhism from the Second Through the Fourth Centuries: The Prefaces of An Shih-kao's *Grand Sūtra on Mindfulness of the Respiration* and K'ang Seng-hui's Introduction to the 'Perfection of Dhyāna.'" In *Papers in Honor of Professor Woodbridge Bingham: A Festschrift for his Seventy-fifth Birthday*, ed. James B. Parsons, 55–126. San Francisco: Chinese Materials Center, 1976.

——. "Shih Seng-yu and His Writings." *Journal of the American Oriental Society* 80, no. 1 (1960): 17–43.

——. "Shyh Daw-an's Preface to Saṅgharakṣa's *Yogācārabhūmi-sūtra* and the Problem of Buddho-Taoist Terminology in Early Chinese Buddhism." *Journal of the American Oriental Society* 77, no. 1 (1957): 1–14.

Liu, Changdong 劉長東. *Songdai Fojiao zhengce lungao* 宋代佛教政策論稿. Chengdu: Ba-Shu shushe, 2005.

Liu, Tong 劉侗. *Dijing jingwu lue* 帝京景物略. Beijing: Beijing guji chubanshe, 1980.

Liu, Xinru. "Buddhist Institutions in the Lower Yangtze Region During the Sung Dynasty." *Bulletin of Sung-Yuan Studies* 21 (1989): 31–51.

Liu, Zhiyuan 劉志遠 and Liu Tingbi 劉廳壁. *Chengdu Wanfusi shike yishu* 成都萬福 寺石刻藝術. Beijing: Zhongguo gudian yishu chubanshe, 1958.

Lizang xindiaoben jiaoji 麗藏新雕本校記. Nanjing: Zhina neixueyuan, 1935.

Loehr, Max. *Chinese Landscape Woodcuts: From an Imperial Commentary to the Tenth-Century Printed Edition of the Buddhist Canon*. Cambridge, MA: Belknap Press, 1968.

Long, Darui. "A Note on the Hongwu Nanzang, a Rare Edition of the Buddhist Canon." *The East Asian Library Journal* 9, no. 2 (2000): 112–47.

Lorge, Peter. "From Warlord to Emperor: Song Taizu's Change of Heart During the Conquest of Shu (965 A.D.)." *T'oung Pao* 91, no. 4–5 (2005): 320–46.

Lou, Burnard, et al., eds. *TEI shiyong zhinan: yunyong TEI chuli zhongwen wenxian* TEI 使用指南: 運用 TEI 處理中文文獻. Taipei: Taiwan E-learning and Digital Archive Program, 2009.

Lowe, Bryan D. "The Discipline of Writing: Scribes and Purity in Eighth-Century Japan." *Japanese Journal of Religious Studies* 39, no. 2 (2012): 201–39.

——. "Texts and Textures of Early Japanese Buddhism: Female Patrons, Lay Scribes, and Buddhist Scripture in Eighth-Century Japan." *Princeton University Library Chronicle* 73, no. 1 (Autumn 2011): 9–36.

Lü, Cheng 呂澂. *Lü Cheng Foxue lunzhu xuanji* 呂澂佛學論著選集. Ji'nan: Qilu shushe, 1996.

——. "Songzang Shuban yinben kao" 宋藏蜀版印本考. In *Dazangjing yanjiu huibian* 大藏經研究彙編, ed. Zhang Mantao 張曼濤, 195–206. 1977; reprint, Beijing: Beijing Tushuguan chubanshe, 2005.

Lü Jianfu 呂建福. "Gaoli wangchao de qirang Fojiao yu dongchuan zhi Mijiao" 高麗王朝的祈禳佛教与東傳之密教. In *Mijiao lunkao* 密教論考, 406–33. Beijing: Zongjiao wenhua chubanshe, 2008. First published in *Bulgyo yonggu* 25 (2006): 139–60.

Lü, Shaoyu 呂紹虞. *Zhongguo muluxue shigao* 中國目錄史稿. Hefei: Anhui jiaoyu chubanshe, 2004.

Lü, Tiegang 呂鉄鋼 and Huang, Chunhe 黃春和. *Fayuan si* 法源寺. Beijing: Huawen chubanshe, 2006.

Luo, Tianyun 羅天云 and Deng, Zhongshu 鄧中殊. "Chengdu Jingzhongsi shi shijie zuizao zhibi Jiaozi de danshengdi" 成都净眾寺是世界最早纸币—交子的誕生地. *Wenshi zazhi* 文史雜誌 4 (2006): 18–21.

Mao, Wen'ao 毛文鰲. "Mao Jin yu senglü zhi jiaoyou ji kejing kao" 毛晋與僧侶之交游及刻經考. *Zongjiaoxue yanjiu* 宗教學研究 4 (2011): 250–55.

Marmé, Michael. *Suzhou: Where the Goods of All the Provinces Converge*. Stanford: Stanford University Press, 2005.

Mayer, Alexander L. "Xuanzang." In *Encyclopedia of Buddhism*, ed. Robert E. Buswell, Jr., 909–10. New York: Macmillan Reference USA, 2004.

Men'shikov, Lev. *Rukopisnaia Kniga v Kulture Narodov Vostoka* (Handwritten books in the cultures of the Orient). Moskow: Glavnaia Redaktsia Vostochnoi Literatury, 1988.

Mingban Jiaxing dazangjing 明版嘉興大藏經. 40 vols. Taibei: Xinwenfeng, 1987.

Mingquan 明佺. *Da Zhou kanding zhongjing mulu* 大周刊定衆經目錄. T 2153, vol. 55.

Mingshi 明史. Comp. Zhang Tingyu 張廷玉 et al.. Beijing: Zhonghua shuju, 1974.

Minh Chi, Văn Tân, and Tài Thu Nguyên. *Buddhism in Vietnam: From Its Origins to the 19th Century*. 1993; reprint, Hanoi: The Gioi Publishers, 1999.

Mirsky, Jeanette. *Sir Aurel Stein, Archeological Explorer*. Chicago: University of Chicago Press, 1977.

Miyazaki, Kenji 宮崎健司. "Nara jidai no Issaikyō ni tsuite" 奈良时代の一切経について. In *Issaikyō no rekishiteki kenkyū* 一切経の歴史的研究, 1–50. Kyōto: Bukkyō Daigaku Sōgō Kenkyūjo, 2004.

——. *Nihon kodai no shakyō to shakai* 日本古代の写経と社会. Tōkyō: Hanawa Shobō, 2006.

Mizang Kai chanshi yigao 密藏開禪師遺稿. JXZ (CBETA) no. 118, vol. 23.

Mizuno, Kōgen. *Buddhist Sutras: Origin, Development, Transmission*. Tokyo: Kōsei Publishing Co., 1982.

Mohan, Pankaj N. "Beyond the 'Nation-Protecting' Paradigm: Recent Trends in the Historical Studies of Korean Buddhism." *Review of Korean Studies* 9, no. 1 (2006): 49–67.

Monnet, Nathalie. *Chine: l'Empire du trait; Calligraphies et dessins du ve au XIXe siècle*. Paris: Bibliothèque nationale de France, 2004.

Morrison, Elizabeth. *The Power of Patriarchs: Qisong and Lineage in Chinese Buddhism*. Leiden; Boston: Brill, 2010.

Mujaku, Dōchū 無著道忠. *Zenrin shōkisen* 禪林象器箋. Ed. Yanagida Seizan 柳田聖山. Kyoto: Chūbun Shuppansha, 1979.

Müller, F. Max, ed. *Sacred Books of the East*. Vols. 1–50. London, 1879–1910.

Mun, Chanju. *The History of Doctrinal Classification in Chinese Buddhism*. Lanham, MD: University Press of America, 2006.

Mun, Gyeonghyun 文暻鉉. "Goryeo Daejanggyeong rijo ui sajeok gochal" 高麗大藏經雕造의史的考察. In *Bulgyeo wa Yeoksa: Yi Giyeong baksa gohui ginyeom nonchong* 佛教의歷史: 李箕永博士古稀紀念論叢, 477–530. Seoul: Hankuk Bulgyo Yeonguwon, 1991.

Murayama, Chijun 村山智順. *Chosen no fūsui* 朝鮮の風水. Tokyo: Ryūkei Shosha, 2003.

Nagai, Masashi 永井政之. "Fu Dashi to Rinzō" 傅大士と輪蔵. *Sōtōshū Shūgaku kenkyū kiyo* 曹洞宗宗学研究所紀要 8 (Oct. 1994): 13–30.

Naitō, Ryūō 内藤竜雄. "Shutsu sanzō kishu senshu nenji ni tsuite" 出三蔵記集撰集年次について. *Indogaku Bukkyōgaku kenkyū* 印度学仏教学研究 7 (1958): 162–67.

Nakajima, Ryūzō 中嶋隆蔵. *Minbanreki kakōzō no shuppan to sono eikyō* 明萬暦嘉興蔵の出版とその影響. Self-published research report, 2005.

——. *Shutsu sanzō kishū—jokan yakuchū* 出三蔵記集—序卷訳注. Kyoto: Heirakuji Shoten, 1997.

Nakamura, Kaoru 中村薫. *Nitchū Jōdokyō ronsō: Ogurusu Kōchō 'Nenbutsu entsu' to Yō Jizan* 日中浄土教論争: 小栗栖香頂念仏圓通と楊仁山. Kyoto: Hōzōkan, 2009.

Nakamura, Kikunoshin 中村菊之進. "Sō Denpoin yakukyō sanzō Yuijō no denki oyobi nenpu" 宋伝法院訳経三蔵惟浄の伝記及び年譜. *Bunka* 文化 41, no. 1–2 (1977): 1–59.

——. "Sō Kaihōpan Daizōkyō kōsei kō" 宋開寶版大藏經構成考. *Mikkyō bunka* 密教文化 1 (1984): 34–50.

Nakanishi, Masayuki. "Kuni no Miya Kuniyoshi ō (Prince)." *Encyclopedia of Shinto*. http://eos.kokugakuin.ac.jp/modules/xwords/entry.php?entryID=489, 2006.

Nanjio, Buyiu (Nanjō Bun'yū). *A Catalogue of the Chinese Translation of the Buddhist Tripitaka*. 1883; reprint, Delhi: Classics Indian Publications, 1989.

Nattier, Jan. *A Guide to the Earliest Chinese Buddhist Translations: Texts from the Eastern Han* 東漢 *and Three Kingdoms* 三國 *Periods*. Tokyo: International Research Institute for Advanced Buddhology, Soka University, 2008.

——. "The Twelve Divisions of Scriptures (十二部經) in the Earliest Chinese Buddhist Translations." *Annual Report of The International Research Institute for Advanced Buddhology at Soka University* 7 (2004): 167–96.

——. "Who Produced the *Da mingdu jing* 大明度經 (T 225)? A Reassessment of the Evidence." *Journal of the International Association of Buddhist Studies* 31, no. 1–2 (2010): 295–337.

Needham, Joseph et al. *The Hall of Heavenly Records: Korean Astronomical Instruments and Clocks*. Cambridge: Cambridge University Press, 1986.

Nguyên, Tài Thu and Tho Thi Hoàng. *The History of Buddhism in Vietnam*. Washington, DC: Council for Research in Values and Philosophy: Institute of Philosophy; Vietnamese Academy of Social Sciences, 2008.

Nie, Furong 聶福榮. "Wanli chao Cisheng Li Taihou chongfo kaolun" 萬曆朝慈聖李太后崇佛考論. M.A. thesis, Jilin University, 2007.

Nozaki, Jun 野崎準. "Nihon no Rinzō nitsuite no oboegaki" 日本の輪蔵についての覚書. *Ōbaku bunka* 黃檗文華 127 (2006–07): 238–39.

Nozawa, Yoshimi 野沢佳美. *Mindai Daizōkyō shi no kenkyū: Nanzō no rekishigakuteki kiso kenkyū* 明代大蔵経史の研究: 南蔵の歴史学的基礎研究. Tōkyō: Kyūko Shoin, 1998.

——. "Mindai Kitazō kō: Kashi jōkyō o chūshin ni" 明代北蔵考:下賜状況を中心に. *Risshō Daigaku Bungakubu ronsō* 立正大学文学部論叢 117 (2003): 81–106.

——. *Risshō daigaku toshokan shozō Mindai Nanzō mokuroku* 立正大學圖書館所藏明代南藏目錄. Tokyo: Risshō University, 1989.

Ogawa, Kan'ichi 小川貫弌. "Gendai Hakuunshū kyōdan no katsuyaku" 元代白雲宗教團の活躍. *Bukkyō shigaku* 佛教史學 3, no. 1 (1952): 1–25.

Oh, Yunhui 오윤희(吳潤熙). *Daejanggyeong, cheonnyeon ui jihe rul dameun geureut* 대장경, 천년의 지혜를 담은 그릇. Seoul: Bulgwang Chulpansa, 2011.

Okabe, Kazuō 岡部和雄. "*Yakukyō to shakyō*" 訳経と写経. *Tōyō gakujutsu kenkyū* 東洋学術研究 22, no. 1 (1983): 13–47.

Okamoto, Keiji 岡本敬二. "Kōrai daizō kyōban no kokusei" 高麗大蔵経板の刻成. In *Chōsen shi no shomondai* 朝鮮史の諸問題, ed. Rekishigaku Kenkyūkai (Japan), 14–23. Tōkyō: Iwanami Shoten, 1953.

Ono, Genmyō 小野玄妙. "Kōrai daizōkyō chōin kō" 高麗大藏經雕印考. In *Butsuden kenkyū* 佛典研究 1, no. 4 (1929). Tōkyō: Taishō issaikyō kankōkai.

O'Rourke, Kevin. *Singing Like a Cricket, Hooting Like an Owl: Selected Poems of Yi Kyu-bo*. Ithaca: Cornell East Asia Program, Cornell University, 1995.

Orzech, Charles D. "Looking for Bhairava: Exploring the Circulation of Esoteric Texts Produced by the Song Institute for Canonical Translation." *Pacific World: Journal of the Institute of Buddhist Studies* 3d ser. 8 (Fall 2006): 139–66.

——. "The Trouble with Tantra in China." In *Transformations and Transfer of Tantra in Asia and Beyond*, ed. István Keul, 310–19. Berlin; Boston: Walter de Gruyter, 2012.

Overmyer, Daniel L. "The White Cloud Sect in Sung and Yüan China." *Harvard Journal of Asiatic Studies* 42, no. 2 (Dec. 1982): 615–42.

Ōya, Tokujō 大屋德城. "Kaiinji kyōban kō" 海印寺經板考. *Tōyō gakuhō* 東洋學報 15, no. 3 (1929): 355–60. Reprinted in Ōya Tokujō, *Bukkyō kobankyō no kenkyū* 佛教古板經の研究, 57–196. Tōkyō: Kokusho Kankōkai, 1988.

——. *Kōrai zokuzō chōzō kō* 高麗續藏雕造攷. 1936; reprint, Tōkyō: Kokusho Kankōkai, 1988.

Pagel, Ulrich. *The Bodhisattvapiṭaka: Its Doctrines, Practices and Their Position in Mahāyāna Literature*. Tring: The Institute of Buddhist Studies, 1995.

Paik, Nak-choon 白樂濬. "Tripitaka Koreana." *Transactions of the Korea Branch of the Royal Asiatic Society* 32 (1951): 62–78.

Palumbo, Antonello. *An Early Chinese Commentary on the Ekottarika-āgama: The Fenbie gongde lun* 分別功德論 *and the History of the Translation of the Zengyi ahan jing* 增一阿含經. Taipei: Dharma Drum Publishing Corporation, 2013.

Pan, Jixing 潘吉星. *Zhongguo zaozhi jishu shigao* 中國造紙技術史稿. Beijing: Wenwu chubanshe, 1979.

Pañcaviṃśatisāhasrikā Prajñāpāramitā. Ed. N. Dutt. Calcutta: Calcutta Oriental Series 28, 1934.

Payne, Richard K., ed., *Scripture:Canon::Text:Context: Essays Honoring Lewis Lancaster*. Berkeley: Institute of Buddhist Studies and BDK America, 2014.

Pelliot, Paul. *Les débuts de l'imprimerie en chine*. Paris: Imprimerie Nationale Librairie d'Amérique et d'Orient, 1953.

Petzold, Bruno. *The Classification of Buddhism: Comprising the Classification of Buddhist Doctrines in India, China and Japan*. Wiesbaden: Harrassowitz, 1995.

Poceski, Mario. *Ordinary Mind as the Way: The Hongzhou School and the Growth of Chan Buddhism*. New York: Oxford University Press, 2007.

Pollock, Sheldon. "Literary Culture and Manuscript Culture in Pre-colonial India." In *Literary Cultures and Material Book*, ed. Simon Eliot, Andrew Nash, and Ian Willison, 77–94. London: British Library, 2007.

Prebish, Charles. "A Review of Scholarship on the Buddhist Councils." *Journal of Asian Studies* 33 (1974): 239–54.

Prip-Møller, Johannes. *Chinese Buddhist Monasteries: Their Plans and Functions as a Setting for Buddhist Monastic Life*. 1937; reprint, Hong Kong: Hong Kong University Press, 1967.

Przyluski, Jean. *Councile de Ra jagr ha: Introduction à l'historie de canons et des sects bouddhiques*. Paris: P. Geuthner, 1926.

Qinggong neiwufu zaobanchu dang'an zonghui 清宮內務府造辦處檔案總匯, ed. The First Historical Archives of China and the Art Museum, The Chinese University of Hong Kong. Beijing: Renmin chubanshe, 2005.

Qishazang 磧砂藏 (copies seen).

——. *Songban Qisha Dazangjing* 宋版磧砂大藏經. 40 vols. Taipei: Xin wenfeng chubanshe, 1987.

——. *Qisha dazangjing* 磧砂大藏經. 5,359 vols. [several cases missing]. Princeton University East Asian Library, Gest Collection.

——. *Yingyin Song Qisha zang jing* 影印宋磧砂藏經. 591 vols. Shanghai: Shanghai Yingyin Song ban zangjing hui, 1933–36.

Qisong 契嵩. *Tanjin wenji* 鐔津文集. T 2115, vol. 52.

Quan Song wen 全宋文. Ed. Zeng Zaozhuang 曾棗庄 and Liu Lin 劉琳. Shanghai: Shanghai cishu chubanshe, 2006.

Quan Tang wen 全唐文. Haikou: Hainan guoji xinwen chuban zhongxin, 1995.

Radich, Michael. "External Evidence Relating to Works Ascribed to Paramārtha, with a Focus on Traditional Chinese Catalogues." In *Shintai sanzō kenkyū ronshū* 眞諦三藏研究論集, ed. Funayama Tōru 船山徹, 39–102. Kyoto: Institute for Research in Humanities, Kyoto University, 2012.

Rao, Zongyi 饒宗頤. "Lun Sengyou" 論僧祐. *Zhongguo wenhua yanjiusuo xuebao* 中國文化研究所學報第 6 (1997): 405–16.

Reader, Ian. "The Rise of a Japanese 'New New Religion': Themes in the Development of Agonshū." *Japanese Journal of Religious Studies* 15, no. 4 (1988): 235–61.

Reischauer, Edwin O. *Ennin's Diary: The Record of a Pilgrimage to China in Search of the Law*. New York: Ronald Press, 1955.

Ren, Jiyu 任繼愈, ed. *Fojiao dacidian* 佛教大辭典. Nanjing: Jiangsu guji chubanshe, 2002.

——. *Zhongguo dabaike quanshu: Zongjiao* 中國大百科全書: 宗教. Beijing: Zhongguo dabaike quanshu chubanshe, 1988.

——. *Zongjiao dacidian* 宗教大辭典. Shanghai: Shanghai cishu chubanshe, 1998.

Rhi, Ki-yong 李箕永. "An Introduction to the Tripitaka Koreana." *International Buddhist Forum Quarterly* 1, no. 2 (1978–79): 5–20.

Ricoeur, Paul. *Figuring the Sacred: Religion, Narrative, and Imagination*. Trans. Mark I. Wallace. Minneapolis: Fortress Press, 1995.

——. "The Sacred Text and the Community." In *The Critical Study of Sacred Texts*, ed. Wendy Doniger O'Flaherty, 271–76. Berkeley: Graduate Theological Union, 1979. Reprinted in Paul Ricoeur, *Figuring the Sacred*, 68–72.

Robson, James. "Talismans in Chinese Esoteric Buddhism." In *Esoteric Buddhism and the Tantras in East Asia*, ed. Charles D. Orzech et al., 225–29. Leiden: Brill, 2011.

Rockstein, Edward D. "The Mongol Invasions of Korea: 1231." *Mongolia Society Bulletin* 11, no. 2 (21) (Fall 1972): 41–54.

Rogers, Michael C. "National Consciousness in Medieval Korea: The Impact of Liao and Chin on Koryo." In *China Among Equals: The Middle Kingdom and Its Neighbors, 10th to 14th Centuries*, ed. Morris Rossabi, 151–72. Berkeley: University of California Press, 1983.

Saliceti-Collins, Anne. "Xi Xia Buddhist Woodblock Prints Excavated in Khara Khoto: A Case Study of Transculturation in East Asia, Eleventh-Thirteenth Centuries." M.A. thesis, University of Washington, 2007.

Salomon, Richard. *Ancient Buddhist Scrolls from Gandhāra: The British Library Kharoṣṭhī Fragments*. London: The British Library, 1997.

——. "Recent Discoveries of Early Buddhist Manuscripts and Their Implications for the History of Buddhist Texts and Canons." In *Between the Empires: Society in India 300 B.C.E. to 400 C.E.*, ed. Patrick Olivelle, 349–82. New York: Oxford University Press, 2006.

——. "An Unwieldy Canon: Observations on Some Distinctive Features of Canon Formation." In *Buddhism Kanonisierung und Kanonbildung in der asiatischen Religionsgeschichte*, ed. Max Deeg, Oliver Freiberger, and Christoph Kleine, 161–207. Wien: Verlag der Österreichischen Akademie der Wissenschaften, 2011.

SAT *Daizōkyō Text Database 2012 Edition* (SAT 2012). Created by the SAT Daizōkyō Text Database Committee, University of Tokyo. http://21dzk.l.u-tokyo.ac.jp/SAT/.

Sawyer, Ralph D. "Martial Prognostication." In *Military Culture in Imperial China*, ed. Nicola Di Cosmo, 45–64. Cambridge, MA: Harvard University Press, 2009.

——. *Unorthodox Strategies for the Everyday Warrior*. Boulder, CO: Westview Press, 1996.

Schifferli, Christoph. "La politique économique des Song du Nord au Sichuan (965–1000)." *T'oung Pao* 72 (1986): 130–60.

Schipper, Kristofer. "General Introduction." In *The Taoist Canon*, ed. Kristofer Schipper and Franciscus Verellen. Chicago: University of Chicago Press, 2004.

Schlütter, Morten. *How Zen Became Zen: The Dispute Over Enlightenment and the Formation of Chan Buddhism in Song-Dynasty China*. Honolulu: University of Hawai'i Press, 2008.

Schopen, Gregory. "Monks and the Relic Cult in the Mahāparinibbānasutta: An Old Misunderstanding in Regard to Monastic Buddhism." In *From Benares to Beijing: Essays on Buddhism and Chinese Religion in Honour of Prof. Jan Yun-Hua*, ed. K. Shinohara and G. Schopen, 187–201. Oakville: Mosaic Press, 1992.

——. "A Note on the 'Technology of Prayer' and a Reference to a Revolving Repository in an Eleventh-Century Indian Inscription." In Gregory Schopen, *Figments and Fragments of Mahayana Buddhism in India: More Collected Papers*, 345–49. Honolulu: University of Hawai'i Press, 2005.

——. "The Phrase 'sa pṛthvīpradeṣaṣ caityabhīto bhavet' in the *Vajracchedikā*: Notes on the Cult of the Book in Mahāyāna." *Indo-Iranian Journal* 17 (1975): 147–81. Also in Gregory Schopen, *Figments and Fragments of Mahayana Buddhism in India: More Collected Paper*, 25–62. Honolulu: University of Hawai'i Press, 2005.

Schmidt-Glintzer, Helwig. *Die Identität der buddhistischen Schulen und die Kompilation buddhistischer Universalgeschichten in China: ein Beitrag zur Geistesgeschichte der Sung-Zeit*. Wiesbaden: Steiner, 1982.

Sen, Tansen. "The Revival and Failure of Buddhist Translations During the Song Dynasty." *T'oung Pao* (2nd ser.) 88 (2002): 27–80.

Seo, Tatsuhiko. "The Printing Industry in Chang'an's Eastern Market." *Memoirs of the Tōyō Bunko* (2004): 1–42.

Sharf, Robert H. "On the Allure of Buddhist Relics." *Representations* 66 (Spring 1999): 75–99. Reprinted in *Embodying the Dharma: Buddhist Relic Veneration in Asia*, ed. David Germano and Kevin Trainor, 163–92. Albany: State University of New York Press, 2004.

——. "On Esoteric Buddhism in China." In *Coming to Terms with Chinese Buddhism: A Reading with the Treasure Store Treatise*, 263–78. Honolulu: University of Hawai'i Press, 2001.

Shen, Hsueh-man. "Praying for Eternity: Use of Buddhist Texts in Liao Buddhist and Funerary Practices." In *Gilded Splendor: Treasures of China's Liao Empire (907–1125)*, ed. Hsueh-man Shen, 81–93. New York: Asia Society, 2006.

——. "Realizing the Buddha's Dharma Body During the Mofa Period: A Study of Liao Buddhist Relics Deposit." *Artibus Asiae* 61, no. 2 (2001): 263–303.

Shenqing 神清. *Beishan lu* 北山錄. 1068. Reprint, Taibei: Wenshizhe chubanshe, 1971.

Shi, Chaoyi. "Huizong and the Divine Empryean Palace Temple Network." In *Emperor Huizong and Late Northern Song China: The Politics of Culture and the Culture of Politics*, ed. Patricia B. Ebrey and Maggie Bickford, 324–58. Cambridge, MA: Harvard University Asia Center, 2006.

Shiina, Kōyū 椎名宏雄. *Sō Gen-ban zenseki no kenkyū* 宋元版禅籍の研究. Tokyo: Daitō Shuppansha, 1993.

Shike shiliao xinbian 石刻史料新編 (Series 1). Taibei: Xinwenfeng chuban gongsi, 1977.

Shim, Jaeryong 沈在龍. *Korean Buddhism: Tradition and Transformation*. Seoul: Jimoondang, 1999.

Shimen zhengtong 釋門正統. Z 1513, vol. 75.

Shimoda, Masahiro. "Some Reflections on the History of Buddhist Canons in Ancient India." In *Indian Philosophy and Text Science*, ed. Toshihiro Wada, 35–57. Delhi: Motilal Banarsidass, 2010.

Shinsan Dai Nihon zoku zōkyō 新纂大日本續藏經. 90 vols. Tōkyō: Kokusho Kankōkai, 1975–89.

Shishi jigu lue xuji 釋氏稽古略續集. *T* 2038, vol. 49.

Shōwa hōhō sōmokuroku 昭和法寶總目錄. Ed. Takakusu Junjirō 高楠順次郎 and Watanabe Kaigyoku 渡邊海旭. 1929–34; reprint, Taibei: Fotuo jiaoyu jijinhui chubanbu, 1990.

Shultz, Edward J. *Generals and Scholars: Military Rule in Medieval Korea*. Honolulu: University of Hawaiʻi Press, 2000.

——. "An Introduction to the Samguk-Sagi—A History of the Three Kingdoms." *Korean Studies* 28 (2004): 1–13.

Siku quanshu 四庫全書, the *Wenyuange* 文淵閣*edition*. 1,500 vols. Taibei: Shangwu yinshuguan, 1983–96.

Silk, Jonathan A. "Review Article: Buddhist Sūtras in Sanskrit from the Potala." *Indo-Iranian Journal* 56 (2013): 61–87.

Sima, Guang 司馬光. *Zizhi tongjian* 資治通鑑. Annot. Hu Sanxing 胡三省. 10 vols. Beijing: Zhonghua shuju, 1956.

Skilling, Peter. "From bKa' bstan bcos to bKa' 'gyur and bsTan 'gyur." In *Transmission of the Tibetan Canon. Papers Presented at a Panel of the 7th Seminar of the International Association for Tibetan Studies, Graz 1995*, ed. E. Steinkellner, vol. 2, 87–111. Wien: Verlag der Österreichischen Akademie der Wissenschaften, 1997.

——. *Mahāsūtras: Great Discourses of the Buddha*. Vol. 2, Pts. 1–2. Oxford: The Pali Text Society, 1997.

——. "Theravādin Literature in Tibetan Translation." *Journal of the Pali Text Society* 19 (1993): 69–201.

——. "Vaidalya, Mahāyāna, and the Bodhisatva in India: An Essay Towards Historical Understanding." In *The Bodhisattva Ideal: Essays on the Emergence of Mahāyāna*, ed. Bhikkhu Nyanatusita, 69–164. Kandy: Buddhist Publication Society, 2013.

Smith, Jonathan Z. "Canons, Catalogues and Classics." In *Canonization and Decanonization*, ed. Arie van der Kooij, et al., 295–312. Leiden; Boston: Brill, 1998.

——. "Sacred Persistence: Toward a Redescription of Canon." In J. Z. Smith, *Imagining Religion: From Babylon to Jonestown*, 36–52. Chicago: University of Chicago Press, 1982.

Smith, Wilfred Cantwell. *What Is Scripture: A Comparative Approach*. London: SCM Press, 1993.

Song huiyao jigao 宋會要輯稿. Ed. Xu Song 徐松. 8 vols. Beijing: Zhonghua shuju, 1957.

Song shi 宋史. Comp. Tuo Tuo 脫脫 et al. 1345; reprint, Beijing: Zhonghua shuju, 1990.

Sørensen, Henrik H. "Astrology and the Worship of the Planets in Esoteric Buddhism of the Tang." In *Esoteric Buddhism and the Tantras in East Asia*, ed. Charles D. Orzech et al., 230–44. Leiden: Brill, 2011.

——. "Esoteric Buddhism Under the Koryŏ in the Light of the Greater East Asian Tradition." *International Journal of Buddhist Thought and Culture* 7 (Sept. 2006):

55–94. Also published in *Korean Buddhism in East Asian Perspective*, ed. Sŭng-ham Yang, Yŏn-sik Ch'oe, and Chong-gŏn Ch'oe, 85–117. Seoul, Jimoondang, 2007.

———. "On the Sinin and Ch'ongji Schools and the Nature of Esoteric Buddhist Practice Under the Koryŏ." *International Journal of Buddhist Thought and Culture* 5 (2005): 49–84.

———. "The Worship of the Great Dipper in Korean Buddhism." In *Religions in Traditional Korea*, 71–105. Copenhagen: SBS Monographs 3, 1995.

———. "Worshiping the Cosmos: Tejaprabha Rituals Under Koryŏ." *International Journal of Buddhist Thought and Culture* 15 (Sept. 2010): 7–26.

Spence, Jonathan. *Return to Dragon Mountain: Memories of a Late Ming Man*. New York: Viking, 2007.

Staggs, Kathleen M. "'Defend the Nation and Love the Truth': Inoue Enryo and the Revival of Meiji Buddhism." *Monumenta Nipponica* 38, no. 3 (1983): 251–81.

Stein Manuscripts. MS. Stein 108, Bodeleian Libraries, University of Oxford. Including: Letter from Aurel Stein to Takakusu Junjiro, June 23, 1924; "Prospectus of the Publication of a New Edition of the Tripitaka in Chinese" by Taisho issai-kyo kanko kwai, undated.

Stone, Jackie. "A Vast and Grave Task: Interwar Buddhist Studies as an Expression of Japan's Envisioned Global Role." In *Culture and Identity: Japanese Intellectuals During the Interwar Years*, ed. J. Thomas Rimer, 217–33. Princeton: Princeton University Press, 1990.

Storch, Tanya. "Dao'an." In *Encyclopedia of Buddhism*, ed. Robert E. Buswell, Jr., 197. New York: Macmillan Reference USA, 2004.

———. *The History of Chinese Buddhist Bibliography: Censorship and Transformation of the Tripitaka*. Amherst: Cambria Press, 2014.

———. "Law and Religious Freedom in Medieval China: State Regulation of Buddhist Communities." In *Religion, Law, and Freedom*, ed. J. Thierstein and Y. Kamalipour, 34–45. Westport and London: Praeger, 2000.

———. "Sengzhao." In *Encyclopedia of Buddhism*, ed. Robert E. Buswell, Jr., 759–60. New York: Macmillan Reference USA, 2004.

Strong, John S. *Relics of the Buddha*. Princeton: Princeton University Press, 2004.

Su, Bai 宿白. *Tang-Song shiqi de diaoban yinshua* 唐宋时期的雕版印刷. Beijing: Wenwu chubanshe, 1999.

Su, Yongqiang 蘇勇強. *Bei Song shuji kanke yu guwen yundong* 北宋書籍刊刻與古文運動. Hangzhou: Zhejiang daxue chubanshe, 2010.

Sueki, Fumihiko. "Building a Platform for Academic Buddhist Studies: Murakami Senshō." *The Eastern Buddhist* 37, no. 1–2 (2005): 8–27.

Sugano, Ginhachi 管野銀八. "Kōrai-ban Daizōkyo ni tsuite" 高麗板大藏經に就いて. *Chōsen shi kōza* 朝鮮史講座, *v. 3 Chōsen shi tokubetsu kōgi* 朝鮮史特別講義, 1923, 219–207 [sic]. 59 pages in total. First published in *Shirin* 史林 7, no. 3 (July 1922).

Sui shu 隋書. Comp. Zhangsun Wuji 長孫無忌. Beijing: Zhonghua shuju, 1977.

Sun, Di 孫覿. *Hongqing jushi ji* 鴻慶居士集. *SKQS*, vol. 1135.

Sun, Yinggang 孫英剛. "Kuada de lishi tujing: Zongpai moshi yu Xifang Sui Tang Fojiaoshi shuxie" 誇大的歷史圖景: 宗派模式與西方隋唐佛教史書寫. In *Bei-mei Zhongguo xue de Lishi yu xianzhuang* 北美中國學的歷史與現狀, ed. Zhu Huizheng 朱政惠 et al., 361–73. Shanghai: Shanghai cishu chubanshe, 2013.

Suzhou fuzhi, Tongzhi 同治蘇州府志. Comp. Li Mingwan 李銘皖 and Feng Guifen 馮桂芬. 6 vols. In *Zhongguo fangzhi congshu: Hua-Zhong difang* 中國方志叢書: 華中地方, 5. 1874; 1882; reprint, Taibei: Chengwen chubanshe, 1970.

Swanson, Paul. "Apocryphal Texts in Chinese Buddhism: T'ien-t'ai Chih-I's Use of Apocryphal Scriptures." In *Canonization and Decanonization*, ed. Arie van der Kooij et al., 245–56. Leiden; Boston: Brill, 1998.

Taishō Shinshū Daizōkyō Kaiin Tsūshin Gappon 大正新修大藏經会員通信合本. Ed. Taishō Shinshū Daizōkyō Kankōkai, no. 1–85. N.p., 1960–179.

Taishō shinshū Daizōkyō 大正新修大藏經. Comp. Takakusu Junjirō 高楠順次郎, Watanabe Kaigyoku 渡邊海旭, et al. 100 vols. Tokyo: Taishō Issaikyō Kankōkai, 1924–32.

Takakusu, Junjirō 高楠順次郎. *Essentials of Buddhist Philosophy*. Westport, CT: Greenwood Press, 1956.

——. *The New Japanism and the Buddhist View on Nationality*. Tokyo: Hokuseido Press, 1938.

Takakusu, Junjirō 高楠順次郎 and Mochizuki, Shinkō 望月信亨. *Shōtoku Taishi Godensōsho* 聖德太子御伝叢書. Osaka: Kanao Bun'endo, 1942.

Takakusu, Junjirō 高楠順次郎 and Watanabe Kaikyoku 渡辺海旭, eds. *Taishō shinshū daizōkyō sōmokuroku* 大正新修大藏經總目錄. Tokyo: Taishō Shinshū Daizōkyō Kankōkai, 1924.

Tamamuro, Fumio. "Local Society and the Temple-Parishioner Relationship Within the Bakufu's Governance Structure." *Japanese Journal of Religious Studies* 28, no. 3–4 (2001): 261–92.

Tan, Shibao 譚世保. *Han-Tang Fo shi tanzhen* 漢唐佛史探真. Guangzhou: Zhong-shan daxue chubanshe, 1991.

Tang, Yongtong 湯用彤. *Tang Yongtong quanji* 湯用彤全集. 7 vols. Shijiazhuang: He-bei renmin chubanshe, 2000.

Tao, Siyan 陶思炎. *Qirang, Qiufu, Chuyang* 祈禳 祈福 除殃. Hong Kong: Sanlian shudian, 1993.

Tekiya, Katsu 的屋勝. "Eiin Sō Sekisha zōkyō bibatsu shū" 影印宋磧砂藏經尾跋集. *Nikka Bukkyō Kenkyūkai nenpō* I 日華佛教研究會年報 1 (1936): 48–166.

ter Haar, B. J. "Buddhist-Inspired Options: Aspects of Lay Religious Life in the Lower Yangzi from 1100 Until 1340." *T'oung Pao* 87, no. 1/3 (2001): 92–152.

——. *The White Lotus Teachings in Chinese Religious History*. 1992; reprint, Honolulu: University of Hawai'i Press, 1999.

Tian, Rucheng 田汝成. *Xihu youlan zhi* 西湖遊覽志. 16th c. *SKQS*, vol. 585

Tokiwa, Daijō 常盤大定. "Daizōkyō chōin kō" 大藏經雕印考. *Tetsugaku Zasshi* 哲學雜誌 XXVIII (1913) and XXIX (1914): 382–83.

Tokuno, Kyoko. "Catalogues of Scriptures." In *Encyclopedia of Buddhism*, ed. Robert E. Buswell, Jr., 116–17. New York: Macmillan Reference USA, 2004.

——. "The Evaluation of Indigenous Scriptures in Chinese Buddhist Bibliographical Catalogues." In *Chinese Buddhist Apocrypha*, ed. Robert E. Buswell, 31–74. Honolulu: University of Hawai'i Press, 1990.

Tong, Wei 童瑋, ed. *Bei Song* Kaibao Dazangjing *diaoyin kaoshi ji qi mulu huanyuan*北宋開寶大藏經雕印考釋及目錄還原. Beijing: Shumu wenxian chubanshe, 1991.

Tsiang, Katherine. "Monumentalization of Buddhist Texts in the Northern Qi Dynasty." *Artibus Asiae* 56, no. 3/4 (1996): 233–61.

Tsien, Tsuen-hsuin. "Paper and Printing." In *Science and Civilisation in China*, ed. Joseph Needham, vol. 5, part I. Cambridge: Cambridge University Press, 1985.

Tsukamoto, Zenryū. *A History of Early Chinese Buddhism: From Its Introduction to the Death of Hui-yüan*. Trans. Leon Hurvitz. 2 vols. Tokyo: Kodansha International, 1985.

Tsumaki, Naoyoshi 妻木直良. "Kittan ni okeru daizōkyō chōzon no jijitsu o ronzu" 契丹に於ける大藏經雕造の事實を論ず. *Tōyō gakuhō* 東洋學報 2 (1912): 317–40.

Tu, Aming 杜正民. "Foxue shuwei ziyuan de fuwu gongneng" 佛學數位資源的服務功能. *Fagu foxue xuebao* 法鼓佛學學報 6 (2010): 118–19.

——. "Foxue yanjiu ziyuan shuweihua zuoye biaozhun yu guifan" 佛學研究資源數位化作業標準與規範. *Hanxue yanjiu tongxun* 漢學研究通訊 (Taibei) 96 (Nov. 2005): 7–16.

——. "Hanwen dianzi dazangjing de zhizuo yuanqi yu zuoye liucheng: yi 'Zhonghua Dianzi Fodian Xiehui' weili" 漢文電子大藏經的製作緣起與作業流程：以中華電子佛典協會為例. *Foxue yanjiu zhongxin xuebao* 佛學研究中心學報 (Taiwan) 4 (July 1999): 347–69.

——. "Hanwen fodian dianzihua: CBETA 2001 nian caiyong de jishu, biaozhun ji jiejue fang'an" 漢文佛典電子化—CBETA 2001年採用的技術, 標準暨解決方案. In *Di sijie zhonghua guoji foxue huiyi: Fojiao yu ershiyi shiji*第四屆中華國際佛學會議：佛教與廿一世紀. Taibei: Zhonghua Foxue yanjiusuo, 2002.

Tushu jicheng: Shijiaobu jishi 圖書集成：釋教部紀事. Z 1661, vol. 88.

Twitchett, Dennis and Klaus Peter Tietze. "The Liao." In *The Cambridge History of China: Volume 6, Alien Regimes and Border States, 907–1368*, ed. Herbert Franke and Dennis Twitchett, 43–153. Cambridge: Cambridge University Press, 1994.

Ui, Hakuju 宇井伯壽. *Nihon Bukkyō gaishi* 日本仏教概史. Tokyo: Iwanami Shoten, 1951.

——. *Shaku Dōan kenkyū* 釋道安研究. 2nd ed. Tokyo: Iwanami Shoten, 1979.

van der Loon, Piet. *Taoist Books in the Libraries of the Sung Period*. London: Ithaca Press, 1984.

Vermeersch, Sem. "Buddhism and State-Building in Song China and Goryeo Korea." *Asia-Pacific: Perspectives* 5, no. 1 (2004): 4–11.

——. *The Power of the Buddhas: The Politics of Buddhism During the Koryŏ Dynasty (918–1392)*. Cambridge, MA: Harvard University Press, 2008.

——. "Royal Ancestor Worship and Buddhist Politics: The Hyŏnhwa-sa Stele and the Origins of the First Koryŏ Tripitaka." *Journal of Korean Studies* 18, no. 1 (2013): 115–46.

Verschuer, Charlotte von. "Le voyage de Jōjin au mont Tiantai." *T'oung Pao* 77, no. 1/3 (1991): 1–48.

Vetter, Tilmann and Stefano Zacchetti. "On *Jingfa* 經法 in Early Chinese Buddhist Translations." *Annual Report of The International Research Institute for Advanced Buddhology at Soka University* 7 (2004): 159–66.

Vimalakīrtinirdeśa: A Sanskrit Edition Based Upon the Manuscript Newly Found at the Potala Palace. Ed. Study Group on Buddhist Sanskrit Literature. Tokyo: The Institute for Comprehensive Studies of Buddhism, Taisho University, 2006.

Vinītā, Bhikṣuṇī (Vinita Tseng). *A Unique Collection of Twenty Sūtras in a Sanskrit Manuscript from the Potala: Editions and Translation*. 2 vols. Beijing: China Tibetology Publishing House/Vienna: Austrian Academy of Sciences, 2010.

Vita, Silvio. "Printings of the Buddhist 'Canon' in Modern Japan." In *Papers from the First Conference of Buddhist Studies*, 217–39. Kyoto: Italian School of East Asian Studies, 2001.

Vorobyova-Desyatovskaya, M. I., ed. *The Kāśyapaparivarta: Romanized Text and Facsimiles*. Bibliotheca Philologica et Philosophica Buddhica V. Tokyo: The International Research Institute for Advanced Buddhology, Soka University, 2002.

Wan xu zang jing 卍續藏經. Reprint of *Dai-Nihon zoku zōkyō* 大日本續藏經. 1912; reprint, Taibei: Xin wenfeng, 1976.

Wang, Bijiang 汪辟疆. *Muluxue yanjiu* 目錄學研究. Shanghai: Yingshuguan, 1995.

Wang, Han 王菡. "Yuandai Hangzhou kanke *Dazangjing* yu Xixia de guanxi" 元代杭州刊刻大藏經與西夏的關係. *Wenxian* 文獻1 (2005): 111–18.

Wang, Jiqing 王冀青. *Sitanyin yu Riben Dunhuangxue: Yingguo Niujin daxue cang Sitanyin kaogu dang'an Riben Dunhuangxue shi wenxian yanjiu* 斯坦因与日本敦煌學: 英國牛津大學藏斯坦因考古檔案日本敦煌學史文獻研究. Lanzhou: Gansu jiaoyu chubanshe, 2004.

Wang, Shengduo 汪聖鐸. *Songdai zhengjiao guanxi yanjiu* 宋代政教關係研究. Beijing: Renmin chubanshe, 2010.

Wang, Wenyan 王文顏. *Fodian hanyi zhi yanjiu* 佛典漢譯之研究. Taibei: Tianhua chuban shiye gufen youxian gongsi, 1984.

Wang, Xiang 王翔. "Beiye yu xiejing: Tangdai Chang'an de siyuan tushuguan" 貝葉與寫經: 唐代長安的寺院圖書館. In *Tang yanjiu* 唐研究 vol. 15, ed. Rong Xinjiang 榮新江, 483–529. Beijing: Beijing daxue chubanshe, 2009.

Wang, Zeqing 王澤慶. "Xiezhouban *Jinzang* muke de zhongyao wenxian: *Diao zangjing zhu chongxiu Dayinsi bei* kaoshi" 解州板 金藏 募刻的重要文獻: 雕藏經 主重修大陰寺碑考釋. *Wenwu shijie* 文物世界4 (2003): 15–19.

Wang, Zhaowen 王肇文. *Guji Song-Yuan kangong xingming suoyin* 古籍宋元刊工姓 名索引. Shanghai: Shanghai Guji chubanshe, 1990.

Weinstein, Stanley. *Buddhism Under the T'ang.* London: Cambridge University Press, 1987.

Welch, Holmes. *The Practice of Chinese Buddhism 1900–1950.* Cambridge, MA: Harvard University Press, 1967.

Welter, Albert. "A Buddhist Response to the Confucian Revival: Tsan-ning and the Debate Over *Wen* in the Early Sung." In *Buddhism in the Sung,* ed. Peter N. Gregory and Daniel A. Getz, 21–61. Honolulu: University of Hawai'i Press, 1999.

——. "Buddhist Rituals for Protecting the Country in Medieval Japan: Myōan Eisai's 'Regulations of the Zen School.'" In *Zen Ritual: Studies of Zen Buddhist Theory in Practice,* ed. Steven Heine and Dale Stuart Wright, 113–38. Oxford and New York: Oxford University Press, 2008.

——. *Monks, Rulers, and Literati: The Political Ascendancy of Chan Buddhism.* New York: Oxford University Press, 2006.

——. "Zen Buddhism as the Ideology of the Japanese State: Eisai and the *Kōzen gokokuron.*" In *Zen Classics: Formative Texts in the History of Zen Buddhism,* ed. Steven Heine and Dale Stuart Wright, 65–112. Oxford and New York: Oxford University Press, 2006.

Weng, Lianxi 翁連溪. *Qingdai neifu keshu tulu* 清代內府刻書圖錄. Beijing: Beijing chubashe, 2004.

Willemen, Charles. "The Prefaces to the Chinese *Dharmapadas, Fa-chü ching* and *Ch'u-yao ching.*" *T'oung Pao* 59 (1973): 203–19.

Wittern, Christian. "Chinese Buddhist Texts for the New Millennium—The Chinese Buddhist Electronic Text Association (CBETA) and Its Digital Tripitaka." *Journal of Digital Information* 3, no. 2 (Feb. 27, 2006). http://journals.tdl.org/jodi/index.php/jodi/article/view/84.

——. "Patterns of Variation: The Textual Sources of the Chinese Buddhist Canon as Seen Through the CBETA Edition." In *Essays on East Asian Religion and Culture: Festschrift in Honour of Nishiwaki Tsuneki on the Occasion of His 65th Birthday,* ed. Christian Wittern and Shi Lishan, 209–32. Kyoto: Editorial committee for the Festschrift in honor of Nishiwaki Tsuneki, 2007.

Wong, Dorothy. "Four Sichuan Buddhist Steles and the Beginnings of Pure Land Imagery in China." *Archives of Asian Art* 51 (1998/99): 56–79.

Worthy, Edmund H. Jr. "Diplomacy for Survival." In *China Among Equals: The Middle Kingdom and Its Neighbors, 10th–14th Centuries,* ed. Morris Rossabi, 17–44. Berkeley: University of California Press, 1983.

Wright, Arthur F. *Buddhism in Chinese History.* 1959; reprint, Stanford: Stanford University Press, 1971.

——. "T'ang T'ai-tsung and Buddhism." In *Perspectives on the T'ang*, ed. Arthur F. Wright and Denis Twitchett, 239–63. New Haven: Yale University Press, 1973.

Wright, David Curtis. *From War to Diplomatic Parity in Eleventh-Century China: Sung's Foreign Relations with Kitan Liao.* Leiden; Boston: Brill, 2005.

Wu, Cheng'en 吳承恩. *Journey to the West.* Trans. Anthony Yu. Chicago: University of Chicago Press, 1977.

Wu, Jiang. "The Chinese Buddhist Canon." In *Blackwell Companion to East and Inner Asian Buddhism*, ed. Mario Poceski, 363-82. Chichester, UK: Blackwell, 2014.

——. *Enlightenment in Dispute: The Reinvention of Chan Buddhism in Seventeenth-Century China.* Oxford; New York: Oxford University Press, 2008.

——. "Finding the First Chinese Tripitaka in Europe: The 1872 Iwakura Mission in Britain and the Mystery of the Obaku Tetsugen Canon in the Indian Office Library." Paper presented at the Third Conference on the Chinese Buddhist Canon, Brigham Young University, Provo, Utah, April 9–10.

——. "Imagining Tripitaka: Legends About the Buddhist Canon in Chinese Sources." Paper presented at the Second International Conference on the Chinese Buddhist Canon at the University of the West, Los Angeles, CA, March 18, 2013.

——. *Leaving for the Rising Sun: Chinese Zen Master Yinyuan Longqi and the Authenticity Crisis in Early Modern East Asia.* New York: Oxford University Press, 2015.

Wu, Jing 吳晶. "Chen Yinke 'heben zizhu' shuo xintan" 陳寅恪"合本子注"說新探. *Zhejiang shehui kexue* 浙江社會科學 12 (2008): 84–88.

Wu junzhi 吳郡志. 1192; 1229. Comp. Fan Chengda 范成大 et al. Reprinted in *Congshu jicheng chubian* 叢書集成初編. Beijing: Zhonghua shuju, 1985.

Wu, K. T. "Chinese Printing Under Four Alien Dynasties (916–1368 A.D.)." *Harvard Journal of Asiatic Studies* 13, no. 3/4 (1950): 447–523.

Wu, Zhijing 吳之鯨. *Wulin fanzhi* 武林梵志. *SKQS*, vol. 588.

Wudeng huiyuan 五燈會元. Z 1565, vol. 80.

Xiao, Mo 蕭默. *Dunhuang jianzhu yanjiu* 敦煌建筑研究. Beijing: Wenwu chubanshe, 1989.

Xiao, Ping 肖平. *Jindai Zhongguo Fojiao de fuxing: yu Riben Fojiaojie de jiaowang lu* 近代中國佛教的復興: 與日本佛教界的交往錄. Guangzhou: Guangdong renmin chubanshe, 2003.

Xie, Jisheng 謝繼勝. "Ningxia Guyuan Xumishan Yuanguang si ji xiangguan fanseng kao" 寧夏固原須彌山圓光寺及相關番僧考. *Pumen xuebao* 18 普門學報 (2003): 99–146.

Xin wudai shi 新五代史. 11th c. Comp. Ouyang Xiu 歐陽修 et al. 3 vols. Beijing: Zhonghua shuju, 1974.

Xin Zhongguo chutu muzhi. Chongqing 新中國出土墓誌. 重慶. Ed. Zhongguo wenwu yanjiusuo and Chongqing shi bowuguan. Beijing: Wenwu chubanshe, 2002.

Xu, Huili 許惠利. "Beijing Zhihua si faxian Yuandai zangjing" 北京智化寺發現元代藏經. *Wenwu* 文物 8 (1987): 1–7, 29.

Xu, Jing 徐兢. *Xuanhe fengshi Gaoli tujing* 宣和奉使高麗圖經, fasc. 17, *Zhibuzu zhai congshu* 知不足齋叢書 vol. 2. *Congshu jicheng chubian* 叢書集成初編. Shanghai: Shangwu yinshuguan, 1937.

Xu, Rucong 徐汝聰. "Yijian zhengui de Zangchuan fojiao zushi xiang" 一件珍貴的藏傳佛教祖師像. *Dongnan wenhua* 東南文化 2 (1999): 99–102.

Xu, Shiyi 徐时儀. "*Kaibaozang* and *Liaozang* de chuancheng yuanyuan kao" 開寶藏和遼藏的傳承淵源考. *Zongjiao xue yanjiu* 宗教學研究 1 (2006): 45–50.

——. *Xuanying he Huilin "Yiqiejing yinyi" yanjiu* 玄應和慧琳一切經音義研究. Shanghai: Shanghai renmin chubanshe, 2009.

Yamashita, Yumi 山下有美. *Shōsōin monjo to shakyōjo no kenkyū* 正倉院文書と写経所の研究. Tōkyō: Yoshikawa Kōbunkan, 1999.

Yamazaki, Hiroshi 山崎宏. *Zui Tō no Bukkyō shi no kenkyū* 隋唐の仏教史の研究. Kyoto: Hozokan, 1971.

Yan Juanying 顏娟英. *Beichao fojiao shike tapian baipin* 北朝佛教石刻拓片百品. Taipei: Zhongyang yanjiuyuan lishiyuyan yanjiusuo, 2008.

Yan, Yiping 嚴一萍, ed. *Baibu congshu jicheng* 百部叢書集成. Taibei: Yi wen yin shu guan, 1964.

Yang, Jian 楊健. *Qing wangchao fojiao shiwu guanli* 清王朝佛教事務管理. Beijing: Shehui kexue wenxian chubanshe, 2008.

Yang, Shengxin 楊繩信. "Cong *Qishazang* keyin kan Song-Yuan yinshua gongren de ji ge wenti" 從磧砂藏刻印看宋元印刷工人的幾個問題. *Zhonghua wenshi luncong* 29, no. 1 (1984): 41–58.

——. "Lun *Qishazang*" 論磧砂藏. *Wenwu* 文物 8 (1984): 49–54.

Yang, Wenhui 楊文會. *Yang Renshan ji* 楊仁山集. Ed. Huang Xianian. Beijing: Zhongguo shehui kexue chubanshe, 1995.

Yang, Yuliang 楊玉良. "Gugong bowuyuan cang *Jiaxingzang* chutan" 故宮博物院藏嘉興藏初探. *Gugong bowuyuan yuankan* 3 (1997): 13–34.

——. "*Qing Longzangjing* de kanshua qingkuang shiyi" 清龍藏經的刊刷情況拾遺. *Gugong bowuyuan yuankan* 故宮博物院院刊 4 (1989): 72–75.

Yao, Mingda 姚名達. *Zhongguo muluxue shi* 中國目錄學史. Changsha: Shangwuguan, 1937.

Yasumaru, Yoshio 良夫安丸 and Masato Miyachi 正人宮地, eds. *Shūkyō to Kokka* 宗教と国家. Tokyo: Iwanami Shoten, 1988.

Ye, Zhi 葉寘 (13th c.), comp. *Airi zhai congchao* 愛日齋叢鈔. Collated by Qian Xizuo 錢熙祚 (d. 1844). Series: *Biji sibian* 筆記四編. Taibei: Guangwen shuju 廣文書局, 1971.

Yi, Chi-kwan 李智冠, ed. *Gayasan Haeinsa ji* 伽倻山海印寺誌. Seoul: Gasan Mungo, 1992.

Yi, Gyubo 李奎報. *Dongguk I sangguk jip* 東國李相國集. Gyeongseong: Joseon Goseo Ganhaenghoe, 1913.

Yifa. *The Origins of Buddhist Monastic Codes in China: An Annotated Translation and Study of the* Changyuan qinggui. Honolulu: University of Hawai'i Press, 2002.

Yim, Deug Guen (Ven. Sung Ahn). "The Enshrinement of the Tripitaka Koreana: Printing Woodblocks at Haein-sa Temple and the Temple's Elevated Status in Subsequent Years." M.A. thesis, University of the West, 2012.

Yong, Heming and Jing Peng. *Chinese Lexicography: A History from 1046* B.C. *to* A.D. *1911.* New York: Oxford University Press, 2008.

Yu, Buhyeon 柳富鉉. "Goryeo Daejanggyeong jeongnyeok sayeo hyeonsang" 高麗大藏經的歷史與現狀. *Daedong munhwa yeongu* 大東文化研究 11 (1976): 56–62.

Yü, Chün-fang. *Kuan-yin: The Chinese Transformation of Avalokiteśvara.* New York: Columbia University Press, 2001.

———. *The Renewal of Buddhism in China: Chu-hung and the Late Ming Synthesis.* New York: Columbia University Press, 1981.

Yu, Jimmy. "Bodies and Self-Inflicted Violence in Sixteenth- and Seventeenth-Century China." Ph.D. diss., Princeton University, 2008.

———. *Sanctity and Self-Inflicted Violence in Chinese Religions, 1500–1700.* New York: Oxford University Press, 2012.

Yu, Kyung-Loh. "A Brief History of the Bureau of Astronomy in the Koryo and Early Chosŏn Dynasties." In *Oriental Astronomy from Guo Shoujing to King Sejong: Proceedings of an International Conference, Seoul, Korea 6–11 October 1993,* ed. Nha Il-Seong and Richard Stephenson, 77–81. Seoul: Yonsei University Press, 1997.

Yuan, Ke 袁珂. *Shanhai jing jiaozhu* 山海經校注. Shanghai: Shanghai guji chubanshe, 1980.

Yuanren zhuanji ziliao suoyin 元人傳記資料索引. Comp. Wang Deyi 王德毅et al. Taibei: Xin Wenfeng chuban gongsi, 1979–82.

Yuanzhao 圓照. *Zhenyuan xinding shijiao mulu* 貞元新定釋教目錄. T 2157, vol. 55.

Yuanzhi 圓至. "Pingjiang fu Chen hu Qisha Yansheng yuan ji" 平江府陳湖磧砂延聖院記 and "Yansheng yuan Guanyin dian ji" 延聖院觀音殿記." In *Muqian ji* 牧潛集, 3.7b–10a and 3.10a–11b. Late 13th c. SKQS, vol. 1198.

Zacchetti, Stefano. "Brief Communication: On the Authenticity of the Kongōji Manuscript of An Shigao's *Anban Shouyi jing* 安般守意經." *Annual Report of The International Research Institute for Advanced Buddhology at Soka University* 5 (2002): 157–58.

———. "An Early Chinese Translation Corresponding to Chapter 6 of the *Peṭakopadesa.* An Shigao's *Yin chi ru jing* T 603 and Its Indian Original: A Preliminary Survey." *Bulletin of the School of Oriental and African Studies* 65, no. 1 (2002): 74–98.

———. *In Praise of the Light: A Critical Synoptic Edition with an Annotated Translation of Chapters 1–3 of Dharmarakṣa's Guang zan jing* 光讚經, *Being the Earliest Chinese Translation of the Larger Prajñāpāramitā.* Tokyo: The International Research Institute for Advanced Buddhology—Soka University (Bibliotheca Philologica et Philosophica Buddhica VIII), 2005.

——. "A 'New' Early Chinese Buddhist Commentary: The Nature of the *Da anban shouyi jing* 大安般守意經 T 602 Reconsidered." *Journal of the International Association of Buddhist Studies* 31, no. 1–2 (2010): 421–84.

——. "The Rediscovery of Three Early Buddhist Scriptures on Meditation: A Preliminary Analysis of the *Fo shuo shi'er men jing*, the *Fo shuo jie shi'er men jing* Translated by An Shigao and Their Commentary Preserved in the Newly Found Kongō-ji Manuscript." *Annual Report of The International Research Institute for Advanced Buddhology at Soka University* 6 (2003): 251–99.

——. "Some Remarks on the Authorship and Chronology of the *Yin chi ru jing zhu* T 1694: The Second Phase in the Development of Chinese Buddhist Exegetical Literature." In *Buddhist Asia 2. Papers from the Second Conference of Buddhist Studies Held in Naples in June 2004*, ed. Giacomella Orofino and Silvio Vita, 141–98. Kyoto: Italian School of East Asian Studies, 2010.

——. "Some Remarks on the '*Peṭaka* Passages' in the *Da zhidu lun* and Their Relation to the Pāli *Peṭakopadesa*." *Annual Report of The International Research Institute for Advanced Buddhology at Soka University* 5 (2002): 67–85.

——. "Teaching Buddhism in Han China: A Study of the *Ahan koujie shi'er yinyuan jing* T 1508 Attributed to An Shigao." *Annual Report of The International Research Institute for Advanced Buddhology at Soka University* 7 (2004): 197–224.

Zanning 贊寧. *Song Gaoseng zhuan* 宋高僧傳. T 2061, vol. 50.

Zhang, Dewei. "The Strength of the Forgotten: Carving the Buddhist Canon in North China Under the Minority Regimes." Paper presented at AAR Annual Meeting, Nov. 20, 2012.

Zhang, Hongwei 章宏偉. "*Fangce zang* de kanke yu Mingdai guanban dazangjing" 方冊藏的刊刻與明代官版大藏經.*Ming–Qing luncong* 明清論叢 5 (2004): 145–207.

——. "Shi zhi shisi shiji Zhongguo yu Chaoxian bandao de Hanwen dazangjing jiaoliu" 10–14 世紀中國與朝鮮半島的漢文大藏經交流. *Guji zhengli yanjiu xuekan* 古籍整理研究學刊 6 (Nov. 2009): 35–47.

——. *Shiliu—shijiu shiji Zhongguo chuban yanjiu* 十六–十九世紀中國出版研究. Shanghai: Shanghai renmin chubanshe, 2011.

——. "Wutaishan fangce cang kanke de shehui ziyuan" 五台山方冊藏刊刻的社會資源. In *Fojiao yu dangdai wenhua jianshe xueshu yantaohui lunwen ji* 佛教與當代文化建設學術研討會論文集 vol. 1, 75–217. Xi'an: Xibei daxue chubanshe, 2013.

Zhang, Shiqing 張十慶. *Wushan shicha tu yu Nan Song jiangnan chansi* 五山十剎圖与南宋江南禪寺. Nanjing: Dongnan daxue chubanshe, 2000.

——. *Zhongguo jiangnan Chanzong siyuan jianzhu* 中國江南禪宗寺院建築. Wuhan: Hubei jiaoyu chubanshe, 2001.

Zhang, Xinying 張新鷹. "Lun *Qishazang* du hou" 論磧砂藏讀後. *Wenwu* 文物 9 (1986): 92–93.

Zhang, Xiumin 張秀民. *Zhongguo yinshua shi* 中國印刷史. Revised and updated by Han Qi 韓琦. Hangzhou: Zhejiang renmin chubanshe, 2006.

Zhang, Yong 張勇. *Fu Dashi yanjiu* 傅大士研究. Chengdu: Bashu shushe, 2000.

Zhao, Sheng 趙昇. *Caoye leiyao: Zhujie* 朝野類要. 諸節. In *Biji xiaoshuo daguan* 筆記小說大觀, series 21. Taibei: Xinxing shuju, 1978.

Zheng, Zhenduo 鄭振鐸, comp. *Zhongguo gudai mukehua xuanji* 中國古代木刻畫選集. Beijing: Renmin meishu chubanshe, 1985.

Zhengshi fojiao ziliao leibian 正史佛教資料類編. Ed. Du Doucheng 杜斗城. Lanzhou: Gansu wenhua chubanshe, 2006.

Zhisheng 智昇. *Kaiyuan shijiao lu* 開元釋教錄. T 2154, vol. 55.

Zhongguo Fojiao renming dacidian 中國佛教人名大辭典. 1999; reprint, Shanghai: Shanghai cishu chubanshe, 2002.

Zhonghua dazangjing (hanwen bufen) 中華大藏經. 漢文部分. Beijing: Zhonghua shu ju, 1984–96.

Zhouzhuang zhenzhi, Guangxu 光緒周莊鎮志. Comp. Tao Xu 陶煦. 1882; reprint, *Xuxiu Siku quanshu* 續修四庫全書. Shanghai: Shanghai Guji chubanshe, 1995.

Zhu, Zifang 朱子方. "Liaochao yu Gaoli de foxue jiaoliu" 遼朝與高麗的佛學交流. In *Liao Jin shi lunji* 遼金史論集, ed. Chen Shu 陳述,vol. 5, 114–37. Beijing: Wenjin chubanshe, 1991.

Zürcher, Erik. *The Buddhist Conquest of China: The Spread and Adaptation of Buddhism in Early Medieval China*. 3rd ed. Leiden: Brill, 2007.

——. "A New Look at the Earliest Chinese Buddhist Texts." In *From Benares to Beijing: Essays on Buddhism and Chinese Religion in Honor of Prof. Jan Yün-hua*, ed. Koichi Shinohara and Gregory Schopen, 277–300. Oakville, Ontario: Mosaic, 1991.

CONTRIBUTORS

LUCILLE CHIA is professor of history at the University of California at Riverside. Her research interests include Chinese book culture and Buddhist publishing in imperial China in particular. Currently she is working on the Qisha Buddhist canon.

CHEN, ZHICHAO 陳智超, the grandson of Chen Yuan 陳垣, worked for the Institute of Historical Research in Chinese Academy of Social Sciences before his retirement. Since 1982, he has been a visiting scholar at renowned universities and research institutes in France, Japan, the United States, Canada, and South Korea. He has published widely on Song and Ming history.

RON DZIWENKA is currently a part-time lecturer in the History Department and the Honors College at New Mexico State University. He received his Ph.D. from the University of Arizona (2010) with a dissertation on the travel of the thirteen-century Indian Monk Zhikong in China and Korea.

HE, MEI 何梅 has been working for the Institute of the Study of World Religions in the Chinese Academy of Social Sciences since 1979. Her academic achievements include compiling and editing the state-run project of the Beijing edition of the Chinese Tripitaka. She also coauthored *Studies of Chinese Tripitaka* with Li Fuhua.

LEWIS LANCASTER is Emeritus Professor of the Department of East Asian Languages at the University of California, Berkeley, and has served as President at University of the West since 1992. He also founded the Electronic Cultural Atlas Initiative. He has published over 55 articles and reviews and has edited or authored numerous books, including *The Korean Buddhist Canon*.

LI, FUHUA 李富華 was a researcher at the Institute of the Study of World Religions in Chinese Academy of Social Sciences until his retirement in 2002. From 1982 to 1994, he participated in the compilation of the Beijing edition of the Chinese Tripitaka. He published many papers on this subject, including *Studies of Chinese Tripitaka*, coauthored with He Mei.

DARUI LONG 龍達瑞 is a professor of Chinese religions in the Department of Religious Studies, University of the West, Rosemead, California. His research focuses on the Chinese Buddhist canon and he has published articles on the Hongwu edition and the Northern Yongle edition. He received a research grant from Princeton University in 2009 and also conducted research at the University of Chicago.

TANYA STORCH is an associate professor of Religious Studies at the University of the Pacific in California. She holds a Ph.D. from the University of Pennsylvania and an M.A. from the University of St. Petersburg, Russia. She has published widely, and her recent work is *The History of Chinese Buddhist Bibliography*.

GREG WILKINSON is an assistant professor of Religious Education at Brigham Young University. He teaches courses on comparative religion and has written on religion in contemporary Japan. His research interests include Japan's new religions, pilgrimage, missiology in modern Japan, and Japanese editions of the Buddhist canon.

JIANG WU 吳疆 is a professor in the Department of East Asian Studies at the University of Arizona. His research interests include Chinese Buddhism, especially Chan/Zen Buddhism and the Chinese Buddhist canon; Sino-Japanese Buddhist exchanges; and the application of GIS tools in the study of Chinese culture and religion. He has published two books with Oxford University Press: *Enlightenment in Dispute* (2008) and *Leaving for the Rising Sun* (2015).

STEFANO ZACCHETTI is Numata Professor of Buddhist Studies at the University of Oxford. His publications include the monograph *In Praise of the Light* (Tokyo, 2005), and several articles. His main research interests include the study of early Chinese Buddhist translations and commentaries, Indian Mahayana literature, and the history of the Chinese canon.

INDEX

CPSIA information can be obtained
at www.ICGtesting.com
Printed in the USA
LVHW030239201119
637929LV00001B/1/P